The New Covenant as a Paradigm for Optimal Relations

The House of Prisca and Aquila

Our mission at the House of Prisca and Aquila is to produce quality books that expound accurately the word of God to empower women and men to minister together in a multicultural church. Our writers have a positive view of the Bible as God's revelation that affects both thoughts and words, so it is plenary, historically accurate, and consistent in itself, fully reliable, and authoritative as God's revelation. Because God is true, God's revelation is true, inclusive to men and women and speaking to a multicultural church, wherein all the diversity of the church is represented within the parameters of egalitarianism and inerrancy.

The word of God is what we are expounding, thereby empowering women and men to minister together in all levels of the church and home. The reason we say women and men together is because that is the model of Prisca and Aquila, ministering together to another member of the church—Apollos: "Having heard Apollos, Priscilla and Aquila took him aside and more accurately expounded to him the Way of God" (Acts 18:26). True exposition, like true religion, is by no means boring—it is fascinating. Books that reveal and expound God's true nature "burn within us" as they elucidate the Scripture and apply it to our lives.

This was the experience of the disciples who heard Jesus on the road to Emmaus: "Were not our hearts burning while Jesus was talking to us on the road, while he was opening the scriptures to us?" (Luke 24:32). We are hoping to create the classics of tomorrow, significant and accessible trade and academic books that "burn within us."

Our "house" is like the home to which Prisca and Aquila no doubt brought Apollos as they took him aside. It is like the home in Emmaus where Jesus stopped to break bread and reveal his presence. It is like the house built on the rock of obedience to Jesus (Matt 7:24). Our "house," as a euphemism for our publishing team, is a home where truth is shared and Jesus' Spirit breaks bread with us, nourishing all of us with his bounty of truth.

We are delighted to work together with Wipf and Stock in this series and welcome submissions on a wide variety of topics from an egalitarian, inerrantist global perspective.

For more information, see our website: sites.google.com/site/houseofpriscaandaquila/.

The New Covenant as a Paradigm for Optimal Relations

Marital Principles Derived from a Theological-Psychological Integration

PABLO POLISCHUK

Foreword by
Ray Pendleton

WIPF & STOCK · Eugene, Oregon

THE NEW COVENANT AS A PARADIGM FOR OPTIMAL RELATIONS
Marital Principles Derived from a Theological-Psychological Integration

Copyright © 2016 Pablo Polischuk. All rights reserved. Except for brief quotations in critical publications or reviews, no part of this book may be reproduced in any manner without prior written permission from the publisher. Write: Permissions, Wipf and Stock Publishers, 199 W. 8th Ave., Suite 3, Eugene, OR 97401.

Wipf & Stock
An Imprint of Wipf and Stock Publishers
199 W. 8th Ave., Suite 3
Eugene, OR 97401

www.wipfandstock.com

PAPERBACK ISBN: 978-1-4982-2612-7
HARDCOVER ISBN: 978-1-4982-2614-1
EBOOK ISBN: 978-1-4982-2613-4

Manufactured in the U.S.A.

Unless otherwise indicated, Scripture quotations are from the New English Translation. NET Bible® copyright ©1996–2006 by Biblical Studies Press, L.L.C. All rights reserved.

Scripture quotations marked KJV are from the King James Version.

Scripture quotations marked NKJV are taken from the New King James Version®. Copyright © 1982 by Thomas Nelson. Used by permission. All rights reserved.

Scripture quotations marked NIV are taken from the Holy Bible, New International Version®, NIV®. Copyright © 1973, 1978, 1984, 2011 by Biblica, Inc.™ Used by permission of Zondervan. All rights reserved worldwide. www.zondervan.com The "NIV" and "New International Version" are trademarks registered in the United States Patent and Trademark Office by Biblica, Inc.™

Scripture quotations marked NLT are from the Holy Bible, New Living Translation, copyright © 1996, 2004, 2007. Used by permission of Tyndale House Publishers, Inc., Wheaton, IL 60189. All rights reserved.

Scripture quotations marked ESV are from the Holy Bible, English Standard Version. Copyright © 2001 by Crossway Bibles, a division of Good News Publishers. Used by permission.

Scripture quotations marked NAS are from the New American Standard Bible, copyright © 1960, 1962, 1963, 1968, 1971, 1972, 1973, 1975, 1977, 1995 by The Lockman Foundation. Used by permission. (www.Lockman.org)

To my wife and covenantal partner Frances

Contents

List of Illustrations   viii
Foreword by Ray Pendleton   ix
Preface   xi
Acknowledgments   xv
Introduction   xvii

PART I: PREMISES AND PRINCIPLES

Chapter 1: Biblical Anthropology and Covenantal Relations   3

Chapter 2: Covenant as a Biblical Paradigm   20

Chapter 3: The Old Covenant as a *Quid Pro Quo*   38

Chapter 4: The New Covenant as a Relational Paradigm   58

Chapter 5: Marriage as Covenant   82

Chapter 6: *Quid Pro Quo* and Beyond: The New Covenant as an Optimal Model   107

Chapter 7: The New Covenant: Made in the Spirit   129

PART II: ACTUALIZING THE PRINCIPLES DERIVED FROM THE NEW COVENANT IN MARITAL TRANSACTIONS

Chapter 8: Empowered by the Holy Spirit to Empower One Another   153

Chapter 9: The Empowered Capacity to Be Unilateral in a Bilateral Deal   174

Chapter 10: Adopting an Unconditional Stance to Optimize Renewed Conditions   191

Chapter 11: Imitating God's Proactive Ways in Marriage and the Church   213

Chapter 12: The Most Excellent Way: Grace and Mercy as Expressions of Love   234

Chapter 13: Covenantal Intimacy and Love   256

Chapter 14: Empowered to Forgive as God Forgave Us in Christ   278

Chapter 15: Letting Go of Offenses and Being Free   292

Chapter 16: Covenantal Renewal as a Way of Life   316

Chapter 17: A Metacognitive-Dialogical Model of Forgiveness   339

Bibliography   353

Illustrations

1. The Human Being in God's Master Design (Fig. 1.1)   9
2. The Spirit's Empowering of Self-Control (Fig. 7.1)   146
3. The Person's Output Empowered by the Spirit (Fig. 8.1)   165
4. Automatic Reactions to Provoking Stressors (Fig. 11.1)   219
5. Mindful Detachment Empowered by the Holy Spirit (Fig. 11.2)   224
6. Changing Automatic Reactions into Purposive Responses (Fig. 11.3)   225
7. Levels of Analysis: Being, Processing, and Behaving (Fig. 12.1)   244
8. The Four Functions of Marital Boundaries (Fig. 13.1)   262
9. Marital Intimacy in Function of Closeness to God (Fig. 13.2)   263
10. Degree of Stability and Satisfaction in Marriage (Fig. 16.1)   332
11. Pathways to Mind Renewal (Fig. 16.2)   336
12. Existential Bracketing of Reality and Mind Renewal (Fig. 16.3)   338
13. Metacognitive Processes in Forgiveness (Fig. 17.1)   341
14. Trialogue: The Internal Dialogues of the Self and the Holy Spirit (Fig. 17.2)   341
15. Processes at Lower Levels: A Feedback Control System (Fig. 17.3)   343
16. Feedback and Empowered Feedforward Control (Fig. 17.4)   346
17. Feedback and Feedforward Control Systems, Reactions, and Responses (Fig. 17.5)   347
18. Empowered Metacognitive-Executive Processes in Forgiveness (Fig. 17.6)   349

Foreword

I AM DELIGHTED TO see the publication of this work coming to fruition. Its long journey started with the insights provided by the teaching of one of Dr. Polischuk's mentors, Dr. Donald Tweedie, at the Fuller Graduate School of Psychology. He was the first to coin the term *covenant therapy* in a couple of articles published by the *Journal of Psychology and Theology* in 1976. Then, the concept was followed by the presentation of a workshop at Andover Newton School of Theology that turned into the invitation to write a seminal article, "The New Covenant as a Paradigm for Family Progress," published with the *Judson Journal* of that institution in 1994. Throughout twenty-five years of teaching courses in Marital Therapy at Gordon-Conwell Theological Seminary, the principles, concepts, and propositions that permeate the pages of this book have been subjected to ongoing dialogical encounters with students, who provided the challenges and opportunities to engage in revisions and refinements of the postulates and their practical applicability to therapeutic situations. This work is the result of years of teaching and research on the subject matter of the New Covenant as a paradigm for relations, coupled to psychotherapeutic endeavors with many individuals and couples who have benefited from the biblical-theological integration espoused here.

I would like to invite the reader to consider the ways in which the metacognitive, integrated view presented in this volume, cast in an architectural design—placing the foundational basis first, followed by a structural framework guiding the building processes, and finishing with overt applicability—may serve as a heuristic device to guide the practical considerations that may apply in relational interactions. I have found that these principles have helped numerous people (clients, parishioners, and students) in their attempts to imitate God's ways in covenantal transactions. Thus, this work does not follow the "how to" style, but rather seeks to follow a scripturally sound ethos, analogous to the Pauline theology found in Ephesians and Romans. In these letters, Paul presents his theological foundations first (e.g., Ephesians 1–4; Romans 1–11) and then follows with admonitions and practical considerations applicable to life under the sun (e.g., Ephesians 4–6; Romans 12–15). Likewise, the first part of this work presents the basic premises, followed by elaborated processes and practical aspects of a covenantal nature.

Foreword

Dr. Polischuk has practiced for many years and found that, beyond psychodynamic and cognitive-behavioral approaches, a metacognitive-dialogical approach (metacognition: to know that we know, to process our processes) could better serve the psychological and relational needs of individuals and couples. While sharing encounters, he also observed that he found it necessary to redefine popular concepts that oversaturate the therapeutic panorama in our present culture, such as "mindfulness" and "spirituality"—reframing and reattributing meaning from a scripturally-based theological perspective without denying their psychological functionality. Mindfulness in this work appears as a sequential construct—detached first, and then purposive in nature: In our attempts to ward off and control the negative reactions that may destroy our fellowship and covenantal intimacy, the empowering of the Holy Spirit allows us as coparticipating humans to engage in a pensive fashion, and then helps us in the purposive, proactive employment of "feedforward" responses that in a superposed fashion allow the enactment of better responses to one another.

The purpose of this book is to provide a solid, basic foundation for the practice of metacognitive-dialogical therapy and counseling, as well as to offer enough information to pastoral counselors and providers of human services and ministry so that they may benefit from the accumulated and consolidated wisdom distilled in the pages of this presentation.

I have been a colleague of Dr. Polischuk in both clinical practice and teaching endeavors at Gordon-Conwell Theological Seminary for the past thirty-five years and see the value of this book, intended to educate, to teach, and to train both the novice and the experienced worker in the field of delivery of human services.

Ray Pendleton, PhD

Director, Masters in Arts in Counseling Program
Gordon-Conwell Theological Seminary

Preface

AT THE SOUTHERN TIP of South America—just above the Strait of Magellan, the islands of Tierra del Fuego and Isla de los Estados, and the treacherous waters around Cape Horn that shiver across the Drake Passage between them and the Larsen Ice Shelf that leads into the Antarctic—is a mountainous region of Argentina known as Patagonia. Here, high in the Andes Mountains, a lone condor, borne up by the power of its ten-foot wing spread, soared loftily from mountain peak to mountain peak; its flight, covering a vast distance, was seemingly effortless, as form and power coordinated in perfect synchronicity.

We viewed that flight in miniature, captured with a cell phone video by a mountain climber pausing on a neighboring peak to witness its splendor. That videographer is the author of this book: The Rev. Dr. Pablo Polischuk.

We think of the condor—form and power working fluidly together—when we think of the present book and the conference that led to our request to publish it with Wipf and Stock's House of Prisca and Aquila Series. Particularly, we think of Pablo Polischuk himself, rising to speak before a standing-room-only crowd at a conference against human trafficking and abuse at Gordon-Conwell Theological Seminary's spacious Alumni Hall and the remarkable response to his presentation.

The audience was comprised of professionals in the field and specialists in related fields—counselors and professors of counseling, as well as leaders of parachurch ministries addressing abuse, and pastors as well as seminarians working with churches partnering with professional, non-profit Christian, and secular organizations as well as the courts and official governmental agencies.

The list of speakers was impressive, informed, and very helpful to all of us working in a variety of ways with human abuse, and the presenters encompassed not only a list of noted counselors but, as well, anti-cult experts, specialists on addiction and addictive behavior, former victims, and among the latter, even a state senator revealing his own poignant ordeal of childhood abuse. The response to each session was fervent, and side conversations broke out everywhere throughout the day.

When Pablo Polischuk ascended the podium, the audience, many of whom were former students, but all of us aware of his expertise, immediately stilled. As we all had hoped, his presentation was astonishing. The only sound now was the clicking of computer keys and the scratching of pencils and pens.

Preface

Every speaker had opened up new avenues of thought for us, but what made his presentation so remarkable was the synergy as he carefully brought all the best of psychological principles, counseling techniques, and theological thought together, a model of action/reflection at its most insightful and effective.

We ourselves were there, not as fellow Gordon-Conwell professors, but because of our three decades of avocational volunteer work as co-founders of Pilgrim Church, a storefront ministry in Beverly, a city on Boston's north shore. Pilgrim's scope includes working with heroin addicts and alcoholics as well as husbands, wives, and children from domestic abuse-ridden households.

Having melded his many years of professional training, hands-on counseling practice, and theological expertise as a seminary professor into one coordinated and powerful presentation, Dr. Polischuk began to reveal his theologically-based approach to needs analysis and counseling for wholeness that was nothing less than astounding in its depth and clarity. He had synthesized all of his tested counseling techniques and his theological and psychological expertise into a set of explanatory charts that addressed foundationally every one of us in our concerns and our specialties. For us, personally, the entire conference came together as he took us carefully through the paradigm—and, judging by the thunderous applause when he closed, the whole scope of the conference came together for many others there as well.

A break was wisely scheduled, and he was mobbed with inquirers. We waited on the outskirts of the crowd, as he carefully invested his attention in each one who wanted to speak with him. We waited until the last one was satisfied, and then we told him how helpful his presentation had been and asked if he would consider publishing this helpful work with us.

The House of Prisca and Aquila series had already released two books from Peace and Safety in the Christian Home (PASCH), *Beyond Abuse in the Christian Home* and *Responding to Abuse in Christian Homes*; another from the director of Canada's the RAVE Project, *Strengthening Families and Ending Abuse*; and several other related books including a Bible study for abuse victims, a couple of books on enriching family life and relations, and a reflection on personal growth after abuse. But what Professor Polischuk had presented in his charts and explanations was clearly the missing element—a careful, sustained theological orientation to negotiating an understanding of the health and wholeness God intended for humanity since the beginning, what healthy human relations should look like now, what exactly the path is to God-centered wholeness, and how to know when we are journeying along it.

One caution: this book is not an "easy read" of pop-oriented psycho-speak and feel-good devotional texts, dumbed down to be perused while one is texting friends; it is an intriguing and engaging study chocked full of information and insight that will enrich and reward every reader who enters it. We think it is interesting enough and original enough and insightful enough to become a standard text for Christians of all denominational persuasions because it spans differences and centers in on the heart of the good news of Jesus the Reconciler applied in the most responsible way, while drawing from the best and most up-to-date of useful psychological theories and techniques and decades of his own active counseling practice. The Alumni Hall that day of the conference held practitioners from a variety of denominational and theological perspectives, but the audience united in its embracing of this healthy and clearly applicable paradigm. All of us seemed to realize it was an approach we need to embrace.

In John 10:10, Jesus contrasted himself with the thief who comes to rob, kill, and destroy—in this context, we might say, the abusing thief who robs our freedom, kills the hope that is within us, destroys our marital bond, and renders our family systems dysfunctional. But Jesus comes that we might have life and have it to the fullest degree. The clear message of the Bible from Genesis to Revelation is for all of us to seek that life now, while it is available to us. This message of God our Creator could easily be lifted out and applied to everyone working in the counseling field, whether a believer in Jesus or not yet one. And a serious means to achieve this goal is this ground-breaking book. It presents God's New Covenant—a scripturally derived, salvific, and exemplary model of relational transactions—as the optimal paradigm for healthy, functional relations applicable to marriage, the family, church, and community transactions. It will reward every moment one invests in it. We see it much like a GPS guiding us through pictures and words down the road to restoration, reconciled to God in faith and families through wholesome, life-enhancing living.

And now a critique of our opening paragraph: as a symbol, the condor is quite inadequate. It is, after all, a type of vulture—a bird of prey a lot like an eagle, despite its majestic flight above the stone mountains and stark plains of the rugged, near-arctic terrain. But, at the same time, it appears to us to be a kind of synecdoche, a representative part of the seemingly entirely impossible task of ministering to human abuse and trafficking victims by people who ourselves are products of a fallen world, trying to negotiate a landscape of the fallen minds of others where victim and victimizer are often one and the same.

Where the analogy might also hold is in the power and the beauty of the God-created strength in the bird as well as in ourselves, a power of coordinated control. The condor rises up and moves across the vastness between mountains because it has been gifted by God with the power to do so. But the power in Pablo Polischuk's paradigm has one further orienting gifting. It has been redeemed by God and can orient itself to the good. This is what makes the paradigm both enduring and life-enhancing—it is a top-down, encompassing, and metacognitive approach to perceive, assess, and enact our relational endeavors under the sun. His insightful system goes from strength to strength—from the application of the best of tested techniques of the artful science of psychology, but all of this enriched by the life-giving message of biblical, theological reflection that come together in a paradigm shaped by the accomplished hands of one who has mastered his craft under the guidance of the Great Master, the one who created not only his and our minds, but the minds of those to whom we hope to bring wholeness and end the cycle of self and others-directed abuse. That is why this book will illumine and equip you with an effective paradigm for understanding and application as it will do for every reader who takes this journey with him.

William David Spencer and Aída Besançon Spencer

Founders and Producers of the House of Prisca and Aquila Series

Acknowledgments

THIS BOOK HAS BEEN shaped and improved by the comments of those readers who take time to assess its content and provide feedback. In terms of its content, I have benefited from the comments, suggestions, and dialogical feedback of literally hundreds of students who have taken my courses (Introduction to Counseling, Marital Therapy, Cognitive Psychology, and Group Dynamics) at Gordon-Conwell Theological Seminary, The Israel College of the Bible in Netanya, and the Ostroh Academy National University in Ukraine. I have been conscious of the feedback provided by my theologically-minded faculty fellows at Gordon-Conwell who are experts in Old Testament, New Testament studies, Theology, and Ministry: Drs. Gary Pratico, Carol Kaminski, John Jefferson Davis, Roy Ciampa, and Raymond Pendleton, among others. I am grateful for the longstanding friendship and valuable feedback provided by Drs. H. Newton Malony and Siang Yang Tan, both from Fuller Theological Seminary, whose critically constructive minds have contributed to the revisions to the manuscript.

Throughout the years of the unfolding of the content of this book, several Byington Fellows at Gordon-Conwell, my research assistants, also contributed with their valuable dialogical interactions. Among such outstanding fellows, Cynthie Quarles Fisher, David Hovis, Rebekah Good, and Aaron Kook have my utmost gratitude for their supportive labors. I am grateful for the encouragement and feedback provided by Drs. Aída B. and William D. Spencer, the co-producers of the House of Prisca and Aquila Series of Wipf and Stock, Publishers, for their appraisal of this work and the invitation to publish it with this reputable institution. I express my deep-seated thanks to Jean Dimock and Esmé Bieberly, who served as editorial sounding boards for many of the stylistic and expressive decisions made as I worked on this book. I also owe a great debt to Frederick Lee, MD, PhD, who, in reviewing the manuscript, provided insightful and helpful suggestions.

Finally, I express my profound gratitude to my wife Frances, for her continuous encouragement, support, and exemplary covenantal faithfulness and love toward my person. The challenges posed to one's living out what one writes about have been graciously empowered by her graceful companionship and loving friendship.

Introduction

COVENANT IS A BIBLICAL theme that runs throughout the pages of God's Word. The terms *testament* and *covenant* are synonymous, and in this work, the New Covenant is adopted as a paradigm—first and foremost, it is regarded as God's redemptive design that is both continuous with and surpassing the Old Covenant in its actualizing power and results. In analogical and exemplary terms, the New Covenant conveys a binding alliance and exudes a relational thrust of a loving nature, and as such, serves as an example to be imitated by God's "dearly beloved children" (Eph 5:1–2), who are engaged in committed, intimate, and accountable relations with one another. Both marriage and the community of believers in the body of Christ—the *ecclesia*—are defined in Scripture as being representative of such committed relations.

A number of scholars have sought to apply covenantal constructs to marriage derived from Scripture.[1] Covenant as an elected—not natural—relationship has been adequately proposed as a comparative basis for the covenantal nature of marriage derived from the Old Testament.[2] Others have employed theological reasoning to assert a notion that presents Christian marriage as a covenantal union before God.[3]

A HIGH CALL: TO IMITATE GOD'S WAYS

The premises underlying the content of this work may be framed in the promise of a New Covenant found in Jeremiah 31, which are interpreted and applied in the letter to the Hebrews (chapters 8, 10). In addition, the Pauline admonition found in his letter to the Ephesians (5:1–2) provides a logical sequel to the promise given as it pertains to the enactment of covenantal terms. As dearly beloved children, believers are admonished to imitate the Father's ways and walk (live) in love. Yet, human attempts to imitate God encounter a big challenge: the enormous gap that exists between the ontological character, functional capacity, and enactive power of God and his creatures renders the fulfilling of this command an insurmountable task for humans to accomplish.

---

1. See, for example, Palmer, "Christian Marriage"; Dunstan, "The Marriage Covenant"; Atkinson, *Caring Enough*; Westcott, *The Concept of Berit*; Hugenberger, *Marriage as a Covenant*.

2. Hugenberger, *Marriage as a Covenant*.

3. See, for example, Palmer, "Christian Marriage"; Dunstan, "The Marriage Covenant"; Atkinson, *Caring Enough*.

Introduction

The transcendent God has chosen to relate to humans in his immanent terms. Yet, the fact that God has chosen to reveal his name and relate to his creatures in this fashion does not give humans the power to ultimately define or categorize his essence. His presence, power, and mysterious ways of transacting are difficult to systematize into categories. The depths of the riches, wisdom, and knowledge of God's judgments, designs, and ways remain inscrutable (Rom 11:33). Consider Paul's prayer for the Ephesians, in which the apostle requests that God may give them the Spirit of wisdom and of revelation in their growing knowledge of Christ so that they may know also what is the hope of their calling, the wealth of their inheritance, and the incomparable power of God acting on their behalf (Eph 1:17–19). The apostle reminded them that they have been treated with a unilateral and unconditional grace dispensed proactively so that they would experience a metacognitive-spiritual enlightenment. Having been empowered by the opening of "the eyes of their hearts," they were now able to have a better glimpse of God's overarching revelation and purpose (Eph 1:17–23).

To our benefit, an incarnated version is available. A supporting, exemplary premise is embedded in the Ephesian text: believers may imitate God and walk in love "as Christ loved the church and gave himself for her" (Eph 5:25). If the divine prototype seems out of reach for struggling humans, Paul offers himself as a concrete model to the Corinthians, worthy of imitation: "Be imitators of me, just as I also am of Christ" (1 Cor 11:1).

METACOGNITION: ADOPTING A HIGHER PERSPECTIVE

Readers are invited to become mindfully aware and consider their covenantal relations in a metacognitive fashion. This book seeks to integrate a theological and psychological basis for living "in God's sight" and patterned after God's terms. It aims to encourage ministers, therapists, and providers of human services in their endeavors with individuals, partners in marriage, family members, and members of a community. It seeks to stir up the metacognitive and dialogical aspects of readers' lives, encouraging their mindful awareness of the interpersonal transactions and processes involved in covenantal deals.

The paradigm derived from the interpretation of the New Covenant as both a salvific design and a relational, exemplary model is better understood if a metacognitive stance—a "higher" perspective—is adopted. Readers are invited to consider a transcending theological view, in which God relates to the human in an encompassing fashion. In this "architectural" perspective, humans are embedded in a thoughtful project that started before the foundation of the world. In such a design, God has envisioned and "preformed" the human according to a prototype—the measure of the stature of the fullness of Christ. In chronological time, the human was formed in the image of God. Due to the fall into sin, the human was deformed—rendered a sinner, depraved and dysfunctional. In a fallen condition, the human needed a redemptive plan designed to re-form what sin had deformed. The re-formed human is then invited to engage in a transforming process by means of the renewal of the mind, which enables the realignment of human character, conduct, and relations with God's eternal purpose. The process of transformation is also guided by the divine thrust that seeks to conform the redeemed human to the image of the prototype—Jesus Christ.

The metacognitive paradigm also invites readers to adopt a higher, detached mindfulness—to engage in thinking about their thinking and to process objectively their subjective processes. As they receive the empowering of God's Spirit, believers are encouraged to engage in purposeful mindfulness as well in order to actualize their empowered capacity to imitate God's ways of transacting in a covenantal fashion.

From a basic *trivial* level (natural, ordinary, or empirical), the challenge to proceed toward a more *translated* or *transduced* level is posed. To transduce is to process reality beyond its trivial impact—a transducer is a device that converts variations in a concrete physical entity into a meaningful signal—in order to derive a more insightful perspective and convey a more meaningful picture. A metacognitive paradigm emphasizes the need to perceive, assess, and appraise reality "from the top" (activating an executive agent at work) in order to be objective about our subjective states. Furthermore, a renewed mindset may engage in a purposive and mindful way—being able to *transform* sensations, perceptions, thinking, reasoning, and feelings into a more adequate assessment, perception, and attribution of meaning to experienced events.

The metacognitive-dialogical emphasis of this work aims at going "deeper" or "higher" in order to delve into and capture more tacit or subconscious levels of processing thoughts, feelings, and behaviors. The term *subconscious* in psychoanalytical language may be translated or reframed as "super-conscious" in cognitive science terms. In analysis, a person engages in introspective musings and deliberations, scrutinizing deep-seated values and attitudes, motivations, and reasons underlying overt behaviors. In cognitive terms, such a process is observed with detached or purposeful mindfulness, as if "from the top," in attempts to be objective about one's subjective states.

A BASIC ADHERENCE TO SCRIPTURE AS TRUTH

Typically, scientists and investigators (bottom-up processors) have followed an empirically-based Aristotelian logic and philosophy (e.g., the British empiricists Locke, Berkeley, and Mill, among many others). Psychologists such as Skinner, Watson, and other behaviorists belong to such club. For these thinkers, the source of knowledge (epistemology) resided in the observable data of the world at large. On the other hand, psychologists such as Rogers, May, Allport, Maslow, and other humanists or existential thinkers followed top-down perspectives proposed by Plato, Kant, and Leibnitz, among others. These thinkers gave credit to the innate human potential to unravel truth, providing the basis for humanistic and existential renderings of diverse "truths."

In a postmodern world, scientists have recognized their own tacit or "personal knowledge" derived from a sort of top-down executive agency at work while doing research, as Polanyi has pointed out.[4] Furthermore, a metaphysical core comprised of beliefs and assumptions has been postulated as residing at the central agency of a person's cognitive processing. This core is surrounded with what Lakatos has called a "protective belt" comprised of cognitive processes and maneuvers that safeguard the assumptions held in the lodged, consolidated metanarratives.[5] The old term *objectivity* has been replaced with a new construct: an exercise in inter-subjectivity. Thus, diverse truths emerge from a socially mediated, participatory hermeneutics that guides the process of scrutiny and the interpretation of the reality being observed. In a metacognitive fashion, scientists may personally recognize the fact that their tacit assumptions emerge from top-down processes, while at the same time they attempt to remain committed to their bottom-up endeavors.

As a respected researcher at Harvard, Howard Gardner has written several books on the subject of truth, ethics, and moral aspects. In his work *Truth, Beauty, and Goodness Reframed*, he advocates the adoption of "truths" as defined in pluralistic terms.[6] According to this postmodern philosophical position, your truth is not necessarily my truth, as we may each start from different epistemological, ontological, and teleological bases. From a theological perspective, and in accordance with an evangelical position, truth is essentially one and ultimately resides in the source of truth, the Lord. In sum, in a postmodern world there is *no place for truth* even in some theological circles.[7] It is necessary and essential to define what truth is in God's terms, and what is worthy of being borrowed from secular veins before we apply or amalgamate it wisely, so as to differentiate it from error.

In the academic communities among evangelicals in the USA (the author is writing as a person embedded in an evangelical community), a conscious effort is made to regard the top-down propositions derived from Scripture as a truthful and reliable basis. At the same time, the academic aim is to engage in bottom-up processes characterized by the painstaking gathering of exegetical, historical, contextual, cultural, and evidential data in attempts to arrive at a fair interpretation of Scripture. In doing so, faithfulness in adhering to the bottom-up processes that try to elucidate, corroborate, enhance, and render more applicable the truth processed in top-down fashion is not just commendable but also essential.

In this book, the paradigm derived from a new covenant promised by God starts at the top, as a God-given design and prerogative. This expressed will is exemplified

---

4. Polanyi, *Personal Knowledge*.
5. Lakatos, "Falsification," 192–94.
6. Gardner, *Truth, Beauty, and Goodness Reframed*.
7. Wells, *God in the Wasteland*.

in God's relational terms, applicable to concrete situations in marriage, family, and community. Yet, although the New Covenant is presented as a paradigm derived from top-down considerations, it needs to be understood in all its ramifications, applicability, and consequences from a concrete, practical, and empirically ascertained experience. Relational processes are observed in therapeutic and helping situations in which the collection of data, the gathering of complaints, the allowance of expressions of concrete pain, suffering, breakdowns, abuses, and dysfunctions, etc., represent bits and pieces to be assessed and interpreted in order to establish a proper intervention. As such, the participant-observer capacities of the pastor, mediator, counselor, or therapist enter with both top-down and bottom-up processes that may lead to an integrated, abstracted, and applicable paradigm.

A metacognitive function is essential in order to be aware of one's cultural bias, cognitive filters, and personal predispositions in approaching subject matter. It is essentially important to be consciously aware of one's own theological premises, values, and practices. Awareness of the ontological and epistemological variables that come into play in research and writing allows for more fairness in the pursuit of truth. Having a sense of one's own tendencies and self-confirmatory biases helps in the process of adopting a fair and open learning stance. That stance is at the core of treating one another with respect and dignity--along social strata, cultural, gender, and situational contingencies.

Such a point of view is coupled with a personal response to God's summoning call in faith and obedience. The awareness, recognition, and impact of God's presence cannot be taken lightly but must be experienced with awe and respect. In order to depart from a top-down process, the therapist, pastor, or mediator by necessity has to metacognitively define his or her bases, premises, tacit understanding of reality, and personal faith in God that seem to qualify all statements, assertions, interpretations, and counsel.

AN OVERVIEW OF THE BOOK

Scripture is the epistemological basis (the source of our knowledge) from which theological postulates and principles are derived. Their proper place is stressed in the first chapter, and the whole book appeals to them--either by quoting them directly or referencing them in principled ways, drawing upon the spirit of the letter. Covenant as a construct appears to be an overarching theme in Scripture, and God's diverse ways of transacting with humans are addressed. The second chapter deals with these ways, providing a relational paradigm. The Old Covenant is set forth in chapter 3 as a preamble to greater things to be revealed, or as a *pedagogos* leading us to consider even better ways of imitating God's redemptive actions. Then, the New Covenant is presented in chapter 4 as the fulfillment of previous covenants, with a superior mediator perfecting our redemption from sin. Such a covenant is set forth as the paradigm

Introduction

for optimal relations between God and humans as well as humans in transactions with one another.

The primary aspect of the New Covenant being stressed is its redemptive nature. Then, in view of God's ways of accomplishing this redemption, the New Covenant is presented as an exemplary paradigm of the Father's ways of relating. It provides a foundational basis for establishing the criteria and the principles of operation applicable to believers transacting in marital and family relations. Of all human transactions, marriage is viewed as a particular covenant, stressed in chapter 5. Readers are reminded that the church at large is seen as the overarching and encompassing context of this particular unit, as well as singles, widows, and any believer without sanguineous or legal ties to a significant other. The community of believers is regarded as the object of God's love and of Christ's redemptive work, being empowered now by the person, presence, and power of the Holy Spirit.

A *quid pro quo* ("this for that") paradigm is offered in chapter 6, as a contract-type deal modeled after the Old Covenant. This deal serves as a preamble to the New Covenant––made in the Spirit––as a better, actualized deal coming from God to humans, described in chapter 7. Chapters 8 through 15 disclose the terms of the New Covenant as topics encompassed in the chapters' headings. God's actions toward us are framed in these covenantal terms: proactive, empowering, unilateral, unconditional, graceful, merciful, intimate, forgiving, and renewing. As dearly beloved children and imitators of God, we who attempt to follow the example of the Son who gave himself for us may learn from such ways and apply them in practical terms. Our marriages, families, and transactions at large may profit from such imitative behaviors. As living systems, marital relations as well as families tend to stagnate, decay, or die unless they are replenished with life-giving elements.

Chapter 16 stresses the need for mind-renewal as a covenantal way of life that allows relations to remain vibrant, alive, and satisfying. To conclude the treatment of the subject matter, chapter 17 presents a metacognitive-dialogical model, applicable to the process of forgiveness and the letting go of offenses. The model delineates componential aspects of the trivial-transduced-translated-transformed processes, synthesized into a whole configuration that represents a hyper-abstracted, metacognitive, and encompassing panoramic view of a Spirit-empowered forgiving process. Partners in relationship are encouraged to be empowered and transform automatic reactions provoked in challenging transactions into mindful and mature responses toward the other. Also, partners are encouraged to be proactive rather than reactive––capable of engaging in unconditional and unilateral dealings without being codependent, enabling, or perceived as weak in character. Partners are encouraged to show grace, mercy, and loving care to each other, transacting from a higher perspective and empowered by the Holy Spirit. The reader is invited to explore the inner workings of the mind that enters into such transactions so as to develop a higher perspective.

In sum, this work represents an abstracted and principled integration between theological and psychological disciplines intended to contribute to the field of human services. Relations in marriage, the family, and the Christian community may benefit from following the patterns proposed in scriptural terms, interpreted theologically, and applied practically in covenantal transactions. It is hoped that providers of human services as well as those in ministry will benefit from the content of this book.

Part I: Premises and Principles

Chapter 1

Biblical Anthropology and Covenantal Relations

THE BIBLICAL-THEOLOGICAL PREMISES THAT underlie the main theme of this book are derived from the New Covenant, regarded as a new, actualizing, and empowering paradigm for optimal relations in marriage and the body of Christ--the ecclesia. Thus, rather than focusing on the political emphasis placed upon covenant as a treaty-document, or its possible cultic dimensions, a relational emphasis is proposed. To that end, marriage, as a relational bond of an accountable, faithful, and loving nature, is framed in biblical anthropology in contrast to secular versions registered in a postmodern world. The sufficiency of Scripture guiding the integration of clinical research and practice is also stressed, with integrative efforts appealing to clinical research and practice.

The approach utilized in this work regards Scripture as the basis from which God's revealed truth is extracted and interpreted. Theological principles derived from such processes are integrated to psychological thought, applicable to the counseling field. Three lines of reasoning underlie such considerations: epistemology (the sources of our knowledge, propositionally revealed truth and empirical research), ontology (the essence or substance of things being investigated), and teleology (the purposive sense of direction). The historical, cultural, and contextual aspects of revealed truth represent the contextual basis to be applied in deriving principles applicable to counseling, psychotherapeutic, and ministerial endeavors.

A Trinitarian emphasis encompasses the relational nature of being a human who is created in the image of God. The relational nature of the Trinity—Father, Son, and Holy Spirit—engaged in eternal *perichoresis* (dancing together within a perimeter) and, existing in hypostatic-ecstatic union (three persons in loving affinity), guides the relational aspects of partners in a marriage covenant. Partners are joined in his presence, live under his authority, and are ultimately accountable to God for how they conduct their covenantal stewardship. Partners are invited to imitate God's loving ways, expressed in the terms of the New Covenant and exemplified in the ways in which Christ gave himself for the object of his love.

At the core, an analysis of human interactions starts with focusing on each interlocutor as a transacting person endowed with some values, attitudes, capacities, and processes of a cognitive and emotional nature. Scripture is taken as the source of data that guides the approach to the relational aspects defining intimate relations. The ontological aspect of a marital relation (the essential basis) and its teleological dimension (its purposive sense of direction) are encompassed in an overarching, metacognitive point of view.

A person enters a covenantal relationship with a counterpart: Is this human being an autonomous agent, devoid of consequential aspects related to life under the sun, or a created being subject to an ultimate source of accountability? This question is important in view of the premises of this work that regard the human as God's dearly beloved child—created, redeemed, and transformed so as to follow after the Father's ways, walking in love. The human is defined as a potential member of God's household, a covenantal partner treated with love, grace, and mercy by an all-powerful God, who introduces his children to a covenantal community and desires the best for them.

As it pertains to covenantal deals, the essential dimensions and purposeful aims of a marital system may be ascertained in terms of the nature of the relationship, the essential character qualities of its parties, the styles of transacting, and the functional value of relating on this basis.

A HIGHER VIEW OF HUMAN NATURE: BIBLICAL ANTHROPOLOGY

This book deals with a relational paradigm and begins by exploring the person as a relational being, a partner engaged in covenantal transactions. A top-down approach endowed with a high view of Scripture defines the human being as created, fallen, and redeemed. Most evangelicals, whether Reformed or Dispensationalist, view the ontology of being human as a creature made in the image of God (*Tselem Elohim*), but in need of redemption due to the fall into sin. Such a natural and negative condition necessitates a transformation in order to fit again into God's eternal purpose and design. Theologies adopting a more liberal stance regard human nature as being neutral or even positive—able to be resocialized, shaped, or adjusted to a positive norm by means of social, educational, or therapeutic endeavors. Many authors have addressed the complexity of what human nature, created after God's image, is all about. The available patristic and reformation literatures, as well as the writings of modern and current theologians, reflect a diversity of opinions on the topic.[1] The stances adopted by the author of this book are set forth in this chapter.

An encompassing perspective on being human is set forth. The reader is invited to step back in time and join God's unfolding plan from eternity to eternity, framed in the context of chronological time and observed from a "higher" perspective. A

---

1. See, for example, Anderson, *On Being Human*; Barth, *Church Dogmatics*; Buber, *Between Man and Man*; Cook and Lee, *Man and Woman*; Grenz, *The Social God*; Grudem, *Biblical Foundations*; Gruenler, *The Trinity*; Panneberg, *Anthropology*; Van Leeuwen, *The Person in Psychology*; *Gender and Grace*; Zizioulas, "Human Capacity."

metacognitive, theological design rendered in a top-down metanarrative is presented here. The synthesized theology running through this work presents several propositions and tenets.

1. *The preformed human.* The human being has been regarded as an object of anthropological, sociological, and psychological study. To these domains, a theological premise is added: the human has been *preformed* "in God's mind" even before the foundation of the world (Eph 1:3–14). Pauline theology points to the notion that God unraveled a mystery and disclosed enough of his design to provide us with a glimpse of his will and purpose; that is, as a designing architect, God had the human in mind before he created the heavens and the Earth. Scripture alludes to Jesus as the Lamb of God, immolated before the foundation of the world (Rev 13:8). Because this event would take place in order to deal with human sin, it follows that sinful humans were proactively included in the design. It was because of sinful humankind that the redemptive event at the cross would take place in due time and at a given place.

    We may muse over the fact that if both the human and the cross were in God's mind and purpose before creation, then Adam may have been patterned after the eternally existing, yet-to-be-incarnated Son. After all, God's mind is not subject to, contingent upon, or restricted by time (past, present, or future). Moreover, Jesus is actually postulated as being the perfect measure of man (generic humankind, as in Eph 4:13). Paul designates Jesus as the "last Adam" and the "second man" (1 Cor 15:45) to emphasize the summing-up and ending-up of the temporal existence of sinful humankind and to introduce the beginning of a new creation. As redeemed creatures, we aspire to grow unto him, to the stature of the perfect prototype (Eph 4:13).

2. *The formed human.* God the creator, redeemer, and sustainer of his created order is the master architect of the universe. God is the designer of all human existence under the sun: its essence, its structural dimensions, its administrative functions—as well as its relatedness to God, fellow creatures, and the cosmos at large. God has chosen to relate in immanent fashion, providing essential and sufficient glimpses of his revealed will and purpose. In God's time and purpose, the human was created after the image of God (*him*, Gen 1:26–27), formed from dust (Gen 2:7), sharing the elements of the created order, and placed at the pinnacle of the created world as a steward of God's domain.

    The creature made in the *Tselem Elohim* is postulated in this work as an embodied reflection of God, endowed with ontological (substantial, essential) potentials resembling those of the creator. Also, this image is grounded in God—a Trinity who is eternally related in hypostatic-ecstatic union (three persons in loving fellowship) and capable of relating in *perichoresis* (dancing together within a defining perimeter) with other fellow humans. Partners in a covenantal relationship may engage in dialogue with God, with each other, and with themselves. They may engage their inner being (a sort of top-down, executive function) in metacognitive ways in order to monitor, assess, and regulate their internal deliberations.

The dialogical-rhetorical self is a major idea in this work, integrated to the research and theoretical musings of psychologists and philosophers.[2] Internal dialogues may assume diverse aspects (e.g., deliberations, rumination, conjectural musings), coupled with internal rhetoric (e.g., self-persuasion, choice-based decisive commands). Both aspects are seen as capacities of the human made in God's image. The dialogical-rhetorical self is presented as a key feature embedded in the capacity to imitate God along proactive, unilateral, and unconditional endeavors, regarded as essential dimensions in covenantal relationships.

Relational humans, who have much in common with the sixth-day created order, were invited to participate in intimate fellowship with God on the seventh day. They are endowed with capacities to serve as administrators of the created order and to exercise a faithful stewardship of God's domain (Gen 2:15–20). A covenant—made with Adam and Eve in the garden (Gen 2:21–25) and ratified after their fall into sin (Gen 3:8–21)—points to a qualified relational bond between God and his creatures, as well as among the creatures themselves. The *verbia solemnia* (solemn oath) implicit in the statement "bone of my bone, flesh of my flesh" may be taken as a covenant-binding element in the presence of an officiating God (Gal 2:23).

3. *The deformed human.* The first couple was not able to stay within God's stipulations and disobeyed his will by doing their own will. Yet, God treated the disobedient and fallen couple with grace and mercy and covered them with the skin of a sacrificed animal. Such a redemptive and restorative cover signified a covenantal renewal after the fall into sin. Thus, the qualification of God's definition of an original covenant is reflected in an ontological design conveying intention, purpose, and will in establishing couples, families, and communities as the text unfolds. The *Tselem Elohim* is reflected in both substantial (ontological, essential) and relational aspects of being human: being and behaving in God's will, able to relate, communicate, love, and engage in functional transactions so as to fulfill a design. Such a design included several clauses: to propagate, socialize, fill the Earth, enjoy fellowship, exert administrative functions, and the like.

Due to their disobedience to God's will, humans experienced a distortion in the original design, becoming *deformed* at the ontological, as well as at the relational or transactional, level (Gen 3). Such a deformed state may be postulated as the ground for dysfunction and pathology, framed in biological terms (e.g.,

---

2. See Hermans, "The Dialogical Self"; "Voicing the Self"; Polischuk, "Perspectives on the Self"; "A Metacognitive Perspective"; Nienkamp, *Internal Rhetorics*.

physical, physiological, biochemical, neurobiological variables) and psychological processes (cognitive, emotive, motivational, and behavioral variables). Negative dialogues (distorted, intropunitive, depressive, anxious in nature) and faulty internal rhetoric (distorted, equivocal self-persuasion) add to the fallen human incapacity to be and to do what God desires.

4. *The informed human.* After the Fall, humans were *informed* of both their sinful state, as well as the possibility of salvation from sin, when God provided them with a redemptive promise (Gen 3:15). The grace and mercy of God did not leave humans abandoned or out of the realm of redemption; instead, they became the targets of God's love in spite of sin. The *informed* aspects of God's revelation and propositions, cast into a redemptive plan, involved the call of Abraham and the establishment of the nation of Israel through whom a savior would come to redeem humankind. God established a covenant with Abraham of extended proportions (Gen 15) and long-lasting effects.

   Such an informed aspect was further exemplified in the giving of the law, codified in tablets of stone via Moses, the mediator of a covenant made with Israel. The Old Covenant was a bilateral-conditional deal in which God and Israel established a special relationship based upon God's prerogatives and commandments for life. This covenant would act as a preamble to new things to come in God's eternal plan disclosed in time.

5. *The reformed human.* In due time, the redemptive promise was fulfilled in the coming of the Son, who, in a unilateral, unconditional, and proactive fashion, provided the basis for human restoration to fellowship with God. The mediator of the New Covenant worked out the redemption of humankind at the cross. Jesus substituted, propitiated, atoned for, and redeemed humans, establishing peace between them and God. Jesus Christ is the "last Adam" (the sum total of fallen humankind) and the "second Man" (the prototype of a new humankind) who established the basis and means by which repentant humans now have the opportunity to be *reformed* (reborn, regenerated) by believing and appropriating Jesus's redeeming work by faith (Rom 3—6). The mediator of the New Covenant, in unity with the Father and the Holy Spirit, has acted in grace and mercy displayed in multiform fashion (unilateral, unconditional, proactive, forgiving, forgetting, empowering, and restorative of a believer's intimacy with God). This manner of love and works represents the redemptive basis for transactions to be exemplarily grasped, enacted, and followed by God's beloved children.

6. *The human as transformed being.* Believers empowered by the Holy Spirit may, through faith and obedience, be *transformed* and resocialized at the core. They are radically changed at the ontological (characterological) level by means of the renewing of their minds and engage in a constant growth process known

as *sanctification* (Rom 6:1–23; 12:1–2). The internal dialogues and rhetoric of redeemed humans receive the input of the Holy Spirit, being empowered along a constant process of alignment, refinement, and faith-based perspective grounded in God's will.

7. *The human being conformed to Jesus Christ.* As believers proceed along their journey, fixing their eyes upon the author and finisher of their faith (Heb 13:1–2), they are shaped by God's grace and power, being subject to vicissitudes and contingencies so as to be *conformed* to the *Tselem Elohim* again. Jesus Christ is set as the prototype of their faith, character, and conduct. God works through and optimizes all contingencies in the process of conforming the believer to the image of his Son. As a supreme sculptor, God chips away the excessive stuff from the block of marble in order to shape his work of art. As a potter, he also adds on the necessary stuff and molds it so the masterpiece is shaped according to his ultimate model: Jesus Christ, the prototype of faith and conduct.

8. *The human glorified.* Finally, the human is glorified (ἐδόξασεν: edoxasen = given proper honor, glory) and provided with an eternal habitat in order to enjoy God and his presence forever (Rom 8:28–30).

Such a basic theological design represents the encompassing context for our specific theme, presenting the premises that underlie all relational considerations between the creator God and his creatures—and between creatures engaged in interpersonal transactions. Made in the image of God, humans may reflect the endowments, attributes, and capacities of the Maker or exude properties of an ontological and relational nature, regardless of the distortions caused by sin. This actualizing capacity is empowered through the salvific work of Jesus Christ and the ministry of the Holy Spirit, accepted by faith and lived out in obedience. An illustration may serve the purpose of encapsulating this biblical anthropology.

Biblical Anthropology and Covenantal Relations

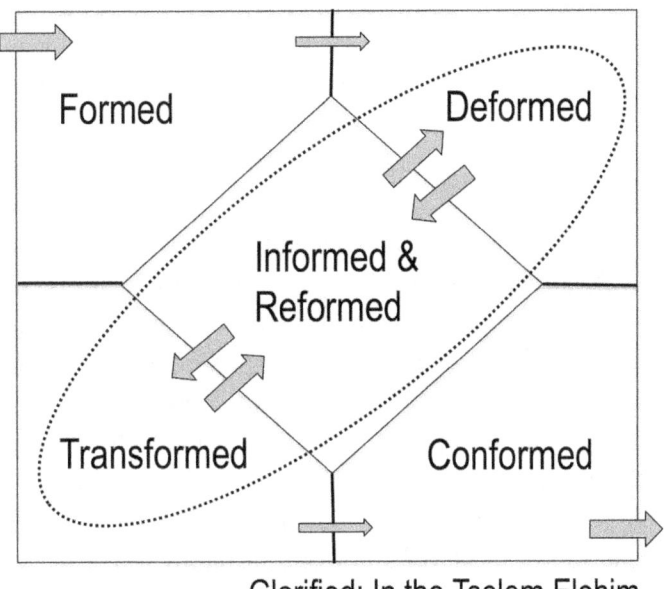

Fig. 1.1: The Human Being in God's Master Design

Putting it all together. The puzzle represents the diverse aspects of God's definition of who the human being is in a larger context of revealed truth. Starting with a proactive plan before the present *aion* (lapse, era, or chronological time), God works at creation, forming the human. The human then falls into sin and experiences the consequences, becoming a deformed being (that is, distorted and dysfunctional as compared to the original design). Proceeding with redemptive acts, God culminates his work (Eph 2:10) in transforming and then conforming the human to the image of the Son (Rom 8:28–30). The end of the story presents the human being as glorified in the next *aion*.

The arrows inside the oval boundary stretch diagonally over three pieces, indicating the ongoing feedback loops engaged by the reformed self in the here and now. These represent the internal dialogues and rhetoric occurring within the self, acting as a top-down executive agency mediating between the deformed self (sinful nature pulling back) and the reformed self (regenerate nature pulling forward). The inner struggles of the self may be seen as being prompted, pulled, and influenced by both sides: the base, sinful, or carnal nature on the one side and the regenerated, empowered, and spiritual nature on the other. Whatever the dialogical self decides in coparticipation with either the flesh or Spirit has consequences in the sight of God.

The notion of a reformed self engaging in internal dialogue appears in Pauline theology in the context of his letter to the Romans; the contrast is presented as "living according to the flesh" (having an outlook shaped by the things of the flesh) versus "living according to the Spirit" (having a perspective shaped by the Spirit) (Rom 8:5–13). The internal deliberations of the reformed self—mediating the internal struggles taking place between the deformed self and the transforming self—may be compared to the textual connotations drawn from Romans 7:7–25. The apostle Paul's shift from a deliberating dialogue to a persuasive rhetoric is noted in verses 24–25: "Wretched man that I am!" Who will rescue me from this body of death? Thanks be to God through Jesus our Lord!"

Made in the image of God humans are endowed with relational capacities. The image of God in the human has been emphasized in substantial terms. The relational definition needs to be stressed as well, for it represents a basic assumption of analogical proportions applicable to human relations.[3] The Godhead (Father, Son, and Holy Spirit) is eternally related in love. Such unity in love is described as a *hypostatic-ecstatic* fellowship (*hypostasis*: substructure, underlying substance, a fundamental reality that supports all that is placed upon; *ek-stasis*: to be or to stand outside oneself, to decenter and move toward the target of one's love) that is engaged in *perichoresis* (*peri*: around or perimeter; and *choresis*: derived from choreography; the term denotes a dance within a perimeter or boundary). The ontological quality of being human reflects or exudes God's relational property. Students interested in the notion of the social nature of the Trinity may consult the works of theologians such as Grenz and Gruenler, among others.[4]

SECULAR NOTIONS OF RELATIONAL TRANSACTIONS

Diverse theories have emerged in the secular field of investigation as it pertains to the nature of being human. From a negative viewpoint, theories have shifted to a neutral position and have finally supplied a more positive perspective. Couples and family therapy followed along such avenues as well. A systematic review of the field of marital and family therapy (MFT) reveals that over twenty diverse systemic therapies have been developed to help distressed couples and families.[5] Most, if not all, therapies derived their existence from bottom-up approaches that attempt to empirically observe, measure, and test hypotheses, as well as develop theories and strategies to be utilized in practice. These therapies were summarized and described by several authors.[6] Interested readers may consult such meta-analytical renderings. The following approaches are presented as examples of the vast domain:

3. Zizioulas, "Human Capacity"; Gruenler, *The Trinity*.
4. Grenz, *The Social God*; Gruenler, *The Trinity*.
5. Tan, *Counseling and Psychotherapy*.
6. See, for example, Goldenberg and Goldenberg, *Family Therapy*; Sells and Yarhouse, *Counseling Couples*; Tan, *Counseling and Psychotherapy*.

- Psychodynamic, Object Relations therapy.[7] This approach may serve as an insightful and foundational perception to have in mind when dealing with issues of the past that impinge upon the dynamics of partners in discord or among family members manifesting dysfunctional patterns springing from unresolved issues;

- Experiential therapy.[8] This approach is really a meta-theoretical take on couples or family work as it delves into the ongoing existential dilemmas—focusing on issues, interpersonal communication, and problematic situations as partners and family members experience them;

- Systemic, Transgenerational therapies.[9] This is a basic take on systems in general and sub-systems in particular, of interest to those who prefer to adopt a meta-cognitive, global stance and approach couples and families as systemic entities to be understood and changed in order to enable their components to develop a contextual perspective, to alter some structures or processes, and to adopt new patterns of a more functional nature;

- Structural therapy.[10] This approach may serve as a functional mapping of systems, allowing for an understanding of how family configurations become dysfunctional and what strategic rearrangements in structures, processes, and functions would have to occur in order to render them more functional;

- Strategic therapy.[11] This approach may be functional in concrete situations dealing with present-day problems, as it focuses on overt behaviors in need of strategies that achieve concrete solutions in a short amount of time;

- Cognitive-behavioral therapy (CBT).[12] These therapies emphasize contracts between marital partners and family members—a relevant topic of interest to this work; these approaches help to operationalize the themes, complaints, and needs of marital partners and family members in discord, casting them in concrete terms, such as antecedents, frequency, intensity, duration, and consequences of behavioral excesses and deficits, and seeking to establish functional *quid pro quo* exchanges of an interpersonal nature;

- Solution-focused therapy.[13] These therapies also emphasize the practical side of covenantal transactions in need of some intervention; they are geared toward

---

7. Scharff and Scharff, *Object Relations Couple Therapy*.
8. Whitaker, *Midnight Musings*; Satir et al, "Family Reconstruction."
9. See Bowen, *Family Therapy*; Boszormenyi-Nagy and Krasner, *Between Give and Take*; Selvini-Palazzoli et al., *Paradox and Counterparadox*.
10. Minuchin, *Families and Family Therapy*.
11. Haley, *Strategies of Psychotherapy*; *Problem-Solving Therapy*.
12. Jacobson and Margolin, *Marital Therapy*; Stuart, *Helping Couples Change*.
13. Berg, *Family Based Services*; de Shazer, *Clues*; De Jong and Berg, *Interviewing for Solutions*.

concrete solutions more than they delve into the past or attend analytically to dynamics in the present;

- Emotion-focused therapy.[14] This approach has served as a corrective measure to the cognitive emphasis that dominated the field for a while; the addition of emotions to the repertoire of therapeutic concerns may be considered as a parallel emphasis to be displayed in theological circles: to add passion and feeling to the cognitive theorizing—an essential component of the basis for covenantal transactions.
- Narrative therapy.[15] These approaches may be functional in considering the personal narratives of partners engaged in covenantal transactions framed in marriage and family systems, as "every saint has a past and every sinner has a future" to be narrated, elucidated, or changed.

Space limitations do not allow for a thorough treatment and appraisal of such therapies. These approaches differ regarding the nature of the human being in relation to self and to others. The psychodynamic approach, including object relations theory, holds a negative perspective on the nature of human beings, who are subject to unconscious forces and behave on hedonistic principles, while avoiding the experience of pain. Systemic approaches regard the transacting humans as persons who developed in a context marked by circular causality, interdependence, and intergenerational transmission of relational patterns, coalitions, triangulations, and the like. Both negative and positive aspects are taken into account, with some leanings toward a pessimistic view that fosters dysfunctions in these systems.

Cognitive-behavioral approaches regard human nature as being neutral or positively endowed and capable of change under some guidance and direction. More recent approaches to MFT appeal to established systemic notions, adding positive perspectives to their views on human nature. Human beings are seen as capable of exercising choice—able to change, engage in creative-problem solving, and search for meaning. Narrative approaches emphasize the change in the accounts of negative, oppressive, and problem-focused stories. Their aim is to empower partners and family members so that they may be able to rewrite such stories in a more constructive way. In doing so, marriage partners and family members may create more positive scripts to live by.

This author adopts both positive and negative aspects to characterize human beings, corresponding to the creation of the *Imago Dei* (Latin for *Tselem Elohim*), who are fallen into sin and then are redeemed and empowered to regain the original design of God. Thus, the approach originates from a top-down perspective, based upon God's revelation and apprehended by means of human endeavors such as exegesis,

---

14. Greenberg and Johnson, *Emotionally Focused Therapy for Couples*; Palmer and Efron, "Emotionally Focused Family Therapy"; Jones, "Emotionally Focused Therapy."

15. Monk et al., *Narrative Therapy in Practice*; White, *Maps of Narrative Practice*.

Biblical Anthropology and Covenantal Relations

hermeneutics, and attribution of meaning (bottom-up processes of an investigative nature). These deductive-inductive efforts are finally systematized into theological and psychological renderings that may serve as contributors to the development of approaches and strategies in therapy, counseling, and guidance.

From a systemic point of view, mutuality and differentiation in couples and families offer an interesting complementarity along structural and functional endeavors. That is, a healthy relationship should allow for interpenetration and conscious reciprocity in intimate dealings on the one side, and the freedom to be and to actualize personal endowments without splitting the fellowship on the other. Forcing couples or families to foster excessive mutuality may lead to rigidity, enmeshment, suffocation, or entrapment. Stressing too much differentiation in the system may foster chaotic anarchy, antinomianism, and isolation/insulation between people in relational transactions.

The same approach to theologically constructed covenants may follow: as paradigms assisting to establish structural and functional ways of relating, the Old and the New Covenants may be considered as being both mutually continuous and uniquely differentiated. On a qualifying note, we may call them paradigms without necessarily boxing God in to categories that limit his greatness, awesome transcendence, and inscrutable wisdom. Too much forced continuity between covenants may naïvely deprive God of his sovereign, transcendent, or mysterious ways of being and relating contextually (as he may consider it necessary in his own counsel in spite of our attempts to define his ways). Too much differentiation between his covenantal transactions may lead to arbitrary or partial views of his designs, conveying a sense of a God who has to change his mind according to whatever dispensation is in vogue. Thus, a paradoxically balanced perspective allows for both continuity and uniqueness in covenantal transactions without violating God's wisdom or logic, which is far above any precarious human endeavor aimed at the philosophical, psychological, or theological pursuit of truth.

THE SUFFICIENCY OF SCRIPTURES AND INTEGRATION OF CLINICAL RESEARCH AND PRACTICE

A relevant question in presenting biblical paradigms integrated to the behavioral sciences pertains to the notion of the *sufficiency* of the Word invoked as a principle of operation. In an encompassing paradigm, questions must be asked pertaining to the *necessity* versus the *relevance* and *functionality* of employing any addenda to Scripture. A multilevel analysis of God's intervention in the cosmos may be helped by the appeal to relevant sources that convey clarifying aspects along the pursuit of truth. Questions arise when a Christian investigator/helper considers a given phenomenon at the core (e.g., clinical depression in a believing wife) and needs to elucidate its etiology. She may assume that her lack of faith, negative perceptions of God, a possible demonization, or some spiritual variable could be responsible for the dysfunction (spiritual etiology), while at the same time, she may entertain the possibility that this matter pertains to the fields of genetics and biochemistry (natural sciences) or to the fields of cognitive or behavioral psychology (social/behavioral science).

God's domain encompasses both particular and general revelation. The Word seems to be silent about medicine, physics, astronomy, mathematics, agriculture, and veterinary medicine, etc. Yet, it is not silent about the nature of personhood or the relational aspects of humankind. We have no specific directives as to how to plant corn in Alaska. The Bible does not provide any particular guidelines to clarify the experimental findings derived from chaos theory. Nevertheless, the Word has a lot to say about how to imitate God in establishing and fulfilling covenants between husbands and wives, parents and children, and members in the body of Christ.

The author subscribes to the principle of the sufficiency of Scripture as it applies to redemptive purposes and to social, relational, and ethical-moral living. Empirical and scientific approaches to the created order that appeal to general revelation do not necessarily appeal to the *sufficiency of Scripture* as a guide. In the case of conducting investigations in astrophysics or thermodynamics, for example, Scripture is not necessarily sufficient to guide such endeavors. This line of reasoning may be used to consider the human at different levels of reality, departing from a genetic, biochemical, neurophysiological, or psychological point of view.

The human is subject to both the created and the transcendent order and may be considered as both a natural entity embedded in the cosmos and as the *Tselem Elohim* (Gen 1—2). The human derives a body from the elements of the created order and a personhood from God, the creator and the postulator of her/his being. Even more so, in a distinct fashion, the human has been given dominion and administrative authority over the created order, endowed with the capacity "to call things by name" (Gen 2:19–20) and to define reality as a scientist. The question is whether the human recognizes God in his investigative enterprise or displaces God with agnostic or arrogant defiance.

The viewpoint adopted in this work is based on God's design and purpose, revealed in the invitation to share in fellowship with God. Scripture is the believer's rule of faith and conduct, regarded as being essential, sufficient, and powerful to accomplish God's design as it pertains to human redemption and lifestyle. It is essential and sufficient in conveying the ultimate teleological destiny of the believer, while providing a useful guide along life's pilgrimage. In the here and now, within a created order and subject to natural laws, the believer receives the general admonition to live mindfully with administrative, economic, and accountable zest. Such a life draws from God-given prerogatives of freedom enacted within his established boundaries.

Our culturally affected, underlying personal motivations and the socialized avenues that we employ in the process of elucidating scriptural truth cannot be ignored. Gathering, abstracting, and consolidating scriptural meaning are necessary dimensions in the elaboration of a model for interpersonal transactions. From a transcendentally given propositional truth, a transduced and applicable model takes form, applicable to our everyday transactions. How conscious we are about the processes we employ to accomplish such tasks depends on the level of metacognitive-dialogical mindfulness guiding our endeavors. Living today based on scriptural principles in view of an eschatological encounter with the Giver of life (That Day, or the day of Christ's return) and bringing that higher view into our relational stewardship in the sight of God are essential dimensions in our covenantal transactions.

Several trends have merged in our times to create a negative social momentum that affects marital and family relationships. The skeptical and agnostic legacy left by the higher criticism of old has challenged the accuracy and veracity of Scripture and its applicability to human behaviors and relationships. These trends still influence our culture with their aftereffects. Moreover, current postmodern trends challenge biblical metanarratives and the universal applicability of truthful principles.

The need for God-given absolutes in establishing an ethical-moral basis for human behavior and relationships is set forth as an essential thrust of Scripture. In a more personal way, our human propensity to reject God's will in order to do our own resonates with the old prophetic statement: "For my people have committed two evils: they have forsaken me, the fountain of living waters, and hewed out cisterns for themselves, broken cisterns that can hold no water" (Jer 2:13, ESV).

On the one side, the currents of this *aion* infuse and foster the forsaking and abandonment of God's normative, ethical-moral basis for interpersonal relationships. On the other, such currents promote interpersonal ways that seem to follow materialistic, hedonistic, and utilitarian purposes that may affect the stability and ultimate satisfaction of marriages and families. Socially and culturally sanctioned narratives have displaced scriptural metanarratives in an attempt to provide particular and personal parameters in defining and enacting relational terms.

In the following chapters, Scripture is taken as the basis for the author's musings, conjectures, and considerations. Efforts are dedicated to present a desirable and efficient basis of faith and normative conduct, drawn from Scripture as they pertain to the New Covenant in Reformed and Dispensationalist theologies. In spite of the differences between these theological interpretations, gleaning from such fields reveals that both traditions emphasize the relevance, applicability, and paradigmatic bases of the New Covenant for present-day relations between God and believers, and believers among themselves.

As to the adoption of some basis for reflections and guidelines for service to those who need help in relational matters, constructs derived from God's revealed ways of transacting with humans will be considered. From the dawn of human history, humans, being relationally created, have established diverse basis for relationships—resorting to contracts, alliances, or covenants. Such paradigms have served to stipulate the terms of interpersonal engagements.

Part I: Premises and Principles

COVENANTAL CONSIDERATIONS

The thrust of this book deals with covenants as the basis for relationships depicted in Scripture, focusing on God's dealings with humans as a main theme. Covenants made with Adam and Eve, Noah, Abraham, the Israelites as a nation, and David's household are examples of these deals. The focus of scrutiny in this work is the New Covenant, promised in Jeremiah 31, and interpreted and elaborated upon in Hebrews 8 and 10, besides other passages. Such a covenant is presented as a paradigm that represents God's ultimate and optimal deal that actualizes all previous covenants in a better way. This covenant—by extrapolation—is applicable to relations in marriage and the family in particular ways. Several principles derived from the New Covenant are elaborated upon and viewed as value-based and practical aspects of God's design pertaining to human relations. They serve as premises for practical considerations that analogically may apply to intimate relations. Theology may inform our psychology and practice.

The considerations are born of a context that, in many ways, is removed from the original settings in which Scripture was given and then compiled in a canon. Thus, some contextual, historical, and background issues will be pursued in this work, so as to provide a better understanding of the themes and topics addressed. Cross-cultural studies offer interesting comparisons in which sacred texts are taken in a theonomous fashion in order to arrive at distinct conclusions. For example, the picture drawn from fundamentalist-influenced peoples (such as those in Sudan, Iran, Pakistan, Egypt, and elsewhere in the Islamic world) renders a reconstruction of beliefs and practices based on interpretations of the Qur'an which present marriage as a hierarchical contract—a "purchase and sale" agreement under a divinely sanctioned social order.[16]

The author has worked among Hispanics and Slavic peoples in the USA and has encountered many experiences of a cross-cultural nature. In the Hispanic world, many texts of the Bible are abstracted and utilized by popular writers in order to entrench patriarchal, hierarchical models of family life among fundamentalists.[17] Hispanics coming to the USA often look with disdain at the perceived laxity in family structures, processes, and norms that characterize marriages and family life in our culture. The same cultural/theological interaction applies in the Slavic world, where male superiority and hierarchy in marriage and the family have been the customary way of defining these institutions for centuries. Based on scriptural interpretations and cultural heritage, traditional Orthodox believers, as well as more recently established denominations, have interpreted and practiced a complementarian or hierarchical model of marital and family relations. Yet, such practices tend to lean toward a more egalitarian partnership when subject to European or American cultural forces with both liberal and evangelical theological interpretations that emphasize equality and mutual respect between spouses.

16. Hardacre, "The Impact of Fundamentalisms"; Haeri, *Law of Desire*.
17. Maldonado, *Even in the Best Families*.

The issue at hand is whether we as humans are open, willing, and able to regard God's Word and Spirit as a top-down agency that defines, establishes parameters, and empowers our relational beings and endeavors. The epistemological question is: where do we get our knowledge from regarding how to function in everyday affairs? How can we ascertain God's will as it relates specifically to human transactions in marriage and the family? Furthermore, do we also extend such concern to the assembly of believers in fellowship, the community we call the church? If we depart from a scriptural basis and adopt a qualified theonomy, this posture may serve as the underlying basis for a normative paradigm. In doing so, we may recognize that, after all, we are humans who attempt to imitate God's ways (Eph 5:1–2). That is a difficult endeavor, since God is incomprehensible, transcendent, omniscient, and omnipotent—and we are not. Imitating God as dearly beloved children necessitates a leap of faith. Paul's appeal to that end defines such imitation as "walking in love."

Thus, we may look at a particular covenant made by God with a person like Abraham; or we may look at Sinai for answers, making allusions to the covenant made by God with the house of Israel; or we may regard Jeremiah's prophetic utterance about a new covenant as the basis for transactions. In such procedures, how would we consider the relationship between the Old and the New Covenants? We may go beyond the *nomothetic* basis of the Old Covenant to a Reformed theological view that integrates both, applying such terms as a graceful paradigm for the church, the "new Israel" of God. Or we may adopt a qualified Dispensationalist distinction emphasizing the dawning of a new era and regarding the New Covenant as a new deal—"not like the old"—and applicable to the believing Gentiles today.

Whether we adopt a Reformed or a Dispensational theological interpretation, we realize that both postures may be able to adopt the New Covenant as a paradigm of relations between God and humans. Both perspectives convey the idea that humans may imitate God's ways as dearly beloved children, following the patterns of transactions characterized by grace, mercy, love, and justice. The old commandment to love God, followed by "and thy neighbor as thyself," merge with the new: to "love as Christ loved us." Imitating God as his dearly beloved children, walking in love, accepting one another, bearing the burdens of one another, and forgiving one another: all of these tenets point to the intricate balance between the aspects of a covenant that tie God and humans vertically (a salvific paradigm), as well as humans among themselves (an imitational example), along a more horizontal line.

The Old Covenant is viewed as a paradigm for establishing and maintaining desirable relations between God and Israel, constituting the norms for the people of God in their transactions with one another. These provisions pointed to ethical, moral, and civil norms applicable to everyday transactions, framed in the premises of this covenant. The New Covenant is adopted as an actualizing and better model for transactions, having continuity with the Abrahamic as well as with the Old Covenant mediated through Moses. This better deal supersedes the terms of previous covenants and actualizes in a more powerful and desirable fashion God's will for his people. It provides a superior basis for relational terms between human beings. That is the thrust of this work, and hopefully the reader will engage dialogically with the subject matter being presented.

INTEGRATIVE EFFORTS

In this work, selected books on marriage and the family written from various Christian perspectives are cited and consulted.[18] The vast literature seems to point to marriage and the family as the primary units of social structures and as agents of the transmission of values and practices from generation to generation. The family unit has been represented as a microcosm of a larger universal, social, ethical, moral, and spiritual order.

Without diminishing the relevance and sufficiency of Scriptures, the integration of clinical research and practice, based upon psychological principles, adds to the content of the chapters dealing with concrete avenues utilized in therapeutic and counseling endeavors with marriages and families. The author has engaged in four decades of laboring in the field of ministry integrated with clinical psychology, serving as a provider of services to hurting human beings in need of guidance, direction, mediation, and encouragement.

Christian integration of theology and psychology is a relatively new endeavor, compared to the diverse interpretations and categorizations that have oversaturated theological circles for a while. This integration is not necessarily unified, but originates from diverse psychological angles, as well as from distinct theologies drawn into the mix. Hopefully, this work represents an abstracted and principled integration between these disciplines aimed at contributing to the field of human services. For the purpose of this work, relations in marriage, the family, and the gathered assembly of those called to belong to the church would benefit from following the patterns proposed scripturally, interpreted theologically, and applied practically in covenantal transactions. It is hoped that providers of human services, as well as those in ministry, will benefit from the content of this book.

This book attempts to provide the basis for reflections and applications in the field of psychotherapy, counseling, mental health, and pastoral ministry. A new, better way of relating is stressed, adopting the New Covenant as a theologically constructed

---

18. See, for example, Tweedie, "Contract Therapy"; Wright, *Marital Counseling*; Adams, *Marriage, Divorce, and Remarriage*; Anderson and Guernsey, *On Being Family*; Balswick and Balswick, "A Theological Basis"; *The Family*; *A Model for Marriage*; Polischuk, "A New Covenant"; Crabb, *The Marriage Builder*; Worthington, *Hope for Troubled Marriages*; *Dimensions of Forgiveness*; Warren, *The Triumphant Marriage*; Hugenberger, *Marriage as a Covenant*; Engelsma, *Marriage*; Friesen and Friesen, *Counseling and Marriage*; Guernsey, *The Family Covenant*; Dobson, *Love for a Lifetime*; Chapman, *Covenant Marriage*; Cloud and Townsend, *Boundaries in Marriage*; Spencer et al, *Marriage at the Crossroads*.

paradigm that goes beyond contracts, *quid pro quos,* and transactions that rely on human efforts and insight. Besides the expected professional qualifications demanded in counseling or therapeutic situations, the appeal is made to consider God's empowering presence and scripturally-based guidance in the process of helping those in need of renewal, restoration, or improvement in their intimate relations. To that end, metacognitive notions saturate the chapters of this work, appealing to the readers' thinking about thinking. Metacognitive-dialogical aspects are delved into, defining the therapeutic terms of interaction between providers of services and those seeking help, between covenantal partners in marriage, and between family members. The self is defined in dialogical terms and is challenged to engage in metacognitive appraisal and control of internal dialogues and rhetoric. Trialogical aspects between the conflicted dialogical self and God are seen as internal engagements of an existential nature. The author hopes that readers will engage him in dialogue—that presence in absence that occurs in the event of reading—and that they also will reflect upon their own internal dialogues and rhetoric in response to the content and thrust of this work.

Chapter 2

Covenant as a Biblical Paradigm

A PARADIGM IS A conceptual model that serves as a heuristic device of an applicable nature. In both theology and psychology, a paradigm serves as a guiding model in the investigative endeavors engaged in by scholars and researchers. It also serves as a basis for delineating approaches and strategies in ministerial, counseling, and psychotherapeutic endeavors.

As a paradigm derived from Scripture, covenant conveys a unifying theme encompassing the binding transactions between God and his people in the narrative of God's revelation. This construct conveys the principles upon which humans may grasp the awesome privilege of relating to a living God and pleasing him in accordance with his will and purpose. The principles derived from this model may be also regarded as the basis for optimal transactions as they pertain to marriage, the family, and the community of faith. In Christian thought, the analogous term *testament* has been adopted to describe or define covenant, and this label has succeeded in a major way: today we refer to the two great divisions of the Bible as being the Old and the New Testaments.

THEOLOGICAL CONSIDERATIONS ON COVENANT

The content of this book follows a logic in which theological propositions antecede practical aspects applicable to covenantal relationships. In Pauline writings, the apostle's exposition of theological premises (e.g., Rom 1—11; Eph 1–3) precedes practical recommendations (e.g., Rom 12—16; Eph 4—6). Exemplary and normative bases are provided for the establishment of practical guidelines of an ethical and moral nature. Following the same line of reasoning, theological considerations derived from God's covenants are presented as the Father's ways of behaving in love, applicable to relations of intimate nature such as marriage, the family, and the community of faith.

In modern times, extensive research on the subject dates back to Wellhausen.[1] His work has been regarded as a starting point for modern research on the biblical concept of *berit*, "covenant." His provocative approach presented a documentary hypothesis based on higher criticism and naturalistic philosophy. Wellhausen denied

---

1. Wellhausen, *Prolegomena*.

the antiquity of the Sinai covenant, regarding it as a non-existing concept until its late deuteronomic development. In his opinion, the construct evolved from and was redefined from a natural (or primitive) bond between God and Israel (similar to a father-son kinship bond); it was then recast into a systematized legalism that emerged in postexilic Judaism, emphasizing the ethical aspects of this deal.[2] Wellhausen's view provoked controversies and divided scholars for many decades. On the positive side, it stirred up a great deal of research on the matter.

Approaching the theme of covenant from a historical perspective, Paul R. Williamson alludes to Cocceius (1603–69) as a pioneer in interpreting the Bible holistically and allocating *covenant* a central place in theology.[3] His review also includes Witsius, who in 1677 produced an important work about federal theology in which the unity of Scripture was postulated and synthesized in covenantal terms.

In his review of the covenant-focused saga, Kitchen gives credit to Mendenhall for drawing from and appealing to extensive non-biblical data used to frame covenants in their historical and cultural contexts.[4] Likewise, Nicholson gave credit to Mendenhall, McCarthy, and Weinfield as major contributors to the field as pertains to the use of ancient Near Eastern texts (i.e., the Hittite suzerainty treaties) as sources of comparison with the covenants of Scripture.[5] Mendenhall regarded covenant as a concept framed in a juridical dimension, while Eichrodt's interpretations of scholarly research promoted a covenant-based theology.[6] Covenant, for him, was not a dogmatic concept underlying the development of a corpus of doctrine, but a code word that signified the typical description of a living process between God and his people. This process had a definite beginning and then unfolded under God's auspices. It provided a glimpse of manifest divine reality unique in the history of religion.

According to Hahn, the manner of distribution of covenantal obligations between parties entering into the deal would be the key to the typology of the covenant.[7] This typology would include 1.) Kinship covenants (also called parity covenants), in which parties of equal status would enter with the assent of having an equal distribution of privileges and obligations; 2.) Treaty covenants, in which obligations were imposed by a superior over an inferior party (such as the vassal treaties of ancient Mesopotamia); and 3.) Grant covenants, in which the superior party pledged privileges and granted them in a unilateral fashion to an inferior party (usually as a response to faithfulness or based upon some qualities deserving recognition or merit). Hahn's meta-analysis of the studies in the field emphasizes a familial or relational factor that seems to integrate

---

2. Hahn, *Kinship by Covenant*.
3. Williamson, *Sealed with an Oath*.
4. Kitchen, "The Fall and Rise."
5. Nicholson, *God and His People*.
6. Mendenhall, "Law and Covenant"; Eichrodt, *Theology of the Old Testament*.
7. Hahn, *Kinship*.

the diverse dimensions related to covenant over the last century, such as the ethical, cultic, social, juridical, and theological aspects embedded in such deals.[8]

As a clarifying note, even the terms used to define such types do not necessarily convey an absolute sense or a discrete meaning applicable to all deals, as sometimes parties of different status may have entered parity covenants as if they belonged to the same strata. As an added note, it is important to ascertain a structural dimension—who pronounces the covenantal oath. In a parity deal, both parties swear an oath; in the treaty-type, only the inferior does so; and in the grant-type, only the superior does so.

The author has had the privilege of working for more than three decades at an institution where scholars such as Drs. Kline, Kaiser, Niehaus, Hafemann, and Hugenberger have made excellent contributions related to the study of diverse covenants. These colleagues approached the subject matter from various positions, emphasizing the distinct yet unified aspects of God's salvific theme. Appealing to extra-biblical sources, as well as to scriptural data, Kline elaborated further on Mendenhall's views and identified the form of biblical covenants with the common Suzerain-Vassal treaties of the Ancient Near East in the 2nd millennium BCE.[9] In comparing the structure of such treaties, Kline suggested the following parallels:

- Preamble (cf. Deuteronomy 1:1–4);
- Historical prologue (cf. Deuteronomy 1:5–3:29);
- Stipulations (cf. Deuteronomy 4—26);
- Document clause (cf. Deuteronomy 27);
- List of gods as witnesses (not registered in Deuteronomy, as there is only one God);
- Sanctions: curses and blessings (cf. Deuteronomy 28; 31—34).

Kline provided insights emphasizing distinctive features of the Old Covenant as a law covenant, based on bilateral stipulations and works applicable to both parties involved (Israel and God) in contrast to other covenants such as the New Covenant. Yet, many reformed theologians after him have regarded the Old Covenant as being fundamentally a contingent order under the administration of the covenant of grace.

The thesis provided by Hugenberger on marriage as covenant, of importance to this work, is supported by his exhaustive exegesis of Malachi 2:14 and a thorough examination of the premises and principles derived from it.[10] His work represents an invaluable source of data on the subject as it draws interesting comparisons between marriage and covenantal elements. Kaiser's emphasis on the New Covenant (based on Jeremiah 31:31–33) as an actualizing expression of the Old also represents a valuable

---

8. Ibid.
9. Kline, *The Structure of Biblical Authority*; Mendenhall, "Law and Covenant."
10. Hugenberger, *Marriage as a Covenant*.

contribution to the premises of this work.[11] His emphasis on the continuity of God's deals, while recognizing the uniqueness of the actualization of the Old in the New, is taken as a corroborating aspect of the New Covenant as a valuable paradigm for the present time.

Niehaus affirms the notion that God has made covenants with humans, and those covenants have been central to the unfolding of redemptive history.[12] In his view, to regard the unity of a theologically constructed covenant as an amalgamated reality seems to rob God's multiform wisdom of uniqueness or particularity in enacting diverse covenants. At the same time, he affirms the notion of God's unifying agenda or program of salvation. This agenda included covenants based on common grace applicable to all—enacted in a particular fashion with a given constituency in a discrete context. Niehaus makes a distinction between the Adamic and Noahic covenants as derived from "common grace," and those made with Abraham, Moses, and David as being peculiar to Israel or its elements.

According to this line of reasoning, the promise made to Abraham was actualized in the giving of the New Covenant. Paul's argument in Romans 9 through 11 was that Israel did not become a party to the New Covenant, although it was promised to them in the OT. As Paul stated, "To them belong the adoption as sons, the glory, the covenants, the giving of the law, the temple worship, and the promises" (Rom 9:4). Yet, Israel rejected their Messiah and his New Covenant. In doing so, they failed to actualize the better deal intended for their good. And as the argument goes, they will not be part of it until they choose to do so; they will then be justified by faith in the only mediator provided by God.

As unifying elements go, the kinship nature of a covenant enters into the definition of most scholars, as well as the invoking of an oath ratifying the deal. At times, one of the parties may be a collective entity (such as the nation of Israel or the house of David). In terms of position, parties were expected to be of equal status so that their obligations would be distributed in equal fashion. Most often, covenants were established with a proactive superior party and a reactive inferior party, characterized by an unequal distribution of obligations.

In sum, not only the paradigmatic construct, but even its definition, as it appears in both the Old and New Testaments (*berit* or *diatheke*), has been a matter of dispute and controversy amongst scholars. It is not the intention of this work to engage in a debate over the diverse, existing definitions or to systematically and painstakingly argue for a given position on the subject to the exclusion of others. Such a task has been pursued thoroughly and rendered in excellent accounts by highly competent scholars from different angles (e.g., Frank Moore Cross, Gordon Hugenberger). The vast domain of material dealing with covenant can be further assessed and pursued

---

11. Kaiser, "The Old Promise."
12. Niehaus, "An Argument"; "Covenant"; "Covenant and Narrative."

Part I: Premises and Principles

by interested students and readers by consulting the exceptional reviews available on the topic.[13]

A main division exists in the field with regard to the thrust and flow of covenantal transactions: these may be unilateral (in the sense of a legal obligation imposed by one party over another) or bilateral (establishing or renewing a relationship between two parties). This work emphasizes God's unilateral thrust to start with, followed by a gracious invitation to engage in a bilateral fashion. Such a perspective should not be confused with the position adopted by those advocating a legal obligation (e.g., Wellhausen, Nicholson). The perspective adopted by this author is that only as an empowered being may the human enter into a bilateral covenant in response to the unilateral, unconditional, and proactive thrust of grace and mercy coming from God. Being redeemed, redefined, and elevated to God's higher transactional plane (regarded as being both in a new position before God and in a new state of redefined being) by God's unilateral, unconditional, and proactive grace, the human may enter into a bilateral deal with God.

COVENANT FRAMED IN THEOLOGICAL POSITIONS

Covenant, as a paradigm derived from Scripture, represents a key aspect of this work. The purpose of this chapter is to glean valuable relational principles derived from this paradigm, which are applicable to remedial, conciliatory, and therapeutic endeavors in the fields of marriage, family, and faith communities.

Covenantal considerations are grouped into categorical systems of interpretation without engaging in the controversies and debates that have characterized the scholarly pursuits related to the topic. Theological positions on covenant may be placed in two big categories: Covenant theology and Dispensationalism. As of late, a third current, known as New Covenant theology, has emerged in attempts to bridge the gap between the two polarities. Yet, it appears that such efforts did not accomplish the ultimate goal of establishing a commonly acceptable synthesis.

COVENANT IN REFORMED THEOLOGY

Covenant notions in Reformed theology have developed in time with roots in the writings of Augustine and John Calvin.[14] Johannes Cocceius (c. 1603–69) is credited with developing a foundational concept of covenant in *The Doctrine of the Covenant and Testament of God* (1648). This theology was clearly expressed in the British Westminster Confession of Faith and further developed by Herman Witsius (1636–1708)

---

13. See, for example, Hillers, *Covenant*; Nicholson, *God and His People*; Hahn, *Covenant in the Old and New Testaments*; *Kinship by Covenant*; Williamson, *Sealed with an Oath*; Kitchen, "The Fall and Rise."

14. Calvin, *Institutes of the Christian Religion*, first published in Latin in 1536.

in the *Economy of the Covenants between God and Man*. In the United States, the writings of Jonathan Edwards followed the same lines of interpretation.[15]

The establishment of seminaries prompted theological research and fostered the defining of doctrinal positions on the matter. Princeton theologians (Charles Hodge, A. A. Hodge, B. B. Warfield, Geerhardus Vos, and J. Gresham Machen) developed systematic notions on covenantal nature framed in Reformed theology. At Gordon-Conwell Theological Seminary, Meredith Kline, David Wells, and Richard Lints, among others, have been the proponents of this system. Well-known Reformed theologians in the evangelical domain include R. C. Sproul, J. I. Packer, John Frame, Sinclair Ferguson, James Boice, and Michael S. Horton, among others.

As a framework for biblical interpretation, Reformed theology emphasizes the relationship between the Old Covenant with Israel as a nation and the New Covenant—promised to the tribes of Israel and specially to Judah, but applicable to both Jews and Gentiles. Covenant theology asserts a distinction between the covenant of grace and the covenant of works. The covenant that God made with Adam and Eve in their pristine purity before the Fall has been referred as "the covenant of works," in which God promised them blessedness contingent upon their obedience to his expressed commands. After the Fall, God continued to promise redemption to human beings who had violated the covenant of works. The ongoing promise of redemption in spite of human sin is defined as the "covenant of grace."

Under the overarching covenant of grace spanning from creation to consummation, the principle at work during the covenant of works was subsumed under the guiding principle of grace—being simultaneously applicable under the Old Covenant. The New Covenant is not actually new in the sense that God changed his mind; its novelty resides in the fact that God would act in a superposed, infusing, and empowering fashion, allocating his law into the hearts and minds of people and deleting their sins and misdeeds. The unaltered covenant that the forefathers broke would be fulfilled and realized by means of God's Spirit by the empowered human, who was able to obey God's commands.

Furthermore, Reformed theology relies on a representative (or federal) concept. As a substitute for all humans, Adam represented humankind in his disobedience and fall, bringing about the consequential condemnation due to sin. On the other side, Jesus's active obedience not only assures all believers that the redemption of sin has been accomplished, but also attests to the fact that they have been reinstated to fellowship with God because Jesus (the last Adam) accomplished the assignment of defeating the devil and granting them an eternal inheritance. The work of Jesus has secured eternally the salvation of the elect before God. This federal representation allows for both the imputation of sinfulness and condemnation in Adam on the one side, and the justification and freedom from sin, as well as the eternal security in Christ, on the other.

15. Edwards, *The Works*.

Part I: Premises and Principles

Reformed theology focuses on the atonement that Jesus accomplished in bearing the sins of his people and being punished for them. The atonement is vicarious and substitutionary. On the cross, Christ took upon himself the negative sanctions of the Old Covenant. He took upon himself the curse that is deserved by all who disobey the law of God. He bore in his body the punishment due to those who violated not only the law of Moses, but also the covenant of works that was enacted in the Garden of Eden. Reformed theology describes "the passive obedience of Jesus," pointing to his willingness to submit to his reception of the curse of God on behalf of sinners.

Beyond the negative fulfillment of the covenant of works, Jesus offered a positive dimension by bestowing the blessing of the covenant of works upon anyone of Adam's race who would put her/his trust in him. Adam was the covenant breaker and failed to gain the favor of God. In contrast, Jesus is the covenant keeper. Covenant theology refers to the "active obedience" of Christ, which includes not only his death, but also his life of perfect obedience—which became the sole ground for justification. His perfect righteousness (gained via his perfect obedience) is imputed to all who put their trust in him. In this view, Christ's work of active obedience is absolutely essential to the justification of all believers.

Readers who are familiar with this approach are aware of the theological divide over the nature, number, and continuity among the diverse covenants. The unified version of God's covenants versus the replacement of the Old Covenant with the New remains a matter of a controversial nature. Scholars such as Dumbrell and Hafemann, among others, advocate for a single covenant encompassing all transactions between God and Adam, Noah, Abraham, Israel, David, and a new covenant with the house of Israel and the house of Judah in times to come.[16] Kline and Niehaus, among others, stress the diverse, relational aspects between God and humans in historical time (God not being subject to such chronological aspects); God has acted according to his designs and agenda.[17] In this view, "God has chosen the manner of his self-disclosure and the degree of his propositional revelation in and for each covenant."[18]

Common grace is postulated as being an overarching and superordinate principle inherently embedded in God's dealings with humans. This grace permeates all covenants enacted according to God's unified purpose, redemptive script, and redemptive path. Such gracious dealings began with the Abrahamic covenant, were foreshadowed in both the Sinaitic and Davidic covenants (fulfilling partial and contextual promises), and received a full actualization in the giving of the New Covenant through the great mediator. In sum, God's unified program of salvation may be considered to be the path to the renewal of all things that were foreshadowed, pointing to the New Covenant as a leading avenue that culminates in the establishment of a new heavens and Earth, and the actualization of a new humanity conformed to the image of the Son.

16. Dumbrell, *Covenant and Creation*; Hafemann and House, *Central Themes*.
17. Kline, *Kingdom Prologue*; Niehaus, "An Argument"; "Covenant and Narrative."
18. Niehaus, "Covenant and Narrative," 558.

COVENANT IN DISPENSATIONALIST THEOLOGY

Dispensationalism is a theological system that began with the writings of John Nelson Darby (1800–82) and was further developed by the Plymouth Brethren movement. This theology was propagated through the development of the *Scofield Reference Bible*, with Cyrus Scofield being its chief editor.[19] Succinctly, this position asserts the belief that, between God's creation and his final judgment, there were seven dispensations (distinct eras) depicting God's dealings with humans. These eras constituted a framework for synthesizing the content of Scripture. The system emphasizes a distinctive, eschatological, end-times perspective, in which the pre-millennial return of Christ and the pre-tribulation rapture of the church will take place, followed by a tribulation period which culminates in the establishment of a millennial kingdom.

Dispensationalists believe that the nation of Israel is a distinct entity from the Christian church, and that God has yet to fulfill his covenantal promises to his elected nation. These promises include the land promises, which, in the world to come, result in a millennial kingdom and the establishment of a third temple in Jerusalem from which Christ, upon his return, will rule the world for a thousand years.

Dispensationalists emphasize the contextual audience to whom these promises were written, regarding Israel as the original recipient. This contextual distinction associates the Old Covenant with Israel, while the New Covenant applies to both believing Israelites and Gentiles united in one body (during the dispensation of grace). The New Covenant will have a future, plenary actualization during the restoration of Israel and the inauguration of the millennial kingdom. Classical Dispensationalists refer to the present-day church as a "parenthesis" or temporary interlude in the progress of Israel's prophesied history. In other areas of theology, Dispensationalists hold to a wide range of beliefs within the evangelical and fundamentalist spectrum.

In this view, the New Covenant promised in Jeremiah 31 stands in contrast to the Old Covenant of Moses, although both were contracted with ethnic Israel. The author of Hebrews cites Jeremiah in chapters 8 and 10 mainly to demonstrate to his Jewish audience that the promise of a second covenant implies that the first covenant was both a shadow of reality and temporary, exhorting them not to rest their faith in the first covenant but to look to the mediator of the new one. According to Darby, the church, as a result of her relation to the mediator of the New Covenant, presently enjoys its spiritual blessings and privileges even though it is not formally under the Old Covenant.

Gentile believers were not necessarily the audience that Jeremiah had in mind. Yet, these believers, as well as Hebrew believers, appropriate the terms of such blessings so as to be able to accept the invitation to approach God's mercy seat, go through the veil, and encounter God because of the redemptive work of Jesus, the mediator of the New Covenant. Darby's notions provided a rationale for a future (and literal)

---

19. Scofield, *The Scofield Reference Bible*.

fulfillment of the promise found in Jeremiah as it pertains to Israel and Judah, as well as being relevant to present believers in the church, who may share the spiritual benefit through their common mediator. In this system, the promises embedded in the New Covenant constitute a paradigm of relations between God and believers in the present age.

Moderate Dispensationalists, such as Chafer (1871–1952), regarded the New Covenant as a revealed deal applicable in two aspects: God's will in saving, preserving, and conforming believers to his Son, guaranteeing them his heaven;[20] and, after that, in effectuating the future salvation of Israel as promised under the unconditional terms found in the prophetic utterances (Isa 27:9; Ezek 37:23; Rom 11:26–7). Chafer also reflected on a dual covenant structure by drawing parallels applicable to both Israel and the church. The restricted promises to Israel (Jer 31:31–34) have an ample range of blessings as these apply to the church (Matt 26:28).

This two-covenant view was followed and expanded by Walvoord and Ryrie, who paid attention to the challenges posed against Scofield's twofold application of one covenant as being inconsistent with the "mysterious" nature of the church.[21] Such challenges centered upon the church being *a mystery unknown to the prophets* so that the New Covenant foretold by Jeremiah was not necessarily geared to the church, but directed to Israel and Judah. Both Walvoord and Ryrie admitted the importance of such criticism as it pertains to the development of a two-covenant view as they worked to establish a consistency in the interpretation of the Hebrews 8 citation. In moderate dispensationalism, the New Covenant applicable to the present church is different than the New Covenant promised to the houses of Israel and Judah in Jeremiah. The Gospel references to the Lord's Supper, along with those made by Paul in 1 Corinthians 11:25, speak of the church's New Covenant. It is this new deal that Paul ministers to both Jews and Gentiles (2 Cor 3:16). In contrast, Paul's reference in Romans 11:27 (a citation of Jeremiah's prophecy) is taken as being distinct from the Jewish New Covenant, which is yet to be fulfilled.

Moderate dispensationalism approaches the book of Hebrews (especially chapters 8 and 10) as being an address to Jewish people. The author shows them "better" aspects applicable to Christianity, which include a "better covenant" made with the church, while admitting that Hebrews 8 and 10 make mention of Jeremiah 31 as pertaining to the New Covenant with Israel to be fulfilled in the future. The confusion or difficulty that emerges from such a position is solved if the passage of Hebrews 8 (a citation of Jeremiah's prophecy) is taken to show that the Old Covenant is not eternal after all. The emphasis of the citation is directed to the words *new* or *better* and not to its content—as applicable to Israel. This theological position asserts that the "better

---

20. Lewis Sperry Chafer, founder of Dallas Theological Seminary; retrieved from http://bartimaeus.us/pub_dom/the_kingdom_in_history_and_prophecy.html (14 January 2016).

21. Walvoord, "The New Covenant with Israel," 25; see also Ryrie, *Basis of the Premillenial Faith*, 118.

covenant" in Hebrews is that which the Lord Jesus established with the church, noting that nowhere in the letter is this covenant explicitly alluded to or exclusively fulfilled among the Jews themselves. Indeed, in the moderate position, this notion is presented as a reason for the lack of appeal to the content of the covenant.

The Dispensationalist position may be considered as being both a redemptive paradigm and a model for ongoing relations between God and his people. Of applicability to this work is the fact that this position supports the use of the New Covenant as the basis for marital, family, and neighborly relationships. These relations are patterned after God and derived from his principles, and they serve as applicable guidelines during the present dispensation of grace.

In sum, Dispensationalists refer to Covenant theology with terms such as *supersessionism, fulfillment,* or *replacement theology* on the basis that it teaches that God has somehow shifted the promises made to Israel and has replaced Israel with believing Christians as his chosen people in the Earth. Covenant theologians counter such claims, denying the notion that God has abandoned his promises to Israel; rather, they see the fulfillment of the promises to Israel in the person and the work of the Messiah, who established the church in organic continuity with Israel, and not as a separate entity replacing his people.

COVENANT AS AN ENCOMPASSING AND INTEGRATED PARADIGM

All told, the debate among reformed theologians and dispensational thinkers is an important issue in the field of Christian thought. Yet, for the purposes of this work, both Covenant theologians and Dispensationalists seem to regard the New Covenant as being primarily a paradigm of salvific proportions, and then as a paradigm for human relations applicable to believers—whether Gentile or Jew—at the present time. As such, the New Covenant represents a model of God's being and actions toward his children.

Reformed theology emphasizes the unity and continuity—as well as the actualization and applicability—of the New Covenant in the present time. Thus, for the purpose of this work, it seems appropriate to assign a prominent role to this covenant in the establishment of intimate relationships, such as marriage, and to derive some principles applicable to family transactions as well. Husbands and wives may follow God's proactive, unilateral, and unconditional thrust so as to be graceful and merciful toward one another. They may dispense forgiveness and let go of their mutual offenses as God forgave them in Christ. The exhortatory premises found in Ephesians 5:1–2, "Be imitators of God as dearly beloved children and live in love" and "Just as Christ also loved us and gave himself for us" are followed by a logical conclusion: husbands are to love their wives "just as Christ loved the church and gave himself for her" (Eph 5:25). Wives may adopt an analogous stance and treat husbands with the same attitude of respect displayed by the church toward Christ (Eph 5:33). This apostolic appeal is embedded in a covenantal paradigm that needs to be taken to heart and engaged in with mindful, behavioral enactments, following the trinitarian model in which partners engage in a loving, interpersonal lifestyle.

After all is said and done, what is the most important question Scripture poses to us? If, as in the case of Peter, we were given the choice between "Who do you say that I am?" and "Do you love me?" what would be our ultimate choice and response? Without denying the importance of ascertaining who Jesus is (a confession of faith), and the scholarly debates on the nature, the intention, and the punctilious details of what a covenant is, this work emphasizes the loving, binding relationship between God and his children—to be enacted by his children amongst one other.

The covenant between Christ (the husband) and the church (the wife) appears as a paradigm, a prototypical model in Paul's mind as he addresses marital relations based upon a theologically interpreted, analogical basis. The apostolic teachings are not intended to replace the tablets of stone, as if these represent a new law. Reading Ephesians 5 with a dogmatic lens may lead to the adoption of a rigid paradigm that causes partners to relate as if they are locked into a grid of some sort. Keeping in mind the contextual background, the social milieu of the time, and the Pauline eagerness to see things done according to God's patterns, the spirit of the letter seems to appeal to the enactment of the grace, mercy, and love necessary for relations of a mutually loving and respectful nature.

Besides marriage, the nurture, care, love, and discipline that parents need to demonstrate toward their children may follow the principles derived from the exemplary character and conduct displayed by the Father toward his children. Likewise, the respect and obedience demonstrated by children toward their parents may follow the example of the Lord's attitude, obedience, and love displayed in relationship to the Father.

As it pertains to pastoral or therapeutic work with couples and families, the Reformed position seems to support and encourage the applicability of a unified covenant of grace as a paradigm of exemplary nature. The principles derived from the New Covenant may illustrate and guide the strategies applicable to a sound pastoral or counseling approach. Covenantal principles may be functionally embedded in the process of helping parties to establish optimal deals in marital or family therapy.

This author follows the argument that considers the New Covenant as God's optimal revelation that actualizes God's purpose embedded in all past covenants. Covenants made with Noah (Gen 7), Abraham (Gen 17), the nation of Israel (Exod 19), Joshua (Josh 24), and David (2 Sam 7) culminate in a paradigm which falls along continuous lines and yet presents an all-encompassing and "better" deal. This reasoning seems to resonate with the arguments provided by the author to the Hebrews. Having in mind the text found in Romans 9 through 11 as an intrinsic part of Paul's unfolding argument and God's historical and future dealings with Israel, the author regards the New Covenant as an actualizing and living expression of God's will in the here and now, as well as a covenant to be actualized with Israel in the future. Yet, such a future scope does not obliterate the claims that pertain to the actual application of the covenantal terms in the present time, as exposed in the letter to the Hebrews.

COVENANTAL MINDFULNESS: DEVELOPING A METACOGNITIVE POINT OF VIEW

In order to actualize the terms of a covenantal paradigm in human relations, it is necessary to develop a proper mindset: to look at the "things above" (Col 3:1–2) and to "get our minds ready for action" (1 Pet 1:13). In the process, we all "with unveiled faces reflecting the glory of the Lord as in a mirror [beholding the face of Jesus Christ who is the true image of God in character and conduct] are being transformed into the same image" (2 Cor 3:18). In terms of interpersonal relations, we are encouraged to "develop the same attitude toward one another that Christ Jesus had" (Phil 2:5).

Stated in interpersonal-neurobiological terms, we need to "align our mirror neurons" with God's loving, graceful, and merciful character so as to be animated by the Holy Spirit's infusion and interpenetration, enjoying an intimate fellowship in love. Partners in marriage may positively change one another as well, by aligning their hearts and minds in love. In the nervous system, this accelerates the conduction of electrical impulses from mirror neurons by improving myelination—the formation of an insulating sheath consisting of a mixture of proteins and phospholipids around the nerve fibers.

Keeping in mind that all covenants in Scripture started with God's top-down, proactive initiative, we need to adopt a higher—transcendent, supra-rational, or metacognitive—point of view in order to be in tune with his design. In Pauline theological terms, we need to avoid being conditioned by our selfish, materialistic, hedonistic, or narcissistic tendencies: "Do not be conformed to this present world" (Rom 12:2). That is, we need to avoid being squeezed into or trapped within the mold of this present age so as to mindlessly follow any voguish trend under the sun.

On a positive note, a metacognitive stance allows us to ascribe a better meaning to our earthly existence. We do so by inviting and being mindful of the transcendent propositions coming from the ultimate definer of reality in order to infuse our trivial pursuits with meaning. Philosophies of life that originate at ground level and develop in a bottom-up fashion (or theologies that naturalize God's propositions in a "demythologizing" fashion) may prove to be inadequate to empower us to do God's will. The attempts to imitate God or to live by the principles of a covenant that originate in a supernatural plane cannot be actualized by following philosophies of life that originate from a bottom-up perspective.

Imitators of the Father's covenantal ways need to develop insights and understanding of such premises by adopting a metacognitive point of view so as to "develop the mind of Christ." An operational definition of such an abstract expression may run like this: To develop the mind of Christ is to experience an alignment of our cognitive-affective-motivational structures and processes so as to be in tune with God's purpose and to adopt a willful disposition to surrender to and obey his designs and will. Such a mindset implies the adoption of an intentional and purposive perspective that may run against a culture of narcissism—characterized by individual choices affected by personal demands or desires. A covenantal mindfulness is to be encouraged in order to build our lives (marriages and households) in tune with God's desires and to accomplish his will and purpose.

COVENANTAL MINDFULNESS: LIFE UNDER THE SUN

The decision to enact a covenant emerges from a position of empowered strength in which a person engages with a willful choice and a conscious mindset. The author appeals to the reader's capacity to invite the transcendental aspects of God's given revelation to all trivial endeavors characterizing human existence. The apostle Paul made a metacognitive assertion to the Galatians, stating that a disciple's predicament is characterized by "living in the flesh by faith in the Son of God" (Gal 2:20). Such an expression can be considered a scriptural baseline in which the coparticipation between natural and transcending reality is possible.

The meaning of "being crucified with Christ" can be elucidated as the decision to place all personal efforts, ambitions, and desires of the self under God's authority. Being in solidarity with Christ in his death also means to place all personal goals and designs under his scrutiny and purpose. This surrender (a living sacrifice) allows a person to experience the presence and power of the Holy Spirit as "being there" in order to deal with the natural dimensions or sinful propensities that characterize her/his struggles under the sun. Thus, a believer's alignment of her/his cognitive, affective, motivational, and behavioral processes may be placed under the lordship of Christ and held in a mindful alignment with God's will, with a conscious awareness of the daily challenges while "living in the flesh" by faith in the Son of God.

The expression that follows in the same verse ("and the world is crucified to me") encourages a believer to regard the cosmos, the *aion* (the world order, the spirit of this age, or the secular fashions) as being devoid of the power to entrap her/his character, mindset, and behaviors. This perception allows the person to declare a personal freedom from both the appeal and the influence of the entrapments of this age. The verse adds, "What now I live in the flesh, I live by faith in the Son of God who gave himself for me" (Gal 2:20). Living by faith is living "as if" one is *getting there* when one is *not there* yet.

The paradigm that develops in this work follows a metacognitive-dialogical reasoning of an intrinsic nature: the eternal order in God's design and purpose supersedes the created order, which is subject to and contingent upon his original intention.

The promise of Jesus to believers was that he would be with them all their days until the end of this age. He also promised the Holy Spirit, a person who would be with them and in them as an empowering agent after his ascent to the Father. A constant, internal dialogue with the indwelling Word and the Holy Spirit allows the realization of God's will in enacting the trivial aspects of everyday life.

God's covenantal terms and principles align and empower our humanly covenanted terms so that we possess a better consciousness in enacting our transactions. Beyond cultural versions of idiosyncratic, socially defined alliances, a covenantal grounding in God's Word provides a better terrain and a better basis for superconscious transactions with one another. Beyond deeply seated personal needs, narcissistic demands, and neurotic trends, covenantal relations may be enacted with accountability before the one who defines marriages and families.

COVENANTAL RELATIONS IN VIEW OF ESCHATOLOGY

In the first chapter, a succinct rendering of biblical anthropology depicted the human as being preformed, formed, deformed, informed, reformed, transformed, and finally conformed to God's image. In this unfolding revelation, covenant as a paradigm appears as an underlying feature present in God's eternal view and design. The mediator of the New Covenant started his salvific journey following this design derived from the top, departing from the right hand of God. Then, from this empowered grounding, the mediator stepped down to a conscious and willful *kenosis* (his "emptiness"—or the accommodation and assimilation of his prerogatives and claims to the human condition). He did so without losing sight of his God-given capacity for assertive dealings and for speaking the truth in love. In like manner, any imitator of God in Christ may derive a principled stance and engage in behaviors that denote a decentered emptiness without masochism, unassertiveness, or codependency.

The redeemed fellowship described by John in Revelation depicts a great multitude comprised of all tribes, tongues, and ethnic groups, worshipping and praising the same Father and common God. These diverse people decenter from their own ethnic, racial, and social particularities and hone in together on God as a focal point, worshipping in unison their creator and redeemer. This metacognitive point of view draws from a future-oriented, honing device: a teleological point of reference or *eschaton*, referred to by Paul as "That Day" (the Day of Christ's return, 2 Tim 4:8). It represents a conditioning and orienting factor "guiding from the future" and providing a sense of direction to the path taken by a person, a couple, or a family system. The picture is one of unity in diversity. Bringing *That Day* to *this day* means that such an eschatological "omega point" may provide a sense of direction and meaning to our social and covenantal relationships right here and right now.

The command of Paul given to the Galatians—to "walk [behave according to a lifestyle] in the Spirit"—involves such a sense of direction, or alignment, with God's expressed commands (Gal 5:16). It also acts as a metronome, marking the tempo of the believer so as to be "in step with the Spirit" (Gal 5:25). This walk (lifestyle) presupposes a purposive end, a destination point at the end of the sojourner's path. Focal awareness directed to That Day brings a convergent point of reference and stirs up a sober mindset by reminding the believer of her/his reckoning or accountability before the tribunal seat of Christ (2 Cor 5:10). Whatever we have done while in the body—good or bad—toward God, others, and especially toward partners and family members will be rewarded (or not so rewarded) in That Day.

Thus, all human transactions—conduct, intention, and influence exercised among/upon each other in the house of the Lord—will be brought into account before the Lord of the house. God is not only the author, but also the overseer and judge of all human transactions. The infusion and feedback of this future point into the present may trigger an anticipatory feedforward process. We may behave proactively in view of That Day and then turn the mindfulness backward—call it a feedback loop—so as to infuse "this day" with a metacognitive awareness. In view of this spiritual reality, we may engage in our daily transactions with meaning and purpose. This worldview represents a so-called "eschatology in the process of being realized" and brings "the presence of the Kingdom" into our present reality.[22]

When a husband relates and behaves toward his wife (actually God's property) in view of That Day, his attitudes and behaviors probably align much better with God's expectations and principles as these pertain to his relationship with his partner (1 Cor 6:19–20). He may become a better steward of his marriage relationship, being more mindful and considering the woman at his side not so much as *his* wife but as God's child: a person who has chosen to enter into and share her life with him in a covenantal partnership under God. Thus marriage is redefined as a privileged, temporal concession: sharing their life under the sun, both are defined as administrators of their relationship under the lordship of Christ.

COVENANT AS A UNIVERSAL PARADIGM

Our postmodern culture may object to the notion that covenant is a paradigm of universal applicability. Yet covenant appears in Scripture as a universal construct, applicable across cultures and ethnic groupings. The particularities of the covenantal arrangements may vary and be culturally contextualized, but the essence of God's redemptive and transacting model in dealing with humans remains a universal propositional truth. The gospel represents good news of a redemptive nature to all the inhabitants of the world, applicable at all times. The New Covenant is a gospel-derived and intertwined concept that frames this redemptive plan in relational terms. It appeals to all nations, ethnic groups, peoples, and tongues as a supracultural paradigm.

---

22. Ladd, *The Gospel*.

The apostle Paul was a prominent Jew and Roman citizen, who wrote a letter in Greek to the ancient Ephesians (modern Turkey), presenting them with three chapters of basic theological principles, followed by three chapters of applicable and practical concerns—including guidelines for marriage, the family, and social relations. He addressed relational issues in a cultural milieu different from his own, and, overcoming his own initial ethnocentrism, he admonished husbands to love their wives "as Christ loved the church and gave himself for her."

Such an admonition was counter-cultural and revolutionary if we keep in mind the time and cultural context of his writing. In reality, his guidance represented a supracultural and metacognitive statement that challenged the Ephesian natural customs at the core. A higher covenantal perspective hit them "from above" and demanded a change in the alignment of their customary ways with God's covenantal terms. The paradigm exposed and elaborated in this work postulates the New Covenant (to be dealt with in chapter 4) as a supracultural construct applicable to Israeli, as well as to Gentile, believers today. Those who follow the Messiah and mediator may derive exemplary principles and guidelines from God's covenants so as to conduct their transactions in ways that honor God.

THEOLOGICAL-PSYCHOLOGICAL INTEGRATION

This work builds upon what has been said and done in the past in the field of covenantal transactions found in Scripture. It also draws from the research findings in the field of psychology. Many efforts have been dedicated to the field of marital and family therapy in order to develop paradigms of a contracting nature, such as the *quid pro quo* approach proposed by Don Jackson, where exchanges of goods and services, as well as privileges and responsibilities, are established between partners in marriage.[23] In such contracts, the mutual exchange is contingent upon adherence to the stipulations of each party. Richard Stuart, Azrin, and many others have employed such contracting aspects in working with couples and families.[24] Studies in the realm of counseling and clinical psychology may serve as means of comparison and contrast to the approach and emphasis of this work.

Cognitive-behavioral therapy often resorts to contracting among partners in need of solutions to their discords and breakdowns. The purpose of such exchanges is to balance obligations and privileges in attempts to arrive at a fair deal, a "win-win" solution between parties. Tweedie applied covenantal principles among Christian couples analogous to the contractual aspects employed in cognitive-behavioral marital work.[25] The employment of some sort of covenant, contract, or mutually agreeable exchange between two parties seems to have characterized human interactions

23. Jackson, "Family Rules."
24. Stuart, "Operant-Interpersonal"; Azrin et al., "Reciprocity Counseling."
25. Tweedie, "Contract Therapy."

since the birth of civilization. In terms of marriage counseling, most Christian writers advocate some sort of viable and fair covenantal arrangement of an equitable nature.[26]

CONCLUSIONS

In sum, covenant as a paradigm for human relations is set forth as God's way of dealing with his children, translated in terms and principles that serve as an underlying basis for defining normative and exemplary patterns worthy of imitation. It promotes and provides optimal guidelines considered to be essential as we attempt to:

- Establish *mutual premises* and grounds for intimate relationships, and doing things according to a mutually held set of principles, values, beliefs, and practices;
- Establish emotional *boundaries* as a perimeter within which persons in intimate relations may think, feel, act, and relate with the certainty that such expressions are framed within an desirable, purposeful, and functional delineation;
- Establish *proper clauses* framed in terms of expectations, rights, and privileges; delineate mutual responsibilities among partners, as well as any transactional features needed along the development and consolidation of interactive patterns and transactions between members of a system;
- Provide the *optimal context* in which ongoing opportunities are allocated for each person in the system to exercise gifts and services toward one another; also promote interactive processes that enhance, empower, or actualize the potentials of the persons in relation;
- Provide *faith, hope, and convictions of reassurance* as these pertain to the continuity and renewal of marriage and the family system in time;
- Delineate *functional roles and adaptive functions* in relationships, framed in stable and flexible terms, that foster a proper differentiation and an enhanced mutuality between partners;
- Provide a *context for communication* and exchange of impressions, ideas, feelings, desires, etc., among partners: who says what to whom, with what effect, how, why, when, and where considered as variables framed in a context of clear and desirable interactions;
- Provide a *sense of protection and safety* in the system that serves as a boundary to ward off undesirable, dysfunctional, or toxic interactions derived from negative currents, pressures, threats, or challenges of a cultural or secular nature.

---

26. See, for example, Worthington, *Marriage Counseling*; *Hope-Focused Marriage Counseling*; Polischuk, "A New Covenant"; Vande Kamp, *Family Therapy*; Crabb, *The Marriage Builder*; Guernsey, *The Family Covenant*; Wright, *Marital Counseling*; Malony, *Win-Win Relationships*; Balswick and Balswick, *A Model for Marriage*; Sells and Yarhouse, *Counseling Couples*.

All of the above relates to the many *opportunities to imitate God's ways* in relating: being and acting in unilateral fashion in view of optimal bilateral deals; behaving in unconditional and yet assertive ways; being proactive versus reactive; acting with grace and mercy, empowering one another; being forgiving and letting go of offenses; and renewing the covenantal terms in an ongoing fashion. These derived principles and considerations constitute the main thrust of this work.

This chapter has emphasized the main premise that covenant is a scriptural paradigm applicable to human relations. The content of this work conveys notions based upon the findings gathered from psychological research and clinical practice integrated with theological principles derived from Scripture. These integrative efforts are framed conceptually without displacing or diminishing the sufficiency and relevancy of God's revealed truth.

Chapter 3

The Old Covenant as a *Quid Pro Quo*

THE OLD COVENANT (ALSO referred to as the Mosaic Covenant or the Torah) defines a specific agreement between God and Israel and stands out as the main theme of the Old Testament. It presents God's statutes and principles—stipulations of a moral, ceremonial, and ethical nature—that were registered in the writings attributed to Moses (the Pentateuch). The engagement starts with God's proposition to Moses (Exod 6:6–8):

> Therefore, tell the Israelites, I am the LORD. *I will bring you* out from your enslavement to the Egyptians, *I will rescue you* from the hard labor they impose, and *I will redeem you* with an outstretched arm and with great judgments. *I will take you* to myself for a people, and *I will be your God*. Then you will know that I am the LORD your God, who brought you out from your enslavement to the Egyptians. *I will bring you* to the land I swore to give to Abraham, to Isaac, and to Jacob—and *I will give it to you as a posses*sion. I am the LORD! (Emphasis mine)

Forecasting the covenantal deal, God addresses Moses in a top-down, unilateral, unconditional, and proactive fashion. God displays his graceful and merciful thrust to his chosen leader. God's desire is expressed in emphatic *"I will . . . "* terms.

The Old Covenant has been the subject of much theological study and scrutiny dealing with its religious, legal, moral, and ethical dimensions.[1] These dimensions are embedded at the core of God's redemptive design, representing a "shadow of reality" (Heb 10:1) and a preamble announcing better things to come: the advent of the New Covenant.

All covenants convey a functional purpose: to engage two parties by means of intentional, interactive elements, seeking to connect these parties in discrete terms. The Old Covenant expresses God's desire to dwell among his children and to guide and protect them. In a unique and countercultural fashion, the God of Israel expresses his desires to engage with his people in love. God's exuding—transcendent yet immanent—presence within his chosen nation bestowed his graceful and merciful character

---

1. See, for example, Mendenhall, "Law and Covenant"; McCarthy, *Old Testament Covenant*; Nicholson, *God and His People*; Kitchen, "The Fall and Rise"; Kaiser, *Toward an Old Testament Theology*; Niehaus, *God at Sinai*; Brueggemann, *The Covenanted Self*; Williamson, *Sealed with an Oath*; Dumbrell, *Covenant and Creation*; Hahn, *Kinship by Covenant*.

upon them, providing his children with the opportunity and means to engage in divine-human encounters and establishing a vital fellowship by means of a mediator. Having such an awesome display of interaction, children engaged in interpersonal transactions would have a pedagogical paradigm to learn from and imitate. Humans would derive social, ethical, and moral principles, applicable to interpersonal transactions and patterned after God's "manner of love."

COVENANTS ANTECEDING THE OLD COVENANT

According to Scripture, several covenants were enacted prior to the giving of the Old or Mosaic Covenant. To start with, God spoke the world into being *ex nihilo* (out of nothing) and placed humans upon his works, addressing them with covenantal terms. The Genesis narrative presents God's transaction with his creatures with an initial preamble that identifies him as the covenanting Lord. Then, a sort of historical prologue follows—the creation narrative—justifying his sovereignty over the created order. The covenantal terms also include stipulations from the granting Lord, cast into commands and sanctions—blessings for obedience and curses for disobedience to his will and design. A relational theme between God the creator and his creatures unfolds in the narrative, cast in covenantal terms.

1. *The Adamic covenant.* An initial covenant took place between God the creator and Adam and Eve as a created couple in the Garden. This deal may be regarded as being the first institutive act involving a divine-human transaction. The covenantal elements present in the complementary nature of the Genesis 1:1—2:3 narrative (a preamble, a historical prologue, stipulations, deposition, witnesses, blessings, and curses) were compared by Niehaus to those present in the accounts of treaties depicting the relationship between a king and vassals of ancient Mesopotamia.[2] The biblical account repeats the creation narrative in Genesis 2 with a purpose in mind, emphasizing the relational dimension by stating, "That is why a man leaves his father and mother and is united to his wife, and they become one flesh" (Gen 2:24). The creating God sets up and presides over the union of two people as it becomes a partnership (a marriage or couple system) with heavens and Earth as implicit witnesses of the deal.

God related to the couple in what may be called a trialogical interaction: first he related in dyadic fashion to Adam, and then to Eve, as his created children. God then related to both as a couple, a system comprised of individuated persons joined in mutual love and destined to become intimately bonded in one flesh. This relationship could be described with a theological term used to define the Trinity: *perichoresis* (interpenetrated movement in love, persons dancing together within a perimeter). This

---

2. Niehaus, "Covenant and Narrative."

union would resemble God's *hypostatic-ecstatic* union (decentered persons exuding and joining one another in mutual love).

The stipulations provided by God defined their status as joint partners or stewards under His sovereign dominion, originally postulated in Eden and then ratified after the couple's fall into disobedience and sin. The expression registered in the encounter between man and woman reads, "This is at last bone of my bones and flesh of my flesh" (Gen 2:23). This pronouncement before the Fall has been regarded as a sort of *verba solemnia* (solemn oath) used in a formula to denote a uniting pledge.[3]

The fall into disobedience and sin disrupted the pristine arrangement with negative consequences for both partners and detrimental effects on their ecosystemic context. The couple's precarious attempts to escape and hide from God, and then cover themselves in shame, are presented as efforts to cope with their failure to stay within the terms of the original covenant. Their conscious nakedness—being in the open, ashamed, guilty, anxious, and aware of their need to cover—resulted in flight responses and defense mechanisms. A psychological reading may indicate the couple's use of projection, blame, rationalization, and justification before God. The covering and restoration of their covenantal deal is also registered as God's loving care for his creatures in spite of their sinfulness.

It is of importance to realize that this covenant has a universal tone as it pertains to a prototypical relationship between Creator and creatures that provides basic premises, principles, and practical considerations as these pertain to marriage, the family, and social relations in community. It points to God's design and will for such institutions, framed in a context of stewardship before his presence and stressing a conscious accountability to his purpose and definite will for humans to enact. The main purpose for humans is set forth: to live not for their own sake, but for the glory of the Creator and to fulfill his desire. In fulfilling this vertical dimension, their fellowship with and love for one another would be augmented and satisfied. The basic covenantal relationship was set forth in marriage: as male and female in a trialogical relationship (between God and man-woman), they would enact their union under the auspices of a sanctioning God and remain accountable to him and his design. Such a union presupposed the individuation of personhood that was necessary to enter into a mutual interpenetration expressed in a marital system that was framed in hypostatic-ecstatic love.

The failure to keep the original terms opened the door for the entrance of sin and brought about the curses that negatively affected the physical, spiritual, and social orders. The curse may be seen as a vehicle of consequential feedback involving creatures that emerged from a given ground of being and deprived themselves of the connectedness to the source that provided them with energy, existential life, and meaning. Disobedience and the fall into sin prompted the consequential mechanism of the curse's thrust that subjected the failing parties to their sources of being. The

---

3. Hugenberger, *Marriage*.

woman was subjected to man's desire, and the man was subjected to a diminished and fragile predicament. As a steward, he would toil over the ground with sweat, engaged in a constant struggle with a medium characterized by thorns and hardships under the sun.

The fall into sin ruined the original design established under pristine conditions: the male's superordinate position as related to the female is presented in the narrative as a consequence of the catastrophic event. Adam's naming (or defining) of his wife as "Eve" (mother of all living) has often been cited as the basis for a hierarchical system in marriage, the family, and human relations in community. This position derives from an interpretation of the pronouncements found in Genesis 3, regarded as *covenantal elements* rather than as *a covenant lawsuit*. The discovery and study of ancient Near East treaties allowed scholars to differentiate the intent of the original terms with the *covenantal lawsuit* as a genre that involved characteristic pronouncements of judgment applicable to those who would fail to keep the terms of a covenant.

Corrective efforts in theological interpretation appeal to the redemptive promise found in Genesis 3:15, where the seed of the woman would crush the seed of the serpent: an allusion of Messianic proportions with redemptive effects, which restored things to the original design of God, including the status/position of the woman. The redemptive dimension appears in the majority of OT prophetic material as well, coupled to the covenant lawsuits applicable to conditions of disobedience. Some scholars have compared the pronouncements found in Matthew 23:13–39 to the last and greatest OT covenant lawsuit.[4]

Regardless of the Fall and its consequences, it is safe to assume that the lawsuit derivatives for the Adamic covenant do not necessarily have an eternal endurance. The couple was reconnected to God and to one another by a redemptive act from God's side (sacrificing an animal for their sakes and covering them with skin). This restitution of fellowship by redemption anticipated the promise of a redeemer who would be there for humans to rely on and who would make them capable of living as imitators of God, walking in love with one another. Redemption would empower God's children regardless of the negative factors associated with sinful nature, which in an antagonistic fashion tends to disrupt human relations.

Although the consequences of disobedience run through human transactional history, the ultimate redemption in Christ has encompassed such consequences and dealt with them, empowering human relations in marriage, the family, and the community of faith to engage in transactions "beyond the curse."[5] That is, redeemed humans in Christ have regained freedom, empowerment, respect, honor, and love for one another. They may now engage in new and better deals, exemplified in the terms of the New Covenant (Gal 3:28).

---

4. Niehaus, "Covenant and Narrative," 539.
5. Spencer, *Beyond the Curse*.

2. *The covenant with Noah.* The biblical narrative presents a dreadful context in which humankind reached excessive levels of sinful degradation and was destined for destruction. In this context, "Noah found grace in the sight of the Lord" (Gen 6:8). God's unilateral, unconditional, and proactive grace prompted the call of Noah, and a covenant was established with him. This covenant (Gen 9:1–17) follows the same dimensional elements that are compatible with the second millennium BCE treaties. Following Niehaus's outline, the elements may be succinctly stated as follows:[6]

- Title: "And God blessed . . . " (9:1);
- Stipulations: "Be fruitful and multiply, and fill the earth" (9:1, 4);
- Blessings: "And God blessed . . . " (9:1–3);
- Curse: Man's blood demanded from man and beast (9:5–6);
- Oath: "I establish my covenant . . . " (9:9–11);
- Sign: A rainbow and an explanation of its meaning (9:12–17).

The relational aspects of God's love for his children are emphasized again. This covenant falls in line with the Adamic covenant, as if a renewal of terms took place in which God addressed issues applicable to all humankind. The common grace of God appears to be the foundation upon which his more particular grace would be provided later on. Yet, the descendants of Noah were less than able to keep God's original intentions, and in their obstinacy were scattered throughout the globe by God's intervention at Babel. The nations that followed deviated from the original ways, engaging in all sorts of behaviors and practices that demonstrated their unwillingness and incapacity to stay in covenantal terms with God. Rather than God engaging in further judgments, a redemptive event took place with his call of a person and the giving of new promises.

3. *The Abrahamic covenant.* As the narrative goes, God's love—displayed in unilateral, unconditional, and proactive grace—was displayed once again. From among the dispersed and rebellious nations, God targeted a person from Ur of Chaldea. With faith and in obedience to God's call, Abraham embarked on a walk with God toward a promised land. He was then shaped by God in an ascending and growing fellowship (registered in Gen 12—14), and at a given time, he developed the capacity to be engaged in a relational covenant with his calling God. A unique deal was established between God and Abraham (Gen 15:7–18; 17:1–4). Again, the dimensions of this covenant seem to follow the lines of the contextual narratives of second millennium BCE treaties and covenants. The ratification of this covenant has been emphasized in which promises were given (descendants, land, and an extensive impact on the world) with the cutting of animals, swearing, and witnesses.[7] The coparticipation between

---

6. Niehaus, "Covenant and Narrative," 541–42.
7. Weinfeld, *Deuteronomy*; Niehaus, "Covenant and Narrative."

Abraham's descendants and God was expected: the land being granted had to be conquered through warfare, with Joshua leading this endeavor. Later on, Moses had to deliver enslaved Israelites from Egypt and give them a covenant at Sinai.

Genesis 17 adds further details related to the Abrahamic covenant. God's unilateral and all-powerful capacity to bless his child (and his descendants) is cast in an epithet as he identifies himself as *El Shaddai* (diversely translated as "almighty," "powerful destroyer," or "God the mountain-one"). Such a descriptive definition conveys God's strong, unshakable capacity to deliver the goods as promised by the one who sits on top of the universe. Readers may compare the diverse texts dealing with the symbolic connotations of these top-down processes coming from the covenanting God interacting with his children. Several "peak experiences" are registered in Scripture. God addressed Abraham at Mount Moriah and delivered his covenant from Mount Sinai. In the New Testament, Jesus shared a glimpse of his eternal glory with three of his beloved disciples at the Mount of Transfiguration and departed from the Mount of Olives, promising to return to the same spot at the end of times.

The readers may note also that all such dealings have a sovereign, unilateral tone and thrust, while, at the same time, seeking to invite believing humans to relate to God in covenantal deals actualized through faith and obedience to his will. Once humans accept the unilateral thrust coming from God in top-down fashion, such persons, couples, families, or communities of believers are able to engage and relate to God in a loving, bilateral fashion.

The redefinition (re-forming the formed, yet deformed, being) and change of name from Abram to Abraham (a defining description of his personhood: from "high father" to "father of multitudes"), as well as the redefinition and change of his wife Sarai to Sarah ("my princess" to "princess of all"), took place. Both husband and wife would be reminded of God's will and loving intentions for them in their future, having a real and concrete manifestation of God's covenantal terms as fulfilled relationally. At times, it may be simply hard to accept God's redefinitions so as to re-attribute meaning to our own designation or to that of our neighbor: imagine a 70-year-old person trying to call his wife by a different name! The changes in definitions seem to have relational connotations with God and with one another; they also extend with radial momentum to include the community of believers.

To affirm the deal, circumcision was established as a sign or seal of the covenant to be re-enacted by all males belonging to his household through the generations. Later on, a converted Gentile (a proselyte) had to go through this process in order to be counted as one belonging to God's people.

A significant dimension of the Abrahamic covenant is emphasized in Genesis 22, where Abraham is commanded to give God his son Isaac in sacrifice. The command was cast against all the promises given, for the nation of descendants would not have a chance to exist if Isaac was taken out of the picture. The blessings of all nations would vanish at Mount Moriah. In this dreadful context, the well-known account is given in which the sacrificial substitution takes place at Mount Moriah. Abraham called the place *YHWH Yireh* or "The Lord Will Provide" (Gen 22:14), a prophetic utterance pointing to the fact that, on that mountain, a temple would be built by Solomon, where the glory of God would be seen in the future (2 Chron 3:1).

Fifteen centuries later, an ultimate substitute—the Lamb of God—would die outside of the wall of the city built on that mountain, and his blood would take the sins of the world away from God's presence (John 1:29). When addressing defiant Jews in his day, Jesus alluded to this event, saying, "Your father Abraham was overjoyed to see my day, and he saw it and was glad" (John 8:56). Other translations say, "Abraham rejoiced at the thought of seeing my day; he saw it and was glad" (NIV).

The relational nature embedded in this transaction may be noted, as Abraham was pushed to the limits of his faith and had to believe in the God who promises above the promises for which he was believing. This existential leap of faith was taken, and God attested to the faithfulness of his child by solemnly swearing by his own name that he would fulfill the terms of his covenant (Gen 22:16). The author to the Hebrews provides an explanatory note in which Abraham's faith is defined as a proactive deed enacted in view of God's power to give him back his son, even from the dead (Heb 11:17–19).

Many scholarly efforts have been dedicated to the Abrahamic covenant, regarded as a key transaction that overarches time and reaches out to Israel and the rest of the nations through the provision of the promised seed of Abraham, Jesus Christ (see Gal 3:29; Acts 3:25; 13:23; Rom 4:13, 16–18). Important as it was, the Abrahamic covenant foreshadowed the Mosaic covenant and anticipated the new one as well. Nevertheless, it was not intended to exert a normative pressure upon believers. The covenantal sign (circumcision) was abrogated once the reality brought by Jesus superseded the shadows of reality. Instead, a new "circumcision of the heart" takes place in the believer (Rom 2:28–29). Everything of eternal import that has been promised in this covenant has been taken up and expressed in a new and better way in the New Covenant, as Paul convincingly argues in his letters.

The Abrahamic covenant reminds individuals, couples, families, and faith communities of the fact that God's grace empowers believers as relational beings. Consider God's promise to Abraham (Gen 12:2–3), and by extrapolation, to his descendants (natural and spiritual):

- "I will bless you" (*being* ontologically blessed by God);
- "I will make your name great and you will be a blessing" (*becoming* a blessing as we grow in faith);
- "All peoples on earth will be blessed through you" (an exuding property of *being and becoming* a growing source of blessing)—so as to be able to exert a social, ethical, moral, and spiritual influence on all peoples.

The Old Covenant as a Quid Pro Quo

This radial and centrifugal expansion is embedded in the Abrahamic covenant so that all families on Earth will pronounce blessings on one another on account of his faithful descendants' being, becoming, and behaving.

THE ESTABLISHMENT OF THE OLD COVENANT

The Old Covenant was given in due time, after Israel's deliverance from slavery and their exodus from a worldly empire. The deal was made as they faced a long, convoluted journey marked by hardships. God and Israel had an encounter of extraordinary proportions, prompted by the unilateral and proactive grace of God. In the midst of a context marked by transitional contingencies, God engaged Israel bilaterally, providing stipulations, promises, and blessings by means of a mediator. Israel was given the opportunity to respond to this deal by accepting God's terms in obedience and engaging the Lord with faithful love as a chosen party entering into a divine marriage deal. In this book, the emphasis is placed on the *relational* dimension of the Old Covenant to be conveyed and apprehended in a faithful and loving fashion.

Old Testament scholars (e.g., Mendenhall, Kline, Kaiser, Kitchen, and Niehaus) have understood and affirmed that the Deuteronomic account follows the literary genre and legal style that characterized the late second millennium BCE Hittite international treaties. The context for such a covenant is presented in the biblical narrative, depicting the nation of Israel as falling short of God's will, descending to Egypt, and becoming slaves of the world's leading empire. For more than 400 years, the Israelites were oppressed and subject to the Egyptian rulers and their culture, norms, habits, and social structures.

The Israelites' mindset was affected by negative contingencies. They were enslaved, degraded, and mistreated for more than four centuries. Psychologically speaking, these oppressive and degrading factors fostered the development of a survival mentality marked by oppositional tendencies, reactionary attitudes, and retaliatory stances. The people of Israel developed a bonded and homogeneous ethnocentricity, characterized by protective and insulating tendencies coupled with an exclusionary stance toward Gentiles. These schemata accumulated and consolidated into an ethnocentric, sociocultural metanarrative.

Conjecturally speaking, the dynamic and ecosystemic forces exerted their effects over the mindset of the wandering Israelites. Years of pilgrimage under harsh conditions fostered the entrenchment of a negative and antagonistic group identity. In functional ways, Israelites developed over-compensatory, "stiff-necked" stances and mechanisms in order to survive. People that were subjected to slavery and degradation often develop both a sensitive and apprehensive stance toward any perceived threatening or top-down authority giving commands. They were imprinted and infused with the derogatory ways and means to which they were subject for such a long time. The negative experiences remained engraved in their mindset as semantic and episodic memories, unconsciously and mindfully carried into their present and affecting their future hopes. These characteristics defined the Israelites that Moses led out of Egypt.

The pressures exerted from their past experiences, framed in terms of a cognitive dissonance, added to a group mindset filled with paradoxes: how could it be possible that a loving and all-powerful God would allow them to be subjected to such an ordeal? If they were the chosen ones, why would such experiences be allowed? Their lack of a secure attachment to the God of their fathers did not provide Israelites with a basis for confidence or a sense of trust. Four centuries of slavery fostered a sense of learned helplessness, and the feeling of having been abandoned by a distant Father did not provide a sense of security, belongingness, or esteem. Such people needed a powerful covenantal deal to establish a new relationship with God their deliverer.

GOD'S INTENSIFIED PRESENCE IN COVENANTAL TIMING

The Mosaic covenant may be depicted as a relational deal with Israel in which God employed an intensified degree of revelation expressed concretely. So far, his presence had been registered in theophanies of a sporadic and intermittent nature. God had visited humans on special and powerful occasions in order to unfold his ongoing, eternal purpose to targeted individuals. Those chosen for such revelations became prototypical examples of God's grace and conveyed intended meanings along redemptive history: 1.) Adam and Eve as the couple under God's jurisdiction and design acting as progenitors of the human race; 2.) Noah as the faithful leader of a family who found grace in the sight of the Lord and was saved with his family in order to fulfill God's purpose in a renewed fashion after the judgment passed on sinful humans; and 3.) Abraham as the founding father of Israel and of all believers who would follow in his steps before God.

The time had come in redemptive history for God to establish a covenant that would provide a concrete expression of his enduring presence in the midst of his people. The covenant was given with pomp, thunder, lightning, and glory, so as to impress the human party with the awesome presence and power of the covenant giver. His desire to dwell among his people was expressed in a command to Moses: "Let them make for me a sanctuary, so that I may live among them" (Exod 25:8).

A definite approach to God was delineated in the context of a tabernacle, with the institution of the priesthood being established in order to serve in favor of the people in the sight of God. By means of the tabernacle (God's first dwelling place), the mediating ministry of Moses, and the priesthood, God would ascertain his covenantal presence in the midst of his people. In all matters of guidance and decision-making, God could be consulted through a mediator making intercession for them. God would be accessed by means of five types of discrete offerings (for sin, guilt, peace, presents, and burnt offerings) in accordance with established guidelines and purposes. The tablets of the law provided a concrete rendering of his will, and all the objects of the tabernacle pointed to the diverse aspects of his character and works.

A BILATERAL-CONDITIONAL PARADIGM

The Old Covenant was given within the context of the ancient cultures. Old Testament scholars have compared the literary form and legal tone of the Mosaic covenant to the Hittite international treaties of the second millennium BCE.[8] Based on Mendenhall's (1954) studies, Kline elaborated on the correlation between the suzerain treaties and several sections of Scripture, describing the essential clauses of the Old Covenant as follows.[9]

- Title/preamble (Exod 20:1; Deut 1:1–5; Josh 24:2);
- Historical prologue (Exod 20:2; Deut 1:6—3:29; Josh 24:2–13);
- Basic commands and detailed laws (Exod 20:3–17; 20:22–26; 21–23; 25–31; Lev 1—25; Deut 1:6—3:29; Josh 24:2–13);
- Deposit of text and public reading (Exod 25:16; Deut 10:2, 5; 31:24–26; 31:10–13; Josh 24:26);
- Witnesses (Exod 24:4—marked by stelae or stones; cf., with those in Gilgal, Josh 4:3–9, and Shechem, Josh 24:27; Deut 31:19–22, 30; 31:26; Josh 24:22);
- Blessings for obedience (Lev 26:3–13; Deut 28:1–14);
- Curses for disobedience (Lev 26:14–41; Deut 28:15-68; Josh 24:19–20);
- Epilogue (Deut 29:2—30:20).

These comparative analogies are drawn so as to capture the contextual ambiance in which God's revelation to humans was provided as a relational deal—to be accepted by faith and obeyed in humble recognition of God's love, grace, and mercy.

The deal starts with God's declaration to Moses: "I am the God of your father, the God of Abraham, the God of Isaac, and the God of Jacob" (Exod 3:6), followed by, "I have come down to deliver them from the hand of the Egyptians and to bring them up from that land to a land that is both good and spacious, to a land flowing with milk and honey" (Exod 3:8). The continuity between the Mosaic covenant and the Abrahamic covenant is reflected in the repeated expression that starts with God's unilateral "I

---

8. The relevance of the Hittite treaty form to OT materials was pioneered by George E. Mendenhall, in "Covenant Forms in Israelite Tradition," 50–76. Meredith G. Kline further provided analytical renderings of the concept in *Treaty of the Great King*, as well as Kenneth A. Kitchen, *Ancient Orient and Old Testament*.

9. Kline, *The Structure*.

will" expressions (Exod 6:6–8). The introduction of a conditional "if you . . . then I . . ." proposal appears as an added feature in a bilateral covenant (Exod 19:5–6):

> "And now, *if you* will diligently listen to me and keep my covenant, *then you will be* my special possession out of all the nations, for all the earth is mine, and you will be to me a kingdom of priests and a holy nation." These are the words that you will speak to the Israelites. (Emphasis mine)

Thus, a sort of a *quid pro quo* was embedded in the tone of the transactional deal. The proactive initiative was God's: "He gave Moses two tablets of testimony when he had finished speaking with him on Mount Sinai, tablets of stone written by the finger of God" (Exod 31:18). The narrative emphasizes God's initiative stated in concrete stones: "Now the tablets were the work of God, and the writing was the writing of God, engraved on the tablets" (Exod 32:16).

These tablets were smashed by Moses in his anger when the people turned aside and worshipped a golden calf: "When he approached the camp and saw the calf and the dancing, Moses became extremely angry. He threw the tablets from his hands and broke them to pieces at the bottom of the mountain" (Exod 32:19). The mediator himself, described as the meekest man on Earth (Num 12:3), broke the tablets in a moment of rage. In sovereign grace and mercy, God commanded Moses to chisel a new set of tablets: "The Lord said to Moses, 'Cut out two tablets of stone like the first, and I will write on the tablets the words that were on the first tablets, which you smashed'" (Exod 34:1). The mediator was instructed by God to coparticipate and chisel a new set of tablets so that God would inscribe his will again.

In anticipation of the next chapter, and in the spirit of the letter to the Hebrews, an interpretative comment is made here. The sets of tablets were deposited within the ark of the covenant, behind the veil of the tabernacle, inside the Holy of Holies. As a symbolic way of anticipating a future event, this intent foreshadowed the person and work of "the seed of Abraham" (also called "the seed of David"). One greater than Moses would contain—incarnate—or guard the law: the mediator of a New Covenant. In contrast to Moses, Jesus Christ would not break the tablets (the Torah), but rather embody and keep it in an intact and perfect way.

The Abrahamic and Davidic covenants presented God's promises, blessings, and inheritance unconditionally, without stating any stipulations. At Sinai, the expectations pertaining to the obedience and faithfulness of the people were set forth. Nevertheless, the law did not include a restriction over against the dispensation of grace and mercy coming from God. The law is God's frame of mind, the structure by means of which the conditions are set forth to evoke the human response to his grace and mercy and to obey his commandments.

The Old Covenant was given in the midst of the exodus experience, demonstrating God's compassion and love for his people (Exod 34:6–7). The law embodied God's grace and mercy in leading Israel—those who were oppressed, insignificant, powerless, and weak—during their exodus. The giving of the Torah is embedded in a redemptive narrative. It embraces both the provisions of God's commandments for his people and the narrative of his saving acts. Law and narrative story are two modes of one and the same top-down agency: the Torah of God's life-giving action. Consequently, belief in God's redemptive story and obedience to God's law were two modes of responding to the Old Covenant. Redemptive and relational aspects are intertwined in the transaction between God and humans.

The subsequent chapters of the Pentateuch contain further dimensions of the Torah. This divinely revealed instruction conveys the sense of a relational binding between the Lord and his people as they journey from Sinai through the wilderness. Keeping in mind Israel's past, affected by their enslaved state with its negative connotations, God deemed it necessary to further stipulate civil, ethical, and moral aspects of everyday life. The Old Covenant is presented in the historical books, providing a dramatic prologue that justifies God's prerogative in providing both stipulations (commands) and sanctions (curses and admonitions for transgression) to his people. A succinct version of these clauses appears in the opening of the Decalogue: "I am the Lord your God, who brought you out of the land of Egypt, out of the house of slavery." As a consequence, "You shall have no other gods before me" (Exod 20:2).

Other commands follow this edict. In a conditional-bilateral deal, the people accepted the terms with Moses officiating as the mediator. This deal was ratified when both the artifacts of the Tabernacle and the people themselves were sprinkled with the blood of sacrificed animals. Moses warned the people repeatedly of the promise of blessing in the land for obedience on the one side, and exile for disobedience on the other. Finally, the testimonial tablets were deposited in the ark of the covenant to be consulted with and appealed to on occasion.

THE OLD AS A FORERUNNER OF THE NEW COVENANT

Why would God give such a covenant if a new one was in the makings, at least in his mind? Why not establish an optimal deal from the beginning, right after the exodus experience? Was God changing his *modus operandi* as the events took place—as if he were subject to human maneuvers or contingent upon their behaviors? Or was God adapting his deals to the progressive unfolding and growth of his people so as to establish a homeostatic equilibrium between their accommodation and assimilation of his ways? We are reminded that God is not bound to a chronological time; he is eternally proactive and omniscient in his designs. God acts in an architectural fashion rather than as a reactive handyman fixing problems. His eternal purpose unfolded in *due time*. Thus, our metacognitive capacity to ponder on such matters may be more accurate if we behold in a better fashion a God whose definitions of reality in space and time are far above our cognitive appraisal.

Part I: Premises and Principles

A glimpse of God's mind may be apprehended from the statement made by Jesus to his disciples, "I still have many more things to say to you, but you cannot bear them now. When he, the Spirit of truth, comes, he will guide you into all the truth" (John 16:12–13). Thus, the answer to our initial questions emerges from the Scriptures themselves, pointing to the Old Covenant as the necessary tutor, a *pedagogos* called to be at our side in conjunction with the Holy Spirit. The Old Covenant was established between God and Israel in the midst of a pilgrimage with their lives filled with vicissitudes; they were leaving behind a background of slavery and oppression and pressing forward to a future to be actualized in the Promised Land. Under these conditions, the covenant became a *pedagogos* (παιδαγωγὸς; in Galatians 3:24, a "mentor"), leading the people in their sojourning along God's expressed will. This mentor would prepare the way for the establishment of a New Covenant. A new and better deal would both epitomize God's redemptive thrust and represent his ultimate transactional paradigm. God's relationship with his dearly beloved children would be optimized and actualized.

The Old Covenant represented a dialectical and dialogical transition until the time for the fulfillment of the promise made to Abraham would come. This promise centered upon a seed (a descendant *in potentia*) from his loins, a redeemer who would once and for all establish a better deal: a New Covenant (Gal 3:19). It provided the basis for the relationship between YHWH and Israel for the next 1500 years, foreshadowing the coming of the Messiah and experiencing the systematization of its content and interpretative meaning. Besides its revealed, redemptive purpose—as far as it pertains to humans relating to God in salvific terms—the Old Covenant would serve a normative and functional guide for exemplary ethical, moral, and civil conduct.

An important expression is found in Matthew 5:17, which states that the "law and the prophets" will never pass away, nor any part thereof. This expression can be understood as being, in fact, a genuine temporal expression. Yet this interpretation allows room for the qualifying of the temporal until all prophecies come to pass, as Gordon, among others, has argued.[10] Within the Old and the New Testaments, "the law and the prophets" renderings of ordinances and prophetic statements are seen as being fulfilled eventfully, elucidated by the post-resurrection apostolic writings that shine light on their meaning. Thus, as many rudiments have "passed away" with the old economy, and everything has become "new" in the present, Christians are not so bothered by circumcision, dietary restrictions, festivals, and the like. By regarding those rudiments as transitional objects, no guilt or shame is experienced in celebrating the freedom and the grace that has brought the meaning of such shadows—symbols and figures—into an actualizing fulfillment in Christ. It is the moral tone of the law that is preserved, rather than the ceremonial or civil aspects, which are considered to be time-bound and culturally-based.

10. Gordon et al., *The Use of Forgiveness*.

The law encompassed God's standards for "walking in love," with a sense of direction and tempo guiding life under the sun. The commandments served as defining elements of a boundary intended to demarcate God's will. They represented a set of codified principles of operation upon which to build. Both individual lifestyle and relational transactions would be actualized in fair, equitable, loving, and peaceful terms. The core of such commandments was expressed in loving God and one's neighbor as one would love oneself. The commandments were accompanied by a number of regulations that set forth the premises for physical, social, ethical, and moral functioning and transactions The regulations of an interpersonal nature and the safeguards pertaining to people's rights and privileges were added in order to define Israel's responsibilities to be and behave as God's chosen people.

HUMAN SENSATION, PERCEPTION, AND ATTRIBUTION OF MEANING TO THE OLD COVENANT

In his account of dialogical nature taking place within and between his deformed and transforming self—mediated by his reformed self—the apostle Paul regarded the Old Covenant as being "holy, righteous, and good" (Rom 7:12). Yet, in his dialogical deliberation, he found that the very commandment that promised life proved to be deadly to him (Rom 7:10). Because of the entrenched sin in his members, this deadly sense became noticeable and salient. As a mirror revealing his imperfection and natural propensity to sin, the law opened the eyes of his understanding, and he saw himself as subject to the law of sin and death. Thus, the expressed values and principles that were sculpted in stone became a rigid standard demonstrating his human incapacity to be and to do what God desires.

The holy, perfect, and good law addresses humans with injunctions that are impossible to obey due to human incapacity, resulting in the sense of being imposed upon by a condemning agency. The sculpted statements are experienced as being rigid and cold—and apparently insensitive to the human struggles for perfection. They seem to come down from a detached and stern Father who appears to be aloof and unavailable. Psychologically speaking, the negative filtering of human perceptions of God and his perfect law are due to the fallen nature of human information processing. The naturally flawed filters that characterize the natural mindset affected by sin render slanted and distorted images of God and his purposes.

The inner rhetoric that emerges in Romans 8 is a metacognitive shift from the internal dialogues shared by the apostle with his audience in the previous chapter. It is set forth, in essential questions, as the antidote to the impossible dilemma: given the sinful predicament in which a person finds her/himself, how can that person be persuaded intrinsically of the fact that she or he is at peace with God? How can that person be secure in God's hands and live free from condemnation, so as to experience the benefits of being an inheritor of God's promises? The Pauline answer is found in the chapter following his dialogical dilemma (Rom 8), in which peace with God, assurance of salvation, and fruitful living may be achieved not by human efforts, but by the grace of God. He has provided the means for a believer to live empowered by the Spirit who animates a new and better covenant.

God's commandments are experienced by a contrite human as being condemnatory injunctions, due to the stipulated consequences associated with trespassing them. The incapacity to remain in obedience to the covenant terms renders a person a prisoner of his own precariousness, being consciously aware of the power of sin to impinge upon and trap his mindset. In relational and natural terms, personal and interpersonal rights, prerogatives, and obligations may become confused. In marital transactions, the balance between offers, demands, privileges, and responsibilities may experience dysfunction.

Allusions made by both Peter (Acts 15:10) and Paul (Gal 5:1) to the law being a "yoke" cannot be ignored. Analogically, as it pertains to human alliances such as marriage, it becomes obvious as to why Paul recommends that individuals "not be unequally yoked" (2 Cor 6:14). Unequal yokes would be characterized by interpersonal dysfunctions such as marital tug-of-wars due to conflictive values, and difficulties in achieving a peaceful lifestyle due to unequal expressions of faithfulness. A lack of synchronicity in transactional mindsets would be reflected in interpersonal styles and customs, adding unnecessary pressures to a couple.

The covenant between a righteous God and an unrighteous people was experienced as being restrictive and oppressive. In time, it became a heavy burden to bear. The readers may remember that the Old Covenant was initially intended to be an instrument of justice, peace, and love. It was intended to promote a good life. Yet, it is due to human incapacity and failure that the Torah's contents and intent may be experienced as oppressive and condemning or as curtailing the person's freedom to exercise her or his own will. Any God-given precept becomes a crushing and appalling instrument as the sinful human is deprived of doing his or her own will and objects to, defies, or disobeys God's will. Those who reluctantly attempt to obey and fulfill the obligations of a covenant may experience a sense of being devoid of joy or fulfillment in the process.

From a believer's perspective, these filtered and slanted versions are the effects of sinful, phenomenological distortions in perception of a God-given reality. Even in the case of the experience of honest believers, the law appears to be a negative injunction against their attempts to do good, judging their lack of perfection. Yet, God's revelation in the Torah may be seen as a provision of standards for life, established to help humans to function according to God's designated will.

Even "under the law," not everyone experienced the same negative impressions of God's revelation. A person like David, endowed with artistic abilities and a sensitive spirit and an eagerness to do God's will, superposed his perceptions over that of his contemporaries and, with a metacognitive perspective, was able to see the wonders of the law. His mindful reframing of experiential vicissitudes allowed him to perceive life contingencies with a sense of God's awe, beyond the entrapments of a legalistic, bogged-down mindset. His faith-based convictions resulted in better attributions of meaning to God's law.

While many of his contemporaries regarded the law as a sort of a steamroller that flattened their hopes, ambitions, and desires, David and other worshippers employed a sort of feedforward control system that acted in superposed fashion, rising above any negative feedback provided by life's stressors. In that way, they would redefine their predicament, and from the dust of their own despair, they would still sing the praises of the law. As a poet, David compared God's words to the taste of honey dripping from a honeycomb, sweet to the taste, and energizing the spirit (Ps 19). He would meditate on the law day and night (Ps 119:97), finding delightful aspects in it (Ps 119:24) and rejoicing in the statutes. The sons of Korah earnestly desired God and his Word, expressing their spiritual thirst in figurative language—as a deer pants for streams of waters (Ps 42:1).

A SYNTHETIC PERSPECTIVE ON THE OLD COVENANT

The scholars of the law have systematized the commandments, regulations, and expectations into 613 statements. For our purposes, we may succinctly summarize the Old Covenant in a few, functional clauses. In sum, we may say that this covenant represented a relational paradigm with these characteristics for the recipients:

- It was given by God in an unilateral fashion, to be engaged with in bilateral encounters between two parties: God and Israel;

- It sprang from the unconditional and steadfast love of God, but was conditionally experienced, contingent upon the fulfillment of the statutes, ordinances, and standards of the law. Obedience to God's decrees would bring the desired blessings promised in the deal;

- Covenant partners assumed full responsibility for their promises, oaths, and actions, without excusing, blaming, projecting, or displacing their accountability;

- Parties entered the covenant consciously, endowed with willful, abnegated, and participatory choices. God never forced any person to participate, but invited them to consider the exercise of the basic choice between principles leading to life or death;

- The deal provided a basis for a stable lifestyle and encompassed all aspects of life: spiritual, ethical, moral, ceremonial, and civil. It was based upon God's definition of reality and appealed to a person's convictions and actions. Human moods and feelings would fluctuate, but the demands of obedience to the covenant remained at the same level. Commandments were firmly sculpted in stone;

Part I: Premises and Principles

- The deal was fair if the parties would fulfill their respective obligations stipulated in what we today call a *quid pro quo*. Equality would be preserved in a protective manner with the rights, prerogatives, boundaries, and expectations of each party held in proper view;

- The deal promoted love for God and the neighbor equitably. The marriage partner was considered to be the closest neighbor of all. To love the neighbor as one's self implied the desire to promote the same benefits for that person as were desired for one's self. Partners would be able to nurture mutuality in love;

- The deal had a continuous relevance. The Israelites would retell the stories of Exodus and the giving of the law generation after generation. Remembering and celebrating the commitments made were essential for the renewal of a vibrant life and service;

- The deal was externally mediated, with objective standards engraved on stone. Retrospectively, this covenant would be regarded by New Testament writers as a tutor, a *pedagogos* that would bring people to the real teacher, who then would allocate them into their hearts and minds.

Nevertheless, this covenant proved to be inadequate, due to our natural tendencies to sin (to miss the mark or to trespass the limits set by God). The failure to keep the covenant resides in human weakness and incapacity to stay within God's defining boundaries. From a human standpoint, the covenant became a rigid paradigm that trapped the person in guilt and condemnation. The contract that started with pomp and ceremony, with the sounds of trumpets and flashes of lightning, turned into a somber mourning. In times of captivity, such as the time of Israel's exile to Babylon, people experienced a sense of defeat, degradation, and despair as they realized that this state was due to their disobedience to God's will.

The potential stability in relations turned into rigidity in roles and functions with little room for flexible alternatives. In time, post-exilic developments associated with the Old Covenant became elaborate with traditions added to the essential commandments. The leaders responsible for the teaching of the Torah systematized and provided the people with interpretations of God's revelation that further added to the repertoire of legalistic injunctions. A ceremonial and ritualized spirit permeated the covenantal interactive routines between Israel and their God, in which the religious form remained, but the essence and life of worship became stagnant.

The intended ecstasy in serving the living God turned into apostasy (*apo-stasis*: a negative movement away from the target of love). What was intended for a decentered service unto the Lord of the house became a self-centered, egotistical exercise in self-righteousness. The Torah's principles aimed at promoting respect, honor, and dignity among equals became elements of manipulation, struggles for control, and hierarchical maneuvers in the hands of the religious leaders. Pharisees and other leaders sought to take personal advantage by using the law to fulfill their own needs.

A review of the scriptural narrative reveals that, in spite of human unfaithfulness and incapacity to stay within the confinements of this covenant, God's faithfulness in keeping his promises endured. Thus, it was not that God was unable to deliver the promised blessings, but rather that human incapacity necessitated the enactment of a new covenant.

The salient feature in the Old Covenant is that God's grace, loyalty, faithfulness, and dedication stand as basic ingredients of this paradigmatic model for relationships. To love purposefully in spite of being dejected or to give unilaterally in spite of being abandoned are hallmarks of steadfast grace and sovereign mercy at work, not an exercise in codependency. As God exercises his willful prerogatives toward his children, we may learn that our loyalty and faithfulness in keeping our covenants with others are predicated upon our capacity to imitate God's ways—that is, to be, to choose, and to regard ourselves as being loyal, faithful, and dedicated children of God. Yet, as the human predicament obviously demonstrates, it is due to the hardness of our hearts that allowances for disengagement or alternative courses of action may take place in our transactions with one another.

We are not God. Thus, we may separate; we may become divisive, unforgiving, step on boundaries, disrupt our harmony, and the like. We may cling to our rights and protect our life space based upon defensiveness, anxiety, or narcissistic needs. In clinical work, the author has witnessed the conflicts experienced by couples due to their inability to remain faithful to their marital covenant with negative consequences leading to separation or divorce. At times, the best, functional paradigm in therapeutic endeavors seeking reconciliation was engagement in a process that barely resembled the Old Covenant—a *quid pro quo* intended to satisfy the needs of both partners—or a deal in which there are no losers but only winners.

Partners joined in unequal yokes, manifesting a lack in the satisfaction of their basic needs or experiencing threats to their self-preservation (as in the case of abusive or manipulative relations), may attempt to enact a contract in which the Old Covenant's dictum "an eye for an eye" constitutes an equitable measure of prevention, protection, and safety. Far from representing a graceful or optimal deal, this *quid pro quo* establishes a barely fair agreement in which partners are neither taken for a ride nor become subject to manipulation or abuse.

The fact that a basic arrangement can be made and preserved so as to guarantee that there will be no losers does not invalidate the possibility for a better deal (to go beyond legalistic or justice-driven contracts). Just as the Old Covenant was a preamble to better things, a *pedagogos* teaching a new and better way of transacting, a preliminary deal may apply in cases where human-disgraced covenants are in need of renewal and restoration. A "buffer zone" is offered between the original covenant state—which has become a disgraced state—and the possibility of establishing a new deal in order to allow room for negotiations. In that zone, reconciling maneuvers between covenantal partners need to be mediated with the aim to establish a new covenant based on love, grace, and mercy.

INTEGRATIVE POSSIBILITIES

The Old Covenant as a paradigm may be taken as a springboard for therapeutic considerations. Secular versions resembling the contractual agreements analogous to the bilateral-conditional aspects found in the Old Covenant have made their contributions to the field of marital and family therapy (MFT). Don Jackson's introduction of a contractual model known as a *quid pro quo*, Jacobson's emphasis on behavioral exchanges between partners, and Stuart's integrated cognitive-emotive-behavioral contracts between partners in marriage have followed avenues emphasizing bilateral-conditional deals marked by fairness, justice, and empathic understanding between contracting parties.[11] From a Christian perspective, Tweedie's proposal for marital counseling, described as Covenant therapy, integrated behavioral principles with scriptural assertions.[12] Other Christian therapists have proposed these mutual exchanges in covenantal terms as well.[13] The conscious integration of proven psychological strategies and theological postulates served as a basis for the development of approaches in working with couples and families.

The Old Covenant provides an ethical and moral basis for the establishment of fair and loving transactions applicable to marriage and the family systems. People experiencing difficulties in their intimate relationships who seek to repair, restore, or renew their marital or familial transactions may profit from counseling approaches that utilize the principles gathered from the paradigm disclosed in this chapter. Again, to reiterate a main point, the Old Covenant model may serve as a *pedagogos* (a mentor or guardian), guiding troubled marriages and families in need of reconciliation and restoration. Analogous to the continuous yet discrete function served by the Old with respect to the New Covenant, when people in discord and disgrace decide to employ a helpful agent, a bilateral-conditional deal may be regarded as a functional paradigm to start with.

The Old Covenant may be adopted as a paradigm for relations, a model to be employed in the attempt to integrate psychological principles applicable to therapeutic approaches in couples and family work. This paradigm points to a triadic engagement comprised of Israel and God, mediated through Moses. Following this viable model,

---

11. Jackson, "Family Rules"; Jacobson and Margolin, *Marital Therapy*; Stuart, *Helping Couples Change*.

12. Tweedie, "Contract Therapy."

13. See, for example, Worthington and DiBlasio, "Promoting Mutual Forgiveness"; McMinn, *Cognitive Therapy Techniques*; Malony, *Win-Win Relationships*; Ripley et al., "Covenantal and Contractual Values."

a couple may engage in transactions, being mediated by a minister-counselor or a Christian therapist who acts as an empowered agent of reconciliation. These trialogical endeavors may take place under God's empowering presence, sanction, and guidance. With metacognitive mindfulness, this triad may engage one another under the auspices of the Holy Spirit present in the sessions—the ultimate overseer of marital and familial deals. Ministers of reconciliation may be called upon to exercise this service on behalf of those who need restoration and renewal, who live under the predicament of failing, broken, or inoperative covenants.

Metaphorical allusions and extrapolations from the statements above may apply to many marriages and families within Christian circles of fundamentalist, orthodox, or evangelical persuasions. In promoting the stability of a hierarchical system, many couples have forgotten that the covenant provided also for partners' satisfaction. Many couples have experienced a procrustean phenomenon—fitting a partner to one's design at the expense of their emotional life. By doing so, they force the other into a tight predicament in which their individuation and vitality have to be curtailed.

Sadly, therapeutic endeavors have witnessed many partners who forcefully edit, attempt to shape into a rigid form, or nullify the differences of each other in order to preserve some systemic stability and achieve a perfect fit. In these legalistic systems, partners may be squeezed into a mold defined by narrow interpretations of the letter, devoid of the Spirit, and using scriptural injunctions in an inappropriate and controlling manner. In terms of covenantal deals, these ways of transacting miss the loving intentions applicable to intimate relations as devised by God.

Legalistic bilateral-conditional covenants foster negative patterns—putting up with one another, being guided by demands, engaging in repetitive routines intended to force a stable equilibrium, and sacrificing satisfaction—that characterize the ethos of many marriages after the honeymoon is over. Entropy takes its toll, and the fossilization of a once-vibrant life occurs. Slowly, insidiously, and relentlessly, many marriages witness the decay of their zest, novelty, creativity, and emotional life. The need is obvious: to take into account the principles of a New Covenant in order to provide couples with the basis for continuous transformation and renewal.

Thus, a *quid pro quo*—a fair, bilateral-conditional deal—is needed when the renewal of a covenant is called for, integrating the paradigm described in this chapter with those elements derived from clinical research and practice. Yet, this deal is seen as a preamble for better things to come—the enactment of a New Covenant.

Chapter 4

The New Covenant as a Relational Paradigm

God's expressed desire to dwell among his people and be accessible to them (Exod 25:8) became a reality as the Old Covenant was established. The relationship between God and humans was transacted through objectivized means—a tabernacle, a mediator, a tribe of priests, and sacrificial offerings. The covenant was given to Israel after the people were delivered from Egypt—from a state of subjugation, degradation, and slavery. These contextual factors exerted devastating and disruptive pressures upon their relations in general, affecting their social structures and interpersonal processes. Having been subject to such contingencies for 430 years, the Israelites needed a fresh frame of reference to serve as a guide for relational patterns as they sojourned in the desert en route to the Promised Land. The Old Covenant served precisely as a framework for Israel to establish fair and mutually satisfying relationships between members of the community.

The Old Covenant established a relationship between YHWH—the holy God—and the not-so-holy nation of Israel. In a sovereign and gracious fashion, God provided his Torah with stipulations and expectations and included obligations and privileges to be enjoyed. These conditional promises were coupled to consequences, contingent upon Israel's obedience to his will. Civil, ethical, and moral standards accompanied this covenant, which were codified by Moses. The deal started with God's unilateral grace, engaging people bilaterally with both parties being joined by Moses the mediator, and was sealed with the blood of sacrificed animals. The Israelites were enabled to access God and relate to him by means of the tabernacle, the priesthood, and the offerings. All these means foreshadowed the coming of a New Covenant.

SCRIPTURAL BASIS FOR THE NEW COVENANT

As a starting point, the promise found in Jeremiah 31:31–34 states,

> "Indeed, a time is coming," says the Lord, "when I will make a new covenant with the people of Israel and Judah. It will not be like the old covenant that I made with their ancestors when I delivered them from Egypt. For they violated that covenant, even though I was like a faithful husband to them," says the Lord. "But I will make a new covenant with the whole nation of Israel after I plant them back in the land," says the Lord. "I will put my law within them

and write it on their hearts and minds. I will be their God and they will be my people. People will no longer need to teach their neighbors and relatives to know me. For all of them, from the least important to the most important, will know me," says the Lord. "For I will forgive their sin and will no longer call to mind the wrong they have done."

Besides Jeremiah's prophetic utterance, other OT passages include Ezekiel 11:19–20 and 36:26–32, where a new heart, a new spirit, and an empowered capacity to walk in God's ways are promised. The terms *covenant* and *testament* are synonymous. The designation *New Covenant* appears in several instances in the New Testament (Luke 22:20, 1 Cor 11:25; 2 Cor 3:6; Heb 8:8, 9:15; 12:24). This designation derives from a translation of the Greek terms καινὴ (*kaine*: new) and διαθήκη (*diatheke*: covenant). Luke, the author of the Gospel bearing his name, Paul the apostle, and the author of Hebrews adopted the term to define a new, actualizing way of considering God's covenantal thrust. Although John does not use the term itself, his account of the person and ministry of Jesus points to the inauguration of a new economy in the actualization of God's eternal plan and purpose as the following section demonstrates.

THEOLOGICAL CONSIDERATIONS ON THE NEW COVENANT

The studies focusing on the New Testament have been subject to a great deal of scrutiny, characterized by controversial interpretations rendered by diverse theologians. These considerations are beyond the scope of this work. Stated succinctly, the *unity* in God's covenantal redemption runs throughout Scripture. God's grace appears as a theme throughout redemptive history—beginning in Genesis 3:15 with a promised redeemer coming to accomplish God's will in due time—and underlines the progressive unfolding of God's eternal design. The New Covenant is not understood as being a *new* covenant (in the sense of a new idea or dispensation), but rather as a new *administration* or actualization of the same thrust of grace embedded in the Mosaic Covenant that preceded the New. In other words, the Old Covenant is seen as being an essentially gracious covenant as well.

Reformed theology carries over the old order into an actualizing new: Israel merges with those Gentiles who believe and accept God's grace; they are inserted into God's family as joint inheritors of the kingdom of God. The Old Covenant is expressed in new and better terms in the New, and so on. Readers who subscribe to a Reformed theology may consult with expositions and notions rendered by scholars of this persuasion.[1]

---

1. See, for example, Kline, *Kingdom Prologue*; Murray, "Covenant Theology"; Robertson, *Christ of the Covenants*; Witsius, *The Economy of the Covenants*; Vos, *Biblical Theology*; Sproul, *What Is Reformed Theology?*; Horton, *God of Promise*.

Part I: Premises and Principles

Dispensational theology regards the Old Covenant as a discrete era during which this deal was the specific means employed to establish a relationship between God and Israel. The New Covenant represents a new dispensation of grace distinct from the Old. Writers who have adopted a dispensational mindset emphasize the *differences* in God's dealings with humankind and the uniqueness of the diverse deals as they pertain to the contextual purpose and meaning of a given era. A dispensation defines the ways in which God acted in history along the unfolding of his redemptive purpose. With each new revelation and disclosure of purpose came a series of new responsibilities and/or privileges, resulting in a new dispensation.

According to Dispensationalist theology, God has separated Israel as a unique and special nation (the chosen ones, the special treasure that God calls "my people"). The church was a hidden dimension even to the prophets of old; because it was located in a sort of valley between the peaks of Sinai and Calvary, it was not perceived accurately. The mystery of the church as the body of Christ came to full view after the death, resurrection, and ascent of the redeemer Jesus Christ. The coming of the Holy Spirit inaugurated the birth of the church, an entity comprised of both believing Jews and Gentiles joined in one body. The event that took place at Pentecost, coupled with the death, resurrection, and ascension of Jesus Christ, marked the beginning of the dispensation of grace: a period that will continue until the second coming of the Lord. In dispensational thought, God's *two peoples* co-exist at the present time: Jews and Gentiles. God's favor is directed toward Gentiles who are given the chance to accept the same Messiah that the Israelites have rejected. After the "times of the Gentiles" are fulfilled, all Israel will be dealt with again and will enter into the eschatological fulfillment of God's covenantal design (Rom 11:25–27).

Dispensational theology has been challenged by those of a Reformed persuasion as a system that categorizes God and splits his sovereign and unified acts into paradigms with many administrations of distinct, even antagonistic schemata in approaching and treating redemptive history. On the other hand, Reformed theology has been challenged by Dispensationalists on the grounds that scholars have lumped all of Scripture into an undifferentiated whole that has resulted in a theologically constructed covenant of grace. This system is challenged on the basis that it seems to squeeze all other expressions of covenantal nature into a box, representing a neat package that does not do much justice to God's sovereign and unique relational expressions.

Those readers who align themselves with a Dispensationalist persuasion may consult the works of Walvoord, Ryrie, and Decker, among others.[2] These authors review the dilemmas and challenges involved in agreeing upon what the New Covenant actually means and present the diversity of interpretations that emerged within this domain.

---

2. Walvoord, *The Millennial Kingdom*; *Prophecy*; Ryrie, *Dispensationalism*; Decker, "The New Covenant"; *Christian Scholarship*.

Simply put, it is quite difficult to define God's way in either case (Rom 11:33–36). Adopting a theological system serves the main function of grasping and preserving truth as given by God and as interpreted by thoughtful humans. It also helps theologians to delineate normative ways in the hopes that those believers who learn from their findings may live according to what they consider to be God's will. Disagreement between theologians may serve a cautionary function to practicing clinicians to carefully consider the fact that, while Scriptures are given, theologies are elaborated with human filtering processes. To faithfully and consciously define and postulate doctrines has important consequences for the body of believers. Let God judge us all at the end: "Blessed is the one who does not condemn himself by what he approves" (Rom 14:22).

This work presents the New Covenant as a relational paradigm, prompting believers to be imitators of God as dearly beloved children and to walk in love after the exemplary ways derived from covenantal principles. To that end, some considerations about the dilemmas that characterized the field were given attention in order to glean positive findings and derive better ways to imitate the Father's covenantal dealings in human relations. In the final analysis, those who imitate the Father's ways are doers of the will of God, not hearers of academic discourse or philosophers engaged in intramural theological sports.

JOHN'S GOSPEL AND THE NEW ORDER

John the Evangelist may be regarded as Jesus's closest friend during his earthly days. As a personal eyewitness, he framed the continuous and actualized aspects of the Old Covenant as he saw them being fulfilled in an incarnated fashion before his own eyes. In John's account, the symbols and shadows of reality receded as the true light disclosed, at full intensity, the actualization and fulfillment of these *pedagogical* means.

John's metacognitive consciousness of God's eternal plan in actualizing a New Covenant may be gathered from his obvious recapitulation of Genesis in his Gospel narrative. The reader may ascertain the personalized tone in this account. For example, "In the beginning God created the heavens and the earth" (Gen 1:1) receives a new light in John's statement, "In the beginning was the Word, and the Word was with God, and the Word was fully God. The Word was with God from the beginning. All things were created by him, and apart from him no one thing was created that has been created. In him was life, and the life was the light of mankind" (John 1:1–4). He ties the relationship of the Father and the Son together in a continuous design.

John's account of the redefinition of the character and behavior of a fisherman called Simon bar Jonah into Peter (John 1:42) echoes the Genesis narrative dealing with Abram (changed to Abraham, Gen 17:5–6), and Sarai (changed to Sarah, Gen 17:15). Just as Abraham of Ur (of the Gentiles) would become the founding father of God's nation, a disciple from Galilee of the Gentiles would become leader in the new assembly (*ecclesia*) of God's people. Although John remains silent on this matter, another evangelist remarks that John's own name was changed by Jesus as well when he received a nickname together with his brother James: "Sons of Thunder" (Mark 3:17). These three friends could be seen as belonging to an intimate circle of privileged fellowship among the twelve disciples. They were granted privileges not accessible to others, such as witnessing the resurrection of a girl, observing Jesus's transfiguration, and being invited to pray with him at Gethsemane.

John's account of the encounter between Jesus and Nathanael reinforces the concept of the New Covenant having a better mediator, who adopted a personalized stance when he introduced a new economy. In a parallel narrative, Jacob's encounter with God in Genesis is echoed in the Gospel. In a transcendent display of God's grace, Jacob had a *kairotic* time with God in which his name was changed (Gen 32:27–28). Originally his name derived from a verb, "covering the heel" (or "may he protect" as a rearguard—an allusion to Jacob grabbing Esau's heel at birth). Later on, upon the discovery of his deceitful maneuvers, Jacob's name was given a negative connotation by a displaced Esau: "'Jacob' is the right name for him. He has tripped me up two times!" (Gen 27:36). Yet, the deceitful Jacob finally received a new name from God himself: Israel, or "God fights" (an indication that he would cease to fight for himself by means of deceitful manners and rely on his God in the midst of his struggles). This change of name prompted a redefinition of his character and conduct.

In John's narrative, Nathanael (given of God) received Jesus's astonishing definition as being a "true Israelite *in whom there is no deceit*"—a contrast posed in reference to the redefined Israel of old (John 1:47, italics mine). The connotations made by John as echoes of Jacob's personal encounter with God receive support in an analogous narrative. Jacob's ladder with angels going up and down was registered as an indication that the eternal and created order, the past and the future, and the divine and the human elements had united at a given spot—Beth-El, or the House of God. In Nathanael's case, Jesus alludes to the same ladder, but adds an enormous distinction in which the eternal, transcendent, and divine presence of God is now actualized in his own person: "You will see heaven opened and the angels of God ascending and descending on the Son of Man" (John 1:51).

Beth-El was an awesome display of God's presence, a phenomenon captured and symbolized in a stone anointed with oil by Jacob. Yet, this apparent and symbolic object (*phenomenon*) was superseded by the reality (*noumena*) of God's kingdom inaugurated in human space and time in a more actualized form: the person of Jesus. God's desire to dwell among his people did not diminish, but increased in intensity and actualizing thrust: God would send his Son, and he would be Emanuel, "God with us." John puts it succinctly: "Now the Word became flesh, and took residence [Gk. ἐσκήνωσεν, "dwelt," or "pitched his tabernacle"] among us" (John 1:14). He is the true temple of the living God (John 2:19). John's editorial comment distinguished the old and the new transactions: "For the law was given by Moses, but the grace and truth came about through Jesus Christ" (John 1:17).

Assuming that the same evangelist wrote the last book of the Bible, John seems to avoid the establishment of a dichotomous mindset between God's transactions registered in both the OT and the NT. An encompassing metacognitive awareness seems to guide him as he casts God's redemptive history with an eschatological omega point at the end of the line. John alludes to the ark, the centerpiece of the tabernacle holding the tablets of the Old Covenant, as a visible object in heaven, thus connecting the Old and the New economies: "Then the temple of God in heaven was opened and the ark of his covenant was visible within his temple" (Rev 11:19).

WHAT IS NEW AND BETTER IN THE NEW COVENANT?

Gleaning after scholars and students of Scriptures, we may present several aspects of the newness of the covenant under discussion.[3]

1. *A new and better path to optimize redemptive contingencies.* Having stipulated the just and reciprocal aspects that characterized the Old Covenant, the New Covenant is presented as a deal that supersedes and surpasses this paradigm when it applies to all its elements—its premises, promises, and lasting results. Scriptures are emphatic in stating that there was no fault in the Old Covenant per se, and that the law remains eternally just, good, and holy (Rom 7). The painful reminder is that we humans were unable to fulfill our part of the bargain: "For he [the Lord] finds faults with them . . ." (Heb 10:8), "for they did not continue in my covenant" (Heb 10:9). Due to the incapacity of the respondents, it became necessary to provide a new deal in which this factor would be taken into account. The author makes the point that this new way of transacting has rendered the old less efficacious: "In speaking of a new covenant, he [the Holy Spirit] makes the first one obsolete. And what is becoming obsolete and growing old is ready to vanish away" (Heb 8:13).

    Jesus alluded to the New Covenant the night he was betrayed. The narrative of the Lord's Supper appears as a preamble to the events that would take place at the cross. The time had come to actualize God's redemptive design. The shadows and symbols of the Old Covenant were given a true meaning by Jesus during the last meal he had with his disciples (Luke 22:15). He took a cup of wine after the supper and overtly stated that it was a new symbol, a guaranteeing seal of a new covenant made "in his blood." The Passover meal had developed several traditions that added further symbolic connotations to the narrative of Exodus.

---

3. See, for example, Anderson, *On Being Human*; Bruce, *The Epistle to the Hebrews*; Newell, *Hebrews*; Owen et al., *Prepare/Enrich*; Pentecost, *Faith that Endures*.

Part I: Premises and Principles

In Jesus's time, the custom included four cups as part of the supper—symbolizing sanctification, judgment or deliverance, redemption, and praise or restoration. It is believed that "the cup of the New Covenant" was the third one (the cup of redemption) offered by Jesus after the supper. He reserved the last cup for a joint partaking with his bride at the celebratory supper of the Lamb's wedding to the church.

The cup was not necessarily a "newer cup" in a material or concrete sense. The wine was not necessarily a beverage of better quality, nor was it different in taste, color, or aroma. The newness resided in the redefinition of the reality shadowed by the cup. Luke registers the words of Jesus as unambiguously stating, "This cup that is poured out for you is the new covenant in my blood" (Luke 22:20). Thus, it is a testimony to the purpose of the symbol: *it is poured out for you* (italics mine). It is a coparticipatory endeavor to be ascertained and accepted (a symbol to "take in" what is poured out for us). Receiving the essential meaning (drinking) of the cup communicates the sense of a deep relationship: we are partakers of the life of Christ. To ingest it in that fashion is to accept in faith and obedience the offer of grace and to actualize God's offer of redemption. In that way, the celebration of freedom from bondage, pilgrimage under the sun, and fellowship at the table of the Lord acquires a new meaning.

The novelty of the covenant resides in the fact that God has established an uneven co-participation that elevates the human to a higher ground of transacting. The Son of God became the Son of Man so we could become the children of God: "But God demonstrates his own love for us, in that while we were still sinners, Christ died for us" (Rom 5:8). God's sovereign will has operated in renewed covenantal—*unilateral, unconditional,* and *proactive*—terms. God's actions spring from a *graceful* and *merciful* intention toward undeserving humans. God's empowering of human faith and obedience invites the believer to engage as a bilateral counterpart. The kenosis of Christ and his redemptive effects need to be seen in conjunction with God's re-forming, redefining, and elevating of the redeemed human as he counts his creature as being "in Christ" (an expression that appears some 120 times in the NT).

2. *A new and better offering with better results.* Contrasted with the repetitive offerings for sin (Heb 10:1–4), the offering of Jesus (Heb 10:5–10) achieved better results. Christ's body was broken for us (rending the veil in two, he opened the way to the Holy of Holies, Matt 27:50–51; Heb 10:20). Then he offered to the Father his blood poured out for us, removing our sin before the Father's presence: he is the Lamb of God who takes away the sin of the world (John 1:29). Now he lives and makes intercession for us as a High Priest (Heb 7:25). The author to the Hebrews presents an argument comparing the sacrifices of old that instituted the

Old Covenant with Christ's sacrificial superiority as the basis for instituting the New Covenant (Heb 9:19–23).

Jesus came to fulfill "the law and the prophets," and in doing so, provided an offering that superseded the five types of offerings (sin, guilt, peace, fragrant, and burnt). The author to the Hebrews (10:1–15) states that the old gave way to the new, introducing the incarnated Son to the world with the expression, "Here I am, to do your will" (10:7). The blood of the New Covenant is presented as being superior and as having lasting effects. These aspects are eminently presented in the address to the Hebrews. In a metaphorical way, the author voices Jesus's blood, which speaks better things than Abel's blood (or bloods, signifying all the potential descendants that were eliminated before they would ever be born), as if appealing to God from the ground, crying for revenge (Heb 12:24). This distinction between the dialogical bloods is not merely semantic or rhetorical; it is a conceptual and principled thrust conveying the nature and the meaning of Jesus's claim before God: grace, mercy, and love at work versus retaliation, revenge, and condemnation.

3. *A better mediator between God and his children.* A mediator is a sort of shuttle diplomat who intervenes on behalf of two parties entering an agreement and represents both sides with a high degree of understanding of their contractual obligations and privileges. The letter to the Hebrews sets Moses as a mediator of the Old in contrast to Jesus, the mediator of the New Covenant (Gal 3:19–20; 1 Tim 2:5; Heb 9:15; 12:24).

On the one hand, Moses is depicted in Scripture as both a great leader and a sinful human. In his attempts to do something for his enslaved people, he killed an Egyptian, (Exod 2:12); he also failed to circumcise his own sons, who were born to a foreign woman (Exod 4:24–26). In moments of frustration, he smashed the tablets of the law (Exod 32:19) and struck the rock instead of speaking to it (Num 20:8–12). His temperamental behavior kept him from entering the Promised Land. He had a speech impediment and would have flunked a course in public speaking as well. He required the remedial help of a better orator (Exod 4:10). His excuses elicited God's stern response (Exod 4:11–17). In sum, a fallible, mortal human was elevated and empowered by God's proactive, unilateral, and unconditional grace so as to become the greatest leader of Israel and the mediator of the Old Covenant.

On the other hand, Jesus is depicted as being a better mediator than Moses. As an incarnated Son, he is a person who understands both sides (divine as well as human) to the fullest degree. He mediates with a full awareness of the character, will, expectations, and demands of God. He mediates with a thorough understanding of the ontological (character), behavioral (actions), cognitive (thinking, reasoning, judgment, decision-making), emotional (feelings), and social (relational) needs and wants of the human. Besides this, he is aware of the temptations to which the human is subject. He not only understands and has empathy, but also advocates in favor of the fragile human before God because he participated in our human nature and was tempted in everything, but did not yield to these temptations (Heb 2:18).

As the mediator of a New Covenant, Jesus intercedes for those who are being set apart for God (Heb 8:2; 10:10, 14). As a matter of fact, he is the *only* mediator perfectly qualified to render such a service. As a faithful Son, he is counted as being worthy of more glory than the glory attributed to the servant of the Old Covenant (Heb 3:3–6). As a result, the admonition is given to pay attention to what the Holy Spirit says above and beyond Moses (Heb 3:7–19), so that we are able to enter into an actualized resting state (Heb 4:7).

4. *A better priest to intercede in favor of God's children.* The New Covenant introduces a better priest, compared to those priests who served in the old system (Heb 4:14–16; 5:1–10; 7:1–28; 8:1–6). He is depicted as being sinless and perfect, eternal, and able to relate to the Father at equal levels. As an officiating High Priest, he "sat down at his right hand" in order to be there for good and to plead our cause. The Old Covenant established a restricted and occasional entrance to the presence of God, allowing the high priest to offer the blood of a representative animal on the propitiatory (*kapporeth* or cover) once a year on Atonement Day. This act was done in a hurry in order to convey the awesome and dreadful aspect of God's distinctive holiness being approached by sinful humans in need of expiation.

The New Covenant offers a new, living, and open way to the presence of God. Having offered himself once and for all time (versus repetitive offerings of old) as a single sacrifice for sins (Heb 10:12a), Jesus Christ *sat down* at the right hand of God (Heb 8:1–2; 10:12b). The High Priest of the New Covenant does not minister in a hurry, but is seated at the right hand of God (Heb 1:3). "But now Jesus has obtained a superior ministry, since the covenant that he mediates is better and is enacted on better promises" (Heb 10:6). As a merciful priest, Jesus sympathizes with human weaknesses and intercedes on behalf of those he has ransomed with his offering (Heb 4:15; 7:25).

5. *A new and better covenantal seal and guarantee.* Christ is also presented as being the *surety* or *guarantee* of this covenant (Heb 7:22). The Old Covenant was sealed with the sprinkling of blood of sacrificed animals on both parties: the objects of God's sanctuary and the people themselves. The evangelists registered the statements made by Jesus at the Last Supper: "For this is my blood, the blood of the covenant, that is poured out for many for the forgiveness of sins" (Matt 26:28); "This cup that is poured out for you is the new covenant in my blood" (Luke 22:20). Paul's appeal in his letter to the Corinthians is regarded as being part of

the institution of the New Covenant seal: "This cup is the new covenant in my blood. Do this, every time you drink it, in remembrance of me" (1 Cor 11:25). This institution also includes the broken bread as a symbol of Christ's body broken for us, the rent veil (Matt 25:51–52; Heb 10:20) that opened living access to the Father. Once accepted, he remains the High Priest of our confession, making eternal intercession for those who believe. Jesus Christ, the High Priest/mediator/guarantor presents this seal to the Father, and then conveys to the human party the efficacy of the new deal (Heb 9:14).

6. *Better promises for empowered living.* Not only a mediator, priest, and guarantor, Jesus Christ is recognized as being the *sovereign head,* granting everlasting covenantal promises to his people (Eph 1:22–23; 5:23; Col 2:19): forgiveness of sins, including the decisive letting go and forgetting of them (2 John 1:12; Heb 10:17–18); reconciliation and peace with God (Rom 5:1); rest from human works (Heb 4:1–11); assurance of an eternal security (John 3:16); and an eternal inheritance with his saints (Eph 1:18). These are far better promises than anyone could have imagined under the Old Covenant deal (Heb 8:6).

7. *A new and better way of access to the Father.* The way traced in the Old Covenant could be gathered from the setup of the tabernacle: a sinner approaching God would place an offering in the hands of the Levites, who would enter through the door of the outer court and place it in the hands of the officiating priest. The priest would then offer the sacrifice at the altar. Priests had to wash their hands and feet at the bronze laver before entering the Holy Place. In the Holy Place, a candlestick with seven branches would illuminate the way to a table with showbread and an altar for frankincense burning in front of the veil. All priests would stop there. Only the high priest would enter the Holy of Holies once a year (Atonement Day) to sprinkle the blood of a sacrificed animal on behalf of the people and atone for their sins on the propitiatory or cover (*kapporeth*) of the ark of the covenant. The ark contained an urn of manna, the rod of an almond tree used in the selection of the priestly tribe of Aaron's descendants, and the unbroken tables of the law.

In the New Covenant, the Lord's statement, "I am the way to the Father" sums up his actualization of all human-made artifacts, symbolic objects, rituals, offerings, and the priesthood. He is the one who descended from heaven, and through his kenosis, he became the accessible door, the altar, the amalgamation of five offerings (sin, guilt, peace, present, and burnt offerings), and the fountain of sanctification of the believer who approaches the Father by faith. He is also the door to deeper encounters with the Father at a Holy Place where his light, communion, and intercession exude and further invite the believer to proceed along a transformative process. It was on the basis of Jesus's sacrifice and through the broken veil that he entered into the Most Holy Place with his own ransoming blood, presented it before the presence of the Father, and atoned for human sin.

As to the symbolic objects within the ark of the covenant, Jesus Christ is the God-elected and appointed High Priest (the almond rod being the symbol of a chosen priesthood). He is the bread that came from heaven (the urn with manna), and he provides us with life. He is the only one who fulfilled the law (the unbroken tablets) and embodied its content, thrust, and meaning. This covenantal stela—now a living testimony placed in the hearts and minds of believers, as well as a testimonial to be read in public—may be appealed to as God's revealed will, directing the right path of his imitating children who walk in love.

8. *A better outcome with better results.* The effect of partaking in this covenantal deal is better than any previous outcome, with the instituted elements acting as a mnemonic device guaranteeing a redemptive fellowship in the Spirit with freedom from sin and empowerment for service. Those who partake of the bread and the cup of the Lord have eternal life, a fact guaranteed by *eating* (or "taking in") the bread (John 6:51) and *feeding* on (or "chewing") the bread (John 6:58). Consider the outcomes and the benefits of the new deal:

> Therefore [as an obvious conclusion to all previous considerations], brothers, since we have confidence to enter the holy places by the blood of Jesus, by the new and living way he opened for us through the curtain, that is, through his flesh, and since we have a great priest over the house of God, let us draw near with a true heart in full assurance of faith . . . let us hold fast the confession of our hope without wavering, for he who promised is faithful. And let us consider how to stir up one another to love and good works. (Hebrews 10:19–24, ESV)

The efficacy of the covenantal grace and the imputation of righteousness as a gift empower the believer to "reign in life through Jesus Christ" (Rom 5:17). Due to these gracious endowments, the New Covenant provides the basis for a lifestyle that seeks to imitate the Father's manner of love and his expressive ways. A believer's empowered lifestyle receives the influx and impetus of God's indwelling Holy Spirit. His grace teaches the believer to engage in relations with a unilateral, unconditional, and proactive stance—and to do so with grace and mercy toward her/his partner, family member, friend, or neighbor at large. This empowerment comes not as an external coating or investment, but begins at the core of the innermost parts of the human being.

The potential capacity of a believer to know God's will can be activated and energized by the Holy Spirit so that she/he may appropriate the spirit of the law—now intrinsically allocated as entrenched dicta—deep within the heart and mind. Then, all human processes—cognitive, affective, behavioral, and motivational—being infused by God's Spirit, may be aligned and empowered in order to engage in intimate fellowship with God. The Holy Spirit may prompt the worshipper's inner dialogues, rhetoric, and decision-making, empowering the person to engage in the enactment of God's designs for her/his life.

9. *A new way of ministering to God and to one another: in the Holy Spirit.* As it pertains to the ministry of the New Covenant, Paul uses an analogy to succinctly present a contrast between the new and the old order. According to the Old Testament narrative, when Moses received the ministry of the law, his face was effulgent—radiant and glorious—for having been in God's presence at Sinai. Upon his descent, he veiled his face so the Israelites would not see his fading glory disappear. As his face became less radiant and more like the semblance of an octogenarian who had spent lots of time under the sun, the people would not have noticed the fading glory.

According to Paul, ministers of the New Covenant serve God with "unveiled faces," approaching him in freedom as they are progressively transformed from one degree of glory to another by beholding the face of Jesus Christ. Paul states that while many still read Moses as if the veil is placed on their eyes, believers in the New Covenant may apprehend the Word as a living expression with open eyes and eager hearts. Those who serve the Lord on behalf of others as servants of this new order may gather insights from Pauline theology:

> Therefore, since we have such a hope, we behave with great boldness, and not like Moses who used to put a veil over his face to keep the Israelites from staring at the result of the glory that was made ineffective. But their minds were closed. For to this very day, the same veil remains when they hear the old covenant read. It has not been removed because only in Christ is it taken away. But until this very day whenever Moses is read, a veil lies over their minds, but when one turns to the Lord, the veil is removed. Now we all, with unveiled faces reflecting the glory of the Lord, are being transformed into the same image from one degree of glory to another, which is from the Lord, who is the Spirit. (2 Corinthians 3:12–18)

A comparison and contrast may be drawn between Old Covenant servants (priests and Levites) and New Covenant servants in their relational styles as these pertain to trialogical encounters between God, minister, and person in need. In contrast to the ministry of the Old Covenant, which is perceived as being detached, impersonal, and focused on ceremonies, rituals, and external sacrifices, the new order appeals to an interpersonal interaction mediated through the Holy Spirit. Pauline theology stresses the ministry of a New Covenant (2 Cor 3:6), in which those who serve through preaching and teaching the Word, counseling, and building the kingdom of God, do so in the power of the Holy Spirit. They have the empowering person and presence of the Paraclete, being equipped to shape up the saints and build the new dwelling place of God (Eph 2:20–22), defined as the body of Christ (Eph 4:12). The relational tone and thrust of the ministry of the New Covenant is exemplified in the fact that Paul, as well as other collaborators, would be ready to share not only the gospel (propositional truth), but also themselves (interpersonal transactions of loving nature):

> [W]e became little children among you. Like a nursing mother caring for her own children, with such affection for you we were happy to share with you not only the gospel of God but also our own lives, because you had become dear to us. (1 Thessalonians 2:7–9)

Sharing good news is essential in spreading God's kingdom; sharing oneself in doing so reveals a new and better way of ministering this good news. It provides a living example of the ways in which God intended humans to relate in love. After all, beyond symbolic or objectivized means, God shared himself with humans by sending his Son. The incarnated Jesus related in such a way that he was nicknamed by his enemies as "a sinner's friend." This principle applies in any ministry dealing with people, including counseling endeavors characterized by sharing life with acceptance and validation.

10. *A new, better way of relating with one another.* God's desire to relate beyond sporadic encounters and to engage in an ongoing manner with his people was expressed in a command given to Moses. He was told to make a sanctuary (tabernacle) for God so he would dwell among them (Exod 25:8); that is, instead of relating in sporadic, intermittent, or unpredictable ways, God desired to lodge and dwell among his children. To that end, special artifacts (acting as transitional objects, shadows, and figures of reality) would be built and lodged in a tabernacle serving as a tent of meeting between God and his people. This dwelling would host the ark of the covenant with the stela within, yet this dwelling (and all the objects of the tabernacle) would be man-made. The artists were empowered by the Spirit of God to accomplish the task (Exod 31:1–6). As material objects, these artifacts were holy (separated, consecrated, and dedicated) only in reference to God's person and were regarded as transitional objects employed in service to a holy God.

In the New Covenant, God's desire to dwell among his people was actualized in the coming of the Son as an incarnated being, the true tabernacle of God (John 1:14; 2:19–21). He became human and dwelled among us as Emmanuel (Matt 1:23). After his work was accomplished, he sent the Holy Spirit from the Father's throne so that the third person of the Trinity would be with us, among us, and in us (John 14:15–25; 16:7–15). The New Covenant actualized God's desire and will in full force, establishing an ongoing and empowered relationship with his people by means of the accomplished work of Jesus Christ and the coming of the Holy Spirit.

The terms of a New Covenant are granted to believers by God, acting as a top-down agent, who offers those who believe in his gospel the opportunity to respond in faith and obedience. The human response emerges from a bottom-up perspective impacted by the Holy Spirit's prompting and call. The entrance to God's fellowship is then experienced as an ongoing transaction held at an elevated level, mediated by the Holy Spirit's infusion, coparticipation, and upward drawing of the person's empowered capacity to relate to a living God. In the process, a cognitive awareness and dissonance may emerge, in which God's sovereign will and the believer's conscious response interact, both being affirmed in a paradoxical yet integrated manner.

Those who are convicted by the Holy Spirit and enter the covenant by faith experience the claims and impact of the gospel as an appeal of unconditional nature. If they accept and enact the covenantal deal, they do so not as mindless, robotic puppets, but as fully conscious beings. This relational encounter with the Father opens the eyes of the heart of the believer and allows the allocation of the laws of God (his conditions of worth, value, and meaning) deep within the mind. The believer apprehends and appropriates the covenantal terms in an existential manner, and her/his participatory faith and obedience catalyze the experience of a bilateral fellowship with God.

PRINCIPLES IN HUMAN RELATIONS DERIVED FROM THE NEW COVENANT

Having defined the novelty of the New Covenant as an optimal redemptive paradigm, we now delineate this model as a paradigm for human relations. Ten aspects of the New Covenant are presented as the basis for the elaboration of sound principles applicable to marriage and intimate human relations such as the family and the community of believers.

This work emphasizes the vital role of the Holy Spirit's person, power, and continuous presence among God's people in the unfolding and actualizing of the covenantal terms. In citing the promise of Jeremiah twice (chapters 8 and 10), the author to the Hebrews seems to bypass the modern scholarly custom of citing human authors. The terms of the New Covenant unfold with an actualized meaning provided by an author who gives *direct credit to the Spirit* in doing so (Heb 8:8; 10:15). This letter was intended for first-century Jewish believers in need of encouragement. Eventually, the letter was "published" in the NT canon for our consumption.

The New Covenant is presented as a paradigm derived from Scripture and applicable to believers, serving as an exemplary and guiding model for relationships patterned after God's ways of engaging in love. In applying these terms, the appeal is directed to husbands, wives, parents, children, and friends in the community of faith: to consider God's exemplary ways and enact them with the mindset demonstrated by Christ toward us (Eph 5:1–2). After all, the incarnated Jesus Christ was the living embodiment of the New Covenant in action. In a previous article, the author delineated the exemplary terms gathered from this new deal.[4] The dimensions of the New Covenant as a paradigm are amplified and dealt with in successive chapters. Here we present them succinctly:

1. *The empowering of the inner being.* In the old economy, the law was consulted with externally and regarded as a standard of comparison and contrast with God's commandments sculpted in stone. Obedience to God's law was regarded as the means to align a person's character formation, conduct, and relations. In time, religious leaders took the 613 derivatives of the law and burdened people with extra injunctions, powering over them with their interpretations. In the new economy, God's law would be placed within human hearts and written upon their minds, empowering rather than powering over the believer.

   In the New Covenant, God's law is intrinsically allocated into the mindset of believers and intertwines with their cognitive processes—thinking, reasoning, perceptions, judgments, attributions, and the formation of attitudes and values in life. God's Spirit also infuses the emotional processes of the believer—sensitivity, empathy, love, and passion. Ezekiel's prophetic statements reads, "I will give you a new heart, and I will put a new spirit within you. I will remove the heart of stone from your body and give you a heart of flesh" (Ezek 36:26). God's Torah is infused into the depths of this new heart (Jer 31:33; Heb 8:10; 10:16) and co-participates with the cognitive-emotive-enactive structures and processes of the believer "filled with the Spirit." At the ontological level, the person is vivified and capacitated by the Holy Spirit in order to be able to do the will of God. An interesting allusion is made by Paul in reference to the ministry of the New Covenant among the Corinthians: "You are a letter of Christ, delivered by us, written not with ink but by the Spirit of the living God, not *on stone tablets* but on tablets of human hearts" (2 Cor 3:3, italics mine).

   Contrary to the human quest for power, control, and manipulation, God's intention is to empower a believer in order that the believer may empower others in a decentered fashion. Husbands and wives are not to power over (subjugate or dominate) each other, but to serve one another under Jesus's lordship. Jesus demonstrated with his own example what it means to empower versus powering over as he came to serve and not be served, to minister life and to empower the weak—keeping the human condition in mind as finite, precarious, and incapable of achieving God's design on natural terms.

---

4. Polischuk, "A New Covenant."

The empowered mindset may be regarded as a top-down executive agency—the inner being endowed with intrinsically emergent properties—that is capable of exuding love in action. By virtue of being moved by the Spirit and following the promptings of the indwelling Word of God, the empowered person may love the neighbor in a decentered fashion without necessarily experiencing a depletion of his/her energy. The proactive enactment of the command to "walk in love"—the engagement of the empowered mindset to love in feedforward fashion—may meet with reciprocity coming from the neighbor. Yet, the feedforward thrust does not depend on expectations of an ulterior nature. In that sense, "he who loves his wife, loves himself" as Paul reminded husbands (Eph 5:28).

Multiple accounts in Scriptures attest to the empowering of the powerless that was dispensed by Jesus. Tax collectors, prostitutes, lepers, outcasts, and those deemed less than kosher received a gracious and merciful treatment from him. A prime example of the shift from the old to the new may be derived from the apostle Paul's experience. Prior to his experience of *metanoia*, the apostle relied on his own power to do God's will, based on his strict adherence to the law. After his encounter with Jesus, he was empowered by the Holy Spirit to do so (Acts 9:17).

Far from diminishing or trapping the other as often happens when powering over occurs, a person empowering the other—a partner in marriage, a family member, or a community friend—fosters fellowship and consolidates the bonds of love. The connotations of the covenant, as exemplary of the ways in which humans are to relate to one another as imitators of the Father's empowering ways, is the subject of chapter 8.

2. *An empowered capacity to engage in unilateral thrust.* As usual, God has acted in sovereign grace, not responding to any human request or answering any human demand. In stating the promises of the covenant, Jeremiah begins each of them with God's unilateral expressions: "I will make . . . I will put my law . . . I will write it on their hearts . . . I will be their God . . . I will forgive, etc." It is not the human invitation that has prompted God's action, but God's uncalled-for decision and design that has poured his loving concern upon each human with redemptive aims and effects.

The covenant is God's design, a plan enacted before the foundation of the world. The mystery hidden for generations has been disclosed and revealed by the Spirit (Rom 16:25; Eph 3:9; Col 1:26). In his book *On Being Human*, Raymond Anderson utilized the concept of covenant to state a theological anthropology in which the human is determined as being in covenant relationship with God.[5] Anderson and Guernsey further elaborated the concept, stating that a covenant originates in a unilateral relation established by God with a community,

---

5. Anderson, *On Being Human*.

Part I: Premises and Principles

summoning a nation to a history of response.[6] This covenant love also provides the foundations for family life (Eph 5:32).

The unilateral thrust engages the human in order to render the deal into a truly bilateral relationship; it summons the human to believe, accept, and obey the terms of the redemptive deal in order to relate in love: "We love because he loved us first" (1 John 4:19). Actually, there is no covenant if two parties are not engaged and interact. Thus, it is not a question of partners of equal status or power being engaged or of exerting equal efforts on both sides. It is a matter of mutual engagement in a relation—even between partners of differential characteristics—and God invites the human to coparticipate in a bilateral deal, responding to his love, grace, and mercy with faith and obedience.

The exemplary aspects of the covenant are derived from God's unilateral thrust. How can husbands, wives, parents, children, or friends imitate this manner of love? Perhaps it is when adverse occasions arise (e.g., in facing uneven and difficult transactions, in prompting the renewal of a stagnant system, or in facing conflictive situations in need of reconciliation or resolution) that this manner of love can be evoked. In these cases, the believer is defined not by circumstances, but by God's empowering to imitate his unilateral ways. Alternatively, these unilateral behaviors may simply emerge as random acts of love that enhance a marriage or a family system when there is no request or demand for such. Chapter 9 deals with these matters.

3. *The empowered capacity to be unconditional.* God's provision of grace and mercy demonstrates that the events and processes embedded in the covenant are markedly slanted in favor of the human regardless of the creaturely predicament. Humans are not in a position to ascertain or fathom what the covenant means to God the maker. It seems to be an ontological attribute displayed in sovereign action. God's all-powerful capacity to act in grace is expressed at times in clauses such as, "If my people, who belong to me, humble themselves, pray, seek to please me, and repudiate their sinful practices, then I will respond from heaven, forgive their sin, and heal their land" (2 Chron 7:14). Yet, in God's conferment of the promises of a New Covenant, the formula "If you . . . then I . . ." does not appear; rather, a unilateral thrust permeates all his statements.

Unconditional aspects are seen in God's ways: in sending Christ, in resurrecting him from among the dead, in the outpouring of the Holy Spirit, and in sending a message of saving nature. God has apportioned the proper payment of all human debts by providing a perfect sacrificial offering, accepting the payment in full, and removing any veil standing in the way of the redeemed as they approach his throne of grace. The only thing for a believer to do is to believe and accept in faith what is being offered in grace. There is no credit or personal merit

---

6. Anderson and Guernsey, *On Being Family.*

in believing, for such a stance of active faith or appropriation demonstrates a dependency upon the one who offers and promises such a covenant. The unconditional thrust is positive, redemptive, and encompasses sinners who are unable to offer anything in return except their faith, love, and devotional obedience. After they are reformed, believers may engage in a bilateral fellowship as they are transformed and conformed along the way.

The unconditional thrust displayed in designing, working out the terms, and establishing this deal between God and humankind does not depend on the sinful party's ability or contribution. The weight of the contribution to the relationship of love and communion between God and the human is unequally distributed to start with and continues in that way throughout the unfolding of the details. The Holy Spirit, nevertheless, enables the human to act on faith and obey God's terms, accepting and receiving the blessings of the covenant. Yet, the everlasting life enjoyed by the person with whom God makes His covenant does not depend upon the merits of this person. In sum, there is no "work" on the part of the human that serves as a condition in order to have the covenant or to enjoy its effects. The resultant works are exuding properties of a new nature that has been empowered in order to produce them. God's unilateral thrust rules out human efforts and merit. The believer cooperates with God in establishing and maintaining the covenant and in experiencing its blessings: peace, safety, assurance, love, and so on.

As these concepts apply to human relations, we are reminded that most bilateral covenants (and especially contracts) appear to be conditional. Nowadays, it is customary for many couples to establish prenuptial agreements stipulating terms in view of a possible separation or divorce. When situations arise and the imperative needs or demands may call for an unconditional stance to be displayed, what are the ways to behave? Can a human be totally unilateral without claiming any reciprocity in return? Can a human engage in a unilateral fashion in order to establish an ambience in which a better bilateral deal may be arranged? These issues are addressed in chapter 10.

4. *The empowered capacity to be proactive.* God's promises and clauses are not contingent upon human acts or willpower. Nothing we do takes God by surprise or catches him off guard. Thus, the covenant is not a reaction to human drama or stimuli in any way. It is the unfolding of a proactive design, an eternal purpose born out of the mindful intention of God who calls things as if they are when they are not yet. The anticipatory pronouncements made in Scripture reveal that it is the good intention of God to bring his children to share his eternity in fellowship and love.

God is out of human time, yet infuses time with his immanence in order to relate to the created order. It is in these terms that we may affirm that the New

Covenant is not the result of God's "fast thinking" (emotional, reactive); instead, it is the architectural, deliberate result of "slow thinking" through *aions*, even before the foundation of the world (Eph 1:3–13). God's design began outside the bounds of chronological dimensions: the incarnation of his Son and his death, resurrection, and ascension were outlined before the foundation of the world in time. The sending of the Holy Spirit and the gathering of a people to form the body of Christ were elements of a mystery hidden for generations, disclosed in due time, demonstrating God's multiform wisdom and power. From God's perspective, we are glorified and sitting in heavenly places with Christ. From our perspective, we wait to see how such pronouncements will unfold, hoping for the best outcome.

Again, the theological abstracts enunciated already (ha'adam being pre-formed, formed, deformed, re-formed, transformed, and conformed back to the *Tselem Elohim*) should not be seen as accidental happenings. These are elements in the unfolding of a unilateral, unconditional, and proactive God acting covenantally. As imitators of the Father's ways and as dearly beloved children, we may gather insights as to how to be proactive in our relational interactions. That is precisely the subject matter of chapter 11.

5. *An empowered capacity to dispense grace.* In the New Covenant, God gives what the human does not deserve: forgiveness of sins, the riches of his grace and mercy, and inheritance in heaven, etc. (Eph 2:1–2). God's grace is manifested in that, while we were yet sinners, Christ died for us (Rom 5:8). Having been rescued from the vain manner of life, which we received from those who socialized us, we recognize that it was the sovereign grace of God that has reached us (1 Pet 1:18–19). The call of God and the proactive preparedness of a convenient path destined to guide the believer to become like Christ in a process of transformation and renewal depend on the energizing power of God, without being prompted by any merit on the human side (Eph 2:10; Rom 8:28–29).

   Marriage and family life offer plenty of opportunities for us to engage in interpersonal dealings as imitators of the Father, framed in covenantal terms. Instead of legalistic injunctions based on a *quid pro quo*, believers in intimate transactions may establish a climate of grace and engage in graceful transactions with one another. Such is the subject matter of chapter 12.

6. *An empowered capacity to show mercy.* In the New Covenant, God spares us from the ultimate consequence or impact of our trespasses, not paying us according to our deeds. While grace is the act of giving us what we do not deserve, mercy is the withholding of retaliatory, justice-based paybacks for our transgressions. God is rich in mercy (Eph 2:4; 1 Pet 1:3), and in spite of our sinful state, he made us alive in Christ by giving us a new opportunity to have a new beginning through a new birth. Grace and mercy are complementary aspects of the love of God

acting sovereignly and proactively. The apostle Paul recounts all the deeds of God toward humans (Rom 1—11); in view of these mercies, we may present ourselves as living sacrifices (Rom 12:1–2). We reciprocate and love God because we have first been loved (1 John 4:19). Thus, we become mutually engaged in bilateral dealings with God only by virtue of his manner of love—empowering, proactive, unilateral, unconditional, graceful, and merciful—in covenanting with us.

Human relations at large, and marriage and family interactions in particular, provide us with multiple occasions to display mercy toward one another. How to display this mercy in imperfect human transactions—in marriage, the family, or friendships bound to challenge one another with stressors—is the main focus of chapter 12, coupled with grace-bound considerations.

7. *Promoting intimacy and fellowship.* The New Covenant as a relational paradigm is optimally expressed in the opportunity to actually know God (Heb 8:11). Having such a High Priest and this new and living way, we are invited to an intimate relationship and fellowship with God. In terms of human relationships, the paradigm allows for intimacy and profound knowledge of one another. As a matter of fact, if we consider the upward move toward God's level, we find that the closer covenantal partners are to God, the closer they become to one another. The need for defensive covers and maneuvers in interpersonal dealings diminishes as a believer accepts being accepted by God and becomes more available to interpersonal transactions of a truthful nature. The possibility of relating in intimacy with unveiled faces and with open honesty becomes a viable option for partners in marriage, family members, and friends in community. Such matters are considered in chapter 13.

8. *An empowered capacity to forgive offenses.* Perhaps the most astonishing expression in Jeremiah's prophecy is the promise that God will actually forgive sins and trespasses by removing them and letting them go. Contrary to the repetitive aspects of the Old Covenant's sacrificial offerings that only *covered* sin with short-lived efficacy before God, the New Covenant dealt with sin once and for all through Christ's efficient and sufficient sacrifice, *removing* sin from God's presence. The New Covenant provides an open and accepting stance toward the sinner who approaches God's throne of grace (defined also as the mercy seat) in order to receive forgiveness on account of Christ's work.

This forgiveness is total and encompassing in view of the redemptive sacrifice of Christ (Jer 31:34; Heb 8:12; 10:17). As it applies to human transactions, instead of being trapped in retaliatory feelings or trying to take revenge in anger, a forgiving stance may be adopted. The paradigm calls for the empowering of a person to forgive the debts and trespasses committed against them. Paul stresses the exemplary ways of the Father as a model for human relations: "Be kind to one another, compassionate, forgiving one another, just as God in Christ also forgave you" (Eph 4:32).

The New Covenant affects persons at the core. The re-forming of the basic structural or ontological dimension of a person's being is necessary in order for this person *to be* an imitator of God. Being a forgiver precedes doing or acting in forgiving ways. Through faith and obedience to God's design, a person may learn to be a mimic of God along a transforming process. As God's law is placed within the heart and mind and the empowering of the Spirit occurs, an empowered, forgiving person is prompted to move in a unilateral and unconditional fashion from within and advance in a process of forgiveness (a cognitive, affective, motivational, and willful process). Finally, the person's empowered structures and processes are manifested in concrete acts of forgiveness.

The New Covenant provides the basis for a metacognitive, dialogical treatment of offenses. Being a forgiver at heart, a person's mindset is prompted to stop automatic retaliatory reactions to offenses by means of a *detached mindfulness*. To develop this objectivity about subjective states is a metacognitive capacity that results from the exercise of conscious awareness and perception under the Holy Spirit's shaping. The forgiving person may ponder and deliberate with inner dialogues, calculating the damage done to his/her person, the cost of forgiveness, and the freedom to be defined by God, not by the offender.

The process of forgiveness involves the appeal to God's empowering in order to monitor, regulate, and choose appropriate responses to the triggering offense. As the process unfolds, the person may engage in decisive and enactive behaviors with *purposeful mindfulness*. Forgiveness is enacted under full awareness of the need to imitate the Father and forgive as the forgiving person has been forgiven in Christ. As compared to the Old Covenant pattern in forgiving—which may be seen as a *strikeover* in editing mistakes or errors—forgiving in a New Covenant fashion may be seen as a *deletion* of these mistakes or errors.

The author proposes a metacognitive stance that enables the person to process her or his own processes in purposeful mindfulness. The person who is being prompted by a top-down executive function and is endowed with a metacognitive, inner rhetoric may persuade herself to imitate God's ways, deciding to forgive as God did. As an insightful and empowered forgiver, the person is not a masochistic pushover or a codependent enabler, but someone who actually understands God's ways of exercising forgiveness as exemplified in the New Covenant. This capacity is due to the infusion of the indwelling Holy Spirit into the Word-bound heart and mind of the believer. Chapter 14 deals with forgiveness as a main issue in relations and expands the incipient concepts enunciated here.

9. *An empowered capacity to let go of offenses*. The Old Covenant stressed the binding elements that reinforced the parties' commitment and steadfastness in fulfilling

stipulated obligations. This covenant allowed for the constant remembering of the wrongs committed by a failing party. Transgressions committed against God stood as barriers in the way of free access to God's presence. The need for repetitious means such as offerings and sacrifices was evident; they were employed in a religious fashion in order to establish peace with God. The author to the Hebrews states that such sacrifices and offerings did not obliterate the wrongful past, but reinforced the negative episodic and semantic memories associated with sinful acts. This remembrance exerted pressures on the sinner's conscience, elevating his need to repent and expiate before God, regardless of all his previous attempts to reach a state of peace.

In the New Covenant, God has promised to adopt a voluntary, retrograde amnesia with respect to our sins and misdeeds. By saying, "I will remember no more" (Jer 31:34; Heb 8:12; 10:17), God demonstrates a proactive, unilateral, and unconditional stance. Letting go of offenses is a new theme; as Paul states, love does not keep an account of wrongs (1 Cor 13:5). The believer receives power to engage her or his capacity to let go of negative memories that underlie and animate the quest for revenge. The forgiver may be endowed with an empowered metacognitive-executive control and, thus, is able to adopt a forgiving attitude. This top-down agency may be engaged in order to monitor, regulate, and let go of the negative ruminations that often accompany the aftereffects of sinful events. The willful process of purposeful forgetting obliterates the power of negative associations and memories and allows for the exercise of freedom from their entrapments. Needless to say, the renewal of the person's mindset facilitates this process.

The binding element of the law was experienced as a burden that was hard to shake off. When a human broke any clause of the contract, the full extent of the penalties would be called upon, placing a heavy yoke on the offender. The many impositions added to the basic tenets of Moses invariably loaded the Israelites with cumbersome regulations that were experienced as an enslaving paradigm. The New Covenant provides the opportunity for freedom: to be and to become Christ-like, to feel and think positively, to forgive and forget offenses, to love as God has loved, and to go beyond the letter of the law without being disrespectful of it. The believer is set free by the work of the mediator (Rom 6:18). The believer experiences, on the one hand, freedom from sin and its penalties; on the other, freedom to approach God and to serve him (2 Cor 3:17).

The ability to exercise forgiveness and let go of offenses—to turn the other cheek when slapped and to walk a second mile when oppressed—is made possible for those who understand the workings of this new deal. Being empowered to reattribute meaning to reality and refusing to capitulate to nonsense, the empowered believer may imitate God as a person defined by God, not by the offender or her/his actions. Again, a free person who chooses to be nice, to forgive, and to forget is not to be confused with being a codependent who naïvely enables nonsensical patterns in relationships. This person should not be seen as an oppressed slave performing under the yoke of a law, but as a free person endowed with total freedom to be and to choose to behave above and beyond the letter of the law.

Letting go of offenses involves the retroactive erasing of negative memories and the establishment of a clean slate necessary to the eventual possibility of writing a new script. A better life-script would guide the establishment of a better lifeline and provide the guidelines necessary to enact a better lifestyle. The transformative development of a new character, behavioral repertoire, and lifestyle may focus on the positive aspects of restoration, empowerment, and proactive pursuit applicable to the promotion of a person's wholeness. This is a crucial issue in interpersonal dealings and needs a thorough treatment, which is given proper attention in chapter 15.

10. *An empowered capacity to experience renewal.* The New Covenant does not grow old. There is no further covenant promised after this deal as it is God's ultimate will, destined to accomplish God's eternal purpose. The eschatological promise states, "And the one seated on the throne said: 'Look! I am making all things new!' Then he said to me, 'Write it down, because these words are reliable and true'" (Rev 21:5). In a way, we may anticipate this renewal in the here and the now in order to "be transformed by the renewing of your mind, so that you may test and approve what is the will of God—what is good and well-pleasing and perfect" (Rom 12:2), or to "be renewed in the spirit of our mind" (Eph 4:23).

The Holy Spirit has been actively administering and actualizing the covenant in an ongoing fashion and will continue to do so in this age until the age to come. There is no entropy, no decay, and no fading glory in this deal. The superlative greatness of God's power continues to exert the redemptive energy that allows for the transformation and conformation of believers into God's ultimate prototype, as they become Christ-like in character, conduct, and relations. Marriages and families, as well as faith communities in need of renewal, may profit from the considerations of this work.

As we examine this topic further, we shall see the implications of the necessity for a dialogical rendering between an old, decaying order and the establishing of a new one. It may be said at this point that the continuity between the Old and the New Covenants are analogical to the continuity between a covenant made between partners whose first love and commitment has failed or was broken, and the renewal of their covenant as a necessity. Through the redemptive work of a mediating experience, based upon the extracted premises, a new deal for a couple in distress is in order—not to destroy or to invalidate their old vows, but to empower, transform, and renew their relationship. A renewed alliance may be based upon the the clauses extracted from the New Covenant. Chapter 16 deals with such matters.

THE NEW COVENANT AND INTEGRATIVE BIBLICAL COUNSELING

The analysis of the New Covenant has provided ten distinct principles of an exemplary nature. Readers may consider the ways in which God has acted and follow Paul's admonition to the Ephesians (5:1–2) to imitate God as dearly beloved children and walk in love; that is, to develop a style of life patterned after God's Word, applicable to marital and family systems, structures, processes, boundaries, and interactive patterns.

The premises and principles explored in this work may serve as underlying assumptions in working therapeutically with partners in marriage, members of families, and relations within the fellowship of believers. Often, what appears to be a Christian counseling approach is the functional adoption of a given secular strategy to which a therapist introduces and quotes Bible verses and perhaps prays during the session. Beyond simply quoting verses in a session or stringing together scriptures deemed appropriate to confront problematic conditions, New Covenant principles may prove to be foundational to a philosophy and praxis of counseling from a biblical perspective. It is desirable for Christian counselors, psychologists, and pastors to be endowed with a biblical-theological mindset and psychological mindedness (metacognitive and dialogical) so as to engage those who suffer or are in need of guidance in a holistic way.

As it applies to a therapeutic profession, the author appeals to an abstracted paradigm over against a method that relies on shopping for Bible verses (at times taken out of context) to be applied in concrete situations. Thus a master-builder versus a bricklayer approach is emphasized. (Note: The author has nothing against a bricklayer's work per se, having engaged in such work himself, helping his father to build a house in his youth.) This work presents a metacognitive-dialogical approach based upon a principled methodology. Beyond "how to" approaches, this work seeks to integrate biblical theology pertaining to the New Covenant—adopted as a top-down revelation given by God to be elucidated by believers—with psychological principles based on both research and clinical practices.

As a final note, the terms of the New Covenant may be understood by those who actually know the Lord, who accept Scriptures as being God's Word, and who are willing and able to follow the exemplary ways derived from the scrutiny, interpretation, and application of the principles gleaned from academic, clinical, and devotional endeavors.

Chapter 5

Marriage as Covenant

Previous chapters have dealt with covenant as a paradigm of a relational nature with both the Old and New Covenants exemplifying God's redemptive design. The superb terms encompassed in the new deal were dealt with in a more particular fashion, considered as being both a redemptive and relational paradigm that superseded the old deal. This chapter approaches marriage as a covenant, defined as a dyadic system framed in a theology of human relationships, derived from scriptural principles applicable to its structures and functions, and patterned after God's intimate relationships with Israel and the church.

MARRIAGE AS A COVENANT IN SCRIPTURAL NARRATIVE

Many authors have regarded covenant as a paradigm used to depict the spiritual and social dimensions of marriage.[1]

The metaphor of divine marriage has a long tradition in scholarly endeavors. The Babylonian, Assyrian, Canaanite, and Hittite cultures that emerged in the ancient world have provided a contextual background for many biblical studies dealing with the emergence and development of the people of Israel and their customs. The anthropological data that has emerged from the study of human relations registered among ancient peoples has enlightened our understanding of marriage as a key social system. The structural organization of marriage and its functions, as depicted in Scripture, show many similarities to those found in ancient cultures.

The ancient concept of "divine marriage" represented a special feature registered in many written accounts found in cuneiform tablets, scrolls, and papyri. Original accounts dealing with relational contracts between parties included the invocation of supernatural beings in sanctioning human transactions. Human alliances followed

---

1. See, for example, Neufeld, *Ancient Hebrew Marriage Laws*; Rabinowitz, "Marriage Contracts in Ancient Egypt"; Baab, "Marriage"; Tweedie, "Contract Therapy"; Dunstan, "The Marriage Covenant"; Atkinson, *To Have and to Hold*; Philips, "The Church of God"; McKenzie and Wallace, "Covenant Themes in Malachi"; McLean, "The Language of Covenant"; Blomberg, *Matthew*; Polischuk, "A New Covenant"; Hugenberger, *Marriage as a Covenant*; Smalley, *The Covenant Marriage*; Ripley et al., "Covenantal and Contractual Values"; Smolarz, *Covenant*; Balswick and Balswick, *A Model for Marriage*; Miller, *Marriage in the Book of Tobit*; Köstenberger and Jones, *Marriage and the Family*.

after the patterns perceived to exist among the alliances among the gods and goddesses themselves. As an example, the laws pertaining to marriage contracts, betrothal, bride price, dowry, wedding feasts, divorce, adultery, and roles such as best man, etc., registered in the codes of Hammurabi provide valuable insights into such issues.[2]

The Jewish roots of the marriage covenant have their origins in the account of a prototypical union depicted in Genesis 2:21–24. Most Christian writers appeal to this narrative with allusions to Adam and Eve as a prototypical couple whose marriage was performed by God himself. Although the term *covenant* (*berit*) does not appear in Genesis 2 and 3, the implied nature of this deal is stressed by the wording of the passage: "Man shall leave his father and his mother and hold fast [cleave] to his wife, and they shall become one flesh" (2:24). The expression has often been associated with a covenantal context, reinforced by the "formula" used in binding relationships of an intimate nature, such as the one found in the Genesis narrative: "This is at last bone of my bones and flesh of my flesh" (2:23). An interesting passage is found in 2 Samuel 5:1, where the people of Israel made a covenant with David in Hebron before the Lord, with the expression, "Behold, we are your bone and flesh." The same event is narrated in 1 Chronicles 11:1, and appears as a ratifying, covenantal expression.

Several prophets (pre-exilic, exilic, and post-exilic) have alluded to God's deals with Israel in covenantal terms. The customary challenges and problems surrounding the study and interpretation of prophetic books are beyond the scope and the intent of this chapter. The reader has to bear in mind that all prophets demonstrated an apparent mission: to afflict the comfortable and to comfort the afflicted. Thus, many negative depictions saturate their accounts, pointing to human failures and unfaithfulness in keeping their covenantal terms with God, followed by the positive aspects emphasizing God's restitution and renewal due to their repentance and adherence to covenantal terms.

1. *Hosea's account.* The first mention of divine marriage found in Hebrew literature is credited to Hosea.[3] For our purposes, we will focus on the living metaphor of a prophet commanded to love an unfaithful wife as being exemplary of God's unilateral, unconditional, and merciful concern for Israel. Most commentators divide Hosea 2 into two sections: the first section is found in verses 2 through 15, where God's statements picture him as the husband of an unfaithful wife, including his mercy toward her and the future restoration of his unfaithful partner. The second section presents allusions to God's removal of his wife's objects of idolatry—worshipping pagan gods, depicted figuratively as adulterous relations with foreign "lovers"—and reinstating his betrothal (original engagement pledge): "I will betroth you to me forever; I will betroth you to me in righteousness and in justice, in steadfast love and mercy. I will betroth you to me in faithfulness.

---

2. See Pritchard, "Sumerian Sacred Marriage Texts."
3. Hall, "Origin of the Marriage Metaphor"; Smolarz, *Covenant*.

And you shall know the LORD" (Hos 2:19–20, ESV). The chapter stresses the bond and the belongingness (or lack of it) as pertaining to marriage language in Scripture. Besides Hosea, other Hebrew prophets addressed the people with covenantal allusions in order to describe the relationship between God and Israel.

2. *Jeremiah's account.* Focusing on the unfaithfulness of the nation and their open disobedience to the terms of the covenant, Jeremiah warns Israel about the invasion, captivity, desolation, and destruction that will take place as a consequence (chapters 2 and 3). The blessings of their youthful alliance (2:2–3) are set in contrast to their recent and current behaviors that describe their unfaithfulness (2:4–13). Their obvious rebelliousness, degradation, immorality, and apostasy will be subject to punishment with devastating consequences as a result. The admonitions that follow in chapter 3 depict Israel as a wife committing adultery with many lovers (3:1–3). The prophet stretches his analogy, including two wives (both Israel and Judah are depicted as unfaithful and adulterous partners) receiving their punishment.

Jeremiah follows the same theme in chapter 13 (vv. 22, 26–27), where other metaphors apply: Jerusalem is depicted as a violated woman experiencing shame for her sins, suffering at the hands of her lovers and being made into a public, shameful spectacle. Yet, with all that, the unilateral and proactive thrust of God is anticipated as well, employing a marriage metaphor where God will forgive her iniquities and restore her into a virgin state (31:3–5). The reader may note that it is in this dreadful context that a New Covenant is promised (Jer 31:31–34). In contrast to the devastating outcomes of the failures to keep the Old Covenant, the New Covenant is forecasted as a better and actualizing deal. In this light, this work regards the New Covenant as a model representing a paradigm for marriage that supersedes the old analogy.

3. *Isaiah's account.* In four instances, the prophet deals with Israel in metaphorical fashion, casting several figures into a domestic drama. Chapters 4 through 66 depict Israel as a nation during and after the exile to Babylon. In the first place, Zion appears as God's wife and the mother of all the Judean children with whom the father is arguing. They have charged God with neglect, abandonment, deportation, and captivity, placing the blame of all such negative outcomes on the Lord. Isaiah presents God's position, proving that it was the children's unfaithfulness and transgressions that brought such consequences.

Isaiah's second allusion to marriage as a metaphor depicts Zion (a mountain representing the city of God's choice or Israel as God's chosen one) as being restored by her husband and able to generate many children again (54:1–10). A third instance employing marriage imagery describes God as the bridegroom of Israel (61:10). To conclude, the prophet employs the divine marriage theme to forecast the restoration of Jerusalem after returning from their exile (62:3–5). Interested readers may consult several available sources dealing with this topic.[4]

4. *Ezekiel's account.* Addressing the people as a fellow partaker of their Babylonian exile, the prophet dedicates two passages to pinpoint their predicament, due to their unfaithfulness to the covenantal terms with God. In chapter 16, Israel is depicted as a child of pagan origin, neglected and left to die, and yet captured by God's unilateral and proactive supervision as he initially passed by her. On a second passing by, God saw Israel as being a grown woman, ready for love, and proceeded to cover her nakedness. Ezekiel 16:8 reads, "Later I passed by, and when I looked at you and saw that you were old enough for love, I spread the corner of my garment over you and covered your naked body. I gave you my solemn oath and entered into a covenant with you, declares the Sovereign LORD, and you became mine" (NIV). This symbolic action (covering) indicated his intention to betroth and marry her, entering into a covenantal relation.

God's redemptive *cover* is a theme that runs throughout Scripture. The reader may compare Ezekiel's allusions to passages found in Genesis 3:21 where God covers Adam and Eve's nakedness; in Ruth 3:9, where Boaz extends his cover to Ruth in a redemptive pledge; and in Hosea 2:5, 9, where God removes his cover from an unfaithful wife.

In sum, Ezekiel's account presents the thrust of God's redemptive and dignifying love for Israel, displayed before the nations of the cosmos (16:14), by washing her and dressing her with precious clothes and royal jewels (16:9–13) and by providing her with the finest food (16:13–14). Then, the prophet proceeds to charge this woman with idolatry as an unfaithful wife taking advantage of her husband's gifts and sacrificing their children to Canaanite gods (16:16–21). Her alliances with foreign powers (Egypt, Assyria, and Chaldea) point to her spreading adultery, seeking the favors and protection of such "husbands" instead of keeping her covenant with a providing and faithful partner.

The prophet delivered a very serious charge, comparing Israel to a prostitute serving the demands of several lovers (16:22, 25). Even more, her character is depicted in lustful, even nymphomaniac, terms (16:31, 33–34). These behaviors deserved punishment (16:35–43). Yet again, God's anger would diminish and calm down (note the rendering of God's emotive aspects cast in human terms, depicting an angry husband) in hopes that the wife's conscious realization of her wrongdoing would emerge, and that she would experience regret, remorse, and repentance before being restituted and restored (16:52–58). Ezekiel ends his charge with the results of this covenantal unfaithfulness (16:59) and with the husband's remembrance of their vows at Sinai, intended to regain their covenantal momentum without denying the reality of Israel's failures.

---

4. See, for example, Hanson, *Isaiah 40—46*; Brueggemann, *The Psalms*; Oswalt, *The Book of Isaiah*.

The passage mentioned emphasizes the binding element of an oath in the context of a covenantal marriage. The metaphor of the harlot closes with the statement in verses 16:59–69, in which God's declarations stand initially in a direct contrast: "You have broken the covenant" versus "I remember my covenant." Later on, the prophet stresses the fact that the covenant that God remembers is the covenant he made in the days of Israel's youth, and that God will fulfill his promises in the future in spite of Israel's unfaithfulness. In covenantal terms, Ezekiel stresses God's declaration of recognition: "I will establish my covenant with you, and you shall know that I am the Lord" (16:62).

Ezekiel 23 appeals to the marriage metaphor again, this time introducing two sisters (Samaria and Jerusalem, capitals of the Northern and Southern kingdoms) in covenant with the same husband. If we adopt a metacognitive view of Scriptures and consider its internal consistency, it is proper to assume that polygamy here serves only an analogical function rather than representing a prototypical or paradigmatic example. The figurative narrative points out that both Israel and Judah had engaged in unfaithful dealings with foreign lovers (Egypt, Assyria, and Babylon as political husbands). Furthermore, the prophet reminds both Israel and Judah that their propensity toward unfaithfulness was not something new, but was part of a rather long history dating from the time of their bondage in Egypt, being abused under their oppressive rulers. This propensity was noticeable before the covenantal "marriage" was established with God at Sinai.

In psychoanalytic terms, the so-called *Stockholm syndrome* may have been at work: the Israelites could be compared to enslaved, victimized, and sexually abused virgins who, after regaining their freedom, were not able to detach from their abusers, but identified with their aggressors and paid an unhealthy devotion to them. Unfortunately, Ezekiel does not end with a positive analogy as it pertains to marriage. He shifts away from the marriage metaphor and employs other analogies to buttress the hopes of redemption and restoration. The visions of a valley full of dry bones coming alive and the power of overflowing rivers coming from God's presence both convey metaphorically the restorative future awaiting Israel.

5. *Malachi's account.* Delivering his charges at a post-exilic time, the prophet addressed the failing priests and leaders of Judah in a dialogical and metaphorical fashion, employing the marriage covenant as a well-known paradigm to make his points. In the passage, the prophet reverses the customary thrust (i.e., the unfaithful wife theme), balancing his negative injunctions by focusing on the metaphor of unfaithful husbands this time. Malachi 2:14 reads, "The Lord was a witness between you and the wife of your youth, to whom you have been faithless, though she is your companion and your wife by covenant" (ESV). The NIV

renders the text as "the wife of your marriage covenant." Actually, most translations seem to render the same concept: marriage—even depicted in negative and failing terms—is framed in a covenantal paradigm.

Hopefully, all the prophetic expressions alluding to marriage as a covenant serve as scriptural basis for the considerations that follow in this work. From the data found in the Old Testament, we may proceed to the allusions made in the New.

NEW TESTAMENT ALLUSIONS TO MARRIAGE

Shifting from metaphorical to actual references to marriage as a covenant found in the NT writings, the words of Jesus, Paul, Peter, John, James, and the author to the Hebrews are presented in a brief review.

From a logical perspective, if the statements made by the ambassadors of a king about his covenantal terms are worthy of respect, much more attention should be paid to the words of the king himself. If prophets were trustworthy conveyors and providers of data on the nature of marriage and its terms, a greater and more powerful definer of the marital system is Jesus himself. His definition of human reality takes precedence over all others as the creator, author, sovereign, and granting Lord who defines the nature of marriage and sets forth its covenantal terms.

Jesus's teachings on marriage. Both Mark and Matthew register the account of his response to the question about divorce posed by the Pharisees (Mark 10:1–12; Matt 19:1–9). His teaching on the subject included "hard sayings" about marriage and divorce and represented a major challenge to his listeners. In what appeared to be an extreme point of view (at least to those who preferred to adopt a relaxed stance on the subject matter), he alluded to a person's intentionally covert or unexpressed lustful thoughts as being functional equivalents to the act of adultery. In these terms, a covetously minded person commits adultery without acting overtly. From a cognitive science perspective, thoughts are implicit behaviors of the mind at work. Of course, this teaching provoked strong reactions in the Pharisees who emphasized external aspects of behavioral nature encompassed in 613 commandments (Matt 5:27–28, 31–32).

First-century Jews were exposed to two main schools of thought on the issue of divorce. On the one hand, Shammai's conservative views allowed the dissolution of a marital covenant solely on the grounds of a partner's unchastity. On the other hand, Hillel's liberal views allowed for divorce on the grounds of any viable cause. Both parties tried to engage Jesus in order to favor one side and create a division between him and his followers. His reply was cast in a rabbinical style, deriving a generalization based on two scriptures. As registered in Matthew 19:4b, he appealed to Genesis 1:27: "Have you not read that he who created them from the beginning made them male and female . . . ?" Then, he continued with the second citation, drawn from Genesis 2:24: "Therefore man shall leave his father and his mother and hold fast to his wife, and the two shall become one flesh" (Matt 19:5, ESV). His concluding principle followed: "So they are no longer two, but one flesh. What therefore God has joined together, let no man separate" (Matt 19:6, NAS).

We learn from Jesus's teaching on the subject that

- God made humanity into two different genders: male and female, as counterparts of each other, and as a relational expression of his image;
- Before this union is to take place, the development of an identity needs to be established in the context of a family system; both differentiation and mutuality are embedded in the process encapsulated in the statements "leaving father and mother" and "cleaving to a partner";
- The design called for two differentiated beings—a *male* and a *female*, individuated from *father* and *mother*—to enter into a monogamous relationship;
- The union of partners would be ratified in their social and emotional bonding and actualized in becoming "one flesh" (an allusion made to a sexual union);
- What God had joined in covenant should not be put asunder by any man.

Theologically speaking, marriage is defined at ontological level as the union of a male and a female before and under God, bonded and held together in hypostatic-ecstatic fellowship after the Trinity—grounded in, exuding, reflecting, and actualizing the *Tselem Elohim* (God's image).

Paul's teachings. St. Paul makes allusions to human marital engagements in 1 Corinthians 7:1–39, which denote the seriousness, stability, and longevity of these covenantal unions. The passage reflects the notion that, even in the Gentile world, these marriage engagements were regarded as covenantal dealings. Marriage ceremonies always included formal or contractual elements that were recorded as public happenings, sanctioned in the presence of witnesses and celebrated by the community. In spite of the passage of time, these elements remain among us in vestigial or overt fashion.

Given his unique call and his ministerial dedication exerted during challenging times, Paul's views on marriage (1 Cor 7:1–16) included a cautionary statement of preference: "It is good for man not to have sexual relations with a woman (lit., "not to touch a woman"). But because of the Corinthians' blatant immoralities, his counsel was that each man should have relations with his own wife and each woman with her own husband (7:1–2). Faithfulness to a covenant partner was expected. When considering the decision to enter into a marriage union, a deep commitment appears to saturate the mindset of the apostle. His admonitions convey a serious and binding sense of mutual duty that goes beyond casual agreements or trivialized contracts.

Once married, partners should fulfill one another's natural desires and not deprive one another of their conjugal rights (partners should "fulfill their obligations" as if they owe and pay a sexual debt to one another). Paul considered a partner's sexual withholding or deprivation to be a cause of temptation—provoking the propensity of an unfulfilled person to trespass the intimate boundaries of marriage in order to satisfy sexual urges in inappropriate ways—seen as a vulnerable spot utilized by Satan himself in his attempts to intrude upon and destroy the union.

In this passage, Paul made allusions to a lifelong commitment to a covenantal bond, reinforcing the depth of such union: "A woman is bound to her husband as long as he lives. But if her husband dies, she is free to marry anyone she wishes, but he must belong to the Lord" (1 Cor 7:39, NIV). Previously, he had stated, "To the married, I give this command—not I, but the Lord—a wife should not divorce a husband (but if she does, let her remain unmarried, or be reconciled to her husband), and a husband should not divorce his wife" (1 Cor 7:10–11). Paul's generic advice to those desiring to marry appears in 2 Corinthians 6:14, addressed to prospective partners considering a transactional engagement: to avoid being mismatched and to pursue and be bonded in an equal yoke (faith and values binding them).

Paul provides further advice to those who are already bonded in a mixed marriage: "To the rest I say—not the Lord—if a brother has a wife that is not a believer *and she is happy to live with him*, he should not divorce her. And if a woman has a husband who is not a believer *and he is happy to live with her*, she should not divorce him" (vv. 12–13, italics mine). Note that Paul adds an editorial comment, clarifying whether he had received these commands from the Lord or was expressing his own opinions on the matter. He wanted to make sure that believers would assign the proper weight to his message and allocate a proper value to their source. He adds, "But if the unbeliever wants a divorce, let it take place. In these circumstances the brother or sister is not bound. God has called you in peace" (v. 15). Paul envisioned the possibility that in such mixed unions, the believing partner could be functional in bringing the unbeliever to faith. Yet, he did not push a dogmatic agenda that would oblige a believer to endure lifelong suffering at the hands of an abuser or to stay in an unhealthy alliance as if such a covenantal deal would glorify God.

As for the structure of this system, scholars have debated as to whether his assertion was rendered as a universal paradigmatic injunction or cast in a culturally syntonic statement: "Now I want you to realize that the head of every man is Christ, and the head of the woman is man, and the head of Christ is God" (1 Cor 11:3). The term used for "head" is κεφαλή (*kephale*), which has been subject to much debate. Given the diverse interpretations of its contextual meaning, arguments in favor of "authority" versus "source" of care, nurturance, etc., have characterized the writings of proponents amongst complementarian and egalitarian positions. The hierarchical aspects that emerged from this passage appeal to the creation story, in which the order or the primacy assigned to the forming of the first of Adam is also used by Paul in his

Part I: Premises and Principles

writing to Timothy (1 Tim 2:9–15). Several authors of this persuasion have presented their views, and the interested reader may resort to these writings.[5]

The egalitarian interpretation of *headship* has regarded this term as the loving attitude and behavior of a husband toward his partner, expressing service, care, protection, and nurturance, etc. The egalitarian camp includes many proponents, such as Paul Jewett, F. F. Bruce, Gordon Fee, Roger Nicole, Aída and Bill Spencer, Ben Witherington, and Katherine Kroeger, among others. An amicable and respectful dialogue between evangelical proponents departing from both positions has been provided by a dialogical rendering by two Christian couples.[6]

Perhaps the most cited NT passage is found in Ephesians 5:22–32, in which relationships are predicated on the premises that believers are imitators of God and are commanded to live a life of love. Love and respect are given as dimensions in a healthy alliance under God, both partners being subject to one another out of reverence for Christ. In his letter to the Colossians (3:18–19), Paul follows the same line of reasoning and appeals to husbands' love and wives' respect as being hallmarks of a covenantal union.

Peter's views on marriage. Peter's account is not as extensive as Paul's. He mainly focused on mixed unions (1 Pet 3:1–7), where wives were encouraged to treat unbelieving husbands with respect in view of a possible change of heart on their part. Again, the allusions are made with strong covenantal tones underlying the obligatory aspects of marriage syntonic with the customs, expectations, and interpretations of God's will as expressed analogically in the covenantal passages related to marriage that we reviewed before. Sadly, such arguments have been often utilized to suppress or oppress believing women into an unhealthy submission within abusive or degrading contexts.

The reader may draw analogies of God's dealings with Israel or Christ's dealings with the church, keeping in mind that it is the husband who in both cases has exerted his unilateral, unconditional, proactive, graceful, merciful, and empowering efforts toward an unworthy wife, a fact that is often missed in situations dealing with domestic oppression or abuse. Often, it is the wife who is pastorally counseled and charged with the expiatory responsibility to "save" her husband by means of an obedient, submissive, and quiet demeanor. As an example of bad hermeneutics applied to Peter's writing, the tacit (or overt) expectation is that her suffering will act in an expiatory fashion toward her husband, which she should gladly endure. The appeal is made here to the correct interpretation of Scripture so as to avoid its utilization as an oppressive or degrading means rather than as a life-giving and empowering Word.

James's metaphorical allusion to a covenantal notion. James resorts to metaphorical language to address faltering believers as unfaithful partners: "Adulterers, do you

---

5. See, for example, J.I. Packer, Elisabeth Elliot, Wayne Grudem, Mark Driscoll, Tim Keller, John F. MacArthur, C.S. Lewis, and John Piper.

6. See Spencer et al., *Marriage at the Crossroads*.

know that friendship with the world means hostility toward God? So whoever decides to be the world's friend makes himself God's enemy. Or do you think the scripture means nothing when it [vainly] says, 'The spirit that God caused to live within us [or the spirit that he causes to live within us] has an envious yearning?'" (James 4:4–5). Scholars have debated the meaning of the passage on the basis of the referent of the word *spirit,* allowing for both a positive and a negative interpretation. This author falls in line with those who consider the "spirit" in this passage to be the intrinsically lustful capacity left by God in the human, a propensity for yielding to temptation until redemption is accomplished. This spirit is the agent responsible for developing a divided mind (James 1:8, 14) and for the engagement in inner struggles mentioned in the context (James 4:1–4).

The author to the Hebrews. After exposing the New Covenant in detail as being God's actualized paradigm for relations, the author makes one brief allusion of a connotative and practical nature: "Marriage must be honored among all, and the marriage bed kept undefiled, for God will judge sexually immoral people and adulterers" (Heb 13:4). The reader may surmise that this exhortation was made in view of the contextual exposition rendered in the previous twelve chapters of the letter. Also, invoking God's judgment as it pertains to unfaithfulness in marital relations seems to ratify the concept of marriage as a covenant before its ultimate overseer.

John's final revelation. Finally, the covenantal analogy receives glorious attention as John's Revelation points out: "Let us rejoice and exult and give him glory, because the wedding celebration of the Lamb has come, and his bride has made herself ready" (Rev 19:7). John then registers the angelic request: "Come, I will show you the bride, the wife of the Lamb!" (Rev 21:9). His allusions to a New Jerusalem, coupled with analogical language describing a bride and a lamb, merge into a composite picture. This compounded and figurative language appears also in the Pauline allegory found in Galatians 4:21–31, where Abraham's partners Hagar and Sarah are compared to Sinai and Jerusalem, with the resulting children born into a slave state under the law (the offspring of the Old Covenant) as contrasted with those born into freedom and grace (the offspring of the New Covenant). From these allusions, we may gather together a picture that allows for a glimpse of God's final purpose in which not only our union with the Son will be accomplished, but also our eternal and secure attachment to our Father, fulfilling his covenantal design with his children.

THEOLOGICAL CONSIDERATIONS

Marriage and the family have been the focus of attention of ministers, educators, and providers of service. Covenant as an analogy for human transactions—marriage in particular—runs deep in Christian thought. Reid presented a covenantal basis for relationships in marriage; Tweedie rendered a version of *covenant therapy* with couples based on an analogy between contracts and covenants.[7] The Old Covenant with Israel has been taken as a model for parenting in which loving care and respect are balanced with discipline and accountability. Scripturally delineated functions also include forgiveness and restitution of covenantal relations.[8] Key covenantal notions represent the basis for a biblical anthropology with God as the postulator of personhood and the human defined as a God-derived entity. Marriage and the family are social institutions that belong to a temporal and secondary order, contingent upon the primary order established by a creating, redeeming, and sustaining God, who intends to bring his children into an eternal state of redefined fellowship with him.

Other authors joined such theological trends. Chartier emphasized God's parenting role, following his actions toward Israel as being exemplary and worthy of imitation.[9] Anderson presented the covenant between God and Israel as a basis for his biblical anthropology and human relations.[10] Anderson and Guernsey further developed the idea of covenant as a unilateral relation established by God with his people Israel, through specific actions by which he summoned individuals and, finally, an entire nation into a history of response.[11] Besides this unilateral aspect, unconditional and graceful aspects were stressed as well.

Focusing upon the language of covenant applied to a theology of the family, McLean has stressed the metaphorical aspects of a covenant in terms of its components.[12] The sociability of persons, the couple as a basic social unit, and the inherent struggles and conflicts that intertwine with harmonious functioning were some aspects presented by the author. Forgiveness was emphasized as a main ingredient in covenantal transactions (to forgive and be forgiven), acting as a reinforcing element of the bonding to each other. The author also emphasized the need for order and law, acting as boundaries that safeguard the enacted covenants. Finally, the memories of the past, life in the present, and anticipation about the future were stressed as time-framed aspects that provide a temporal awareness to those who live in a covenant relationship. Along the same lines, Intrater (1989) regarded covenant relationships as characterized by love, seen as a more excellent way to interact as partners in marriage.[13]

In an article on the New Covenant as a paradigm for family progress, this author presented ten principles derived from Scripture and interpreted as basic ways in which God has acted toward humans.[14] The appeal was made for humans to consider and act toward each other in God's manner of love exemplified in covenantal terms.

7. Reid, *Marriage Covenant*; Tweedie, "Contract Therapy."
8. Gangel, "Toward a Biblical Theology."
9. Chartier, "Parenting."
10. Anderson, *On Being Human*.
11. Anderson and Guernsey, *On Being Family*.
12. McLean, "The Language of Covenant."
13. Intrater, *Covenant Relationships*.
14. Polischuk, "A New Covenant."

Balswick and Balswick integrated a Christian perspective on the contemporary home based on social sciences, clinical insight, and biblical theology.[15] The authors drew from covenantal themes and integrated them with systemic approaches in marriage and family therapy. In line with covenantal principles, Engelsma stressed the fact that marriage was a counterpart to the mystery of Christ and the church, expressed as a covenant-bond in Scripture and history.[16] Burke alluded to happiness as predicated upon both love and commitment enacted in marriage.[17] Guernsey expanded the model from marriage to the family covenant, stressing love and forgiveness as essential dimensions in the Christian home.[18]

In terms of marital stability, Lowery highlighted a covenant basis for staying together for life.[19] In terms of marriage processes, popular authors have emphasized covenant models for building communication and intimacy in marriage.[20] Judith and Jack Balswick developed a model for marriage built on four premises: covenant, grace, empowerment, and intimacy.[21] Yarhouse and Sells based their approach on scriptural passages (e.g., Ruth 1:16–18; Eph 5:21–33; 2 Tim 1:5) with an emphasis on dependency on God, mutuality, self-denial, perseverance (resiliency), and integrity as key factors in healthy Christian couples and family relations.[22]

In terms of its universality, Witte and Ellison have compared marriages as described in Jewish, Christian, and Muslim understandings.[23] Their work, *Covenant Marriage in Comparative Perspective*, brings together scholars from diverse religious traditions, comparing marital contracts and covenants. Their efforts sought to elucidate various facets of marriage from the perspectives of both jurisprudence and religion, producing an integrated picture of the legal and spiritual dimensions of marriage. In chapter 1 of that work, Novak reviewed the Jewish dialectic between contract-covenant among Jewish marriage considerations.[24] Of interest to Slavic readers that belong to an Orthodox perspective, Harakas presented an excellent work dealing with marriage as a covenant before God; Lawler presented a perspective of marriage as a covenant among Roman Catholics.[25]

---

15. Balswick and Balswick, *The Family*.
16. Engelsma, *Marriage*.
17. Burke, *Covenanted Happiness*.
18. Guernsey, *The Family Covenant*.
19. Lowery, *Covenant Marriage*.
20. See, for example, Smalley, *The Covenant Marriage*; Chapman, *Covenant Marriages*.
21. Balswick and Balswick, *A Model for Marriage*.
22. Sells and Yarhouse, *Counseling Couples*.
23. Witte and Ellison, *Covenant Marriage*.
24. Novak, "Jewish Marriage," In *Covenant Marriage in Comparative Perspective*, 26–52.
25. Harakas, "Covenant Marriage," In *Covenant Marriage in Comparative Perspective*, 92–123; Lawler, "Marriage as a Covenant," In *Covenant Marriage in Comparative Perspective*, 70–91.

Part I: Premises and Principles

My colleagues at Gordon-Conwell, Aída and William Spencer, in collaboration with Steve and Celestia Tracy, have provided an important work dealing with marriage from both egalitarian and complementarian perspectives.[26] In a dialogical fashion, couples in conversation provide insight into gender roles and decision-making in marriage and intimacy. Tim Keller, a graduate from the same institution and now a popular pastor in NYC, has produced an excellent book for married people, *The Meaning of Marriage: Facing the Complexities of Commitment with the Wisdom of God.*[27]

Usually, scholars have adopted a retrospective approach in their considerations, going back to Genesis, the law, the prophets, and New Testament studies on the subject. Extending a theological vision geared toward a more eschatological perspective, Smolarz has provided a study with a special reference to the book of Revelation.[28] In his work, covenant draws from the metaphor of divine marriage throughout Scripture. His approach interacts with the writings of the Old Testament, those of the intertestamentary period, and New Testament studies, following an eschatological point of reference that guides marriage considerations as they apply in the here and now.

All in all, the research and notions provided point to important theological implications that are embedded in any consideration pertaining to Christian marriage or family system. Some elements or dimensions of abstracted meaning are further delineated in the following pages.

COVENANTAL ELEMENTS IN MARRIAGE

Several notions appear as dimensions in marital transactions extracted from scriptural data and interpretation. A succinct review is presented here.

On leaving and cleaving: readiness for marriage. Many customs surrounding marriage developed among the contemporaneous cultures of the Middle East where Abraham lived before experiencing his call to establish his family and settle in a land promised to him. In ancient times, the physical configuration of Mesopotamian houses indicated that, in most circumstances, extended families resided together. So, the expression "man shall leave his mother and his father" refers not so much to a geographic distancing, but to the principle of a *transfer of allegiance* (defined in cognitive-emotive and behavioral terms) from parents to a spouse so as to establish a new unit. Likewise, "to cleave to his wife" is an expression that describes the interpersonal intimacy that should characterize a marriage partnership, being inaugurated and constantly enhanced by means of a renewed sexual intimacy.[29]

---

26. Spencer et al., *Marriage at the Crossroads.*
27. Keller, *The Meaning of Marriage.*
28. Smolarz, *Covenant and the Metaphor of Divine Marriage.*
29. Blomberg, *Matthew,* 290.

Marriage vows: oaths and verbia solemnia as marital pledges. A key principle is found in Ezekiel 16:8, where metaphorical language is used: *"I gave you my solemn oath and entered into a covenant with you . . . "* For most Israelites familiar with such writings, marriage was not considered to be just a simple social contract, but an oath before God, a committed relationship bound by the steadfast love of God. Under such auspices, the key ingredient of marriage was a mutual commitment under oath made before God and witnesses. The rights and privileges of the participants entering into a covenant were obviously held in mind, but subordinated to the encompassing desire to obey God and his commands. God's love and presence above and among them, which never ceases nor diminishes its binding power, was considered the binding element par excellence.

Scholars have argued over the place and importance allocated to *verbia solemnia* in marriage. It appears that it was an intrinsic part of Israelite marriages, a solemn declaration of mutual obligations, commitment, and responsibilities constituting an oath, supporting the argument that marriage is a covenant patterned after God's deals. Some biblical data supports this notion (Gen 2:23; Hosea 2:4, 17–19; Prov 7:4–5). Besides this, keeping in mind Israel's customs dating from the second century BCE, the apocryphal book of Tobit (7:11–12) registers a marriage with an oath ratifying the contract.

The treatment of this source by Miller provides insights into the nature of marriage oaths in Israel, including the notion of *verba solemnia* and God's designs and presence in such covenants.[30] Further data gathered from extra-biblical sources dealing with *verbia solemnia* was presented by Hugenberger, who appealed to the writings registered in papyri found at Elephantine and Wadi Murabbat.[31] The Elephantine Papyri (c. 200 BCE) are a collection of ancient Jewish manuscripts dating from the 5th century BC. They come from a Jewish community at Elephantine, an island in the Nile at the border of Egypt and Nubia. The Murabbat papyri (c. 600 BCE) were found at a cave in Murabbat at Khirbet Mira, north of the Kidron Valley south of Qumran. Both accounts support the utilization of *verbia solemnnia* in the arrangements of marital transactions of the time.[32]

On a negative, yet wise, note, the author of Proverbs reminds the youth about the wisdom of keeping covenantal matters in place before God as it pertains to temptations of a sexual nature. The warning directed to a young man when encountering a "wayward wife" was to preserve his integrity by avoiding her. Otherwise, she could lure him with her seductive words as a wife "who has left the partner of her youth and ignored the covenant she made before God" (Prov 2:17–17).

Engagement: betrothal and the bride-price. In Scripture, the engagement of a couple was totally binding. Either his parents or the man himself would designate a

---

30. Miller, *Marriage in the Book of Tobit*, 121.
31. Hugenberger, *Marriage as a Covenant*.
32. Ibid.

woman to be his wife, and would freely offer the prospective bride an article of some worth in the presence of witnesses. Her acceptance of this item would indicate some sort of explicit deal, called *erusin* (betrothal). This practice is mentioned in the narrative of Abraham arranging the marriage of his son Isaac to Rebekah, instructing his steward to offer valuable gifts to her (Gen 24). Arranged marriages were characterized by strong covenantal elements, cast in *verbia solemnia* (solemn vows) before the parties came together to consummate their union. As far as covenantal parties are concerned, Baab identified them to be the families of both the groom and the bride.[33] For McKenzie and Wallace, a covenant was made between the prospective husband and the father or brother of the bride-to-be.[34] Atkinson stressed the idea that the parties were the man and the woman entering marriage.[35]

Textual references found in Deuteronomy 22:23–29 deal with sexual encounters between a "virgin pledged to be married" and a man who sleeps with her, whether consensually or forcefully. To be pledged in marriage had the force of a binding covenant. Only death or divorce would break it, even when the couple had not yet consummated their sexual union. Thus, a pledged person who willingly or consensually had sexual relations outside of such a bond would be put to death as this event would be considered an adulterous act, even when the marriage ceremony had not taken place yet.

If the pledged woman was raped, and had no access to any help, only the man performing the sexual act would be stoned to death. In contrast to a person who is engaged, a single person would be confronted by the community and forced to deal properly after the sexual event was discovered, paying fines and even marrying the person with whom the sexual union took place. Whether the marriage should occur in such case was a questionable matter, subject to the will of the father of the female. The wishes of the female would be considered as well. (See Exodus 22:16–17: "If a man seduces a virgin who is not pledged to be married and sleeps with her, he must pay the bride-price, and she shall be his wife. If her father absolutely refuses to give her to him, he must still pay the bride-price for virgins.") Anachronistic as it sounds to a postmodern audience, such were the contractual facts in those days.

In time, the practice was codified in the Talmud (c. 1st century BCE–6th century CE) as a strongly pledged deal (betrothal), a state in between marriage and what today we call "engagement." Marrying without this agreement was considered immoral, and breaking a betrothal required a formal divorce as any violation of betrothal was considered adultery. Even though the marriage has not yet been consummated, if a man and woman were betrothed, they were considered to be husband and wife respectively. Thus, the promises made in this engagement represented a much more serious business than our present-day engagement practices. In order to betroth a woman, a man

---

33. Baab, "Marriage."
34. McKenzie and Wallace, "Covenant Themes."
35. Atkinson, *To Have and to Hold*.

had to pay a given sum (*mohar*, or bride-price). Readers interested in such matters may consult the works of Neufeld, Rabinowitz, Philips, or Smolarz, among others.[36] Rather than being a "purchase and sales" agreement, it appears that this bride-price was a sort of guarantee that ensured the comfort and security of the bride.[37]

In some cases, other forms of payment or gifting were administered, as in the case of Jacob working seven years for Rachel (Gen 29:18–20). The *mohar* could be regarded as a seal ratifying a covenantal marriage. The story of David and Michal is significant. The daughter of the king would be given to David in betrothal to be married if he would defeat a giant, bringing his head as a trophy to Saul (1 Sam 17). As the story continues, "When the time came for Merab, Saul's daughter, to be given to David, she was given in marriage to Adriel of Meholah" (1 Sam 18:19). Michal, another daughter, was in love with David, and Saul gave David a second opportunity to become his son-in-law. This time, the bride-price was a hundred Philistine foreskins (1 Sam 18:20–27). To gather this odd payment, he had to kill one hundred men from the enemy camp and circumcise them. In the meantime, Michal was given away to Paltiel, and as a "consolation price," David took both Abigail and Ahinoam as his wives (1 Sam 25:40–44). After a long while, resolving his unfinished transaction, David demanded the right to reclaim his first wife—promised in engagement by Saul, who broke this pledge without any right to do so—and he got her (2 Sam 3:14–15).

The New Testament story of the virgin Mary, betrothed to Joseph, a righteous man, is significant in that it reveals the same arrangement followed from ancient days. Mary and Joseph, defined as being engaged, were called *husban*d and *wife* before they consummated their marriage (Matt 1:16, 18–20, 24; Luke 1:27; 2:5). Consider these statements: "While his mother Mary was pledged to be married to Joseph, but before they came together, she was found to be with child through the Holy Spirit. Because Joseph, her husband to be, was a righteous man, and because he did not want to disgrace her, he intended *to divorce her privately*" (Matt 1:18–19, italics mine). The angel reminded Joseph, *"Do not be afraid to take Mary home as your wife"* (italics mine). Although they were not technically *together*—there had been no wedding feast or sexual union (Matt 1:20, 24–25)—they were married. Their betrothal was considered a serious matter, a covenant, binding the couple. This union could only be broken by either the death of one partner or divorce on the grounds of unchastity, following the laws found in Deuteronomy 22:13–21.

The apocryphal book of Tobit (chapter 8) alludes to marriage contracts in which some details are given succinctly. The father "gave his daughter away" by formally taking her hand and leading her to her husband with the words, "Here she is: take her." Then, the father would bless them both. The husband and his wife would write a formal marriage contract, validating it with seals. A public feast would follow, sometimes

---

36. Neufeld, *Ancient Hebrew Marriage Laws*; Rabinowitz, "Marriage Contracts"; Philips, "The Church of God"; Smolarz, *Covenant*.

37. Emmerson, "Women in Ancient Israel."

for several days. The institution of a "best man" appears as well in Judges 14:11, which narrates Samson's wedding feast. A twist in the story appears as his betrothed wife was given away to his best man, contrary to law and custom (Judg 14:20).

As an additional note, these facts are considered the main reason why more attention has been given in the Bible to the problem of adultery than to the temptation of engaging in premarital sexual promiscuity. As most people were promised, pledged, or contracted for marriage at an early age, there was nothing practiced in the ancient world comparable to our modern (or postmodern) practice of dating. Dating, as we know it, is defined as a progressively intimate relation in which a gradual and mutual exposure to one another's attentive behavioral experiences takes place, on a less-than-committed trial-and-error basis, characterized by a casual and investigative stance, and eliciting passions that cannot be righteously fulfilled. These dating behaviors had no place in ancient or biblical societies. Sexual temptation experienced by most men involved adultery more than premarital sex, as most of the available women were already married or pledged in marriage. Even in Jesus's terms, "You have heard that it was said, 'You shall not commit adultery.' But I tell you that everyone who looks at a woman with lustful intent has already committed adultery with her in his heart" (Matt 5:27–28, ESV).

A union with covenantal ratification. The question of the ratification of a marriage covenant has been the object of controversial discussions as well. An oath was considered to be an intrinsic part of a covenant, and the absence of this data in some narratives led some scholars to question the notion of marriage being an actual covenant.[38] Yet, in arguing for the tacit or implicit presence of an oath, other scholars have alluded to rites more than actual oaths as being ratifications of a covenant.[39] Some have regarded the delivery of a bridal gift or bride-price as the anticipatory seal of the covenant.[40] A common meal (Exod 24), the placing of one's hand under the thigh (as an act of acknowledgement of subordination to a deal, Gen 24:2, 9), and the erection of stones as landmarks of a pledge (Gen 31:45) are examples of such rites. The vows of consent between a husband and wife have also been regarded as the sealing formula.[41]

Processions, ornate wedding clothes, and maidens of honor are mentioned as special features in Psalm 45, a wedding song. It was expected that invited guests would wear appropriate wedding clothes (Matt 22:11–12). According to custom and tradition, the assembly of the families and the wedding feast followed. It was regarded as an occasion to celebrate with gladness and joy (Jer 7:34; 16:9). A wedding meal would bind the families entering into the deal (Gen 29:27; Judg 14:12; Rev 22). Finally, the consummation of the marriage would take place in a nuptial chamber (Gen 29:23).

---

38. Milgrom, *Cult and Conscience.*
39. McCarthy, *Treaty and Covenant,* 91.
40. Burrows, "The Basis for Israelite Marriage."
41. Dunstan, "The Marriage Covenant"; Atkinson, *To Have and to Hold.*

Some scholars have regarded the sexual union to be the key factor in sealing a covenant.[42] Marriage seems to be a covenant because it is a *relationship* between *non-relatives,* which involves *obligations* and is established through an *oath*. Since these three ingredients are clearly present in marriage, it follows that the sexual consummation may represent the binding element—a concrete seal of a social, cognitive, emotive, and spiritual transaction. In the case of a single man who engages in sexual relations with a woman, the law demanded that he should be forced to marry her because of the magnitude of this act (Gen 24:67; 29:21–28; Exod 22:15–16; Deut 21:10–14; 22:28–29; 25:5, among other texts). The sexual act was not casual, frivolous behavior. The term "taking" (as when Isaac took Rebekah) signifies a sexual union in Gen 24:67. Also, "going in to her" (Gen 29:21) has the same connotation (as when Jacob asked Laban for Rachel). It is on the weight of evidence of such passages that the implication of the sexual union being an oath-like sign has been drawn.

Furthermore, the verb "to know" in Hebrew is used for intercourse (Gen 4:1, 17, 25; etc.), as well as for covenantal recognition. God acknowledges the human, as in "before I formed you . . . I knew you" (Jer 1:5). The human is invited to acknowledge (to know) God in covenant as well (Jer 9:5; 31:34). Some texts are intentional in the identification of both covenantal and sexual overtones as an oath sign, such as Hos 2:22: "I will betroth you to me in faithfulness, and you shall know Yahweh." Yet, whether this seal applies to any and all—to committed or one-night-stands, to serious or trivial sexual activities among people in a postmodern world—remains a debatable matter. On the other hand, it points to the seriousness of becoming "one flesh" in a marital covenant because it acts as a corroborating oath of some sort.

The provision of a cover as a marital pledge. Being covered runs as a redemptive, safeguarding, and empowering theme throughout Scripture (Gen 3:21; Exod 21:10; Ruth 3:9; Hos 2:5, 9; Luke 15:22; Rom 13:14; Gal 3:27). Kline discusses the image-investiture and covenantal aspects of the cover God spread over the primordial couple.[43] The features of the passage after the Fall are presented in sequence. The couple runs away from God's presence and will; they hide and manifest anxiety, guilt, and shame. They are depicted as being in need of redemption and restoration. At this juncture, God intervenes by shedding the blood of an innocent animal and covering the couple with its skin. The event of covering the couple's nakedness testifies to God's unilateral, unconditional, and gracious care in forgiving and restoring the couple before his presence.[44] An interesting remark is provided, in which the singular form "skin" is used, so as to embrace the couple with a single covering element. The unity of male-female bonding in covenantal marriage was reaffirmed, restored, and renewed by a gracious God.

---

42. See, for example, Palmer, "Christian Marriage"; Hugenberger, *Marriage as a Covenant*.
43. Kline, *The Structure of Biblical Authority*; *Kingdom Prologue*.
44. Kline, *Kingdom Prologue*, 150–51.

Part I: Premises and Principles

The narrative in Genesis points to nakedness as a deeply conscious realization of personal precariousness and exposure to scrutiny or as the impacting outcome of having sinned by disobeying God's will. Having their eyes opened, both husband and wife experienced guilt (the ontological awareness of being in the wrong and having done wrong) and shame (the conscious realization of being caught with their leaves down, being exposed in their basic faultiness and lack of perfection). In relational terms, nakedness conveys a strong connotation of being exposed as sinners in need of a cover, prone to employ flight reactions, and defensive maneuvers.

The covering or spreading of a garment upon a person in the OT can be seen as a symbolic counterpart of God's redemptive covering. This emblematic propitiation is coupled with a solemn oath, such as the one registered in Ezekiel 16:8. Other passages that pertain to this theme include the redemptive covering of Ruth by Boaz: "Spread the corner of your garment over me, since you are a guardian-redeemer of our family" (Ruth 3:9b). This narrative refers to the redemptive custom of the time and is not intended to extend a forced interpretation as to who covers whom today.

Also, we may surmise that the NT parable that includes the covering of the prodigal upon his return was a restorative act done by a gracious and forgiving father who provided him with a new garment (Luke 15:22). The Ephesians passage (chapter 5), in which we are admonished to be imitators of God as dearly beloved children and to walk in love, is followed by the exemplary love of Christ for his church, which he redeemed with his covering act. This redemptive cover includes men and women gathered as the church under the lordship of Christ.

The apostle Paul used a metaphorical covering ("put on Christ") to convey the effects of the redemptive and empowering work of Jesus Christ on behalf of the believer: "Put on the Lord Jesus Christ, and make no provision for the flesh to arouse its desires" (Rom 13:14). The apostle reminds the Galatians that their identification with Christ covers them before God: "All of you who were baptized into Christ have clothed yourselves with Christ" (Gal 3:27). Protection, care, provision, as well as redemption and empowerment, are meaningful aspects embedded in these covering events.

As it pertains to human relationships, a lot of controversy has surrounded the issue of headship in marriage and the community at large. The terms itself has been subject to diverse interpretations (authority versus source), and the issue of "covering the head" or being covered has received a great deal attention from both the egalitarian and hierarchical interpretations.[45] The covering as examined here represented simply a historical reference to customs derived from the ancient world, as these applied to pledges in marriage, seen as covenantal dimensions of love, redemption, protection, and security.

---

45. See, for example, Sproul, *Knowing Scripture*; Fee, *The First Epistle*; Spencer, *Beyond the Curse*; Grudem, *Biblical Foundations*; Spencer et al., *Marriage at the Crossroads*.

MARRIAGE AS AN ENDURING YET CONTINGENT ORDER OF UNIVERSAL NATURE

In our postmodern world, traditional views of marriage and the family have been challenged, discredited, abandoned, or redefined. Trade books offer a plethora of "how to" approaches and concrete guidelines without much regard for theological basis.

Even among psychologists and researchers in the domain of human relations, a great amount of "psychobabble" seems to characterize secular versions of marriage and family dealings. Strategies and approaches, as well as remedial advice, are often offered without any anchor points or absolutes. The recent rulings in the USA on gay marriage and debates on family-related issues have placed marriage and family at the forefront of the public eye. In anticipatory fashion, Köstenberger and Jones argued for a return to biblical essentials as these apply to marriage and the family.[46] More so than at any point in history, the authors argue that we are now confronted with the need to carefully define the meaning of marriage and family on a theological, ethical, and moral basis.

Universal versus particular premises for relations. In a postmodern world, it has become difficult to postulate metanarratives, absolutes, or universals applicable to human relations. Thus, tribalism, intersubjective hermeneutics, and private "truths" dominate the field of social relations, with pressures to be open and accept diverse transactional models applicable to discrete populations. At mundane and peripheral levels, some cultural customs established by means of socialization may apply without any concerns. A cultural expectation, such as husbands giving wives flowers and chocolates on Valentine's Day, seems to be a given in American culture. Due to globalization and accessibility to cross-cultural information, variants of this custom have experienced an expansive effect, entering into the ethos of many other cultures.

A more debatable aspect involving egalitarian versus complementarian structures for marital relationships represents a bigger challenge to the mindset and the ethos of diverse cultures, including American evangelicals. Traditional versus postmodern trends, hierarchical versus egalitarian stances, and close-minded versus open-minded debates characterize our present ethos. Although some aspects have been reformatted to keep up with the times (the old Jewish matchmaker now has become eHarmony), other aspects are not so contextually adaptable: arranged marriages may be still applicable in some cultures, while in other settings such a practice would be abhorred.

Unique features (idiosyncratic) may be ascertained from particular marital covenants within the confinements of discrete cultures as these pertain to their customs and relational patterns. Also, differential aspects may be gathered by observing the structures and functions that apply to marital covenants within a specific group as compared to another ethnic or cultural population. A major question arises from such observations: Are humans so intrinsically diverse, finding it necessary to adopt unique

---

46. Köstenberger and Jones, *Marriage and the Family.*

or particular ways applicable to their tribes, *ethnes*, or cultures? Or are they able to merge into some universal, unified patterns of interpersonal transactions? Can the principles derived from the New Covenant be considered as universal and optimal for marriage and the family? Particularities applicable to a given population, associated with peripheral and trivial matters, may be cast into differential categories without altering essential aspects of a given universal order derived from Scripture. This work emphasizes the adoption of principles derived from Scripture, universally applicable to a "new creation"—redefined in Christ—and considered the people of God (2 Cor 5:16–17). To such a person/culture, universal virtues—such as respect, dignity, justice, love, care, and empathy, among others—apply across the board.

The author has taught graduate courses and conducted workshops in marital therapy in diverse cultures and can testify to the need for both: particular aspects relevant to Hispanic, Slavic, Israelite (Jews who follow the Messiah and Christian Arabs), or American cultures coupled with the universality of the biblically-derived basis that applies to all believers in the world.

The New Covenant as a universal paradigm for marriage and family transactions. The main thrust presented in this work elaborates upon an abstracted outline rendered by this author, enunciating principles derived from scriptural and psychological data patterned after an encompassing, eschatological design and representing the basis for imitating God's loving manner of relating.[47]

The comparative and evaluative emphasis that points to the New Covenant as being especially "better than" the old one unfolds in terms of its empowered unilateral thrust that may lead to the establishment of better bilateral deals. The unconditional nature of this covenant provides the establishment of better conditions applicable to fair and loving transactions. Also, due to its proactive empowerment, this new way of interacting with one another may foster better responses (versus reactions) on each partner's side. The graceful and merciful aspects of this covenant may enable partners to forgive one another in a better fashion and let go of their mutual offenses. The openness and honesty that exude from being dealt with by God's cleansing Spirit invites them to intimacy and to the renewal of encounters with steadfast love. These features comprise a new and better way of relating, imitating the Father's ways. The New Covenant is rendered as a relational paradigm in which God has acted on behalf of the human in an extraordinary, supracultural fashion, setting the example for Spirit-empowered human transactions.

The top-down, idealistic terms derived from Scripture need to be infused into and balanced with the bottom-up, empirical, and realistic aspects, taking into account human frailty, incapacity, and precariousness in attempts to imitate the Father's ways. Scripture alludes to the New Covenant as being "made in the Spirit," so as to set forth the top-down principle of empowering human efforts to accomplish God's designs,

---

47. Polischuk, "A New Covenant."

will, and purpose which are exemplified in covenantal deals. These terms will be dealt with in detail in the following chapters.

Paul's theological basis for his appeal to the Ephesians in chapter 5 follows some reasonable logic: A basic premise embedded in the command "Be imitators of God as dearly beloved children" is followed by a minor, exemplary premise: "As Christ loved the church and gave himself for her" (Eph 5:1–2). As a conclusion, husbands must love their wives as he did, and wives must respect their husbands as Christ demonstrated his respect for the Father. Parents should treat their children as administrators of God's grace and imitators of his love and discipline. Children should obey their parents as this stance and behavior is commendable in the eyes of the Lord. Bosses and employees should follow along lines of respect, dignity, and mutual stewardship under God's dominion.

Many writers appeal to Paul's statements made in Ephesians 5, but do so by resorting to his conclusions instead, and at times bypassing the major and minor premises. We cannot take conclusions and present them as basic premises without violating some logical sequencing. If we do, we engage in solipsistic, axiomatic, and self-confirming hermeneutics. We "prove" what we intend to prove in *a priori* fashion—a style known in psychology as the "Rosenthal effect," being unconsciously guided by a "self-confirmatory bias" in thinking, reasoning, and judgment.[48]

We need to establish God's top-down propositions of an encompassing nature first in order to then present some particular principles derived from them. Therefore, as a consequence of this top-down ontological basis, and following God's pattern, the right conclusions follow: Husbands love their wives; wives respect their husbands; parents train their children with love and discipline in the Lord; children obey their parents; and the relational aspects between old masters and slaves (modern employers and employees) are all set forth as the *expected ways of being and behaving* on the basis of the premises outlined. They represent the exuding properties of living in the Spirit of the letter based upon God's basic propositions.

Beyond marriage, the paradigm widens as friends and relatives, as well as the members in the body of Christ, are encompassed. Given the contemplation that all human transactions in the here and now finally will end up before God, the Father of all, who is in all, and through all (Eph 4:6; 1 Cor 15:28), it is imperative to have a progressive, future-oriented eschatology in mind. As stewards of God's property—which includes created beings—we shall account to God for our relational administration. We shall render an account of all our relational transactions with one another (2 Cor 5:10). Thus, "imitating God" and "walking in love" propel a believer centrifugally, decentering the self toward others and moving from egotism to social interest. This decentered imitation of Jesus's mindset applies to every believer in particular, and then expands to marriage and the family system. It also radiates out to include

---

48. Rosenthal, *On the Social Psychology*; Mahoney and DeMonbreun, "Confirmatory Bias"; Meichenbaum, *Stress Inoculation Training*.

meaningful friendships and the local community of believers (the house of the Lord). This paradigm expands and extends to the whole household or dominion of God (the cosmos with its human relations—singles, widows, separated or divorced believers, employers, employees, etc.).

INTEGRATING COVENANTAL NOTIONS AND MARRIAGE CONTRACTS

In our culture, marriage is regarded as being both a contract and a covenant. In colonial New England, based upon the Reformed theology brought by the Puritans, covenantal laws applied to marriages.[49] In recent times, the state of Louisiana enacted the first modern covenant marriage law.[50] In actual terms, what sounds like a covenant is in reality a contract between mutually agreeing parties. Arizona followed with similar laws in 1998, and Arkansas in 2001.[51] (These laws postulate a two-tiered system in which couples may choose to enter a contractual marriage characterized by a set of minimal formalities and the possibility of a no-fault divorce.)

On the other hand, a covenant marriage has been defined as being a stringent and permanent deal in which a couple receives some detailed counseling from a religious or professional counselor and swears an oath with binding pledges. Both partners enter the alliance having a full knowledge of the nature and purpose of their pledges before God, as well as the privileges and responsibilities spelled out in their covenantal clauses. Promises and pledges made to each other include mutual honor, love, and care for one another for the rest of their lives. Only serious faults would allow for divorce, such as adultery, capital felony, malicious desertion, and/or the physical or sexual abuse of a spouse or their children.

This book deals with marriage as a covenant, implementing an underlying philosophy aligned with a long tradition held among Protestant, Catholics, and Orthodox believers. The covenantal emphasis of this work is not a legalistic one, but derives from a biblically based paradigm for relations in hopes to actualize God's design within an atmosphere of grace, following God's principled ways as understood by this author.

Integrative scope and efforts. In the field of marital and family studies, several authors and clinicians have contributed to the idea of marital contracting, establishing *quid pro quos* and transactional analysis. Object Relations theory, based upon psychoanalytical grounds, emphasizes the notion that the need for a satisfying relationship with a significant other is the fundamental motive of human existence.[52] Efforts in this

---

49. Morgan, *Puritan Family*; Johnson, "Marriage as Covenant," In *Covenant Marriage in Comparative Perspective*, 124–52; Stackhouse, "Covenantal Marriage," In *Covenant Marriage in Comparative Perspective*, 153–81.

50. Witte and Ellison, *Covenant Marriage*.

51. Spaht, "Covenant Marriage Seven Years Later."

52. Framo, *Family-of-Origin Therapy*; Scharff and Scharff, *Object Relations Family Therapy*.

domain are dedicated to help partners become aware of unresolved issues from the past involving their families of origin, fostering their understanding of these patterns and promoting change. Biblical-theological considerations act as points of inferential connectedness for the formation of a metaphysical and metacognitive core of beliefs and principles from which to derive abstractions with practical applications in mind. In so doing, a conceptual integration is sought with sound psychological theory, especially with those aspects dealing with family systems and couples therapy.

Bowen's System theory and practice have been seminal in prompting several approaches in marital and family therapy.[53] Systemic aspects move beyond immediate symptom reduction, focusing on several processes aimed to increase marital resilience and prevent future symptoms through the facilitation and development of intimacy, problem solving, and mutual satisfaction to be experienced by both partners. Bowen studied dysfunctional cycles of behavioral interchanges between spouses, and between parents and children, stressing the need for proper differentiation and individuation within the mutuality of the system. In his intergenerational approach, Ivan Boszormenyi-Nagy emphasized the ethical dimension in marriage and the family in terms of trust, loyalty, entitlements, and indebtedness toward one another.[54] His systemic approach seeks to preserve a sense of fairness and foster the balance between partners' satisfaction and the fulfillment of their obligations toward each other.

Regulatory aspects merging with systemic thinking appear in the form of structural therapy, focusing on how families are organized and what principles govern their transactions.[55] This view pays attention to the structures encompassing family roles and rules, and the alignments and coalitions that emerge from the system's dynamics. These functions interact and are enacted within the system's boundaries. Marriage is a subsystem embedded in the family's configuration. This therapy aims at the reorganization of rigid or maladaptive structures and processes in order to allow for the establishment of better relations. Systemic theory has provided a great deal of insight into approaches utilized in marriage and family therapy, helping in the understanding and changing of transactional patterns in need of adjustment, renewal, or restoration. Integrative efforts between systemic theory and Christian principles have proved to be of functional value.[56]

Of interest to the investigations in the area of marriage contracts, Don Jackson has provided a paradigm for couples and family deals known as a *quid pro quo* ("this for that") based on fairness, equity, the exchange of privileges and obligations, and the setting of boundaries and proper expectations.[57] Neil Jacobson made significant

---

53. Bowen, *Family Therapy*.
54. Boszormenyi-Nagy and Krasner, *Between Give and Take*.
55. Minuchin, *Families*.
56. Balswick and Balswick, *A Model for Marriage*.
57. Jackson, "Family Rules."

contributions to the field of marital therapy with his behavioral contracting.[58] Richard Stuart has left an integrative legacy, dealing with insight, behavioral exchanges, and emotive tones in contractual arrangements.[59] Don Tweedie coined the term *Covenant therapy*, presenting contracting aspects that integrate psychology and theology, applicable to marriage.[60] His approach, among others, will be considered in the following chapters in the attempt to integrate such efforts with theological principles.

It is possible to have a contract without necessarily establishing a covenant before God, as most unions in a secular society attest. In these cases, the choice to live together is made on a personal basis or as guided by civil-societal expectations. Those entering such contracts appeal to human counterparts as witnesses or enter into their interpersonal arrangements on a purely trial-and-error basis. A covenantal relation, on the other hand, does not exclude the notion of entering into a contractual deal, which may prove necessary due to the human inability to behave with an ongoing, God-like, transcending point of reference. Thus, quite often a *quid pro quo* within a covenantal relationship is necessary and may be seen as a functional preamble to establish new and better deals.

---

58. Jacobson and Margolin, *Marital Therapy*.
59. Stuart, *Helping Couples Change*.
60. Tweedie, "Contract Therapy."

Chapter 6

Quid Pro Quo and Beyond

The New Covenant as an Optimal Model

MARRIAGE IS A COVENANTAL deal, enacted in good faith and established on premises of a fair, equitable, and mutually satisfying nature. Yet, a covenant may be violated or abrogated and become inoperative, due to the unfaithfulness or incapacity of one or both partners to keep their promised terms. A disgraced condition calls for a mediating endeavor that would restore a sense of justice, fairness, and stability on both sides of the deal. This chapter presents an approach to marital counseling derived from the systematic renderings of the theological principles extracted from both the Old and New Covenants.

A *quid pro quo* is a bilateral-conditional contract that may serve as a preamble to the establishment of a new and better covenant. A dialectic process may be engaged between the original covenant (compared to the Old Covenant, established on a bilateral-conditional basis) that has been broken, and a new covenant (compared to the New Covenant, characterized by a climate of forgiveness, grace, and mercy) in order to promote the establishment and actualization of better terms.

CONTEXTUAL CONSIDERATIONS

The Old Covenant—a bilateral-conditional covenant between God and Israel—established a mutually satisfying relationship. It was introduced with celestial lightning and thunder at Sinai. Yet, in time, its glory faded away, and it was experienced as a heavy yoke for Israelites to bear. Likewise, a marriage that usually starts with pomp and ceremony may experience an entropic decay characterized by dysfunction and despair. Restoration and renewal in Israel's case was always predicated upon its repentance and return to the faithful ways delineated in the original covenant.

Before the establishment of any kings in Israel, the book of Judges depicts Israel's cyclical patterns of disobedience, defeat, and degradation, followed by repentance, restoration, and renewal. The establishment of the royal households and the priestly ministry in Israel did not help matters, as we may judge by the failures of the people to obey the covenantal terms. Several prophets denounced the infidelity of Israel (God's "wife") and called the people to repent and obey the terms of the covenant. In the midst of Israel's exile in Babylon—a direct consequence of their disobedience—the prophet Jeremiah announced the coming of a New Covenant. God's unilateral and proactive will provided the hope needed in such a deplorable context. Analogically, a decaying marriage in need of restoration and renewal may be offered the hope of a new deal and summoned to a negotiating table in order to engage and establish a better covenant.

The medium employed by God to deliver the basic terms of the Old Covenant was a concrete object—two tablets of stone—that conveyed a sense of durability and permanence. It could be defined as being a rigid or static deal, yet it conveyed a dynamic and vital sense of connectedness with God, the giver of the covenant. Due to the fact that the tablets would be deposited within the ark in the Holy of Holies, it was necessary to expand its influential and normative power to the whole nation and to re-enact and renew its terms on diverse occasions.

In contrast to the exceeding availability of scriptural data today, the limited accessibility to the tablets posed the necessity of renewing the covenantal terms in public gatherings. As a matter of fact, the covenant was renewed at Shechem (Josh 24:1–28) and then at Gilgal (1 Sam 11:14–12:25). The Torah was rediscovered in the times of Josiah, bringing a revival in Israel's spirituality (2 Chron 34:1—35:19). After a remnant's return from their exile in Babylon, Ezra narrated the rediscovery and renewal of the written covenantal terms. As registered by Nehemiah (8:1–13), people were read these terms with interpreters aiding in the understanding of the expressions and meaning of the Torah.

Throughout Israel's history, the Old Covenant has experienced diverse interpretations ascribed by rabbis and Jewish scholars, who added a wealth of opinions and conjectural meanings to the content of the law. It is safe to say that the trend has continued until our days, and that Jewish people still deal with all the implications of this process. It is with profound respect that believers today—as "children of Abraham," according to the promise of the New Covenant—need to approach these sacred texts and derive principles of the Word as expressed in the covenant of old. At the same time, believers enjoy the benefits that resulted from the actualizing power of the New Covenant.

In Israel's case, a renewal of the covenant was necessary due to the fact that the initial agreement had experienced repeated failures in its binding power, resulting in a relational degradation. It was a good idea to bring the covenantal parties together in order to engage in a new and better transactional deal. Although Jeremiah's promise of a New Covenant was given to the houses of Israel and Judah, these houses have not yet actualized the promised terms in full. By rejecting their Messiah and ignoring his offers, they forfeited their opportunity to enter into the promised new deal. The hope is that one day they will do so. Extrapolating from these theological reflections, we may consider an application of scriptural principles to our present-day relationships: in the case of believers experiencing failures in their original covenants, the restoration and renewal of their promises and pledges becomes an obvious necessity.

ENTROPIC FACTORS AT WORK

Marital transactions may be affected by many variables. Failures in communication, lack of attention to one another's needs, unfaithfulness, manipulation, and abuse are some of the negative factors in any marriage. Based on his longitudinal research with couples, Gottman (2000, 2007) found several factors associated with decay in the integrity and stability of marriages. He calls these the "four horses of the apocalypse": negative pronouncements, contempt, stonewalling, and defensiveness. Researchers from the Mental Research Institute in Palo Alto have pinpointed the presence of ironic patterns at work, employed by partners who, in their attempts to solve their problems, paradoxically foster, reinforce, and maintain these problems repetitively.[1] Family Systems therapists have emphasized the fact that the lack of differentiation and mutuality between partners leads to dysfunctional, negative, or codependent patterns in marriage and family relationships. These patterns effectively erode mutual empathy, love, and attentive care.[2]

To arrest the entropic forces mentioned and provide guidelines for healthy transactions, marriages in need of help may receive practical guidance from pastors, counselors, or therapists acting as mediators of better covenants. These helpers may empower partners engaged in counseling by providing glimpses of hope along the efforts to restore and renew their covenants. Failures in covenantal transactions that have resulted in marital dysfunctional patterns represent a challenge facing every counselor and therapist working with hurt and hardened hearts and minds. Therapeutic endeavors aimed at the restoration and renewal of marriage covenants may begin with the envisioning of the possibility of establishing a *quid pro quo*—defined in this work as a bilateral-conditional contract of a fair and equitable nature—patterned after the Old Covenant.

BILATERAL-CONDITIONAL APPROACHES IN THE FIELD OF MARITAL THERAPY

In the secular field, Don Jackson introduced the concept of a bilateral-conditional paradigm—the already-mentioned *quid pro quo* ("this for that")—carried into therapeutic practice at the Marital Research Institute of Palo Alto.[3] The rules of this deal were based on the notion that marriage is a voluntary relationship, permanent in nature (supposedly a lifetime contract), that unfolds within the context of a life-space marked by exclusive boundaries—no third parties allowed. The bilateral-conditional contract was conceived as a functional paradigm intended to guide a goal-oriented

---

1. Watzlawick et al., *Change*.
2. See, for example, Bowen, *Family Therapy*; Framo, *Family-of-Origin Therapy*; Johnson, *The Practice*.
3. Jackson, "Family Rules."

relationship along many mutual tasks to be carried out on a long-term basis. In order to enact and actualize the terms of a *quid pro quo*, partners were led to establish a process marked by fairness, justice, respect, and dedication to mutual gains.

After Jackson's initial endeavors, interactive deals of a bilateral-conditional nature have been prevalent in the literature dealing with marriage conflicts.[4] Cognitive-behavioral approaches have utilized some form of behavioral exchanges among couples, family members, and even groups.

In the Christian field of marital therapy, Don Tweedie adopted the *quid pro quo* strategy, reframing the concept and casting it in Christian terms as *Covenant therapy*.[5] Personal communication and sustained exchanges with Tweedie (as one of the author's mentors during his graduate years) have influenced the content of this work. The paradigm described in this chapter follows Tweedie's line of reasoning and goes beyond his notions. This author regards the establishment of a *quid pro quo*, not as a final goal to strive for, but as a preamble to the development of better deals. A bilateral-conditional contract is presented as an initial, transitional phase along a process designed to foster a climate embedded in New Covenant terms—grace, mercy, flexibility, and proactive deals of a unilateral-unconditional nature besides the establishment of fairness, justice, and peace. The quid pro quo is regarded as a set-up for preliminary dimensions to be established before the adoption of a new way of imitating God's ways of transacting with one another. Encouraging a dysfunctional couple in despair to engage in the enactment of a better deal—springing from unilateral, unconditional, proactive, and gracious attitudes—is not an easy task to accomplish. Partners who have been hurt, abased, or who have treated one another with contempt tend to be defensive and less prone to receive and follow these suggestions. Yet, the possibility exists among those who, having a glimpse of what God's presence and power can do if given a chance, may be open to establishing a preliminary preamble to a better covenant.

THE *QUID PRO QUO* AS A PREAMBLE TO A NEW COVENANT

The initial stage of the proposed approach focuses upon the need to solve interpersonal difficulties at preparatory phases. The establishment of some general guidelines is essential to that end. Schematically, the process is similar to the avenues employed by Jackson, Tweedie, Haley, Stuart, and Boszormenyi-Nagy and Krasner, among others.[6] The author emphasizes some specific refinements that run along covenantal prin-

---

4. See Azrin et al., "Reciprocity Counseling"; Stuart, *Helping Couples Change*; Gottman et al., "Behavior Exchange Theory"; Jacobson and Margolin, *Marital Therapy*; Madanes, *Strategic Family Therapy*; Boszormenyi-Nagy and Krasner, *Between Give and Take*, among others.

5. Tweedie, "Contract Therapy."

6. Jackson, "Family Rules"; Tweedie, "Contract Therapy"; Haley, *Problem-Solving Therapy*; Stuart,

ciples, elaborated below. In order to establish a quid pro quo, the following variables need to be taken into account.

1. *Level of entry*

If we draw analogies from Scripture, it is fair to assume that the Israelites who had been subject to a long period of oppression, subjugation, and degradation (a very disgraceful set of contingencies) were not ready for a new covenant yet. It would stretch their capacities to behave as God's ultimate design called for; rather, they needed a deal that would provide boundaries and norms for living as pilgrims entering into a new, promised land. Also, the covenant would serve as a *pedagogos*—a tutor that would teach them the ways of God—after they settled in that land. During his ministry among his people, Jesus reminded his disciples about the promise of the Father—the New Covenant—pointing toward its fulfillment after his redemptive work was accomplished.

Conflicting parties experiencing the negative effects of broken covenants, having invalidated their original deals, need to establish some basis for better operations—a strategic preamble—that will prepare them to envision an engagement to be enacted along better transactions. At this level of entry, a mediator may prove to be useful in establishing some bilateral-conditional guidelines for the couple. He or she needs to demonstrate a trustworthy, caring, and empathic relationship with the couple in order to act as a mediator between them. Then, he or she may guide the couple along some principles:

- Enabling and encouraging the couple to investigate and ascertain what is their main complaint—the chief problem affecting their being and relating. Both partners may be encouraged to render their versions of experienced reality—the problem(s) as they see, feel, and think about it (them);

- Sometimes, a problem looms too large to be approached at first sight. In this case, the mediator helps the partners to break down the chief complaint into its components; then, they define and establish one problem at a time in order to focus upon it in a more precise manner;

- The mediator adopts a metacognitive-dialogical stance (that is, a detached, yet mindful and purposive stance as a participant-observer in the process). Without missing a bit of either the content (*what is* the problem being described) or the process (*who says what to whom, how, and with what effect*, including his/her own countertransference in the process), the mediator engages in dialogue with both partners. Assuming that the Holy Spirit is present in the session, the engagement may be regarded as being not just dialogical, but "trialogical";

Helping Couples Change; Boszormenyi-Nagy and Krasner, *Between Give and Take*.

Part I: Premises and Principles

- From an observing-participatory vantage point, the mediator may analyze and ascertain the couple's difficulties and engage the transactional patterns employed by the couple—verbal and nonverbal, especially their communication patterns. Besides reflective listening and feedback, the mediator may help along the communications process and recast any faulty patterns into more appropriate ones. The mediator may ascertain whether the couple's covenant is in need of remediation, reframing, rebuilding, or renewal;

- Throughout the process, the mediator fosters an open, honest, and clear understanding of the expressions of each partner rather than allowing for dysfunctional aspects to dominate the session—such as mind-reading activities, projections, blaming, excusing, and the like;

- Following the vast amount of empirical research findings related to the need to engage in more positive versus negative expressions among couples, the mediator seeks to foster the couple's insightful awareness into their expressive patterns. The mediator seeks to empower the couple's mindfulness—their metacognitive perception—so that they become more objective about their intersubjective transactions;

- In sum, partners may be empowered to seek to remediate their negative interactions—contemptuous, judgmental, abusive, and the like—and change these into positive transactions. This process may foster the establishment of a climate of acceptance, good faith, and tolerance toward one another and open a way for the procedures that follow.

2. *Defining accurately the issues and the problems*

In many instances, a proper definition of a recurrent problem represents the beginning of a good negotiation. It is important to establish grounds for transactions to be engaged in good faith, giving the benefit of the doubt and seeking the benefit of both partners entering the deal. Well-defined initial complaints may be expressed in harsh, hurtful, or unrefined terms. It is the task of the mediator to help both partners refine their expressions. From negative complaints and demands of a judgmental or opinionated nature, partners may be coached and learn to address one another in a more reflective, objective fashion. The emotional toning down of expressive interactions may receive a great deal of help from mediators who, without censoring their expressions, may funnel the communication process into a more graceful and amicable transaction. After a proper interactive atmosphere is established, further guidelines follow:

- The mediator encourages the partners to state their complaints, excesses, and deficits in assertive, yet loving and positive ways, rephrasing if necessary in order to provide a model for the partners to follow—"speaking the truth in love" (Eph 4:15).

- A basic condition, applicable to the session, is stated and agreed upon by the mediator and the couple in the triad: *own your own thoughts, feelings, and behaviors. Do not project, blame, defend, or rationalize. Be fair and intentional in establishing good terms of mutual concern;*

- The mediator coaches the couple to be specific and concrete; that is, both partners agree to render any abstract or general statement in concrete terms. Problems may be cast in terms of their *frequency* (how often they happen); their *intensity* (how much, how big, how profound, how impacting, at what level, etc.); their *duration* (how long they have been there); their *antecedents* (what happens before the problems occur); and their *consequences* (what happens after the problem emerges). These five variables may encompass all behaviors, attitudes, and transactions that are brought up and described by the couple. These concrete expressions facilitate the perception and definition of the issues to be dealt with;

- The mediator will not allow long storytelling, litanies of complaints, or endless charges to be delivered against each other. Rather, the mediator will provide helpful coaching to keep the expressions of partners brief, concise, and understandable. These succinct expressions tend to foster dialogue and help in the translation of complaints and requests, without engaging in detached yet accusatory storytelling or the monopolizing of the encounter by one partner;

- At this juncture, it is necessary for the mediator to foster a mutual responsibility to communicate truth in love, encouraging partners to stick to the issues and to avoid detours and unconscious or purposive sabotaging of the process through stonewalling and the use of defensive maneuvers.

3. *Setting appropriate targets and goals*

In career guidance circles, the statement applies, "If you don't know where you are going, you will not get there." In couples therapy or any mediating counseling, it becomes necessary to state specific goals that encompass the needs and desirable outcomes as expressed by both partners. The same applies in family systems and group dynamics.

- The goals of a marital system may be set to accomplish tasks and to maintain the system as a vital one. Thus, not only is the accomplishment of tasks deemed necessary, but the maintenance of the system as well—in terms of cohesiveness, stability, morale, empathy, attentive care, and intimacy, etc.;

- Some goals may be absolute ("we both will be faithful to one another," or "we shall be and will remain Christian believers"), while other goals may be directional ("we shall date once a week," or "we shall communicate with empathy and in positive terms");

- The accomplishment of these task-oriented goals and the maintenance aspects of the system may be measured over a baseline of actual behaviors, attitudes, or patterns. This baseline may be established by concrete measures of frequency, intensity, and duration of stated behavioral goals. Changes in antecedents and consequences may be registered as well. These baselines may serve as anchors or levels of comparative measure along the way.

4. *Establishing the terms of a quid pro quo*

- The mediator encourages the expression of the thoughts and feelings of each partner, while reminding them that they are the owners of this feelings—addressing concerns on a first-person basis and rendering their requests and demands appropriately without projecting, displacing, accusing, or degrading one another;
- Furthermore, the mediator reminds the couple to keep discussions "solution focused," rather than employing the session to proliferate further accusations, snowballing, or catastrophizing their predicament;
- The next, crucial issue at this phase is to foster a compromise, bargaining with requests and demands already expressed, chunked, or encapsulated into, at the most, three clauses. Give-and-take procedures follow, with partners being encouraged to be flexible as they bargain in order to give room while taking and establishing some ground as well;
- The fostering of mutuality is essential: the couple may be encouraged to think in terms of fairness, equality, and justice. After all, the second commandment reminds the couple to love their neighbor as they love themselves. In the attempt to establish a *quid pro quo,* the dictum for the hour could be, "No losers, but both winners." The mediator may remind the couple of the fact that, if one of them feels like a loser in the transaction, this feeling will permeate their interactions until they both feel like losers. In the end, it is not fun to live with a loser or to be a loser in marriage: only a win-win solution is desirable;
- The exchange of demands and requests may be framed in bilateral, conditional clauses: "If you . . . then I . . ." or "I will do this for you, and will expect . . . from you." Partners choose from among their complaints, requests, or demands and focus on a couple of workable petitions, expressed as requests. These terms may necessitate some mutual refinement, redefinition, and accommodation on both sides to establish equilibrium between the requests and/or the demands made of each other. The mediator's role is one of gentle yet assertive coparticipation with the couple in order to ensure the establishment of more functional transactions;

- At this juncture, the exchange may be coached and empowered by the mediator to follow a more gracious, positive line: "*What would make your day?*" "*What would you do for your partner that will indicate your willingness, ability, and choice to satisfy their needs?*" This prompting may change the tone of a *quid pro quo*: "*Choose those behaviors and attitudes—translated into requests or privileges—that would please you and fulfill your needs, desires, hopes, or plans. State these in a reflective manner in order to be heard by your partner. Then she/he will have the wonderful opportunity to grant them as privileges to you*";

- The mediator coaches partners to decenter and focus on the other: "*Allow your partner to choose one, two, or three behaviors/issues that would please him/her. At the same time, say to yourself, 'What does he/she want that I can offer as a privilege?'*" Then, coach partners to translate the other's requests/demands into possible privileges that they may offer to the other in an equitable, fair, and mutual way. In sum, the mediator fosters a golden rule to be activated: do unto to your partner as you would have them do unto you;

- Provided that the partners are willing, able, and decisive about engaging in fulfilling the terms of a bilateral-conditional contract, they may be encouraged to do so on a discrete, temporal basis. Making tentative, specific agreements with a time-limited framework has proven to be a successful approach in cognitive-behavioral marital therapy. A weeklong tentative deal, for example, is feasible, functional, fair, and empirically measurable;

- The mediator may encourage communications such as the following: "Each of you ask the other for feedback on how pleasing each of these items would be if they were done. Each of you explain how difficult it would be to carry out the items you have listed in the responsibilities statement of your contract. Each of you rank the degree of desirability of your privileges, and the difficulty of fulfilling the requests and/or demands made of her/him. Each of you negotiate and specify the terms of how, how much, when, where, with whom, etc., applicable to each responsibility and corresponding privilege stipulated in your contract. Remember that compromise is essential and that bargaining represents an attempt to be empathic, fair, open, and flexible";

- Through this mediation, the fair exchange of mutual requests and privileges—accommodating and establishing equity among partners—fosters the feasibility of a positive *quid pro quo* between those in partnership.

- The establishment of a tentative contract is to be understood by both to be a guideline for their actions with concrete homework assignments that emerge from their mutual requests and expected privileges. The mediator may help along the establishment of these homework assignments in each case—understood by both, concretely stated, and providing guidelines for action;

- Further eliciting of conscious awareness, metacognitive stances, and mindfulness may be encouraged: "Once you have made the contract, ask yourselves: 'Am I ready to do this? Am I willing to do this? Is this in my agenda for today/for this week? Is this good for me? Does it represent love and respect for my partner? Can I commit myself to the fulfillment of my promises?'" The mediator encourages partners to keep working until they are sure that they will be committed to the terms for one week in order to restate, renegotiate, or refine the contract in stepwise fashion.

5. *Coaching along the way*

As in the case of God's dealings with his children, we need to be there for one another along any covenantal journey. In God's case, we count on his omnipresence, immanence, and constant care. We do not have a deistic philosophy in mind in which God acted as the initiator of a covenant, propelling the deal and then absenting himself from his created order. It is our understanding that God never left to chance a design that he planned before the foundation of the world. From Genesis to Revelation, God is there to back up his terms. His covenants—seen as continuously ongoing, unified, yet discrete in nature—were enacted with purposes in mind, being actualized under his jurisdiction, presence, and power. As human mediators, we do not have this capacity, nor do we possess these characteristics and powers. Yet, human mediators need to mindfully attend to the bilateral-conditional covenants made by partners seeking their help to ensure their successful enactment. An ongoing participation and guidance along the covenanting or contracting endeavors are needed.

- Mediators should not leave things to chance. Feedback is essential to ensure that the terms of the contract will be followed, safeguarded, and fulfilled. Thus, checking in and then providing feedback as to how things went, as well as paying attention to the contractual process—who did what to whom, with what effect, etc.—are items in the agenda of the ongoing sessions with the couple;

- Correcting the terms, aligning the attitudes and behaviors, and expressing the feelings associated with the process are essential components of the feedback loops engaged in the sessions with the couple. Toning-down or augmenting the requests also contributes to this corrective, aligning feedback, with assiduous encouragement to keep up with the program;

- Once the couple has learned to transact in an open, fair, bilateral-conditional fashion by means of a mediator, they are encouraged to transact with one another on their own. That is, they are to establish mini-contracts on a weekly basis, in which they enact their terms, concretize their expectations, postulate their consequences and privileges, and see how they grow and succeed along these mutually arranged *quid pro quos;*

- Even as they are successfully managing such deals, it is functional for the couple to check in with the mediator on a stipulated, temporal basis to ascertain and reinforce their positive dealings;

- After learning, practicing, and experiencing the benefits of new patterns and better transactions, the consolidation of gains along the projected goals should be evident and a time of "overlearning" (nailing the nails over and over until they are flat, leveled with the board) may prove useful. As the partners act on intuition (defined as an abstracted, tacit, personal knowledge chunked from a vast array of experiential knowledge carried into ongoing practice), this consolidated, tacit, personal knowledge allows for better grounds to be established, fostering better deals.

6. *Opening up the possibilities to go beyond a quid pro quo*

The Old Covenant lasted 1500 years until the promised seed of Abraham came to fulfill and actualize its terms in full (Gal 3:19), becoming the mediator of a new, better covenant (Heb 9:15). Thus, the old deal was an essential, vital paradigm acting as a forerunner of better things to come. As a *pedagogos*, the old led to the new. Perhaps, in a similar fashion, a humanly established *quid pro quo* may imitate the old, yet functional ways of doing things until the couple is ready to proceed beyond legalistic terms and engage in better, more gracious terms. A dialectic tension between legal demands and gracious privileges is necessary to start with as an entry level for those who, embedded in their dysfunctions, dilemmas, struggles, and frustrations, come for help.

Honeymooners seldom come to therapy—although some do, as seen in cases where a partner discovers in a hurry that the person they married, now emerging from the false facade of their projected persona, is not the real deal. Those who come for help somehow have failed to keep the promises made to each other in time. Their original marriage covenant somehow has been broken, invalidated by one or both partners, and they experience the entrapment of demands and expectations (*you ought . . . you should . . . you better do . . . you better not try that*—and the like). Before grace may abound and mercy flow, dysfunctional couples need to establish a *quid pro quo* to set some safe, fair, functional, and preliminary terms. Then, with better attitudes, stances, and feelings, the couple may be ready for a new deal.

- After several weeks (in some cases, months), the *quid pro quo* may prove to be legalistic, routine-oriented, or fallible. Partners may experience entropic tendencies due to their past negative history or dealings, or they may shrink from their zestful ways due to anxieties about the future. The encouragement to renew their minds, to refresh their terms, or to reframe their deals should be provided by the mediator. Even with that, a legalistic sense may develop;

- A dialectical process allows for the development of insights into what is possible through structured fairness and a graceful, merciful deal with a unilateral, proactive, and empowering spirit. The tension generated by legal aspects versus graceful ones presents questions, which may be properly addressed by the mediating counselor;

- A climate of renewal is fostered: Hearts and minds are taken into consideration, and efforts are dedicated to the restructuring of thoughts, attitudes, feelings, and motivations held by the partners. A dictum employed by Dr. Tweedie (one of my mentors) in his brand of contract/covenant therapy (and adopted by the author on numerous occasions) has been the following: *"Wells run dry; sewers never stop. Whenever you tap into a sewer system, it stinks. We are here to dig up new wells with cleaner water."* Thus, it is important to encourage the renewal of minds and behavioral efforts to establish better deals in approximation to higher goals held by the couple;

- Fostering a climate of grace is a process that stresses the giving of privileges to the other whether they are merited or not. This is the nature of grace, which points to the delivery of benefits, blessings, and positive reinforcement to the undeserving ones. To this grace, *mercy* is coupled, representing the notion of not paying the other with retribution or applying a deserved penalty for a perceived wrongdoing;

- Thus, the approach draws from a dialectical process in which there is an interplay between the actual fulfillment of a preliminary law (established as a *quid pro quo* between the partners in dispute) and the climate of grace which ultimately allows for the establishment of the basis for a new deal;

- Growth in insight and awareness of what is needed to transact in a better fashion necessarily appeals to a higher order, to the empowering from God's presence and power, and to the establishment of a paradigm after the New Covenant.

7. *Beyond a quid pro quo: Fostering a new and better covenant*

Ascertaining the level of readiness of the couple is essential. Motivational interviewing may help with this assessment: Are they willing to go beyond a *quid pro quo*? Are they ready to engage in a more demanding process? Is that registered in both of their agendas for here and now? Do they see the necessity, the goodness, of establishing a better deal? If the answer to these questions is in the affirmative, then a better deal may be established without the dangers of fostering codependency, manipulation, naïve idealism, or super-spiritualism. The following possibilities comprise the terms of a New Covenant and will be expounded in subsequent chapters.

Fostering a unilateral initiative leading to better bilateral deals. Partners entangled in bad contracts, who feel that they have been mistreated and taxed beyond their strength, will not appreciate the request to extend grace and mercy and forgive the offenses committed against them. In their minds, to do so represents an exercise in masochism, victimization, or a display of nonsensical weakness. As it is, they may express themselves as being stretched beyond their capacity to be elastic and flexible any longer. They are ready to snap, not to bend even more. The task of a mediator is thus a difficult one, given the expectations of fairness, justice, and retaliation for perceived wrongdoing. Yet, the establishment of a climate of grace is not just recommended, but functional, desirable, and essential if any new covenants are to be established at all.

The notion of *unilateral dealings* has been proposed by Torrance as the basic ingredient of a covenant of grace in contrast to bilateral contracts, which are enacted in more legalistic terms.[7] This corrective notion may be perceived as a healthy one as most therapists (and some theologians) have interpreted the meaning of marriage covenants exclusively from an initial, bilateral consideration. The perspective of this work regards the New Covenant as fostering a unilateral and proactive initiative, which may lead to the enactment of new and better bilateral deals. This possibility emerges from an unconditional stance, provoking the establishment and acceptance of mutually acceptable conditions.

The New Covenant serves as a way to invite each partner to unilaterally, unconditionally, and proactively engage in relational matters as an imitator of the Father's ways. Those who engage in a unilateral way may do so in view of promoting the experience of a better bilateral deal. As the apostle Paul reminds us, we may engage this capacity, which emerges from the thrust provided by the love poured into our hearts by the Holy Spirit (Rom 5:5). It is on this basis that a believer is capacitated to take the initiative, to be proactive, and to engage in unilateral deals without necessarily waiting upon the other to show up or make a move. This proactive initiator is not bound to situational contingencies or reactive to them, but is free to be a loving person and to act in love. The way to act lovingly toward, to empower, to forgive, and to let go of the offense committed by the other are all dimensions encompassed in the New Covenant as a paradigm for relations. Chapter 9 deals with this subject matter in more detail.

T*he capacity to be unconditional* is fostered as well. Maturity allowing, efforts are dedicated to empower the partners to give with grace from an energized posture, not as subject to the other's control. The avoidance of traps represented by challenging formulae such as, "If you . . . then I" is desirable. The reinforcement of unconditional notions is sought, which may open up avenues for the partners to be gracious, proactive, and motivated to act in freedom.

Assertiveness has a place in speaking the truth in love. Direct talk is needed if the misunderstanding of motives or actions proves to be disruptive and dysfunctional. Dialectically speaking, a counselor should not rule out the possibility of setting conditions if things deteriorate into negative deals—as when the partners forget that they are attempting to transact in a new fashion and resort back to their quid-pro-quo mentality. Thus, if the partners are not mature enough or insightful about the terms of a new covenant, they may resort to the fair, egalitarian, and reciprocal deals that

---

7. Torrance, "Creativity Research in Education."

safeguard their intentions to be mutual—both winners and both willing to keep trying to establish better deals.

Proactive versus reactive stances and movement along dedicated behaviors are encouraged, guided by the goal of establishing an expected growth in grace, fostering a positive ambiance, and a mutual engagement endowed with faith and hope. The dispensing of mercy to grace and the careful consideration of the issue of forgiveness among hurting people are challenging processes to be enacted, especially if partners tend to be reactive toward one another's attitudes and behaviors. These processes are taken into consideration in the chapters that follow. Schematically, we may postulate forgiveness as an event which is funneled into an ongoing process, counting the cost of trespasses against each other, the hurts and pains, the broken promises resulting in dejection, disillusionment, and despair. All these issues are taken into account in a sober, insightful, and empowered climate of tolerance of ambiguity in view of better resolutions, forgiving, and forgetting so as to set new deals based on a qualified existential, yet constructive paradigm. Besides forgiveness of wrongdoing, restitution, fairness, and justice—coupled with grace and mercy—are stressed again. Chapter 10 deals with this subject matter in more detail.

The fostering of intimacy becomes a challenge in situations where much ground has been eroded by hurts, pain, dejection, and manipulation. Working with defensiveness, lack of trust, guardedness, and retaliation proves to be a difficult task for any mediator. Yet, intimacy cannot grow in an atmosphere characterized by these stances, attitudes, and feelings. Thus, concurrent with the efforts to establish grace, the avenues to follow include unilateral dealings; unconditional stances; forgiveness and forgetfulness; the fostering of openness, trust, and vulnerability; clear and honest communication; and understanding of each other with empathy. Chapter 13 deals with this subject matter in more detail.

Empowering one another results only when struggles for control, manipulation, and supremacy give way to mutual respect, the fostering of growth on both sides, and the opening up of avenues to become the persons God has intended to enter into a covenant before His presence and sanctioning power. Empowering could be described, taught, and conveyed as the capacity to actualize potentials given by God: to feel appreciated, accepted, and validated by one another. This is the subject matter addressed in chapter 8.

Beyond retaliation. The capacity to act with grace is a feature of an empowered attitude and decision to act as an imitator of God. The principles enunciated in previous pages are the basis for concrete operations during interventions. Thus, counselors and therapists seeking to help people along covenantal paradigms applicable to interpersonal transactions need to be versed in such principles in order to set up a climate of grace, regarded as a basic and appropriate premise for their helping occasions. The Holy Spirit may empower partners to let go, to abandon retaliation, and to experience freedom from anger, revenge, and bitterness. Not letting go of one's negative metanarratives (seen as deeply embedded schemata of intrapsychic weights or as active dimensions that feed feelings of victimization, rumination, and morbid rehearsal of traumatic events) results in self-abasement and intropunitiveness. These factors are seen as being impediments to the efforts of a victimized person to engage in a process of forgiveness. These are sensitive aspects to be dealt with in any mediating effort, not easily apprehended by those who feel victimized and desire some vengeful satisfaction based on the old dictum: "An eye for an eye, a tooth for a tooth."

Empowering the dispensing of grace and mercy. Besides being holy and mighty, God is also revealed as gracious and merciful, as exemplified in covenantal relationships. In dealing with humans, God's unmerited favors and encompassing forgiveness are basic themes that permeate his covenantal transactions. God's loyalty to the created order and his manifestations of concern and care extend beyond the ability of humans to stay within God's established boundaries. Grace may be defined as unmerited favor dispensed toward the undeserving ones. God has acted on behalf of humans in a proactive, unilateral, unconditional, and graceful manner—all that "while we were yet sinners" (Rom 5:8).

Being gracious reveals the level of maturity present in a person. The fruit of the Spirit (defined in concrete manifestations of love, joy, peace, goodness, patience, faith, meekness, and self-control, according to Galatians 5:22–23) acts as an indicator of the quality of being, the ontological, sub-structural character of openness, the person, translated into processes of cognitive, affective, and behavioral nature. In concrete terms, being gracious necessitates these attributes of the Spirit coparticipating with the human character to render it capable of transacting with flexibility and a nonjudgmental disposition. At the same time, this character formation allows for the speaking of truth in love in order to avoid misconceptions and misperceptions that might arise from the display of grace on the part of the unilateral-unconditional person.

Hopefully, both parties in the covenant experience a mutual growth and emerge at similar levels of spiritual sophistication, emotional growth, and behavioral willingness to be fair, egalitarian, and empowering of each other. Thus, the covenant in time becomes bilateral-unconditional as Balswick and Balswick have pointed out.[8] In counseling couples, encouraging the exercise of practical love requires considerations beyond retaliation, aiming at the capacity to act with grace and forgiveness. Chapter 12 deals with grace and mercy as expressions of love.

Forgiveness within covenants. Most of the time, transactions registered in counseling deal with events and processes of a hurtful nature that necessitate forgiveness between partners. This forgiveness is conceptualized at times as either a series of events or as a process. In terms of the New Covenant, the Father promises to forgive and forget the sins committed by powerless humans based upon his provision: having placed all the sins of the world upon the propitiatory offering of the Son, and regarding Jesus as the perfect substitute for sin, God has accepted the sacrifice at the cross as

---

8. Balswick and Balswick, *A Model for Marriage*.

full payment for the redemption of those who place their faith in the person and the work of Jesus. God's forgiveness is perfect, encompassing, efficient, and sufficient for any transgressor who repents, has faith, and obeys. By extending this forgiveness, God acted unilaterally and proactively. It is this paradigm that St. Paul appeals to when he admonishes disciples to "forgive one another as God forgave you in Christ" (Eph 4:32; Col 3:13).

The parable of two debtors also stands as a powerful reminder: a creditor forgave a debtor an enormous amount of money. He in turn, upon being forgiven, bumped into one of his debtors. This debtor was unable to fulfill his small obligation to the previously forgiven creditor. The creditor forcefully demanded payment of the small debt contracted by his debtor, and when he failed to received it, acted very harshly. Hearing the news, the bigger creditor confronted him, and then acted in a manner that conveyed a retributive justice without mercy. This measure was taken in light of the inability or unwillingness of the creditor to learn from the lesson of grace dispensed toward his precarious person (see Luke 7:36–50).

Jesus made it clear: whatever debts are contracted among humans pale in comparison with the debts humans have contracted with God by being sinful and acting upon it. Thus, the perceived injustices among humans are flat versions compared to the vertical dimension of indebtedness before God. Humans tend to minimize sinfulness toward God through rationalizations, intellectualizations, and excuses; a failure to comprehend the effects of depravity allows for humanistic doctrines and a propensity to aggrandize human goodness and benevolence. Thus, to appreciate the grace dispensed toward us (in being forgiven by God), a strong statement in the Lord's Prayer reminds us of our reciprocal necessity to imitate his ways: "And forgive us our debts *as we forgive our debtors*" (Matt 6:9–13; Luke 11:2–4, italics mine).

The terms of a New Covenant as a paradigm for human transactions stress the importance of forgiveness of offenses. It is fair to state that, as preliminary considerations are taken into account in the assessment of marital dysfunction, no shortcuts are taken to sabotage the working through of disagreements, hurts, and trespasses against one other. As Augsburger pointed out, people have to develop insights so as to care enough to forgive, and care enough not to forgive as well.[9] It sounds paradoxical, but a proper emphasis needs to be placed upon knowing what a person needs to forgive, rather than naïvely dispensing forgiveness as a blanket that covers the unknown. This knowing is predicated upon the full realization of the wrongs committed, the extent of the damage done, and the consequences of the contracted debts in terms of hurt, pain, disappointment, disillusionment, and the like. Thus, if a conscious realization takes place, the person willing to forgive does not act in naïve or ameliorative ways, but counts the cost of letting go. The person engages in costly grace. Chapters 14 and 15 deal with these matters in more detail.

---

9. Augsburger, *Caring Enough*.

DEALING WITH DIFFICULT CASES

Often the counseling encounters that take place in Christian settings, involving well-intentioned but less-than-wise efforts advocating forgiveness, have regarded such as an event of an existential and sporadic nature. The expectation underlying this act usually fosters the emergent pardoning and the erasing of all offenses on the spot, hoping that even the vestigial signs of any wrongdoing would disappear in a condensed moment without any process-like work. In a way, that is how God does it. Humans, on the other hand, need to be empowered by the Holy Spirit with a unilateral, unconditional, proactive love endowed with grace and mercy in order to be willing and able to imitate God at that level. Otherwise, humans undergoing and processing their victimization, abuse, neglect, or degrading circumstances may be subject to further damage by being pushed to forgive with negative consequences. Many cases may be cited in which the offenses that have been committed against a partner needed a thorough processing before forgiveness took place.

Cases involving physical or sexual abuse, unfaithfulness, negligence, and emotional abasement deserve full attentive treatment. Imagine a woman battered by a partner for many years or sexually abused by a relative (who has developed numerous symptoms that denote a severe psychopathology) being confronted with the admonition to forgive. Imagine a faithful wife who has been hurt by many affairs committed by her husband being told to stick around and remain submissive, to suffer vicariously and as an expiator, and to be patient until God does something with her husband. A husband who suffers from his partner's treatment to the point of being clinically depressed may be advised to suffer for God's sake. And so on.

In many cases, this abuse impinges upon the marriage relationship, affecting the levels of trust, intimacy, and openness to engage in transactions of a jovial or enjoyable nature. The author has dealt with cases in psychotherapy in which such persons were counseled to endure suffering and were obliged to forgive a perpetrator of abuse or domestic violence "then and there" in the pastoral session. Forgiveness was treated as an event, applicable to the forgiver, who had to let go of the offenses and had no further claims against the perpetrator. Often, victimized people are counseled to repress any negative, residual connotations that might follow after such a "forgiving" event. It is fair to say that these individuals were abused again, this time by a well-intended but naïve counselor. A lot of restorative work needs to be done before any *quid pro quo* may be suggested or established in such difficult cases.

Forgiveness is a process that necessitates attention and coaching and will be dealt with further in chapter 14. God counted the price of forgiveness; as Bonhoeffer put it, it is costly, not cheap grace that saves us.[10] So it is with a human forgiving another: she or he must count the cost of letting go of offenses as God did. Any human involved in a process of forgiveness will experience emotional, cognitive, and physiological drain-

---

10. Bonhoeffer, *The Cost of Discipleship*.

age; depression; anxiety; and post-traumatic stress, etc. Before couples work may be done, the counseling process must allow the victims of domestic violence to engage in individual therapy in order to be able to restore their image and integrity, as well as their capacity to exercise trust and intimacy. In most cases, the abusers are coached to participate for some time in an anger control group with accountability to allow for the reestablishment of trust. Both victims and perpetrators of abuse deserve an empathic attention and understanding, a listening ear without judgmental connotations, and a safe context. The hurting ones need to be provided with an empowering presence in order to grow in grace and mercy and develop enough stamina to bear anxiety, depression, and other emotions associated with their negative contingencies.

Yet, such cases are not doomed to perpetual victimization if the persons are encouraged to grow into a position of personal strength and dispense grace, being empowered and energized to enact the terms of forgiveness after the patterns of God in the New Covenant. This forgiveness is an outgrowth of being empowered and freed to act as imitators of God. In these cases, the unilateral, proactive, and empowered capacity transcends human nature that is characterized by vindictiveness, retaliation, and anger. Letting go without any strings attached is only a possibility when the person is nurtured into the imitative aspects of following God's ways of doing things. In dispensing grace and mercy, the metacognitive, insightful person is not disempowered in the process. This stance allows no room for the development of a sense of divine unfairness. The conviction and confidence placed upon the perfect justice of God becomes a resting platform for inner peace only if the person is able to locate him/herself in an eschatological paradigm in which God sees perfectly all aspects of negative contingencies and has the final word and judgment.

The possibility of "setting oneself free" exists, in that by enacting forgiveness and dispensing grace liberally as a function of a conscious realization of being empowered by God to imitate such stances and behaviors, the bars are removed from one's jail, so to speak. Che Guevara used to encourage Cuban peasants with a slogan: "You have nothing to lose, except your chains." The dictum has elements of truth that may apply in the case of those whose anger, bitterness, retaliatory feelings, and quest for revenge hold them captive to their own negative emotions. These feelings vanish only when those who feel oppressed coparticipate with a liberating Spirit, letting go of human offenses in the presence of God, the greatest creditor who forgave all human debts and offenses in Christ.

The realization grows along definitions of being "named after God," rather than being defined by negative circumstances or trapped by somebody else's past or present obnoxiousness, wrongdoings, abuses, or neglectful behaviors. This is a crucial set of principles, not easily understood by hurting persons or by abused victims. The treatment of such conditions necessitates tuning in to the feelings, predicaments, and emotional struggles of these individuals. The promise of freedom is to be taken as a "being-in-becoming" without necessarily leaning toward a realized eschatology (things are done, fulfilled, in such a manner that there is no need of treatment, elaboration, or even mention of negative past experiences) or toward a futuristic eschatology (someday God will make things all right; in the meantime, let us teach people to praise God when they are sexually molested, physically abused, etc.).

Although possibilities do exist to praise God in everything, and actual accounts of suffering people who praise God in spite of all imaginable adversities can be gathered, an accountable therapeutic endeavor needs to adopt a stance in which an "eschatology in the process of realization" guides the pathways. This eschatology considers that the person is empowered and set free to behave in grace, mercy, and forgiveness, yet is not able to do so perfectly in the here and now without struggles. In due time, the person will be able to do so by the grace of God so that encouragement along such lines is both necessary and desirable.

Again, in terms of a New Covenant paradigm, hurting parties may resort to expressions of hurt, pain, frustration, anger, and the natural tendency to cry for retaliation and revenge before God and before mediators acting as counselors and therapists. Beyond these expressions, the introduction of the climate of grace and the development of insight and awareness of the capacity to be empowered so as to restructure the meaning of reality and to allocate a new understanding of being redefined by God, fosters a setting of freedom from external impositions and abasements, as well as from shame, guilt, and self-condemnation "from within." The aim of this type of intervention is to foster the experience of freedom before God, which is reinforced in transactional terms between the partners and witnessed and encouraged by the helper.

CONCLUDING REMARKS

In the conduct of therapy or counseling, those who help partners to develop better covenants may resort to encouragement along graceful lines and promote a "feedforward" stance that serves as an excellent ground for transacting. Feedback is essential to communicate thoughts and feelings as responses go, but promptings made along proactive behaviors are features that "complete" the interactive endeavors in any communication and transaction. This demeanor evokes concrete, anticipatory manifestations—attending to needs before they are expressed as requests or demands and fulfilling opportunities aimed "to provoke to love and good works" (Heb. 10:24); that is, to plan ahead so as to attend the needs of one another, regarding them as privileges to be conceded and proactively fulfilling those expectations that the other was dreaming about or wishing for.

A lot of research and teaching goes on in the area of spirituality at the present. In this paradigm, a sign of maturity and spiritual development may be defined as the capacity to target the other's needs, requests, and demands before they are actually expressed and without necessarily expecting anything in return. This is to behave in a unilateral, unconditional, proactive, graceful, and loving fashion without any ulterior motives and without employing a defensive maneuver known as a "reaction formation" (behaving unconsciously in an opposite and apparently magnanimous manner from what one really would like to do, which naturally emerges from a reactive, retaliatory, or negative way). The fruit of the Spirit may be manifested in concrete, everyday living—not just in a neo-monastic atmosphere or in an isolated detachment from life's struggles.

We may have grown accustomed to the notion that humans are incapable of doing anything in grace if we are endowed with a basic, cynical philosophy of life. Trapped in an entropic, solipsistic, deterministic context, what can a human do to behave in freedom with dignity, love, and grace? The human has to invite the transcendent into the trivial aspects of everyday living, practicing the presence of God's Spirit in order to enact the terms of a New Covenant, which are engraved in heart and mind. These terms allow for the experience of freedom and renewal. In affect-qualified terms, a person's solipsistic system may be infused with emotional *negentropy* (a double-negative term indicating negative entropy, defined as the vital force needed to rejuvenate and vivify a decaying system) in order to render it vibrant, empowered, and functional.

Strength in weakness is a paradigm cited by St. Paul when he addressed the issue of being ministers of a New Covenant with analogies drawn from being "jars of clay with treasure within" (2 Cor 4:7). The infusion of the spiritual into the natural, empowering the weak aspects of humanness, refers to the Spirit's enabling of our natural incapacity to become capable and functional for the purposes of God. It is through the renewal of the mind that a person is transformed into a capable being that enacts covenantal terms with optimal results. Thus, not only partners in transaction need to be addressed in this fashion, but also those who aim to help as mediators or ministers of a New Covenant. These ministers need to pay attention to the New Covenant paradigm in the first place. In this fashion, the therapeutic communication is not just based upon the "letter"—on concepts or constructs—but on the sharing of life, the utilization of the empowered self in terms of exuding God's presence and positive influence.

In a final analysis, the empowering of believers is made possible because Jesus inaugurated the "promise of the Father"—the new deal to be brought by the Holy Spirit's empowering (Luke 24:49). The same concept is reinforced in Luke's citation of the promise made by Jesus: "You shall receive power and you shall be my witnesses" (Acts 1:8). We are encouraged to trust and wait upon God, to receive the power of his Spirit, to be empowered by God with his gifts, and to bear his fruits in ministry as those who present a vivid example of what the love, grace, and power of God can do among us.

Renewing the clauses of the covenant. Because human transactions experience a diminishing quality as they are subject to natural processes in time—sameness, monotony, diminished zest, entropy, and decay in energy—the notion of renewing a binding covenant is a sound one. The renewal of covenantal clauses depends on partners' ability and willingness to be creative, spontaneous, and free to think, feel, and behave in good faith with positive intent and the aim of mutual satisfaction. In most cases where stability is stressed, it must be noted that satisfaction should be a highly correlated goal to have in mind. The prospect of living together for a long time should be accompanied by the notion that this longevity is a desirable, pleasant, and satisfactory experience in intimacy.

The capacity to restructure the functions and roles within the dyadic relationship is to be ascertained as the dimensions of flexibility, amplitude in loving acceptance, validation, and support of one another are key variables in the process of renewal. As those who treasure something of value and as "containers" of a "new wine," the ontological being of a person needs a readiness to withstand the stressors of life. The analogy drawn from Scripture alludes to the fact that "no one pours new wine into an old wineskin" (Matt 9:17). The problem with old wineskins is not that they have lost their fashionable image or their designer style, but that the flexibility, stress tolerance, and capacity for expansion needed to remain intact and accommodate, assimilate, and equilibrate to one another as new challenges exert their pressures is lacking.

Many internal aspects brew or ferment with expansive pressures that tax the holding capacity and viable permanency of many couples. Old wineskins stand for those structures (as well as the people who comprise them) that are rigid, inflexible, dogmatic, and narrow-minded. These "old wineskins" have no tolerance for ambiguity, paradox, or newness within the challenges and adventures in living. We learn from physics that whatever material does not bend, expand, accommodate, assimilate, or equilibrate to the demands exerted upon it tends to break. Partners in marriage (and those who attempt to help them) cannot ignore this metaphor, for anyone subject to the pressures of everyday living may become an old wineskin.

The capacity to reattribute meaning to reality in order to refresh the diverse aspects of romanticism, fun, relaxation, and satisfaction in general is desirable. This disposition needs to be introduced into the transactions of the partners to remind them about their creative capacity, derived from God. God creates *ex-nihilo* (out of nothing). Humans create in a secondary sense, employing something to achieve their masterpiece. It is the privilege and responsibility of helpers to encourage the partners to discover the available resources within and around them and to engage in creative dealings in order to foster intimacy, pleasurable endeavors, and zest in life. Covenantal renewal is the main topic of chapter 16 of this work.

Follow up. As mentioned before, after deals are established in a structured manner, the couple may be coached to establish their new covenants in a gradual, ongoing fashion. In this way, their capacity to think, feel, and act creatively in a unilateral, unconditional, proactive, and gracious manner can be ascertained "from the sidelines" as the counselor provides them with corrective, positive, and challenging feedback. Thus, a shaping may take place in which ultimate targets are well defined and perceived as being optimal, eschatological, and purposive. These directional goals are brought back and stipulated in present, concrete, and reachable terms. These objectives may be established gradually within a context of guided reinforcement, encouragement, and support.

Marital counseling at this juncture becomes more than just a tune-up of the system because a process is enacted in which the sounding board or checkpoints provided along the way act as a mirror for the couple's alignment with God's designs, propositions, and desires. Finally, recommendations are given to the partners to keep building, enhancing, and enriching their marriage for as long as they live together.

Chapter 7

The New Covenant: Made in the Spirit

THE NEW COVENANT HAS been defined in chapter 4 as being both a redemptive and an exemplary paradigm for optimal relations. As it pertains to its basic premises, binding promises, mediator, guarantee, and results, the writer to the Hebrews demonstrated the superiority of the New Covenant as compared to the Old. In Paul's argument to the Corinthians (2 Cor 3), these features have been ascribed to the actualizing role of the Holy Spirit—the third person of the Trinity—who empowers its terms and enables the human to enter into an open, free, and intimate deal with God. The efficacy of the New Covenant is based upon the work of Jesus at the cross and his resurrection and ascension to the Father—from whose presence the Holy Spirit descended to inaugurate the new deal and guarantee its fulfillment. The major thrust of this chapter focuses upon the Holy Spirit's person, presence, and power as he energizes and capacitates believers to grasp, appropriate, and enjoy the results of the New Covenant.

The Holy Spirit is presented as the one who testifies today of the priestly office of the mediator before the Father, invites the believers to enter into God's domain to serve in his presence, and assures them of their eternal predicament as inheritors of God's kingdom. The Holy Spirit empowers those who enter into a newness of life to live out the terms of the New Covenant. God's manner of love and transacting are abstracted in exemplary principles, applicable to human transactions as we strive to imitate God's character and conduct in marriage, the family, and the community of faith. The relational aspects of these intimate relations are mediated through the empowering and enabling agent of the new deal, the Paraclete (defined as the one called to be at our side to help us at all times).

A COVENANT MADE IN THE HOLY SPIRIT

In the letter to the Hebrews, the author makes several appeals to the Old Testament writers employing a unique style, superseding human amanuenses with the expression, "As *the Spirit says*" (Heb 3:7; 10:15, italics mine). In modern scholarship, if an author cites a concept expounded by a previous scholar, the citation must give proper credit to the original source. Yet, in citing Jeremiah, the author of Hebrews omitted the prophetic source (as well other prophets, psalmists, and even Moses), ascribing the testimony directly to the Holy Spirit: "The Holy Spirit also testifies to us about this. First he says, 'This is the covenant that I will make with them'" (Heb 10:15). It is significant that neither the author nor those who are cited are mentioned in the letter. The implicit credit for this extraordinary exposition (rendered in a superior Greek, as compared to the rest of the NT) is assigned solely to the Holy Spirit, the co-author of Scripture who inspired (God-breathed and infused into the human amanuensis) the original script. Scripture is Spirit-breathed and infused into the cognitive processes of all amanuenses who registered God's Word; it speaks as the vicar of Christ and the voice of God to the church, even today.

The reader may notice that this author holds not just a high view of Scripture, but an even higher view of the Holy Spirit (the author who inspired the original script), who is there to back-up, unfold, elucidate, and illuminate the minds of faithful readers at the present time. It is of utmost importance to regard the Holy Spirit as the one who brings the New Covenant to actualization and fruition in the lives of those who want to imitate God in their human transactions. To that end, it is important to mark a major difference between the Old and New Covenants. The editing note in the Gospel of John states that the Holy Spirit *had not been given ye*t under the Old Covenant (John 7:39, italics mine). His coming in power had to await the accomplishment of the redemptive process—the death, resurrection, and glorification of Christ. Upon that basis, the Holy Spirit would be poured down (a metaphor for his top-down, infusing, interpenetrating, or immanent presence—and his transforming power) upon the believers at Pentecost (Acts 2:1–34; 17–18; 33).

The exalted Christ gave this gift (a person, as he himself is also called God's gift to us) to the church from the Father's throne (Acts 2:33). This is not to deny the presence and ministry of the Holy Spirit from the beginning of time (Gen. 1:2) or the empowering anointing of the agents of the theocracy of old—priests, judges, prophets, and kings under the Old Covenant. Even artists such as Bezalel and Oholiab were filled with the Holy Spirit, who empowered them with the ability and intelligence to express their art. They were endowed with creative knowledge and expert craftsmanship in order to devise all the artistic designs in the making of the Tabernacle (Exod 31:1–6). God expressed his will in multiform fashion: in creating the things of the world, in tablets of stone, in scrolls of prophetic expressions of the Word, in magnificent works of art, and in metaphorical, symbolic ways.

DEPICTIONS OF THE PERSON OF THE HOLY SPIRIT

To be grasped by human cognitive and emotive capacities, the Holy Spirit is depicted in anthropomorphic (cognitive, emotive, and behavioral) terms. To translate transcendental aspects to ordinary humans, the Bible presents expressions about the person and the power of the Holy Spirit in analogical language. As a top-down executive agent, the Holy Spirit "came upon," "descended" upon, and was "poured out" on believers (Acts 2:17; 10:44–45; 18; 19:6; 33). Believers were "baptized" into the Spirit (John 1:33; Acts 1:5) and "filled with" the Spirit (Acts 2:4; 4:8, 31).

Personal attributes are ascribed to the Spirit in psychological/spiritual renderings of a cognitive nature. Scripture employs anthropomorphic terms to ascribe humanlike qualities to the Holy Spirit. He speaks, reminds, teaches, directs, and guides (John 14:26; 16:13–14). The emotive or affective aspects are also set forth as the Spirit may be grieved (Eph 4:30), resisted (Acts 7:51), or lied to (Acts 5:3). The willful characteristics are conveyed in the transactions of the Spirit with believers in that he gives gifts for service (1 Cor 12), guides their walk (John 16:13), directs their path with a sense of direction and tempo (Gal 5:16, 18, 25), prohibits an apostle from going into given places (Acts 16:6–7), and mediates between the Father and those who at times do not know how to pray (Rom 8:26).

Not only is the spirit of the letter placed within human hearts and minds, but God's love is as well (Rom 5:5). Thus, the terms of the New Covenant are embedded, intertwined, or infused with God's personal power and love in more actualized ways. Just as the Old Covenant was given with tangible (and yet metaphorical) signs, so was the New Covenant—with manifestations such as the sound of a violent wind, tongues of fire, and speaking in diverse tongues at Pentecost (Acts 2:1–4). The Holy Spirit, as the author and enabler of the new alliance, is presented in terms that convey his cognitive, affective, and willful aspects and his redemptive, transforming, and conforming power.

Also, in at least one instance, zoomorphic terms are utilized, in which a dove rested upon Christ at his baptism with the clear indication that it was the Holy Spirit who would inaugurate and empower his ministry (Matt 3:16–17).

Scripture employs abstract constructs of a phenomenological and symbolic nature. One of these is the wind or breath of God, which indicates his dynamic, empowering thrust. He gives strength to the weak and animates the fainthearted. He bends and moves people in God's direction as well. The wind of God filled the house that hosted the gathered disciples at Pentecost (Acts 2:2).

Another symbol used in Scripture is the anointing oil. The anointing of priests (Exod 30:30), prophets (1 Kgs 19:16), and kings (1 Sam 10:1) was done to convey the notion of the Spirit's presence in these inaugural and empowering endeavors. A horn with oil was a symbol of power; the pouring of oil upon the heads of those chosen to minister as mediators, announcers, and leaders indicated God's credentialing of these people for works that they would enact before his presence and in favor of his people. Oil has been utilized in conjunction with blood in the purification of priests (as well as utensils of the tabernacle), as a sign of consecration, dedication, and sanctification before God in his service. In the NT, oil is also associated with a healing unction used by elders when praying and laying hands upon the sick (Jas 5:14–15).

Jacob's stone (a simple, natural object) became "the house of God" by virtue of the outpouring oil anointing the natural element. In kairotic fashion, Beth-El amalgamated the human and the divine, the past and the present, the sinful and the angelic, and the trivial and transcendental dimensions of reality. Symbol and reality were catalyzed in a transcending event, mediated through the anointing of a stone. Things in themselves are not necessarily sacred (although customarily we may refer to Israel as the "holy land") or endowed with intrinsic meaning. It is the presence of the Holy Spirit that sanctifies people or objects and allocates true meaning to mundane reality.

Water has been used as an analogical picture depicted in diverse forms, such as floods, rivers, rain, and dew. The Spirit inundates, provides life to dry landscapes, germinates life, allows for growth, and fosters the development of fruits. The Spirit acts as a cleansing agent as well, removing impurities and sanctifying people and objects. Isaiah alludes to the overflowing of water upon dry land as representative of God pouring out his Spirit upon Israel: "For I will pour water on the thirsty land, and streams on the dry ground; I will pour out my Spirit on your offspring, and my blessing on your descendants" (Isa 44:3). Ezekiel presents an increasing flow of salutiferous waters emanating from God's throne and covering the land as an allusion to God's overwhelming redemptive acts through the Spirit toward Israel (Ezek 47).

The prophet Hosea wrote that God refreshes Israel "from above" with rains: "As surely as the sun raises, he will appear; he will come to us like the winter rains, like the spring rains that water the earth" (Hos 6:3). Not only would God bless them in due season, he would also refresh them on a daily basis as alluded to in his expression, "I will be like dew to Israel" (Hos 14:5). Water as a symbol points to the Spirit's gestating, renewing, refreshing, cleansing, and quenching power. These dimensions are necessary in an intimate relationship, providing the essential elements that facilitate, enhance, satisfy, and fulfill partners engaged in transactions of a stressful, challenging, or exhausting nature. In the last day of the feast of the tabernacles, while everyone present in the temple was expecting a jar of water to be poured before the altar in commemoration of the pilgrimage through the desert, Jesus stood up and cried, "If anyone is thirsty, let him come to me and drink" (John 7:37). Jesus appealed to human thirst for meaning, righteousness, satisfaction, and blessedness in life. John indicated that this expression referred to the promise of being filled with the Holy Spirit, which would come after Jesus was glorified (John 7:39).

The Holy Spirit is also depicted symbolically as descending tongues of fire (Acts 2:3). Fire is employed as a symbol of the Spirit's actions, metaphorically burning, melting, and purifying the hearts and minds of followers who receive the energy and dynamic power to live as God commands. Upon his call to ministry as a prophet, Isaiah's mouth was touched with a burning coal as a sign of God's cleansing of his speech (Isa 5:6–7). Initially, after God's summoning call, the prophet rendered excuses, claiming to be a person of unclean lips, belonging to a company of people whose expressions were less than desirable. The remedy for these inadequacies and dysfunctions was a touch from God's Spirit, cleansing and redirecting the flow of communication in more functional and desirable ways. Likewise, many husbands and wives and many parents and children may benefit from the Spirit's purifying power interacting and intertwining with their dialogues to change their negative, contemptuous, and abasing expressions into words of engaging love, saturated with peace, and sharing life.

Fire coming from above consumed Elijah's sacrifice offered to God at Carmel in a symbolic and powerful display. Burnt offerings were customary in Israel's worship. As an offering burnt at the tabernacle, a thermodynamic phenomenon would take place with heat and smoke ascending to the atmosphere. This naturally reduced, transduced, transformed, and exuding property (smoke arising upward) conveyed a more transcendent meaning in which the offering enacted by mere humans would become an exuding property of an expiatory and atoning nature, ascending to God as a reconnecting and redemptive transaction. The event, charged with spiritual meaning, was grasped phenomenologically and connected the offering person with a receiving God. Again, many partners and family members may benefit from surrendering to the purifying, cleansing, and warming effects of the Holy Spirit in their daily transactions with one another.

These expressions convey the Holy Spirit's properties or acts attributed to his person, presence, or power. These symbols, figures, and metaphors are not to be confused with the actual person of the Holy Spirit. Often, the casual or passionate use of effusive rhetoric in stressing the presence and activity of the Holy Spirit may obscure the awesomeness of his being by focusing on sensations or by describing physiological states, effects, or phenomenological signs of some sort. It is essential to remember that the Holy Spirit is a person to be related to in a personal way.

THE PRESENCE AND INDWELLING OF THE HOLY SPIRIT

Analogical language is employed to convey the Spirit's coparticipation with the human. The "indwelling" of the Spirit appeals to spatial/temporal considerations to convey states of heart/mind and processing levels of reality. This indwelling is referred to as the *arrabon*—a down payment granted as a sample of a greater being whose awesome presence humans cannot comprehend or contain in its fullness (Eph 1:13–14). This down payment (or guarantee) was promised by Jesus himself (John 14:16; 16:3) and was partially given to the disciples after the resurrection as he "blew upon them" (John 20:22) with the same breath infused into the first man (Gen 2:7). The reader may connect this notion to Ezekiel's vision, in which the Spirit metaphorically blew upon scattered dry bones and made them alive again, as a prophetic message about Israel's restoration (Ezek 37). It is safe to say that God is alive and well, and his inspiring and revitalizing breath (*ruach*) or wind (*pneuma*) still breathes upon the church today and indwells believers, who are described as temples in which such divine presence abides (1 Cor 3:16; 6:19).

The Holy Spirit has been at work since the beginning of creation. We are not denying the personal regeneration and sanctification of those who had profound encounters with God during the days of the Old Testament. Yet, according to Peter's sermon, it was at Pentecost that Joel's prediction was realized (Acts 2:16–21). Ezekiel, a contemporary of Jeremiah, in speaking of the everlasting covenant of peace that God would establish, alluded to the Spirit as the activating agent of a new deal (Ezek 16:60; 34:25; 36:25–29).

Furthermore, Paul alludes to a different principle, operating apart from the works of righteousness, when he claims that the New Covenant is "of the Spirit" (2 Cor 3:6). The vital agent of creation, redemption, justification, and sanctification is the Holy Spirit, who acts throughout covenantal transactions from the beginning to the end, encompassing the human in a coparticipatory fashion.

This author surmises that, as a companion of Paul until the end (2 Tim 4:11), Luke had plenty of opportunities to dialogue with the apostle on a day-to-day basis. Gathering from this longstanding schooling in theology, the physician Luke presents a sophisticated account of the coming of the Messiah after 400 years of prophetic silence. In his gospel, the introduction of the good news and the announcement of the birth of Jesus Christ are saturated with references to the Holy Spirit.

- John the Baptist, the heralding precursor to the Messiah, would be "filled with the Holy Spirit" since birth (Luke 1:15);

- John's mother, Elizabeth, had the distinct honor of being presented as the first person in the NT who was "filled with the Holy Spirit" upon hearing the virgin Mary's greeting (Luke 1:41);

- The announcement made by the archangel indicated that the Holy Spirit would "come upon" a young virgin, Mary, and gestate the body of Jesus (Luke 1:35);

- Simeon, a righteous and devout man who was waiting for the consolation of Israel, had the privilege of being "under the influence" of the Holy Spirit. In his account, Luke registers that "the Holy Spirit was upon him" (Luke 2:25) and that the Holy Spirit "revealed to him" that he would not die before he had seen the Lord's Christ (Luke 2:26). Furthermore, Luke adds that, "moved by the Holy Spirit, he went to the temple courts" (Luke 2:27) to take Jesus in his arms and express praises to God (known as the *Nunc Dimitis*).

It was fitting that the Holy Spirit—the inspiring, overseeing author of the Old and New Covenants—would connect all events and create a continuous revelation of these transactions through powerful acts, such as the gestating, infusing, and guiding people along God's redemptive plan. The Paraclete was promised by Jesus himself

The New Covenant: Made in the Spirit

(John 14:15–27; 16:5–16) and would empower the believers in a new fashion, enabling them to fulfill the terms of a new deal coming from God.

THE PRESENCE AND ACTS OF THE HOLY SPIRIT IN THE CHURCH

In his second writing (Acts, or The Acts of the Holy Spirit through the Apostles), Luke's narrative depicts the church as coming to existence by virtue of the Spirit, who became the vicar of Christ on Earth until his second coming.

- The Promise of the Holy Spirit's coming was given by both the Father and the Son: "You will be baptized with the Holy Spirit" (Acts 1:4–5, 8);
- The Holy Spirit "descended, came upon" believers at Pentecost (Acts 2:1–4), narrated as a direct reference to Joel's prophecy (Acts 2:17–18);
- This presence would extend beyond Pentecost: "The promise [you will receive the Holy Spirit] is for you . . . for your children . . . for all who are far off . . . for all whom the Lord our God will call" (Acts 2:38);
- Peter was filled with Spirit (Acts 4:8);
- The Holy Spirit inspired Peter's sermon at Pentecost (Acts 4:8);
- The Holy Spirit was present in the assembling of the disciples (Acts 4:31);
- The Holy Spirit was present in the judgment of Ananias and Sapphira who "lied to the Holy Spirit" (Acts 5:3, 9);
- The first deacons (serving ministers) were selected on the basis of being "filled with the Holy Spirit and wisdom" (Acts 6:1–6);
- Stephen, the first martyr, was "filled with the Holy Spirit" (Acts 7:55);
- After Philip's work in Samaria, Peter and John were sent there and prayed for the converts that they might receive the Holy Spirit, for he had not yet fallen on any of them, but they had only been baptized in the name of the Lord Jesus. Then they laid hands on them, and they received the Holy Spirit (Acts 8:12–17);
- The Holy Spirit led Philip to join the Ethiopian eunuch returning from Jerusalem. "And the Spirit said to Philip, 'Go over and join this chariot'" (Acts 8:29). "And when they came out of the water [after baptizing the eunuch] the Spirit carried Philip away" (Acts 8:39);
- The Holy Spirit filled Saul [Paul] after his experience in the road to Damascus (Acts 9:17);
- The Holy Spirit addressed Peter, directly guiding him to encounter Cornelius (Acts 10:19–20);

- While Peter was preaching at Cornelius's house, "the Spirit fell on all who heard the word." Given the visible/audible manifestations, Luke registers Peter's words: "Can anyone withhold water for baptizing these people, who have received the Holy Spirit just as we have?" (Acts 10:44–48). Note an interesting fact: Cornelius and his household were "baptized with the Spirit" before they were baptized in water;

- The Holy Spirit was present at the church in Antioch (Acts 13). While the prophets and teachers were worshipping the Lord and fasting, the "Holy Spirit said, 'Set apart for me Barnabas and Saul for the work to which I have called them'" (Acts 13:1–2). Note the personal pronouns and the willful, intentional tone of the Spirit in addressing the congregation of believers and calling, empowering, and sending the first missionaries;

- Converts of these missionary endeavors (disciples) were "filled with joy and the Holy Spirit" (Acts 13:52);

- The Holy Spirit was present at the first council (Acts 15). The first encyclical letter counted on such presence: "For it seemed good to the Holy Spirit and to us . . ." (Acts 15:28). Note: We seldom write letters like that. Perhaps it is because we tend to ignore the fact that the Holy Spirit is there, present, witnessing our deliberations, and prompting us with corrective yearnings;

- Paul, Timothy, and Silas were "forbidden by the Spirit" to speak the word in Asia (Acts 16:6), and when they attempted to go into a given region, "the Spirit of Jesus did not allow them" (Acts 16:7). Note that stopping and prohibiting the apostle, utilized by the Spirit as a guiding principle, is as good as providing a positive sense of direction;

- The Holy Spirit was present at Ephesus. When Paul laid hands on the believers, "the Holy Spirit came on them" (Acts 19:1–7);

- The Holy Spirit foretold Paul's sufferings (Acts 20:23); these afflictions were also brought to mind through a prophet: "Thus says the Holy Spirit, 'This is how the Jews at Jerusalem will bind . . . and deliver [Paul] into the hands of the Gentiles'" (Acts 21:11).

THE HOLY SPIRIT'S CONTINUOUS PRESENCE AND POWER

Paul's writings are full of allusions to the person, power, and presence of the Holy Spirit. Note such references in the letter to the Romans (Rom 1:4; 7:6; 8:1–17, 23; 26–27; 9:1; 15:13, 19, 30). The first letter of Paul to Corinthians refers to the presence of the Holy Spirit as being in their midst (1 Cor 2:4, 10–16; 3:16) with the connotation that believers are living temples, indwelled by the Holy Spirit (1 Cor 12:3) and

The New Covenant: Made in the Spirit

gifted by him (1 Cor 12:4–11). Note the following expressions: "To each one the manifestation of the Spirit is given for the common good" (1 Cor 12:7, NIV). "All these [the gifts—word of wisdom, word of knowledge, faith, healing, miracles, prophecy, tongues, interpretation] are the work of one and the same Spirit, and he distributes them to each one, just as he determines" (1 Cor 12:11, NIV). "For we were all baptized by one Spirit so as to form one body—whether Jews or Gentiles, slave or free—and we were all given the one Spirit to drink" (1 Cor 12:13, NIV).

In the second letter to the Corinthians, Paul and his companions are defined as being ministers of a New Covenant, serving those who believe. Those believers are in turn defined as letters, "written *not with ink but with the Spirit of the living God, not on tablets of stone but on tablets of human hearts*" (2 Cor 3:3, italics mine). Paul proceeds to describe the new ministry empowered by the Holy Spirit in contrast to the Old Covenant (2 Cor 3:6–18). The old way is described as being veiled to those who reject the Messiah. In a bold contrast, even Moses—the mediator of the Old Covenant—is described as veiling his face in order to conceal from Israelites the obvious sight of the fading glory of his face as it would diminish in radiance, and his shining glory would come to an end. The ministry of a New Covenant is depicted in terms of its outcomes both in the character and the conduct of those who serve as ministers: their service is empowered in an ongoing and renewable basis. It fosters an open stance as the person is free to approach the Lord with an unveiled face, beholding the unfading glory of the Lord and being progressively transformed into his likeness.

Allow me to draw a conjectural analogy from interpersonal neurobiology: perhaps the mirror neurons of the believer are aligned with the effulgence, radiance, and awesome re-socializing power of the face of Jesus, apprehended by faith and merged within love. Perhaps (again, these are the author's side notes, conjectural as they may be) not only the ontological being is transformed by the renewal of the mind (Rom 12:1—2), but even the production of oxytocin, the activation of the amygdala, the cingulate gyrus, and the myelination of mirror neurons running along new neural pathways. In terms of an expanded attachment theory (and thousands of research articles focusing on mother-infant bonding), having such powerful, resocializing prototypes as the Father and the Son and being enabled by the Holy Spirit, a person beholding with unveiled face the Lord shining in a New Covenant may be progressively conformed into the object of his/her worship: the image of the Son (2 Cor 3:18; Rom 8:28–30). In terms of social learning theory, observational and vicarious learning from actual, symbolic, or imaginary models represents a powerful basis for imitational endeavors leading to the acquisition and reinforcement of desirable character traits and self efficacy.[1]

To the Galatians, Paul's admonishing words are conveyed with rhetorical questions: "Did you receive the Spirit by the works of the law or by hearing with faith? Are you so foolish? Having begun by the Spirit, are you now being perfected by the flesh?"

---

1. Bandura, *Social Learning Theory*.

(Gal 3:2–4, ESV). Connecting his argument to the Abrahamic covenant, he proceeds: "Does he who supplies the Spirit to you and works miracles among you do so by works of the law, or by hearing with faith—just as Abraham 'believed God, and it was counted to him as righteousness?'" (Gal 3:5–6, ESV). The whole letter is a warning to persevere in faith, to rely on grace, and to not turn back to the old ways that would never save them from their predicament. He reinforces his appeal with an allegory (introducing Sarah, Hagar, Sinai, and Jerusalem as prototypes, following a rabbinical way of teaching). In this allegory, the allusion is made to believers being children of the promise, appropriating by faith the provisions of a new deal and being free from bondage in order to serve God in a new and better way.

Keeping up with the Spirit is the theme of Galatians 5, where walking with both a sense of direction and cadence in the Holy Spirit (5:16, 25) are proposed. Along this journey, believers are to sow to the Spirit (dedicate their efforts to surrender to, invest in, and merge with God's Spirit) in order to reap (obtain the desirable outcomes of God's promises) in due time from the Spirit (Gal 6:7–10).

In Ephesians, the eternal design and will of God are displayed in chapter 1, with the assurance that believers are "sealed with the promised Holy Spirit," who is regarded as the guarantor of the believers' inheritance until they acquire it (Eph 1:13–14). Paul's prayer for the Ephesians is that God would give them "the Spirit of wisdom and revelation in the knowledge of him" in order to enlighten their perception, assuring them of their hope and of their inheritance of God's riches. The letter stresses the introduction of believers into the body of Christ, who is the head, granting them all the benefits of a New Covenant. Jews and Gentiles join as fellow citizens and members of the household of God, having access in one Spirit to the Father and being built into a dwelling place for God by the Spirit (Eph 2:4–22).

It is the Holy Spirit who has revealed this mystery, hidden for generations and manifested now through the actualizing of God's eternal design in Christ and the results of his work (Eph 3:13). It is through his indwelling in the hearts of believers that the Holy Spirit strengthens them (Eph 3:17), uniting them in one body under the Lord (Eph 4:3) and sealing them for the day of redemption (Eph 4:30). The Holy Spirit is also depicted as a "sword" in spiritual warfare terminology (Eph 6:17), amalgamated to the Word of God. Believers are counseled to "pray at all times in the Spirit" (Eph 6:18); that is, believers may resort to a higher transducer, a more accurate and powerful interlocutor, offering themselves to his care and coparticipatory intercession in order to experience his empowering presence while they dialogue with and appeal to the Father.

Thus, this presence is postulated as being there, as the vicar of Christ on Earth, in the here and the now, until he comes back. As the Father acted (and still does) in history, and as the Son became flesh and dwelt among us, so the Holy Spirit came to be with and in us—to abide until the end of this age. John provides an eschatological picture wherein the indwelling Holy Spirit joins the bride in inviting Christ back to Earth (Rev 22:16).

The letter to the Hebrews presents syllogistically the arguments of Christ's superiority to all the created order: angels, Moses, Joshua, the tabernacle, the offerings, the priesthood, and the way to access the Father through a new, open, and living way. The focal theme of Hebrews is that Jesus is the mediator of a New Covenant. Conceived by the Holy Spirit, Jesus was led by the Spirit throughout his life and ministry to offer himself to God. Upon his death and resurrection, Jesus would ascend to the Father to sit at his right hand and intercede for us (Heb 7:25). As a high priest, he lives forever and has a permanent priesthood, characterized by holiness, blamelessness, and purity. Having been set apart from sinners and being exalted above the heavens (Heb 7:26), he mediates from this position. From this state/position, he sent the Holy Spirit to be with and in us, as promised (John 14:16). Pentecost as an event was the fulfillment and ratification of the new transaction, inaugurating the life of the church. The Holy Spirit sent by Jesus from the Father's throne came with visible and audible signs, announcing the dawning of a new era in which God the Spirit would be actually present—guiding and empowering those who enter into a new transaction by faith.

The old transaction between God and people was established in stone as a concrete, binding stela and a tangible reminder of God's will and love. The inscribed tablets were a testimonial and a mnemonic device. As we recall, the original tablets were broken by the "meekest man on earth," the giver of the law, the mediator of the Old Covenant. Under God's order, the second set was deposited in the ark within the veil in the Holy of Holies. The command to place the tablets of the law within the ark points to the notion that the eternal truth—expressed in concrete commandments engraved in stone as a tangible script—would be kept intact and find actualization in the one who came to fulfill all promises and obey the Father's will.

After all, the tabernacle was a shadow or figure of better things to come. The tabernacle, in sum, was outlined as having an outer court with its door, the altar, the five types of offerings, and the bronze fountain; a Holy Place with its candelabra's light, the bread of the presence, the altar burning incense, and the veil; and the Holy of Holies with the propitiatory covering the ark, which contained the jar of manna, the branch of an almond tree that came to life and gave fruits overnight, and the unbroken tablets in the ark. All these artifacts were a shadow of the reality that was to be fulfilled in the person and work of Jesus Christ.

Metaphorically, the deposit of the unbroken law within the ark points to the fact that the law was totally fulfilled by Jesus Christ. He is the only one who actually kept it in its real significance. The purpose of the law was Jesus Christ, who epitomized God's expressed will in incarnated fashion. His challenge to the religious leaders of his day was "Can any one of you prove me guilty of sin?" (John 8:46). The Gospel narrative affirms that no one did. His impeccable life had a purpose: to become our substitute, to die for us, to resurrect, to present himself as the perfect sacrifice (Heb 9:10), and to reconnect us with the Father, acting as a better mediator on our behalf (Heb 3:3–6; 8:1–6).

It is through the eternal Holy Spirit that Jesus offered himself as the unblemished sacrifice whose blood cleanses our consciences from acts that lead to death so we may serve the living God (Heb 9:14).

> For by one sacrifice he has made perfect forever those who are being made holy. The Holy Spirit also testifies to us about this. First he says, "This is the covenant I will make with them after that time, says the Lord. I will put my laws in their hearts, and I will write them on their minds." Then he adds, "Their sins and lawless acts I will remember no more." (Hebrews 10:14–17, NIV)

The apostle Paul presents the Holy Spirit as the one who not only actualizes the effects of the new alliance, but also empowers those who choose to live under these new terms. The apostle regarded himself and those who ministered at his side as being "competent as ministers of a new covenant—not of the letter but of the Spirit" (2 Cor 3:6, NIV). He reminded the Corinthians that they were now children of God, the "result of our ministry, written not with ink but with the Spirit of the living God, not on tablets of stone but on tablets of human hearts" (2 Cor 3:3, NIV). The apostle pinpoints the difference between the script itself and the author of the script, as God's presence, will, and Word are placed in human hearts by means of the Holy Spirit (Rom 5:5).

THE CREATIVE, REDEMPTIVE, SUSTAINING, AND TRANSFORMING POWER OF THE HOLY SPIRIT

Employing metaphorical language may lead to the perception that the Holy Spirit is just that—a force, an influence, or an ethereal universal spirit permeating God's universe. Yet, as already noted, Scripture presents the Holy Spirit as a person. The presence of the person of the Spirit was postulated directly, promised by the Father and the Son. He is stated as being there from the start as a proactive generator of life and as an agent of change through time. All the indications in Scripture point to the fact that the Spirit is present today, active in accomplishing God's will among and in us. It is important to reiterate the fact that the Holy Spirit is the third person of the Trinity. Being God, the Spirit is not subject to human manipulation as we do not bring or make the Spirit come down by our own efforts, acts, or tactics. As a matter of fact, the Spirit acted in spite of Peter's initial attitude or behavior, registered in Acts 10. This promised agent needs to be recognized, realized (not as a theological construct to be reified, but as God with, among, and in us), and obeyed in submission.

The Holy Spirit is a powerful person at work; he was present and coparticipating in creation (Gen 1:2), infusing with life the material dust from which Adam was formed (Gen 2:7). God's breath on dust combines the highest and the lowest elements in the created human, animating the person as the Imago Dei.

From the beginning, the Holy Spirit witnessed the Fall and its results. Now he deals with the fallen human, incubating and gestating the capacity of the human to respond with proactive grace, producing repentance from sin, calling into conversion unto Christ, saving, and regenerating a new life. The Spirit coparticipates in each person's growth as a proactive initiator of a new lifestyle.

The Author acts in grace and mercy, prompting the human to respond to this summoning. As the Word is planted in hearts and minds, the "soil" becomes more receptive to it, more absorbing of it. The believer, interacting in coparticipation with the Spirit, experiences the germinating of God's Word in the capacities of cognitive, affective, and motivational structures and processes, becoming productive and fruitful. The power to live according to God's Word is given by the Author, who energizes the human to be and to do what God desires.

The Spirit generates fruits in the believer who surrenders to his action and is willing and able to follow his directions. A natural fruit is the natural outcome of the timely interaction between the epigenetic potential embedded in the seed and the proper environment (soil). Seed and soil enter into a gestating, coparticipatory process that unfolds in time under optimal contingencies. Also, a fruit is the emergent property of an established tree that in due time produces a desirable byproduct. It is the final outcome elaborated by means of epigenetic forces regulating the bottom-up processes moving upward from the root (embedded in the chemical nutrients of the soil) in interaction with the ecosystemic contributions of photosynthesis and irrigation. Pruning is a process that fosters the production of better and more abundant fruit.

A spiritual fruit may be seen as a conjoint endeavor in which the seed of the gospel and the soil of the believer's ontological ground of being act in accordance. The Holy Spirit interpenetrates and aligns the cognitive, affective, and enactive structures and processes of the human and proactively infuses (indwells) the human, prompting the person to respond to the intentions of God and produce the expected qualities of character (e.g., love, peace, joy, etc., as outlined in Galatians 5:22–23). The fruit of the Spirit may be also defined as the exuding property that conveys the desirable character qualities found in a person who is rooted in God's Word and lives by the Spirit in accordance to God's will.

In human relations, it is through the Holy Spirit's energy, direction, and thrust that the believer may demonstrate the qualities of character needed to enact the terms of a New Covenant. In order to adopt a positive dispositional attitude and move in a unilateral, unconditional, and proactive fashion toward the other (a partner, a neighbor), the person needs to draw from the Word and the Spirit as she/he attempts to imitate the ways of the Father. It is by means of the indwelling and directing Spirit that the person may be empowered in order to act with grace and mercy, dispense forgiveness, and let go of any offenses committed against her/his person. The empowering of the Spirit enables the person to empower his/her partner and seek the benefits for the other above and beyond his/her own. The mindful intimacy experienced by a partner with the indwelling and dialogical Spirit is the empowering capacity to prompt, exude, spread, and infuse the same quality of caring togetherness toward a human counterpart.

The obvious outcomes of this coparticipation are evident in a transforming character in the process of being conformed to the image of the Son (mirroring his character and conduct), marked by love, joy, peace, patience, kindness, goodness, faithfulness, gentleness, and self-control (Gal 5:22–23). Any "evidence-based" counseling needs to rely on the empirical observation of the emergence and continuity of such traits, regarded as characterological properties demonstrated toward a partner in marriage, a family member, or a fellow member in the community of believers.

Beyond the factors that apply to marital and family relationships, the Holy Spirit endows the community of believers with gifts (1 Cor 12:4–11), allowing for a concerted effort by the body of Christ to be and to do what God has intended. Rather than relying on natural endowments or giftedness, a believer may ascertain what the Spirit has allocated into her/his service in order to administer these gifts with humility, accountability, and responsibility. These gifts are not necessarily bargained for by the believer—who, narcissistically, may seek the more outstanding or powerful ones—but are given by the Spirit to members of the body of Christ as he wills and desires.

The Holy Spirit is the agent of illumination and insight. He is the same person who hovered over, inspired, and illuminated the mind and heart of Moses, the prophets, the psalmists, and apostles—as well as conceived the writing of the original Scripture. The same Spirit is present in the act of reading, meditating on, and digesting Scripture today. By his will and grace, the disclosing of the veil of our natural fading and inadequate grasp of spiritual reality is possible and the opening of the eyes of our hearts as well so that we may understand with all the saints the design and the love of God for our lives (Eph 1:17–19). The Holy Spirit may provide us with insightful perceptions of revealed truth. The appeal to the Spirit in the process of extracting truth (exegesis) and interpreting it (hermeneutics) allows for an insightful process that goes beyond the analytical work and interpretation arrived at by human cognition. The meaning, veracity, and relevance of Scripture come alive when the Holy Spirit is given ample room to endow us with the word of wisdom, word of knowledge, discernment of spirits, and the rest of the gifts.

The Holy Spirit provides strength—the power to be, to do, to think, and to feel in renewed and more functional ways, beyond human willpower. This energy activates the zest and intrinsic motivation to do what is appropriate and pleasing to God, stretching us beyond the natural capacities of our human nature. The Holy Spirit separates the human from the entrapments and patterns of this world, sanctifying the believer. Sanctification simply means that those who accept the summoning call of God and enter into a New Covenant transaction with him are separated from the entrapments of the world (its values, natural customs, and lifestyle patterns); they are also dedicated to and inaugurated for God's service, being empowered to do so in a consecrated way while sojourning under the sun.

If the identity of a person is gained "in Christ," integrity is achieved by becoming like him; intimacy is the sharing of self with others as Christ did, and industriousness is the expected fruit of doing his works. Being filled (clothed/empowered/invested) with the Holy Spirit empowers us for the tasks of ministry/service (Eph 4:11–12). Gifted persons (apostles, prophets, evangelists, pastors-teachers) equip (mend, set things straight, compose, or prepare for service) the saints for the work of ministry so that believers edify the body of Christ. The tasks of teaching, shaping, discipling, counseling, guiding, reconciling, mediating, comforting, supporting, nurturing, praying, interceding, and being there for one another are all aspects of the ministry done in the Spirit.

The Holy Spirit makes us "ministers of a New Covenant" (2 Cor 3:6, NIV), endowing and empowering us with a unilateral capacity to bless, to give, and to be there for others, decentering from our narcissism. After God, as beloved children, we may say, "I will do . . . I will take the initiative . . . I will bless . . ." without any ulterior motive or personal expectation.

As the promoter of proactive stances, the Holy Spirit will challenge those of us who are naturally reactive and prone to retaliation to become more graceful and merciful. We may give others what in our estimation they do not deserve. We may not retaliate (pay them in negative ways) with a response that in our estimation we think they deserve. As ministers of grace and mercy, we may be free to love and do good works, promoting a ministry of justice and equity. This ministry in the Spirit becomes an open, honest, life-sharing endeavor instead of a display of detached professionalism or the fulfillment of perfunctory tasks. This ministry promotes reconciliation among one another, mediating in God's ways of resolving conflicts and promoting peace. A minister of the New Covenant seeks to establish freedom from sin and entrapments resulting from negative past experiences and to empower those who are weak or unable to stand for themselves.

The Holy Spirit provides the intrinsic capacity to love (Rom 5:5). All human transactions may receive the energizing capacity of this outpouring to become more proactive and unconditional, as the power is given to love not just those who are naturally lovable, but even to those who are difficult to engage. At times, loving "in spite of the other" is a necessity in the body of Christ, as well as in family transactions. These endeavors are not necessarily an exercise in masochism, codependency, or false humility, but true expressions of a new-covenantal nature animated by the Holy Spirit who pours love into human hearts so that we may imitate God in our daily walk.

The personal power of God, the Holy Spirit, pours into our hearts not only the demands of the law, but the power to enact them. Not only are norms intrinsically allocated, but the capacity to enact them is provided as well. Thus, the covenantal transactions are not regulated by a "cut and dry" dicta, but by a personal rendering of the Spirit's loving power infusing the human to be and behave in ways that resemble God's ways of being and doing.

The ministry of the New Covenant, as Paul stated, is actualized by reliance on, coparticipation with, and surrender to the person and the acts of the Holy Spirit—who enables his ministers and engraves living letters on the tablets of the hearts of those who accept the gospel (2 Cor 3:3), qualifying them to engage in works of service (2 Cor 3:8). The concepts presented in this work emphasize the leading presence and power of the person of the Holy Spirit, actualizing the distinctiveness of the New Covenant without denying continuity with the Old, which we may regard as a preamble or *pedagogos* to this new or better deal. Jeremiah's prophecy (31:31–32) states that the New Covenant is "not like the covenant I made with their fathers." The author to the Hebrews recapitulates this prophecy in chapters 8 and 10. A distinctive thrust is stressed, pointing to a deal that will be more empowering and accomplish God's will toward humans optimally.

Along such distinctiveness, the apostle Paul defined himself and his fellow workers as being "ministers of a New Covenant" in 2 Corinthians 3:6. In his defense against some accusations made by the Corinthians, Paul asserted his call to serve and made analogical comparisons between the Levites of old and his own ministry (see 1 Cor 9:1–27). This service unto God and fellow human beings was neither an upgrade of the old, nor a patchwork of some sort, but a new way of understanding the tasks to be performed before God and the transactions to be made among humans. It was "new wine in new wineskins," endowed with emergent properties that would allow the faithful human to do God's will as prompted from "within" and as empowered by a new principle of operation: the Holy Spirit at work.

A Christian who is dedicated to social services, even if he or she is not officially ordained into priesthood or ministry, may nevertheless be "ordained by God" to do his/her service to those who need help along the way—provided this person has the qualifications to do so. Many believers who work as professional therapists and counselors may consider themselves as scripturally based servants of grace and mercy, empowering people and relying on both their training and the Holy Spirit to fulfill God's call in their lives.

COVENANTAL PARTNERS AND THE HOLY SPIRIT

In Pauline writings, a heavy dose of theology usually precedes the practical applications pertaining to human relations. Theological premises and propositions found in Ephesians 1—3 precede the practical advice given to believers. In Romans, eleven chapters present a theological basis before giving some admonitions as to how to behave. Likewise, in view of the lengthy exposition on the person, presence, and power of the Holy Spirit, partners in marriage, members of a family, and friends in community may consider how this "agent" may empower them in their attempts to actualize their covenantal terms. Partners in covenants may greatly benefit from grasping biblical-theological truth, regarded by Jesus as the solid ground upon which to build their spiritual, social, and personal houses. Beyond our natural efforts, power is given to be and to do what is desirable and lovingly right before God.

A METACOGNITIVE-DIALOGICAL MODEL: EMPOWERED TO IMITATE GOD'S WAYS

The propositions, principles, and expectations derived from the exemplary aspects of God's covenant appear to be an impossible task to accomplish. As a matter of fact, to imitate God is not a natural propensity of the fallen human. Yet, the empowering of the Holy Spirit makes it possible for believers to engage in coparticipation with God's design to accomplish his will and purpose. To engage in love, with peace and joy, demonstrating patience, kindness, goodness, faithfulness, gentleness, and self-control requires the empowering of the Spirit. The capacity to be unilateral, unconditional, and proactive—and to do the right things at the right time in accordance with God's purpose and design—necessitates the internal guidance and energizing thrust of the Spirit. These character traits and behavioral enactments appear as dimensions of the fruit of the Holy Spirit (Gal 5:22–23).

A modest attempt to delineate how this empowered capacity may be fostered is presented in a diagrammatic form (see Fig. 7.1). A more thorough explanation of the metacognitive-dialogical model appears in the final chapter of this book (chapter 17, exemplified in the process of forgiveness). The reader is invited to consider this diagram to acquire a better understanding of the empowered process. We may depict the Holy Spirit as infusing, "in-merging," or entering into the human heart and mind to empower a person's cognitive-affective-motivational structures and processes at an ontological (essential, substructural) level. Of course, a flat, two-dimensional rendering will undoubtedly fail to convey all the intricate complexities of the divine-human encounter. Yet, this illustration may serve as a viable explanation of this complex process.

At the top of the picture, the infusion of the indwelling Spirit is presented as evoking the indwelling Word at the ontological basis: the core metacognitive-emotive-enactive schemata of consolidated metanarratives comprised of basic beliefs, values, and attitudes. In the graphic, the arrows going up and down at the middle of the upper box indicate the ongoing coparticipation between the divine Spirit and the human executive agency—the core inner being endowed with metacognitive values and beliefs consolidated in metanarratives.

Part I: Premises and Principles

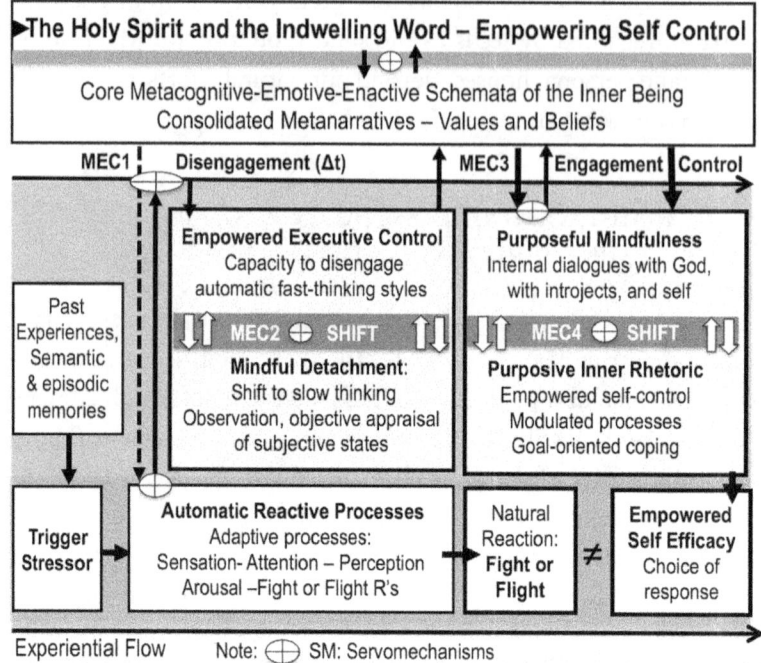

Fig. 7.1: The Spirit's Empowering of Self-Control

The person that is impacted by a partner's challenge (an offense, a discrepancy, a dysfunctional pattern, an attitude of contempt, an act of stonewalling, a negative comment, etc.) also receives an influx stemming from the past (an addenda of negative schemata residing latently in the deep structures of semantic and episodic memories). Many events that "are there" as consolidated metanarratives charged with unfinished transactions, unresolved issues, faulty attachments, semantic and episodic memories, etc., may be evoked automatically. These further contribute to the reactive momentum, and once triggered, prompt an automatic fight-or-flight reaction (the sequence occurring at the bottom level of the graph).

The Metacognitive-executive control system (MEC). A believer who is endowed with the indwelling Word and is under the jurisdiction of the indwelling Holy Spirit may experience an infusion by a transcending—yet immanent—higher power into his or her natural system. The author appeals to both the presence and power of the Holy Spirit and the indwelling living Word of God. In coparticipation with the believing human, this *perichoresis* (interpenetration) may be actualized in existential terms. Beyond the neurobiological and physiological apparatus, the higher cortical functions of the human are indwelled with the empowering from God's side. Call it an empowered "metacognitive executive control" system (MEC)—provided that the person believes in the actual presence of the person and the power of the Holy Spirit and appeals to him at a critical moment (call it a Δt, or a split-second happening). The metacognitive executive control (MEC1) may be engaged, activated by the indwelling Spirit who

The New Covenant: Made in the Spirit

empowers the believer's top-down executive agency so that he or she may be able to apply a clutch (a mechanical device designed to disengage a motor from a driving train) to the naturally reactive aspects of an ongoing experiential flow. That is, the person may detach mindfully and be able to disengage the automatic, fast-thinking processes coupled to his or her natural reactions to stress.

Contrary to popular concepts and philosophies about mindfulness proposed by Zen practitioners that permeate our culture, this author regards the construct as a Spirit-empowered capacity to consciously disengage an ongoing reaction, to experience the impact of stressors in a calm state, and to then shift and turn attention to a purposeful response. In other words, the MEC may be regarded as a human function empowered by the Holy Spirit that enables the believer to engage in a self-controlled manner. Mindfulness is the interplay between detached observation (adopting a calm, relaxed, consciously controlled mindset) and purposeful engagement in internal dialogue (deliberative, ruminative, etc., in nature), as well as in internal rhetoric (persuasive, decisive self-talk); it is the ability to be aware of one's processes and modulate, regulate, and control them.

Thanks to this initial MEC1, a person may disengage from automatic reactions and engage in a more detached, slow-thinking process. After that initial shift, the person may be able to shift again and employ a more purposive, metacognitive control over his or her thoughts, feelings, and behaviors. Being empowered, the person may engage in a more objective appraisal of her/his subjective states; that is, the person may be able to briefly observe, assess, and appraise her/his predicament in a more purposive and mindful engagement.

After the initial infusion of an empowered capacity to apply the MEC "clutch" and disengage automatic fight-or-flight reactions of an organismic nature, the person may appeal to the indwelling Spirit and Word by employing a feedforward loop going upward (to the upper box). This interpenetrated fellowship allows for an empowered capacity to shift again (by means of the metacognitive executive control, now labeled as MEC2) and engage in purposeful mindfulness. At this juncture, internal dialogues may take place, which are charged with deliberations, conjectures, debates, etc. These internal dialogues may be established between the self and God, with introjected others, and with self (the objective, observing, or mindful dimensions of the self in dialogue with the subjective states or dimensions of the reactive self). Arguments and counterarguments—challenging, confronting, reframing, and trying to make sense out of whatever is going on—seem to characterize these internal dialogues.

The change from a person's natural propensity to engage in automatic, conditioned reactions to mindful responses demands the control of this natural propensity and a disengagement from automatically elicited internal dialogues. The shift to mindful, internal rhetoric (self persuasion) may take place as these processes are metacognitively halted and disengaged. The capacity to do so is attributed to the indwelling Spirit and Word, postulated here as empowering the metacognitive executive control (now labeled as MEC3) of the human, leading to the person's own internal persuasion (rhetoric). This inner rhetoric enables the person to aim at some viable attitude or disposition in order to act as an imitator of God.

The persuasive rhetoric may draw from the Spirit-empowered capacity to address oneself with regulated, modulated, and positive coaching, aligning possible responses with what would resemble a God-like way of transacting. At this juncture, as far as responses go, the insightful and empowered person may mindfully and purposefully choose to be unilateral, unconditional, proactive, graceful, and merciful, not being subject to the original stressors that provoked the initial reaction. Thus, rather than reacting with emotionally charged fight-or-flight behaviors, the person may respond in a consciously mindful and self-controlled way.

In short, the above diagram may be seen at three levels of analysis: at the bottom level, the processes may be regarded as being the typical ways in which the organismic reactive systems behave once they have been triggered by any stimulus. At a middle level of processing, the person's metacognitive, dialogical, and rhetorical processes take place. The person may employ a shift from the initial reaction, choosing to employ a more detached and mindful stance, and then shift again to a more purposive engagement. The vital appeal to the upper level is necessary, resorting to a dimension in which the Holy Spirit and the indwelling Word operate and affect the mind and heart of the person, empowering her/his ontological structures (inner being). Being endowed with this empowering capacity, the person may be objective about subjective states of mind and heart and engage in slow, deliberate thinking.

By virtue of practicing the spiritual disciplines applicable to the growth, development, and consolidation of the fruit of the Spirit, a disciple like Timothy is encouraged by the apostle to "train yourself in godliness" (1 Tim 4:7), in order to be better prepared to modulate and respond to life's stressors and challenges with purposive mindfulness. By "disciplines" we mean the assiduous engagement in "seeking and beholding the face of Jesus Christ" (mindful meditation), spending time in his presence in prayer (formal or existential), and reading and engaging with Scripture in dialogue (listening to God's voice with the awareness of the Holy Spirit being there to elucidate it; meditating on, pondering, and treasuring the Word in the heart and mind). On the negative side, it also helps to avoid being squeezed into the mold of this present age (Rom 12:1–2). In this manner, the person's growth takes place as the self is offered as a living sacrifice before God in an ongoing fashion with thanksgiving, praise, and worship. Beyond events, the process of being transformed and conformed into the likeness of Christ is guided by the ultimate goal in this growth: to resemble him and to do his works (Rom 8:28–30).

The shift from automatic reactions to purposeful responses takes place along a process (as a feature of "training in godliness" or character formation), characterized by a shaped sequence under the person's metacognitive-executive control (MEC). Being provoked, hit, or challenged by a stressor, the person starts processing this contingency with an initial mindful detachment (MEC1), then engages with purposeful and conscious internal dialogues (MEC2), and finally appeals to the regulation, modulation, and choice of responses (MEC3) under the auspices of the Spirit in coparticipation with human faith and obedience to God's ways. That, in essence, is the metacognitive-dialogical rendering of the psychological understanding of self-control—the fruit of the Holy Spirit in action.

EMPOWERED BY THE HOLY SPIRIT TO ACTUALIZE THE TERMS OF THE NEW COVENANT

In sum, the essential difference between reacting in an automatic, negative fashion and responding in a modulated, controlled manner resides in the capacity of a partner to engage her/his metacognitive-executive control system (MEC) with the awareness, coparticipation, and empowering of the indwelling Spirit and Word. Doing so enables the partner to be able to engage in empowered internal dialogues and rhetoric, arriving at rational and functional responses—as opposed to behaving at primitive, natural, or reactive levels.

As partners in marriage recapitulate the terms of a New Covenant empowered by the Holy Spirit, they are reminded that his person, presence, and power is there to:

- Capacitate partners to adopt a proactive stance, being endowed with good intentions and planning events, situations, and privileges to provoke one another to love and good works;
- Enable each other to take unilateral initiatives when necessary, being able to dispense grace and mercy as prerogatives of being imitators of God;
- Empower partners to behave in unconditional ways if necessary in situations that demand that they be the bigger, better, or more mature person in order to break a gridlock in communication or to go over a defensive impasse in more functional ways;
- Show grace toward a person who does not necessarily deserve it;
- Show mercy to a person who has failed to live up to the terms of a covenant;
- Dispense forgiveness to a partner, acting as God acted toward him or her in Christ, without being a codependent person;
- Let go of offenses, not keeping an account of evil;
- Empower, rather than power over, the other;
- Foster intimacy, daring to be open, honest, and transparent; accepting and being accepted; loving and being loved;
- Renew the terms of the covenant made before God so as to be always fresh, revitalized, and energized with creativity and zest.

Part I: Premises and Principles

Relations in Christ may and can be actualized by means of this empowering. There is hope for troubled marriages, provided that partners are willing and able to engage in metacognitive-dialogical considerations under the auspices, guidance, and overseeing presence of the Holy Spirit.

Part II: Actualizing the Principles Derived from the New Covenant in Marital Transactions

Chapter 8

Empowered by the Holy Spirit to Empower One Another

POWER IS A CONSTRUCT used in a variety of ways and is ascribed diverse meanings and connotations. The origin of the term is an alteration of the Latin *posse* (be able), conveying a sense of capacity or ability to do something or to behave in a particular way. In the social realm, power is an ever-present dimension framed in a sentence: who says or does what to whom, and with what effect. It is a central feature in the domains of leadership, politics, government, economics, and education. It appears as a major issue cast in terms of social authority and control at work in family systems and marital relationships. In sum, interpersonal power is the faculty to influence the behavior of other people in purposive ways and gear the course of interacting events and processes in a given direction in order to accomplish desirable or intended outcomes.

Metaphors derived from physics often apply to psychological processes, including those at work in human relations. In physics, power is the amount of energy consumed per unit of time. To empower is to provide or allocate energy to a system in order to achieve a desirable effect or result in time. In the fields of mechanics and hydraulics, to empower is to provide a system with a combination of forces and movement (acceleration and momentum) that would actualize its potential energy in kinetic fashion, propelling its dynamic capacities to achieve some results or outcomes. Analogically speaking, to empower someone is to behave purposefully in order to bestow, foster, or reinforce the actualization of her/his potentials, endowments, gifts, plans, or desirable purposes.

Interpersonal empowerment refers to the capacity, intention, and purposive mindfulness provided by a given person who, being endowed with delegated, achieved, or projected power is able and willing to confer, share, or delegate this influential energy to a beneficiary of it. The aim of this empowering attitude is to enable the targeted person to develop a potential capacity, to enhance a gift, to accomplish a task, or to achieve a desirable purpose. For partners transacting in a covenantal marriage, to empower one another is simply to demonstrate mutual acceptance, respect, validation, and love for one another. Beyond "powering over," parents may empower their children by fostering their physical, intellectual, social, and spiritual growth. They do so by providing the milieu, means, and encouragement necessary for children to

Part II: Principles Derived from the New Covenant in Marital Transactions

develop and consolidate their capacity to balance their individuation and their mutuality in the context of the family system.

BIBLICAL NOTIONS OF POWER

In theological terms, power is the ability provided in grace and mercy by an omnipotent God that enables the human to do the right thing by his standards and to achieve his will. God's power is aimed at empowering the human to achieve the potential for which he or she was created, redeemed, and provided with a sense of destiny before the Lord. The privilege and opportunity to fulfill God's will as it pertains to human relations are predicated on the promises given in the New Covenant, based upon the premises disclosed in this work.

The words for power used in the NT are *exousia* (ἐξουσία: power as authority) and *dunamis* (δύναμις: power as energy, a dynamic force at work). In the context of the ancient world, *exousia* represented the power of choice or the liberty to do what one is pleased to do. It expressed the physical power or the mental ability with which a person was endowed. It also represented the delegated, ascribed, or projected authority (influence) and the right (privilege) to exercise it. The subjects of a lord, or those living under the governmental or administrative power of a given ruler, had to obey the stipulations provided by those in power. Regal authority, honor, dignity, and other attributions of power have traditionally been symbolized by the use of some visible signs, such as a crown topping the head of the ruler.

In the ancient world of Abraham, the veiling of women was a symbol of submission to the authority of their husbands. This custom prevailed through many centuries, reflected in the Hebrew mindset and culture. During the times of the apostle Paul (who wrote to people in Corinth, a Greek city with Roman influence), the covering of a woman's head with a veil was a symbol of submission to a husband whose authority over his household was culturally and ecclesiastically sanctioned (1 Cor 11:2). Of interest to readers of this work, the same apostle reminded the Galatians that "in Christ" the differential aspects of this "powering over" had to be reframed and renewed in view of the fact that the New Covenant brought an equalizing dimension to human relations:

> For all of you who were baptized into Christ have clothed yourselves with Christ. There is neither Jew nor Greek, there is neither slave nor free, there is neither male nor female—for all of you are one in Christ Jesus. And if you belong to Christ, then you are Abraham's descendants, heirs according to the promise. (Galatians 3:27–29)

The covenantal aspects in marital relationships are further elaborated in the letter of Paul to the Ephesians, where human relations are framed in analogical terms, derived from God's ways of relating and Christ's sacrificial and empowering love for his bride, the church.

The second term for power (*dunamis*) has been used in Scripture to denote a sense of exerting the capacity to move, achieve, or accomplish some desirable tasks. It may be seen either as an inherent endowment residing in a person or entity by virtue of its nature or an exertion with which a person or entity performs great works (such as miracles). It also refers to the power and resources arising from numbers, such as the power consisting in or resting upon powerful armies. Among business people, the *Wall Street Journal* is regarded as being a powerful newspaper due to the fact that a great number of influential investors and people interested in financial matters subscribe to it. Thus, the term applies to the energy or capacity of a person, group, or entity to achieve projected goals. Modern derivatives may be seen in the labels applied to an explosive capable of a rapid, instant impact (such as dynamite) or to a dynamo representing a constant source of power.

These New Testament concepts denote a construct of a structural nature (who is who, or where a person fits in an organizational chart), applicable to relations and an empowered capacity to animate interpersonal transactions, and aimed at accomplishing desirable results (who does what to whom, and with what effect). Power may be considered as the top-down executive capacity of a person to exert authority (influence, jurisdiction, or control) over others. From the author's perspective, power is the capacity to love, to serve, to accomplish goals, and to fulfill God's revealed agenda for human interactions. In sum, power is the ability to imitate God as dearly beloved children and walk in love, living out the terms of a New Covenant.

The Trinity—the granting Father, the risen Lord, and the actualizing Holy Spirit—is depicted as *being* powerful, as *demonstrating* power, and as *bestowing* or *granting* power upon the human. God's power—both positional and energetic—is demonstrated in great fashion through his creative, redemptive, transforming, renewing, and sustaining works registered in Scripture. The empowering of patriarchs through his covenantal calls, and the empowering of priests, prophets, and kings through their anointing to accomplish God's will by serving on behalf of his people testify to God's delegating authority.

Jesus's power is also depicted in Scripture when he commissioned his disciples after his resurrection: "All authority [ἐξουσία] in heaven and on earth has been given to me" (Matt 28:18). His authority was demonstrated even before his death and resurrection as attested in the gospels. Both his authority and energy were displayed over nature (Matt 4:34–41), over sickness (Mark 2:1–12; 8:22–5; Luke 17:11–19), and over death (John 11:1–54). This power was exerted over the spiritual world as well (Mark 5:1–17). God's power acted on Jesus's resurrection (Eph 1:19–20), raising him from the dead and bestowing upon him a name above all names—*Kyrios*, the Lord—representing *the* maximum authority (see Phil 2:1–11).

Part II: Principles Derived from the New Covenant in Marital Transactions

The gospel is depicted as being the *power* (δύναμις) of God to save the human from sin (Rom 1:16). After his ascent, Jesus sent the promised Holy Spirit: "But you will receive power (δύναμιν) when the Holy Spirit has come upon you, and you will be my witnesses in Jerusalem, and in all Judea and Samaria, and to the farthest parts of the earth" (Acts 1:8). The Holy Spirit came with force upon the disciples (Acts 2:1–4) in order to empower them to be his witnesses, to do the right things, and to act as representatives of a new brand of priests and prophets (1 Pet 2:9). The Holy Spirit is not to be confused with an abstract concept of a powerful nature—a sort of esoteric flux permeating the universe—but is to be recognized as a person who is powerful, acts with power, and empowers the believer.

POWER AND DELEGATED AUTHORITY

The Lord himself, as the author and finisher of the New Covenant, assured his disciples regarding the power bestowed upon him by the Father: "All authority [power] has been given unto me" (Matt 28:18). Then, he promised to empower his disciples so that they would carry on the task of making disciples of all nations. Beyond this inner circle of followers, the promise of the Holy Spirit was given to those who would believe through generations (Acts 2:39). Thus, the Holy Spirit is the empowering agent of the New Covenant, promised by the Father (Luke 24:49) and the Son (John 7:37); he is the third person of the Trinity, active in the world today.

Those who believe and accept God's terms enter into a binding fellowship with him; they are adopted into his household and are redefined at ontological, positional, and relational levels. Being reformed (regenerated) and embedded "in Christ" defines their justified, acceptable, and validated standing before God. God's power restructures the ontological-relational dimensions of those who believe by changing their hearts and minds and by placing his laws within them by means of the Holy Spirit. God's children under the Old Covenant who felt powered over by the commandments of the Torah, especially as interpreted and applied by the doctors of the law, would now experience the indwelling of God's power intrinsically as the Holy Spirit enabled them to do his will in a more graceful, freeing, and loving way.

Religious leaders at the time of Jesus *powered over* people by placing heavy burdens on them. People's predicament under the Torah was registered as a negative system of indictments, experienced as a heavy yoke placed upon their necks by those who, even as ministers of the Old Covenant, were unable to bear it. The apostle Peter's reference to this concept is found in his address to the religious leaders of Jerusalem on the occasion of the first council held in that city:

> After much discussion, Peter got up and addressed them: "Brothers, you know that some time ago God made a choice among you that the Gentiles might hear from my lips the message of the gospel and believe. God, who knows the

heart, showed that he accepted them by giving the Holy Spirit to them, just as he did to us. He did not discriminate between us and them, for he purified their hearts by faith. Now then, why do you try to test God by putting on the necks of Gentiles a yoke that neither we nor our ancestors have been able to bear? No! We believe it is through the grace of our Lord Jesus that we are saved, just as they are." (Acts 15:7–11, NIV)

Those who are "born of the Spirit" receive the fresh promises delivered by the mediator of the New Covenant: "Take my yoke on you and learn from me, because I am gentle and humble in heart, and you will find rest for your souls. For my yoke is easy to bear, and my load is not hard to carry" (Matt 11:29–30). Thus, a new sense of freedom and dignity derive from following Jesus. The believer's personhood is now grounded on new premises and promises. Those who believe, "receive him" by faith, and obey him are given the *right* (ἐξουσίαν: power, authority) "to become the children of God" (John 14:13). The term used by John refers to the authority or weight granted to those who enter into a covenant with God, being especially endowed with moral influence or spiritual power.

In their gospels, Matthew (10:1), Mark (3:15), and Luke (9:1) employed both terms to express the concepts of power (δύναμιν) and authority (ἐξουσίαν). Scripture affirms the fact that, having called his disciples, Jesus gave them authority (ἐξουσίαν) over unclean spirits so they would be able to cast them out and to heal every disease and sickness (Matt 10:1; Mark 6:7). Luke alluded to the fact that Jesus delegated and invested upon them the power (*exousia*) "to tread on evil forces" (symbolized as "serpents and scorpions") (Luke 10:19). Matthew registers Jesus's commissioning words to the twelve, delivered with empowering tones: "heal the sick [ἀσθενοῦντας θεραπεύετε, *asthenountas therapeuete*], raise the dead; cleanse lepers, cast out demons. Freely you received, freely give" (Matt 10:7–8).

In John 10:18, Jesus assertively affirms his jurisdiction over his own actions, will, and intention, which he received from the Father. Likewise, empowered disciples may feel both secure and assertive about their convictions, status, capacities, and endowments. From a natural perspective, Pilate thought that he had the authority to set Jesus free, and he addressed Jesus with naïve one-upmanship: "Don't you realize I have power either to free you or to crucify you?" To which Jesus answered, "You would have no power over me if it were not given to you from above" (John 19:10–11, NIV). From a metacognitive perspective, Jesus responded assertively, stressing the fact that the governor's authority was a concession allowed by a higher power, and that he himself was in control of his own life—which *he freely gave* for humankind at the cross.

Paul stressed the fact that his delegated apostolic authority was an empowered capacity to build and to serve others—not a prerogative to control or manipulate them (2 Cor 10:8; 13:10). Yet, although Paul was endowed with a delegated apostolic authority, he did not take advantage of it to impinge upon, demand, or claim his apostolic rights, such as the right to be attended to or to be supported by the church. He did not use this privilege, but worked with his own hands, demonstrating an exemplary "servant leadership" worthy of imitation (Acts 20:33–35; 2 Thess 3:8–9).

Examples of delegated authority are registered in Scripture, such as the hierarchical relationship between a master and his servants (Mark 13:34) or Roman emperor and his centurion (a commander of a hundred soldiers). In the case of a centurion encountering Jesus, the notion of being *under* a higher authority empowered the commander to exercise authority *over* others. That is precisely what the centurion recognized in Jesus: he perceived his power and authority as being endowed, delegated, or bestowed upon him by a higher authority—a powerful source, namely God. Jesus had demonstrated that he was subject to the Father's will. The Roman centurion understood this principle, invoking it on behalf of his sick servant:

> I did not even consider myself worthy to come to you. But say the word, and my servant will be healed. For I myself am a man under authority, with soldiers under me. I tell this one, "Go," and he goes; and that one, "Come," and he comes. I say to my servant, "Do this," and he does it. (Luke 7:7–8)

Jesus praised the faith of this man as he understood that Jesus had all authority and power because he was subject to a higher command, just as he himself was. Living under the authority of a top-down agency with granting power allows for the exercise of authority over others.

In today's egalitarian, democratic culture, it is not popular to preach, teach, or counsel about living "under authority" of any sort. As prodigal sons and daughters, we are prone to claim our own rights, to reject God's authority in order to live in our own desires, and to do our own thing. Scripture makes allusions to the original rebellion of an archangel against God's authority, who aimed with a defiant, dejecting, and obstinate attitude and was cast down to Earth as a result. The prophet's expressions in voicing the archangel Lucifer's statements are marked by narcissistic self-centeredness, registered as internal dialogues: "You said to yourself, '*I will* climb up to the sky. Above the stars of El I will set up my throne. *I will* rule on the mountain of assembly on the remote slopes of Zaphon. *I will* climb up to the tops of the clouds; *I will* make myself like the Most High!'" (Isa 14:12–15, italics mine). (We may add, "I will take a selfie picture and send it all over the world.") Since his fall, after being cast down and becoming the "prince of this world," the tempter of human beings wants to be imitated by his followers, appealing to human egocentrism. Needless to say, Lucifer's rebellious and selfish stance has gained a lot of followers and sympathizers among humans across the ages and cultures, reflected even among our own communities of faith, couples, and families.

Pauline advice and command is for both husbands and wives to be "subject to one another" based upon a major premise: "out of reverence for Christ" (Eph 5:21). The basis of marital transactions is a mutual submission in love, both living under the lordship of Christ. The *dominion* of Christ has a different connotation today as compared to the original setting in which the term was used. The readers may note that the United States was born out of a premise—no taxation without representation—which was based upon principles of fairness, justice, and equal rights. The consequential rejection of the British royal authority followed with the establishment of a democracy that, so far, has been functional among us. As members of a democratic culture, we do not bow down to any royalty. Nevertheless, we may bow down before other sources of power that define, control, and establish the trends that pressure and squeeze us into our cultural world. The idolatrous elements that permeate our culture and our person (economic status, prestige, fame, attributions of success, or the self as the ultimate source of authority) may be implicitly or explicitly regarded as exerting some authority over us.

THE EXERCISE OF POWER AND AUTHORITY

Authority is often used for power that has been legitimately delegated or ascribed by social structures endemic to human relations. As such, the exercise or the administration of power may be seen as being good and just or as evil and unjust. In social systems and corporate organizations, power may be described as flowing downward (the superior influencing the inferior) or upward (the subordinates influencing the decisions of those in power or leadership). Hierarchical systems are set up in ways so that those above (defined as those who are superior or have more authority) influence those below (those who are inferior or endowed with less authority). Egalitarian systems seek to establish an even flow of equitable power, mutually influencing one another.

The capacity to adopt a higher perspective and to perceive things from a "superior plane" frees a person from a narrow, culturally embedded definition of personhood and allows for a reframed perception of being "in Christ," which yields a renewed vision of both men and women as new creations embedded in Christ and grounded in a defining God (Gal 3:28).[1] This position empowers men and women to feel securely attached, to be humble before the Lord, and to be bold in their actualization of their freedom in Christ. In Paxson's emphasis, the Holy Spirit is the indwelling, infilling, cleansing, controlling, guiding, and anointing person at work in the life of both genders, who are joint inheritors of God's kingdom. Under this authority, men and women are less prone to assume one-upmanship over one another, being eager to serve one another in love and with respect.

Again, to power over is to exert influence upon another, to control some aspects of the other, or to place burdens on another. Examples of "powering over" may be found in dictatorial systems, demagogic manipulation, hierarchical setups, abusive situations, and covert manipulation in passive-aggressive situations. In all cases, the

---

1. Paxson, *Life on the Highest Plane*.

unequal distribution of power (control or authority) is a key variable. How this distribution originates is another question. The rich, despotic, forceful, or controlling parties have something in common: they have access to resources and mechanisms to exert their influence and to act in a top-down fashion toward those considered their inferiors.

In terms of structural aspects observed in relational configurations, hierarchical systems tend to foster powering over one another as those in control of physical, financial, and social resources exert their authority over those lower in rank or status. Their decision-making capacity receives the support and reinforcement derived from their relative status. The social power at play in dyadic relationships or in family systems may be assessed at different levels. The referential, social, or relational power may be delegated, achieved, projected, or despotically established.

- *Delegated power.* A person is conferred status by means of a higher referential, defining entity, divinely or socially bestowed upon the empowered person who, as a consequence, exerts power over those under such authority. Sanctioning by a divine authority may allow for the establishment of a hierarchical structure; humanly constituted powers (such as a democratically elected official) may also allow for respectful structures, characterized by representative, federal, or elected authority. God or cultural sanctions are taken and displayed in ascriptions made to the authority of parents over children or some headship of husbands over wives as found in hierarchical interpretations of scriptural passages. Egalitarian systems see the application of scriptures defining both partners as being redefined ontologically and relationally in Christ as co-heirs of grace and empowered by the Spirit. Both partners consider themselves as being endowed with delegated and referential sources of power to engage in mutual submission to one another;

- *Achieved power.* The person "gathers" or "earns" power on the basis of an overt display of influential character traits and personal behaviors. A person achieves power that emerges from a long sequence of interpersonal attitudes and behaviors, resulting in a social influence of a positive and benevolent nature and worthy of respect and honor. On the other hand, this interpersonal power may acquire a negative or fearsome quality and convey a sense of fear. This negative display leads to defensiveness, avoidance, fearful submission, or covert hostility. Husbands or wives may exert these emergent properties, acting on the basis of their achieved power—be it positive or negative. On a negative note, this power emerges as a result of the conditioning process established between a fearful, submissive, codependent, or needy partner and a dominant, controlling person who is prone to usurp and control the other in a disrespectful, demeaning, or despotic fashion. On the positive side, a person's admirable character qualities and exemplary conduct may emerge and consolidate into an established social, spiritual, and emotional power. These may be features that characterize a servant-leader who is not despotic or controlling, but loving and caring;

- *Projected power.* This kind of power may be seen as the "halo effect" observed as the result of the projected attributions cast upon a person who does not necessarily possesses this power, but is approached and treated as if he or she does. The unconscious wishes, needs, desires, and fantasies of those who want this person to possess the desirable qualities, endowments, and authority enter into play, regardless of whether reality corresponds with their projections. Many individuals experience the need to have a person to securely attach to, depend on, and be grounded in as a source of nurturance, care, protection, and security. On a negative note, a person may be negatively perceived and regarded as being despotic by those who, due to their own unfinished transactions, negative experiences, or traumatic memories, may project negative attributions that are not necessarily present in this person;

- *Despotic power.* A person may impinge upon and impose his or her authority over others without this power being delegated, elected, or projected upon by them. Usually those who are bigger, stronger, or more dictatorial exert their influence unfairly upon those unable to match their thrusting control. Sometimes, partners complement one another in a dysfunctional way: sadistic partners often find masochistic counterparts, and partners whose character shows weak or wavering traits may seek those who demonstrate stronger, controlling stances.

THE HUMAN TEMPTATION: A PROPENSITY TO POWER OVER

Struggles in relationships started after the fall into sin. The pristine transactions were interrupted and distorted after the quest for conscious power took place; following the desires of the eyes, the flesh and prideful ambition became the definers of reality. When partners enter any transaction, the interactive nature of the relationship allows for the development of mutual comparisons, expectations, and demands from each other. These terms denote the quest for the mutual satisfaction of basic needs. The lack of attention to these needs often results in a partner's complaints, insults, injuries, struggles, and violence. In attempts to establish satisfactory transactions, partners may engage in dysfunctional, manipulative, or controlling endeavors.

These transactions aggregate and foster the development of the need for social influence—inherent, allocated, attributed, or projected—which may result in power struggles. Given the natural propensity of humans to define one another and to establish grounds for personal space, expectations, and rights, the emergence of struggles for control are common experiences in human transactions. The anxiety of being found precarious, unacceptable, and faulty is coupled with our basic needs for

Part II: Principles Derived from the New Covenant in Marital Transactions

acceptance, validation, worth, and esteem. In some, the will to power over is more evident, springing from characterological traits and/or socialized attitudes and behaviors. These needs may underlie partners' attempts to control and predict the outcomes of their transactions.

The struggles for personal control may assume many forms. Attempts to know what is going on in the mind and heart of the other and to predict their behaviors are features of the quest to control the anxiety of the unknown and unpredictable. Knowledge about and control of interpersonal circumstances, added to the predictability of possible relational outcomes, are variables that reduce anxiety in partners. Also, the ability to define reality provides a sense of control to the definer. Thus the attempts to define one another (as in labeling or editing one another) are a constant temptation, inherently present in interpersonal relations. To feel secure and protected against any eventual threat or stressor demands the establishment of good personal boundaries. Hence, partners attempt to establish their life-space or emotional territory, marking and securing it by means of defense mechanisms. These defenses protect the ego from emotional harm; yet, carried to extremes, they may isolate or insulate partners from one another and diminish the establishment or consolidation of their intimacy, openness, and connectedness.

Believers under a New Covenant do not experience God's power as something to be afraid of; rather, they are empowered to enter the presence of God through the new, open, living way of access traced by Jesus, the mediator of a New Covenant (Heb 10:19–22). This empowering is not predicated upon human will, effort, or achievement, but is an endowment from God's grace, mercy, and love. Such empowering prompted the author of Hebrews to admonish his readers to "provoke one another to love and good works" (Heb 10:24). Those who have been empowered by God may engage in a mindful and proactive thrust toward one another; that is, they are empowered to behave with mutual encouragement, fellowship, love, and good deeds. Examples of such empowering of one another can be found in the works of Christian authors writing as partners.[2]

The difference between the Pharisees's powering over and Jesus's empowering is obvious. This difference is observed in the manner in which the interpreters applied the law and the way in which Jesus taught. While Pharisees were biased interpreters of the law, Jesus was the giver, the author, of such dicta. Jesus's teachings were pointedly contrasted to the usual style employed by scribes, rabbis, and priests: "You have heard . . . but I say unto you" (Matt 5:38–48). The Pharisees were prone to impose their interpretations on people by exercising referential authority, placing burdens on people that they themselves could not carry. On the other hand, Jesus came to take people's burdens upon his shoulders and appealed to those who felt burdened with his invitation: "Come unto me, and I will give you rest" (Matt 11:28). He expressed

---

2. See, for example, Jack and Judith Balswick, *A Model for Marriage*; Aída Spencer et al., *Marriage at the Crossroads*.

his assessment of the human situation and the entrapments of sin by becoming the substitute for all sinners—taking the burdens off the shoulders of repentant sinners, lifting them up, and setting them free.

THE HEADSHIP NOTION AMONG US

We may accept authority as a valid concept in interpersonal relations patterned after God's display and exemplified in the submission of the Son, as well as in the effacing tone of the Holy Spirit, sent in the name of Jesus by the Father. Yet, analogies break down when we face the difficulties present in theological interpretations of "headship" (a sort of interpersonal authority), evidenced in the discrepancies amongst scholars and practitioners on this topic. A passage that offers this challenge is 1 Corinthians 11:3: "But I want you to know that Christ is the head of every man, and the man is the head of the woman, and God is the head of Christ." The rest of the passage (1 Cor 11:4–16) elaborates on such matters.

As it applies to the headship construct, the term *kephale* (κεφαλή), translated as "authority" (as well as "source"), has been the subject of many debates in the field.[3] Both egalitarian and complementarian positions have stated their arguments based upon the same construct, and the interested reader may consult the existing works in the field.[4]

In any case, the servant-leader model may appeal to both perspectives if the model of headship displayed by Christ serves as both as a paradigmatic authority and a service-oriented dedication to be taken into account. Students and interested readers may gather from this work that the crux of the matter—beyond theological arguments—consists of the need for both husbands and wives to be imitators of God as beloved children and to be subject to one another out of their reverence for Christ. Having this transcending perspective—a metacognitive viewpoint—allows for purposeful mindfulness, a super-consciousness of living under God's dominion.

Both husbands and wives need to realize that they do not own one another, but are responsible to administer their relational dyad as stewards before God. Both will render a full account of whatever they have done to one another on "That Day." That is, whatever a husband or wife does toward his or her partner—God's property given for a time under the lordship of Christ—he or she will account to God for at the end of their joint endeavor (2 Cor 5:10).

---

3. We have dealt briefly with such matter in previous chapters. The references in the NT are many and are provided here for the sake of interested readers: Matt 5:36; 6:17; 8:20; 10:30; 14:8, 11; 21:42; 26:7; 7:29–30,37; Mark 6:24–25, 27–28; 12:10; 14:3;15:19,29; Luke 7:38; 7:46; 9:58; 12:7; 20:17; 21:18,28; John 13:9; 19:2, 30; 20:7,12; Acts 4:11; 18:6,18; 21:24; 27:34; Rom 12:20; 1 Cor 11:3–5; 11:7; 11:10;12:21; Eph 1:22; 4:15; 5:23; Col 1:18; 2:10; 2:19; 1 Pet 2:7; Rev 1:14; 4:4; 9:7,17,19; 10:1; 12:1, 3; 13:1, 3; 14:14; 17:3,7,9; 18:19; 19:12.

4. See, for example, Grudem, *Biblical Foundations*; Balswick and Balswick, *A Model for Marriage*; Spencer et al., *Marriage at the Crossroads*.

Part II: Principles Derived from the New Covenant in Marital Transactions

Husbands are encouraged to *give their lives* for their wives in a loving fashion. This analogical command—to imitate Christ's giving of himself for his bride—to love their wives as Christ loves the church—goes beyond "being nice" or "helpful" in their treatment of their partner. Those who love, give: The Father loved the world so much that he gave His only begotten Son; Christ loved the church so much that he gave himself for her; the Spirit loves and gives gifts to the body of Christ. In line with these relational matters, the apostle addressed wives with the instruction to respect their husbands, demonstrating a loving attitude instead of treating them in a contemptuous, demeaning, rejecting fashion. In short, partners were advised *to empower*—not to *power over* one another.

The Balswicks deal with these matters along egalitarian lines with an emphasis on empowering versus powering over one another.[5] Rather than seeking to repress, subjugate, or control a partner's being with controlling attitudes and behaviors, both husbands and wives may consider the freeing, actualizing, and empowering capacity given by God's Spirit to imitate the Trinity's loving, covenantal ways of relating. Rather than appealing to Scriptures as weapons or as instruments to cajole one another, partners may share the life and love that exudes from God's living Word. Rather than employing proof-texts as weapons to dominate or as lever points to buttress their self-gratification, partners are to empower one another with the spirit of the letter.

BEING EMPOWERED BY GOD IN ORDER TO EMPOWER

The teachings of Jesus point to God's desire to relate to humans in empowering ways. Through parables, Jesus taught about the vitality of being empowered to be and to do God's will. He presented the picture of a vine and its branches as a symbol of the necessity of the human to be grounded in him in order to be vitally able to produce the desirable, expected fruits. In a direct fashion, he applied this metaphor to the human predicament: "Without me you can do nothing" (John 15:5). The need of the believing human to *abide* (to remain connected, to lodge, to establish residence) in him is axiomatically stated.

The point made is that the person entering into a covenant with God requires the vital "sap" (the Holy Spirit and the living Word) flowing through his cognitive, affective, motivational, and enactive substructures and processes. Dynamic feeding upon the Word—the absorbing, digesting, elaborating, and transforming aspects of this spiritual metabolic process—is vital in nurturing and energizing the human grounded in God. To actualize this potential, the believer is commanded to abide in him (co-participating in interpenetrated, *perichoretic* fashion) and to remain open and available to the empowering Spirit and Word which flow through his cognitive-affective,

---

5. Balswick and Balswick, *A Model for Marriage*.

motivational, and enactive processes as a living and efficacious agent of sustenance, transformation, renewal, growth, and fruitfulness.

An analogy may be drawn from feedback control systems, depicted in a diagram involving the natural flow of processes in a closed system. They receive the input from internal (interoceptive) or external (exteroceptive) sources, such as the impingement of negative forces at work, temptations, or challenging stressors, and they also receive the feedforward input of a superposed variable—the influx and empowering of the Holy Spirit so as to change the output of the system. It is through coparticipation with the Holy Spirit that a person may change a natural reaction into an empowered response (Fig. 8.1).

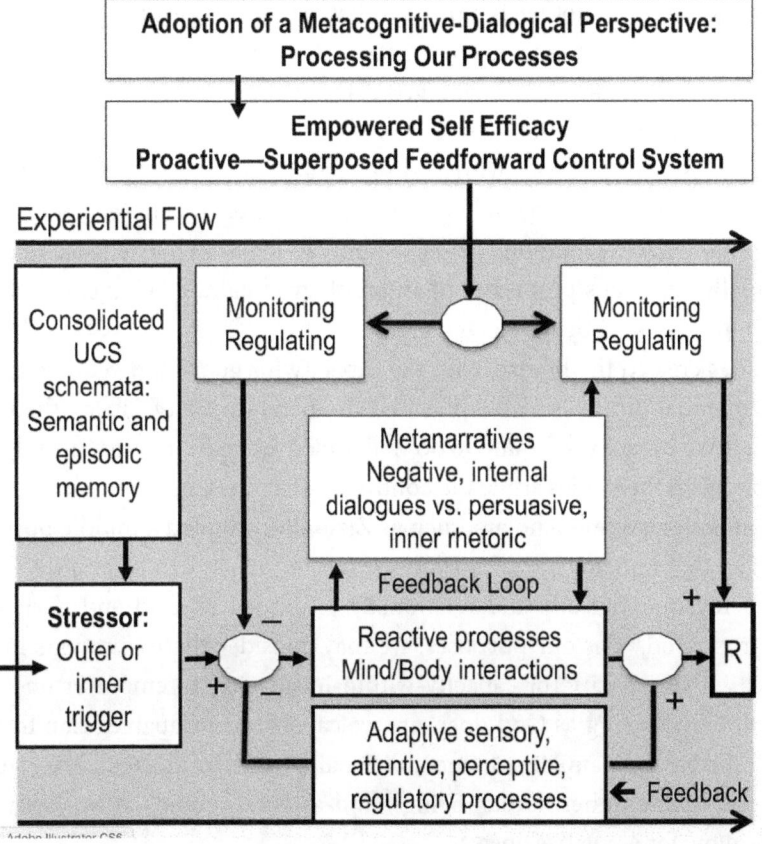

Fig. 8.1: The Person's Output Empowered by the Spirit

This model will be further elaborated in this work, dealing with empowered forgiveness (chapter 15). The illustration presented here is a preview of the postulated manner in which coparticipation with the Holy Spirit enables a believer to accept the challenge to be an imitator of God and to walk in love—not subject to circumstances or vicissitudes, but living by faith—and to enact the terms of the New Covenant: to be and act in a unilateral, unconditional, proactive fashion as a free, empowered, and mindfully purposeful person. The empowering of God is not only an individual matter, but also a communal endowment. The Spirit dwells corporally in the body of Christ; the Spirit abides in the living edifice comprised by believers, defined as "living stones" (1 Pet 2:5). From the root up, the sap of the vine runs through all the branches and enables the living organism to produce fruit. What we gather from this description of reality *from Jesus's perspective* is that we, as a church community, are not capable of exuding a natural, autonomous existence as envisioned by God. His intention is not to foster independent spirits, but to ground us in him, vitally connected to the author and finisher of our salvation that we might exude the properties of the one who is the source of our life, who feeds and sustains us, and who empowers us so that we may be fruitful.

Empowering one another is a process that gathers momentum from the sum of the diverse dimensions expressed covenantally. Acting in a unilateral, unconditional, and proactive fashion, and displaying grace and mercy in doing so, conveys a sense of respect, care, and dedication to one another. Being able to forgive and let go of offenses, while fostering intimacy with openness, transparency, and honesty allows us to empower one another. Covenantal love sets partners free to behave in ways that defy common, mundane expectations (and even human logic) as they engage one another with mutually conscious properties of an ontological nature, being energized by the Holy Spirit to empower the other.

God has created the human with the capacity for good, and yet, due to the Fall and consequential sinfulness, what prevails is human incapacity. Liberal theology emphasizes human capacity to be and to do well under optimal circumstances; Reformed and fundamental theologies argue the contrary—that humans are totally incapable of doing what is right. Some scholars, such as Zizioulas, adopted a middle position and would argue that humans have "capacity within incapacity" to be and do what God desires—being ontologically and relationally grounded in God and deriving their capacity from God.[6] For our purposes, we may consider these questions in light of the capacity or incapacity (or capacity-within-incapacity) to empower one another. In terms of empowering as God does, are we capable or incapable? Can the human take the initiative to be unilateral, unconditional, proactive, graceful, and merciful in order to empower another human being? God-assisted systems at work, enabled by the Spirit, allow for a positive answer.

When the original automobiles came on the scene, they were wonderful machines that facilitated human needs for mobility and transportation. Yet, in terms of technology, they demanded some effort such as in turning and braking. The advances in technology facilitated both by means of power-assisted steering and brakes. In a systemic fashion, the driver applies a foot to the brake pedal and hands to the steering wheel, but the engine provides the energy to do the power-assisted braking and

---

6. Zizioulas, "Human Capacity."

turning. The coparticipation of the purposive human with the power system allows for the optimization of the driving experience. The engagement may be judged to be minimal at the human level, yet it is maximized by the energy provided by the systemic connectedness to the engine. Likewise, we may say that the human possesses "capacity within incapacity" to advance in transactional endeavors with a sense of direction and tempo to do what is right, acceptable, and honorable, as well as the potential to stop on time when facing temptations to do evil. These God-assisted steering and brake systems are empowered by the Holy Spirit in coparticipation with human partners.

INTRINSIC EMPOWERING OF THE HUMAN HEART AND MIND

God's covenantal promise states, *"I will put my laws into their hearts."* That is, the conveying of his expressed will no longer will be something extrinsic, engraved on stone, but will be placed in the tablets of human hearts. If I paraphrase this as a clinical psychologist, I might say that the coparticipation between the Holy Spirit within and the human emotive, sensorial, willful, and enactive processes takes place as the believer surrenders and obeys God's summoning call. Then, the mindfully engaged affect of the person is prompted and propelled toward love—of both God and neighbor—as exuding properties of an ontological nature as the Holy Spirit "pours" such love "into the heart" (Rom 5:5).

Covenantal love is not a forced or fabricated emotion gained through willful, legalistic, or humanistic endeavors. It is the "fruit of the Spirit" (Gal 5:22–23) that emerges as a spiritually natural consequence of being filled with the Holy Spirit in coparticipation with the human believer. The heart of the person is empowered, energized, or "converted" to respond as a top-down, empowered, executive agent. This empowered capacity emerges from the new birth (born of the Spirit) and is strengthened as the believer grows spiritually, becoming more able to regulate her or his emotive, sensible, and empathic functioning.

The admonition to imitate God as beloved children and to walk in love derives from the great commandment. The command to love God with all our hearts, minds, and strength is posed to human beings as subjects, as children, or as individuals who possess the capacity to respond to God's command as free agents. Just as God loves in ecstatic fashion, so humans are commanded to come out of themselves and refine the focus of their attention, faith, and obedience as they respond to God's summoning call.

The command to obey and follow God's ways may appear as a legal injunction to behave; that is, to engage in acts of love based on the notion that love is an act of the will—an event or a series of events. Yet, if we look deeper, loving God and the neighbor can be seen as processes of a cognitive, emotive, and enactive nature, underlying the loving events or behavioral enactments. Moreover, love in essence is allocated deeply in the sub-structural, ontological being as a capacity of *being*, prompting the production of processes of *becoming* a loving person and culminating in acts of love (regarded as fruit or evident works).

An act of love (an event) differs from engaging in a loving process, which unfolds as the result of an attitude, a characterological stance, or a dispositional trait that emanates from an ontological or sub-structural (hypostatic) ground of being. That is, *being a loving person at the core* (sub-structural, ontological level) allows for thinking along loving terms, feeling with loving affect (process level), and behaving in loving ways (overt, observable, or trivial level).

God's granting terms include a major promise: "I will write them [my laws] upon their minds." The empowering of God through the Holy Spirit energizes the cognitive capacities of the believer—mindful awareness, attention, perception, reasoning, attribution of meaning, learning, judgment, and decision-making. These cognitive processes receive the influx of the empowering Spirit: they are interpenetrated, illuminated, and capacitated to engage in higher abstractions and metacognitive levels of discerning—defining reality in a better fashion. The believer's mind is enabled to develop and consolidate beliefs, attitudes, and values in alignment with God's living Word. The indwelling Word capacitates the believer to develop principled norms for living, adequate mental habits, and proper relational stances.

The coparticipation between the interpenetrating Holy Spirit and the human spirit (the inner being as a willing, mindful, and dedicated respondent) allows for spiritual growth, character formation, and maturity. God's empowering is evident in the character qualities of being and in the conduct displayed in concrete behaviors. The renewal of the mind (Rom 12:1–2; Eph 4:23) is effectuated by the intrinsic interaction of the surrendering person and the Spirit—placed within and guiding the cognitive structures, processes, and events. The capacity to live existentially, currently, and actually (as if every day is a new opportunity to engage in proactive, unilateral, unconditional, and loving behaviors) is a potential to be actualized. This realization is achieved by the ongoing "girding up" (tightening or having a grip over) of one's mind. Being metacognitive about one's mindful processes allows for a focused, purposive, and conscious engagement in relations (1 Pet 1:3; Eph 4:23).

BEING IMITATORS OF GOD: EMPOWERING ONE ANOTHER AS GOD DOES

As gathered from the above considerations, to empower is to sanction, capacitate, or authorize a person to be, think, feel, or do what is commendable. Furthermore, to empower is to foster and encourage someone to reach some aim or to reinforce the attitudes, feelings, or endeavors of another along the way to his or her actualization of potential.

God, by virtue of being omnipotent, omniscient, transcendent, and immanent, could choose to power over the created order. The flooding experience in Genesis points to the fact that God can and does display a "powering over" paradigm. If God now chose to ride on a steamroller and flatten everybody, that would be God's prerogative. Yet, God has chosen to bless and to love, to lift and to empower us to stand before His presence as upright creatures made whole through the work of Jesus Christ. Scripture states that one day God will power over creation—not with a flood, but with fire—to create a new heaven and a new Earth. As a matter of fact, that is the eschatological promise: a day will come on which God will power over all creation in an overt, absolute fashion. Nevertheless, God has chosen to covenant in ways that empower us in the here and the now, enabling us to engage in our precarious transactions until "That Day" on which all His children will enjoy a permanent attachment in love with the eternal Father, actualized in a new economy.

In view of God's eternity, how can a father or a mother empower a son, a daughter? How can a husband or wife empower a spouse? How can a minister empower a disciple, a follower of Jesus? How can a member of the body of Christ empower another? These are valid questions to be answered on the basis of a deep understanding of covenantal terms framed in the effort to imitate God as beloved children. Whatever the assignment of position in a relational system is, the same covenantal principles of empowering apply—whether that system is a marriage, a family, or the fellowship of a church community. Power struggles may exist within all three domains, and the desires to control may be present in all. As principles go, instead of burdening and powering over, husbands are to lay down their lives for their wives as Paul reminds us in Ephesians 5. The principle applies not only to marriage, but also to the relation between parents and their children, and between believers who also have to lay down their lives for one another (1 John 3:16).

Loving as Jesus does conveys a sense of trust, peace, and confidence, enabling the other to reach out, to try harder, and to extend beyond the customary aspects of ordinary endeavors. Love in action serves as an energizer in transactions. Well-being may be fostered if two conditions are met: the absence of evil and the presence of goodness. As far as empowering goes, the absence of evil may be seen when the charges one may have against the other are dropped, when burdens placed upon the other are lifted, or when an undesirable thorn in the flesh is removed. The presence of goodness may be seen in the enactment of purposeful behaviors aimed at blessing, reinforcing, or providing satisfaction to the other. Proactively planning endeavors that will "make her day" or "fulfill his needs" may assume all sorts of forms, according to the expressed needs of wives and husbands. To do so in a truly unexpected, unilateral, and unconditional fashion boosts the power of these actions. To surprise one another with spontaneous, random acts of love breaks us away from deadly routines, customary expectations, and boredom.

Part II: Principles Derived from the New Covenant in Marital Transactions

An empowering stance fosters meaningful moments and happenings, providing energy for consistent behavior within a constantly renewed fellowship. This empowering may be a tacit, underlying basis for operations of a daily nature, conveyed through nuanced communication with more positive and fewer negative expressions of a reinforcing nature. The empowering of one another may assume behavioral tones, enacting a repertoire of well-intended actions, aimed at reducing stress, burdens, and expectations as they pertain to the other person. A husband can empower his wife by being proactive, thoughtful, and purposeful in setting contingencies to facilitate and fulfill her life's desires, goals, and achievements as a person.

As a note of interest, marriage covenants among humans differ from the typological marriage covenant between Christ and his bride in terms of the disparity between their ontological status, their contributive power or efforts, and their perfection-status interacting along their partnership at work. In egalitarian models, two humans start from the same basis: Both partners are made in the *Tselem Elohim*, and both are counted as sinners due to the Fall. Both then proceed along God's design: being reformed, transformed, and conformed to the image of the Son. Both are receptors of grace and mercy and stand on the same footing before God, being defined in Christ. As such, their cultural and social differences vanish (Gal 3:28). As they engage in a marriage covenant, both are subject to one another out of reverence to Christ (Eph 5:21).

To empower is not just an event or a series of events, but a process. It represents a stance, an attitude of mind and heart that is conveyed with respect, sincerity, and integrity. To empower is to decenter from one's needs, wants, and claims and enable the other in order to foster the possibilities of her or his endowments, gifts, or efforts to be engaged in a more adequate, functional, or purposive fashion. Thus, to empower is to provide positive reinforcement by purposefully conveying a positive attitude, sharing, rewarding, enhancing, or uplifting the other.

To empower is also to remove perceived or actual hindrances experienced by the other to allow her or him to experience more freedom, lightness, peace of mind, rest, or relaxation. To empower is to lift the burdens of the other and bear them with and for the other. A sense of joy or happiness may result from this empowering. With empathic understanding, a partner may assess the possibility and need to "be there" for the other when noticing his or her predicament in facing a challenge or any endeavor that demands effort, energy, courage, or dedication. The challenge in such cases is to consistently express a respectful attitude along the way—without conveying any kind of demeaning or patronizing stance.

Redefining and recasting codependency and triangulation. In the domains of systems theory, structural and strategic approaches, as it pertains to family and couples work, it is customary for counselors and therapists to emphasize the establishment of boundaries, the differentiation of partners, and the mutuality of transactions. The fear of enmeshment and codependency runs high in the American way of doing things, so as to avoid negative buzzwords and concepts such as "codependency" and "enabling" in transactions. Due to the fact that many people in relationships suffer from oppression, manipulation, neglect, and abuse, counselors and therapists are prompt to take care of therapeutic business by empowering such people with insight and cognitive-behavioral strategies in order to ward off possible entrapments in codependency and enablement. Yet, at times, these efforts may miss the point when it comes to a true realization of a more graceful, merciful, and empowering endeavor prompted by a conscious adherence to God's principles found in covenantal expressions.

Codependency has been adopted as an undesirable trait to be addressed in therapy, empowering people to be free, unbound, and assertive with the ability to set limits. A person who engages in codepedent behaviors that reinforce maladaptive patterns is defined as being an enabler. We would not label the Spirit as being a codependent although he is an enabler—of desirable behaviors. The Spirit coparticipates with the human without losing freedom or dignity; the Spirit is free, unbound, and willing to be in us. Moreover, the Spirit enables us to do what we cannot do for ourselves. If the same Spirit abides in both partners, and both partners abide in Christ, the possibility exists that both will exert a positive influence on each other. We have defined this condition as being interdependent after the *perichoresis* of the Trinity. As a matter of fact, to allow oneself to be influenced by the other is stated as being one of the several positive factors enunciated by Gottman in his extensive research with couples in his "love lab" at Washington University.[7] Thus, without denying the need to address the negative connotations of codependency as it appears in therapeutic renderings, we may reframe this concept and redefine codependency in positive terms. In this case, interdependence is the condition in which the variations due to one variable positively affect the variations of another variable. Mutual feedback and reciprocity may create a positive momentum, allowing for a deeper alliance and a more powerful thrust animating the relationship.

The same argument applies to "triangulation" in marriage. This term has been defined in systems theory as the condition in which a partner who is experiencing difficulties with the other tries to engage a third party in order to "triangulate" him or her in a manipulative, advantageous, or unfair fashion. This triangulation confers a dysfunctional, precarious, and unfair sense of stability to the manipulative partner. The therapeutic aim is to "de-triangulate" the couple and to encourage them to engage in dyadic relationships of a functional nature. Yet, in a covenantal marriage, invoking the presence of the person, the power, and presence of the Holy Spirit into the partnership does not necessarily produce such negative connotations. In times of distress, partners do not seek the help of the Spirit in order to manipulate or control one another, but to enable their joint efforts and arrive at desirable solutions. This redefined triangulation renders it a contingency in which both partners are empowered by a transcendent—yet immanent—third party so as to experience a new and better partnership.

7. Gottman et al., *Ten Lessons*.

Part II: Principles Derived from the New Covenant in Marital Transactions

CONCLUSION: EMPOWERING ONE ANOTHER

In practical terms, to empower is a stance/process to be enacted behaviorally in an ongoing fashion. In daily transactions, partners may proactively decide to engage in mindful endeavors, imitating God's ways:

- When, due to any negative contingency or event, one notices any hint of disappointment, dejection, despair, or defeat in the semblance, attitude, stance, or disposition of a partner, one determines to be emotionally, cognitively, and behaviorally there for him/her;

- To provide a sense of hope, faith, and courage to be, think, feel, or do something positive in order to respectfully assist, promote or enable a partner's thoughts, attitudes, feelings, and behaviors. To support a partner in his/her attempts to cope with or resolve a situation, providing interactive presence and respectful, non-opinionated feedback throughout the deliberations arising through dialogue;

- To be there as a soothing, validating presence when a partner experiences anxiety, dread, or fear associated with negative contingencies, challenges, or demands. To be a sounding board for her/his musings, conjectures, worries, and concerns;

- To adopt a detached, yet mindful, non-judgmental stance in listening to accounts of anxious metacognitive styles—such as threat monitoring, worrying, anticipatory musings, and catastrophic thinking. Then, to purposefully and mindfully engage in fostering faith, hope, and either fight or relaxation responses versus anxiety;

- To listen attentively and empathically without necessarily providing direct opinions or judgments, but engaging the partner's capacity to reason, employ logic, regulate, and modulate emotions, and engage in desirable coping styles;

- To be there as a sounding board when a partner experiences depressive feelings, concerns, or behaviors. To offer a supportive presence, accepting and validating the person's state in order to mindfully engage his/her capacities to capture, define, challenge, or reframe negative thoughts, reasoning, or judgments. To aid in the process of addressing negative inner dialogues and styles of thinking—ruminations about negative events, attributions of personal failures, inadequacies, etc., guilt feelings associated with such, or shameful considerations about inadequacy, incompetence, etc.;

- To be there without pushing too much (no singing to the afflicted heart, as it is obnoxious to do so, according to Proverbs 25:20) and without reinforcing depressive concerns either;

- To provide a positive yet respectful presence, aiding in the process of challenging and replacing negative views of the self, the world, the future, and to provide mutual encouragement, faith, and hope.

In sum, it is through the empowering of the Holy Spirit that a partner in marriage or a member of a family transacting with other members may be:

- Able and willing to be and act in a unilateral fashion if necessary and functional;
- Able and willing to be and act in an unconditional fashion, if necessary;
- Proactive in dealings, anticipating and planning ahead;
- Able to dispense grace to undeserving others, empowered as a free agent;
- Able to show mercy toward the offending parties without feeling like a loser;
- Able to forgive as God forgave in Christ;
- Able to let go of offenses and move on freedom, not keeping an account of evil;
- Able to convey respect, honor, dignity, acceptance, and validation to the other;
- Able to invite and foster intimate deals with a sincere attitude;
- Able to renew and live existentially every day—not trapped in meaningless, mindless, and deadly routines.

These are the terms of a New Covenant in action, and partners under the auspices of the Holy Spirit and wise in the Word may engage in imitating the Father's ways in a practical, ongoing fashion.

Chapter 9

The Empowered Capacity to Be Unilateral in a Bilateral Deal

To enter into a covenant is to share or to cut a treaty, alliance, or contractual agreement between two parties. Covenants are bilateral in nature, except in cases involving a granting disposition on the part of a giver offering benefits without claiming any reciprocity. In particular, marriage was defined as being a special covenant before God, where two parties mutually bind themselves in an agreement of profound significance. Obligations are mutually pledged and accepted, and privileges are promised on both sides. In that way, the deal resembles a parity covenant between equals.

It is within such covenants that plenty of opportunities arise for the terms to be disregarded, neglected, or violated by one or both partners. In these circumstances, a partner's empowered capacity—prompted by a metacognitive stance endowed with grace and mercy—to engage unilaterally emerges as a possibility to be enacted. The decision of a partner to act in a unilateral and proactive manner is a necessary step in the process of effecting a desirable change in a system experiencing dysfunction, failure, or brokenness. A willful partner's unilateral stance and initiative (born out of grace and mercy) are functional and necessary in the case of realigning an original commitment gone astray, reconciling a discrepancy in expectations and their fulfillment, or redirecting a course of action that deviated from original plans. Such endeavors may prove to be essential in attempts aimed at restoring the covenantal terms and achieving a better bilateral deal. The "bigger person" may employ "I will . . ." statements of a unilateral nature rather than "If you . . . then I" statements that apply in bilateral deals.

A WORD ON UNILATERAL COVENANTS

God's unilateral covenants are exemplified in his deals with Noah, Abraham, and David. In Noah's case (Gen 9:9–17), God promised that never again would all life be destroyed by water. This deal also had a "sign" (a rainbow in the sky) that would remind Noah's descendants of God's unilateral covenant. In Abraham's case, as the deal was cut, only God passed through the split animals with his flaming torch. A promise was made to bless Abraham personally, to make him a blessing to others, to multiply his descendants, to make a great nation out of him, and to grant him land.

A sort of *verba solemnia* was pronounced, as God told Abram that he could "know for certain" (perhaps covenant terminology to attest to the seriousness of the oath) that God would deliver his promises. In ratifying his covenant with Abraham, God's expression, "'I solemnly swear by my own name,' decrees the LORD" appears as a binding covenantal oath (Gen 22:16).

In Abraham's day, a covenant could be established between two individuals as in the case of Abraham buying a plot or a cave for the burial of his wife Sarah from a Hittite lord. In ancient Mesopotamia, treaty-type covenants existed in which a conquering king (suzerain) would offer protection to a subjugated king (vassal). In return, the vassal king would send the suzerain a yearly tribute. Also, in those days, certain covenant ceremonies involved each party presenting a representative (a substitutionary animal), cutting it in half, and placing the parts opposite to each other to make a way for the parties to go through. Each party would walk between the split animals proclaiming their part of the covenant and making an oath (a way of saying "So may I be split if I do not fulfill the terms of this covenant"). Ceremonially, the animals added a symbolic reminder of the consequences that would follow if the terms of the covenant were violated.

In the covenant with Abraham, only God went through the split animals. Abraham fell asleep and woke up with God's presence certifying the terms of a unilateral, unconditional, and proactive covenant. God entered into a relationship with Abraham by mercy and grace, and the only thing Abraham did was to believe God and accept the promise by faith.

God initiated the relationship and desired a response to his unilateral grant: "I will confirm my covenant as a perpetual covenant between me and you. It will extend to your descendants after you throughout their generations" (Gen 17:7–8). Note the pronouns: *your* God, *their* God. A personal, as well as communal, aspect is stressed—a differentiated, yet mutually binding promise. The promise itself is an *unconditional* proposition. This covenantal theme runs throughout Scripture (see OT references, including Gen 17:6–8; Exod 20:2; 29:45; Lev 11:45; Ps 124:1–5; Jer 32:38; Ezek 11:20; 34:30; 36:28, etc., as well as NT references where God is *for us* in Rom 8:31; 2 Cor 6:16–18; and Rev 21:2 ff.).

God's commitment in covenant involved more than a particular expression bracketed in space and time. The unilaterally given promise encompassed the totality of God's redemptive process, conveying a sense of God's omniscient foreknowledge of an unfurling design exemplified in the election of Abraham and his Israelite descendants, and the future inclusion of Gentiles who by faith would jointly comprise the body of Christ, the church. This eternal design unfolds in Scripture as an actualizing process including the forming and re-forming of the fallen human through God's calling, justification, transformation, conformation to his standard, empowering perseverance, and final glorification.

Part II: Principles Derived from the New Covenant in Marital Transactions

Covenantal terms have been abstracted and synthesized, conveying the unifying theme of God's divine presence and fellowship: "My presence will go with you" (Exod 33:14); "I will be with you" (Isa 43:2; Matt 28:20); and "I will dwell among them" (Exod 25:8) are ongoing scriptural expressions, as well as promises of divine protection, supply of needs, healing, empowering, and so on. God's relentless pursuit of his people with grace, love, mercy, and blessings is embedded in his encompassing design. The names of YHWH, being so diverse, reveal the same thrust: "I AM the Lord your provider" (Gen 22:14); "I AM the Lord your banner" (Exod 17:15); "I AM the Lord your healer" (Exod 15:16); and so on.

IS THE NEW COVENANT UNILATERAL OR BILATERAL?

Reformed theology appeals to the bilateral bases of covenant at large, while at the same time emphasizing the unilateral thrust displayed by God in matters such as the believers' election, their call to belong to God's people, and their empowered perseverance which capacitates them to remain secure in God's will and eternal purpose. The blessings of the covenant apply in the present to both Jews and Gentiles. The initial, unilateral thrust of God's grace is responded to by the Spirit's empowering of human repentance and faith, by means of which the believers enter into a covenantal transaction. Such a living relationship is experienced as being positional, existential, and bilateral in nature. The believing human seeks to love and obey, to be thankful and to persevere, all in a living transaction that seeks to please and glorify God. As the Reformed catechism puts it, the chief purpose of humans is to glorify God and to enjoy him forever. Of course, God's unilateral deals in the here and now are not ruled out, as God may sovereignly intervene in the course of personal, corporate, and universal history as he pleases.

Believers who adopt a Dispensationalist position regard the New Covenant as originating with God as well. This covenant appeals to the same salvific basis: God's unilateral grace in sending Jesus to be the savior of sinners—whose person and work achieved our redemption. Also, it relies on his blood shed at the cross, considered as being the ratifying element of the covenant, presented by the mediator to the Father on our behalf. The appropriation of the terms of the covenant is contingent upon the believer's repentance, faith, and obedience to God's call. The believer engages in a bilateral relationship with God through the mediation of Jesus, empowered by the Holy Spirit. The believer strives to persevere in faith and seeks to please God in worship and service.

In Dispensationalist terms, if a "second round" of covenanting history is to take place in the future between God and all Israel, this deal will be initiated once more by God's proactive, unilateral, and unconditional will in action. This prompting will be responded to by a repenting nation that will finally accept their delivering Messiah. In any case, this book is not about eschatology, but focuses on how to derive analogies from the New Covenant in the present in order to live a life characterized by walking in love. The unilateral thrust to accept, validate, love, challenge, correct, and edify one another is to be adopted by any faithful believer who is willing, able, and ready to see that *in Christ* (a new creation) there is no Jew or Gentile, no slave or free, no male or female, and hopefully, no Reformed or Dispensationalist claiming one-upmanship, as the monopoly of absolute truth belongs to Jesus alone.

As an exemplary covenant, the manner in which God acted toward the human may be adopted and followed by all believers who may enter into an intimate and loving covenantal relation such as marriage. Both partners may imitate God as dearly beloved children and walk in love, taking the initiative to serve, care for, or bless one another. Members of a family likewise may follow unilateral initiatives when needed or demanded by challenging circumstances. Parties entering into a community covenant—whether Jews or Gentile followers of Jesus—may see themselves as enacting unilateral terms in the hopes of promoting positive, functional, and desirable interactions of a healthy, bilateral nature. Whether they understood such terms as being preliminary and anticipatory enactments of the real fulfillment of the promised covenant in some future day or simply actualized these covenantal terms in the present, the functional value appears to be the same. In both cases, beyond academic or scholarly debates, disciples live as imitators of God and glorify him in engaging in deeds of a loving nature in the here and now.

HUMAN CAPACITY WITHIN INCAPACITY TO BE UNILATERAL

A unilateral (one-sided) contract is a deal in which one party (the granting or giving person) makes a promise in exchange for an act (or abstention from acting) by another person (the recipient of the grant or gift). If the receiver acts on the giver's promise, the giver is legally obligated to fulfill the contract, but a receiver cannot be forced to act (or not act) because no return promise has been made to the giver. After a receiver has acted upon the terms of this contract, only one enforceable promise exists: that of the giver.

As an example of a unilateral deal, a reward may be offered or stipulated, such as, "Anyone who returns my lost cell phone will get a hundred dollars." The person offering the reward cannot demand or claim anything from anyone to fulfill the reward offer. The responsibility rests on the side of the person making the offer, both to promise and to deliver the promise. Receivers are not obliged to do much, except to fulfill the terms of the promise if they want to receive the reward. In extreme cases, a potential receiver can sue the offering party for breach of contract if the person does not provide (pay the promised amount) after the receiver has fulfilled the contract's requirements (to give back the lost cell phone to the giver).

Part II: Principles Derived from the New Covenant in Marital Transactions

The basic distinction between God's deals and parity covenants is that the covenantal transactions originating from God are endowed with a unilateral and proactive energy. As God engages the human, the response of a believing person acting in faith and obedience turns the covenant into a bilateral deal. Slanted as it may appear, this transaction is regarded as desirable by God, who exceeds in grace, mercy, faithfulness, power, love, and justice far above the human party.

The New Covenant has been presented as being unilaterally established, but bilaterally engaged as a believer responds to these terms. It expresses God's desire to have fellowship with us and invites us to enter into such a deal. The notion of entering a unilateral covenant in the absolute sense of the word is really a contradiction in terms. A covenant is essentially an agreement between two or more parties, assuring a fair, just, peaceful, and life-enhancing deal. It is necessary that both parties entering the transaction adhere to the stipulations, demands, and privileges outlined in the clauses of a contract. The nature of a *quid pro quo* is based on the understanding that *both* parties feel like winners. Neither partner wants to be taken for granted—but to be treated fairly and reciprocally. Thus, the logical expectation is that a good deal would be characterized by bilateral and conditional transactions.

Problems arise because of the human incapacity to remain perfectly within the stipulations and expectations of a *quid pro quo*. Human beings are subject to the entropic and negative effects of the "law of sin" that impinge upon their deformed state of being. It is only through the redemptive power of God's covenant that human reformation, transformation, and renewal are possible. The doctrine of human depravity—as stated in both Reformed and Dispensationalist perspectives—is the one that receives most empirical evidence. Therefore, it is virtually impossible to expect the enactment of a perfect covenant between humans prone to sin, as one or both parties eventually will fail to fully enact its terms. From any reasonable perspective, in spite of pledges, promises, wishes, and desires, it seems quite difficult to envision a perfect or fair contract being flawlessly enacted due to human weakness. The wish is there, but "the flesh is weak."

We are reminded that even the most perfect law, given under optimal circumstances by the greatest mediator of old, was broken. Moses, the lawgiver (defined as the "meekest man" on the planet), was the first to break the law: he smashed the God-given tablets. After God's call, Moses fasted forty days and nights and was given the two tablets of stone with God's inscriptions of the Ten Commandments. With an effulgent face—radiating the glory of God—he came down Mount Sinai in order to mediate a covenant between God and humans. This covenant was described as being a perfect deal by David (Ps 19:7); the apostle Paul refers to it in the same terms (Rom 7:12). Yet, in the context of these awesome circumstances, Moses, after witnessing the orgiastic display of the Israelites who had made a golden calf for themselves in his absence and had given themselves to all kinds of excesses, lost his temper and broke the law.

God's covenant with Israel was a display of graceful nature, although it appeared to be predicated on their behavioral and attitudinal obedience to the given commandments. Scripture reads, "Now if you obey me fully and keep my covenant, then out of all nations you will be my treasured possession" (Exod 19:5–6). God's will was to bless the people and to finally redeem them in spite of their disobedience, defeat, and degradation. In covenantal terms of old, the positive outcomes of obeying them would result in God's blessings. These terms were stipulated and enacted as a bilateral, conditional deal.

The Old Covenant made it simple: those who would obey and remain in the terms stipulated by God would be blessed and have positive results as God's care, protection, and provision would flow in a graceful fashion toward them. On the other hand, disobedience would bring curses and negative consequences. Gathering the people at the foot of Mount Sinai, Moses mediated the terms of a covenant to them, reading the terms as if these came directly from the mouth of God. The response to the commandments was affirmative with the Israelites giving their oath to do everything God told them to do. Moses took the initiative to seal the transactions with blood, sprinkling the objects pertaining to God's side; also the people gathered in order to ratify the deal. The nature of the event could be described as a bilateral, conditional covenant involving God, Israel, and Moses as a mediator.

The law was perfect, holy, and good. The terms were fair and just. The conditions set forth were aimed at the optimization of contingencies to allow humans to obey and walk in God's ways. Nevertheless, due to human weakness and their propensity to disobey and rebel against God, the covenantal terms were broken repeatedly. God acted in history with consequential chastisement—to treat Israel with grace over and over. The covenant proved to be a preamble, a foretaste of better things to come from God's side. In the writings of Paul to the Galatians, the law is compared to a *pedagogos* (a tutor who brings the child to the real master). Its main purpose, or end, was Christ: his person and work, which actualized a better covenant. It was given until "the seed of Abraham" would come and display in incarnate fashion what God's will required in the covenant.

A reading of Romans indicates that God acted unilaterally throughout history, but especially in sending the Son to this world (no one asked for him or brought him down); God acted without relying on a human counselor in sending Jesus to the cross (even when we were sinners, far away from God, in darkness). God acted unilaterally in resurrecting him from the dead, even as humans were totally ignorant as to what was happening and had no power to do anything about it. The human contribution was negative, defined in terms of disobedience, degradation, scorn, and the like. The picture presented in the second chapter of Romans is a bleak one: a deformed human totally incapable of reaching out to seek God or take any initiative to connect with him in a covenant.

Part II: Principles Derived from the New Covenant in Marital Transactions

Human depravation—a doctrine ignored by most psychological systems—is depicted in the first two chapters of the letter, concluding with the verdict, "All have sinned, and come short of the glory of God" (Rom 3:23). As a consequence, all are excluded and far away from God's premises and promises. Then, righteousness *apart from the law* is imputed to those who believe, and they are justified by faith so as to have peace with God (Rom 4; 5). God's salvific act re-generates the believer and re-forms what sin has deformed. Then, the process of re-socialization (sanctification or transformation of being) is depicted as a result of engaging with God in coparticipation with the Spirit (Rom 6). The struggle between the incapacities of the sinful nature and the empowering aspects of God's Spirit is presented in vivid detail (Rom 7). The apostle Paul conveys an introspective glimpse of his internal dialogues between the deformed and transformed self, mediated by the empowered and metacognitive, re-formed self, concluding with a victorious tone in chapter 8. Paul invites the believers to see the effects of God's covenantal redemption: they are freed and empowered to live as empowered beings, free from condemnation and secure in Christ.

In a parenthesis—skipped by replacement theologians, emphasized by Dispensationalists—Romans presents a challenging section (chapters 9—11) in which the sovereign and unilateral acts of God are displayed, stating the restoration of His people as a promised fulfillment of the New Covenant. Warnings and exhortations are given to the Gentiles, especially those in the capital city, the center of the empire. Paul stresses the need to remain in faith, obedience, humility, and the fear of God. Believers are not to take God for granted, boast about their status, or diminish the value and intent displayed in God's grace, mercy, and love in electing his own.

The explanations about God's sovereign plan with respect to Israel and the Gentiles sets the framework for more practical implications in chapter 12. Based on an understanding of such mercies, we believers are exhorted to present ourselves as living sacrifices and to be transformed by the renewal of our minds (Rom 12:1–2), so as to do the works of God and fulfill the terms of his covenant. The theology of the cross, and the praise and worship surrounding it, come after the humans are approached with the message of the gospel and understand the salvific move as coming from God unilaterally in grace and mercy. Humans then respond to this message with faith and obedience, enacting a bilateral covenant.

The letter to the Ephesians presents even more directly the unilateral dealings of God, who acts on our behalf in a "top-down" fashion. It starts with God's intentions and will to bless the human even before the foundation of the world, making sure that we are seated in heavenly places in Christ (chapter 1), then commanding us to walk (chapter 4), and finally admonishing us to be firm against all odds (chapter 6).

Examples of humans engaging unilaterally, unconditionally, and proactively can be found in scriptural accounts. The case of Job is a good illustration: he presented sacrifices and offerings to God on behalf of his children ahead of time, just in case they detoured from God's ways and committed sinful acts (Job 1:5). Pointed aspects of a unilateral, unconditional, and proactive nature are gathered from Luke's account of Jesus's intercession for Peter before the disciple would deny him three times (Luke 22:31). The unilateral, steadfast love of the mediator of a New Covenant for his own is succinctly described: Jesus is the one who *"loved them to the full extent of his love"* (John 13:1). Extending his unilateral capacity toward us and binding us in a bilateral way, Jesus sets forth a "new commandment"—to love one another as he did (John 13:34). It is proper for us to imitate his ways according to John; in his words, we "ought to lay down our lives" for one another as Jesus did for us (1 John 3:16*)*.

It has been argued that the Greeks had several terms for the concept of *love*. At a basic level, *eros* represented a passionate, energetic, yet demanding love, drawing the object of desire toward one's side. An attachment that would indicate a more rational passion was expressed with the term *philos*, as in philosophy (love of wisdom), philanthropy (love of humankind), and so on. The term *agape* conveyed a more disinterested, unconditional, and unilateral quality, such as the love described by St. Paul in 1 Corinthians 13. Love is described as being deep, powerful, relentless, steadfast, enduring, patient, kind, positive, and willful. Yet, *agape* does not foster naïveté, codependency, or masochistic stances in the believer; rather, it is exuded as a result of the coparticipation of the Holy Spirit and the faithful, obeying person. It is the concrete enactment of covenantal terms by an empowered, free, and willful person imitating God's ways.

EMPOWERED UNILATERAL PARTNERS IN BILATERAL COVENANTS

As already stated throughout the book, most contracts among humans are of a bilateral, conditional nature.[1] Establishing a *quid pro quo* is an equitable deal as it offers two parties the opportunity to engage in transactions of a win-win nature. The arrival at these possible outcomes may be the result of fair bargaining, flexibility, accommodation, assimilation, and equilibration between parties. This state of affairs represents a successful outcome even in the most secular therapeutic work. Many times, due to difficult contingencies encountered between conflicting parties, a bilateral-conditional contract is the most desirable outcome that can be achieved with Christian couples and families in therapy. A *quid pro quo* is a commendable, praiseworthy, and desirable setup.

When a person engages in a bilateral and conditional contract, three factors enter into the equation: uncertainty, unpredictability, and lack of absolute control over their interdependent purposes and fate.

---

1. Lederer and Jackson, *The Mirages of Marriage*; Tweedie, "Contract Therapy."

Part II: Principles Derived from the New Covenant in Marital Transactions

- A partner can never claim absolute certainty that the other will deliver the promised goods; also this partner is not necessarily sure that she or he has the capacity, disposition, or energy to accomplish the promised clauses made to the other;
- The lack of predictability means that the bilateral covenant as a system is subject to anticipatory anxiety and stress. A marriage contract conditions the parties to relate in covariance, subject to circular feedback loops and constant vigilance that the fairness, justice, and equanimity of the contract transactions are enacted as promised;
- A partner's well-being is contingent upon the other's stances, movement, dealings, and expectations. The purposes of both partners may be orthogonal to each other, and the fate of their marriage rests on their mutual endeavors extending into the future. Lack of absolute control over these variables makes the bilateral conditional covenant less than secure.

In time, an interdependent contract of a bilateral and conditional nature may become stiff, legalistic, binding, and tedious. We are reminded that even the bilateral-conditional aspects of the Old Covenant, originally given as principles for life, became a deadly burden and a heavy yoke that was impossible for failing humans to bear. The terms of the covenant became an instrument that demonstrated in obvious ways the incapacity of humans to stay within the stipulations proposed by God. Sadly, in human terms, contracts of a bilateral and conditional nature are made to be broken.

As reviewed in chapter 5, marriage is a bilateral covenant made between two people who exchange privileges and responsibilities (e.g., vows) through a mediator (minister) before some witnesses (family members, friends, and congregation). It resembles somehow God's paradigm in the Old Testament, stipulating privileges on one side and responsibilities on the other. It sounds like a *quid pro quo* of some sort. Among Christians, partners pledge and expect to remain sexually faithful to each other. The vows exchanged between them stress a concern about mutuality—to be there for each other through it all, for better and for worse, in sickness and in health, through thick and thin. This arrangement conveys mutuality and fairness, although on many occasions some attention needs to be paid to the deal if any violation, unfaithfulness, abuse, or neglect of the terms renders the relationship dysfunctional or unfair.

THE NEED FOR UNILATERAL INITIATIVES

The need for a unilateral stance arises when the covenant fails, due to the incapacity of one or both partners to remain faithful and deliver all the promises made in mutual accord. In failing covenants, the more capable, able, and willing party may choose to adopt a unilateral position and initiative in order to engage the other with the intention to engage in a restorative or renewing work. The unilateral initiative frees a partner who is willing and able to challenge a deplorable status quo and prompt the enactment of a better, desirable deal. An ongoing saga runs through Scripture where God repeatedly takes a unilateral initiative and calls Israel to repentance from their sinful ways in order to restore their fallen state. God's unilateral prompting addresses their inadequacies and failures, pinpoints the causes of such unfaithfulness and idolatry, and promises to restore their condition as partners if they repent, turn around, and re-enact the terms of the covenant. Of course, in God's deals, the human element comes short of ever taking an initiative, since the comparative levels of the engaging parties are obviously slanted: God is omnipotent, omniscient and faithful, and the human is weak, clueless, and unfaithful.

This distinction is essential to a fair understanding of the possibility among equals to imitate God's unilateral deals, especially as demonstrated in the New Covenant. The occasions that would call for such a unilateral initiative on the part of a partner are born out of the necessity to take an initiative when negative contingencies affect the deal and it becomes dysfunctional or fails to express faithfulness, loving care, attention, and so on.

- The unilateral decision and initiative begins with a willing, able, and proactive partner seeking to engage a not-so-willing, not-so-able partner in correcting, restoring, or rendering more functional a failing covenant when needed;
- The hope in all these cases is that such a unilateral initiative will engage and prompt the less committed or able party to at least react to after being incited or provoked to love and good works;
- The hope is that this unilateral stirring will lead to the recognition of the need to establish a more functional bilateral deal;
- The unilateral initiative may emerge and proceed from a well-intentioned and good-natured person with an adequate ego, strength, and willpower. Theoretically (and hopefully from a reality-based possibility), a believer has the advantage of being empowered by the Holy Spirit and endowed with the Word dwelling intrinsically in heart and mind to engage in a unilateral fashion. The energized believer may adopt and enact a unilateral initiative if needed—without being counted as being a codependent, weak, enabling, or dysfunctional, naïve person.

Again, although the establishment of the New Covenant appears to be a unilateral initiative coming from God's side, its operation and manifestation seek to engage the human in a bilateral fashion. No demands or conditions are set forth in the gospel, which is the proclamation of grace and mercy from above. God begins with unilateral offers and grants the undeserving salvation, giving us what he demands; that is, the Son has finished all and has accomplished his will. It is through the merits of Jesus that regeneration, faith, and conversion for the human become a possibility. It is the Holy Spirit who applies the effects of his merits. Yet, the New Covenant's demands emerge

Part II: Principles Derived from the New Covenant in Marital Transactions

so as to prompt human coparticipation, engaging his rational and moral nature. God deals with the human as a being created after his own image, rendering him/her an accountable being, capable of responding in a conscious, responsible fashion. The human enters the covenant freely and willingly, departing from sin. Likewise,

- The unilateral disposition to behave described in the examples above is in accordance with the counsel given by the author to the Hebrews; it is meant to initiate loving behaviors, provoking one another to love and good works (Heb 10:24). In the long run, nevertheless, the aim is to establish a more desirable and fair bilateral covenantal relationship;
- Partners need to consider the advantage of being "on the same page" as two unilaterally aimed people: this partnership becomes by necessity a relationship characterized by bilateral transactions.

The will of God is revealed clearly and beautifully in the New Covenant, displaying a work of grace that reflects itself in the human consciousness and stimulates the will of a disciple to greater activity. The covenant of grace does not nullify people but lifts them integrally, enhancing their faculties and powers—heart, mind, will, and strength—so as to be able to imitate the Father's ways. Yet, it is simply hard for any human partner to take the initiative to go beyond expectations, to move above the stipulated terms without being perceived as less assertive, less powerful, or lacking in control. The natural propensity in most marriages is to wait for *the other* to make a move, characterized by the formula, "If you do this . . . then I will . . . " This formula has the power to foster defensiveness, guardedness, cynicism, and wait-and-see stances, which in turn, challenges the other to become more adamant or demanding. In sum, it traps a person in a dependent posture.

The issue at the center of these anxieties appears to be the power held by, or perceived to be held by, the other partner's side. This quest for control becomes a central feature in marital dealings and may represent the need to be secure or to experience the privileges envisioned in the original covenant. It is in times of distress, when a marital partner experiences contempt, hurt, pain, or dejection associated with the other, that it becomes difficult for a hurt partner to be unilateral and move beyond the impasses generated by these contingencies. Partners are prone to get stuck in ruts, engage in dysfunctional habits, and fail to draw upon and display an ongoing unilateral attitude and initiative.

The capacity to be unilateral is a quality of character empowered by the Spirit and the indwelling Word, which enables partners to be metacognitive and adopt a higher perspective about their relationship. Beyond *quid pro quo*s or contracts of a bilateral-conditional nature, partners are invited by an all powerful God—who empowers through the Holy Spirit—to dare to believe in, accept, and enact the terms of a New Covenant in practical ways. Yet, according to covenantal history, it took 1500 years to enact a New Covenant after the Old was given. In God's timing, the old ways acted as a preamble or a forerunner of a new deal before a more gracious paradigm was introduced.

ADOPTING A METACOGNITIVE-DIALOGICAL STANCE

A hallmark of the New Covenant is the capacity to engage in unilateral and unconditional transactions as God does. In marriage, who will be the first to take this initiative when parties are in conflict? Who will break the ice, go over the hump, or conquer the impasse? Will this person be labeled as an enabler or regarded as a codependent who cannot suffer a state of ambivalence, incongruence, or stress? Can that person afford to face the criticisms of a narcissistic culture that regards such behavior as a display of weakness, originating from neurotic, pseudo-masochistic feelings and demonstrating the hallmark characteristic of being a pushover?

When a person experiences pain, hurt, anger, or frustration due to unfair dealings or any negative transaction, engaging in unilateral and unconditional dealings demands a more transcending point of reference. The need to adopt a distinct vantage point arises in order to define the self as being free, above circumstances, and aimed with choice. A metacognitive perception is what is needed in order to engage in inner dialogue and deliberate about what needs to be done when a challenging occasion is presented. Once a partner decides to take a unilateral initiative, internal dialogues may flood his/her mind—with God, with the partner in mind, with significant others, and with the self—characterized by ambivalent ruminations, anticipatory anxiety, musings about just retributions, and other styles of thinking. A metacognitive capacity to mindfully detach from these dialogues may take place, prompted by the empowering Holy Spirit and engaging in internal rhetoric (self talk of a persuasive nature), characterized by a mindful decision to act with grace and mercy toward the other.

A metacognitive-dialogical stance presupposes having a good grasp of one's self-image, esteem, and efficacy. Having been defined by socializing agents first, and then by peers, culture, models, and the cosmos in general, it is a challenge to stand up and be defined by God as a new creation in Christ (2 Cor 5:17). And yet, having received abundant grace and righteousness as a gift, this person may "reign in life through Jesus Christ" (Rom 5:17). A person empowered by God's grace and in control of his/her thoughts, feelings, and action may engage in a forward move without being defined by the other—or by any set of contingencies surrounding the self. Thus, the person may act *as if* he or she is free and above natural expectations because he or she *is free indeed* to move on better and higher grounds.

Again, to engage in such unilateral and unconditional dealings does not negate the reality of the conflict; rather, it establishes an accurate assessment of the damage done with a metacognitive awareness of the negative and unfair dealings committed against the self. Given the human predicament, an offended person is prone to act with natural fight responses—anger, revenge, retaliation—and fail to display conciliatory behaviors with peaceful outcomes in mind. Yet, unilateral and unconditional dealings are predicated on the capacity to "put the self to death with Christ" (Gal 2:20) and to be alive and well, empowered to engage in freedom. This "putting the self to death" is not a suicidal wish or a neurotic, intropunitive stance, but a mindful choice employed to suspend personal rights and prerogatives in order to act as an imitator of God with grace and mercy. This stance does not obliterate the demands for fairness and justice; it simply sets the tone and the ground for better negotiations that may follow.

The empowering of a partner's cognitive processes (thoughts, reason, judgment, attribution of meaning, memory) by the Holy Spirit needs to be invoked and take place. The restructuring of cognitive processes fosters the capacity to reattribute meaning to what is being experienced from a metacognitive—higher, insightful, spiritual—point of view without losing the grasp on reality testing. It is not a question of over-spiritualizing, denying, or repressing reality. It is the reframing of a partner's perception into a more accurate, God-defined perspective in order to allocate a different meaning to the transaction. It helps a great deal to perceive and to act *as if* one has the freedom to proceed along—and sometimes *in spite of*—the other. In that way, the other does not condition one's stances or attitudes or rule over one's feelings. The actions of the other do not determine one's behaviors because one remains free to think, feel, and act in unilateral ways if/when needed.

The person has to intrinsically sense the fact that he or she is not alone, but is accompanied by the Paraclete who is not just outside watching, but is indwelling and infusing the right perspective into the mind and heart, providing power and suggesting the right avenue to do the right thing before the eyes of an all-encompassing God. *A partner behaves in the sight of God*, bypassing the naturalness of our often futile and vain endeavors. His inspiring, infusing, empowering presence can move the self toward the object of love (even when it is perceived to be unlovable)—beyond legalistic injunctions, propositional pressures of the moment, or any other externally mediated prompting.

Besides cognitive restructuring—a process that includes reappraisal and reframing of experienced reality—the emotional processes have to be reckoned with. Sensibility is not lost in these unilateral and unconditional dealings. Emotions may range from mild anxiety to terror; from sadness to despair; from annoyance to murderous drives; and from aggravation to a thirst for revenge. Yet, without employing psychological defenses such as denial or repression, the person may face the reality of his/her predicament. Without resorting to rationalization and intellectualization to ward off the anxiety that arises from these conflictive situations, an empowered person may engage consciously and properly. This person may *stop, think, internally dialogue and deliberate, reframe, internally persuade self to imitate God, and act* instead of reacting. The motivation to extend unilateral and unconditional dealings is a chief property of the regenerated and renewed person, who now may display the capacities of his/her transformed and empowered self, animated and guided by a higher principle of operation. Beyond retaliation and revenge, the unilateral person may respond with grace and mercy.

By providing a New Covenant, God anticipated in a unilateral way the real needs of those targeted as objects of love. In doing so, the most fundamental aspect was to communicate empathic love, engaging the dearly beloved children in gracious and caring ways, protecting and providing the essential and empowering guidance to live a life worthy of their call. Those who understand the terms of a New Covenant may dedicate efforts to imitate God and behave toward the spouse, the child, the parent, the sibling, or fellow members of the body of Christ in ways that will pleasantly surprise them and convey a sense of dedication devoid of ulterior motives.

To anticipate and do good things without being asked may be the most beautiful gift we grant one another, provided that these things are not just our projections of what the other should have, experience, or achieve. Humans do not possess an omniscient capacity to anticipate all actual needs of their counterparts as God does. Yet, those who imitate God try by all means to address and actually behave in unilateral ways while having an accurate perception of their neighbor's real needs and desires. True intimacy—knowing and being known—allows for such mutual knowledge and anticipatory gifting.

ADOPTING A UNILATERAL THRUST IN CONCRETE SITUATIONS

Unilateral initiatives are facilitated and are easier to enact if a metacognitive perspective is adopted. This posture may be described as a deliberate openness to, and keen awareness of, God's empowering presence, while being mindfully objective about one's subjective state. To process one's own processes and to check one's underlying motivations appeals to the capacity to be mindfully detached from the entrapments of any situational demands or constraints. Furthermore, a metacognitive-dialogical stance engages purposefully one's own inner reflection and dialogue (pondering, deliberating), considering the possible ways and means to attend to a given interpersonal challenge, dedicate conciliatory efforts in a conflictive situation, or surprise a partner with a positive behavior.

In a metacognitive-dialogical stance, a shift from one's pensive internal dialogue to inner rhetoric is essential. This inner persuasion originates from an empowered, top-down executive agency, fostering the capacity to decide to act in a unilateral fashion. One aspect of the fruit of the Holy Spirit (Gal 5:22–23) is the empowered capacity to exercise self-control. The empowered person is able to act along independent lines, not being subject to negative circumstances, environmental contingencies, or the attitudes and behaviors of a counterpart engaged in covenantal dealings. The intrinsic capacity to act in unilateral ways is a hallmark of being unbound, not subject to external vicissitudes or contingencies. A free person is able to engage in purposeful endeavors and act in intentional ways in control of his/her responses. This attitude (an attribute of *the mind of Christ*, as in Philippians 2:5) is called for when a covenantal relationship experiences troubles due to interpersonal struggles arising from negative contingencies—ranging from minor offenses to major failures—that affect marital stability and satisfaction.

The occasions to display unilateral deals are many because marriages are prone to experience problems in their structural configuration (who is who in the system, relating to whom outside the system) or in the unraveling of processes—communication; roles played by partners (chosen, established, imposed, delegated, etc.); satisfaction of needs (love, esteem, respect, acceptance, validation, etc.); and the like. These occasions are challenges to be addressed in a functional fashion. To avoid misunderstanding on this topic, some reality testing is called for in order to ascertain what a unilateral deal is *not*:

- The decision to be and act in a unilateral fashion should not be confused with weakness, codependency, or naïveté. It is not the urge of a marital partner to be squeezed into a mold defined by the idiosyncratic expectations or demands of the other;

- Unilateral stances are not emergent properties of intropunitive stances, attitudes, or beliefs. It is not a masochistic posture or the display of neurotic overcompensation derived from a lack of ego strength, weakened stamina, or insecurity;

- To be unilateral is not to adopt a propitiatory or an expiatory stance based upon guilt, manifesting the need to redeem the other in neurotic attempts to redeem oneself. The need to be needed may prompt such attitudes and behaviors due to a person's equivocal quest for self redemption, acceptance, or approval;

- It is not a display of benevolent dictatorship: giving what one thinks or regards as being essentially good for the other, rather than respectfully ascertaining what the other actually needs, desires, or expects. Nor is it behaving narcissistically in anticipatory and proactive ways, regarding oneself as being magnanimous toward the other, but missing and not addressing what the real concerns or requests of the other person truly are.

Distortions and dysfunctions in structural systems often need the unilateral initiative of a partner, as when the other assumes excessive control and exerts his/her authority in ways that may affect the mutuality of the system or unbalance the fairness of the original set up of the couple. Often, a more sensitive partner will notice the deterioration of the couple's harmony and engage in an appraisal of the system in order to restore it to a desired state. This partner—being metacognitive—is the one who may engage the other in a unilateral fashion, hoping to establish the grounds for a better deal. To do so, the person has to start by asking: *Am I willing? Am I able? Is this in my agenda? Am I ready?* Affirmative answers will allow the person to engage in true unilateral dealings, acting in a deliberate way with conscious awareness of being free, willing, and able to engage in such endeavors.

The mature and caring partner usually takes the unilateral initiative in a dyad that is experiencing problems. It is important to note whether she or he starts to move from a choice-based stance versus a codependent one. The able person may engage in appeals to God in prayer, in intercessory petitions, and in attempts to see the establishment of a better milieu and ambiance. The appeal is made to a higher order of accountability—a transcending being who is the author and finisher of the faith and practice of both partners—bound in covenant during their pilgrimage under the sun. This higher perception allows a partner to be mindfully unilateral and empowered to speak the truth in love, holding the partnership accountable "in the sight of God." The unilateral initiative has ultimately a desired goal in mind: to engage in a better bilateral partnership that demands mutual, responsible efforts in order to foster the renewal and restoration of the intentions stated in the original covenant.

Attempts to remediate any failures in communication often necessitate the initiative of one, if not both, partners. Breakdowns in communication occur when any variable that enters into the process (who says what to whom, how, why, when, where, and with what effect) allows for the misunderstanding of messages. Misperception of one another's attitudes and behaviors, as well as misattribution of their meaning, contributes to failures in transactions, leading to distancing and separation between partners. Judging one another, versus assuming good faith and giving the benefit of the doubt, exacerbates the process. The obvious need is to break a stalemate, wherein a couple's position counts as an impasse in which, while neither partner is necessarily "in check," they cannot move except into the position held by the other. In such cases, the unilateral disposition can be either a codependent, enabling behavior (reacting in weakness) or a truly unilateral response—emerging from freedom of choice, empowered stances, grace, and mercy.

Distanced partners engaging in stonewalling, defensiveness, negative deals, and contempt—the "four horses of apocalypse," according to Gottman—often require the insightful "aha" experience of one partner (if not both) to initiate unilaterally exemplary conduct that will convey a positive, conciliatory, non-defensive message endowed with an open, respectful, and engaging stance.[2]

Special instances involving failures in transactions due to a partner's dysfunctional attitudes or behavior often necessitate the unilateral initiative of the other—a more stable, mature person—willing to engage in better, functional deals. Yet, the relational patterns posed by a problematic partner (e.g., struggling with depression, anxiety, or being incapacitated in some fashion) often demand extra efforts and place burdens on the shoulders of the unilaterally concerned and caring partner. Often the formula employed in many marriage ceremonies ("for better or *for worse*") becomes an issue in counseling that deals with these difficult situations. In these stressful relationships,

---

2. Gottman, *Marital Interaction*.

Part II: Principles Derived from the New Covenant in Marital Transactions

a person (either by choice or by necessity) needs to regard him- or herself as being able and willing to work along an agenda set by the circumstances and stresses of the moment. In such cases, a "stress inoculation training" paradigm may be employed in a cognitive-behavioral fashion. That is, the able partner needs to inoculate self with the reality of possible suffering—preparing a mindset to face negative contingencies ahead of the game so as to be ready if the occasion calls for it. Supportive work with the willing-able partner becomes a necessity in order to prevent a burnout syndrome that may result from the extra efforts employed along the way.

The process of "arming oneself with the thought of possible suffering" is what St. Peter alludes to in his letter, preparing believers for eventual suffering on account of their faith (1 Pet 4:1) so that they might be metacognitively ready for action versus being defeated by stressors. This unilateral disposition may facilitate the process of "being there" for the other and remaining objective and empowered (by means of supportive fellowship and personal attention to his or her own mental health) so as to be of help to the other.

In sum, God's unilateral and unconditional dealings are obvious features registered in Scripture. Being on the receiving end, a human may love God in return and, in an imitational fashion, extend the same manner of love toward others. Unilateral and unconditional acts of love enacted by willing and able partners may not only ameliorate and lower marital defenses, stonewalling, and retaliatory dealings, but also establish a climate of grace, mercy, and good faith.

Chapter 10

Adopting an Unconditional Stance to Optimize Renewed Conditions

From the outset, the New Covenant is introduced with God's unilateral initiative, marked by a series of pronouncements indicating God's proactive and unconditional thrust ("I will . . . "). As the covenant unfolds, these premises provide an optimal ground for bilateral conditions to be established. This chapter appeals to partners in covenantal relations to envision the possibility of engaging in unconditional transactions patterned after God's ways. Many opportunities in intimate transactions call for such endeavors.

An initial question may be posed: is it possible for humans to engage in unconditional deals without being prompted by any ulterior motives? Social conventions are framed in conditional terms. Human existence begins with a newborn coming into this world as a needy, fragile creature. The common expectation is that those who procreate will take care of the newborn with some level of unconditional love, expressed through nurturing care and protective endeavors. In terms of reciprocity and mutuality, the newborn is the recipient of services and goods without offering much in return. As the person matures, more accountability and responsibility are demanded of the individual, and these are framed in conditional terms in the context of marriage, family, community, and society at large.

FACTORS INFLUENCING RELATIONAL MATTERS

A general assessment of family systems across cultures demonstrates that acceptance, validation, protection, safety, and rewards, etc., are all predicated on some tacit or explicit expectations. The norms of a family system develop as social, cultural, and spiritual regulations that establish, maintain, support, and provide guidelines applicable to the structures and the functions of the system. These implicit or explicit norms may be regarded as contingencies that foster and empower the life of the system, framing the boundaries in which differentiation and mutuality are established in a stable, satisfactory climate.

A marital system is predicated upon the readiness of both partners to engage in a covenantal transaction. Each prospective partner "leaves father and mother" via differentiation, becoming individuated, empowered, and mature, and "cleaves to

Part II: Principles Derived from the New Covenant in Marital Transactions

his partner" in mutuality—a fusion of persons into a relational system without the loss of their integrity. Hopefully, the dyadic relationship will be regulated by a set of conditions and enacted within agreed-upon parameters. Due to the fact that human nature has experienced a disturbance in the original design due to sin, the propensity to engage in advantageous, self-centered, or manipulative ways remains a distinct possibility.

In simple terms, a bilateral-conditional arrangement seems to prevail in most systemic human transactions. Unconditional initiatives emerge as necessary endeavors in covenantal transactions when dysfunctional patterns affect the stability and/or satisfaction of the marital dyad. These measures represent a remedial mindset seeking to renew or restore a desirable relationship—not to be imposed upon unwilling partners or to be employed in an indiscriminative or wholesale fashion—in efforts dedicated to resolve conflicts or to move beyond an impasse. Often, a partner's unilateral initiative may prove to be impractical or dysfunctional, due to predisposing factors present in the character of the other partner—unfair, self-centered, and narcissistic, among others. Unilateral initiatives may be the starting point in a partner's efforts to establish a better bilateral-conditional contract with his/her partner. The law given to Israel—the Old Covenant—was the best *pedagogos* given to a nation in need of interactive structures, guidance, and protection. After all, all human systems devoid of transactional conditions represent a utopian notion, an unrealistic setup, or an anarchic, antinomian state of affairs.

Whether on purpose (mindfully) or unconsciously (mindlessly), marital and family systems differ in terms of the degree, amount, and nature of transactional conditions, aimed either to foster a climate of mutual acceptance and validation between their contracting parties or to promote a sense of lack of worth, esteem, or efficacy. Conditional clauses are framed into explicit norms and expectations, utilized to regulate the interpersonal transactions in a given system. If these conditions are rigidly imposed, they tend to create difficulties in establishing a climate of grace or in providing a sense of security, acceptance, or efficacy in the developing offspring of such systems. Often, a demanding and insensitive partner may appeal to Scripture in an unfair way—imposing or demanding in the attempt to squeeze the other into a mold derived from personal, convenient, or idiosyncratic interpretations and applications of the Bible. In cases of parental physical or sexual abuse—or neglect of any kind—the offspring of these parents may develop a sense of insecurity and inadequacy in their own attachments. Insecure attachments fostered under these circumstances may result in detrimental consequences later on in life, carried over into future attachments and relations.

Secure versus insecure attachments in childhood have been the subject of much research.[1] Attachment notions were extrapolated and applied as foundational aspects

---

1. Bowlby, *A Secure Base*.

in emotion-focused marital therapy.[2] These studies support the observation that secure attachments tend to foster trust, positive self-esteem, personal worth, and a sense of acceptance and validation based on unconditional dealings in favor of the developing child. Conversely, insecure attachments are associated with conditional, unstable, and dysfunctional socialization patterns. Theoretical aspects dealing with separation issues (proper or improper detachment from a source of nurturance, security, and comfort), coupled with attachment issues (secure or insecure unions), provide an important basis for the considerations addressed in this work and represent important developmental features affecting adult relations, especially in the areas of marital satisfaction and stability.

A person who experiences secure attachments to start with, and then experiences the empowering validation and reinforcement in the process of individuation—separating, detaching well, and differentiating self from his/her family of origin—has better chances to establish secure attachments later on in marital and family relations. However, failure to properly separate from love objects may produce anxiety and related syndromes in the developing person. In spiritual terms, attachment to God in Christ and being indwelled by an empowering Spirit allows a person not only to stand alone, but also to be ready to engage in fellowship.

Fair expectations and conditions in covenanting terms may be applied in a functional fashion as marriage and the family relations are concerned. When a person decides to leave father and mother (to differentiate or individuate) and become one flesh with a partner (to form a mutual union), some anticipatory anxiety may surge in the person's heart and mind. The consciousness of entering into a lifelong covenant with somebody yet to be known challenges our sense of autonomy and independence, as well as our sense of personal control. Separating from what is known and facing the unknown always pose a challenge to us, due to our innate need to know, control, and predict some aspects of our future life. These conditional expectations are related to the main variables that exacerbate a partner's anxiety as these relate to the future: lack of knowledge, lack of control, and lack of predictability. Thus, the need for conditional clauses in covenantal dealings typically emerges, based on fears of uncertainty and unpredictability embedded in human transactions.

A person facing the unknown requires some reassuring basis that may provide her or him with a sense of security, satisfaction, and comfortableness. Conditions of worth emerge in reference to the selection of a desirable, prospective partner. Desirable factors may include character traits; intellectual, emotional, and behavioral features; tastes; hobbies; philosophy of life; faith; values; etc. The utilization of computer-assisted matchmaking testifies to the need for predictability and success in relationships sought by those attempting to find the love of their life.[3] Neil Warren, the developer of the popular eHarmony matchmaking Web site, based his approach

2. Johnson, *The Practice*; Greenberg and Goldman, *Emotion-Focused Therapy*.
3. Warren, *Finding the Love of Your Life*.

Part II: Principles Derived from the New Covenant in Marital Transactions

on factors such as character traits, values, attitudes, expectations, and conditions of worth entering into dating relations.

The computerized approach is based upon data gathered and factored empirically, allowing a person seeking the love of his or her life to define hoped-for features in a prospective partner in order to predict a good match. This popular approach is a matchmaking paradigm for prospective partners seeking to set up a positive relationship based on empirically derived, conditional clauses to be fulfilled in desirable ways. Of course, it all depends on the honesty and truthfulness of those who fill in the forms to present themselves as desirable "partners to be."

At the beginning of any relationship, more faith than experience seems to guide both partners' transactions. Often, faith may be mixed with idealized, wishful thinking, projecting fictional aspects onto the *imago* of the relationship. As time goes on, reality-based experience seems to erode such positive, idealized perceptions. With the passage of time, the interpersonal experiences accumulate in consolidated scripts, and their actual or real impact may diminish the partners' faith in each other. Several factors—entropy, stagnation, satiation effects, and routines devoid of love—tend to decrease the level of vitality in a marriage.

A diminished level of loving interactions—reflected in lower frequency, intensity, or duration of loving, caring, attentive behaviors—may prompt a couple to consider using a conditional deal to regain positive momentum. Negative feelings associated with lack of respect, honor, and dignity (conveyed attitudinally or behaviorally) often elicit concerns in a partner who desires to set up some conditions to reestablish mutual, satisfactory covenantal terms. Complaints and demands expressed in couples therapy often result in a set up in which conditional love, attention, respect, and validation seem to be a starting point before the more ideal, desirable terms of a New Covenant can be enacted. Couples experiencing these anomalies often need to appeal to a bilateral-conditional *quid pro quo* in order to establish some grounds for peace, functionality, or mutual satisfaction.

Partners who are experiencing difficulties in their transactions and have lost their faith and trust in each other often resort to a conditional formula such as, "If you ... then I ..." and place the responsibility on the other to do something on their behalf before moving on to fulfill the promises made to the other. Being unable or unwilling to take a unilateral, unconditional, or proactive initiative, they want safeguards and guarantees before they engage in any bilateral-conditional deal. In setting up such grounds for transacting, each person depends not only on his or her own capacity to deliver the goods (or on the degree of his or her commitment to the relationship), but also on the attitude, personal characteristics, and behaviors of the other.

The formula "If you, then I" that initially represents a fair and equitable deal may become a vehicle for repetitive transactions that, due to the repeated failures experienced in the attempts to keep the *quid pro quo*, may entrench a couple's demanding, conditional, and dysfunctional system. The essential condition set forth by the initiating or complaining party is obvious: *if the other* fulfills the terms of the deal, *then* the person may move toward the fulfillment of those behaviors expected from him or her as well. Quite often, the formula moves away from a personal, unilateral stance and fosters an increase in the expectations placed upon the other—elevating the bar so that the other has to jump higher in order to meet the ongoing demands.

UNCONDITIONAL INITIATIVES AND CONDITIONAL CONTINGENCIES IN COVENANTS

The New Covenant has been cast primarily in unconditional terms at its onset (Jer 31:31–37; Ezek 16:60–62; 37:28; Isa. 81:2). Jeremiah's prophecy was given under deplorable conditions with Israel in exile due to their sinfulness and disobedience to God's covenantal terms. This initial thrust engaged the human in order to elicit a response to God's desire to restore and relate to his creatures as intended in the original design. Due to human incapacity, precariousness, and weakness, God always judged it necessary to set forth his stipulations for humans to obey after engaging in a proactive, unilateral fashion. Thus it is fair to say that God-given covenants always included obligations, keeping in mind the maximum benefits for the obeying humans.

At Eden, the conditions were stipulated with regard to the human administration of God's domain. Toiling in the garden and acting as stewards of God's property were conditional clauses stipulated in a contractual transaction with a "job description" provided by the giver of a privileged context to those receiving the charge. The deal had a lot of beneficial consequences predicated upon obedience to God's design, as well as detrimental consequences associated with disobedience. A plentiful provision of sustaining and nurturing items were offered for humans to partake from except a prohibited tree, set as a condition for obedience, faithfulness, and dependence upon God's will and design. Obeying God was set forth as a condition. This command was not given to satisfy God's needs, but to prevent humans from experiencing negative consequences. Yet, left to their own choice and design, the couple disobeyed God's terms due to the lust of the eyes, the desires of their flesh, and their prideful quest to become like God. The narrative registers the detrimental consequences affecting human history since then.

After the fall into sin, it was God who, in a unilateral and proactive initiative, sought the drifting runaways and asked the question "Where are you?" (Gen 3:8–10). It was God who found them and set conditions after their encounter (Gen 3:14–19). After the consequential aspects related to their failure in keeping the covenant were declared, it was God who took the initiative to cover them with a redemptive mantle (Gen 3:21). In that way, God ratified his initial covenant with the couple and empowered them to keep going on as stewards of His domain. Thus, in a conditional covenant, an unconditional display of grace and mercy made its appearance, demonstrating the character of a loving God who provided the means for a covenantal restoration to take place.

Part II: Principles Derived from the New Covenant in Marital Transactions

In the case of Abraham, the unilateral, unconditional, and proactive thrust of God's call elicited a faithful response on his part. The summoning call came at a time when Abraham was described as being ungodly, demonstrating God's grace and mercy toward him. Being impacted by this unilateral thrust, Abraham's faith led to his obedience to God's call, engaging him in a bilateral fellowship. This partnership unfolded through a lifestyle characterized by a faithful dependency on God who calls into existence the things that do not exist (Rom 4:17). The response in faith and obedience actualized the terms of a covenant, but the fact remains that it was God's unconditional thrust that initiated the transaction and evoked the faithful response of the human.

In setting the terms of an unequally binding covenant with Israel, humans did not contribute to the planning design or to the initial thrust employed to execute it. God's reminder to the people reads, "I lifted you on eagles' wings and brought you to myself" (Exod 19:4). Then, God adds, "And now, *if you* will diligently listen to me and keep my covenant, *then* you will be my special possession out of all nations, for all the earth is mine, and you will be to me a kingdom of priests and a holy nation" (Exod 19:5–6, emphasis added). Faithfulness, steadfastness, and perseverance are expectations framed in terms of a covenantal response to God's summoning, unilateral thrust. This invites humans to enter into a truly bilateral deal as counterparts; they are not regarded as robots or zombies, but as fully conscious, accountable, and responsible beings called into an intimate deal with God.

In giving the Old Covenant, two parties entered the transaction. God gave the Torah in the context of great promises, all of which were born out of God's unconditional "I will take you to myself for a people . . . I will be your God . . . I will bring you to the land . . . I will give it to you as a possession" (Exod 6:6–8). God set forth conditions of worth by stipulating the main clauses: The Israelites were not to have any other gods, and they were to keep always the decrees engraved in the tablets of stone. God reminded Israelites that YHWH (I Am that I Am) is their holy Lord and judge, and that they are his obedient people. The covenantal dynamic was rendered in a basic premise: God makes his covenant, and his people respond with faith or unbelief, obedience or disobedience. As consequences go, they receive blessings or curses, salvation or condemnation.

Blessings, endowments, and consequential states of heart and mind are associated with faithful obedience to God's terms. They emerge and flow from intimate relationship as exuding properties of a grounded, relational dynamics. They are the offspring of the mutuality or interdependence of differentiated beings. Technically and theologically speaking, that is the precise meaning of establishing a *hypostatic-ecstatic* fellowship characterized by *perichoresis* after the pattern of how the Trinity relates (see John 17:21). Human obstinacy, defiance, disobedience, and rebelliousness are factors that stop this flow of blessings and disrupt intimate dealings with God. As far as covenants go, God remains faithful to his promises; it is the human who is unable to stay within the terms of the deal and fulfill them to perfection. And as human covenants go, marriages are not exempt from mishaps and disappointments, necessitating a renewal and transformation of the partners' hearts, minds, and wills on an ongoing basis.

THE NEW COVENANT AS A PARADIGM IN ESCHATOLOGICAL CONTEXT

In giving the New Covenant, God's unconditional tones resonate as introductory premises that disclose a fresh, revitalizing, and actualizing deal. These premises and promises seek to engage those who accept the terms by faith and surrender to God's design, providing them with optimal contingencies, which are set forth as guidelines for enacting God's will and assuring human satisfaction.

As seen in previous chapters, the debates about the New Covenant are plentiful in terms of defining who the targeted partners are and its fulfillment in space and time. We have paid some attention to both Reformed and Dispensationalist positions, but have regarded the debates on such matters as belonging to the theological domain. For obvious reasons, these escape a fair and thorough treatment due to the nature, scope, and space limitations of this work. In pragmatic terms, we have adopted and applied the New Covenant as being in continuity with all previous covenants. We also have regarded the New Covenant as a new deal, distinctly pertaining to God's people here and now—comprised by both believing Jews and Gentiles. This consideration is framed within the context of God's mysterious ways, challenging us to remain humble in our claims and approaches and extract the best possible principles in order to be able to imitate the Father's ways, exemplified in his covenantal transactions with humans.

In the New Covenant, God acts in a unilateral, unconditional, and proactive fashion, engaging and empowering people to accept, obey, and enact his ways. His grace, mercy, and love are bestowed upon the human and leave no room for merits to be displayed or accrued by the human, who is regarded as an unequal partner in the covenant. Yet, with all that, the nuances and direct expressions registered in Scripture point to stipulations, expectations, and desirable conditions to be accepted, obeyed, and enacted in order to be in fellowship with the covenanting God.

The unconditional terms of the New Covenant are treated in this work with purposive mindfulness, avoiding an extreme emphasis that might convey a sense of disregard to God's warnings pertaining to perseverance in faith and obedience. Obvious questions arise: If the New Covenant sounds so unconditional in its thrust, should the believer relax his or her coparticipation with God as a partner or take God's grace for granted? Or should the believer mindlessly, if not purposefully, engage in sin because God's grace is so abundant? Should a believer persist in sin because he or she is not under the law, but under God's grace? As Paul the apostle would emphatically and

Part II: Principles Derived from the New Covenant in Marital Transactions

vehemently put it, *Not at all! By no means!* (Rom 6:2, emphasis added). A believer's perseverance is, after all, a hallmark of having been elected.

Although there are no conditions set forth in Jeremiah's promise, repeated twice by the author in Hebrews 8 and 10, plenty of scriptural references are registered to warn any pretentious, conceited, or entitled human. Even those Israelites addressed by Paul's rhetoric, who apparently claimed an ethnocentric monopoly of interpretation of God's truth, needed to pay attention to the voice of the Spirit in calling people to persistent faith and obedience. In other words, having being elected, called, or drawn into God's fellowship by the Holy Spirit, a believing person cannot boast in this standing, but must humbly praise God who acted in unconditional grace and mercy.

In a challenging passage (Rom 9–11), which often receives a diminished emphasis due to the adoption of given theological positions, the apostle Paul engages dialogically with Gentiles who were saved by grace and entered into a covenantal deal by the sovereign act of God with admonitions and warnings:

> Now if some of the branches were broken off, and you, a wild olive shoot, were grafted in among them and participated in the richness of the olive root, do not boast over the branches. But if you boast, remember that you do not support the root, but the root supports you. Then you will say, "The branches were broken off so that I could be grafted in." Granted! They were broken off because of their unbelief, but you stand by faith. Do not be arrogant, but fear! For if God did not spare the natural branches, perhaps he will not spare you. Notice therefore the kindness and harshness of God—harshness toward those who have fallen, but God's kindness toward you, provided that you continue in his kindness; otherwise you also will be cut off. (Romans 11:17–22)

Pauline warnings are there to challenge the tendency of those who receive a covenant born out of God's side—his unilateral, unconditional, and proactive side—with idiosyncratic logic, interpretations, and theological assertions. The passage that follows the one just cited reads:

> For I do not want you to be ignorant of this mystery, brothers and sisters, so that you may not be conceited: A partial hardening has happened to Israel until the full number of the Gentiles has come in. And so all Israel will be saved, as it is written: "The Deliverer will come out of Zion; he will remove ungodliness from Jacob. And this is my covenant with them, when I take away their sins." (Romans 11:25–27)

A series of connotations may be drawn from these three chapters, in which God deals with Israel and the Gentiles and reminds us of his covenantal promises to be fulfilled in due time. From this author's perspective, whether we subscribe to a Reformed theology (that regards the covenant as being in vogue with the unified people of God comprised by both Jew and Gentile believers) or to a Dispensationalist view (that by extrapolation anticipates the future fulfillment of the covenant as being applicable to believers in the here and now), the New Covenant applies to "whosoever believes in Him" (the mediator) in the present.

Adopting a strong stance with conviction and security based upon God's election and grace is commendable as the emphasis is placed on God's side of the equation. To this conviction, the emphasis of a believer's coparticipation with God as a response to grace with an assiduous attention being paid to the conditions set forth in the New Covenant is, paradoxically, commendable as well. To remain in faith and obedience and to persevere until the end are assertions derived from Scripture, which we do well to pay attention to with humility and thanksgiving.

The context in Romans 9 through 11 seems to leave room for an actual fulfillment of this covenant with the house of Israel and the house of Judah in the future. God knows. We try to know—or think that we know—and debate with each other. In spite of distinctive theological positions competing for hermeneutical supremacy, we may faithfully regard the New Covenant as a deal to enter into, actualize, and enjoy in the here and now.

Debates aside, the main point is that God's sovereign grace and mercy are the loving ways that his children need to faithfully follow after and imitate as they walk in love. After this possibility is actualized, we may set some interpersonal conditions of a functional, desirable nature as well.

THE SCRIPTURAL ADMONITION TO ABIDE (REMAIN) IN CHRIST: COVENANTAL UNION

Jesus's admonition in the parable of the vine and the branches is repeatedly stated: "Abide [remain, reside] in Me" (John 15:4–10, NKJV). Is this an unconditional and irresistible placement or a faithful condition to pay attention to? Being intrinsically united with Christ is a result of God's unilateral and proactive grace—to be accepted by faith by the participating human who chooses to obey. The conditions of permanence, adherence, and fruitfulness are actualized by means of God's gracious and merciful empowering of the human incapacity, experienced as gifts from God. Perseverance—to abide, to remain, to reside in Christ—is stressed in this passage repeatedly, and it appears as a condition born out of God's desire to engage the human in a covenantal fashion.

In human terms, to "fall in love" (why do we not say, rather, to "be ecstatically elevated in love"?) seems to be a kairotic event. Experientially speaking, "it happens" as people relate, discover one another, and lower their defenses so as to know and be known at intimate levels. The process that leads to these pointed "aha moments" (or to a gradual "sliding down" into a *love state* of heart/mind/will) may be explained in psychoanalytical, hedonistic, social, or pragmatic terms. Beyond that event, *to remain* in love is a process that needs assiduous attention. As a matter of fact, this process is marked by conditional expectations of an implicit (tacit, or unspoken) or explicit

Part II: Principles Derived from the New Covenant in Marital Transactions

(spelled out, or scripted) nature. These conditional aspects need to be mindfully attended to by both partners, with dedication and perseverance, in order to establish and sustain both satisfaction and stability in marital relations. Needless to say, the opportunities to be and act in an unconditional fashion arise within such a context, especially when the expected conditions and stipulations are not adhered to, fulfilled, or satisfied by one or both partners.

We have seen both YHWH and Israel and Christ and the church metaphorically cast in the OT and NT covenantal marriage narratives. For our purposes, if New Covenantal terms are patterned after the relationship between Christ and the church, several factors appear as being of utmost importance: 1.) The manner of agape love (decentered, ecstatic, seeking the benefits of the other) that binds partners; 2.) The security and permanence of such attachments; and 3.) The evidence of fruitfulness or the behavioral repertoire of a positive nature expected from partners. Although the New Covenant is given unconditionally, God-given conditions apply in the unfolding of its terms among humans that enter into a relationship with God. Thus, the applicability of its principles to marriage needs to be qualified: human partners need to accept, adopt, and remain in covenantal terms—framed in conditions such as faithfulness, mutual care, and reciprocal love.

The apostle John's emphasis on a mutually bonding connectedness in love is a key feature in his writings. In his Gospel, the words of Jesus are registered by the apostle as being, "Remain in me, and I will remain in you. Just as the branch cannot bear fruit by itself, unless it remains in the vine, so neither can you unless you remain in me" (John 15:4). A series of qualifying statements are provided by Jesus (emphasis added):

- "The one who *remains* (abides, resides) in me—and I in him—bears much fruit" (v. 5);
- "If anyone does not *remain* in me, he is thrown out . . ." (v. 6);
- "If you *remain* in me and my words *remain* in you, ask whatever . . ." (v. 7);
- "Just as the Father has loved me, I also have loved you; *remain* in my love" (v. 9);
- "If you obey my commandments, you will *remain* in my love, just as I have obeyed my Father's commandments and *remain* in his love" (v. 10);
- Finally the same thrust that started the admonitions finishes the sequence: "This I command you—to love one another" (v. 17).

As for the hope provided by the secure attachment between Christ and his disciples, the deep interpenetration desired among the disciples is registered in the priestly prayer in John 17: "Holy Father, keep them safe . . . so that they may be one just as we are one" (v.11). Then, he adds, "That they may be one just as we are one—I in them and you in me—that they may be completely one, so that the world will know that you sent me, and you have loved them just as you have loved me" (John 17:22–23).

This thought is further elaborated in John's first letter: "That you may have fellowship [communion or genuine association] with us (and indeed our fellowship is with the Father and with his Son Jesus Christ)" (1 John 1:3). An undeniable consistency between faith and works is expected: "If we say we have fellowship with him and yet keep on walking [conducting ourselves, behaving] in the darkness, we are lying and not practicing the truth" (1 John1:6). Evidence of faith at work is expected: "But if we walk in light as he himself is in the light, we have fellowship with one another" (1 John 1:7). A metacognitive reflection is provided: "Now by this we know that we have come to know God: if we keep his commandments" (1 John 2:3). Inconsistency becomes an obvious feature in relational terms: to know God and not keep his commandments does not make any sense (1 John 2:4). On the other hand, "But whoever obeys his word, truly in this person the love of God has been perfected. By this we know that we are in him" (1 John 2:5). Thus, "The one who says that he resides in God ought himself to walk just as Jesus walked" (1 John 2:6).

> See what sort of love the Father has given to us: that we should be called God's children—and indeed we are! For this reason the world does not know us: because it did not know him. Dear friends, we are God's children now, and what we will be has not yet been revealed. We know that whenever it is revealed we will be like him, because we will see him just as he is. And everyone who has this hope focused on him purifies himself, just as Jesus is pure. (1 John 3:1–3)

Further evidence is presented that "everyone who has been fathered by God does not practice sin, because God's seed resides in him, and thus he is not able to sin, because he has been fathered by God" (1 John 3:9). The person who keeps his commandments resides in God, and God in this person: "Now by this we know that God resides in us: by the Spirit he has given us" (1 John 3:24). Addressing the community of faith, John declares, "Dear friends, let us love one another, because love is from God, and everyone who loves has been fathered by God and knows God" (1 John 4:7). Then he adds, "In this is love: not that we have loved God, but that he loved us and sent his Son to be the atoning sacrifice for our sins" (1 John 4:10). Based on such premises, the conclusion follows: "Dear friends, if God so loved us, then we also ought to love one another. No one has seen God at any time. If we love one another, God resides in us, and his love is perfected in us. By this we know that we reside in God and he in us: in that he has given us of his Spirit" (1 John 4:11–13).

The reader is encouraged to follow John's argument (1 John 4:15–21) with a sense of the interpenetrated fellowship of God and all believers, predicated upon the conditions of being loved and loving in return. The same is followed in his second letter: "Everyone who goes on ahead and does not remain in the teaching of Christ does not have God. The one who remains in this teaching has both the Father and the Son" (2 John 9). Thus, *to remain*, or *abide* in Him is to experience an ongoing, interpenetrated union with Christ.

Part II: Principles Derived from the New Covenant in Marital Transactions

Union with Christ assures a believer of having an eternal security anchored in his work of grace. Couples entering into a covenantal relationship with one another, unfortunately, do not have the same certainty in temporal terms, judging by the rates of divorce among believers. Thus, the appeal to the New Covenant as a paradigm for marital relations should not ignore the fact that human fallibility and the capacity for unfaithfulness represent a perennial challenge to the life of a marriage. The need for constant attention and renewal is obvious—to remain in love and keep the terms of a covenant made before God. As a matter of fact, marriage belongs to the contingent order—encompassed within our lifespan under the sun—although it is subject to a divine order in terms of responsibility and accountability before God. According to Scripture, human covenants are dissolvable by death or by unfaithfulness; a third option appears to abrogate a marital deal as well—the unbelieving partner chooses to depart, leaving the believer in a state of freedom from the obligations and prerogatives of the original covenant.

As stated before, the verb *to remain* (*meno*) indicates a close, intimate (and permanent) relationship between the believer and God. A safe assertion is that every genuine Christian has this type of relationship. Yet, a great deal of deliberation has taken place in the theological arena, centered on the concept expressed in the verb *abide* or *remain* in reference to the possibility of being cut off, pruned away, or discarded as a branch of the vine. Those who remain in Christ belong to a special class of believers who are firmly established in Christ. Yet, due to differences in theological interpretations, different meanings emerge: on the one side, believers may consider themselves to be the elected ones, placed in the vine by a sovereign God, securely attached, and allowing growth to happen. On the other side, believers may regard themselves as the faithful ones hanging on to the vine as a condition to maintain their status, with their security being contingent upon a continuous process of abiding by faith.

In human practical and empirical terms, marriage covenants tend to lean more toward the conditional aspect of "remaining" in a secure attachment with both partners demonstrating faith, obedience, and perseverance in keeping covenantal terms, rather than expecting such secure terms to be there by virtue of having elected to be together. Due to the sinful propensities of human nature, every day may offer the potential for a disaster to happen, unless both partners "remain" in their stated covenantal terms.

Covenantal analogies applicable to marriage also offer logical challenges. Although "once married, always married" may be a doctrinal view adopted by many believers, dissenting partners contemplating separation or divorce do not seem to follow the same logic in their covenantal dealings. There is no such thing as "eternal security" in earthly marriages. Christian marriages do dissolve, even among the best evangelical couples—as anecdotal evidence, experiential data, and empirical studies show. After their covenantal commitment is established, no husband or wife would allow their partner to enjoy a single life—behaving as he or she pleases with respect to other possible non-covenantal persons—no matter how unilateral, unconditional, graceful, or merciful they think they are. A faithful partner wants to be sure that his or her counterpart actually perseveres and behaves according to their covenantal expectations.

THE CAPACITY TO ENGAGE IN UNCONDITIONAL INITIATIVES IN RELATIONAL TRANSACTIONS

Needless to say, covenants among humans rely on bilateral-conditional transactions. Whether transactional conditions are written and recorded or conveyed in tacit, non-verbal manners, these terms are necessary to safeguard the fairness, mutuality, and health of a relationship. In most situations, conditions prevail as intrinsic ingredients of any recipe for accountable, responsible, and desirable relationships. Whether implicit or explicit, conditions are deeply engraved in the heart and mind with expectations as to their mutual fulfillment. The same commandments engraved on tablets or stone are now written on human hearts and minds so that God's principles for life remain essentially the same: to love God with all one's heart, mind, and strength is of primary importance. It then follows that one is to love the neighbor as one loves him- or herself.

Partners in covenant may have their conditions cast in vows, pledges, or contractual agreements, whether these are written on a parchment or pronounced as *verbia solemnia*. Yet, when these vows are broken and the need to restore a marital fellowship is evident, partners may be encouraged to adopt a unilateral-unconditional initiative to start with. This possibility is predicated upon the premise that believers are commanded to be imitators of God. Scripture registers the fact that God addressed the human incapacity to be reciprocal in fulfilling covenantal expectations and terms by exuding a lavish display of grace, acting in unilateral-unconditional ways—consistent with his loving nature and purpose. God's desire is to re-engage, restore, and renew a permanent state of fellowship with the human.

As relations consolidate and unfold in time, stipulations and expectations of a conditional nature may experience changes, due to the ongoing aspects of growth or decline in attention, care, concern, and love for each other. Partners in marriage experience numerous challenges and consequently experience diminishing levels of vitality, satisfaction, and dedication to each other. Complaints about each other's deficits and excesses, failures in communication, employment of defenses, negative comments, contempt, and stonewalling indicate the need for attentive tune-ups or even overhauls to the marital system. These contingencies point to the need to employ measures to ensure some renewal, restoration, or rebuilding of the relationship. We have approached this subject in chapter 6, in establishing an adequate bilateral-conditional contract (*quid pro quo*).

Nevertheless, there are disturbing occasions in which the call for a partner to be proactive, unilateral, and depart from an unconditional basis becomes a necessity.

Part II: Principles Derived from the New Covenant in Marital Transactions

Transactions are mediated by means of feedback loops—predicated on negative signals that indicate the need to attend to some aspects of the transaction in order to correct and align the interactive flow in the right direction. To proactively anticipate the possibility of negative contingencies, partners may be encouraged to employ a feedforward thrust—a superposed control system acting over and beyond negative contingencies—in order to correct and redirect any disturbing aspects that arise in the marital system. These feedforward occasions are not mandatory (as in legalistic or despotic transactions), but are born out of the necessity to correct the negative feedback loops that appear as repercussions of the failures to keep the terms of the original deal. A visual aid may help to elucidate this concept, and readers may also, to that end, refer to the illustration depicted in a previous chapter (Fig 8.1).

The unilateral, unconditional, and empowered capacity of the person may be evoked by the top-down decision of his or her metacognitive-executive control. This capacity is best activated and evidenced if the person behaves under the auspices of the Holy Spirit, willing and able to engage as an imitator of God. Being endowed with a full consciousness of the reality of any wrongdoing committed against him or her, the empowered person becomes mindfully aware of the situation that demands this gracious and merciful stance. Also, reality testing is an essential factor in employing unconditional measures in order to avoid a codependent transaction that may further enable an offending partner along his or her dysfunctional ways. That is, an insightful partner will assertively speak the truth in love while remaining a loving, faithful person acting in a unilateral and unconditional fashion.

To be and act in an unconditional manner is easier when a relationship is healthy and functional and partners experience mutual satisfaction. These factors foster and energize the creativity of partners to engage in random acts of love, surprising one another with favors, attention, and spontaneous behaviors. Small or not-so-small gifts may be dispensed "out of the blue" and for no reason. Action may be performed that proactively anticipate the needs of the other. All these behaviors may be actualized in freedom, for they represent conscious choices devoid of ulterior motives that are aimed with the intention to cause the partner to feel "on top" of trivial ways of behaving.

The reader is challenged to think of these possibilities and act in such a way so as to feel in tune with a giving God, loving as he does and acting unconditionally as an imitator of the Father. As Christ offered himself for his bride, so a husband can be prompted by the Holy Spirit and his own commonsense to love his wife because this is the way to be and behave. Relational occasions upon which an unconditional posture may be employed are many. Needless to say, it becomes more difficult to be unconditional when things are not so peaceful, functional, or desirable in a relationship. Here are some examples in which a partner has the choice to be reactive and retaliatory—to pay an eye for an eye, acting in a fair and reciprocal manner—or to dispense grace and mercy unconditionally:

- Being impacted by grace and mercy, filled with love, a person may decide to engage in random acts of a noble, enhancing, reinforcing, or helpful nature—approaching the other with respect and seeking to fill a need, fulfill a desire, or facilitate an endeavor undertaken by the other. The person may act as if he or she possesses what it takes to be kind and benevolent—without any ulterior motive or expectation in mind;

- Operating from a "higher plane" or metacognitive stance, a partner may consider him or herself to be the recipient of God's love, grace, and mercy and decide to love the other in imitation of Christ's love for the church—without the expectation of return and without secondary narcissism (loving the other because one has the need to be the object of the other's love and receive it in return);

- When considering the possible contingencies that may impinge upon and render the state of mind of one's partner difficult (such as being depressed or anxious, experiencing trauma, being afflicted with losses, etc.), one's unconditional disposition may be displayed—realizing that the other does not have the capacity, energy, disposition, or willingness to be an equal contributor and being mindful about the lack of reciprocity coming from the other's side. One may decide to act unilaterally, providing an empathic presence and exercising care and concern concretely because *that is the thing to do* under such circumstances. It is the proper way of imitating the Father's ways;

- Appealing to a metacognitive, unconditional stance, in which tolerance for ambiguity and frustration may overcome the urge to retaliate, a partner may decide to engage in random acts of love, grace, and mercy. A partner may do so just because these are intrinsically good ways of imitating God's treatment of sinners, including his or her own self. As God does, an empowered person acting unconditionally may "shine" and "rain" upon a partner, regardless of the merits or the qualifiers applicable to the other;

- In conflictive situations or in an impasse, a partner may employ mindful detachment and engage his or her metacognitive-executive control in the problem-solving process. The capacity to 1.) Observe objectively and monitor ongoing transactions as they happen; 2.) Take a positive, unilateral initiative; and 3.) Decide on a given course of action, are all ingredients that merge in a problem-solving process. A great deal of help comes from adopting an unconditional stance to start with. An empowered partner may promote a non-judgmental and conciliatory atmosphere, behaving in the direction of a possible positive outcome without using the "If you . . . then I . . . " formula;

- With a metacognitive stance, a partner may decide not to remain trapped in the other's negative, defiant, obstinate, etc., dispositional attitude, but to adopt an attitude of self-efficacy and control. A partner may choose to be free, willing, able, and internally persuaded in order to bless, give, share, or help the other, based upon his or her own initiative when there is no perception of any reciprocity;

- Adopting an unconditional stance allows a partner to be mindfully aware of his or her own motives: even if one thinks of oneself as magnanimous or exorbitant in dispensing an unconditional favor, grace, or positive behavior, the need arises for a metacognitive-dialogical assessment to take place: to check if any unconscious ulterior motives underlie or enter into the process being enacted and to ascertain the true nature of imitational endeavors after God's heart. It is quite easy to be unaware of one's deep-seated secondary narcissism (*I love myself in loving you, hoping that you will reciprocate my love so I get what I want*) or an inauthentic philanthropic display covering a tight, resentful core attitude (a *reaction formation* in psychoanalytical terms);

- Check if a "reaction formation" is at work: a defense mechanism of the self that represents a diametrically opposite behavior, enacted unconsciously in order to mask the actual or real feeling that one has for the other. An example of a reaction formation may be seen in the expression, "I really hate you, but Christ in me loves you, so let me hug you." This behavior may cover up real feelings of a negative nature toward the other by dispensing overt goodness and behaving "unconditionally" in (apparently) altruistic ways in order to present oneself as a spiritual Christian;

- In exercising unconditional love, one has to be mindfully aware of the possibility of being neurotically driven by the *need to be needed*. There is some intrinsic reinforcement in being counted as being an altruistic person; thus, a partner's need to be needed may seek opportunities to do something good for his or her partner. An unconscious motivation may underlie a partner's overt behaviors, such as being a rescuer, a savior, or a caretaker. Although ultimately there is nothing wrong with being nice, it is simply proper to check our motives in these transactions. Are we behaving in a decentered way, on behalf of the other, or in a self-serving fashion? Furthermore, as Jeremiah put it, "The human mind is more deceitful than anything else. It is incurably bad. Who can understand it?" (Jer 17:9). From a metacognitive-dialogical perspective, we may pray with the psalmist: "Examine me, and probe my thoughts! Test me, and know my concerns!" (Ps 139:23).

CONFRONTING DIFFICULT SITUATIONS

Many marital and family systems experience difficulties that necessitate the intervention of a counselor. These difficulties may be due to the display of a person's abnormal, dysfunctional character traits and negative attitudes, which may disrupt the harmony of the couple or family system and pose challenges for a partner or family member to deal with. These traits and dispositions seldom offer any basis for mutual, fulfilling covenants. Being (or remaining) in such a relationship often necessitates an initial thrust and movement of an unconditional nature toward the difficult partner, provided that the imitator of God is a person capable and willing to extend a mindful expression of grace and mercy with the aim to establish better, fair, and functional transactions.

The attitudes and behaviors of an offending partner may trigger a crisis/challenge in a faithful person who has usually shown the capacity to engage in unconditional behaviors in the past. Gottman's research has shown that the presence and expression of negative relational patterns such as defensiveness (e.g., denying wrongs, rationalizing, or excusing maladaptive behaviors); stonewalling (e.g., entrenching and not being available to transact in a fair fashion); contempt (e.g., showing disdain, acting in rejecting ways toward a partner); or negative expressions (e.g., accusations, judgments, connotations, or demeaning, abasing, or degrading behaviors toward a partner) naturally would elicit negative feelings and defensive dispositions in any faithful person's case.[4]

The clinical observation of the author, registered in many therapeutic instances dealing with couples in conflict, allows for the following assertion: the lack of empathy and understanding demonstrated by an offending partner, coupled with an uncaring, insensitive attitude, stance, or behavior, renders it extremely difficult for any partner to elicit an unconditional behavior. A difficult partner's resentment, obstinacy, or defiance that conveys an angry detachment, passive aggressiveness, or active obnoxiousness may trigger natural and automatic negative reactions as well. These negative contingencies, repeatedly experienced, may trap a sensitive person's spirit in ways that simply render it difficult for this person to be and act in unilateral, proactive, and unconditional ways toward the offending party.

Readers may refer to the illustration found in chapter 7 (Fig 7.1) to have a better understanding of the following paragraphs. Often, as these patterns appear, the metacognitive-executive control of the reasonable, willful, able, and unconditionally endowed person must be engaged. First, the person needs to adopt a posture of detached mindfulness in order to be able to stop a natural, negative reaction from snowballing. Then, a stance of purposeful mindfulness follows in order to engage in the slow thinking, monitoring, and regulating of the inner dialogues that emerge from experiencing problematic transactions. After the initial buffering of the automatic reactions and the engagement in deliberative, ruminative, emotionally charged dialogues, the person—with the assistance of an empowered, metacognitive-executive mechanism—may shift to his or her inner rhetoric and persuade him/herself to be, think, and act in a mature, assertive, or rational way.

The modulation of one's responses may be empowered and assisted by the Holy Spirit and the indwelling Word. The person responding in this way—being able and willing—may then employ an unconditional response, if needed, and engage in an

---

4. Gottman, *Marital Interaction*.

interactive process without necessarily supporting or validating the partner's defensive, negative, or dysfunctional style of behaving.

The unconditional response superseding the natural reaction is not necessarily a "given," but it may represent the outcome of "training in godliness" (as the apostle Paul recommended to his disciple Timothy). This training may be seen as being a process of acquiring good habits by means of purposive mindfulness, involving the proactive engagement in a metacognitive rehearsal of functional coping styles. Some of the functional and desirable habits in training in godliness may be defined: stress inoculation training, anticipation of predictable and repetitive dysfunctional patterns, and the consideration of alternative manners of behaving as an imitator of God ahead of the game, etc.

The person trained in godliness may resort to a variety of coping styles of thinking, already consolidated and abstracted into her or his tacit knowledge and allocated deeply in the structures of the mind. In this way, "speaking the truth in love" becomes a possibility, representing expressions drawn from the empowered ontological substructures and processes, which finally "show up" as responses or coping styles consciously chosen. Then, the faithful, loyal, and loving partner may consciously adopt a top-executive stance and mindfully detach from possible emotional entrapment. The partner is endowed with the capacity to behave with mindful purposefulness in order to conquer a reactionary mindset; the retaliatory dictum, "an eye for an eye," is superseded by a decision to imitate God, and say, "I will do this . . . " This partner chooses to engage as a free agent, empowered to speak the truth in love, to state options, and to address the other in an assertive, yet loving fashion. To "turn the other cheek" or to "go the second mile" should not to be interpreted as a subjugated attitude leading to codependency or masochism; rather, it is an exercise in freedom and dignity, empowered by a higher order of conditioning—the Holy Spirit who indwells the responding person.

Serious mental health issues on the partner's side that demand ongoing attention, sustained care, or the fulfillment of unfair expectations (which may be irrational, bizarre, or inordinate in nature) may tax a partner's capacity and willingness to think, feel, and act unconditionally. Human patience and tolerance for ambiguity and stress have their limits. Many relationships break down under such conditions, and marital separation seems to be a way of coping with inordinate stress. In cases in which partners decide to stay and work at it, grace and mercy are necessary features to be present in the transactions of a faithful, patient partner. Coaching, setting limits, and providing a strong frame of reference to the offending party also becomes a necessity in order to provide a sense of fairness, justice, and peace of mind to the willing partner. In any case, the necessity to provide an ongoing, empowering energy and a renewed disposition to keep transacting existentially in such occasions is an obvious feature of these dysfunctional dyads. The need to bracket painful reality moment by moment in order for a willing partner to be replenished and persevere in arranging fair deals (marked by longsuffering and forbearance) is an essential reality to behold, a condition to be consciously stressed in these cases in order to offer support to the healthy partner.

It is a very challenging task to be, think, feel, and act in an unconditional fashion. The top-executive functions, the metacognitive and dialogical processes of the person engaged in such endeavors, are affected negatively by the perception of uneven and unfair demands placed upon her or his shoulders. Besides, she or he may experience biochemical, physiological, cognitive, and emotional changes associated with physical-emotional fatigue and burnout. The necessity for the attention and treatment of such uneven conditions is obvious. Supportive therapy coupled with insightful and cognitive-behavioral approaches is often necessary to regulate the biopsychosocial and spiritual capacities on both sides of a partnership in order to engage in mutually acceptable covenantal terms.

In human terms, it is difficult to be unconditional when a partner has violated the covenantal terms in any blatant, unfair, dishonest, or unfaithful fashion. In situations that involve failures on the part of the other—such as acting in undesirable, disappointing, and unethical ways or engaging in an unfaithful or immoral fashion—any suggestion or appeal made to the forgiving person to engage in an unconditional fashion has to be framed within some conditions that may ensure a degree of fairness and care for the giver of grace and mercy. Conditions do apply in such cases, geared to safeguard the fairness, justice, and reciprocity that apply to any covenant of worth.

- In such cases, a cautionary stance is necessary in order to consider the recasting and re-enactment of the terms of a covenant: conditions have to be stipulated to allow the offending person to recognize, regret, experience remorse, repent, and decide to work along restorative, reparative, and redeeming lines. These conditions may help the repentant person to seek help, to work on a reparative endeavor, and to decide to re-engage in a better covenant aimed at faithfulness, respect, honor, and the dignity of the union. Chapter 14 deals with the nature of the process of forgiveness that may apply in such cases;

- Obviously, when trust has been violated and needs to be re-established, some conditions need to be placed in order to guide the reparative aspects of a broken covenant. It takes time and efforts exerted by the offending party to convey to the offended one the possibility of engaging in a forgiving process leading to a healing state. Both common sense and restitution-based notions apply, aimed to protect and provide a framework to rebuild trust and faithfulness;

- In working toward the reparation and renewal of a damaged covenantal union, the formula "If you do this, then I will do that" may apply in view of the circumstances that led to mistrust or that demonstrated a repeated inability to stay in mutual accord or fulfill the basic expectations established at the onset of the covenant. Chapter 6 addresses such *quid pro quo* issues. The legal/formal or functional formula "If you, then I" may gradually change into more unconditional tones if trust, honesty, respect, honor, and dignity are restored. These efforts take time, willingness, empowered ability, and constant accountability;

- If forgiveness has taken place and the capacity to let go of offenses has been displayed, then the need to adopt and renew an unconditional stance is called for. This disposition will help the forgiving person to not regurgitate or ruminate upon the past failures that have been already dealt with and forgiven. "Sewers never stop flowing"—and tapping into negative memories may constantly afflict the forgiving party, leading them to rehearse these memories obsessively and become upset, angry, etc. Chapter 15 addresses such issues;

- The person trapped in this dilemma needs to see the benefits of adopting a unilateral and unconditional stance in order to let go and be set free. It is necessary for the partner who is willing and able to be based on an appropriate principle: choosing not to consider the failing partner's unfairness, unfaithfulness, or damaging behaviors as the qualifying or defining parameters of her/his being or emotional freedom.

- The unconditionally minded person may employ a sort of "emotional override"— a superposed feedforward control system—in order to consider him- or herself as being defined in God's (and one's own terms) and to adopt an assertive stance. This posture allows for "speaking the truth in love" and exercising the prerogative to confront the perpetrator of the offense in order to engage in a conflict-resolution process;

- An attitudinal and behavioral demonstration of regret, remorse, and repentance on the perpetrator's side is of great help along the forgiveness process. In witnessing these attitudes and behaviors, the challenge is posed to the offended partner to be able to set conditions, yet at times, to be and to act in an unconditional fashion, imitating the Father's ways in forgiving and letting go in order to be free to act in love.

- To be unconditional, and to act on that basis, are possibilities within the scope of God's grace and mercy because the person recognizes that he or she has been the recipient of God's love, grace, mercy, forgiveness—and has also promised to let go of his or her own offenses. The call to imitate such ways is the real challenge to be enacted—at times, even "in spite" of the other's character traits, conduct, or influence.

The statements above are not comprehensive or exclusive. The propositions are given so that a person may be able to adopt a metacognitive stance to be employed in cases in which the structural and the functional aspects of a marital or family system seem to be dysfunctional and do not allow for a natural disposition to be emotionally free or to act on a mutually established basis of a proactive and unconditional nature. The statements above emphasize the fact that a partner is not necessarily bound, impeded, or curtailed by the character traits, behaviors, or attitudes of the other. Rather, an empowered partner may be free to display a graceful, merciful, proactive, and unconditional initiative toward the other because she or he imitates the Father. Having said that, in many dysfunctional and abusive cases, a believing partner has to exercise the conscious choice either to stay in this entrapment or to seek freedom and abrogate an already broken covenant.

THE OTHER SIDE OF UNCONDITIONAL BEHAVIORS

At times, in a surge of energy, a person may decide to act unconditionally—philanthropically, magnanimously, or disinterestedly—and grant a privilege, gift, or endowment to a partner. These behaviors may emerge from a sincere, open, and mindful person in whom the empowering of the Spirit has allocated the energy to act in a unilateral, proactive fashion. Yet, the same overt behaviors, under some circumstances, may be questioned and assessed. Psychoanalytic theory tends to view a lot (if not all) of these endeavors as being unconsciously motivated. The overt, unconditional behaviors may represent defensive maneuvers aimed to cover up some deep-seated needs, narcissistic in nature, or tinted with some ulterior motives. To give or grant something to somebody, without expecting any accountability on his or her part, conveys a degree of naïveté, carelessness, or irresponsibility. Thus, a person behaving in this unconditional way may be counseled to search deep within, in a metacognitive fashion, and ascertain what motivates him or her to do so. The well-known defense mechanisms may be at work: denial, repression, suppression, reaction formation, altruism, or any other styles of behaving unconsciously. On the other hand, the unconditional thrust may be born out of a purposeful mindfulness and enacted under the monitoring, regulation, and prompting of the metacognitive-executive agency, emerging from the top of the higher cortical (and spiritually empowered) processes.

With such considerations in sight, it is possible for a believer to act in an unconditional fashion when the circumstances demand such a stance. Aimed with the right motives, the person may dispense grace and mercy concretely. We have explored these contingencies in view of a sound theological basis, integrated to psychological principles and appealing to human common sense. This manner of loving the neighbor may be proactively attempted in concrete situations. The reader is encouraged to actualize this potential under the auspices of the empowering Spirit, who is always there to enable the human believer to imitate the ways of God.

Part II: Principles Derived from the New Covenant in Marital Transactions

CONCLUSION: UNCONDITIONAL THRUST, LEADING TO PROPER CONDITIONS

This chapter has attempted to show God's unconditional ways, as well as the conditions placed by God for the benefit of humans entering into covenantal transactions.

In his letter to the Ephesians, Paul reminds us that "we were dead in trespasses and sins" when God's grace came to us. Can anyone—including God—place any conditions before a dead person? Can we expect anything from somebody totally incapable of enacting a response? A principle emerges: we can place conditions on somebody to the extent that such person is able to grasp, understand, and be willing and able to respond to them.

The nature of God's unconditional deals is evident, since the appeal of His grace acted toward the human who was "dead in trespasses and sins" (Eph 2:1). In this state of non-being, no responsiveness, reciprocity, or possibility of grasping and obeying any conditions could be expected. God has provided the unilateral and unconditional thrust, giving a new life and then re-formatting and empowering with life the newly-born human—and allocating faith in order to listen, receive, and obey God's summoning call. Yet, because the design calls for an encounter with dialogue, fellowship, and communion with God, the address is made as if the human is a free agent, responding to such grace. Communion and the experience of love happen to humans because they have the potential and capacity to relate back, to respond to God's unconditional grace and mercy as free agents. The call to remain in faith and to obey God's will is there, set forth in invitational terms toward a loving encounter in the present—and to persevere in spite of all challenges facing such relationship—until God's appointed time for the eternal and inseparable encounter takes place.

Thus, although unconditionally given to people who initially were unable to enter into the deal, the covenant stipulations are offered to vivified people, setting forth the expectations and appeals to adhere to them with faith, hope, and love—coupled with obedience, fear of God, perseverance, thanksgiving, and praise. These theological musings may underlie the basis of a marital covenant as well; partners who are alive by the grace of God do well to consider their union not merely as a casual contract, but as a covenant before God with all the implications that apply to such a paradigm. It is hoped that some glimpses of the possibility of imitating God as beloved children resonates with the readers' understanding of grace and the concrete ways in which this imitation may take place in daily transactions with partners, family members, or friends in community. The appeal to be unconditional is there: when the occasion arises, to enact in these terms, hoping for optimal conditions to follow out of love, grace, and mercy—and to be set as guiding principles of marital and family life.

Chapter 11

Imitating God's Proactive Ways in Marriage and the Church

PROACTIVE STANCES HAVE BEEN emphasized in the world of business, social relations, and intimate transactions. Appealing to a wide audience, Covey placed this characteristic mode of thinking and behaving as the first among seven habits of highly successful people.[1] Needless to say, to be proactive is not a new concept. God, in due time (Heb 1:2) revealed himself in a proactive fashion, conveying a design that anticipates and takes care of his created order ahead of time (Eph 1:1–14). Biblical-theological considerations are presented to start with in order to elaborate principles applicable to our efforts to imitate God's proactive love. The eternally existent, omnipotent, and omniscient Creator has provided humans with a particular revelation (Scripture) in order to be known, to engage with, and to offer the opportunity to serve and fulfill his eternal purpose and good will. The apostle Paul encourages God's children to adopt a proactive disposition and to enact this mindset in proactive behaviors. He does so by encouraging us to be imitators of God (Eph 5:1) and to adopt the same attitude toward one another that Jesus Christ has (Phil 2:5).

GOD'S COVENANTAL PROACTIVE THRUST

God's proactive thrust is said to originate "before the foundation of the world" (Eph 1:4). The eternally proactive design has been unfolded before us, addressing us as co-participants in a covenant that was enunciated ahead of chronological time—not as a reaction to human contingencies, but as a purposive and intentional plan. Of course, our way of experiencing and measuring chronological time does not help matters. For an eternal "I AM," the past and the future pose no problems. God is not subject to our limitations in temporal or spatial terms. God's proactive stances and dealings are a hallmark of the one who has everything under control and sets the course of events according to his will, causing things to be and defining reality in terms yet to be grasped by mortal beings.

God preformed the human—a masterpiece in his eternal design (Eph 1:3–14) that, in due time, was formed from dust, received God's breath, and became a living soul. The human was formed into his image (*Tselem Elohim*). Scriptures affirm the

---

1. Covey, *The Seven Habits*.

Part II: Principles Derived from the New Covenant in Marital Transactions

preexistence of Christ, allowing us to infer that Adam was created after some prototype already figured in God's eternal design. Adam was formed after the image of the prototype, the measure, the perfect standard set by God to behold and imitate. In due time, Jesus took human form "after Adam" in order to become an empathic, faithful, and perfect representative before God that he might redeem the fallen human. Yet, this redemption was not a reactive deal, contingent upon human disobedience and the fall into sin; rather, it was a proactively planned feature: Jesus Christ "had been slain before the foundation of the world" (Rev 13:8).

The fall of humankind into sin rendered the human's formed state into a deformed (dysfunctional, distorted, or degraded) condition. Yet they were not abandoned to destruction, but were informed about a redemptive possibility cast in a promised re-formation and a restoration of the fallen/deformed state through "the seed of the woman" (Gen 3:25). God acted in history by sending his Son, born of a virgin, who accomplished the eternal plan—outlined before the foundation of the world—by dying, resurrecting, and ascending to the presence of the Father. Scripture affirms that Jesus intercedes for those who believe and accept God's news until he will come back to reign with them. This work is able to re-form the believer who accepts such good news by faith and in obedience to God's design (Rom 3—6). God empowers the redeemed human by transforming his or her being by means of the renewal of the mind and surrender to God's will (Rom 8:12). God continuously optimizes contingencies in order to conform the redeemed believer into the image of the Son (Rom 8:29–30); God works proactively in such a way that all things work together for the good of the believer in this conforming process.

THE NEW COVENANT CONVEYS GOD'S PROACTIVE INITIATIVE

Examples of God's proactive disposition and thrust are revealed and rendered as propositions throughout all the covenants registered in Scripture. In a special way, the New Covenant promised in Jeremiah 31, and restated in Hebrews 8 and 10, provides a series of promises to the houses of Israel and Judah. Note the expressions (emphasis added):

- "Behold, days are coming, declares the LORD, when *I will make* a New Covenant . . ." (Jer 31:31);
- It follows, "This is the covenant which *I will make* . . . *I will put* My law within them and on their heart *I will* write it . . ." (Jer 31:33);
- "And *I will be* their God . . ."(Jer 31:33);
- "For *I will forgive* their iniquity, and their sin *I will remember* no more" (Jer 31:34, NAS).

Imitating God's Proactive Ways in Marriage and the Church

The repetitive emphasis in the declarations ("I will") permeates the gracious and merciful terms of the promises. As in a granting covenant, God proactively extends his sovereign will into a design, marked by unilateral and unconditional tones. Jeremiah delivered the promise of this New Covenant while the Old Covenant was in vogue, in spite of the impending exile of Israel and the captivity in Babylon that would last seventy years. Despite the imminent gloom and doom of his time, the visionary prophet saw the day in which God would faithfully act—"as usual" and according to his nature—in proactive fashion again.

Anticipating the future, and delving into the *not-yet*, God calls things as if they are already there (Rom 4:27). God the creator, redeemer, and sustainer of the universal order has proactively revealed his eternal purpose with the end result in mind. In his omniscient wisdom, transcendence, and unlimited capacity to exercise jurisdiction over space and time, God has revealed his overarching design by providing a proactive glimpse of his will. In a particular way, this will is embedded in the promises we find in the New Covenant. By extrapolation, God's pronouncements—starting with "I will"—may be imitated in an exemplary fashion. In that way, transactional endeavors may be characterized by proactive, rather than reactive, attitudes and behaviors among partners or family members.

Jesus, as the mediator of the New Covenant, acted proactively. He came to enact the terms of God's covenant of old, but also to institute a new deal, actualizing and perfecting an unfolding design. Scripture provides us with a preview of what would be his eternal disposition and priestly ministry after accomplishing the task set before him. Jesus Christ is our substitute, who died on the cross for us; he resurrected and ascended to the Father. He became the perennial mediator of the New Covenant on our behalf. During his earthly ministry, Jesus provided glimpses of the empowered effects of the terms of a New Covenant in concrete deals. An example of Jesus's proactive care and concern for his disciples—addressing Peter in particular—is found in the narrative of his final discourse, registered in Luke 22:31–34:

> "Simon, Simon, pay attention! Satan has demanded to have you all, to sift you like wheat, but I have prayed for you, Simon, that your faith may not fail. When you have turned back, strengthen your brothers." But Peter said to him, "Lord, I am ready to go with you both to prison and to death!" Jesus replied, "I tell you, Peter, the rooster will not crow today until you have denied three times that you know me."

Jesus predicted Peter's trials ahead of time and responded to the apostle's objections and unwise assertiveness, forecasting his triple denial, as well as anticipating his restoration to fellowship with him. In a way, Jesus inoculated stress into his disciple's mind in order to foster the acquisition of a metacognitive defense mechanism to enable the disciple to regain momentum after his downfall and to cause him to be restored to fellowship (a narrative registered in John 21). Jesus introduced the possibility of a future, redemptive contingency in the mind of Peter who, in spite of his failure, would be able to be restored. In a proactive manner, Jesus prepared the apostle for the destructive forces of Satan acting against him.

In his Gospel, John provided an interesting account in which Jesus prepared fish for breakfast to tired, undeserving disciples who had abandoned the ministry bestowed upon them (John 21). Anybody cooking for eight people knows that it takes some planning and preparation to do so. Rather than chastising his friends, Jesus prepared breakfast for them at the lakeshore. The Lord's attitude and behavior were not born out of a bilateral, conditional, or retaliatory reaction to human weaknesses and failures. In John's narrative, Jesus's unilateral, unconditional, proactive, graceful, and merciful love for his own was exemplified in the simple act of feeding them. An editing note by John (13:1) reminds the readers of his Gospel that Jesus, who knew that his time had come to depart from this world to the Father, and "having loved his own who were in the world, he now loved them to the very end" (or "to the full extent of his capacity," "completely," or "to the uttermost degree").

Pauline theology emphasizes God's proactive design as it pertains to our being, position, and essential union as residing "in Christ" (an expression that occurs 120 times in the NT, mostly in Pauline writings). This expression has been the subject of much consideration and diverse interpretations of its meaning.[2] In sum, the expression "in Christ" defines believers as God's ultimate expression of well-being, security, assurance, and eternal destiny with him: "For we are his workmanship, having been created in Christ Jesus for good works that God prepared beforehand so we may do them" (Eph 2:10). Three aspects extracted from this verse stand out: We have been created by God; we are God's special workmanship so that we would engage in doing loving, good works; and these good works God has set forth ahead of us in a proactive and intentional way.

For a person to become and act proactively, he or she needs to be socialized to that end, and employ insight and dedication in pursuing a desirable goal. This person will demonstrate both a character and a behavioral repertoire marked by insightful, anticipatory, and planning traits. The image of God in the creature—defined as being a reflection of God's character and works or an exuding property emerging from being grounded in such a Being—allows for the notion that humans can and should be imitators of a proactive God. Being born again of the Holy Spirit, believers may be resocialized by the same empowering agent. The premise of this book is that, as beloved children, we are to imitate the Father and walk in love. To be proactive is to exude deep-seated values that underlie the behaviors and attitudes entering into play when a believer engages people, situations, problems, or projects with mindful anticipation, insight, and purposefulness.

---

2. Barth, *Ephesians*.

THE NATURAL REACTIVITY OF THE CREATED HUMAN BEING

As creatures, we come to this world in a precarious, fragile, and finite condition, subject to the care and will of progenitors and caretakers. We are born into a social context saturated with the transactions of other humans subject to the same context and predicament to begin with. From the start, we are naturally prone to think, feel, and act in reactive terms—to be safe and secure as we interact with stressors. Thus, we are endowed with the innate capacity to be reactive, adjusting to the ongoing impact of the environment and becoming conscious of our finitude—subject to entropy, decay, and constant threats to our well-being. Our fragile predicament calls for defenses against the anxiety of non-being, the threat of life's challenges, and multiple stressors beyond our control.

The innate reactive capacity may be defined as the tendency to engage (mindlessly or consciously) in a fight-or-flight response after being triggered by some sort of challenging stimulus—or prompted by a perceived request, demand, or stress impinging on the organism (body/mind). The eliciting trigger may be external, coming from the world outside the skin as many physiological examples demonstrate: Our pupils are reactive to light; a desirable object is reacted to with desire, manifested in accelerated heartbeats. The provoking/evoking stimuli can also be internal: Being hungry drives us toward some food; experiencing a thermal sensation of being cold prompts us to seek some blankets; feeling hurt by somebody's attitude may provoke a reactive depression; a negative memory, a flashback, or a fleeting thought of an anxious nature may elevate our blood pressure or elicit a ruminative, internal dialogue.

Paradoxically speaking, being reactive may respond to a quest for tacit, implicit, subconscious, or anticipatory proactivity. The conscious or unconscious quest for security, belongingness, safety, acceptance, validation, and other intrinsic needs elicits our natural defenses. The need to know, control, and predict to some extent what the future looks like renders us defensive, apprehensive, anxious, and eager to do something in order to have peace of mind and security. Thus, to be reactive is to display the human capacity for self-preservation and protection when facing any stressor.

Reactions could be considered as springing from diverse sources of activation. Reflexive, automatic behaviors of an organismic nature are coupled with processes mediated through the autonomic nervous system (ANS), and to higher cortical processes involving styles or patterns of thinking and feeling that have become habituated and emerge in a customary or repetitive manner. Willful behaviors may be considered to be reactive when these are engaged in a conscious, willful, and purposive way, triggered by negative challenges. Negative processes of a cognitive nature (thoughts, reasoning, perceptions, attributions of meaning, memories) and an emotive nature (feelings, sensibility) enter into play and respond to actual triggers (people, happenings of a challenging nature) or to the upsurge of internalized objects or events (introjected others, traumatic memories).

The unconscious adoption of the ideas or attitudes of others may exert influence and power upon a person's mindset: inner dialogues that emerge as self talk—deliberations, musings, conjectures, ruminations, and the like—as well as diverse voices charged with episodic and semantic memories acting as "presence in absence" when brought to mind. These interoceptive musings may trigger anxiety, depression, post-traumatic experiences, and other reactions "from within" the person.

Human fragility, entropy, and decay, springing from the existential angst of realizing our own finitude and mortality or from the fear of non-being, result in defensive maneuvers. Attempts to control and predict contingencies are aimed toward feeling safe, secure, accepted, validated, relevant, or meaningful. Many endeavors are geared to ascertain the possibilities of our survival in a cosmos perceived to be stressful, hostile, or challenging. Human development is surrounded with contingencies that foster reactive stances. The birth and entrance of an infant into a challenging world starts a developmental process of adaptation marked by organismic efforts to accommodate, assimilate, and equilibrate as he or she is placed under the care of other anxious humans.

AN ANALYSIS OF REACTIVE PHENOMENA

A person under stress or facing a challenge tends to react in a conditioned, learned, or automatic fashion—the so-called fight-or-flight reaction. These learned or conditioned reactions to stress need to be moderated and regulated in order to become more adequate, objective, and rational, placed under some cognitive executive control. A metacognitive stance helps the processing human to regulate and modulate such responses, engaging with slow thinking and elaborated coping styles.

The necessary self-control or self-efficacy needed to respond functionally and adequately to any challenges or stressors is not a natural endowment; rather, it develops with some training or shaping. Since the days of behavioral, simple S-R (stimulus-response) postulations and paradigms in learning theories, a lot of research has been conducted, which has expanded our understanding of the ways humans process information and respond to life's challenges. Even at basic levels, observing human behavior in interpersonal transactions poses a difficult dilemma—how do we elucidate what is a cause, and what is an effect?—since most interactive patterns tend to be circular and repetitive, becoming customary and stereotyped.

As complex organisms, humans have the intrinsic capacity to process information in a naturally automatic, experientially learned, and abstracted fashion. The organismic system of a human being reacts automatically (unconsciously, according to Freud, or super-consciously, according to cognitive scientists) when activated by a stressor, trigger, or challenging situation. As seen throughout this work, human relations offer plenty opportunities to engage reactively, being triggered by an array of interactive stressors. A graphic illustration may elucidate these matters.

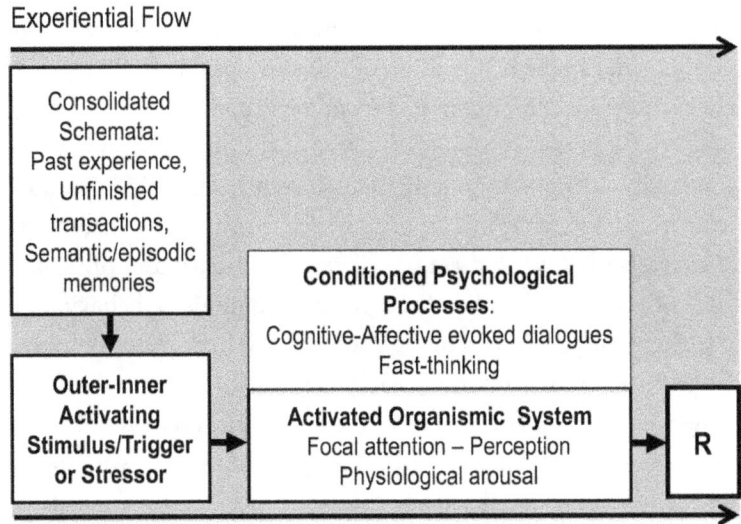

Fig. 11.1: Automatic Reactions to Provoking Stressors

Human reaction time (RT)—or the time-lapse between being provoked by a stressor or stimulus and reacting to it—has been a subject of experimental psychology since the middle of the nineteenth century.[3] Reaction time is affected by many variables, such as the level of arousal or state of attention,[4] age,[5] gender,[6] personality types,[7] as well as anticipatory readiness to respond.[8] In general, the average RT responses range from 150 to 300 milliseconds, depending on the variables mentioned above. In sum, it is doubtful that any person under any circumstances may prevent a natural reaction to stimuli impacting the reactive organism. Thus, we catch ourselves after we have been triggered by a stressor and engage in fight-or-flight reactions. Natural and automatic reactions pose a challenge to humans who desire to regulate, modulate, and control them.

Any stressor or stimulus that activates a reactive thought, feeling, or behavior may challenge the organism from within (interoceptive) or impact the system from the outside (exteroceptive). In the biblical vignette presented by Jesus, a person who

3. Deary et al., "A Free, Easy-to-Use."
4. Welford, "Choice Reaction Time."
5. Lajoie and Gallagher, "Predicting Falls."
6. Welford, "Choice Reaction Time"; Der and Deary, "Age and Sex Differences."
7. Brebner, "Introduction"; Welford, "Choice Reaction Time."
8. Welford, "Choice Reaction Time"; Gottsdanker, "The Attaining"; Jakobs et al., "Effects of Timing."

receives "a slap in the face" (an external contingency acting as a negative stimulus) naturally produces an automatic, negative retaliation (an overt, automatic fight reaction). The reaction in this S-R paradigm may be also cast as being the result of a mediating process going on in the mind or heart of the person seeking retaliation. The provoking event (S) engages the organism's cognitive, emotive, and behavioral processes (O) that enter in the justification of a reactive payback (R) supported by the Old Covenant dictum: *An eye for an eye, a tooth for a tooth.*

The mindset of a person, although reactive at the core, is also endowed with a constructive capacity, being able to anticipate, forecast, and rely on probabilities of an alternative nature. A person may engage in self-construed demands of a perfectionistic and excessive nature that act as triggers for the arousal of negative sensations, thoughts, or actions. Obsessive thoughts and compulsive behaviors may act as self-induced triggers that evoke reactionary stances and behaviors. Ontological dread (existential angst) may come from the past (as guilt, shame, unfinished transactions, unresolved anger, etc.) and from the future (as anxiety, awareness of lack of predictability and control)—and be experienced in the present, mixed with anger, fear, depression, and the like. Existential aspects that are processed by a sensitive, pensive, introspective, or perfectionistic person may trigger reactions of a negative nature.

REACTIVE THOUGHTS AS IMPLICIT BEHAVIORS OF THE MIND

In customary language, the definition of *behavior* is an act of a discrete nature, differentiated from thoughts or feelings. Yet, we may expand the definition. A lustful thought (an interoceptive or internal trigger that is entertained), according to Jesus, constitutes a "mindful act" of adultery. In this way, Jesus redefined lustful thoughts as being implicit or tacit behaviors of the sinful mind. The reactive process triggered by an external stimulus incites the interoceptive process of the mind at work—a mindful or intentional musing not yet overtly actualized is still an implicit behavior of the thinking mind. Consider this statement: "Whoever looks at a woman to desire her has already committed adultery with her in his heart" (Matt 5:28).

The statement indicates that the anticipatory lustful thought already conveys the intent of committing a "virtual adultery," and—from a metacognitive and higher perspective—is counted "as if" the person already has engaged in this transgression, violating the expectations and commands to that effect. Such a person has objectivized the woman, intruding into her virtual boundary—usually without her awareness, assent, or consent. In coveting the woman, the lustful person has regarded her as a sexual entity to be used in self-fulfilling terms. The object of desire, once registered by the covetous person—by means of perceptive awareness of physical reality, or internal imagery retrieved from memory—triggered his appetitive stances, which in turn led to consummatory reactions actualized in his carnal mind.

A person may sin purposefully or by accident—by not being on guard or by being caught in the entanglement of his or her own desires. A given thought or an image may "arise from within the heart" unconsciously or be proactively elaborated on in order to fulfill an inner desire, causing the human to engage in his or her innate propensity to sin. Alternately, the lustful thought may be a reaction, provoked by the sight of a desirable person, which appeals to the sinner's capacity to react to a triggering stimulus. Paying attention, experiencing a sensation, reinforcing a perception, allocating attribution of value and meaning to a desirable object, and experiencing the urge of a lustful reaction are intertwined, parallel processes, chunked and chained in numerous feedback loops of a cognitive, emotive, physiological, biochemical, and enactive nature.

The natural or automatic reactions, once evoked, in turn provoke further internal struggles and dilemmas. In the case of a super-conscious believer, the lustful thought—whether a reaction to an external stimulus or an anticipatory internal trigger—often culminates in a secondary reaction of a guilty nature. The person may condemn him- or herself for sins committed "mindfully" that never actually took place in the concrete, observable world. Obsessive thoughts about hurting somebody or addictive thoughts about having a prohibited substance testify to that fact: thoughts are implicit behaviors of the thinking mind that may evoke guilt, shame, anger, and other emotions. In some cases, behaviors are enacted in attempts to ward off these inner dynamics, as seen in obsessive-compulsive cases of hand washing or repetitious prayers aimed to seek absolution from a given sin, etc.

In terms of overt, external triggers, it is relatively easy to observe the reaction of a wife to her husband's blunt behavior (such as an insult, a provocative action, or looking at another woman). Internal triggers are more difficult to elucidate. Biochemical or physiological sensations, as well as cognitive processes (thoughts, memories, internal dialogues) or emotive states (unattended or unresolved feelings), may elicit reactions of a negative nature. Often, these are regarded as etiological factors causing anxiety, worry, depressions, or unrest in a person.

Sometimes these originating "causes" do not appear as obvious to an external assessor. Even the person experiencing them may not necessarily be conscious of these built-in, automatic, or organismic-subceptive processes. A stimulus may be experienced or responded to without being brought into awareness—the mind may apply unconscious strategies to protect the person from undesirable effects associated with reactions to the triggering stimulus. Usually, a person becomes aware of reacting to bothersome events or people only after the reaction has taken place. As observed in clinical settings, when it comes to cognitive, emotive, or behavioral feedback loops between partners engaged in conflicting dialogues, these seem to run in endless pathways animated by covert causes, representing unfinished transactions stemming from the past, conditioned habits at work, present circumstances that are consciously challenging, or future anticipations of a negative nature.

Part II: Principles Derived from the New Covenant in Marital Transactions

THE CONCEPT OF FEEDFORWARD CONTROL

We are used to the concept of feedback loops. For instance, we employ biofeedback gadgets to provide feedback to the person about his or her biological systems, such as muscle tension related to stress and anxiety (measured in microvolts, captured by electrodes pasted to the forearm or forehead muscles, and transduced into a signal that the person can read, monitor, and change by educating his or her autonomic nerve system). Feedback loops are affected by disturbances, and control of these can be achieved after the disturbance has made an impact, forcing the system to react in some fashion in order to correct the effects of the disturbance. Thus, a feedback controller cannot do anything until the system has been affected by a disturbance, being reactive in nature. In contrast to feedback control, feedforward control acts the moment a disturbance impacts the system without having to wait for the effects of the upheavals, deviations, or disturbances, allowing the top-down controller to cancel the effects of such inconveniences.

A feedforward control system is a concept derived from control systems engineering. Mechanisms are planned to supersede and regulate the disturbances created by external contingencies that may upset the natural flow of events in a system. Temptations may be defined as disturbances in the flow of a believer's life—coming from external sources or from the internal propensity to engage in sinful thoughts. The disturbances coming from our own sinful nature interact with the sensations, organismic processing, and basic hedonistic tendencies coming from our natural, human predispositions. To ascertain these, we need to be metacognitive about our own processes: to think about our own thinking and process our processes mindfully. This capacity allows us to employ feedforward control systems—endowed with purposeful mindfulness—that may act in a superposed fashion and modulate our responses to the tempting, negative disturbances. The reader is invited to think of him- or herself as a person that engages life's challenges "from the top," as a metacognitive-executive, feedforward controller. The person endowed with a metacognitive-executive control (or MEC) may exercise this faculty with the aid of the Holy Spirit, who empowers his or her inner being. The MEC enters into play, eliciting a feedforward control—a proper response—superposed to the disturbance in the natural, referential flow (the natural, sinful reaction triggered by the tempting stimulus). Acting as a feedforward regulator, the person's MEC engages his/her capacity to mindfully detach from the automatic reaction and then shift into a purposive response in order to cancel the effects of the disturbance. A graph depicting these processes appears in chapter 8 and may be helpful here (see Fig. 8.1).

Imitating God's Proactive Ways in Marriage and the Church

SHIFTING FROM REACTIONS TO PROACTIVE RESPONSES

A vignette taken from the Sermon on the Mount depicts the natural, organismic, and automatic propensity to react to a slap in the face. This natural reaction is countered by Jesus in a challenging statement: "But whoever slaps you on your right cheek [a backhand slap—a major insult in those days], turn the other to him also" (Matt 5:39, NAS). This proposition challenges the notion that a human is inexorably trapped by his nature to engage in a predictable, reactive behavior. Somehow, the same human may be empowered and adopt a metacognitive posture so as to be willing and able to deliver a mediated, regulated, and controlled response under the jurisdiction of a top-down agency—call it *self-control under the empowering auspices of the Holy Spirit*.

The automatic reaction may be stopped by means of a metacognitive-executive control (MEC), a sort of stop sign allowing for a small bracket of time to enter into play with detached mindfulness in which a shift from fast thinking (automatic, emotional, reactionary) to a more pensive, rational, empowered dialogue may take place.[9] An internal dialogue with self may emerge, triggered from within and based upon consolidated values and empowered premises allocated in the person's heart and mind. After stopping the flow of natural events and deliberating with internal dialogue, the MEC of the person may shift again, this time changing the content and emphasis from inner deliberation to a persuasive internal rhetoric.[10]

The empowered person may "come to his empowered senses" and decide to respond in a way that demonstrates an exercise in self-control: turning the other cheek. This is not an exercise in masochism or ego-weakness, but a response under the auspices and empowering of a higher conditioning order—the Holy Spirit indwelling the person, setting the person free from retaliation and from anybody's control over his emotions, thoughts, or reactions. Call it a *proactive principle of freedom and flexibility* that enters into play in order to shift one's automatic, fast-thinking reactions into purposive responses. Following the flow of experiential impacts and the human reactions to them, a diagram introduces the infusion of an empowering agent—the Holy Spirit—who activates the metacognitive-executive control system (a top-down agency) in order to detach mindfully from automatic reactions already in process, utilizing feedforward control.

---

9. Kahneman, *Thinking, Fast and Slow*.
10. Nienkamp, *Internal Rhetorics*.

Part II: Principles Derived from the New Covenant in Marital Transactions

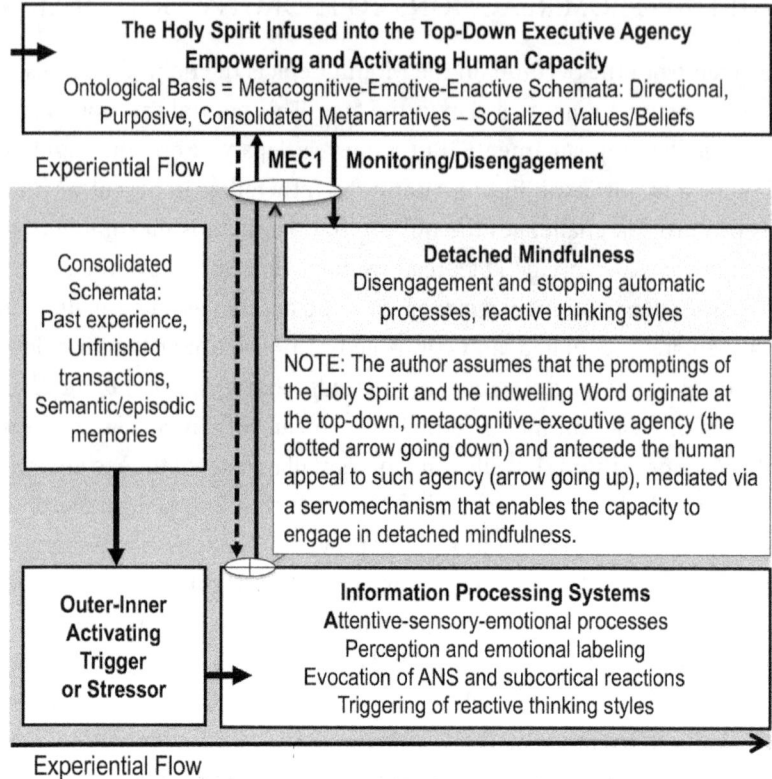

Fig. 11.2: Mindful Detachment Empowered by the Holy Spirit

The model presented here seeks to illustrate the ways humans process information. The reader may follow the flow of happenings in the heart, mind, and will of a person who, in a metacognitive-dialogical fashion, may be empowered by the Spirit and the indwelling Word to engage top-down executive control mechanisms in order to change automatic reactions and engage in self-controlled responses. The reader may refer to the illustration presented in chapter 7 that deals with the Holy Spirit's empowering of the believer's top executive functions (Fig. 7.1), stressing the enabled capacity to shift from reactions to responses—a variant of this diagram is presented here for reinforcement purposes. Note that the lower level depicting the organismic reactions are now infused and dealt with by an empowered self-control in order to engage in proactive and purposive responses.

Imitating God's Proactive Ways in Marriage and the Church

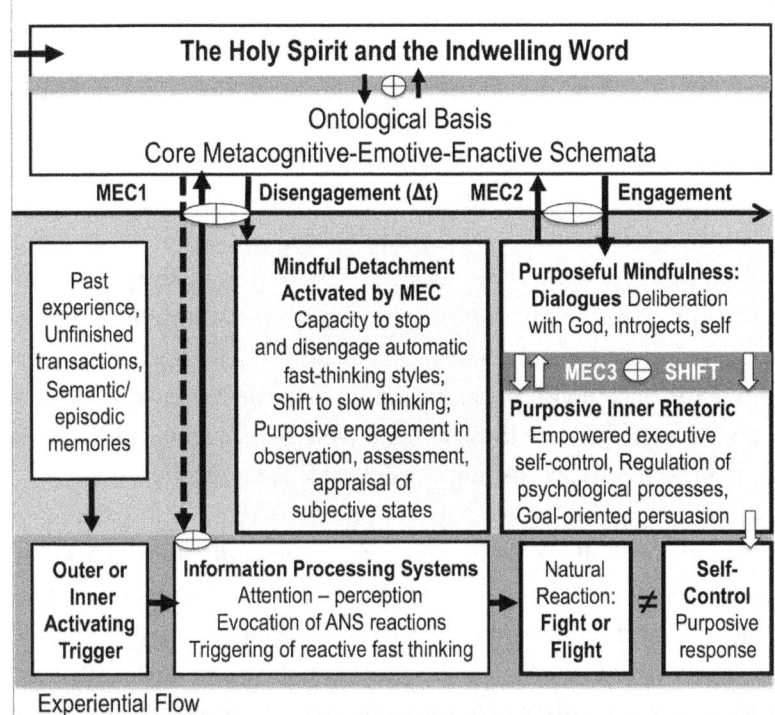

Fig. 11.3: Changing Automatic Reactions into Purposive Responses

An understanding of this process may help when transacting with difficult people or situations in order to turn automatic reactions into modulated responses. Being proactive in foreseeing difficult engagements or in facing challenging encounters may act as a sort of "stress inoculation training" that prepares the mindset of a person proactively. This attitudinal disposition enables the person to cope in a better way when encountering stress.

To shift from reacting to responding is a good start. The aim is to proceed toward imitating God proactively. The elements of a truly proactive disposition may be outlined, keeping in mind that, as in "mental chemistry," the total is more than the sum of its parts.

The model offers a comprehensive, architectural view of the processes involved in developing a proactive stance. Beyond stimulus-bound reactions, the empowered person may envision the capacity to be emotionally free and see beyond the limitations of concrete or particular events of a conditioned nature. This model encourages the reader to see him- or herself as less restricted by a conditioned (stimulus-response), linear logic and consider the possibility of engaging in more creative, divergent, and abstract reasoning. This paradigm emphasizes the utilization of top-down, metacognitive processes that allow for a more encompassing, global perspective that may foster the enactment of proactive responses.

Part II: Principles Derived from the New Covenant in Marital Transactions

Being proactive involves thinking ahead, as well as processing processes (being mindful, planning, designing, and elaborating concrete avenues, means, and strategies of action). Proactive endeavors are guided by the perception of the foreseeable consequences of projected actions: being mindful of the possible consequences, feedback, reactions, or responses associated with a given plan of action. A humble recognition of the big gap that exists between humans and God has to be considered. In God's case, transcendence, omnipotence, and omniscience—not bound to time or space—are factors that represent a top-down agent with perfect knowledge of actual, future contingencies and the differentiation between reactions and responses to disturbing challenges. These factors are dimensions of God's knowing what will be and providing all contingencies to accomplish his ends. In our case, the more we are able to know, control, and predict (within our limits) the possible consequences of our actions, the better the prognosis for accomplishing our desirable goals will be.

In our case, anticipating with a hope that is anchored on faith-based, hypostatic, sub-structural premises allows us to have a proactive attitude, which fosters inner dialogues and deliberations that may guide the employment of internal rhetoric, expressed in mindful pronouncements and decision-making. We may define faith-based responses as feedforward control systems employed by our metacognitive-executive agency, acting in a superposed fashion over the negative feedback control registered in our processing negative signals of a disturbing nature.

To be proactive is to act in faith (calling things to be, regarding them as being there when they are not there yet). Humans are advised not to count chickens before they hatch; yet, God does it because he knows. It is only through "possibility thinking" (hopeful versus wishful, desirous, or fictional) that a human can dare to do so. To be proactive conveys a positive stance—of being in tune with reality and in control of personal responses to life challenges. It differs from being negatively anticipatory as experienced in anxiety conditions. To clarify, not all behaviors that on the surface appear to be anticipatory, forecasting, or premeditated are necessarily proactive in a functional way. Most clinical anxiety is anticipatory as in social phobia, agoraphobia, panic attacks, and obsessive-compulsive traits. The person in these cases attempts to ward off anxiety by engaging in efforts to control some aspects of his or her life, and quite often resorts to defensive maneuvers such as avoidance, flight responses, or inaction. Perceiving negative outcomes before facing real threats serves as a self-fulfilling prophecy, where thoughts, feelings, and behaviors follow a well-rehearsed mechanism geared to follow a negative, self-confirmatory bias.

The person may feel defeated before a fight or a failure before taking a test. A wealth of literature dealing with interventions along cognitive-behavioral endeavors is available, representing approaches to help anxious people (endowed with automatic negative thoughts, reasoning, perceptions, judgments, and memories) toward a rational living with more personal control and adequate prediction about safety, and even enjoyment, in daily life. In such cases, efforts aimed at the reframing of negative patterns are necessary, where a cognitive-behavioral intervention may help to ascertain and define these patterns to begin exercising some purposive control and redirection toward positive comebacks and planning.

INTIMATE RELATIONS AND REACTIVE STANCES

At the core, intimate relations provide the context for optimal expressions of love, care, empathy, and the like. Yet, they also pose a challenge to a person's image, integrity, esteem, and efficacy due to the anxiety of being exposed "in the open" and running the risk of being exposed, judged, or rejected by the other on account of some imperfection. Reactive stances against strangers or enemies are expected. They are easier to envision and adopt as functional measures in order to feel safe and secure. Yet, it is in the intimate arena that reactive stances emerge as defense mechanisms, employed to ward off the fear of being known at the core.

As it pertains to our intimacy with God, the closer we come to his presence, the more spots we see in our fallen character under his light. The account in Genesis 3 depicts the first couple's reaction to God's summoning voice as he sought them after their joint fall into sin. Both partners demonstrated a basic reactive stance, negative in nature: being afraid, they ran away from God and hid among the bushes, covering their shame with fig leaves. This "flight response" shows the couple's reactive aspects—an anxious state of mind mixed with guilt and shame, channeled into the employment of defenses designed to ward off their sense of precariousness, inadequacy, and dread. The narrative depicts an anxious mindset derived from the recognition of their failure to stay within God's covenantal expectations. The trespassing of boundaries prompted the couple to recognize their wrongdoing with a sense of guilt, as they became aware of the consequences of their disobedience. A sense of shame also emerged, as a result of being exposed and discovered in a faulty, precarious state.

The notion of "falling in love" with an ideal person seems to defy logic since all have sinned and come short of the standards of perfection desired by God. Thus, the encounter happens between two people covered with fig leaves, and at best, covered by the skin of a sacrificial substitute (covered by the mediator's propitiation). Yet, due to our natural tendencies to relate, falling in love seems to be guided by some desirable template, projected ideally and held in mind, which satisfies a person's longings, desires, expectations, wishes, and so on. The incipient relationship may be cast in Buber's descriptive "I—It" dyad.[11] In this type of relationship, "It" represents and matches the perfect template tacitly held in the mind of the self-centered beholder.

Clinical observation and experience show that, after many interactive experiences, familiarity tends to breed contempt for the same realized object in most relations. Once the relationship is established with the unfolding "real person" ("I—Thou"), the

---

11. Buber, *I and Thou*.

Part II: Principles Derived from the New Covenant in Marital Transactions

ongoing interactions provide plenty of opportunities to evoke anxiety—the fear of being known at the core, unmasked, and caught with the fig leaves down. The anxiety of being exposed as having an undesirable thought or feeling or engaging in any negative behavior produces a sense of guilt (having done something wrong) and a sense of shame (being exposed as a faulty person).

It is safe to assume that, prompted by their need to somehow predict and control possible outcomes of their actions, anxious or guilty humans try to avoid the consequences of breaking a covenantal deal (an ultimate state of separation). In the case of the first couple, separation from God due to sin was a dreadful experience to go through. In psychoanalytical thought, separation anxiety represents the basis of all anxieties. This state of being is characterized by a personal lack of safety, security, acceptance, validation, and sense of belongingness.

The natural reaction of the first couple at the garden is prototypical of the rest of humankind. The reactive behaviors were directed in both directions: toward God (running away, hiding among bushes, employing rationalization, projection, blame, and the like) and toward one another (covering themselves with fig leaves and being unable to face one another in the open). From the beginning, reactive stances and behaviors appeared as instinctual defenses as partners were challenged at primary, self-centered, narcissistic levels. These stances appear to be essentially (ontologically) embedded in the nature of the human being, underlying the tendency to react in any interactions demanding accountability, responsibility, and commitment. Reactive predispositions often characterize intimate relations in marriage and the family.

Reactive stances predispose a person to seek an advantageous position in a challenging encounter in order to be in control and define the situation, the other, and the event at hand. Yet, paradoxically, being reactive places a person in a trapped, defensive, or insecure position. In short, the reactive person feels "under the circumstances" and conditioned by the attitudes or behaviors of others.

Marital relations suffer quite a lot due to the presence of ongoing, reactive codependency issues among partners. Plenty of clinical and popular literature exists concerning partners that enter present-day relations as "Adult Children of Alcoholics" (or whatever condition is perceived to be the result of exposure and development in a system with toxic parents, borderline conditions, etc.). These works emphasize labels such as "victimization" and "codependency" as hallmarks of those who grew up with this predicament. The positive aspects of such groups and movements seem to foster a quest toward freedom, differentiation, assertiveness, and mental health. Yet, at times, they appear to reinforce less than responsible stances in those who become reactive and blame their antecedents in an ongoing feedback loop.

To delve into the past is essential, and to develop insights pertaining to the negative factors that resulted in dysfunctions in adulthood is necessary in order to achieve emotional freedom. Yet, in some cases the person may get stuck in the analytical process and use his or her cognitive gains and explanatory insights to rationalize an ongoing reactive, defensive stance.

Thus, to be free and open to engage in proactive endeavors requires the reframing of thoughts, perceptions, attributions of meaning, and judgment. A great deal of psychotherapy, counseling, and group work are dedicated to restorative endeavors aimed at the restructuring of cognitive, affective, and behavioral processes that will empower the victimized person. The goal in these cases is to empower the person to be renewed, to have a new beginning, and to envision a better outcome in his or her existence. To be proactive necessitates 1.) The empowering of cognitive-behavioral-motivational processes; 2.) The acquisition of positive stances; and 3.) The purposeful coaching of the individual so that these stances eventually become more "natural."

Psychologically-theologically speaking, to be proactive in relations is to operate from an empowered top-executive, mindful, or metacognitive disposition—to think about our thinking and to process our processes ahead of time, keeping in mind a comprehensive picture of the systemic interactions and challenges. It is to look beyond the entrapments of a current state or ongoing problem, and envision possible solutions. In hockey terminology, as Wayne Gretzky put it, it is to skate in the direction of where the puck will be—not where the puck is.

To be scientifically accurate, the argument can be made that a hockey player is constantly reacting to the game in process with focal and peripheral awareness, with tacit, intuitional, and super-conscious concentration, and with the use of abstracted, experiential knowledge when making adjustments—thanks to feedback loops and feedforward control systems. Yet, within the flux of the game, the expert player's global consciousness of what is happening prompts the engagement of his or her metacognitive processes and triggers fast thinking (chunked from a vast array of prior experiential rehearsals), leading to proactive choices geared to modulate his or her reactive, instinctual knowledge of the game.

Thus, to be proactive (even within a reactive situation) is to see, anticipate, plan, and design contingencies ahead of time in order to act having in mind the possible consequences of our actions. In Christian terms, having positive directional goals aimed at the possibility of resolving matters provides a sense of direction and cadence as a person "walks in the Spirit" and engages in loving endeavors.

To actualize the terms of a New Covenant is to be free, unilateral, unconditional, walking in love with a graceful and merciful mindset, empowering, forgiving, and willing to let go of offenses. How do we develop a proactive stance? What is it gained by being proactive in our interpersonal dealings? The thrust of this chapter is to encourage God's dearly beloved children to concretely imitate God's proactive ways in our human transactions.

The Holy Spirit aids us in our inadequacies, acting as a promoter, prompter, and energizer, empowering us from within. Allocated in hearts and minds, the Spirit enables cognitive-affective processes and endows the person with the right motivations,

Part II: Principles Derived from the New Covenant in Marital Transactions

providing the energy to proceed toward others lovingly, regardless of their actions or triggers. The perception of the other—a partner, family member, or friend in a community—as God's creation, bearing God's image (whether acceptable or questionable on the basis of a human display of goodness or obnoxiousness), allows for an interaction with this person on a metacognitive, empowered basis. The infusion of the Spirit enables the person's conscious motivation to engage in a unilateral, unconditional, and proactive fashion toward the other as an object of God's love, who then becomes the object of the love of a human being imitating God's ways. In that fashion, partners in a covenant are encouraged to take the initiative in provoking one another to love and good works. Some examples are provided.

- In any impasse or difficult situation, partners in relation are encouraged to "come to their senses" (recognize the reality of their situation; experience regret, remorse, and repent); they are then coached to envision, forecast, and assume responsibility for personal choices, as well as consider the possible consequences that follow them;

- Partners are encouraged to catch themselves—to become consciously aware of their reactionary attitudes, stop their maladaptive, fast thinking, emotional reactions, and shift to modulated, slow thinking processes under the empowering of the Holy Spirit—using their metacognitive-executive control (MEC) to achieve this goal;

- Partners are encouraged to persuade themselves to seek to be empowered by the Holy Spirit and adopt a mindful stance, engaging in concrete planning of the desirable behaviors and processes to be enacted;

- This mindful stance needs to focus on an eschatological perspective: having a metacognitive view of *That Day* conditioning *this day* and seeing their relationship as a stewardship endeavor before the Lord, to whom both shall give account of how they treated one another in the here-and-now—not as "owners" but as managers of their relationship administering "God's property";

- To that end, partners in covenant need to elucidate their values and clarify their deeply held attitudes and beliefs connected to their life goals as a couple. As couples keep two processes simultaneously in mind—the accomplishment of joint tasks and their own maintenance—a sort of couple's "mission statement" emerges in their development, a common bank of values and beliefs serving these goals;

- Such a proactive vision allows for a mutually reinforcing renewal of personal resources, energy, and healthy habits, fostering a sustainable lifestyle. Proactively designing the engagement through joint prayers, shared scriptural insights, planned activities, and recreational endeavors, etc., enhances the establishment of a common platform, the life-space of being partners in covenant;

- Being proactive allows partners to set priorities guiding the planning and execution of daily, weekly, and long-term tasks. A proactive stance helps avert crises, allowing for more predictability, control, and management of daily challenges;

- In terms of conflict resolution, a proactive disposition and thrust fosters a couple's striving for a mutually beneficial solution. If both partners value and respect one another and allow themselves to be influenced by each other with openness, acceptance, and validation, then a projected "win-win" goal in conflict resolution is feasible;

- A proactive stance fosters the renewal of a partnership by "provoking one another to love and good works." That is, rather than leaving things to chance, couples may adopt a purposive disposition to love and encourage one another to behave in the right way. This love may be manifested in concrete aspects, such as in seeking first to understand the other, and then to be understood by the other;

- A proactive partner uses empathic listening so as to be genuinely influenced by the partner, which in turn may provoke the other to reciprocate and adopt an open mind so as to be influenced as well. This disposition of the mind and heart creates an atmosphere of caring and allows for positive problem resolution;

- Provided that a person is not narcissistically biased or lacking some objectivity about inner or subjective states, being proactive serves a function: it convinces the person with this attitude of his or her own capacity, self-efficacy, and esteem. In a way, observing one's own behaviors and attitudes allows for the chunking of observed experiential habits into consolidated units of self-perception, self-esteem, and efficacy. One may feel better about oneself by considering, through inner dialogical deliberations, the observed results of one's actions, leading to changes in perceptions and feelings;

- Partners may learn to adopt a positive, unilateral attitude while engaging in bilateral dialogue, anticipating and perceiving possible consequences of the interactions as they happen, being mindful of how the communication moves (or should be geared) toward a given direction;

- Partners may be coached to be observers of their engaged dialogue, in tune with the feedback, reactions, or responses of each other in order to make purposive, functional, and corrective adjustments and to envision a positive outcome or a joint solution;

- Based on some knowledge, awareness, or assessment of the needs of the other person, partners may learn to anticipate and provide practical helps or take some action intended to supply these needs—as God does: "Before they even call out, I will respond: while they are still speaking, I will hear" (Isa 65:24);

- In sum, to be proactive is opposite to being reactive (retaliatory, revengeful, defensive, or trapped by the attitudes or behaviors of the other person). It is to consider oneself free to think ahead, to be empowered to plan the possible avenues or course of action to be taken, to identify and prevent potential problems, and to envision a mutually satisfactory solution—without being codependent, weak, or controlled by anything or anybody.

CONCLUDING REMARKS

All of the above considerations have a main target in mind: to be imitators of God, and to "spur one another on to love and good works" (Heb 10:24). This text appears in the context of the exposition of the New Covenant and its effects on the believer. Practical ways of enacting such premises in action can be considered.

Ascertaining the needs of a partner is to decide to attend to these in an anticipatory fashion (rather than being asked or demanded of—and being reactive to these negative injunctions). Being mindful about a partner's challenges enables us to offer support, encouragement, or presence before the partner calls these challenges to our attention. This anticipatory stance and thrust demands empathic understanding of situational contingencies that comprise the flow of mutual experiences. To be proactive is to be mindful and plan to engage in good works—positive endeavors that take into account the needs and benefits to be experienced by the other. It is to take the initiative in setting contingencies that will foster and reinforce the satisfaction of one's partner or family member. To be proactive is not to behave as a "benevolent dictator"—imposing one's own taste or style in addressing the needs of the other. It demands knowledge, insight, and wisdom to plan according to a partner's preferences and enjoyment.

With a renewed mind, a person may engage in random acts of love, mercy, and grace "out of the blue" (the metaphoric blue may stand for earthly endeavors being infused by heavenly quality by inviting God's transcending reality into the mundane aspects of life). These may break the monotony of routines, the entropic tendencies of repetitive "sameness" in interactions, and the satiation effects due to them. In the words of a psychiatrist friend, "If you renew your mind, you never go to bed with the same person." Thus, even at intimate levels, being proactive helps us enact creative, fresh impressions (like Monet's repetitive, yet uniquely distinct renderings of the same reality captured in a new light), deal with an existential appraisal of one another, and facilitate interactive transactions proactively.

Those who are prone to write lists may jot down a few positive, purposive "things to do" for an unsuspecting partner in the following day, week, or month. In some cases, these behaviors may surprise and amaze a partner—or perhaps provoke questions if these behaviors are perceived to be unusual. Also, the giver may witness the positive response of the receiving partner whose jaw may drop in wonder or astonishment.

Imitating God's Proactive Ways in Marriage and the Church

Partners in covenant may become aware and mindful about the communication processes, the interactive patterns, and the feedback loops that take place between them and bring these in prayer to God. A faith-based, purposive attitude helps to entrench and consolidate the principles of the New Covenant in the heart and mind of the proactive believer and facilitates the enactment of planned behaviors. The desired change—from being a reactive to a proactive person—is greatly empowered by the adoption of a metacognitive awareness: we relate and behave in the sight of God, who observes his dearly beloved children and is always ready to assist them, and in coparticipation with his Holy Spirit—the powerful, resocializing agent shaping the believer's cognitive, emotive, and motivational structures, processes, and behaviors.

The suggestions above are not conclusive. There is room for a vast domain of creative endeavors that believers may engage in, following the principles enunciated so far. Preaching, teaching, and counseling on the basis of the New Covenant is good; engaging in and doing such is even better. The infusion of a God-given capacity to human incapacity is essential to optimize contingencies in the process of realizing or actualizing the potential to imitate God along loving works toward others or even the self. A person endowed with this power may resort to random, spontaneous acts of love toward others or plan ahead in order to engage in a number of behaviors aimed to empower, bless, help, or connect with the other in a free, positive, and purposive fashion.

Chapter 12

The Most Excellent Way: Grace and Mercy as Expressions of Love

IN PREVIOUS CHAPTERS, WE have emphasized the capacity to be and act in an empowered fashion, being provided with the necessary energy by the Holy Spirit in order to imitate the challenging ways of the Father. Then we stressed the covenantal capacity to be and act unilaterally in order to establish better bilateral covenants of a fair nature. Also, we emphasized the capacity to be and engage unconditionally in order to set better conditions in covenantal deals. Following the same reasoning, rather than being reactive and acting in a retaliatory fashion, we have emphasized the empowered capacity to be and act proactively—not being subjected to negative contingencies, but being free to be who God intended us to be and to act in freedom and with dignity.

In defining marital relationships, Balswick and Balswick have stressed covenant, grace, empowerment, and intimacy as the four vital components in an ever-deepening process framing marriages and families.[1] If these variables are present, and the relationship was initiated by a covenant made in good faith before God, people in interaction experience a movement toward maturity. Most authors who appeal to covenant as a paradigm allude to the fact that the model originates with a loving and gracious God, with the consequential following of those who are defined by God as beloved children.[2] The key aspects of grace and mercy are discussed in this chapter in view of God's covenantal actions in human history—to be imitated by humans.

COVENANTAL LOVE: THEOLOGICAL CONSIDERATIONS

God is (essentially, substantially) love—as the apostle John has stated repeatedly in his first letter. We may employ semantic terms to state that God *has* love or that he *acts lovingly*, but at the ontological level, God *is* love. When God displays this attribute of

---

1. Balswick and Balswick, *A Model for Marriage*.
2. See, for example, Intrater, *Covenant Relationships*; Polischuk, "A New Covenant"; Hugenberger, *Marriage as a Covenant*; Burke, *Covenanted Happiness*; Guernsey, *The Family Covenant*; Chapman, *Covenant Marriage*; Balswick and Balswick, *A Model for Marriage*.

The Most Excellent Way: Grace and Mercy as Expressions of Love

being in an actualized, working fashion, it becomes a display of amazing grace and mercy.

The love of God is the basis of all the considerations presented in this work, exemplified in the terms of the New Covenant. God has acted, acts, and will act in proactive, unilateral, unconditional, graceful, and merciful ways because these qualifiers denote God's essence and mode of operation. God's empowerment, his forgiveness, his willingness to let go of offenses, his fostering of intimacy, and his renewing of the mindset of believers are exuding properties demonstrated toward those who believe; they are vivified along their journey of faith and obedience to his will.

The New Covenant as a paradigm of a loving, gracious, and merciful nature has been the subject matter of diverse systems of Christian thought in terms of its nature, its place in God's time, its applicability, and its results.[3] Two major currents have provided interpretations that have been chunked and represented mainly in Covenant Theology and Dispensationalism.[4] In spite of differences in the perspectives adopted by these systems, readers need to keep in mind that all covenants were born out of God's love—for humankind and/or for a special community—and unfolded in space and time by a God who escapes such dimensions and is above them. "For God, then, any event is at once future, present, and past. So, for example, the institution of the New Covenant was for him at once future, present, and past."[5]

In brief, Covenant Theology stresses the *unity* in God's purpose as it relates to covenants dealing with human redemption. Unmerited, undeserving grace abounds, sovereignly enacted toward the human. Dispensationalism stresses the New Covenant as a graceful deal given to us in view of a future, discrete time, yet applicable in this present age. As such, it is a distinct deal, superseding the Old Covenant. Room for further fulfillment as it applies to Israel's future is allocated in this perspective.

For our purposes, it is fair to say that God's love, grace, and mercy abound—whether in in a distinctive, yet continuous form, or integrated with all covenants made throughout human history. The common denominator is that all systems regard God's manner of love to be of utmost importance in order to understand his designs. It is of utmost importance for *all children at all times* to imitate this manner of love, regardless of the frame in which love is perceived, systematized, or exemplified.

Readers may be reminded of the statement made by Mr. Iaccoca, the CEO of General Motors: "The most important thing is to keep the main thing the main thing." So, what is the main thing of the New Covenant? To relate to God in love, to live for the glory of God, and accomplish his purpose; to actualize our intimate relatedness to God as imitators of God at the core and to process life's offers and challenges mindfully, wholeheartedly, and willfully, as God does. The terms of the New Covenant embodied in action may be seen as the actualization of God-given potentials—to be,

---

3. Bogue, "Jonathan Edwards"; Showers, *There Really Is a Difference!*; Niehaus, "Covenant."
4. Showers, *There Really Is a Difference!*
5. Niehaus, "Covenant and Narrative," 537.

Part II: Principles Derived from the New Covenant in Marital Transactions

to process, and to do what God has designed and revealed in an encompassing paradigm. Beyond debates and interpretative conjectures pertaining to the New Covenant, the main point remains firm: God has lavished his love upon us; then, we are imitators of God as beloved children and must *walk in love*.

A glimpse of covenantal history gives us a sense of God's love as a common denominator running through transactions at all times. The original covenant with humankind started at Eden, and then was renewed after the fall into sin as God covered graciously the fallen children. Consequences and stipulations were provided, but God's essential love, marked by grace and mercy, was there in spite of human failure. Noah, for instance, "found grace in the eyes of the Lord" and was mercifully rescued from the destructive flood (Gen 6:8). The Abrahamic deal is a reminder of God's love, grace, and mercy as well (Gen 15:18–21). Years later, it was through the grace and mercy of God that the Old Covenant (the Mosaic law) came to Israel. It served Israelites as a *pedagogos*—a mentor and benevolent guide—and also as a mirror that made them aware of their sinful condition (Gal 3:19; Rom 3:20). The covenant reminded them of their incapacity to be and to do what God desired and expected from them. In Pauline theology, it is through the graciously given law that every person's mouth is silenced (Rom 3:19), as they are held accountable to God, unable to provide a rational defense against God's indictment (Rom 3:20).

The Old Covenant *became* a ministry of condemnation that brought death (2 Cor 3:7–11), though not because of a morbid or cruel intention underlying its basis. The commandments were given for life, peace, love, and justice in all human transactions.[6] However, the God-given Torah became a yoke and a burden only because human nature was incapable of fulfilling its demands—and sinful people experienced that burden. Any person looking at this mirror would become aware of their deformed, depraved natural predicament. The inherent propensity to offend God was exposed and clearly condemned by these dicta (Rom 7:24).

Yet, God's love, grace, and mercy shine in the darkness: the mirror of the law (clearly revealing our inadequacies as a super-conscious "retina display") is also the *pedagogos* that brought us back to the real teacher and savior of our lives (Gal 4:1–7). Jesus Christ, as the mediator of a New Covenant, has fulfilled the law and represents the embodiment of God's expectations and desires. He took our place as a substitute before God and offered himself as a propitiatory offering. He intercedes for us before the Father as a priest. It is through him that we are justified, accepted, and validated by the Father, being adopted into God's household as beloved children. His gracious and merciful work presented a new, living, and open way to the Father as we are reconnected with God in the realm of a new creation.

The author adopts a perspective in which the continuity of God's love, grace, and mercy are embedded in both the Old and the New Covenants, representing a unified design revealed on our behalf. God is immutable, transcendent, and free of space-time

---

6. Kaiser, "The Old Promise"; *Toward an Old Testament Theology*.

limitations, yet his covenants apply to humans bound to space and time in ways that necessitate a relational accommodation, assimilation, and equilibrium with God's deals. His design is not an inexorable paradigm of detached, mechanical characteristics, but rather a relational thrust of love, grace, and mercy, passionately engaging us, from Genesis to Revelation. There is room for specific, space-time adjustments as the many covenants registered in Scripture attests, but these need to be seen as embedded in a grand design in which the main theme is love, lavished upon us in grace and mercy, and yet to be fulfilled at the end of times.

In sum, we have a loving, giving God: "For this is the way God loved the world: He gave his one and only Son" (John 3:16). Christ the Son loved us so much that he gave himself for us (Eph 5:1–2). The Holy Spirit loves us and separates us to be saved by the grace of God and regenerates us by giving us a new birth (1 Pet 1:2–3); he sanctifies us (Rom 15:16; 2 Thess 2:13); gives us gifts (1 Cor 12:7–11); and empowers us to live in ways that please God (Rom 8:9–11). The Spirit intercedes for us before the Father as well (Rom 8:26).

Grace and mercy are set in juxtaposition to God's condemnation and payment for sin. Grace is the stance and act of giving a person something undeserved, such as forgiveness, restitution, restoration, and a new start. Mercy, on the other side, is not paying that person his or her "wages" with condemnatory consequences—something that the offending person actually deserves. Perhaps it is easier to consider ourselves as the recipients of an undeserved gift; it is a bit more difficult to recognize God's mercy because that vividly denotes our state, worthy of condemnation and punishment. Yet, both sides of the coin need to be appreciated in their full meaning.

The premise that runs through this book is that as God did it, so we must do it. God's covenantal transactions, especially in the New Covenant, comprise a paradigm for human relations, whether it be marriage, the family, fellowship in church, or caring for God's creatures in general. Grace and mercy are expressions of a loving nature needed at all levels of human transaction. We humans provide plenty of opportunities to stretch each other's patience, tolerance, peace, and capacity to remain in stable and satisfying relations. These negative contingencies are derivatives of the fallen condition—the deformed state of humankind subject to sin and depravity. The doctrine of depravity derives from the Augustinian concept of original sin, which entered the world as a consequence of the Fall. Every person born into the world is subject to the law of sin and death, and apart from God's grace, is totally unable to follow God and obey him. Thus, the doctrine of depravity is the one that receives the most empirical validation among humans, as denoted by the news being broadcast through its various channels. Furthermore, the need for so many books, articles, guidelines, laws, codes, workshops, teachings, and seminars dealing with human relations points to the fact that we are not there yet.

It is fair to assume that only when a person becomes aware of the utter impossibility to stand before God on his or her own—under the penalties of the broken law—does grace become a "sweet sound." The deep awareness of precariousness, finitude, entropy, and despair, coupled with the sense of being condemned and not meeting God's expectations, prepare us to receive the grace and mercy springing from God's love toward us. It is when we see our nakedness and abandon the efforts to cover ourselves with fig leaves that we allow God to cover us with a more perfect cover. In view of these theological considerations, partners in marriage and family members may encourage one another along the attempts to imitate such a loving, giving God.

GOD'S MANNER OF LOVE: UNCOMMON AND CHALLENGING

The apostle John has provided us with an encompassing, key description in his Gospel, which appears in the introduction of the most quoted verse of the Bible: "For God *so loved* the world . . ." (John 3:16, emphasis added). The adverb used by John, οὕτως (houtos), can refer to the *degree* to which God loved—that is, to *such an extent*, or *how much*; or to the *manner*, that is, the *style* in which God loved the world, i.e., by sending his best, ineffable gift: his own Son (2 Cor 9:5).

The apostle alludes to this concept again in his first letter: "See what sort of love the Father has given to us: that we should be called God's children—and indeed we are!" (1 John 3:1). St. John judged it necessary to emphasize the *kind* of love (*agape*) that God has demonstrated on our behalf as something out of the natural and ordinary. Paul ran out of Greek superlatives when, in his prayer, he described the love of God to the Ephesians: "That you may be able to comprehend with all the saints what is the breadth (*platos*) and length (*mekos*) and height (*hypsos*) and depth (*bathos*), and thus to know the love of Christ that surpasses knowledge . . ." (Eph 3:18–19). It is interesting to note that instead of providing a three-dimensional spatial metaphor, Paul emphasized a four-dimensional model, dividing the vertical axis into height and depth. The object of these dimensions does not appear as an obvious point in the passage, and diverse interpretations have been rendered.[7] Perhaps these dimensions reflect both the super-conscious/supra-rational and the subconscious polarities encompassing the incomprehensible, awesome display of the love of Christ for us. It stretches from the highest mountain to the lowest valley and transcends any horizontal interpersonal boundaries, stretching from the nearest to the farthest relational objects.

In principle, to imitate God's loving grace and mercy means to consciously seek to align our attitudes and behaviors toward one another in like manner. In order to avoid the entrapments of a narcissistic culture, we need to remind ourselves of this imperative when we transact with one another in the contexts of marriage, family, and the community of faith. As we experience difficult situations and engage in stressful

---

7. Lincoln, *Ephesians*.

interpersonal interactions, it is necessary to engage a metacognitive, top-down executive perception. From this perspective we may see the possibility of interjecting "God's manner of love" and treat one another with agape-like grace and mercy.

A metacognitive perspective may help us to develop a renewed insight and a deeper understanding of what it means to be a couple engaging in a marital covenant, parents dealing with children, or children transacting with parents. A mindful awareness of "who is there" to transact with becomes a vividly clear and focused picture, charged with a sense of purpose and given a higher meaning. We are reminded to consider our partner, one another, and our neighbors as objects of both God's love and ours. Those whom God loved so much become the object of our love as well.

God's loving *manner of transacting* is expected from those who were lavished with this love by God. His love should not be seen as just a globalized or esoteric wrap-around, but a passionate "I—Thou" type, a thrust that takes into account all the peripheral details of his universe, from galaxies to a sparrow falling to the ground.[8] In a focal and mindful manner, his love is directed to every person made into his image. Thus, redeemed husbands, wives, parents, children, brothers, sisters, and friends may learn to imitate God's mindful, purposive, intense, and dedicated love.

Imperfect human relations always offer the opportunity to engage in remedial ways, seeking to reestablish the stability and/or satisfaction of a system. Intimate transactions between proactive and willing partners and their reactive and unwilling counterparts necessitate the infusion of grace and mercy—an empowered, loving capacity to be dispensed toward the ones who are not so responsive, reciprocal, or fair in their transactions. The basis for this possibility is God's love, the source of grace and mercy—poured into the heart of believers by the Holy Spirit (Rom 5:5).

GOD'S LOVE INFUSES HIS COMMANDMENTS

Sinful humans prone to defy and rebel against any authority do not necessarily like or desire to be commanded (told) what to do or what not to do. An intrinsic defensiveness is elicited when a commandment is given, unless we as believers perceive a greater principle that operates behind the command. It is only when we consider God's commandments as being expressions of his love that we may surrender to his grace, have faith in his design, and obey his will. In response to a question posed by a young person, "What is the greatest commandment in the law?" Jesus answered, "Love the Lord your God with all your heart, with all your soul, with all your mind, and with all your strength." Then he added, "Love your neighbor as yourself" (Mark 12:30–31).

---

8. Buber, *I and Thou*.

Part II: Principles Derived from the New Covenant in Marital Transactions

The New Covenant infused the Old with an actualizing meaning, exemplified in a narrative found in Matthew 9. Jesus was having a meal at Matthew's house after the tax collector's call and conversion. In those days, tax collectors were the epitome of undesirable and despicable characters who were abhorred and rejected by kosher Jews. Many of his friends—tax collectors and sinners—came and ate with Jesus and his disciples. When the Pharisees (considering themselves as the guardians of the law) saw the unusual gathering, they criticized Jesus and complained to his disciples, questioning his behavior. In his response to their judgmental attitude, Jesus cited a statement found in Hosea 6:6, "Go and learn what this saying means: 'I want mercy and not sacrifice'" (Matt 9:13). This response was directed to the interpreters and guardians of the Torah to realign their understanding of its intention and purpose: to live in a faithful and loving relationship with Yahweh, not to simply keep punctiliously the letter of the law devoid of its true spirit. Matthew's account presents the author of the law addressing those who had distorted his original design and purpose in its revealed and scripted form.

The same Gospel presents another glimpse of the Torah's intention (its "main thing") as applied to human endeavors. The same company of critics complained to him about his disciples, who in their hunger, ate from a grain field on a Sabbath. Their charge was, "Look, your disciples are doing what is against the law to do on the Sabbath" (Matt 12:2). Jesus's response to the experts in religious law was based on a scriptural account, alluding to David's understanding of God's love, mercy, and grace. Being hungry, he and his companions entered the tent of the testimony and ate from the sacred bread, which was against the law for him and his companions to eat. Citing Hosea again, Jesus added, "If you had known what this means: 'I want mercy and not sacrifice,' you would not have condemned the innocent" (Matt 12:7). Remaining faithful to the Torah and showing respect toward its intended meaning, Jesus emphasized the relational aspect of covenantal faithfulness, love, and mercy over the form of the letter and its ritualized habits.

Hosea's account has been translated in the NET version as "For I delight in faithfulness, not simply in sacrifice; I delight in acknowledging God, not simply in whole burnt offerings." Other translations render the same passage as "'For I desire mercy, not sacrifice, and acknowledgment of God rather than burnt offerings" (NIV). The noun *checed* used here has been translated in many ways, signifying favor, mercy, covenantal mercy, lovingkindness, loyalty, or faithfulness, among other meanings. In Jesus's perception, the guardians and experts in religious law came short of demonstrating mercy toward their fallen neighbors. If grace is to bestow a favor upon those considered unworthy, mercy is the withholding of a well-deserved punitive retaliation or chastisement. In displaying a judgmental, callous insensitivity to "tax collectors and sinners," the Pharisees demonstrated their utter ignorance about their own sinful predicament before God and their need for grace and mercy.

The emphasis and thrust of Hosea's statement (cited twice by Jesus) conveys God's desire for a covenantal relationship characterized by faithfulness and love more than a ritualized service displayed in attempts to fulfill the OT laws and demands. To offer anything to God is to go beyond extrinsic rendering and present ourselves as "living sacrifices" (Rom 12:1–2). Decentered love targeted upon the desired object of love is not a mindless act or a performance-oriented ritual displayed at given times, but a concrete expression of a deeply felt surrender to His will in daily life. It is the unfolding of a steadfast, loyal, and conscious dedication that characterizes a "new" and "better" covenantal relationship.

The terms of the New Covenant are infused with good news—the gospel. It is by means of the gospel that such terms are proclaimed. It is not customary for marriage counselors or family therapists to equate these terms: covenant and gospel. Granted, proclamation (*kerygma*) is not the same as therapeutic counseling, and usually therapy is not considered to be evangelistic in nature. Yet, providing good news—whether directly or indirectly—to a person, a couple, or a family does offer an embedded message of reconciliation, forgiveness, restoration, and fellowship with God and with one another.

A close examination of their mutual essence and meaning may illustrate our understanding. A major premise is set here: the thrust, content, intention, and expected results of the covenantal nature are all embedded in the proclamation of the gospel. The apostle Paul called it "the power of God for salvation" (Rom 1:16) that is delivered in grace and mercy, expressing the love of God lavished upon undeserved humans (John 3:16). The gospel discloses the mystery of God—the intentional, proactive, unilateral, and unconditional calling of a people based upon premises and actions beyond our ability to accomplish or realize. Accepting the good news by faith and living in obedience actualize the terms of God's covenantal offer of love. Thus, we have good news for couples in distress who need to actualize a redemptive process.

This message conveys all the characteristics outlined in the chapters unfolding the details of the relational deal between God and humans. In imitating God, partners in covenant may realize the simple, yet impacting thrust of the manner of love exuded in the gospel. In sum, husbands and wives in marriage need to see themselves as messengers of good news toward one another, as providers of a positive message of redemption, support, and empowerment. God's love is the primary reason why the gospel came to us. It was God's desire to establish a covenantal relationship with us by redeeming, sanctifying, and drawing us into his eternal fellowship. This eschatological view is stressed in order to align all our relational endeavors with one another in God's sight, keeping this transcending finishing line in mind as we run our faithful race.

From an abstract rendering of the construct *love* (as many times we do, engaging in academic and Bible studies, focusing on terms such as *eros*, *philos*, or *agape*), we may mindfully consider the concrete aspects of love in action. After all, love is a verb, not just a concept. The incarnation of Jesus is the most concrete expression of God's love for us. His death at Calvary is the epitome of substitutionary, redemptive, and transforming love. Jesus *gave himself* for his future bride (Eph 5:2). The intentional purpose and hope of the gospel was succinctly cast: a positive outcome of this love is framed in a New Covenant "so that everyone who believes in him will not perish but have eternal life" (John 3:16). Forgiveness, acceptance, validation, security, stability, and satisfaction are all chunked in the promised outcome. Jesus is not only the mediator of this deal (Heb 9:15; 12:24); he is also the guarantor of it (Eph 1:14). The good news is also that this covenantal love (*agape*) has to be transduced, incarnated, and translated into *our* concrete behaviors of an interpersonal nature, applicable to marriage, the family, and the community of believers.

A characteristic of the good news is that from God's perspective, the human is the focal point of love and is accepted "as is" in a precarious, ungodly, and undeserving condition. Analogically, Scripture encourages us to adopt and enact relationally the same stance. Partners regarding one another as targets of love may exude their capacity to imitate God and behave as Christ did, conveying good news—in diverse forms—to one another.

A NEW COMMANDMENT: TO LOVE ONE ANOTHER AS JESUS DOES

The law was summed up in two great commandments: to love God with all our heart, mind, and strength, and then our neighbor as ourselves. Building upon and moving beyond the sense of reciprocal or mutual love—a feature in bilateral deals after the Old Covenant—the new commandment given by Jesus conveys a greater demand of imitational nature: to love *as Jesus did* (and does). In his words, "I give you a new commandment—to love one another. Just as I have loved you, you also are to love one another. Everyone will know by this that you are my disciples—if you have love for one another" (John 13:34-35). In order to obey this command, we must develop a higher, top-down mindset that resonates with the giver of the command. That is, we need to elevate our perceptions and in metacognitive fashion adopt the mind of Christ—his attitude and disposition. In Jesus's case, the giver did not depend on the receiver's merits or worth, but superposed his mercy in a loving initiative—not rejecting, despising, or chastising, but reaching out to the fallen human.

The apostle John reminds us of the meaning of the new commandment: "We have to come to know love by this, that Jesus laid down his life for us; thus we ought to lay down our lives for our fellow Christians" (1 John 3:16). We, as imitators of God, and following the example of Jesus, are to decenter and lay down our lives for our fellow believers. Furthermore, John explains the meaning of this initiative, alluding to the fact that if one sees a needy person and "shuts off his compassion against him, how can the love of God reside in such person?" (1 John 3:17). The new commandment

The Most Excellent Way: Grace and Mercy as Expressions of Love

in action goes beyond words and is concretely manifested in overt behaviors (1 John 3:18).

In order to love as Jesus did, we need to have "the mind of Christ." The expression is found in Philippians 2:5: "Let the same mind be in you that was also in Christ Jesus." The encouragement is given as an introduction to the verses that follow—presenting the *kenosis* of Jesus and his top-down approach in actualizing our redemption. The apostle's appeal is to develop the same attitude, motivation, and intentional mindset that was exemplified by Jesus—not clinging to his status of being equal to God, suspending his own prerogatives, decentering from his privileged position, becoming a servant, and reaching down to us. In other words, we need to align our cognitive processes—thinking, reasoning, perception, attribution, and judgment—with those of the Lord (as extracted, interpreted, and defined from the biblical data). Then, we may allocate the same value and meaning to our interpersonal transactions—marriage, family, community—as Jesus does, and imitate his manner of love. Our loving, graceful, and merciful thrust needs to be interpenetrated by the Holy Spirit, who may condition and direct our thoughts and feelings as we relate to one another and imitate God's ways.

Thus, partners intending to form permanent, stable, and satisfactory covenants need to frame their stances toward each other in a manner characteristic of the New Covenant's good news—embedded in God's love. The marriage terms encompassed in God's love need to be refreshed, renewed, and existentially actualized in order to avoid distorting the content and intention of the central message. Otherwise, God-given news becomes inoperative—and even condemning—bad news. That is the argument presented by Paul in Ephesians 4: based upon God's love and Christ's work, and applied by the Holy Spirit, believers are to actualize their potential to live as God has designed. The same applies in Paul's argument in Ephesians 5: God's love and Christ's exemplary character and work are the basis for the believer's imitation and walk in love.

At times, cross-cultural differences are taken as premises to argue about the functional applicability of covenantal terms, often yielding to cultural pressures to behave according to the patterns set by the prevailing societal or tribalistic standards. It is of interest to this work to consider that, as a Hebrew of Hebrews and a Roman citizen, the apostle Paul wrote in Greek, addressing believers in Ephesus (modern Turkey), giving instructions pertaining to covenantal relations patterned after God's will. In doing so, the apostle crossed the prevailing ethnocentric and cultural barriers of his time, addressing those Ephesians as being redefined in Christ with a universal message of restoration and renewal. In the apostle's view, they were part of a new creation and living under the lordship of Christ—far beyond their cultural and customary of ways of relating in their marriage and family systems.

The love exemplified by Jesus has a universal appeal and transcends cross-cultural barriers. The apostle Paul reminded husbands in Asia Minor to love their wives *as*

Part II: Principles Derived from the New Covenant in Marital Transactions

Jesus loved the church—to the point of giving his life for her—and as imitators of God's loving ways (Eph 5:25; 5:1). We must be reminded that these believers were not Jews or Greeks, although such cultures might have been represented in Ephesus as well. To love as God does, as Christ does—in every culture, in every age—is a command leading to a behavioral display under the regulation of deeply renewed, underlying processes (Eph 4:23—being renewed in the attitude of our mind) that emanate from deeply regenerated, metacognitive, executive, ontological structures.

Thus, beyond acting in loving ways or thinking and feeling in loving terms, to *be a loving person* rests at the core of obeying the command to love as Jesus did. The same applies to mercy: "Be merciful, just as your Father is merciful" (Luke 6:36). Thus, it is an imperative necessity to regard love, grace, and mercy as ontologically entrenched, emergent properties of a cognitive, affective, and enactive nature that exude from the "inner being"—the substructures of being human (Eph 3:16–17). An illustrative picture may serve to underscore these notions.

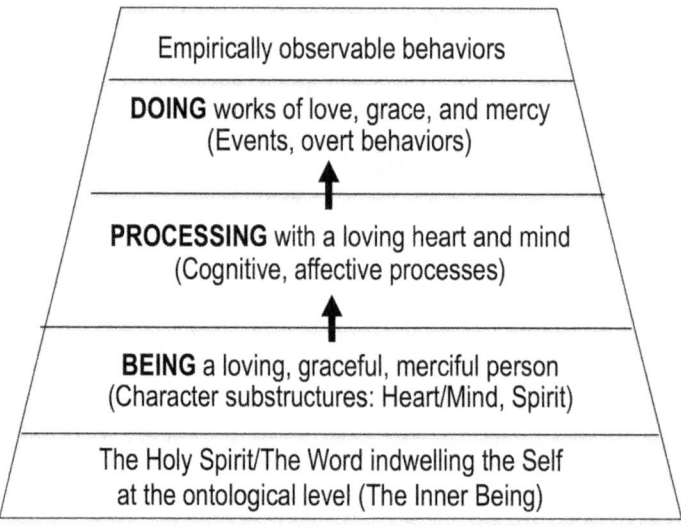

Fig. 12.1: Levels of Analysis: Being, Processing, and Behaving

Imitating God's grace and mercy presupposes a proactive stance, directed unconditionally toward the objects of love in our lives. Whether husbands or wives, parents or children, brothers or sisters, or friends in the body of Christ, we are framed in God's design as imitators of God's character and ways, walking in love and dispensing grace and mercy. That is, we are to plan ahead to give the necessary grace to those who do not deserve any gift, break, or favor. Also, we are to withhold any retaliatory punishment toward those who deserve a chastisement for their attitude, behavior, or trespasses committed against us.

Many therapeutic efforts have been dedicated to emphasize a quest for individuation and differentiation between partners entangled in codependent systems.[9] These efforts sought to balance the processes of individuation and mutuality, to foster the establishment of proper boundaries, and to promote freedom and assertiveness in transactions. The need for bilateral-conditional contracting has characterized most of the efforts dedicated to these ends. The Christian community is not immune to dysfunctional patterns in relations, and these need to be addressed in proper ways. The interplay between justice and love—expressed in graceful and merciful terms—is a major factor in dealing with Christian couples and families.

We may be reminded that in natural terms, human love appears to be conditional, seeks bilateral reciprocity, and is often reactive, contingent upon some demonstration of love on the neighbor's part to start with. Demonstrating love toward a given person and experiencing rejection from that person usually elicits some feelings of disappointment or frustration in us. We tend to diminish our affect toward the offending party in order to protect our integrity and avoid any further hurt. We feel offended and are prone to retaliate in less than loving ways. Yet, we are reminded of the fact that God's love has reached us in our detached, rejecting, and ungodly state: "For while we were still helpless, at the right time Christ died for the ungodly. (For rarely will anyone die for a righteous person, though for a good person perhaps someone might possibly dare to die.) But God demonstrates his own love for us, in that while we were still sinners, Christ died for us" (Rom 5:6–8).

Scripture depicts us as the object of God's love. In a natural (unredeemed) state, we are less than admirable or desirable objects. Due to the deforming, degrading, and devastating effect of human sin, God's targeted object has been described as being "dead in your transgressions and sins" (Eph 2:1). Addressing the Ephesians, Paul reminded them that God took the initiative to rescue them from this state (inert, shut down, unable to reciprocate). They were counted as being estranged from God and unaware of his presence, will, or purpose (Eph 2:2–4). The Ephesians (like the rest of us) had deliberately crossed God's boundaries and purposely challenged his will. They committed errors and made mistakes in their judgment with detrimental consequences. They had "missed the mark" set by God and fell out from the way. Gentiles at large were "dead in trespasses, lapses, and sins," and in spite of this fact, God acted in love, grace, and mercy toward his object. Likewise, we may imitate God and mindfully set our minds on the object of our love—our wife, husband, child, parent, etc.—and act as God did, with an empowered initiative that does not depend upon the moves of the other.

---

9. Beatty, *Codependent No More*; Norwood, *Women Who Love*.

Part II: Principles Derived from the New Covenant in Marital Transactions

AN EXPANDED VERSION OF LOVING EXPRESSIONS

The emphasis given to the "five languages of love" in our present-day evangelical culture has been the object of much attention.[10] Once the concept was popularized in the field of marital relations, it was expanded to a wider audience—children, adolescents, men, women, singles, people in the marketplace, and even the military. These languages include words of affirmation, quality time, giving/receiving gifts, acts of service, and physical touch. Chapman describes these as expressive and receptive factors present in good relationships. Although the systematic application of this paradigm may be useful, we need to pay attention to the fact that it is not as simple to apply the five languages in a wholesale fashion as it sounds. Language is commonly defined as the method or system used in human communication, expressed in verbal, written, or behavioral ways. Partners actively and selectively interpret their messages or languages, and several barriers may intervene between senders and receivers of data. Also, the interaction of these variables is not as predictable as we would like it to be, and only can be explained after the fact.

The five languages abstracted by Chapman may be expanded and regarded as the expressive aspects of love comprising the fruit of the Holy Spirit—the evidential byproduct of having been infused and empowered with Spirit by God. The fruit of the Holy Spirit is the array of manifested qualities of character and conduct exuded by an empowered believer—subsumed under the love construct. The faith and obedience of the believer—surrendering to and being filled with the Holy Spirit—produces essential, motivational, and behavioral outcomes of an enhanced nature. This amplified version of loving expressions derives from Pauline theology, extracted and interpreted from the passage found in Galatians 5:22–23. The well-known text may be interpreted as representing an array of nine qualities running in sequence or a better definition of love, punctuated so as to emphasize the fact that *love* is *the* fruit of the Spirit. If we read "love" followed by a colon—*love: joy, peace, patience, kindness, goodness, faithfulness, gentleness, and self-control* [emphasis added]—we may derive eight dimensions of the same fruit.

The basis for this notion may be found in the letter to Galatians, where Paul's emphasis on the work of the Holy Spirit is contrasted to the demands of the law as these pertain to human efforts to be and to do what God desires. The eight exuding properties of love are framed in the context of a New Covenant. The Old Covenant, given as an external set of commandments, did not have the power to tame or subdue the works of the flesh (Gal 5:19–21). The New Covenant, made in the Spirit and infusing power into the hearts and minds of believers, fosters the production of the desired fruit: the exuding properties of the empowered character and conduct of believers who are filled with the Holy Spirit. These are:

10. Chapman, *Covenant Marriage*.

- Joy: manifesting cheerfulness; extending a favorable disposition of gladness in interpersonal transactions;

- Peace: fostering a climate of tranquility; seeking harmony and concord; promoting the cessation of hostilities; securing safety in relations;

- Patience: conveying an attitude of being long-tempered; embracing steadfastness, endurance, and long-suffering in interpersonal dealings; demonstrating tolerance for ambiguity and frustration; persevering through difficulties in transactions;

- Kindness: a benevolent attitude that supplies the needs of the other and avoids harshness in transactions; a service-oriented stance that expresses moral integrity, excellence, and uprightness in relations;

- Goodness: an intrinsic quality of character patterned after God's uprightness, expressed in acts of kindness and beneficence (versus self-righteousness) toward one another;

- Faithfulness: a quality of being that precedes doing good works; fidelity in relationships; a dispositional attitude that stretches forward, envisions the fulfillment of, and trusts in God's preferred will as it pertains to human relations; a confident stance of a proactive nature in interpersonal transactions;

- Gentleness: a quality of peaceful mildness; a regulated and modulated exercise of power in responding to others; being good-natured and exuding affableness in ways that facilitates communication;

- Self-control: the display of temperance in relations; the virtue of a character that regulates, modulates, and exercises dominion over his/her reactions, desires, and passions; analogous to the concept of self-efficacy in psychology.

The apostle Paul concludes with the assertion that "against such things there is no law" (Gal 5:23b). That is, the believer under the New Covenant is empowered to exude love as a free, willing, and able person—far above and beyond any injunctions, demands, or reproaches of legalistic nature.

EXPANDING EVEN MORE THE CONCEPT OF COVENANTAL LOVE

Love is the core thrust, the causative force behind covenantal transactions. It subsumes all other principles and becomes manifest as the incarnation of the abstract truth given by God, enacted in deep encounters with God and with one another. Being unilateral, unconditional, and proactive in relating to a partner are expressions of agape love. Forgiving and letting go of offenses are hallmarks of those who love a transgressor in God-like manner, imitating the Father's powerful stances in conveying

Part II: Principles Derived from the New Covenant in Marital Transactions

grace and mercy toward an offending party. Listening with empathy—and affirming, validating, and empowering rather than powering over a partner—are capacities to be actualized.

An expanded—yet concrete—way of actualizing our potential to love as God does may be drawn from the classic passage found in 1 Corinthians 13:4–8. From Chapman's five languages of love, expanded to eight dimension of love as being the fruit of the Holy Spirit, we may postulate fifteen descriptions of practical agape love derived from the passage. Adopting an axiomatic stance and regarding Jesus as the incarnation of love and the epitome of its concrete display allow for the substitution of the noun *love (agape)* with the actual *person* of Jesus, the *logos* made flesh. We may ascertain how this superposed reading fits him in terms of ontological, essential characteristics of being—from which his "doing" shows forth:

- *Jesus is patient*—not impatient, impulsive, or reactive in transactions;
- *Jesus is kind*—benevolent, not mean or spiteful toward the other;
- *Jesus does not envy*—not discontented or coveting someone else's assets;
- *Jesus does not boast*—does not display achievements, possessions, or abilities, and does not seek self-satisfaction or gratification;
- *Jesus is not proud*—not arrogant, but modulates his personal displays of character and conduct with humility;
- *Jesus is not rude*—not harsh or obnoxious, but gentle, affable, empathic, respectful of the other;
- *Jesus is not self-seeking*—not egotistical, but decentered, considerate, and outreaching to the other, seeking the best possible benefits for the other;
- *Jesus is not easily angered*—demonstrates longsuffering, tolerance for frustration and ambiguity, and does not react inappropriately to negative contingencies;
- *Jesus keeps no record of wrongs*—lets go of offenses against his person, does not regurgitate negative memories or dwell in the past;
- *Jesus does not delight in evil but rejoices with the truth*—takes no pleasure in witnessing the misery of others, neither causes others to suffer in a sadistic fashion, but celebrates dignity, fairness, and accurate renderings of reality in a positive fashion;
- *Jesus always protects*—provides a cover, buffer, or shield against possible threats to the safety, dignity, or freedom of the other;
- *Jesus always trusts*—gives the benefit of the doubt to the other, assumes good faith in transactions, considers the other as worthy of confidence;

- *Jesus always hopes*—expects the best possible outcomes, projects possibilities of goodness, does not give up or diminish the probabilities of experiencing a better deal;
- *Jesus always perseveres*—sticks to his goals, remains faithful and loyal to his promises and commitments, and is dedicated to see the optimal outcomes in all his projected endeavors;
- *Jesus never fails*—has the willingness, ability, and power to accomplish God's will, the capacity to remain on target and deliver the goods promised to the other.

These fifteen expressions are concrete, operational definitions of covenantal love that fit perfectly the character and conduct of Jesus. They are exuding properties of his being and doing. For the believer, these descriptions represent the hallmarks of being an imitator of the Father's ways, following the example of Christ, and demonstrating grace and mercy toward a significant other. We are all, as disciples of Jesus, called to imitate this covenantal love.

Often in workshops, seminars, and marriage retreats with couples, the author has conducted an exercise, reading in public this passage and superposing his own name into the text (instead of "love" or "Jesus"). In that way, the reading goes, "Pablo is patient . . . is kind . . . does not envy . . . does not boast, etc.," in the presence of Frances, his wife, and the audience as witnesses. In doing so, the author places himself in front of the mirror of the Word, consciously aware of his shortcomings, inadequacies, and lack of perfection. The need for grace and mercy becomes obvious to him. Then, the appeal and request is made to those partners that participate in the retreat to face each other and replace the noun *love* in 1 Corinthians 13 with their own names. As partners read this passage to one another with attentive mindfulness, they may mirror and note their own fitting (or not) into these concrete definitions. This exercise usually ascertains the degree to which those of us who claim to imitate God as beloved children actually exude these qualities—and how much we need to polish our character and conduct.

It is encouraging to grasp the truth that any believing person who keeps his or her covenantal terms is endowed with the same certainty that characterized Paul's assertion: That person resides in God, and God resides in him or her (1 John 3:24). The permanence of the reciprocal relationship between God and the believer is emphasized (see the same statements made in 1 John 2:6; 4:12–13, 15–16). "Dear friends, let us love one another, because love is from God, and everyone who loves has been fathered by God and knows God" (1 John 4:7). The first thrust of this statement gives the causal reason why the readers ought to love one another: because the impetus or exuded capacity proceeds from God's Spirit, empowering the human to imitate the Father. The second clause adds this thought: everyone who loves is fathered by God and knows God, reinforcing the notion that a reciprocal and filial relationship does exist.

Part II: Principles Derived from the New Covenant in Marital Transactions

LOVING IN TOUGH TIMES

As stated before, to dispense mercy is to have compassion and to not pay someone what she or he deserves. It is an unmerited letting go of the proper administration of justice. It is the dropping of all charges and penalties that correspond to the offender of God's righteousness, standards, and demands. In his mercy, God did not count our predicament as something to despise, but saved us (Eph 2:4; 1 Pet 1:3).

Covenantal transactions pose a challenge to marital partners as people in intimate relationship never fail to hurt one another with attitudes or behaviors. These offenses may be overt or covert, conscious or unconscious in nature. Broken promises and vows, and failures to fulfill each other's expectations, affect the stability and satisfaction of partners. Disappointment, dejection, and despair result from trespasses against one's person or boundaries ("sins of commission") or from failures to keep the promises made to each other ("sins of omission"). Needless to say, covenantal transactions necessitate both grace and mercy to maintain the stability and satisfaction of marriages and families.

To dispense grace toward a person who has offended one's being requires a conscious realization of the damage done. It demands a reality check to ascertain the impact to oneself as a "narcissistic injury" has entered into the process. From minor offenses to major ones—such as betrayal of trust—it becomes difficult to deal with one another when a person has been hurt at the core. The sense of being degraded—dejected, depreciated, or diminished—is difficult to ignore. Often, the impact of the offense is magnified, and a snowball effect increases the sense of devastation. Naturally, the individual affected resorts to protective maneuvers that appear to spring automatically from the self-preserving defenses of one's being.

When the person feels the angst of humiliation or when feelings of revenge overtake an otherwise tranquil state of mind, it is simply difficult for this person to think in graceful terms. When an awareness of the devastating effects of abuse, neglect, injury, hurt, or pain appears to control all considerations, only God's empowering through the Holy Spirit enables a person to engage in a process of forgiveness based on grace and mercy. The natural propensity of the human is to retaliate, or at least to aspire to have some sense of justice being done.

Throughout human history, diverse philosophies have developed in the attempt to ward off these natural tendencies. Stoicism, for example, teaches a brand of self-control that denies suffering, pain, or stress—or at least ignores these natural characteristics of humans. The Christian response to offenses, trespasses, and the like, is not to ignore the offender, but to deal appropriately with him/her. Natural propensities are placed under the auspices of the empowering Spirit in order to learn to respond after testing reality—accepting the challenge, dealing with retaliation at the core, and choosing to respond in a purposeful way. The strength of the empowering person and presence gives us the capacity to live the terms of a New Covenant and to imitate God, who has been offended by humanity from Adam to the last existing being. Yet, he says, "And of their sins and misdeeds, I will remember no more."

Understanding the premises of the New Covenant allows us to decide to act by faith and to be empowered by the Holy Spirit, to take initiatives of a unilateral, unconditional, and proactive nature in our daily transactions, and to practice the dispensation of grace and mercy. The opportunities to engage in these ways are there, every day, in every household, in every congregation. We do not have to look very hard or very far to encounter situations in which our boundaries have been trespassed upon or challenged. In our transactions, we are subject to failures and dysfunctions on a daily basis.

Plenty of contingencies characterizing trivial encounters between people call for grace and mercy. As believers, we may be triggered or challenged to elicit responses that should reflect our regenerated and empowered state and our deep understanding and grasp of God's love, grace, and mercy—to be concretely dispensed in imitational ways. Having such a metacognitive mindset is advantageous because our graceful works are not the result of forced compliance with a law, nor do they result from sporadic, precariously drawn efforts. Rather, they represent the exuding properties of well-adjusted and empowered individuals, who have been treated with love, grace, and mercy themselves. Doing good works springs from being a loving person at the core, engaging in cognitive and affective processes, and demonstrating this attitude of the mind-heart in overt actions.

Scripture appeals to figurative language to convey deep, spiritual truth. The analogy of botanical growth applies in the case of the person manifesting the "fruit of the Spirit," interpreted as being the emergent properties of love which are the result of coparticipation between the divine seed and the human soil. Furthermore, the fruit of the Spirit manifested by the believer depicts the array of exuded traits or characteristics of the person infused by God's Spirit, actualizing the terms of the New Covenant. The list of nine descriptive attributes of character in Galatians 5 starts with love at the core. Perhaps we may interpret the rest of the descriptors—joy, peace, patience, kindness, goodness, faithfulness, gentleness, self-control—as amplified aspects or dimensions of love as well.

Thus, reliance on the Holy Spirit as an empowering agent for the actualization of human potentials enacted in faith and obedience is an essential feature of the capacity to live out the terms of a New Covenant. Transactions between intimate people may draw from the Spirit so that they may be empowered to think, feel, and act in desirable ways before God. Couples, families, and friends in fellowship who live under the auspices of the Holy Spirit may abandon their efforts to control or abase one another in any way; instead, they realize the fact that all those who relate to them are children of God, loved by him and brought into their life-space.

Connecting in a Spirit-empowered manner allows for true fellowship in love.[11] Connectedness may be affected by negative patterns of relating and by conflicts arising

---

11. Crabb, *Connecting*.

Part II: Principles Derived from the New Covenant in Marital Transactions

from stresses impinging upon our relations. At times, the tasks and demands placed upon partners in covenant may be experienced as heavy burdens. It takes some effort to reframe negative contingencies so that doing what is right before God is sensed, not as a heavy burden, but as a privilege before an overseeing Spirit. Depending upon and drawing energy from this vital person, presence, and power allows those engaged in intimate relations to connect in a better fashion and bear the burdens of one another. Conflict-resolution paradigms may draw from such influential aspects of grace and mercy—beyond relying on demands for fair and just attempts to establish a *quid pro quo* on behalf of two self-centered individuals.

ASSESSING OUR MOTIVATIONS IN DISPENSING GRACE AND MERCY

Imitating the Father's ways in human transactions is possible only because of God's infusion of power into the believer's motivation to do so. To dispense grace and mercy toward others is the right thing to do, predicated on the capacity to behave according to God's will and to utilize his power to achieve his purposes. Yet, in doing so, it is necessary for us to check our motivations because as humans we are prone to deceive ourselves and behave in ways hidden from our sight (Ps 19:12). It is in his light that we see reality as defined by God (Ps 36:9). Why would we display a willingness to offer something undeserved or dispense an unmerited favor to an offending party? The answers to "why" questions are not necessarily functional or correct. Consider the following possibilities:

- Ulterior motives: we need to ascertain whether we assume a top-down position and condescend or patronize the other, whom we may consider to be lower than ourselves or beneath our dignity. Perhaps we experience a sense of well-being for being altruistic in demonstrating our goodness, or we are drawing attention to our magnanimous capacity to rise above expectations. We may expect to receive grace and mercy in return in order to feel accepted, validated, or secure; etc.;

- Unconscious motivations: we need to check a possible need to expiate ourselves by treating the other with grace and mercy, with the hope that some reciprocity from a higher order will come our way (God forgiving us and granting us grace and mercy in view of our disposition to engage in these behaviors toward someone else);

- Fulfilling a commandment: we need to ascertain whether we are prompted by a sense of obligation, behaving under constraints to obey an injunction or internal command ("I ought, I must, I should"). Paying dues often involves an action taken with a reluctant attitude, a resentful heart, or a forced will; we may feel pressured to comply under a sense of obligation. Dispensing a privilege, on the other side, may be an act of a unilateral and unconditional nature in which we do not expect anything in return;

- Codependency: we must ascertain whether we engage in a naïve dispensing of grace and mercy because these behaviors maintain some dysfunctional status quo in our relations—for instance, to preserve a dysfunctional marriage or to avoid the anxiety generated by changes that may occur in the structures or stability of a dysfunctional system.

The reader may engage in some scrutiny and ascertain whether grace and mercy flow from an empowered heart and mind, being mindfully aware of the reasons to behave in such a manner and counting the consequences of doing so. In more positive fashion, being empowered by the Spirit and based upon the Word, a person may engage in acts of grace and mercy that spring from a loving disposition of character. Examples of these occasions are presented here:

- A partner has failed to live up to the terms of the covenant. The range is wide open; from minor offenses to major breaks in faithfulness, the violation of trust, attentive care, empathic understanding, or the fulfillment of needs require the dispensing of a great deal of grace and mercy. If any attempts are made to renegotiate, reconnect, restore, or renew a broken relationship, concrete steps need to be taken by a proactive, loving, graceful, and merciful partner—provided that these steps are taken in full consciousness as he or she is empowered by God's Spirit to act in freedom and dignity;

- A partner behaves in negative ways—including verbal and nonverbal dejection, contempt, insults, offenses, and abuse—which do not deserve any reinforcement or tolerance. In these instances, the capacity to confront—to speak the truth in love—is called for. Dispensing grace and mercy does not preclude or exclude a partner's freedom to speak the truth in love and be assertive in dealing with the other. The undeserving partner may be treated lovingly while the confrontation takes place; love and justice are simultaneously held in sight. The graceful and merciful partner engages the other in full consciousness of doing so in the sight of God, who is the ultimate perceiver and judge of all covenantal transactions. The empowered person may employ feedforward control systems to superpose and respond to negative contingencies aimed with a higher, metacognitive perspective and remain in control of his/her responses. A free, insightful, and empowered person does not operate out of a conciliatory codependency or a self-deprecatory submission to nonsense. He or she behaves mindfully, willingly, and hopefully, envisioning better results;

- When engaged in disputes or disagreements that disrupt the amicable, peaceful, and caring ambiance of the couple, both partners need to "come to their senses"—to become mindful of what is going on at the moment in order to stop these negative, reactionary contingencies and engage in modulated responses toward one another. The intromission/introduction of love, grace, and mercy from a top-down executive agency is necessary to stop the negative flow and redirect the process toward a more functional transaction.

In sum, as an expression of love, grace is called for when anomalies and failures in keeping the terms of a covenant act in destructive ways, granting a favor to an undeserving partner. Mercy is called for when a partner is tempted to retaliate and get even with the offending other; not punishing the partner is a feature empowered by the Holy Spirit—not an exercise in weakness or codependency.

CONCLUSIONS

This chapter has emphasized the need to imitate God's loving manner in covenantal relations. The concrete dispensation of grace is essentially an exuding attitude of the heart and mindset, aimed at granting something to an undeserving person. Mercy, on the other hand, is the compassionate attitude displayed in letting go of offenses without retaliating in any punitive way against the offending person. It is the consciously enacted thrust of forgiveness, in which we choose not to apply any punishment that an offending person actually deserves. This stance is possible through the empowering presence and power of the Holy Spirit, aiding the metacognitive-executive control of a person.

Many interpersonal, transactional occasions arise in which a transgressor who has done damage to a covenantal deal is present. The resulting disappointment, disillusionment, and betrayal usually evoke a stance of righteous indignation, aimed at the administration of justice and the punishment of the transgressor. Mercy is the ability to see our own faulty predicament before a holy and righteous God, to recognize the manner in which God has dispensed his mercy upon us, and to drop the stones with which we might apply our justice. Being driven by our righteous indignation against an offender evokes strong reactions in us. Yet, we may transform our reactions into responses by appealing to a principled command to confront the offender, deal with the offense, and adopt a graceful and merciful disposition to forgive and let go.

The metacognitive-executive function (alluded to in previous chapters) may enable us to ponder over a principle involving the Father and the Son: The finger of the Father wrote on tablets of stone, "You shall not commit adultery" in order to safeguard covenantal relationships (Exod 20:14). A woman who broke this commandment was caught and brought to Jesus by the experts in the law, who came with stones in hand. On this occasion, the finger of the Son wrote something in the dust that confronted the experts in the law. Whatever he wrote stopped these justice-driven, self-righteous people as they apparently saw their own precariousness and transgressions, obliging them to drop their condemning stones. Showing grace and mercy toward the offending woman, Jesus set her free as well. His parting words were, "I do not condemn you

The Most Excellent Way: Grace and Mercy as Expressions of Love

either. Go, and from now on do not sin any more" (John 8:11). The same finger may address our own predicament, for "by the standard you judge you will be judged, and the measure you use will be the measure you receive" (Matt 7:2).

The enactment of this high standard is achievable under the auspices of the Spirit who produces the desired fruit: love, expressed in self-control or efficacy. As a result, dispensing mercy is not an extraordinary event, but the capacity to imitate God, being free, conscious, and empowered to do so. Such is the *manner of love* that enters into play under the terms of the New Covenant. Many occasions arise in intimate relations to engage in dispensing mercy.

- In receiving a defeated, degraded prodigal upon his return;
- In restoring a fallen brother;
- In dealing with a partner's moral failures;
- In interpersonal dilemmas due to characterological inadequacies or deficiencies;
- In resolving conflicts, struggles, and impasses;
- In treating a partner who suffers from a condition not under his/her control (a biochemical imbalance, a neurobiological aberration affecting thoughts, feelings, behaviors, etc.).

The reader may add a litany of interpersonal occasions to this display of mercy. Instead of being reactionary people, engaged in endless feedback loops triggered by negative contingencies, we may be proactive and even anticipate the challenges of every day with feedforward control, engaging in "stress inoculation training" beforehand. In that way, we may be better prepared to exude graceful and merciful properties that reflect that we are endowed with God's love at ontological levels. Thus, our essential qualities, our characteristics at the root level, may be concretely manifested at the top level as byproducts of our coparticipation with the Holy Spirit.

The dispensation of mercy should not be seen as an extraordinary feat or an unusual way of behaving. Rather, this exuding property is a hallmark of those who grasp the Father's way of being and doing things. The self-control needed to enact what a believer knows, assents to, and *needs* to do in dispensing mercy depends on the believer's surrender to and coparticipation with the empowering, indwelling Holy Spirit as we obey the indwelling Word. Having "the mind of Christ" (Phil 2:1–11) is an essential, ontological necessity: let your mind (heart, soul, strength) be aligned with God's perspective and with his lavish, self-giving love. Rather than being trapped in the currents of this age (*aion*), the apostolic appeal is for us to be transformed by means of the renewal of our mindset in order to discern and follow a higher perspective—a metanarrative that aligns with God's loving, graceful, and merciful deals exemplified in the New Covenant.

Chapter 13

Covenantal Intimacy and Love

". . . because they will all know me, from the least of them to the greatest," declares the LORD. (Jeremiah 31:34, NIV)

To truly know and to be truly known: that is what intimacy is all about. The etymology of the construct *intimacy* may be traced to its Latin origin, *intimare*, which means "to put in" or to allocate within a frame of reference. Thus, it may be seen as a state of affairs marked by the process of allowing someone else to enter one's lifespace and establishing a close union with a deep sense of association and familiarity characterized by privacy. Intimacy is a stable and satisfactory state of being in love—a process that goes beyond a so-called "falling in love" event—experienced as an ongoing, dyadic interpenetration unfolding in a shared life-space.

INTIMACY: BEING IN LOVE—TO KNOW AND BE KNOWN

Intimacy has been emphasized as an essential ingredient in human relations, friendship, and, especially, as the most important aspect of conjugal love.[1] The opening of the inner boundary allows for the sharing of oneself at the core level of interpersonal grounding, lowering the defenses, and regarding vulnerability as an appropriate stance. This calculated risk is predicated upon the knowledge of the other with a willingness to abandon a guarded attitude and to orient oneself toward the other in trust, openness, and the desire to know and be known, to love and be loved. Waring and Reddon, among others, have constructed instruments to measure intimacy, based upon operational definitions of this construct.[2]

These measures represent the attempts to assess the degree to which people open up to one another and establish a mutual life-space, endowed with the right ambiance—love, grace, and mercy, coupled with mutuality, justice, stability, and satisfaction.

---

1. Augsburger, *Caring Enough*; Polischuk, "A New Covenant"; Chapman, *Covenant Marriage*; Balswick and Balswick, "A Theological Basis"; *A Model for Marriage*.

2. Waring and Reddon, "The Measurement of Intimacy."

Our cultural trends seem to place a great value on developing intimacy as the rationale for maintaining marriages satisfactorily, as we see in the numerous attempts to promote this state of affairs through marriage enrichment encounters, workshops, and self-help books. From practical considerations about stability and functional aspects based upon economic necessities, the relational emphasis in marriage has shifted to personal satisfaction, with personal needs for intimacy representing a core aspect of a meaningful existence.

THE THEOLOGICAL BASIS OF INTIMACY

As seen in previous chapters, biblical anthropology points to the human being as a creature made after God's image (*Tselem Elohim*). The merging of the first couple, or the genesis of intimacy, derives from an interpretation of the statements found in Scripture—that a man should "leave father and mother" and then "cleave to his wife" in order to "become one flesh." This oneness is predicated on the process of individuation and differentiation of a self "coming together" with another differentiated and individuated self. As the Trinity related intimately in love in a positive movement and thrust, even before the foundation of the world, humans were created to actualize an analogous capacity for relationship in love. God's eternal intimacy never ceased either to be or to be enacted. It was there at the beginning of creation; it was active in the process of effectuating human redemption and in sustaining the created order; and it remains active in his renewing endeavors.

God's creatures, made in his image, may be defined in terms of both ontological and relational capacities. As differentiated beings, partners grounded in love are able to engage in a dialogical fellowship and relational companionship patterned after God's design and purpose. As God relates eternally in an intimate, hypostatic-ecstatic fellowship, partners made in the *Imago Dei* are endowed with the potential capacity to relate at intimate levels, being capable of "dancing together" within the boundaries of God's design and will.

The fact that the effect of human sin has established a distinction and infused a state of alienation between dyads and family systems is undeniable. The term *apostasis* (moving away from the object of love) may be employed to denote the rupture of ecstasy or the negative detachment, isolation, and distancing between partners who "fell out of love." A distinction can be made: steadfast love embedded in accountability and responsibility characterizes true intimacy in stable and satisfactory dyadic relations. Lust is the condition in which more precarious, unstable, and sporadic relationships are sought to fulfill the demands for intimacy and satisfaction, devoid of any responsibility or accountability to the other.

After the entrance of sin into the world, God took the unilateral initiative to seek after his fallen creatures and engage them in merciful and gracious ways. The restoration and renewal of intimate deals between God and his creatures, as well as

Part II: Principles Derived from the New Covenant in Marital Transactions

creatures among themselves, were established on the basis of covenantal transactions that sought to engage in love within stipulated boundaries and expectations. Although all previous covenants pointed to the restoration and establishment of fellowship with God, it was through the redemptive work of Christ and the efficacy of the New Covenant that true intimacy with God has been restored.

The actualization of this binding condition may be a challenging experience for the autonomous, apostatic, and self-centered human, who still has to "taste" God's salvific and redemptive goodness. Yet, the potential and capacity for this state of intimacy with God is postulated in Scripture. The invitation is given to draw near and to establish a profound fellowship with God in Spirit and truth. The conditions are given as well: to repent (experience a radical change of mind), to have faith in God's provision (his Son and his sacrifice), and to obey God's will. Thus, openness to God's deal, demonstrating vulnerability in recognizing a need for forgiveness of sin, and exercising honesty and trust in approaching God as forgiven, accepted, and adopted children are the ingredients of the process by which a person can experience the presence of God by active coparticipation in faith and obedience. Being God's dearly beloved children, named after God, does not represent an abstract rendering of reality, but rather a solid basis for actualizing the predicament of being imitators of God and engaging in intimate deals after his manner.

In the context of the New Covenant (Heb 10:15–18), God has provided a new, open, and living way of access to His presence (Heb 10:19–22). God has eliminated all barriers created by the entrance of sin, dispensing grace, mercy, and love in forgiving our sin and casting what we have committed against him into oblivion. God has provided a new mediator (Heb 8:6; 9:15), an intercessor who advocates our cause and defends us against any accusations or destructive forces before his presence (Heb 7:25). Jesus Christ—the author and finisher of our faith (Heb 12:2)—has entered the heavenly realm with his own blood to offer his priestly service on our behalf.

The Old and the New Covenants come together in the letter to the Hebrews with the invitation to appropriate the effects of Jesus's work: now we can come and freely approach the "throne of grace" (Heb 4:16) or the "mercy seat" (Rom 3:25; Heb 9:5), both descriptive terms of the propitiatory *kapporeth* or atonement piece. The solid gold cover of the ark of the covenant, adorned with cherubs witnessing the sacrificial blood being sprinkled every year during the Day of Atonement (Heb 4:16), was a symbol of better things to come: Jesus fulfilled such shadows of reality in his death and resurrection, ascent, and priestly intercession for us. It is on this basis that we are invited to approach God and enjoy a deep, personal fellowship. We are challenged to proceed along our journey, running our race—a positive, ascending course (following an asymptotic curve), marked by successive approximations to our ultimate destiny—to be with God and enjoy him forever.

In metacognitive-dialogical fashion, we may realize that being accepted as we are—being known in an actual fashion, including a full disclosure of our makeup, and being thoroughly assessed in our predicament and inner struggles—is an awesome and dreadful fact, a declaration coming from God with impacting proportions. We become mindful of an empowering covenantal principle at work: We are being loved in a purposeful way, and we have to learn to do the same—to love, accept, and validate one another in intimate fellowship as God does. The theological premises are obviously there—to be taken as the basis of our efforts and utilized in our attempts to imitate the Father's covenantal ways. To truly know and to be known by a partner is a challenging proposition—made possible by the empowering of the same Holy Spirit that brings us closer to the Father's manner of love.

Scripture declares that to know God is the highest privilege granted to humans as we are invited to participate in God's fellowship. This privilege is the only valid reason for boasting above the possession of wisdom, riches, or power (Jer 9:23–24). The knowledge of God allows for a powerful truth to register in the capacity of a believer to grasp spiritual reality: The inaccessible God becomes accessible; the transcending Being becomes an incarnate, down-to-earth Savior and sends his Holy Spirit to dwell in us and empower our walk. The omnipotent and omniscient God dwells among us and infuses our temporal existence with meaning, providing insight and power to live according to his design. God, having spoken in the past through many prophets, at many times, and in various ways, finally has spoken *in his Son* (Heb 1:1, emphasis added), who is the radiance of God's glory and the exact representation of his being (Heb 1:3). The Son made the Father known, assuming an incarnational mode of an exemplary nature. Thus, knowing Jesus is equated with knowing the Father as Jesus himself said: "If you really knew me, you would know the Father as well. From now on, you do know him and have seen him" (John 14:7). Jesus claimed to be not only the way to the Father, but the actual expression of the Father, to the point of amalgamating a perceptual definition of God available to humans: "The person who has seen me, has seen the Father" (John 14:6–8). The eternal Word became flesh and dwelt (pitched his tent) among us, and, according to a faithful witness, "We have seen his glory, the glory of the one and only, full of grace and truth, who came from the Father" (John 1:14).

THE BOUNDARIES AND THE LIFE-SPACE OF INTIMACY: PERICHORESIS

Bringing oneself and someone else into a common, private life-space represents a challenge. On the one hand, the risk of being known at the core—the anxiety of being discovered as less than perfect; the inconvenience of having to share goods, time, and concerns; and the necessity to bargain in order to have some sense of equity, fairness, and justice in getting what one wants versus the wants of the other, among many other factors—face the person entering into an intimate alliance. On the other hand, the lack of knowledge, safety, trust, predictability, and control add up as challenging factors that pertain to the person still to be known. Besides, a state of equilibrium

Part II: Principles Derived from the New Covenant in Marital Transactions

necessitates a fine balance between their individual differentiation (versus isolation) and the quest for mutuality (versus enmeshment). Intimacy also is predicated upon a process of balancing accommodation to, and assimilation of, each other's character, conduct, influence, and styles of thinking, feeling, and doing things.

In a theological way, boundaries are the limits within which a dance between partners takes place. The term *perichoresis* (*peri*: as in perimeter; *choresis*, as in choreography) has been a useful construct used in theology to denote an interpenetrated relatedness animated with *hypostatic* (hypostasis: essential, ontological personhood), *ecstatic* (ek-stasis, a decentered movement, moving toward the object of one's love), synchronic dynamics between the three persons of the Trinity. In the case of a marital dance, a man and a woman created in God's image—whose essential ontological or substructural personhood is endowed with the capacity to decenter and merge into the object of their mutual love—relate in love and actualize their union as a counterpart to God's design and purpose. Boundaries should be regarded as the defining and protecting will of God, the creator, redeemer, and sustaining Lord of life, rendered concretely in expressed commandments—engraved in the tablets of stone, as well as written in parchments by God's amanuensis (Moses, the prophets, the psalmist, the apostles, and the evangelists, etc., who under the inspiration of God's Spirit, provided us with Scripture, the living Word of God). In the New Covenant, this will and purpose is engraved by the Holy Spirit in the hearts and minds of God's people, an inward feature aligned in full correspondence with the already-revealed truth in Scripture.

To ensure the stability and satisfaction of a marital covenant, the establishment of a defining and protecting boundary is essential. It is of outmost importance for a couple to trace their boundaries in accordance with God-given parameters—that is, to establish principles to live by in accordance with the expressed will of God rather than choosing to do "their own thing" in an idiosyncratic or culturally conditioned fashion.

The trends in the contemporary United States seem to disregard the long-held, Judeo-Christian basis for marriage, fostering a variety of paradigms based on personal idiosyncrasies, natural tendencies, political demands, and antinomian defiance of any divinely-inspired dicta. The trends of this age (Rom 12:1–2) exert pressures on the mindset of believers; the fashions and trends of the cosmos seem to derogatorily define a Christian marriage as anachronistic, politically incorrect, dogmatically fossilized, and offensive to a postmodern philosophical and practical ethos. In a post-Christian environment, believers in marriage are regarded as couples whose perimeter is too tight and closed, and as dancers engaged in traditional perichoresis devoid of openness, freedom, creativity, and the like. As choreography goes, believers are regarded as mindless people who resemble marionettes behaving according to the pulls and twists of strings attached to a higher puppeteer (a stern, stiff God) who directs their movements. Yet, this perception is a matter of definition: who defines whom, and from what perspective. The same applies if Christians define those who are not following God's ways.

Believing Christians who hold on to an evangelical position tend to regard the postmodern smorgasbord of ideas applicable to marital unions as dyadic relationships patterned after each person's will and desire, disregarding any transcendental or revealed perspective on the matter. From this perspective, unbelieving couples have their spiritual eyes blinded by the natural consequences of sin and are, consequently, devoid of spiritual insight coming from God's revelation. Through natural, carnal lenses, these couples think that they are sophisticated dancers, endowed with complete freedom to move as they design with their own rhythm and passion. These dancers ignore the fact that, in reality, their movements are affected by the trends of a culture that has rejected God's truth; they are controlled by strings attached to a defiant, rebellious, and evil puppeteer—the god of this age—whose movements seem to be exceedingly free, extravagant, sensual, idiosyncratic, and filled with fun. The boundaries of the natural life-space in which the unbeliever's *perichoretic* dance is enacted seem to be flexible and permeable, allowing for the intrusion and influence of whatever elements appear to support, nurture, and reinforce a self-serving, sinful lifestyle. At the end, all dancers will be judged and allocated an eternal reward. Yet, this judgment is not left to believers, but rather to God, to whom we all shall account for our dancing stewardship.

The marital union of believers—joined in an equal yoke—is demarcated and defined by a perimeter surrounding their joint existence, qualified in terms of alignment and correspondence with the will of God. This marital boundary may be compared to the semipermeable membrane surrounding the cytoplasm of a living cell. The functions of this membrane include the protection of the cell from its surroundings and the exchange of substances between the cell and its environment. A cell membrane, in simple terms, 1.) Regulates the ingestion of nutrients; 2.) Elaborates these elements and facilitates the expelling of any waste produced in intracellular metabolic processes; 3.) Stops any toxicity that could harm the cell; and 4.) Facilitates the sharing of nutrients to other cells. The living unit exists, renews its functions, and grows in relation to other systems by means of the effective set-up of a semi-permeable, specialized boundary.

Part II: Principles Derived from the New Covenant in Marital Transactions

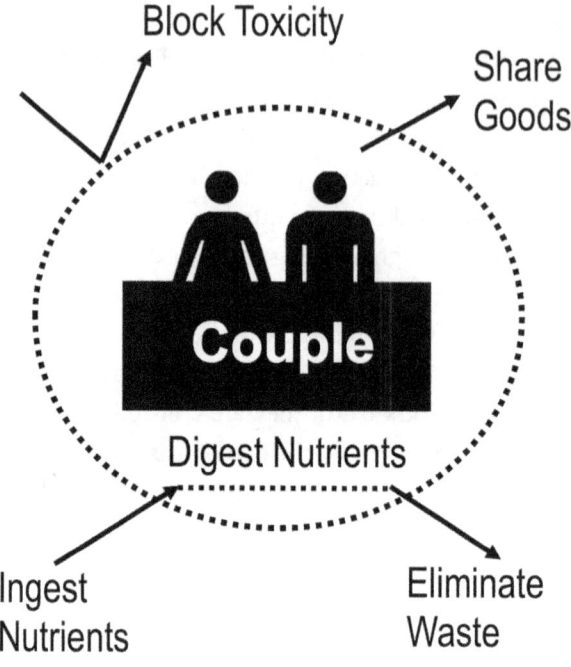

Fig. 13.1: The Four Functions of Marital Boundaries

In marriage, differentiated partners—each person surrounded with a personal boundary—come together and encounter one another in order to form a system—a marital unit surrounded with a boundary. As they come to know and experience one another, their intimacy develops in function of their ongoing, mutual exchanges of an interpersonal, interactive nature. Intimacy develops as the cognitive-emotional state of perichoresis, experienced within the boundaries surrounding a couple. Intimacy is a mutual state of being-in-relation, and a process of ongoing cognitive-emotive interpenetration characterized by love, grace, and mercy.

Intimacy is not a static condition. Partners seeking to establish intimacy are characterized by a quest to know and be known, to understand one another and establish an ongoing, deep fellowship. Intimacy may be seen as the fostering and nurturing of the accommodation to, assimilation of, and equilibration with one another's mind and heart. It is the ongoing process of openness to one another—decentering from one's self and holding on to the other as a fused, embedded, and desired "love object" (using the terminology of object relations theory) without losing one's individuation. To be intimate is to open up the boundaries of one's life-space and to thrust ecstatically toward the other, regarding this person as an intrinsic component of one's ontological being, intertwined with and residing tacitly as a permanent object. This fusion—merging with one another without loss of individuation or integrity—fosters a positive attribution of meaning and value to both partners.

To know and to be known in a deep sense, thoroughly and empathically, provides the dialogical/affective person with a sense of closeness, trust, and peace. Intimacy strengthens a partner's assurance of being accepted and validated by the other. Being joined in an equal yoke provides a sound foundation to a couple, due to the fact that their relationship is framed within God's boundaries. Their core values and beliefs are anchored on the same basis of faith and conduct.

INTIMACY IN FUNCTION OF CLOSENESS TO GOD

The closer each partner is to God, the closer the union to one another becomes. Growing in faith, hope, and love before God allows for a couple's growth along the same dimensions. An illustration of this construct may be rendered. The author's Argentinian version of *perichoresis* is represented by the intimate interpenetration of a dyad in motion: it takes two to tango. Furthermore, it takes a lot of practice to do it well.

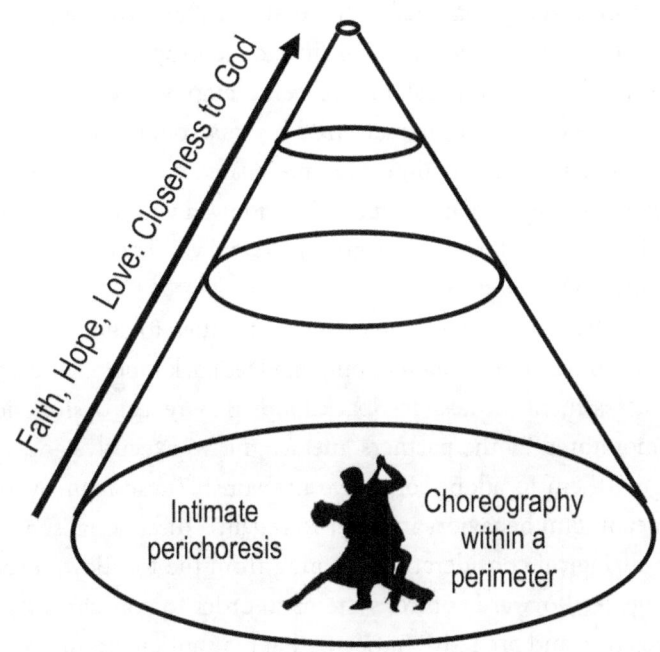

Fig. 13.2: Marital Intimacy in Function of Closeness to God

In ascending fashion, the marital life-space becomes smaller as the invitation to dance together at higher levels is offered. That is, the growth in faith, hope, and love—which are correlated to closeness to God—results in the increase of interpersonal intimacy. Obviously, the closer the dancers are to God, the closer to one another they become.

God's intimate hypostatic-ecstatic union is a paradigm for social relations, and in particular, for intimate partnerships such as marriage. God's love, truth, and perfection are characteristic of this definition of *being-in-relation*. With humans, these characteristics experience a different expression. Due to the Fall, an *apostatic* movement has occurred, with the intrusion of negative contingencies affecting the life-space and boundaries of intimacy, evoking doubt, guilt, shame, and anxiety in the relational systems. These contingencies enter into the relational dynamics of couples, families, and groups. Due to the original break in fellowship, humans tend to resort to inauthentic facades in order to relate to one another. The Jungian persona—a mask, rather than the authentic self-in-relation—appears to be a built-in feature of interpersonal transactions. Intimacy in marital covenants suffers when partners resort to inauthentic or dishonest ways of relating in attempts to ward off the anxiety of being caught with the fig leaves down and exposed to one another in the raw. Human experience quite often registers an obvious lack of adequate trust, honesty, acceptance, or capacity to relate without employing some defensive barriers or covers.

The remedial aspects of redemption need to be stressed. What Zizioulas called "capacity within incapacity" may define the dialectical and dialogical experience of a believer who, being sinful and aware of finitude, entropy, and imperfection, is at the same time mindful of the possibility of being empowered by God's Spirit, able to engage in intimate covenants characterized by trust, openness, honesty, and non-defensive sincerity.[3] Intimate encounters are predicated upon the willingness of both covenantal partners to be open and vulnerable, endowed with interpersonal trust and a mutual confidence derived from being grounded and validated by a gracious, merciful, accepting, and loving God.

Couples in interaction provide many opportunities to send and receive negative signals to one another, registered as ongoing feedback loops that demand mutual attention. The assessment of these feedback loops may reveal dysfunctional contingencies to be monitored by the partners' metacognitive-executive and spiritual sensors, encouraging them to adopt corrective measures. These maneuvers are geared to engage in meaningful behaviors in order to regain a directional sense of purpose. Metacognitive-dialogical considerations coming from the top-down executive functions may engage feedforward control systems in order to consciously superpose an anticipatory, positive, and proactive initiative that may anticipate and correct any disturbances affecting the intimacy of the partners ahead of time.

The same metacognitive-control system may boost an "upward" movement of augmented hypostatic-ecstatic proportions toward God, the overseer of the dyad in relation. If both partners in such a dyadic relationship are joined and live mindfully "in the sight of God," they may experience an upward movement toward God, which

---

3. Zizioulas, "Human Capacity."

in turn reduces their interpersonal life-space and makes it more intimate. This process may allow them to have a growing sensation of being fused with one another without experiencing any loss of personal integrity or individuation. Partners may actualize their capacity to relate to one another without erecting isolating barriers or defensive stone walls intended to hide or protect against possible breakdowns in their intimacy.

In providing a depiction of the possibility of an upward perichoretic movement leading to a sense of deeper intimacy, multilevel definitions of this construct may apply as well. A growing sense of intimacy may be defined as follows.

1. *A mutual feeling of closeness with spiritual-cognitive awareness of agape love at work.* A profound sense of intimacy involves the spiritual awareness of being close to God and one another, assessed in a cognitive-emotive fashion and promoting an enactive capacity to concretely love and to be loved, to know and to be known. It exudes a reciprocal love, a complementary mood, and a metacognitive-sensitive awareness of desiring the same benefits for the other that one desires for self. Furthermore, it goes beyond, regarding the other as the primary object of one's concern, above one's own needs, wants, or desires.

    Taking the agape-love of God as a paradigmatic feature that saturates the dealings occurring in a New Covenant in action, it is important to comprehensively integrate God's knowledge of the human. That is, to love and to know are amalgamated, not bifurcated in this paradigm. Often, in human terms, a person loves someone's persona—a projected, idealized, presentable mask—and attaches his affect to a character not actually known to him. With no experience, hope and faith are the variables that support intimacy at work. Then, as experience accrues, hope and faith seem to diminish. As the person acquires more knowledge of the other, an entropic tendency seems to direct a process of diminishing attachment with negative outcomes: knowing too much may lead to loving less.

    To be known by God—and to be loved by him—represents a unique feature: the sense of intimacy on the human side increases with time and experience, strengthening hope and faith. This unique feature is built into the New Covenant ("and they shall all know me . . ."). Thus, a believer's intimacy with God represents a sound basis for interpersonal transactions at concrete levels of human relations. In marriage, this fellowship increases in depth (or height) as the couple increases their joint commitment, worship, and service to God, having more opportunities to imitate the exemplary transactions between Jesus and the church, of which marriage is a shadow, a copy of reality.

2. *A metacognitive awareness of a state of being.* Intimacy with God and openness to intimacy with a significant other in marriage may be seen as encountering one another at deep levels and remaining in love. Thus, "being in love" is a condition preferred to the popular concept of "falling in love," which presupposes a person's tipping over and ending up in a bonded state. The popular euphemism denotes

an event—not a process—that describes a person being drawn by his/her senses toward a love object and being pulled down into a state of passion without necessarily being committed or accountable to the attracting object. Falling in love does not necessarily assure a continuous process of faithful, dedicated renewal leading to a consolidated union.

Being in love may be seen as an optimal state of continuous, emotional interpenetration. To elaborate and set this notion in a more spiritual, theological, and metacognitive perspective, this state may be defined as a condition in which both partners experience a deeply shared life-space, continuous in time, and permeated by an atmosphere of surrounding peace, joy, and satisfaction. This mindful state transcends time-space boundaries and is marked by the experience of the "presence in absence" of a loved partner—even when the significant other is not physically there, but remains present as a deeply entrenched and amalgamated love object. The loved person is engraved in the heart and mind of the beholder. In other words, the loved one is internalized (introjected) in a cognitive-affective fashion and remains (abides) in the consolidated perceptions and personal metanarratives of the beholder. The image (the schematic representation residing in the implicit, semantic, and episodic memory of the person) dwells in this mindful state. Because there is no need to perform in order to be accepted, validated, empowered, or secure, *being* in such a state allows for the cessation of any activities perceived as necessary *to become* intimate. An emergent sense of trust, confidence, and assurance adds to this state of well-being. The energy in this state is employed in the actual enjoyment of "being there," and then in envisioning loving, proactive behaviors to be enacted in the other's favor.

We may postulate that "being in love" and living in intimacy would allow a person to dedicate efforts to maintain this hypostatic-ecstatic unity, to renew his or her cognitive-emotive processes (heart and mind) in order to maintain the relationship in a vital and vibrant mode, and to experience the ongoing "being-in-the-process-of-becoming" even more intimately. On the other side, anxiety, stress, concerns about possible losses, or existential dread about love not being reciprocated would render a person less than peaceful and relaxed in reference to a state of being in love. Thus, love may be regarded as a life-giving principle, charged with energy (libidinal, according to Freud) that promotes, incites, and stirs up passions, feelings, and behaviors. These energized/exuded manifestations may be exuded in radial fashion across his/her concentric spheres of relatedness.

3. *Companionship: A shared experience of a steadfast nature.* The construct of marriage as companionship appears in Scripture, denoting a deep association marked by a covenant. Malachi 2:14 (emphasis added) states, "The Lord has been witness between you and the wife of your youth to whom you have been faithless, although *she is your companion* and your wife by covenant." God has

created humans as social creatures, and in the case of marriage, has designed the relationship as primarily a covenant between companions before God. A companion is a person who shares the experiences of another, jointly sojourning the vicissitudes of life and being there throughout all circumstances, especially when these are unpleasant or unwelcome.

Covenant includes a companionship dimension—a feature that appears to be embedded in all intimate unions. In a negative description, an Old Testament passage makes allusion to an unfaithful person who forsakes a long-term covenantal companion, a "strange woman"—an unfaithful person or adulteress, destitute for breaking the normal expectations regulating marital relations in Israel—who "forsakes the *companion of her youth* and forgets the *covenant* of her God" (Prov 2:17, emphasis added). The word translated "companion" denotes a close proximity, association, or union between covenantal partners. This closeness involves cognitive, affective, and behavioral connotations of affinity, togetherness, and joint venturing framed in covenantal terms made before God himself.

4. *Identity grounded in intimate fellowship.* Partners who are believers share their identities—both defined in natural terms and in Christ. When spiritual perceptions are accurate, regarding the other as someone whom God has created, loved, and allocated as a joint inheritor of life fosters respect and trust. A perception of the other that regards this partner as "God's property" will result in a conscious administration, a sober stewardship, and an accountable lifestyle. In this paradigm, intimacy with accountability actualizes a loving covenant; on the other hand, intimacy without mutual accountability becomes lust, manipulation, or exploitation of each other. Spiritual affinity, sharing values and joint prayers, devotions, musings, and participation in worship as intimate partners represent basic foundations for stability and satisfaction in marital covenants.

Beyond events that exemplify intimacy in concrete, operational terms, companionship denotes a structural capacity to remain faithfully there for one another. The basis of intimate deals is characterized by steadfastness, loyalty, covenantal commitment, and ongoing care. The behavioral connotations of intimacy include attentive support; demonstrative care, steadfast loyalty; and mutual reciprocity. Cognitive connotations of intimacy may be gathered from the presence of proactive thinking, positive reasoning, and accurate perceptions of each other. Couples may draw from the bank of shared memories and derive satisfaction from their shared, meaningful accounts.

The affective expressions of intimacy emerge from dispositional tendencies that emerge from the couple's deep-seated values and beliefs. These may be manifested in peaceful, joyful, benign concern, as well as steadfast love. Dispositional

Part II: Principles Derived from the New Covenant in Marital Transactions

tendencies to be graceful, merciful, forgiving, and restoring/renewing of the terms of a covenant add to these affective considerations.

5. *Sexuality within God-established boundaries.* The gift and stewardship of sex are wonderful features of "becoming one flesh" in marriage.[4] God-given principles are intended to guide covenantal partners in the way they relate to one another in fulfilling the tasks of life—procreation, mutual satisfaction, and reinforcement of one another's personhood. Intimacy of a sexual nature represents a pinnacle of physiological, emotional, and insightful corollary to empathic encounters of an intimate nature. Sharing mindsets and values, as well as emotional experiences of a loving nature, enhance sexual intimacy and satisfaction. These factors augment the sense of knowing one another and being known at honest, unmasked levels.

DISTORTIONS IN INTIMATE RELATIONS

As stated before, intimacy is best fostered in a climate in which openness and lack of defensiveness has been established. Complements to such stances are trust, faith in each other, and confident hope, based upon a positive attitude. This climate tends to diminish the need for self-protection, reassuring rather than rendering defensive a vulnerable person. Vulnerability under these conditions is not a state of weakness, but represents the strength of a system that allows human beings to be less hypocritical, drop their fig leaves, and accept each other's humanness without judgment.

Distortions in the pursuit, establishment, and enactment of intimacy happen. Under normal conditions, we assume that these anomalies are not intentionally planned. Such distortions may due to unconscious motives and the needs or expressions of learned dysfunctional patterns. These distortions often elicit anxiety and fear in partners who become conscious of their presence and appeal to defensive maneuvers to ward off their feelings and negative reactions. In situations of abuse or neglect that diminish intimacy—harshness, manipulation, exploitation—the survival stances of an individual seeking a safe place and escape these conditions are marked by defensiveness, guardedness, and flight reactions. A person who stays in a negative predicament, from which no escape is possible, develops what Seligman has coined as "learned helplessness."[5] That person may stay in an unsatisfying—yet stable in a chaotically enmeshed, dysfunctional sense—marriage, and give the appearance of togetherness under pressure. Often, a longstanding array of internalized voices, dialogues, and relational patterns render this person intropunitive, encumbered with a sense of shame and guilt and a lack of self-worth and efficacy.

The biblical narrative states that God's love, mercy, and grace encountered human incapacity in their attempt to cover themselves, accepting them in spite of their

---

4. Penner and Penner, *The Gift of Sex*; Smedes, *Sex for Christians*.
5. Seligman, *Helplessness*.

faults and re-establishing a covenant. Yet, the same narrative tells us that it is due to sin, to the Fall, that humans have an intrinsic need to cover up, to hide, and to be less than open and honest with each other. It is noteworthy that as the only couple in the garden, in possession of a large, open-air bedroom, our ancestors still had the need to cover their shame, their guilt, and their awareness of finitude and precariousness from each other when they opened their eyes after sin entered the world through their disobedience. Thus, even in the most optimal of situations, human beings are intrinsically aware of their need to establish boundaries to protect their internally shared lifespace. These personal boundaries (within the couple's systemic boundaries) would be less than open and more invulnerable to each other's accessibility. Perhaps it is safer to assume that a couple's intimacy falls somewhere in between the extremes of total invulnerability and wide-open vulnerability, coupled with their manifested degrees of accountability and responsibility to one another.

Several distortions and dysfunctions of what a desirable intimacy should be may prevail in dyadic relationships, due to multiple, negative influences and destructive forces at work (e.g., of sin, socialization, culture, personal choices, and general aspects of the human incapacity to fulfill God's designs). We may postulate the following anomalies.

1. *Symbiosis.* When a person fails to individuate properly, lacking differentiation from his or her family of origin, an array of needs remains to be satisfied, usually in less than healthy ways. As attachment theory has pointed out, insecure attachments foster a number of dysfunctional patterns in adult relations. The proneness to engage in a clinging fashion and to fuse into the other person manifests itself as a neurotic trend called "symbiosis." Insufficient differentiation of the person allows for a basic overlap in which a symbiotic entity is fostered, pressing for conformity and forced compliance with every expectation and claim of the other. To the untrained eye, the couple's picture appears on the surface as a jointed, mutual, "velcro-type" union, but at deeper levels it may reveal a partner's basic separation anxiety with neurotic fears of abandonment. The lack of self-efficacy may also lead a partner to avoid exposure to stressful and challenging aspects of life, demonstrating a clinging adherence to the other. *Enmeshment* is another term used in family systems theory to indicate this state of being.

2. *Fusion with loss of integrity.* If symbiosis is entrenched at deeper levels and encompasses the lifestyle of a couple, the relationship may be said to be a fused one. To fuse is to confuse intimacy with a total amalgamation of oneself to the other, to the point of having no ground to define and postulate one's identity or worth. If a partner's boundaries are totally permeable and allow all kinds of input coming from the other—opinionated, negative, or toxic—to define his/her being, this person will experience difficulties in assessing his/her own integrity—the quality of being morally upright, honest, and free to speak the truth in love. The concept

Part II: Principles Derived from the New Covenant in Marital Transactions

of "enmeshment" without a differentiation of the self characterizes those couples who merge without having graduated emotionally from their families of origin, or who have not developed enough maturity to recognize the desirable side of their differences, idiosyncrasies, uniqueness, and individuated ways of being and doing things.

3. *Neurotic codependency.* Codependency is a condition of excessive emotional or psychological reliance on a partner in which an enabling person reinforces interactive patterns that bolster the other's abnormal or irrational behaviors and maintain a state of dysfunctional steadfastness. Typically, an enabler becomes codependent with a partner who requires support due to an illness or addiction.

    Those partners who did not emancipate properly are prone to give themselves to attachments in which the price for acceptance and validation is the abdication of any recognizable need, want, or desire of their own in order to qualify as being lovable. The relationship becomes a slanted covenant, based on the terms dictated by the controller for accepting or validating the other. At times, as gathered from clinical experience, even though couples fused with a strong neurotic attachment may seek help to remediate their suffocating, manipulative, and dysfunctional patterns, they tend to abandon marital therapy because they fear that a third party will try to separate them by means of intrusive interpretations, allusions, or splitting remarks. A neurotic bond becomes unhealthily stronger than a quest for freedom to be, think, or express themselves in an open and honest fashion. As the title for Watzlawick's book, which deals with the pursuit of unhappiness in dysfunctional family systems, indicates, "The situation is hopeless, but not serious."[6]

4. *Objectivizing the other in order to fulfill one's quest for intimacy.* Clinical work has shown that partners with inadequate personality development, inferiority complexes, unresolved authority problems, separation anxiety, or who suffer from deprived aspects in their backgrounds manifest a tendency to possess, control, and manipulate the significant other in a self-serving manner. Possession, manipulation, and control of the other characterize these deals. This "intimacy" turns into a procrustean box, a yoke, and a desire to monopolize and objectivize the other totally, depriving this person of life, movement, freedom, and dignity.

    Partners who do not reach such levels of manipulation and quest for control may still be less than mutually respectful, demonstrating a lack of trust, jealousy, and a constant pressure for reassurance from the other in attempts to gratify their own needs. These attitudinal stances and behaviors tend to depersonalize the other, rendering this person as an object of gratification, lust, pride, or servitude. Narcissistic characters tend to "reflect themselves on the other" without giving them value or status as an equal partner. The person controlling and "possessing"

---

6. Watzlawick, *The Situation is Hopeless but not Serious.*

the other may be trapped into a projective, delusional, solipsistic, or self-centered quest for lust, but lack the correspondence, affinity, empathic care, or mutual reciprocity coming from the insignificant other.

Independent, super-assertive, or ambitious persons tend to enter marital relationships as if they need to compete, wrestle, or establish some turf in which the other has to be a willing, acquiescent, and accommodating partner. People with unresolved issues with authority figures in their past, or people with histories of abuse, neglect, loss of grounds, manipulation, and deprivation tend to fight for safe territorial gains. Sometimes, as witnessed in psychopathological accounts of aggression mixed with sex, the augmented libidinal energy in the fighting systems is transduced into sexual passion. The vehement and intense endeavors become the appealing and reinforcing elements, but are often devoid of empathy, care, concern, or respect for the integrity of the partners. This extreme, utilitarian, sadomasochistic activity may be the expression of a narcissistic centripetal force that animates this type of relation, defined in an idiosyncratic and abnormal fashion.

Partners may try to encase, trap, and assimilate the other into their private life-space, without any regard for the needs of the other; they demand that the other accommodate and fit perfectly in their territory without losing an inch of their own. No bargaining is fostered, and demands are made without allowing any concessions on their part, while expecting everything from the other. Extreme cases of depersonalization of a partner resemble the quest of inadequate personalities attempting to have a sex slave instead of a mutual partner. Levy, in his book *Love and Sex with Robots,* argues that the entities we once deemed cold and mechanical will soon become the objects of real companionship and human desire.[7] Human interactions with robotic technology will allow a person to have an ultimate sex slave at the command of a self-serving master. This is a trend that epitomizes the objectivizing of desire into a personally driven, self-satisfying, lustful control, without any regard for true interpersonal intimacy.

5. *Addiction.* Quite often, coupled to the previous category, but not necessarily bordering on such aggressive, painful, degrading, or manipulative states, the longing for intimacy is distorted along sensual and sexual lines that acquire a pseudo-relational quality. A partner may seek personal satisfaction either in a solipsistic fashion, as in pornography, or by finding extraneous companions to fulfill his or her basic drives, which actually fall out of the scope and boundaries of God's intentions for intimate relations such as marriage. A sense of false intimacy results from the deviation and departure from a true love object, employing defenses such as denial, suppression, or repression of the demands set in a covenantal

---

7. Levy, *Love and Sex with Robots.*

accountability, and a personal choice to pursue transitional objects without any regard for interpersonal accountability.

The displacement of true love objects occurs with the sensual person placing the thrust onto visual images, virtual experiences, or actual people that provide a self-centered, sensual, and sexual fulfillment. Lust versus love is the hallmark of these detoured processes. Schaumberg deals with the realities of sexual addiction, which he terms "false intimacy," and offers suggestions and guidelines framed in Christian perspectives for recovery.[8]

ASSESSING BARRIERS TO INTIMACY

How does a couple foster intimate transactions when hurts, pain, disillusionments, rejection, and the like have affected the openness, receptivity, and connecting capacities of one or both partners? Guardedness, defensiveness, mistrust, and isolation are common defenses employed to safeguard the integrity of those hurt by negative past experiences. Unresolved anger and resentment add to these factors, making it difficult to establish proper grounds for intimacy.

Fostering intimacy necessitates a basic knowledge of the destructive elements affecting the dyadic system in order to establish optimal conditions for couples to develop, grow, and consolidate their connectedness. The negative factors affecting intimacy are many; a sample of these elements is provided here.

1. *A partner's negative misperception and misattributions of the other's attitudes, dispositions, and behaviors.* These may be consolidated impressions of a stereotypical and repetitive nature as perceived on the "receiver" side (e.g., dejection, negative remarks, stonewalling, inattentiveness, defensiveness), which erode the foundations of an intimate relationship. A partner's processing style of thinking may add a negative tone to his or her own attitudes and feelings. As a result, due to his/her self-confirmatory bias, a partner may project negative features on the other, distance him/herself, and reject or displace the other from their intimate space. Often, a replacement of the other takes place—the love object is replaced with other objects, processes, or items that supply his or her needs for intimacy. If the negative impressions of a partner are confirmed—being put down, abased, ridiculed, or diminished in any fashion—these reality-based experiences militate against the establishment or renewal of intimacy. A person experiencing a lack of acceptance, respect, and validation may, in a defensive or offensive style, distance him/herself and become unresponsive to any attempts made by the other to connect; or, the individual may detour into an unfaithful pattern leading to a false sense of intimacy in order to satisfy his or her longings for a fulfilled lifestyle.

---

8. Schaumberg, *False Intimacy*.

2. *Negative attitudes held against the other.* The filtering processes and self-confirmatory biases born out of repetitive, negative contingencies, consolidated in transactional patterns, enter into play with detrimental effects on intimacy. Feelings of resentment, coupled with a lack of forgiveness on account of negative events (i.e., hurts, abusive happenings, traumatic memories, etc.), remain as unfinished transactions; these tend to show up repeatedly in an ongoing fashion. Not being able to let go of offenses; ruminating and brooding over negative transactions; and fostering frustration, anger, and even revenge mean that these events are recapitulated as "presence in absence." Hurts and pain stemming from the past tend to harbor antagonism and fighting stances, and these become impediments in the process of establishing or maintaining intimacy.

3. *Maladaptive habits that irritate or exasperate the other.* Whether consciously or mindlessly done, a partner's personal habits and behaviors that annoy the other have a negative effect on the couple's level of intimacy. Verbal insinuations and nonverbal attitudes that convey doubts about the integrity of a partner tend to undermine and erode the level of trust and intimate bonding between partners. Habits are automatic ways of behaving—negative patterns manifested systematically in repetitive and predictable behaviors or manifested sporadically with unpredictable annoyance. These need to be assessed in a fair fashion. In cognitive-behavioral approaches, behaviors may be operationalized into assets, excesses, and deficits. Assets are things done right and need no remedial action. On the negative side, excesses—defined as negative attitudes or behaviors of an undesirable, unnecessary nature that happen frequently, that are too much to take, or that last too long to put up with—need to be assessed and dealt with. Deficits, on the other hand, are defined as those attitudes or behaviors demonstrated by partners that fail to meet the demands of the other or to attend to their needs in an adequate fashion. A partner's needs that are not properly satisfied become complaints, which, if not attended to, augment in tone and intensity, becoming demands or insults, often ending in violence. Obviously, the basic attention to needs would prevent this escalation into dysfunctional behaviors that impinge upon and destroy intimacy.

4. *Defense mechanisms.* Any person experiencing an attack, a threat, or a challenge to his or her well-being would naturally react with some defensiveness. Most of the time, these defenses are unconscious maneuvers to protect the self against anxiety. Common defenses have been addressed by Anna Freud, who provided a catalogue of psychoanalytical terms still in vogue among us.[9] Classical defenses include the denial of actual feelings or of problems that are obvious to a partner, as well as rationalization of obvious problems in need of resolution, avoidance of

---

9. Freud, *The Ego.*

accountability or remedial action, projection, and blame versus acceptance of the ownership of problems and dysfunctions.

These are just a few examples of such unconscious defense mechanisms. At times, the overt manifestation of behaviors does not correspond to the tacitly held feelings of anger, anxiety, or hurt; in such cases, a person may employ a reaction formation, exemplified in attempts to engage in a proper behavior in lieu of a true, inappropriate reaction. Realizing the upsurge of anger against a partner, a person may hug and kiss rather than hurt or be obnoxious to this partner. To protect against personal abasement, manipulation, or control, as well as basic anxiety, the appearance of guardedness and protectiveness characterizes the posture of the defending partner.

5. *Interpersonal stress may provide the ground for unfair fighting and lack of empathy in transactions with a residual negative aftermath.* Quite often, the needs of a couple are translated into complaints, then into requests, and finally, into demands and insults. The ways in which people in conflict resolve their difficulties is important, as any unfairness or injustice left over will be taken up the next time around. The employment of guilt as a weapon or control system may signal a precarious way of handling stress in intimate transactions.

6. *Physical/physiological impediments.* At times, handicaps, dysfunctions, and impediments act as obstacles to intimacy, as in the case of an illness affecting emotional or cognitive processes with the resulting lack of clear communication, empathic understanding, and mutual validation. The employment of some drugs and medicaments may affect cognitive-affective states, as well as behavioral repertoire. In her work, *Disorders of Sexual Desire*, Kaplan has provided important contributions, pinpointing the many factors that diminish the first phase of sexual encounters, anteceding performance and orgasm.[10]

7. *Mental illness.* The presence of some dysfunctions or illnesses such as bipolar disorder, depression, panic disorder, schizophrenia, paranoia, or character pathology affect the relational quality of a couple, including their communication patterns, states of mind, and feelings. A hypoactive desire, the lack of zest for life and pleasure due to depression, or inordinate sexual demands due to manic episodes may affect intimacy as well. The inability to relax and enjoy each other due to excessive anxiety impinges upon the need for tranquility, peace, and relaxation within a couple's life-space. Defensiveness, projection, denial, splitting, and blaming may affect a sense of intimacy in the case of character disorder. Obsessive-compulsive aspects impinge upon relaxation, calmness, relaxation, trust, acceptance, and enjoyment of each other.

---

10. Kaplan, *Disorders of Sexual Desire*.

8. *Distortions in fulfilling basic needs.* In natural terms, intimacy is reflected in two acts that generate and sustain life: sharing a meal in fellowship with someone at the table, and having intercourse in bed. Scholars remind us that the Hebrew word for "knowing" is "to have intercourse with." In psychological terms, food and sex are the most powerful activators and reinforcers of human behavior. These factors convey the simple notion that humans are finite, needy, and necessitate the ongoing replenishment of their needs. The need for food and sexual fulfillment reflect a natural state of being—formed, yet deformed, and in need of reformation and transformation characterized by weakness, entropy, and hedonistic drives (the pleasure principle Freud wrote so much about). They happen to be very close at the neurophysiological level in the septal region of the brain—in the limbic system at the hypothalamic location. They were in much demand at the lustful Roman parties of old. Succinctly, both the bed and the table represent aspects of human fellowship, communion, and mutual satisfaction of basic needs. Both can be seen as weak points as well: soldiers stop and eat even in the midst of a war in order to replenish energies to keep fighting. Obsessive-compulsive overachievers still need to go to bed to allow the brain and the rest of bodily functions to be restored, realigned, and recuperated.

In more adequate—reformed, transformed—terms, the act of having a deep encounter (being in one accord and in one place) and sharing a meal at the table appear together at the Lord's Supper. Besides such transcendent encounters practiced by the fellowship of believers, the common assertion that "whenever two or three Christians are gathered, there is coffee and donuts among them" seems to describe the habitual practices that add flavor to otherwise sober and sacred endeavors. The author to the Hebrews reminds us that the marriage bed has to be kept undefiled (Heb 13:4). Covenantal transactions of loving, ethical, and moral rightness need to be preserved in the fellowship at a communion table, keeping the *koinonia* of the church undefiled as well.

CONCLUSION: FOSTERING INTIMACY

All intimate transactions amongst humans reflect the possible existence of barriers impinging upon, intruding into, or blocking the development, maintenance, and renewal of intimacy. Yet, covenantal transactions may help people to anticipate these, to inoculate stress ahead of time, and to count the cost of mutuality, stability, and satisfaction. A disposition to be there for each other—to bless, to give, and to demonstrate attentive care—does foster an ambiance of intimacy. In view of the main premise of this work, intimacy is best fostered if the terms of the New Covenant—chunked into ten principles—are expressed in concrete behaviors. That is, intimacy increases if the other nine factors are at work—engaging with *unilateral, unconditional,* and *proactive* mindfulness; dispensing *grace* and *mercy* in love; *forgiving* one another and *letting go* of offenses; *empowering* versus powering over one another; and renewing the covenantal vows in an ongoing fashion.

Needless to say, it is the Holy Spirit who empowers partners to enact these principles in concrete behaviors. Relying on the person, presence, and power of the Holy Spirit allows people in relationship to be constantly transformed and renewed in the spirit of their minds, inviting the transcendent into all aspects of everyday life. The establishment, growth, and enhancement of intimacy may be fostered in a proactive fashion. A few suggestions are provided here to that end.

- Openness to one another. Partners that allow themselves to be influenced by the other do better, foster more communication, and enhance positive feelings.[11] Thus, rather than closed defensiveness, guardedness, or emotional unavailability, the willingness and disposition to be there—accessible, inviting, posing no barriers or impediments to the other—foster a sense of "being known" and ready to know the other;

- Honesty and transparency. These may be anxiety-provoking stances to adopt, especially if transactions and patterns of defensiveness have elevated the need to protect the self from any perceived rejection, dejection, or contempt. Honesty and transparency are difficult to enact, due to the fact that the basic anxiety of being known at the core—without facades—appears to be a built-in feature of our deformed state of being in need of redemption and transformation;

- Trust building. The stages of human development postulated by Erikson start with trust versus mistrust, a crisis to be resolved earlier in life in order to function properly later on.[12] Placing too much trust in others may be seen as naïveté; demonstrating too much mistrust in others may be considered a paranoid state. Thus, a healthy balance between these polarities needs to be achieved by partners, especially in cases in which one or both come from dysfunctional systems that have impinged upon the development of trust. Intimacy increases when trust is continuously fostered by faithful, honest, and transparent dealings with one another;

- In a unilateral, unconditional, proactive way, each partner may promote the sharing of experiences of a mutual, satisfactory, and personally relevant nature—respecting the tastes, values, preferences, and styles of each other;

- Praying together: listening to one another's concerns, petitions, praise, and thanksgiving before God helps a couple consolidate their mutual concern for each other, their family, and their friends. Intercession on behalf of others helps

---

11. Gottman and Silver, *The Seven Principles*; Gottman et al., *Ten Lessons*.
12. Erikson, *Childhood and Society*.

a couple recognize the level of empathy that both display in a decentered way before God. The same applies to prayerful thanksgiving for the blessings enjoyed, the accomplishments made, the goals reached, etc., as they jointly recognize God's intervention, support, deliverance, help, and empowering presence;

- Planning together—whether budgeting along money matters or envisioning fun times or vacations, purchasing goods or services, hosting a meal, or any activities that the couple may envision and work toward. Brainstorming, developing creative ideas, and sharing mindsets keeps a couple focused on common targets and directs their mutual honing in on these objectives;

- Sharing great ideas and trivial ones. Life offers plenty of everyday activities that may be chunked into an interpersonal, joint "bank" of small pockets of intimate, shared "secrets," not available to anyone else. This special bonding that develops and consolidates along mundane aspects of life seems to provide grounds for higher perspectives and goals and allows the couple to accrue a "joint bank account" of an experiential nature to draw from.

As a final note, intimacy—defined as interpersonal interpenetration or perichoresis—affects partners in profound ways. Researchers in the field of interpersonal neurobiology remind us that cells that fire together wire together. This axiom has been attributed to Hebb, rephrased as "neurons that fire together wire together" by Carla Shatz, and popularized by Siegel.[13] It is interesting to entertain the notion that partners relating in love have the opportunity, the power, and the privilege to affect one another's minds and brains. Their hearts may "fire together" and reinforce their love for one another, and their mindsets may align cognitive processes as well.

If the findings in the field of interpersonal neurobiology prove to be accurate, it will be feasible to offer a reliable explanation that corroborates the notion that intimate partners affect one another in a holistic fashion. That is, not only do their cognitive-emotive expressions align with and mirror each other's thoughts and feelings, but also the neurobiological substrata and biochemical activities underlying these processes experience positive changes. A partner's brain that is perceiving, beholding, and internalizing the image of his/her counterpart may be transformed at structural levels, consolidating the pathways of mirror neurons associated with cognitive, emotive, and motivational features. Readers are invited to ponder over a Pauline theological notion, dealing with our reformed self "becoming" Christ-like: "And we all, with unveiled faces reflecting the glory of the Lord [or "we all with unveiled faces beholding the glory of the Lord as in a mirror"], are being transformed into the same image from one degree of glory to another" (2 Cor 3:18). In an analogous fashion, beholding one another as covenantal partners—without any barriers or facades—does foster a mirroring effect, which enhances mutual attachment, empathy, and love.

13. Hebb, *The Organization of Behavior*; Shatz, "The Developing Brain," 63; Siegel, *The Developing Mind*.

Chapter 14

Empowered to Forgive as God Forgave Us in Christ

> For I will forgive their wickedness and will remember their sins no more. (Hebrews 8:12, NIV)

> Father, forgive them, for they do not know what they are doing. (Luke 23:34, NIV)

> Be kind to one another, compassionate, forgiving one another, just as God in Christ also forgave you. (Ephesians 4:32)

THE TERMS OF A New Covenant include both the promise of God's forgiveness of our sin and the willful letting go of our transgressions, remembering them no more. The mediator of the New Covenant has accomplished the work of our redemption and offers us a new, open, and living way of access to the Father. From God's side, forgiveness is the act of absolving our sins and misdeeds; from our side, it is the state of being pardoned and set free from sin and from the entrapments that naturally encumber us—the impediments to the actualization of our potentials to be and to do what God desires.

The proposition to imitate the Father's way of forgiving is a challenge posed to believers due to the fact that his process involves the abandonment of retaliatory urges, as well as the dispensation of grace and mercy toward offenders. To forgive as God does—in a metacognitive, proactive, and deliberate way—stretches our human capacities. It is by faith in God's ultimate justice and reliance on the empowering of God's Spirit that we may realize and deal with our precariousness and incapacity to obey the command. Our faith and obedience to God's summoning word allows for the process to be actualized and experienced in existential fashion. Once envisioned and enacted, the process of forgiveness opens the door to the experience of peace, freedom, fellowship, and walking in love as beloved children.

FORGIVENESS IN NEW COVENANTAL TERMS

Several terms dealing with forgiveness appear in the New Testament. The verb *aphiemi* (lit., "I send away, release, remit, forgive, permit, leave, forsake, let alone") and its derivatives occur often, related to concepts such as cancelling debts, pardoning, or delivering someone from some charges or penalties.[1]

The evangelist Luke uses the term to convey the notion of being released from servitude, as well as being set free from oppression: "He has sent me to proclaim *release* [*aphesis*: release, deliverance] to the captives and the regaining of sight to the blind, to set free [*aphesis*: deliver, release] those who are oppressed" (Luke 4:18, emphasis mine). The idea of *aphesis* in this text corresponds closely to the significance of the Feast of Jubilee, which in the LXX is called "the feast of *aphesis*," where slaves were set free. John uses this term assertively: "But if we confess our sins, he is faithful and righteous, forgiving us [lit., that he might forgive us, or take away from us] our sins and cleansing us from all unrighteousness" (1 John 1:9). The neo-testamentary emphasis stresses that God has forgiven, pardoned, and let go of our sins as if they were never committed and has remitted the penalty that would apply as a result of our transgressions.

Other terms are used, such as *apoluo*, from *apó* ("away from") and *luō* ("to loose, release, discharge, dismiss"). The term implies the release (annulment) of an existing bond, specifically used of divorcing a marital partner (Matt 1:19; 5:31–32; 19:7–9; Mark 10:2–12; Luke 16:18). The only text in which *apoluo* is translated "forgive" is in Luke 6:37: "Judge not, and ye shall not be judged: condemn not, and ye shall not be condemned: forgive, and ye shall be forgiven" (KJV). This line of reasoning is similar to Matthew's expression: "Forgive our debts as we forgive our debtors."

Yet another neo-testamentary term, *charizomai* ("I show favor to, forgive"), denotes the action of extending grace, showing kindness, or granting forgiveness to an undeserving person.[2] All in all, the ground of our forgiving one another is established on the recognition of the unmerited, undeserved love that God lavished on us. The New Covenant makes provision for an encompassing—unilateral, unconditional, proactive, and empowering—way of forgiving one another: "For I will be merciful

---

1. The terms *aphiemi* (ἀφίημι) occurs approximately 142 times, translated in forty-six passages as "forgiveness," as in Matthew 6:12: "And forgive us (ἄφες) our debts, as we ourselves have forgiven (ἀφήκαμεν) our debtors." In Matthew 6:14-15, "For if you indeed *forgive* (ἀφῆτε) others their sins (trespasses), your heavenly Father will also forgive (ἀφήσει) you." A derivative, *aphesis* (ἄφεσις: deliverance, pardon; used six times as "forgiveness"), is used in the context of the Lord's Supper. The "cup of the covenant" is offered by Jesus to the disciples with the words (Matt. 26:28): "For this is my blood, the blood of the covenant that is poured out for many for the forgiveness of sins."

2. The term appears twenty-three times and in twelve passages, and is translated as "forgiving," or "pardoning" (as in Luke 7:42, "And when they had nothing to pay, he frankly forgave [*charizomai*] them both"). Students of Scripture may consult with texts such as 2 Corinthians 2:7: "You should rather *forgive* [χαρίσασθα] and comfort"; Eph 4:32, (χαριζόμενοι ἑαυτοῖς καθὼς) trans. "be kind, tenderhearted, *forgiving one another*; as also God forgave (ἐχαρίσατο) you in Christ"; and Col 3:13—"forgiving one another [χαριζόμενοι ἑαυτοῖς] even as the Lord forgave you" (all emphases mine).

Part II: Principles Derived from the New Covenant in Marital Transactions

toward their evil deeds, and their sins I will remember no longer" (Heb 8:12; 10:18). God reconciled us to himself in Christ, "not counting people's trespasses" (2 Cor 5:19). Having been treated by God in that way, we are to imitate him: "Forgiving one another, *just as God in Christ also forgave you*" (Eph 4:32, emphasis added).

The normative nature of the command to forgive is drawn from God's exemplary way of doing things. God grants forgiveness on the basis of the work accomplished by the Son, the perfect offering, the guarantor, the mediator of the New Covenant who did not just cover our sins, but removed them from God's sight. The expiatory, redemptive *covering* of sin before God was typified in the Old Testament, and its *removal* is stressed in the New Testament—a fact based upon the accomplished work enacted by Jesus Christ: his impeccable life, his death, his resurrection, and his intercession for us before God. The basis and the results of such an accomplished feat are cast in terms of a New Covenant between God and sinful humans in need of forgiveness. It is along these premises that those who believe and trust God are commanded to be imitators of God and walk in love as Christ did (Eph 5:1–2). Believers are summoned to mimic God and enact the ways in which God has acted toward them, dispensing forgiveness to one another.

Forgiving as God has forgiven us demands a conscious realization that God's forgiveness was not a spontaneous, whimsical act derived from sloppy oversight, denial, or rationalization of human sin. Rather, the sin of the world, from the First Adam to the last existing person on planet Earth, was placed upon Jesus, the Last Adam—the one who summed up all humankind's transgressions and misdeeds and became the ultimate substitute before God. God did not spare his own Son, but gave him up for us (Rom 8:32). The one who knew no sin was made sin for us, so the righteousness of God would be manifested (2 Cor 5:21).

He bore the sins of the world in his body, being nailed to the cross for us. The demands of justice were satisfied before an ultimate judge, and the finished work testifies that, with one offering, he made perfect those who approach God through this pathway. Grace and mercy flow from the cross as a consequence of having removed sin from God's presence, making peace and establishing fellowship again. This forgiveness in Christ involves the substitutionary work of Christ, the atonement for sin (the payment of our debt, the acceptance of such payment, and the canceling of it), the removal of sin from God's sight and presence, and the freedom to access God again in love.

From God's side, forgiveness is the dispensation of grace and mercy upon offending humans that springs from God, the forgiver. This ontological quality of character and demonstration of graceful behavior are the exemplary basis for God's children to imitate as they relate to one another. From the human side, forgiveness is the capacity to imitate the Father's ways, enacted in concrete terms—a process marked by emergent properties of an empowered character, willing and able to let go of offenses according to the expectations of the forgiving Father. God, who gives the command to forgive, provides the capacity, the energy, and the guidelines necessary to obey this command. The human needs to recognize the necessity of coparticipating with God's Spirit along this endeavor.

GOING IN DEPTH: FORGIVING FROM THE EMPOWERED HEART/MIND

Forgiveness may be defined concretely, as witnessed in a display of overt actions. At deeper levels, it involves a complex array of thoughts, reasoning, memories, feelings, attitudes, etc., that enter into play (engaging in a forgiving process of a cognitive, emotive, motivational, and enactive nature). At an even deeper, ontological level, forgiveness represents a characterological trait, an exuding property of the renewed heart/mindset: being a forgiving person. Of course, "being" is defined not as a static entity, but as a person in the process of *becoming* Christ-like. At the root, *being a forgiver* translates into attitudinal, perceptual, mediating, attributive, and emotive processes that finally culminate in enacted behaviors. The level of difficulty in forgiveness goes up as we go down deep: at a surface level, it seems to be easier to behave in forgiving ways. As a person becomes metacognitively aware of his/her underlying thoughts and emotions, it becomes more difficult to engage in the actual forgiving processes. And, needless to say, it is even more challenging to be a forgiving person at the core—always able, willing, and ready to forgive.

"Father, forgive them, for they do not know what they are doing" appears as a forgiving event registered as one of the seven expressions of Jesus from the cross—pleading to the Father on the perpetrator's behalf. At a natural level, the Roman soldiers knew how to crucify, and the Jewish leaders knew how to condemn somebody claiming to be a Messiah. Thus, the expression goes beyond a trivial connotation to a more transcending exclamation to the Father—the only witness who knew precisely what was going on. Yet, such an event is predicated on the foreknowledge of the Son in fulfilling an eternal plan, on his perfect understanding of sinful nature blinded by sin, and on his substitutionary capacity in offering of himself to the Father. Thus, the forgiving event was an expression of a concrete nature registered by the evangelist, yet it was exuded as a synthesis of a great deal of cognitive-emotive-motivational processes that unfolded in space and time and were synthesized in a kairotic fashion. These processes emanated from Jesus's being—his forgiving character and his essential quality of being the forgiving one.

In human terms, telling somebody to forgive—because God says so—may be a difficult assignment as humans do not possess impeccable traits or a perfect capacity to process all the cognitive-emotive-motivational aspects involving the offender, the offense, and the offended party as Jesus did. Although quite often pastors tell an offended person to forgive (and quote Scripture to affirm such an event), this wholesale expectation to automatically dispense mercy and grace does not appear to have substantial human resources from which to spring. That is, the person may not be able to grasp all the intricate aspects of the process of forgiveness that need to take place. Perhaps, in a sincere or forced fashion, the person forgives in order to obey a command, but without any insight as to what enters into play "underneath" this behavior.

As a process, forgiveness necessitates changes in cognitive, affective, and behavioral structures, processes, and events. It involves the cognitive assessment of the hurt and the connotations associated with the perceived harm. The process involves ruminative thoughts, which at times may assume obsessive proportions and provoke deep-seated negative feelings. An offended person is prone to repetitively recount memories of a painful, anger-provoking, and undesirable nature. The negative attributions of meaning associated with the damages done to one's self-image and esteem provide a morbid quality to the array of entrenched memories of offenses. The emotional connotations associated with these cognitive processes may be described as feelings of anger, injustice, pain, hurt, and shame, which are coupled with the perceptive, attributive, and enactive considerations.

Approaching forgiveness as a command to be obeyed could be outlined along three levels of analysis: overt behaviors, underlying processes, and deeply consolidated structures. Beyond eventful or surface considerations, forgiveness is a process emerging from deeply seated convictions. It is an attitude of the mind that deals with emotive and motivational upheavals caused by the intrusion of obnoxious elements into a person's mediating and attributive processes. It may be regarded as an emergent property of the ontological being subject to injustice, injury, or aggravation of any sort with a willful capacity to deal with the offender and ultimately let go of the offense.

THE COMMAND TO FORGIVE ONE ANOTHER

Jesus commands us as believers to forgive one another (Matt 6:12; 14–15); the apostle Paul follows the same lines, exhorting believers to forgive as we have received the forgiveness of our sins in Christ (Eph 4:32; Col 3:13). Forgiveness is a simple command, yet a complex process to actualize. The simple admonitions given by well-intentioned friends and caretakers who, stereotypically, quote scriptural injunctions (e.g., "Turn the other cheek," "Forgive and let go; it's good for you," "Forgive: after all, it's a command, not an option"), seem to run along the biblical commands to do so. It is not a matter of making something simple into a complex philosophical endeavor, but the fact is that commands tend to elicit adverse reactions in a person. St. Paul shares this in Romans 7, where a simple command ("Do not covet") provoked him to engage in an internal dialogical struggle between his deformed, natural self and his regenerated, transforming self.

The command to forgive may be followed with metacognitive-dialogical, purposeful insight—or by a robotic obedience without insight or deliberate mindfulness. To behave without insight is simply a legalistic act, going through the motions because it is the thing to do. To have insight and not behave in a forgiving fashion provokes guilt—the guilt of knowing what to do but not being able or willing to do it. To develop a metacognitive, insightful perspective about the offense and still be free, open, able, and willing—empowered to engage in a process of forgiveness in a unilateral, unconditional, and proactive manner—is the appropriate way to go without feeling like either a masochist or a codependent enabler.

Simple admonitions to forgive without providing encouragement to embark in a mindful process seems to be right at a surface level; yet, these may leave the forgiving person trapped in internal struggles: ruminations, conjectures, and musings saturated with feelings of unfairness and frustration. The commandment to forgive seems to encapsulate Jesus's ultimate concern, aimed at freeing the offended human by exercising an empowered, graceful, and merciful response. In giving this commandment, Jesus presented a basic promise: we were forgiven by an all-powerful, holy God. Thus, we must forgive because we were forgiven. The parable of the two debtors is a powerful reminder of this premise (Matt 18:23–25).

The commands found in the gospels and in Pauline thought are not to be taken in isolation or out of context. The granting of forgiveness is not simply an overlooking of the trespasses of the offender, but the thoughtful enactment of proper principles applied in the process of forgiving one another. If we consider passages such as Luke 17:3–4 and Matthew 18:15–17, we may develop a heart of wisdom:

> Watch yourselves! If your brother sins, rebuke him. If he repents, forgive him. Even if he sins against you seven times in a day, and seven times returns to you saying, "I repent," you must forgive him. (Luke 17:3–4)

The process may be summarized in four steps: 1.) The offense committed is registered as a fact; 2.) The rebuke or assertive confrontation by the offended party is encouraged; 3.) The offender's stance is assessed and ascertained, cast in a conditional clause—"if" the offender repents, "then" a response follows; and 4.) The forgiveness *must* be dispensed by the offended party. Thus, in line with the teachings of old, this NT passage is very instructive as to the process of forgiveness amongst one another. See Proverbs 27:5–6: "Better is open rebuke than hidden love. Faithful are the wounds of a friend, but the kisses of an enemy are excessive [not to be trusted]." The forgiving person needs to adopt a metacognitive stance and trust that both the monitoring of the actual fruits of repentance and the shaping of the character of the offender are in the hands of God, and that the responsibility and control for these desirable qualities of being and behaving are not placed within the offended party's own hands, but remain on God's side. In Luke 17, the disciples' reaction was "Increase our faith!"

The narrative found in Matthew 18:15–17 describes a forgiving process that involves some sequential steps:

> If your brother sins, go and show him his fault when the two of you are alone. If he listens to you, you have regained your brother. But if he does not listen,

Part II: Principles Derived from the New Covenant in Marital Transactions

take one or two others with you, so that at the testimony of two or three witnesses every matter may be established. If he refuses to listen to them, tell it to the church. If he refuses to listen to the church, treat him like a Gentile or a tax collector.

The narrative may be abstracted in three stages, wherein an initial approach calls for a direct, private confrontation of the offender by the offended party. If this respectful and discreet line of approach is disregarded with contempt, a rebuke or assertive confrontation may take place in the presence of a witness. If the perpetrator of the offense further entrenches himself in defensive maneuvers and shows no signs of repentance, a third stage calls for the community of believers to be involved. The desired stance, attitude, and response would involve regret, remorse, and repentance, followed by an eager desire to restitute, re-align, and restore the relationship. The forgiver may assess and ascertain the fact that the offender has repented and made peace with God and with the offended party. The knowledge and certainty about this assessment is desirable and functional in promoting the person's capacity to relinquish his/her urge to retaliate and let go of the offense.

The basic premise found in Ephesians 5:1, "Be imitators of God," coupled with the qualifying statement, "as Christ also loved us and gave himself for us," becomes the prompting element in the process, which allows for the unilateral, unconditional, and proactive thrust aimed at "forgiving one another as God forgave us in Christ." These terms underlie the process to be applied in concrete, interpersonal situations, seeking to actualize the Christian potential to do what God has intended us to do.

The Holy Spirit is the key element in the enactment of covenantal transactions, for God has already demonstrated that human capacity falls short of fulfilling his will and desire. The efforts to regulate the quest for revenge and change automatic reactions into purposive responses of a controlled nature need the influx of the Holy Spirit. In an analogous fashion, this coparticipation between the Spirit's "in-merging" and human will may be compared to a "power-assisted" brake system, as well as a power-steering control directing the process. Instead of maneuvering based on human willpower, the empowering/assisting of the Spirit in enacting the right thoughts, feelings, and behaviors framed in a new deal in human transactions is provided.

When his disciples asked Jesus to "teach us to pray," he actually gave them a paradigmatic example (we call it the Lord's Prayer). In this model prayer, he taught, "Forgive our debts *as we forgive our debtors*" (emphasis mine). From all the scriptural data and context, we know that God is free to exercise his divine prerogative and forgive in a unilateral, unconditional, and proactive manner; yet, God is free to set up conditions as well: "*If my people*, who belong to me, humble themselves, pray, seek to please me, and repudiate their sinful practices, *then I* will respond from heaven, *forgive their sin*, and heal their land" (2 Chron 7:14, emphases mine). God has revealed his intention to relate in an intimate, personal fashion with his people and expresses a desire to see the human response exuding from a purposefully mindful stance. As free agents, endowed with executive functions and metacognitive-dialogical capacities, humans need to imitate the Father's ways and forgive as he forgave—especially in new covenantal terms.

Can humans imitate God at this level of forgiveness—letting go of offenses? Can conflicting parties consider the possibility of behaving before an ultimate perceiver of reality, a perfect judge of all transactions, who will demand an account of our conscious, deliberate, and willful stewardship of relational matters?

The Old Covenant was framed in love, grace, and mercy with a forgiving God designing its terms. Yet, it also demanded human fairness, justice, and restitution, besides loving our neighbor as ourselves. The statement "an eye for an eye, a tooth for a tooth" could sum up a bilateral, conditional, just, and mutually acceptable transaction between equals in the sight of God. The New Covenant does not invalidate the Old, but fulfills it and provides the life-giving power to enact the will of God "from within." To initiate a process of forgiveness along a new deal allows for the possibility of behaving in a unilateral, unconditional, and proactive fashion. A person who decides to adopt these stances must ascertain the reasons behind the decision to forgive the motives of this thrust.

In metacognitive-dialogical terms, the person considering the need to forgive may ascertain his or her internal dialogues associated with the offending event. These dialogues may be deliberative, ruminative, and conjectural in nature. Then, applying a conscious monitoring and control, the person stops his/her self-talk, and shifts and engages in internal rhetoric (persuading self to decide to forgive and enacting this decision). Otherwise, the person engaged in forgiving, without appealing to an insightful and purposeful basis, may engage in erroneous processes with equivocal outcomes.

The forgiving person cannot fail to acknowledge the basic New Covenantal premise underlying the process and consider the opportunity to imitate the Father's ways: "I have already been forgiven by God, and I am expected to imitate these ways. I will do so in freedom, being empowered to do so by the Holy Spirit and aimed with the indwelling Word of God—not as a masochist, push-over, or codependent enabler." If these principles are ignored, the forgiving process may be engaged with wrong, dysfunctional, or inadequate motives.

Diverse conditions may emerge as a result of blind obedience to a command: a self-righteous attitude, expecting or claiming some prideful recognition with regard to performing a magnanimous act, a tacit sense of super-spirituality, or humanistic pride may be fostered. Likewise, the establishment of naïve codependency, behaving without insight, fostering masochistic feelings and entrapments into ironic processes that support the dysfunctional transactions instead of solving them or of learned helplessness, fostering a sense of martyrdom, victimization, or depression may develop. To "forgive" these ways does not solve anything, but fosters more of the same repetitive patterns.

Part II: Principles Derived from the New Covenant in Marital Transactions

In the context of the connotations derived from the New Covenant, the command to forgive (love, grace, mercy in action) may impact the sensibility of an offended person, eliciting confusion and perplexity as to how to behave or respond to an offending brother. After listening to Jesus, who doubled the standards (as in the second-mile account, or turning the other cheek after being slapped once), Peter could assume that his willingness to be perfectly gracious would be in tune with the demands of the Lord. The apostle approached Jesus with the question: "Lord, how many times must I forgive my brother who sins against me? As many as [or up to] seven times?" (Matt 18:21; Luke 17:4). Matthew's narrative couples Peter's question with his projected answer, a feature that needs a contextual explanation. The Babylonian Talmud—known to the Jews of the time of Jesus—had set up an upper limit to forgiveness of deliberate acts with three times as the maximum allowance (cf., Amos 1:3, 6; 2:6). Peter's inquiry, marked by a generous, higher frequency count, exceeded the cultural expectations of his day. Perhaps the apostle expected a pat on the back or some positive appreciation of his graceful inquiry. Yet, the answer was unexpected, perplexing, paradoxical, and puzzling: "Not seven times, I tell you, but seventy-seven times!"

Thus, rather than counting the frequency of forgiving behaviors, Jesus advocated an ongoing, repetitive, and process-oriented stance to be adopted with reference to forgiveness. Even more, the allusion pointed to the adoption of a forgiving character: to *be* a forgiver rather than forcibly enacting behaviors to be counted. Jesus's metaphorical, hyperbolic frequency (7 x 70 = 490 times) may be regarded as a preview of the forgiving terms of the New Covenant. Humans relating in covenantal terms must always be ready to forgive one another (Luke 17:4) as God forgives them (Matt 18:35), demonstrating a new orientation to interpersonal transactions (Matt 18:15).

The apostle Paul reminds us in Ephesians 4:32, "Be kind to one another, compassionate, forgiving one another, *just as God in Christ also forgave you*" (emphasis mine). To do so in this manner is to imitate the Father's ways as exemplified in new covenantal terms. A simplistic view cannot capture the complexity of feelings experienced or adequately help people struggling with distressing aspects arising from deeply felt emotions associated with offending events. The construct *forgiveness* may be approached from diverse angles as it pertains to its phenomenology (what forgiveness looks like to a person); its ontology (the nature, essence, or substructure underlying the process or events); its epistemology (where we gather the information and knowledge about the construct and its surrounding ramifications); and its praxis (how to engage in the process of forgiveness). Besides, the reasons and motivations to forgive could be explored, as well as the obstacles that may emerge as impediments along the way of forgiveness.

The reader is invited to delve into a metacognitive-dialogical model of forgiveness, presented at the end of this work in chapter 17. The model appears at the end as a summary of the thrust of the New Covenant enacted in the process of forgiveness, following the command to do so as God's dearly beloved children.

HUMAN DEFENSES: OBSTACLES TO FORGIVENESS

Obstacles in the way of being a forgiving person—and consequently to engage in a cognitive, affective, and enactive process of resolving/letting go of offenses—reside in the anticipated fears of aggravating the situation even more. Personality factors may play into the responses to aggravation, transgression, and offenses. In the experience of the author, when dealing with numerous cases involving the need to forgive, characterological features such as flexibility, empathy, meekness, and goodness seem to facilitate the process; on the other hand, neuroticism (anxiety, apprehension, obsessions, compulsions) and dysfunctional features of character (borderline, narcissistic, histrionic, antisocial, obsessive-compulsive personality disorders) produce difficulties of various degrees in the process of forgiving, and even more, in the letting go of offenses.

The fear of doing the wrong things—condoning the wrongdoing, having to reconcile and repair a bad relationship, or not allowing justice to be done—and becoming a codependent with the offender figure among the obstacles to forgiveness. The fear of letting go and forgetting the offenses committed against us appears to be based on the perception of fostering nonsense and betraying our sense of justice. The apprehension about being or becoming an enabler, a codependent, or a masochistic person looms over the horizon. Thus, it seems better to the person, in his or her wounded estimation, to remain in control of a defensive, retaliatory, or even aggressive posture against the offender.

"And forgive our debts as we forgive our debtors" refers to sins committed against us as if they are debts contracted—something that has been taken away from us. Dispensing forgiveness is personally experienced as a decision to cancel a debt, as if someone took something from us: money (an unpaid debt); a state of mind (something has been done that robs us of our peace); heart (our sensitivities have been offended by abandonment or neglect); an unfulfilled request or expectation (a broken promise or covenantal vow).

As we cancel the debts of our debtors or let go of offenses, we set ourselves free. This concept is hard to grasp at first, especially if we regard the debt as being offensive enough to destroy a state of peace, joy, security, or any other positive description of well-being. Letting go of this damage is felt as a double impact on the self (being harmed, yet not free to retaliate), which makes this process even more offensive. A person who experiences a sense of having been taken advantage of may be trapped in anger and its manifestations—feelings of resentment, rumination, and retaliation—and fail to obey the command to forgive. This failure to obey is not due to the believer's lack of knowledge. A victimized person's passion may override his/her reason and block his/her capacity to forgive—in spite of knowing that the command comes from the highest source—because his/her mood and disposition has been negatively altered.

Part II: Principles Derived from the New Covenant in Marital Transactions

The forgiving process also depends on the nature of the injury and the effects on the person. A narcissistic injury (being hurt at the core of a person's ontological, essential being) is not a matter of a casual nature. The self, subject to such an injury, may wrestle with the perception or the fact that his or her pride, self-esteem, self-image, dignity, or reputation have been trampled on, and his or her self-respect may stand in the way of forgiveness. Loss of face, shame, self-pity, and a sense of martyrdom may develop if an injured person is not able or willing to share his or her story, unload, and process the offensive happenings.

FACILITATING FORGIVENESS: THE OFFENDER'S ATTITUDES AND BEHAVIORS

In both pastoral and clinical settings, this author has for many years stressed a process that involves a sequentially logical paradigm following a reality-based approach to healing in relationships. Usually the admonitions are given to the offended party (a victim) to forgive a transgressor. The offended party may feel offended again, this time by the insensitive, un-empathic command given—if it is not accompanied by metacognitive, empowered coaching. Furthermore, because the process involves also the responsibilities and demands for fairness and justice that enter into play, it is necessary to address the issue of the offender: Where is he or she? What is his or her attitude, disposition, or stance? Is that person available, willing, and able to engage in a process that takes into account the reality of the offense, its ramifications, and the sensitivities of the offended party?

It is fair to say that working with an offender seems to be a more challenging task compared to the attentive care dispensed to an offended victim. Besides the defensive stance of the offended party, the countertransference of the provider of services may enter into play in a negative or judgmental way against the offender. The process of forgiveness engaged on the side of the offended partner needs to run in parallel—in a constructive and confrontational fashion—in the case of the offender. This person may be addressed by speaking the truth in love and should be treated as a person in need of forgiveness as well. If an offender is willing and desires to be forgiven, this person may be coached to take some initiative in order to be willing and able to engage in counseling.

The counselor needs to be sensitive to the process going on with the offended partner in order to promote the right ambiance and context for this person to be ready to engage in the process and empowered to extend her or his forgiveness to the offender. The capacity to be and act in a unilateral, proactive, conscious, and deliberate fashion is stressed to avoid codependent traps that may further victimize the offended partner. On the other hand, the offending person needs to adopt a new covenantal attitude and engage in unilateral, unconditional, and proactive initiatives, approaching the offended party along the following principles:

1. *Reality testing.* The offender needs to accept the reality of having done something wrong, of having offended a person by his or her attitudes, behaviors, or stances. The individual must accept the fact that, due to these contingencies, the covenantal aspects of the relationship have been affected, offended, and damaged.

2. *Responsibility.* The offender has to accept his or her responsibility in hurting, offending, or damaging the relationship, as well as the person that feels hurt, having been offended.

3. *Regret.* The offender must engage in cognitive appraisal, recognition, and re-experiencing of wrongdoing that has caused pain, hurt, or aggravation to someone. He or she has to demonstrate an accurate perception of what has been done toward the other.

4. *Remorse.* The offender must convey his or her experience of the feelings associated with the cognitive recognition of wrongdoing. Guilt, shame, abasement, and pain are not to be selfishly or conveniently ameliorated before dealing with the issues that resulted in the dysfunction, destruction, or invalidation of the covenantal transactions with the other.

5. *Repentance.* The offender must demonstrate an active engagement in turning away from wrongdoing, changing the directional thrust of his or her attitudes and behaviors or changing his or her mindset. This process involves the willful decision to face the reality of the offender's wrongdoing and his or her decision to do good versus rationalizing, intellectualizing, repressing, suppressing, projecting, or defending in any way the offending contingencies.

6. *Restitution.* The offender needs to exercise efforts in doing what is right, conveying a remedial disposition and a behavioral demonstration of his or her willingness to repay for tangible losses to the offended party. These efforts involve the disposition to make things right, augmented by the connotation of good faith, going beyond the expectations of the hurt person.

    Payment of debts and restitution enter into play in each case involving interpersonal transgressions. In a comprehensive coverage, the sins committed by a partner against the other were covered by the death of Christ, and these may be dealt with by both sides approaching God's throne of grace. Yet, to be fair, the sins against one another require forgiveness and restitution before approaching God. Zacchaeus, the tax collector mentioned in Luke 19, realized his sin and confessed it to Jesus (recognizing that he had taken advantage of the people whose taxes he was collecting). Jesus attests to the tax collector's "saved" state when he made explicit his intent to make restitution (he would give half of his possessions to the poor, and would give back what he had stolen from people in quadruple amounts). Zacchaeus was freely forgiven by Jesus; also, his victims were compensated by means of restitution. The argument may be made that confession to God alone is all that is necessary for forgiveness before God; yet, as the second commandment indicates, loving the neighbor means that an offended party must be addressed as well to establish fairness and equitable justice.

Attending to the needs for justice and fairness in human transactions is the basis for any civil justice, remediating the effects of faulty transactions in need of repair or restoration. David's prayer of confession in Psalm 51 where he states, "Against Thee, Thee only, have I sinned," may be interpreted in ways that lead to unfinished transactions between humans in need of justice and fairness. Ultimately, all sin is committed against God, the one to whom confession must be made. Yet, the command registered in James 5:16—to "confess your faults to one another"—should be interpreted as following the just, fair, and normative process of interpersonal forgiveness in the fellowship of believers. The confession of the sin(s) of an offender before the elders and the empathic understanding of the impacted, offended parties was not ignored by James, but was attended to fairly.

7. *Restoration.* The offender needs to demonstrate efforts to set the relationship with the offended person on the right course, regaining a positive momentum, reestablishing the right premises, or rebuilding the broken aspects of the relationship. Needless to say, restoration of marital and familial relationships is the aim of pastors, counselors, and therapists that engage in Christian endeavors, dealing with broken, dysfunctional, and divorcing cases. This is possible if forgiveness has taken place and parties are willing, able, and ready to engage in this process under some objective guidance, empowered by the appeal to the Holy Spirit and the Word of God.

A new basis needs to be laid—especially the basis of a New Covenant—as outlined and unfolded in the various chapters of this work, offering a better model for new transactions. The "letting go" of offenses by the offended party is a must—a preliminary clearing of the debris of the ground of new transactions, free from old impediments and free to establish new structures and processes. This stance and disposition to work has to be corresponded with the offender's eagerness to engage in restitution, going beyond *quid pro quo* efforts. The offender needs to demonstrate a unilateral, unconditional, and proactive initiative directed toward the empowering—not the powering over—of the partner. The repentant, regretful, remorseful, and ready-to-restore person has to be mindfully aware of the consequences of attitudes and behaviors displayed toward the renewed covenant in order to do the right things with attentive, caring empathy and respect.

8. *Renewal.* The offender needs to consider and engage in efforts to make things new, creatively seeking to go beyond the customary aspects that allowed for the negative contingencies associated with wrongdoing. The lethargic, routine-based

aspects of the relationship need to be revitalized. The renewal of the mind allows for the transformation of the offender's being, enabling him or her to pursue a life of spiritual integrity, faithfulness, freedom, and flexibility, while fostering the actualization of potentials allocated by God.

CONCLUSION

The paradigm outlined in the diverse dimensions may be helpful to psychotherapists, counselors, and pastors in their attempts to help a person struggling not only with the issue of forgiveness, but with the offender as well. It seeks to empower both partners to take a proactive and empowered initiative and engage in a process that is both therapeutically significant and biblically sound. Recognizing the fact that we often "trespass" covenantal limits against God and our neighbor with whom we share a covenantal relationship allows us to see forgiveness as the means to restore both our relationship with humans that we have offended and our relationship with God, the ultimate overseer of such transactions.

In sum, this chapter has attempted to present forgiveness as a process that may be empowered by God's Spirit as the author and enabler of new covenantal transactions. God's agents—the Holy Spirit and the Word—may endow a struggling human being with the capacity to be unilateral, unconditional, and proactive; aimed with grace and mercy; capable of letting go of offenses; walking in love; and imitating God as a beloved child. A better understanding of the imitational way of forgiving as God does relies on the empowering of the inner being (the top-down executive agency) by the Holy Spirit and the indwelling Word. A metacognitive-dialogical model of this process is postulated and hypothetically diagrammed at the end of this work (chapter 17).

Chapter 15

Letting Go of Offenses and Being Free

> For I will forgive their wickedness and will remember their sins no more. (Hebrews 8:12, NIV)

> Let this mind [the same attitude] be in you, which was also in Christ Jesus. (Philippians 2:5, KJV)

CHAPTER 14 DEALT WITH God's love, grace, and mercy in dispensing forgiveness for human sins and trespasses. This feature stands out as a main expression embedded in the New Covenant as the fulfillment of the shadows, types, and figures of the Old Covenant: beyond covering them before God, the Lamb of God has taken away the sins of the world. Having removed them from his sight, God remembers them no more. Likewise, those who, as beloved children, imitate the Father are also commanded to forgive one another just as God forgave us in Christ (Eph 4:32; Col 3:13). Moreover, this chapter deals with the complementary aspect of forgiveness: the capacity to engage in a metacognitive, unilateral, and unconditional process of letting go of the offenses committed against us; that is, to decide to enact a willful remission, a conscious and deliberate forgetfulness regarding the offenses committed against us. As Paul reminds us, love keeps no record of wrongs (1 Cor 13:5).

From a natural, human point of view, not to retaliate against an offender takes effort. To let go of a debt (operationalized in terms of transactions, such as being robbed of respect, dignity, honor, justice, etc.) contracted by an offending partner (defined as a debtor who took advantage, whether intentionally or unintentionally) is a challenge to the reactionary stances of an offended partner. Whether these be trivial hurts or narcissistic injuries, letting go of "debts" calls for a thorough grasp of a metacognitive, God-empowered process in order to avoid misconceptions or further victimization. This process—letting go of what is owed—is not intended to foster a forgiver's emotional bankruptcy, but seeks to promote a paradoxical replenishment of emotional and spiritual assets in the forgiver's account. As it pertains to this work, empirical findings have pointed to the willingness to forgive and letting go of offenses as characteristic features of long-lasting first marriages.[1]

Negative contingencies have the power to mnemonically trap our mindset in cognitive-emotional styles, such as rumination, regurgitation of wrongdoing, brooding, and victimization. Having been hurt, humiliated, or offended in any fashion may render a person a victim of injustice, wrongdoing, and unfairness, trapped in rumination and brooding with anger. After an event of an offensive nature, equity and fairness in relations demand a series of conditions to be set in place: the resolution of the conflict, the establishment of justice, and the restoration of peace of mind with promises and guarantees of safety, security, and stability.

How do we let go and forget the memories associated with offenses? How do we avoid engaging in retaliatory or vindictive ruminations, obsessive thoughts, or evil desires of a harmful nature against the offender? This chapter deals with a reality-based, metacognitive stance needed in order to be able to dispense grace and mercy. It proceeds from a biblical-theological understanding of the process of letting go. It allows for the conviction and feeling of *being* imitators of God, willing and able to advance from a solid *ground of being*—a secure attachment to God. The process of letting go of offenses is analogous to taking a leap of faith, springing from a secure basis and aimed with an empowered, unilateral, unconditional, and proactive stance. Thus, this leap of faith is taken in a mindful, metacognitive fashion—"from the top," not from under the oppressive, negative circumstances. It is important to see one's self as a *forgiver* defined by God and in full control of one's reactions and responses; that is, to perceive one's self as having the choice to count the cost of forgiveness, to engage in intrapsychic dialogical struggles, and to remain free from the potential entrapments of the negative contingencies to which the self has been subjected. It is necessary to perceive one's self as not being defined or imprisoned by the offensive vicissitudes. In order to be imitators of God and let go of offenses, a sort of metacognitive-executive control mechanism has to enter into play, enabling the believer to engage in this process—empowered by the infused Holy Spirit and the indwelling Word of God.

TO FORGIVE *AND* FORGET?

The Judeo-Christian tradition has regarded forgiveness as a major issue, dealt with in conceptual, theological, and practical terms. This chapter addresses succinctly the continuity and differentiation between forgiveness as understood under both Old and New Covenant terms. In the last three decades, mental health researchers and practitioners have joined the forgiveness topic and field; theologians have been working for a long time along these endeavors. Forgiveness has become a topic of both psychological research and therapeutic approaches. Yet, attempts to define and specify the meaning

---

1. Fennel, "Characteristics of Long-Term First Marriages."

of forgiveness have not provided a cohesive rendering of the construct. Despite a lack of consensus, some agreement exists in regarding forgiveness as a construct distinct from forgetting or pardoning. At this junction, a differential definition and attribution of meaning may be postulated: the New Covenant goes beyond simply forgiving. It addresses the need to engage in mindful forgetfulness and let go of offenses as God did: "Their sins and their lawless deeds I will remember no longer" (Heb 10:17).

For a transgressor, this clause is music to his ears: it sounds like an unusual, most wonderful statement coming from God. The omniscient and omnipotent God—the one who can truly scrutinize, bring matters to light, judge fairly, and establish justice has promised to develop a voluntary, super-conscious, retrograde amnesia with respect to our sins. The Lawgiver who has pronounced the verdict (we are condemned because of sin) is the same Savior who declares us righteous and free. The same finger that engraved in stone the fate of an adulteress wrote on dust something that convicted her accusers and allowed the transgressor to be forgiven and go free. This account of the adulteress—brought to Jesus by the experts in the law and the righteous Pharisees who confronted Jesus with a challenging question, "Moses has commanded us to stone her; what do you say?"—is an example of an understanding of the purpose of the law and the dispensing of grace (John 8:3–11).

God's promise of letting go of our sins stands above and beyond the popular saying, "I'll forgive, but will not forget." For believers to imitate God at that level is another story. The challenge to engage in "willful forgetting" is posed in Scripture, not as a utopian principle, but as an emergent property of being empowered to enact a practical necessity. Needless to say, it is not a question of God being *unable* to remember, but rather *choosing* not to do so. To forgive *and forget* are both intrinsically intertwined in the New Covenant, offered as exemplary ways for humans to imitate the Father in dealing with one another's offenses. For humans—husbands, wives, parents, children, siblings, and friends—to let go of offenses may prove to be not only the good and acceptable will of God, but also the freeing avenue to experience peace of mind and reinforce mental health.

Although forgiveness and active forgetfulness have been regarded as human virtues or strength of character, the process should not be defined in isolation, devoid of a situational context.[2] The contextual nature of forgiveness and letting go cannot be ignored. There is a need to pay attention to the particularities of an offensive event or an ongoing process, for the intensity and extent of the offending stressors may impact different individuals in different ways. Offenses affect people differentially at multiple levels—ontological, cognitive, emotive, and motivational—and at particular states of mind. Each person's self-image, esteem, integrity, honor, and dignity have to be assessed in the aftermath of a given offense. Experiences of shame, guilt, empathy, and other emotive processes may inform the process of forgiveness.[3]

2. Wade and Worthington, "In Search of a Common Core."
3. Konstam et al., "Toward Forgiveness"; Tangney et al., "Assessing Individual Differences."

DIVERSE PERSPECTIVES ON LETTING GO OF OFFENSES

As of late, the psychological field has emphasized forgiveness, but not much emphasis has been placed on willful forgetfulness except as it may be applied on functional grounds—if that complementary aspect helps the person to be free from rumination, brooding, or negative consequences of a psychosomatic nature. The fears of fostering codependency, further victimization, or degradation of the offended person have guided the initial efforts of researchers and practitioners in addressing the process of forgiveness. Some research has alluded to the enactment of forgiveness as a possible expression of naïve or immature defense mechanisms at work. The findings pointed to the possibility of reinterpreting overt behaviors; the letting go of offenses may not represent virtue or strength of character, but a decision based on a fear of confrontation, an unwillingness to acknowledge one's anger, or a need to overlook one's values and beliefs in the service of convenience.[4]

Granted, forgiving somebody does not necessarily demand an engagement in naïve, superficial, or forced interactions with the offender. Yet, at the core, not letting go appears to be a sort of unfinished transaction that leaves a residual "debt" in the offended party's account. Researchers and therapists have realized the need to go beyond the offense and to let go of it. The literature in the field indicates that in order to achieve this desirable outcome, several methods based on diverse philosophies have been resorted to. Secular ways of coaching may be outlined, aimed at enabling and supporting the efforts of a person who needs or desires to let go of offenses to feel free from anger, resentment, or retaliation. The reader may compare and contrast, assess and judge whether these approaches are compatible with a Christian perspective. Perhaps these philosophical and methodological grounds may show what letting go of offenses *is not*, according to a New Covenant thrust.

In the psychological field, cognitive therapies often have appealed to stoic notions in attempting to capture, challenge, and change the cognitive attributions to experienced reality in order to change the feelings associated with such.[5] In sum, stoic philosophy teaches that emotions of a destructive nature (such as anger, resentment, revenge) result from errors in judgments springing from the mortal mind, and that a person of intellectual stature and moral perfection should not experience or give room to such emotions. Centuries ago, philosophers such as Seneca and Epictetus emphasized the fact that we are not perturbed by things themselves, but rather by the view that we adopt about such circumstances. A person of virtue should be immune to misfortune or offensive behavior.

Needless to say, Christian principles of forgiveness and letting go differ from purely stoic assertions. Christians do experience pain, hurt, and suffering as they are offended (and contrary to a Stoic, they may say "ouch"), but they are encouraged to

---

4. Sandage et al., "Toward a Multicultural Positive Psychology."
5. Beck, *Cognitive Therapy*.

Part II: Principles Derived from the New Covenant in Marital Transactions

deal with the reality of pain and suffering, being empowered by the Spirit to act in grace and mercy toward the offender and setting themselves free as they let go of real offenses to their real selves. Stoicism borders on denial and rationalization—varieties of the ego's mechanisms of defense postulated by Anna Freud.[6] Thus, instead of being trapped into longstanding labels (victims, survivors, or martyrs), believers may be empowered to see themselves as fighters, overcomers, and free agents, living above the entrapments of an unforgiving nature.

More traditional psychoanalytic interpretations have been rendered in attempts to explain what—on the surface—appears to be forgiveness and forgetfulness. In general, the psychoanalytical field has regarded symptoms (events of an emotional nature that appear on the surface as psychological or psychosomatic expressions) as responding to deeper dynamics, mostly unconscious in nature. Forgiveness (as an event) may be seen as an enactive expression, a manifestation of an unconscious nature utilized as a defense to ward off anxiety, pain, or hurt. Forgiveness as a process may be seen as a continuous expression of characterological defensiveness, affected by intropunitiveness, negative perceptions, and attributions of meaning, which respond to the reality of being trapped into an ongoing predicament of pain and suffering. Some of these defenses may be outlined in the following manner:

1. *Denial.* Offenses produce emotional pain and hurt, anger, and resentment. They leave a sense of unfinished transactions, a sort of "presence in absence" experienced as pending debts contracted against the ego, creating a vacuum in the heart and mind. One of the major defenses of the ego to counter these emotions is denial. It brushes the reality of the damage done to the self away from the consciousness to avoid the experience of anxiety, hurt, or pain. Denial ignores the impact, consequences, and aftermath of negative transactions.

    Letting go without processing the offense ignores the rights, prerogatives, and privileges of the offended person. It does not help matters on the side of the offender either, as lack of proper attention to the offensive matter seems to reinforce the unjust concept that the offender may actually get away with murder. A psychoanalyst or psychodynamic therapist will seek to empower a patient to develop insight in order to be free to choose, to enjoy a more functional lifestyle, and to live in a mindful state. Denial seldom exists as an isolated defense; other mechanisms appear to emerge as being associated, as depicted below.

2. *Repression.* Offenses trigger reactions in a person's ego, which may be implicitly censored at pre-conscious levels by means of repression so that the retaliatory evocation remains below consciousness. Any emergent feelings of anxiety that are repressed remain as latent and unresolved issues. The offensive residues may bother the person, but repression is engaged as censorship of the person's apperceptive or subceptive awareness—having a hunch, but not being consciously

6. Freud, *The Ego.*

open, willing, or able to define or explore it. In Freudian terms, what we call forgetfulness is simply repression—the hurtful, revengeful, anxiety-provoking "stuff" is there, afflicting the person and emerging symptomatically to the surface.

3. *Suppression.* If the offensive trigger evokes a response that bypasses the repressive censorship, letting go of the offense may be achieved by placing a conscious lid on any boiling emotions such as anger, hurt, pain, shame, etc. The unfinished transaction may emerge in internal dialogues and mental struggles, involving cognitive styles such as brooding, rumination, and regurgitation of negative memories, etc. This mechanism does not remove the negative aspects that run at an unconscious level. It simply applies libidinal energy to keep the offenses under a lid, draining a person's emotional power in order to fuel that effort.

4. *Rationalization.* To rationalize is to find logical reasons to explain any painful reality that provokes anxiety, pain, or hurt. Letting go of offenses may assume this form, as the individual finds reasons for why the offense was committed in the first place, excuses the offender, and perhaps takes on some blame for allowing this offense to happen. The person may appeal to a higher perspective, and in a detached fashion, stoically ponder the virtue of letting go of the trespasses committed against the ego.

5. *Intellectualization.* The person may deal with any emotional connotation felt at the core in purely cognitive terms, not allowing the sensitive, affective loads to bear any weight in the decision to let go. The person may find solace in resolving his or her cognitive dissonance by means of a mode of resolution seeking an intra-psychic consistency—in quest of some functional equivalents to translate otherwise hurtful emotional events into abstract, detached categories, or to adopt an overarching, encompassing explanation that serves the purpose of adaptation to incongruent or dissonant aspects of experienced reality associated with narcissistic injuries.

6. *Reaction formation.* An honest, well-intended, yet naïve Christian may say, "I really hate your guts, but Christ in me loves you; let me hug you in his name." The person may do the opposite of what his or her internal impulses are dictating at the moment in order to convince self that he or she is exercising a controlled response. Perhaps in the process the person may think of him- or herself as noble or magnanimous being, while covering his/her real sensations, perceptions, and definitions in order to feel at peace.

Besides these defenses, some traits of character manifested in styles of relating may be mentioned as these represent dysfunctional interpretations of what letting go means. In more pathological cases, the person that lets go of offenses without processing (not counting the damage done or sharing any feelings with anybody) gets something out of the negative experience. The person may do so because at some basic, essential level (character-bound) a dysfunctional aberration of normal processes has taken place, emerging as a pathological masochism. The psychoanalytic literature provides glimpses of this pathological condition, described as a tendency to derive pleasure from getting hurt or experiencing pain in order to get excitement and meaning. Often this tendency appears in sexual dysfunctions characterized by the experience of pleasure in being dominated, humiliated, or having pain inflicted by someone in a close relationship. Letting go of offenses in this manner is simply reinforcing the dysfunctional patterns in which a sadist and a masochist establish some mutuality.

A condition known as "learned helplessness" also appears to be associated with faulty patterns of letting go of offenses. Seligman's studies on the subject shed some light on a condition in which a person, being subject to persistent negative contingencies, may eventually give up trying to escape and develop a sense of helplessness.[7] This passive attitude and response spring from a negative, trapped mindset, shaped and consolidated in function of the attributions of meaning given to negative life events. Victims of extreme circumstances of entrapment (physical, sexual abuse), or who live under manipulative conditions of a pervasive and sustained nature, tend to develop such mindset. The learned helplessness metanarrative then forms part of the person's make-up. As a matter of fact, some research supports the notion that individuals whose tendency is to forgive their abusive partners are also inclined to return to or remain in abusive relationships.[8]

DIVERSE STYLES AND STRATEGIES IN LETTING GO OF OFFENSES

Along philosophical and pragmatic lines, diverse avenues of reasoning have provided grounds for a diversity of manners employed in letting go of offenses:

1. *Mindfulness.* The cultural trends in the United States pertaining to health, mental health, and human relations have been influenced a great deal by Zen Buddhism, especially in terms of meditational practices and mindfulness. In short, mindfulness is the capacity to detach, observe oneself and one's vicissitudes in a nonjudgmental fashion, and go with the flow without engaging in fight-or-flight responses. In terms of forgiveness, mindfulness allows the person to adopt the stance of a detached observer, to let go of negative feelings associated with offenses, and to remain as a person positioned above such circumstances. The mindful process may be actualized by the person who lets go and adopts a detached state of mind that allows for the control of automatic responses to stress,

---

7. Seligman, *Helplessness.*
8. See, for example, Katz et al., "Individual Differences."

hurt, and pain. Several psychological approaches in therapy utilize this avenue (e.g., Dialectic Behavior Therapy; Acceptance and Commitment Therapy).

2. *Existentialism.* The possibility of active forgetting may be considered as a purposeful attempt to *relegate the past to the past* rather than being a passive, inert processor that "lets go" of bothering stuff (a nonchalant, *laissez faire* attitude). Thus, a mindful choice may be called upon to reject being bound to the past and to be fully engaged in the present moment. To remain focused on the past renders any attempt to move forward into the future a nearly impossible task. An existential approach seeks to achieve a balanced perspective by means of choice: forgetting balanced out by active remembering—in other words, to engage in a mindful choosing of when to forget and when to remember. Thus, by choosing when and when not to invoke the past, a person declares his/her freedom in the here and now, being free to engage in whatever decision is functional. Rumination and brooding leaves a person in the past, allowing negative memories to define and control a person's present and making it difficult to advance to the future.

Active forgetting is the empowered choice to reject the ruminative style employed in processing the wrong and to move forward into a more affirming future. The wronged individual is then able to go on in life and even choose to let go of offenses, relating with his or her transgressor without carrying unresolved feelings from the past. Of course, qualitative aspects of the nature and extent of transgressions call for choices to be made on the basis of the person's willingness, ability, and freedom to do so. Forgiveness and active forgetfulness are both ultimately choices to engage in. Letting go is a decision to release the self from past hurts and to move forward into the future. To take an existential leap of faith is not necessarily an impulsive act of irrational nature. It is a conscious and deliberate "jump" that springs from the ground of *being*—being a free, decisive, and willful person—in facing the unknown with risk and hope. It is based on the choice to be a person defined by principles and convictions, one who is neither defined by the offense nor subject to the offender's grip, opinion, behaviors, or choices.

The existential leap supersedes the offender in a metacognitive fashion without ignoring his being or doing. The target or destination of the leaper is not the offender himself nor the offense, but the existential bracket of time-space where the person wants to be free, above and beyond both the offender and the offense. The leap is endowed with a higher perspective and an empowered sense of well-being. Obviously, those trapped in trivial processing of reality at concrete levels, subject to empirical validation and demanding guarantees of well-being at the end of the jump, may choose not to engage in this process. They may remain existentially trapped and aware of it by choice.

Part II: Principles Derived from the New Covenant in Marital Transactions

3. *Positive psychology.* The shift to a positive psychology has emerged as a movement that focuses on building human strengths and civic virtues.[9] In this domain, the new perspective on forgiveness involves a willingness to let go of offenses and relinquish resentment—both of which are regarded as important components involved in the process of forgiving. Nevertheless, the traditional cautionary aspect remains: to forget is not to overlook, justify, condone, or excuse an offense.[10] To let go in that way is to disrespect, disregard, and minimize the seriousness of interpersonal transgressions, regarding them as trivial or unimportant. Naïve letting go may be seen as an immature defense, which neither helps in the resolution of negative feelings, nor conveys honesty, truthfulness, and fairness. Most researchers regard forgiveness as a process that includes the confrontation, recognition, and acceptance of a major premise: Forgiveness may be granted, but the offending behavior has to be condemned.

Integrating Christian faith with these positive trends, Worthington and Wade have described the absence of forgiveness as characterized by resentment, bitterness, and even hatred, coupled with a purposeful avoidance or retaliation against the offender.[11] Besides retaliation, seeking revenge or justice was added to this description. On the other side, forgiveness was defined as a process facilitated by empathy, resulting in a choice to relinquish the unforgiving stance and seek a possible reconciliation with the perpetrator. However, positive aspects are not devoid of cautionary considerations as these pertain to individual (e.g., victims of abuse or violence) and societal cases (e.g., genocide). To encourage or advocate wholesale forgiveness in a naïve or wholesale fashion may reinforce injustice and foster further victimization. The roles of choice, willful consciousness, ability, and perception of functional outcomes may be taken into consideration.

4. *Legalism.* In pharisaical terms, a person animated with an obedient attitude and eagerness to do the will of God may do so on the basis of legal requirements as against graceful principles. That is, the person may follow the command to forgive and let go as an injunction of an obligatory nature, devoid of an understanding of choice. A combination of dedicated zest, denial, suppression, and stoicism, aggregated to the desire to be perfect and to imitate God without any excuses or qualifiers, may be at work as amalgamated processes. In such a case, duty-bound behaviors take priority over any processes involving deliberation, inner dialogues, or perceptions of possible repercussions on both sides—the offender and the offended. Blind obedience to commands, unquestioning allegiance to

---

9. McCullough and Witvliet, "The Psychology of Forgiveness"; Seligman, "Positive Psychology"; see also Lamb, "Forgiveness Therapy."
10. Enright and Zell, "Problems Encountered."
11. Worthington and Wade, "The Psychology of Unforgiveness."

principles, and demanding leaps of faith serve as the basis for operations of a legalistic nature.

Beyond the humanistic and religious efforts described so far, forgiveness may be seen as a process envisioned from a metacognitive-dialogical stance empowered by the Holy Spirit and the Word of God: the person may depart from a top-down perspective and engage higher cortical processes, empowered by God's presence and power. In doing so, the forgiver may engage the metacognitive-executive control systems (higher cortical levels integrated to the infusion of the Spirit) and monitor the automatic flow of reactive, fast-thinking emotional processes. Rather than engaging in angry, negative, or retaliatory internal dialogues, the forgiver may adopt a detached mindfulness and observe, assess, and spread these dialogues before God and the observing-objective self, and engage in internal dialogues of a better quality. The indwelling Word may enter into play, infusing these dialogues with scriptural assertions. The Spirit-empowered metacognitive-executive control system may allow for the shift from internal dialogues to internal persuasion/rhetoric with positive commands addressing the process itself. And, contrary to secular trends, the believer may be internally persuaded to let go of offenses, and imitating God, engage in willful forgetfulness, remembering them no more. This power-assisted process may be postulated as being an enactment of faith endowed with a willful, deliberate, conscious, and existential choice of a renewed nature.

THEOLOGICAL BASIS FOR LETTING GO OF OFFENSES

A better way of letting go may be envisioned, springing from biblical-theological considerations. John the baptizer came announcing the Messiah, and his words at the baptism of Jesus were, "Look, the Lamb of God who takes away the sin of the world!" (John 1:29). It is of significance that the last of the prophets of the old system introduced the Messiah who would fulfill the shadows, figures, and symbols that characterize the Old Covenant. John pointed to God's provision of a lamb—alluding to the fact that he would not just cover the sins of the world (the blood sprinkled upon the propitiatory, the cover of the ark of the covenant, or the blood of sacrificed animals), but *remove* them and eliminate the ultimate barrier standing between God and those in need of grace and mercy.

It is indicative that the author of Hebrews presents Christ as the fulfillment of all the OT figures: he is the mediator of a New Covenant, the door of access to the Father, and the altar, who subsumes all five offerings into a perfect one and offers his own blood in propitiation for human sin, making a perfect atonement (Heb 10:10). He is the fountain of cleansing, as well as the light of the world (John 8:12), the bread of life (John 6:35), and the one who intercedes before the Father (Heb 7:25) as the

Part II: Principles Derived from the New Covenant in Marital Transactions

chosen priest who was cut early in life, came to life again, and produced fruit before the Father (Heb 8:1).

At the moment of his death, the veil of the temple was torn in two from top to bottom (Matt 27:50–51). The author to the Hebrews takes this event to signify that Jesus Christ opened a new, living way to the Father through the veil of his flesh (Heb 10:19–22). The text reassures believers that "we have confidence to enter the sanctuary by the blood of Jesus" (Heb 10:19). Furthermore, it is by a "fresh and living way that he inaugurated for us through the curtain, that is, through his flesh." And, "since we have a great priest over the house of God," the astounding invitation is given: "Let us draw near with a sincere heart in the assurance that faith brings . . ."

The New Covenant, as understood in terms of atonement, propitiation, and acceptance of the ransom from sin and the penalties that follow, brings freedom. On the one side, we have freedom from sin—its effects and entrapments. On the other, we have freedom to access, to know, and to have intimate fellowship with God. Both aspects are the results of the person and the work of Jesus Christ, the author and finisher of our faith, and the mediator of the New Covenant.

The previous chapter dealt with the treatment of forgiveness as extracted from the Greek verb *aphiemi*, which conveys the notion that "something has been *sent away*"—the remission, forgiveness, or release of someone from an obligation or debt has taken place or will take place. The expression "*aphesis hamartion*" or forgiveness of sins (properly, the act of letting them go as if they had not been committed) is a statement that comes from God's proposition to undeserving humans.

It is hard to imagine that a sinful human, imperfect and struggling in the here and now, receives the offer to come near to God openly; from the human perspective, one approaches God by faith, *as if* nothing stands in between. From God's perspective (and propositional statement), *nothing actually stands in between*. This freedom of access to one another may translate to interactive aspects of fellowship with other humans—especially relating in marriage and the family.

THE NEW COVENANT AND LETTING GO

The promised New Covenant is the unfolding truth proclaimed by Jesus, who alluded to the fact that knowing this truth will set us free (John 8:32). How this freedom is appropriated and actualized is the great question facing a believer. On the basis of the completed work of Jesus Christ, the effectiveness of the New over the Old Covenant needs to be stated as it pertains to the offer of freedom from condemnation and from the deserved punishment due to sin. The removal of sin and the provision of freedom from a guilty conscience before God were effectuated by Christ's sacrifice as it was superior to the effectiveness of the sacrifices of old (Heb 9:14). The symbols and shadows of reality faded away as Christ's work dealt with the ultimate barrier established by sin, allowing the redeemed human to enjoy a restored fellowship with God.

Freedom from sin and freedom to access God are predicated on the peace with God established by Jesus on our behalf. Potentially, a restful state of mind emerges from the attributions of meaning given to the deeply-allocated assurance of being forgiven and set free at the ontological, intrinsic level, to be experienced in coparticipation with the Holy Spirit—the internal witness who establishes this rest for the human soul. Positional reconciliation and peace with God is the condition that has been effectuated by the sacrifice of the Son and established as the outcome of this effective deal before the Father (Rom 5:1; 2 Cor 5:19; Eph 2:15–18). The third offering registered in the levitical system was a peace offering. This offering was based upon the effectiveness of two previous ones: the sin offering (dealing with the root, the ontology of being sinners) and the guilt offering (dealing with the effects of sin, the sinful deeds) (Lev 3:1–17). The peace offering would allow a person and his family to eat in the vicinity of the temple—sharing a portion of the offered sacrifice and partaking in fellowship with God in a symbolic, edible fashion. It was judged to be in good taste to fellowship with God after human sins and trespasses were expiated and cast away.

Covering up versus removing sin. The two modes of dealing with the treatment of offenses (sin)—the OT "covering up" and the NT "taking away"—have been compared by Margalit with the process of writing, in which an author may either cross over or delete a given sentence.[12] Crossing over a faulty sentence leaves the original script intact but clearly provides the indication of its faulty quality, exposed to be seen by the readers. In a way, it represents an overtly exposed cover-up—left there intentionally by the author. To delete means to erase the error, taking it away from the reader's sight. It is as if the reader never knew that the error was committed in the first place. The New Covenant promises a deletion, not just an exposed cover-up.

No doubt, the OT treatment of offenses was effective in its way, but the NT treatment of offenses does better. Humans engaging in new covenantal transactions may learn how to let go as God did instead of covering up. It is unfortunate that psychologists not trained in, nor committed to, a sound theological perspective, fail to ascertain the value of expiatory, redemptive, and empowered aspects of forgetfulness, confusing it with a negative defense mechanism (e.g., "avoidant" coping styles, dysfunctional in nature). Some researchers seem to give credit to letting go of offenses in both "covering," as well as "deleting," ways.[13] Rather than dichotomizing the ways employed (good/bad, functional/dysfunctional, true/false, authentic/inauthentic, etc.), more nuanced and adaptive ways are emphasized in the process of forgiveness. Dismissing offenses and moving forward may act as functional coping styles in preserving a relationship, regarded as being important to the forgiving-deleting person if enacted in a conscious, willful fashion.[14]

12. Margalit, *The Ethics of Memory.*
13. See, for example, Cosgrove, "When Labels Mask Oppression"; Cosgrove and Flynn, "Marginalized Mothers"; Fine, *Disruptive Voices.*
14. Cosgrove and Konstam, "Forgiveness and Forgetting."

Part II: Principles Derived from the New Covenant in Marital Transactions

Letting go of one's prerogatives—not clinging to one's status or rights—comes before letting go of offenses committed against us. Before God would forgive our sins and let them go, he let go of the most precious, dear, beloved Son; God did so for us (Rom 8:32). "For God so loved the world that he gave his one and only Son" (John 3:16). After that, God would give us anything else—not only blessings, but also a merciful suspension of penalties, forgiveness, and the cleansing (deleting) of our scribbled, sinful tablet.

The example of the Son follows: he gave himself for us when we were yet sinners (Rom 5:8). He did not count being equal to God as an excuse to claim his rights and prerogatives or to remain in his privileged status and position (Phil 2:5–11). He took the leap, departing from his secure position, and became one of us; he partook of our human condition with empathy in order to save us. First, he let go of his prerogatives and rights, having a bigger picture in mind: a vast congregation of redeemed sinners. Then, from a position of power, dignity, and love, he took the brunt, absorbed the hits, and died for us in order to accomplish his goal. He eliminated all barriers and reconciled us to the Father, letting go of our offenses (deleting them), and opening a new, living, and free way to the throne of grace.

Decentering from our interests in being properly attended and restituted, and focusing on the benefits to be gained by the offender, represent aspects of self-denial—exemplified in the kenosis of Jesus in Philippians 2. Thus, letting go of offenses means to deny one's self, decenter, and think of the other—the offender who does not deserve this break. It also means to have a metacognitive perception of ultimate design in mind, as well as the eternal consequences of our actions in the here and the now.

It is of extreme necessity for a husband, a wife, a parent, a sibling, or a friend to realize this profound and challenging truth: he or she has to suspend the prerogatives, rights, and privileges of the self, and in a decentered way, think of the other as an object of redemption, a target of grace and mercy. An empowered, metacognitive perception is needed in order to act in freedom—not in codependency or weakness. Forgiveness and letting go (as God did with us in Christ) goes against all the dictates and expectations of a culture that advocates personal rights and prerogatives, supporting an individual's egocentric, selfish, and assertive stance. Our culture stresses the need to establish boundaries and protective fences in order to safeguard the integrity, safety, freedom, and peace of the individual residing within these limits. Yet, scriptural truth tells us that dying to self—letting go of one's pride, prerogatives, rights, hurt, pain, revenge, and retaliation—comes before any attempt may be made to let go of the other's offenses.

Again, the forgiver willing and able to let go of offenses should not ignore the fair basis upon which all human transactions have been established in a covenant inscribed in stone: respect, dignity, equity, and justice coupled with love, grace, and mercy. These tenets represent the foundational basis of a free, democratic society. Yet, with all that, the New Covenant goes beyond retaliation and revenge, without denying the normative basis for fairness, justice, and equity. From a metacognitive perspective—processing mindfully the forgiving process from a higher, top-down point of view—letting go of offenses is the dispensing of grace and mercy in addressing the aftermath of offensive dealings committed against the self. The forgiving process starts with the decision to imitate the Father and the Son: it demands the abdication and willful abandonment of one's rights, prerogatives, and personal guardedness in order to take a leap of faith and engage in the process.

Due to the residual feelings that linger in the heart and mind of an offended person—hurt by a partner that becomes an "enemy"—it is difficult for a wounded self to accept the Pauline challenge—"Let the mind of Christ be in you" (Phil 2:5) as it applies to this process. Yet, the same attitude that moved the Lord to take his own leap of faith and let go of his position, status, and privileges makes it possible to decenter and consider the possibility of loving even an enemy. Jesus initiated the process from a higher perspective and secure attachment to the Father; he outstretched his grace and mercy and bridged the biggest gap in order to reach out and land on our side, forgiving and letting go of our sin. We may imitate his forgiving love and let go of offenses in concrete ways if we are securely attached to the Father and empowered by his Spirit to do so.

THE PROCESS OF LETTING GO

Voluntary forgetfulness may be dissected into componential elements in a feedback loop that involves complex interactions among the offended and the offender—in presence or absence. Who forgives whom, why, how, when, and with what effect are operationalized variables that enter into play in a feedback loop that may be framed in the following analysis:

- The *awareness* and *evidence* of being triggered or provoked by an offensive event, person, or stressor (a behavior, attitude, stance, introjected object, flashback, etc.). These triggers may be captured, operationalized, and measured (in terms of frequency, intensity, and duration); the organismic valuing system encodes this data in order to process it further along cognitive-emotive lines.

- The *relevance* of the impacting information must be relayed to the person's higher cortical functions, as well as to the emotional processing centers. Parallel processes with distributed functions enter in an interactive fashion. This information is not relayed in the raw-data form captured by sensory organs, but in a contextualized form that makes it emotionally resonant (the evoking signal is transduced so as to be processed in a different mode: cognitive-emotive-enactive). New avenues of research are providing some notions as to the biochemistry, neural pathways, mirror neurons, and complex interactions within integrative-interpersonal neurobiology that enter into play in the neuroplasticity of the brain. These complex processes are chunked, establishing a level of resonance, empathy, and meaningful attribution to the experience at hand.

- The *consequences* of the impact of a stressor being processed—the awareness of being upset and the attribution of meaning to the offending event—involve the eliciting of internal dialogues: deliberations, rumination, obsessive thoughts about the negative experience, and the associated feelings of anger, depression, and anxiety, among others. These internal processes may gather an increased momentum and trigger fight-or-flight reactions.

- The *decision to respond* is predicated on the acquisition of insight and the perception of possessing the freedom to engage as an imitator of the Father. The offensive event provides the opportunity to take a given course of action or to choose a path. Hopefully, the forgiver experiences an insightful moment when he or she can shift from internal dialogues to internal rhetoric (self talk, persuasion) in order to make a deliberate choice to respond (i.e., forgive). This choice is greatly assisted by the empowered, top-down executive function that regulates the enactment of a behavioral response.

- Beyond events, *forgiveness and letting go are sequences in an ongoing process*. Further internal dialogues and deliberations may take place in the person's psyche—related to the need to let go as a proactive, unilateral, unconditional choice. The anticipatory anxiety or fear of being weak, codependent, enabling, etc., may assault the mindset with defense mechanisms or elevate the natural reaction to retaliate.

- Forgiveness is a *costly process*; a sort of "counting the coins" to build a forgiving fortress becomes necessary. Also, inoculating stress to self is required in order to be ready for suffering—to face the internal struggles and feedback loops that would inundate the mind with doubts and uncertainties about future repercussions, etc. After this stress inoculation and preparedness to do the right thing, letting go may be experienced as an exercise of an empowered willpower to act in freedom and dignity in imitation of God as a beloved child. Letting go of the person's offenses acts as a deliverance from one's entrapment in anger, pain, dejection, etc. Thus, the person that forgives and lets go of the offense actually sets her- or himself free.

- The enactment of this interpersonal (or interactive) behavior may be personally assessed and ascertained in a metacognitive fashion: the top-down executive function of the person allows for the *processing of the forgiving process*—thinking about one's thinking, learning about one's learning—and benefiting from the objectively observed feedback loop (the sequence of processes described above, from being triggered to responding with forgiveness).

- Every forgiving/letting go response (a segmented or bracketed behavior along a continuous, cyclical, or reverberating process) that evokes, stimulates, or reinforces new behaviors that lead the individual to approximate a desirable/optimal (or functional, adjusting) outcome acquires an *intrinsic value* and provides a *sense of accomplishment* or *well-being*, i.e., an existential awareness and anticipation of reaching a goal by means of the exercise of self-control.

Having these considerations in mind, a new look at the well-known text found in Romans 8:28 may emerge. Every contingency (trivial or earth-shaking, good or bad) counts in the process of becoming the person one wants to be. After all, the verse is a preamble to Romans 8:29–30: the formed, deformed, reformed, and transforming human is now being conformed to the image of Jesus Christ. Within this process, God works through all contingencies in order to achieve this higher goal. The myriad of ongoing feedback loops may be seen as learning opportunities to shape up our destiny and to change our character, conduct, and influence. Being a reformed forgiver—being transformed in the process of becoming a forgiver as God is—may be examined within the bracket of a single forgiving event or contingency. Yet, this microanalysis must be embedded in the flux of chronological time, registering the believer's growth process. The secular notions advocated by psychologists, such as the will to power (Adler), self-actualization (Maslow), or self-efficacy (Bandura) may be parallel constructs that allude to a believer's relentless pursuit of authenticity—the drive to excel and accomplish the most desirable goal: to become Christ-like.

The proactive, purposeful unfolding of a lifestyle, endowed with a sense of direction and tempo, may be metacognitively "sliced" in an existential *kairos*. A person may bracket a contingency and regard it as a componential experience captured along a lifeline. This abstracted experience may be directed and referenced to a bigger, metacognitive goal (an ultimate, ideal, or higher design). As a believing Christian runs the race and looks up to the author and finisher of our faith, he or she may consider any and all contingencies experienced in this life as an infinitesimal portion of eternity. In view of God's time, rather than sojourning through life as a reactive organism, trapped by and subject to its contingencies, the individual may consciously behave in the here and now with freedom and dignity. He or she may be mindfully aware of the opportunity to live in a more empowered, efficacious, controlled, and faithful manner.

THE HOPEFUL RESULT OF LETTING GO: FREEDOM

In considering the ramifications of covenantal transactions among humans, freedom is a vital principle of operation that facilitates the ways in which husbands, wives, parents, children, siblings, and friends in the household of faith conduct their interactive endeavors. Several aspects of freedom may be envisioned.

Part II: Principles Derived from the New Covenant in Marital Transactions

1. *Freedom from entrapments.* One of the last expressions from the cross was "It is finished" (*tetelestoi*, a term used on the sign posted on top of the jail of a person whose sentence was completed in full, and upon which the person was set free). The term denotes that our past has been effectively dealt with. Having collected all sin and paid for it at the cross, Jesus removed the barrier between God and humans, exemplified in the rending of the veil of the temple. God judged that as the Son had offered himself in perfect fashion and procured a complete atonement, eliminating all vestigial signs of sin before God, there was no reason for this veil to be standing in between.

   The truth of the gospel stresses the fact that God has accepted the sacrifice of the Son; the intercessory blood offered by the Son on our behalf is before the celestial throne, and we are summoned to believe and appropriate by faith this truth. Then we have nothing to do, nothing to add, but simply receive God's gift by faith to be free from sin. It appears too good to be true, and that is amazing grace. Yet this grace is not cheap, as Bonhoeffer has written, but costly: it cost the blood of Jesus.[15] The sinner receives grace, forgiveness, mercy, and freedom from negative memories, from self-pronouncements of an injunctive nature, and from the experience of self-condemnation. "Indeed, he who did not spare his own Son, but gave him up for us all—how will he not also, along with him, freely give us all things?" (Rom 8:32).

   Any entrapment that appears to render the human a prisoner or victim of some sort may be confronted and dealt with by faith and obedience to God's freeing design. The coparticipation of the empowered human in the process is essential as the offer of grace and mercy has to be believed, apprehended, and actualized. The human, in turn, may imitate God's way in setting the offender free—and free himself in the process.

   In Jesus's parable of the two debtors (Matt 18:21–35), the unforgiving person is the one who is cast into prison and remains there until he pays the last coin of his debt. Having been forgiven an insurmountable amount by the master, this person was not willing or able to forgive his debtor a small amount and sent him to jail. The master acted accordingly, allowing the unforgiving person a taste of his own medicine. He would remain trapped until he paid his own debt—something impossible in the parable's terms. The teaching is obvious: In view of God's forgiveness, we must forgive our debtors; otherwise, we remain trapped in our quest for revenge, besides being held accountable to God for our failure to do so. This entrapment may be seen from a higher perspective—acting before a holy God who forgave us when we were totally unable to pay our own debts.

   From a bottom-up, interactive, human standpoint, we may feel unable to imitate the Father in dealing with a fellow sinner who asks for our forgiveness. As a matter of fact, lack of forgiveness fuels a deeply entrenched resentment,

---

15. Bonhoeffer, *The Cost of Discipleship*.

which locks up the person's capacity to be free, peaceful, and joyful. Internal dialogues may assume obsessive proportions, with endless feedback loops reinforced by repetitive tapping into long-term and short-term memory banks. We remain trapped in retaliatory attitudes, re-experiencing our hurt, trauma, pain, anger, depression, and anxiety. We may choose to set ourselves free by setting the offender free, removing the bars from our own jail by dispensing grace, mercy, and letting go of offenses. Thus, to forgive and to willfully forget are both intrapersonal and interpersonal dealings. They involve a change in cognitive processes and structures (thoughts, reasoning, perceptions, judgments, memories); in emotional processes (sensibility, affect, emotions); and in behaviors (doing the right thing, letting go of negative attachments and connotations, adding positive aspects, and creating new schemata and memories).

Due to the intrapsychic nature of these processes, the offended party may experience emotional freedom as the process of letting go moves along the experiential flux in time, casting away the offenses committed against the self as God does. This freedom may be experienced by the dispenser of grace and mercy, whether the offender is present or absent, repentant or not, alive or dead. Although the offended person cannot control or predict much of what goes on outside his or her skin, it is the "world within the skin" that can be healed through an intrapsychic regrouping, renewal, and transformation.

2. *Freedom from rumination.* Rumination has been labeled as a "style of thinking" by Wells in his metacognitive therapy for depression and anxiety.[16] Letting go of persistent, cyclical, convoluted, and negative ruminations may be postulated as a hallmark in the process of active and purposeful forgetting. To refrain from engaging in this style of thinking allows for a buffer zone in which positive regrouping and healing may take place. By means of a metacognitive-executive control mechanism (MEC, in chapter 17 of this book), a person may shift from rumination to internal rhetoric in order to persuade him- or herself to do what is right: dispense grace, mercy, and forgiveness. Some studies have demonstrated the association that exists between the frequency, intensity, and duration of ruminations with higher levels of revenge and avoidance of the motivation to let go and be free.[17] The content of these metanarratives may also play a role as the need for revenge has been regarded as an active ingredient in this style of thinking. Letting go of self-inflicted entrapments reinforced by ruminations is a longstanding biblical principle as the parable of the two debtors has shown.

3. *Existential freedom: freedom of choice in letting go.* The author's musings are shared here as a backdrop to a metacognitive-dialogical model of forgiveness and letting go. This model is elaborated in chapter 17. Christian faith has been

---

16. Wells, *Metacognitive Therapy.*
17. See, for example, McCullough et al., "Vengefulness."

integrated to an existential position in which faith in God (not faith in faith) is a matter of personal conviction, passion, and essence. This stance does not necessarily deny a reasonable process of a cognitive-emotive and enactive nature. A discourse about God as the ground of our being allows for a definition of the believer as *being* an imitator of God.[18] As such, the believer may choose to be unilateral, unconditional, proactive, graceful, and merciful—thus free to choose to let go of offenses. Forgiveness represents a paradox to a pensive believer that demands the choice of taking or not taking an existential leap of faith. Sin (an offense in the abstract) has to be reasonably and justly punished; yet sin (the offense experienced) has to be forgiven and let go.

To forgive and let go in order to be free demands the exercise of a deliberate, conscious, and willful choice of some sort. Yet in letting go of offenses, the forgiving person has no further claims against the offender; the one who lets go relinquishes control over the consequences of this decision. This person has no foreknowledge of what will happen on the other side of the transaction. Lack of control, knowledge, and predictability are conditions that foster anxiety or dread (existential angst) in the mindset of the forgiver.

In this framework, forgetfulness may be seen in the context of the connection between faith, passion, and possibility. In order to take a leap of faith and let go, the person must fix the eyes on a higher target, "jumping over" the offense and the offender and focusing upon the summoning God who—from the other side of the gap—commands us to forgive and let go as he did. To jump, the person must depart from the border of the cliff—the limit of God as the ground of being. In jumping by faith, the person behaves "as if" the faith-medium is as solid as the evidence-based ground of departure because it is connected essentially to the same postulator: God who calls things to be as if they are there when they are not. Landing on the other side of the gap (after superposing a feedforward control system over the endless feedback loops of rumination), one hopes to be received by the hands of the summoning God. One also hopes to be approved in this imitational endeavor.

The call for the purposefully imaginative (mindful) task of surrendering to a higher design (God's command to forgive and let go of offenses) involves the suspending of one's justice-driven, upright, moral judgment to engage in a better offer of a gracious and merciful nature. The intrinsic, paradoxical qualities of a leap of faith enter into play in the event/process of forgiveness: letting go of something (the administration of retaliatory justice) while holding on to a better possibility as an outcome (freedom for self and the other, imitating God). Taking this leap and letting go of offenses demands an active faith that goes *against* moral reason (i.e., why should one let go of wrongdoing done against one's self?),

---

18. See, for example, Kierkegaard, *The Concept of Anxiety*; *The Sickness unto Death*; Finch, *A Christian Existential Psychology*; Malony, *Christian Existential Psychology*.

as well as faith that goes *beyond* reason, emerging as a higher, metacognitive perspective of an existential nature. Yet this existential stance is not a baseless "faith in faith," but rather faith in God who summons his child to imitate him and forgive as he has done. No wonder the apostle Paul referred to the gospel as "foolishness" to the Greeks—the philosophical, empirically minded, thinking ones, who could not fit such a message in a rational box.

Being anchored in a faith-based ground of being (in God) and facing a challenging abyss (the dreadful prospect of forgiving and letting go of offenses) is not necessarily an irrational act; rather, it is a paradoxically existential way to "jump" and act beyond the limit of the solid cliff's edge. In enacting forgiveness, one cannot predict the response of the offender. The leap has to be taken in faith. Yet, one may question, why jump into an unknown vacuum? Lacking concrete evidence, reason cannot proceed on such new "ground" but must yield to faith—the hypostasis (ὑπόστασις: substance, support, substructure, steadiness; hence, *assurance*, as in Heb 11:1)—with the metacognitive conviction that God is here witnessing the jump. The reader may deduce that the letting go of offenses is *done before God, based upon* God's summoning Word, and bypassing the offender—not being bound or defined by the perpetrator or by the offense. The forgiver's aim is to obey and please God, the ultimate judge who will pronounce the final verdict and administer the proper justice.

Acting on the basis of an existential connectedness with God who has been, is, and will be there—and upon the belief that His living Word and promises (including commands) are beneficial—the believer may be able and willing to take a forgiving leap of faith. Sometimes, as in the case of Abraham, the command ("give me your son") goes against reason and every promise, obliging the believer to take a "higher" jump. Then he or she must hang on with passionate conviction and surrender to God—the one who gives the promises—rather than to the promises he has given. For this faith, Abraham was commended and called God's friend. Perhaps, this relational friendship is *the* most important definition to any imitator of God who follows in the footsteps of Abraham's faith.

Even dreading the unknown and unpredictable aspects in forgiving and letting go, the believing forgiver may act *as if* he or she is free, above and beyond the entrapments of the offender and the offense. Beyond reason and cognitive analysis, passion in imitating God is an intrinsic part of the leap—the command to forgive and let go. The believer jumps with passion, superseding the hurt and pain of the wrongdoing experienced—and does so by faith in the summoning, invisible God who is there in the act of obeying. One bets everything on that passionate conviction; otherwise, if there is no ultimate observer witnessing the process, one may be resigned to jump into a vacuum and crush every bit of faith-based conviction against nonsense. If the promising God does not actually exist—if he is not there to begin with, or does not care about the process of letting go—why engage in such nonsense? Yet, as the believer holds on to the conviction that God is there and witnesses the process, the command to jump (to forgive and let go of offenses) encourages the believer to connect the dots between the basis and the outcome of the process of letting go without being irrational.

4. *Freedom to take risks—yet acting on faith—in God's sight.* Often, this question comes to mind: *If I forgive, will my partner realize the extent of my effort? Will anybody be a witness to my process?* The intrinsic need to be seen, recognized, and validated by a counterpart becomes a conditioning factor if we attempt to engage in a difficult process of forgiveness. Whether we count on an actual person being there or an imaginary crowd of witnesses—or most especially, God's overseeing sight—this deeply felt need underlies much of the forgiving process. Otherwise we feel alone, not totally understood in our struggles. Forgiving an offending party becomes quite painful and awkward if there are no witnesses, no superposed objective feedback, and no counterpart to appraise the act/process. It takes faith and conviction, as well as a detached and purposeful mindfulness, to engage in internal dialogues and persuade self that one is doing the right thing in letting go.

From a natural perspective, letting go of hurts and pain without being recognized and supported may become a lonely endeavor prone to derail into feelings of self-pity, martyrdom, or masochism. Yet, letting go of offenses in the presence of God—the ultimate perceiver and overseer of all transactions—may be experienced as a supervised endeavor, apprehended by faith and sensed at an intrinsic level. To know that we are being observed and counted as imitators of God by the ultimate judge serves as an affirming and actualizing context for our focused endeavors along interactive transactions with humans in the here and now.

Letting go of offenses evokes anxiety in the forgiving person as the consolidated bank of memories of the account of wrongdoing represents a sort of defensive basis to protect the self from any future abuse, manipulation, or harm. Even thinking anticipatorily about doing so may evoke physiological sensations of unrest, cognitive processes of a negative nature (uncertainty, lack of control, lack of predictability, doubts about doing the right thing, etc.), and emotional feelings such as anxiety and depression. The anticipation of letting go of offenses prompts many questions related to self, the other, and the contextual, social "witnesses"—family, fellowship, and the community. If the damage done is considered to be of profound impact (call it a narcissistic injury, cutting into the essence of being), letting go becomes more difficult. If the social "crowd of witnesses" is there as presence in absence, what others will think about dispensing this freedom may be a negative factor: the person who lets go of transgressions may be seen as being weak, naïve, or codependent—or be treated as a fragile person who capitulates to nonsense. This perceived and projected social influence may exert undue pressure upon the forgiving self. Again, it takes courage to be a forgiver, and letting go must be seen as a process that emerges from ego strength, not from weakness.

When a person lets go of offenses, he or she has no control over the responses of the person being forgiven. In the best case, the offender may recognize the grace and mercy being dispensed and demonstrate gratitude and appreciation to the forgiver. The forgiven may give some tangible evidences to that end, offering some restitution. In this case, the experiential feedback loop reassures the forgiver of the sense that she or he has done the right thing. Moreover, the person may experience an intrinsic satisfaction and positive feelings associated with the perception of positive outcomes that result from the process (e.g., the redeeming experience has produced some fruits of repentance and change of character on the other side). Besides an honest spiritual attribution and affirmation, some rationalization and justification usually enter into the scene, defending the self against possible negative afterthoughts and aftereffects.

On the contrary, if the forgiven person remains unresponsive, obstinate, malicious, or unchanged, the forgiver may experience doubts about having done something embedded in codependency. The forgiving partner may have a sense of futility, interpreting the offender's negative attitudes and behaviors as being damaging, hurtful, or degrading. The investment made in the process has no positive dividends, and as a result, feelings of dejection and contempt may emerge. In intrapsychic fashion, the forgiver may have a sense of intropunitiveness, chastising self for having further reinforced nonsense and dysfunction on the partner's side.

In the worst possible case, the offending party may remain manipulative, demanding, and continue to transgress. The offender may continuously degrade, demean, and abase the forgiver in words or deeds. In this case, letting go of repeated offenses seems an absurd process as there is no redemptive quality in providing grace to a person who has no receptive willingness or ability—and shows no reciprocity. Doing so appears to be similar to Jesus's allusion of throwing pearls to the swine. Thus, it is necessary to adopt a higher perspective, a metacognitive stance that accounts for the fact that the person who lets go proceeds from a position of freedom and self-control, being empowered by the Holy Spirit and the Word.

5. *Increase in self-efficacy and personal self-control.* Benson's research, writing, workshops, and efforts to train people in the relaxation response have been with us for some time.[19] It is interesting that in the process of learning to control the autonomic nervous system (ANS), slow and controlled breathing plays a major

---

19. Benson, *The Relaxation Response.*

role. It balances the oxygen and carbon dioxide mix in the lungs, affecting the brain and facilitating the letting go of muscle tension. The person training in relaxation breathes in and out slowly (six or seven seconds/breath) while concentrating in a focal manner on the process of letting go of tension, coupled with the process of exhaling; the letting go of air being associated with the letting go of tension (or offenses held in the mind). In this process, a forgiver remains in control of the world within the skin—even if the world outside the skin remains unresolved, obnoxious, negative, or unfair.

The forgiver realizes that he or she is not defined by negative external circumstances, vicissitudes, or contingencies. A Christian believer adds to the process the conviction of being defined by God as an imitator, willing to follow the Father's way of dispensing grace and mercy and letting go of offenses. In this case, the person is set free to act as an imitator of God in Christ, offering unilateral, unconditional, proactive, graceful, and merciful outreach. This endeavor is not to be confused with codependency, masochism, or "push-over-ism." Rather, it is the empowering of the Holy Spirit that allows the forgiving person to be in control of his or her responses and to decide to act on the basis of being perceived by an ultimate judge, who will take into account every human transaction.

6. *Freedom to approach and deal with one another.* The New Covenant states the condition gained through the mediator on our behalf: we are free to access the throne of grace (Heb 4:16; 10:19–22) with confidence, full assurance of faith, and even boldness. We realize that the Spirit is the one who leads us to such an encounter and provides freedom and confidence (2 Cor 3:4). If God removed all barriers so that we may engage with intimacy, we may analogize and consider the ways in which we may foster approaching one another in freedom as well. Since the Fall, intimate partners have engaged in setting limits and barriers to intimacy because of the pervasive effects of sin altering the open and free access to one another. From cover-ups (fig leaves) to blame, projection, and struggles for one-upmanship, intimate partners experience the need to establish protective boundaries to feel safe, secure, and protected from harm.

Disobedience to God's will (eating from a prohibited tree) impacted the first couple with devastating effects; the consequences of further damage due to abuse, neglect, offensive behaviors, etc., in everyday transactions add to these negative effects. Setting up proper boundaries is a necessary feature in human transactions—to safeguard our intimate life-space against hurts, pain, dejection, unfaithfulness, and the like. Boundaries are functional demarcations in family systems, acting as limits around a life-space where we can develop in the process of differentiation and individuation as opposed to being controlled, trapped, or enmeshed in codependency and abuse. Boundaries are also necessary to demarcate our God-defined characteristics of being, thinking, feeling, and doing things as persons of worth. These topics have received a great deal of attention in the last decades.[20] Yet, a proper insight into the role of boundaries in the process of forgiving and forgetting needs to be understood. This process necessitates the lowering of a partner's defenses, allowing for a deliberate and conscious vulnerability to start with. Any restorative process or rebuilding of fellowship demands the lowering and removal of barriers and the proper attention to God-given guidelines emphasizing conciliatory endeavors.

CONCLUDING REMARKS

Forgiveness, letting go of offenses, restitution, restoration, and renewal are the means to foster the freedom of approach to one another in dialogue. Accessing one another through a new, open, and living way is analogous to the way we approach God: we do so by adopting a metacognitive stance, reminded of God's own willingness to dispense unilateral, unconditional, and proactive grace and mercy. We may do so while remaining firmly established on the ground of our being—in control of our cognitive-emotive processes, giving the benefit of the doubt, and assuming good faith on the other's part as well.

To conclude our reasoning: The psalmist David was able to sing, "How blessed is the one whose rebellious acts are forgiven, whose sin is pardoned! How blessed is the one whose wrongdoings the LORD does not punish" (Ps 32:1–2). The psalmist in a New Covenant may add to the lyrics, "How exceedingly blessed is the one who lets go of the rebellious acts, the sins, and wrongdoings committed against his/her person!" Because, after all, as Jesus himself has said, "It is more blessed to *give* than to *receive*" (Acts 20:35), including the dispensing of forgiveness and the letting go of offenses.

---

20. Cloud and Townsend, *Boundaries*; *Boundaries in Marriage*.

Chapter 16

Covenantal Renewal as a Way of Life

I will give you a new heart, and I will put a new spirit in you. I will remove the heart of stone from your body and give you a heart of flesh. (Ezekiel 36:26)

Look, I am about to do something new. Now it begins to happen! Do you not recognize it? Yes, I will make a road in the desert and paths in the wilderness. (Isaiah 43:19)

... to be renewed in the spirit of your mind. (Ephesians 4:23)

EVERY LIVING SYSTEM UNDER the sun tends to decay and die. In human relations, a sort of "psychological entropy" enters into play: the vibrant notes of a nuptial march, the exuberant feelings of ecstasy experienced during a honeymoon, and the loving behaviors that characterize a couple's new beginnings tend to fade away in time. The accommodation, assimilation, and equilibration that enter into play between partners engaged in an adaptive process consume emotional energy on both sides with a consequential decay in zest and novelty. A natural entropic tendency (borrowing from the field of thermodynamics) inexorably slows down the dynamic momentum of the interactive system, leading to the ultimate rest—death—unless some infusion of energy takes place. A couple comprised of believers living in a toxic cultural ecosystem—the *aion*, characterized by postmodern, antagonistic trends and cultural patterns permeated with the spirit of this age in rebellion against God—experiences pressures that negatively affect and permeate their mindsets. In the words of Christina Maslach (one of my professors at UC Berkeley and a leading researcher of what is known as the "burnout" syndrome), "We cannot ignore the vinegar in which cucumbers become pickles."

A person's socialization in a given milieu shapes her or his worldview and the ways in which the acquisition of knowledge and the attribution of meaning to reality take place. Descriptions and explanations of social reality are given according to these lenses. Such a culturally embedded condition has often been illustrated by the fact that a fish does not know what wetness is all about—or dryness either, for that matter. Having been born and raised in this medium would deprive the fish of having a metacognitive awareness, unless somehow the fish is elevated to a superior plane and observes the pond from above. Likewise, the naturalness with which any person in a given cultural milieu ascribes meaning to her or his reality and engages in transactions appears to be conditioned by the contextual medium in interaction with her or his constructive mindset. We are reminded in previous chapters that Paul the apostle prayed for the Ephesians so that their perceptive capacities would be opened, illuminated, and able to see things from God's perspective, inviting a transcending point of view into their mundane existence.

Partners in marriage and members of a family system are exposed to, affected by, and embedded in an imperfect cosmos. They are impinged upon, subject to the natural entropic forces present in their cultural context, which affects their character, conduct, and interpersonal relations in negative ways. Partners and family members are prone to experience a constant, pervasive decay in their commitments and dedication to one another. Thus, marriage and family systems need the revitalization of their structures and processes in order to remain alive, zesty, and functional. To grow a marriage in today's culture is like growing coffee in Boston: difficult, but not impossible. As someone who has actually grown coffee—and drunk it—at home in South Hamilton, Massachusetts, the author can attest to this possibility.

Even the Old Covenant needed the revitalized and renewed establishment of a New Covenant, not because of God's failure to keep up with the revitalizing process, but because of the human inability to renew their part of the deal that rendered those terms inoperative. The new system has a built-in feature that assures a living continuity: the promise of the Holy Spirit—a person whose ongoing presence, indwelling, and empowering would animate both the participants and the terms of the covenant. In this way, the Holy Spirit capacitates, transforms, and conforms the human partners as they proceed along their journey, abiding in God's eternal design.

AN EXPANDED BIBLICAL CONTEXT FOR COVENANTAL RENEWAL

God is eternally the same, yet he gives expressions of newness, renewal, and vibrant life throughout the ages. Thus, instead of a static rendering of God's being and action, the revealed script points to an ever-living being: "'The days are coming,' declares the LORD, 'when I will make a new covenant with the people of Israel and with the people of Judah'" (Jer 31:31, NIV). "See, the former things have taken place, and new things I declare" (Isa 42:9, NIV). And then, "Behold, I am doing a new thing; now it springs forth, do you not perceive it?" (Isa 43:19, ESV). Those who wait upon the Lord can renew their strength as well (Isa 40:29–31). Redeemed and regenerated believers grounded in God may experience the transformation of their being by means of the renewal of their minds (Rom 12:1–2; Eph 4:23). The appeal to be transformed is given in the context of the admonition to surrender our bodies to God's will, as living

Part II: Principles Derived from the New Covenant in Marital Transactions

sacrifices (i.e., an ongoing, day-to-day experience), in order to experience renewed transactions with God framed in his will, set forth in a New Covenant. The transformation and renewal of a life of love and fellowship are features embedded in a dynamic, ongoing spiritual process.

The relationship between the old order and the new needs to be considered in light of the coming of the Messiah, his redemptive work, and his role as the mediator of a New Covenant. His preaching of good news to those who were supposed to be the guardians of truth—the definers of God's revelation and will—is presented in Scriptures as an appeal to the transformation and renewal of covenantal terms. In time, God's given principle of life, the law, had become a set of codified dimensions representing an instrument of condemnation and death, according to Pauline theology.

The accumulated traditions and customary practices of rabbis and priests were recast in such a way that the vibrant, life-giving principles became paradoxically obsolete terms, conveying duties and demands devoid of joy. The ways of interpreting and handling the Word given by God often deviated the original intentions into static, regulatory commands that have obliterated a true grasp of God's given intentions. Jesus came to change all that: he brought a transforming, renewing message, providing the true meaning to the expressions of old. The author of the Torah was the expert interpreter that brought the true meaning, the spirit of the letter to life.

Jesus appealed to a parable to point out this fact: "No one sews a patch of unshrunk cloth on an old garment, for the patch will pull away from the garment, making the tear worse. Neither do men pour new wine into old wineskins. If they do, the skins will burst; the wine will run out and the wineskins will be ruined. No, they pour new wine into new wineskins, and both are preserved" (Matt 9:16–17, NIV). This dual metaphor was conveyed by Matthew, registering the words of Jesus as an illustration used to convey a wonderful truth. Old garments and old wineskins contrasted to new ones are the main point: renewal is necessary, not just a patching of the old system. A New Covenant was needed, not just a patching of the Old.

The attempt to repair an old garment by means of patching it with an unshrunk piece would cause a bigger tear. Instead, the need for a new fabric was evident: a new intertwining of fibers was postulated as a better way of doing things, establishing firmness, functionality, and desirability. The old fabric comprised of Jewish threads—the Torah engraved in stone, intertwined with rigid human regulations—could not deal with the demands for flexibility, openness to experience, and adaptation to a new order in which the new, Gentile threads he same Torah intertwined with Spirit placed within human hearts and minds—were invited to coparticipate and belong to the same garment. The old mindset was not willing to be interwoven with those regarded as undesirable, unclean sinners, now invited to be partakers in God's joint design.

The metaphor dealing with new wine poured into new wineskins conveys the same truth. In NT times, containers for carrying various fluids were made out of goat skins. French oak was not yet in vogue. After a chosen animal was killed, the head

Covenantal Renewal as a Way of Life

and feet were cut off, the carcass was skinned, and the skin sewed up (fur side out), sealing the orifices except the neck. A special tanning process was employed to minimize the disagreeable taste. New wineskins were used for new wine while it was still fermenting; old wineskins contained the old wine. If new wine was poured into an old wineskin, the gases formed in the process of fermentation would expand the skin beyond its elasticity, bursting it open and wasting the drink.

As to the main issue, the style of the wineskin is not in question; rather, it is the flexibility of the container—its elasticity and capacity for adjustment—that matters. The new wine's effervescence and expansion exerts stressful pressures against the wineskin's limits. It is the capacity for accommodation, assimilation, and equilibration with a demanding, effervescent element that is put into question.

The illustrations show that the newness of the message introduced by Christ, with the consequential new lifestyle based upon a renewed mind and heart, could not be easily allocated in a static, rigid matrix. The New Covenant inaugurated by the Holy Spirit cannot simply be a patch applied to an old system, which became inoperative due to human failures to adapt and do the will of God. The need for renewed containers to receive and employ this new outpouring of grace, mercy, unconditional love, and powerful presence was something that not too many people were able to digest when Jesus brought such good news.

New garments and new wine are allusions to a new order, a new economy, and a new transaction being brought by God in Christ. In sending the Son as the Messiah to bring redemption to us and to actualize the potential for which we were created, God acted in history in a powerful fashion. Jesus Christ brought the message of life and hope, based on grace and mercy. Having demonstrated that no one can be saved by the works of the law, as all stood condemned and destitute (Rom 3:23), a righteousness apart from the law is now imputed to those who believe in the person and the work of the Savior (Rom 3:21). The gospel is the new, effervescent, and dynamic power of God given as a message summoning humans to believe and accept by faith (Rom 1:16). The new wine by necessity demanded new wineskins: openness to the message, acceptance of the claims, and amplitude of heart and mind to receive, obey, and live according to these claims.

In a somewhat analogous fashion, the renewal of an old covenantal relationship becomes necessary when partners find themselves in an entropic arrangement. Perhaps the relationship remains stable, but the satisfaction, life, and joy of living in covenant have disappeared, and only the routines and duties remain; staying together is just an obligation. In such a case, a covenantal renewal is needed so that the original intentions for which the relationship was established are empowered and revitalized.

The terms of the New Covenant are inscribed on a new medium, moving from tablets of stones to human hearts and minds. God's promise is, "I will put my laws in their minds and I will inscribe them on their hearts" (Heb 8:10). As stated before, the message of old was codified in stone—something rigid, impersonal, and detached. Not

Part II: Principles Derived from the New Covenant in Marital Transactions

much flexibility was allocated once the engraving of the commandments took place with the finger of God succinctly outlining the basic norms for life. It was an external system to be consulted with and interpreted by those able to discern its meaning. Somehow, it felt distant, markedly separated from those who had to abide by its contents. The accompanying legal context added a series of commandments subordinated to the ten, plus ritualized manners, which ruled a person's lifestyle.

The impossibility of keeping the law was exemplified in a simple act. The lawgiver, Moses, who has been described as "the meekest man on earth," lost his temper and smashed the tablets (see Num 12:3). So, even the meekest of all men broke the law. He had to go back to square one, up the mountain, and come back with a second set, which he placed into the ark of the covenant as God instructed him. The ark was a symbol of Christ, the only one who kept the law of God.

The law was the key factor in the Old Covenant. This covenant was conditional, binding people to God by means of obedience, faith, and works. Intended for life, the law became paradoxically an instrument of death. It was rather condemning, for no one was able to stay within the parameters delineated by God. There was no escape from its injunctions, no avoidance of its demands, and no possibility of justification by works—no matter how hard a person tried. It became an instrument of death, according to Paul, because no righteous person was found, not even one, who could boast of having kept all the law. The infringement of one commandment rendered a person liable and condemned.

People under the law were not satisfied with these regulations and sought to add some more. Life became regulated totally by a sort of tyranny of mandates characterized by "ought," "should do," and "do not" injunctions. Human traditions were added by a sequel of interpreters and scholars and became part of the ethos of the Israelites by the time Jesus came to them. The Babylonian Talmud, a later development of Jewish scholarship, is an example of these collected interpretations and additions. Such human commands, teachings, and rudiments, as Paul said to the Colossians (2:16–24), have a good appearance and convey dignity, but are unable to save, redeem, or render any lifestyle functional, due to sinful human nature which cannot abide by such external regulations.

Jesus came to his own people, but his own received him not (John1:11). They were trapped into rituals and ceremonies that were meticulously regulated and punctiliously observed in attempts to systematize God's will. He and his disciples quite often were accused of transgressing these regulations. They did not wash their hands properly before eating. Jesus healed several people on the Sabbath, which infuriated the religious of the day. While John the Baptist's disciples were fasting, Jesus and his disciples were having a party! Jesus talked to women freely, taught them his truth, and hung around sinners most of the time. Such an *avant-garde* person did not fit the old matrix. Both his epistemology and his message of grace were too revolutionary. His concepts were too much to grasp for those accustomed to the old ways, to the routines and rigid patterns.

The prophet Jeremiah saw the day in which God would make a New Covenant—not like the old one, but a radically new economy. God's sovereign purpose would be fulfilled in us, apart from the law (Rom 3:21), in spite of our inability, frailty, and sinfulness. God would supersede the Old Covenant with something new: The New Covenant is not just a new, remedial patch to fix an old rag; it is something new to strengthen the fabric of our new being. The New Covenant is not a paradigm provided to domesticate our wild flesh, but a transforming design that renders us new creatures. These theological considerations represent the ground for the appeal to the New Covenant as a paradigm of a relational nature—especially in dealing with marital renewal.

THE NATURAL MIND AND THE NEED FOR RENEWAL

To renew is to resume some originally planned and intended endeavor, regaining sight of an intended design. In order to engage in this process, some redirection and realignment is necessary. Also, the refinement of ways and means being utilized is important so as to reach a desirable state. Living organisms (including humans engaged in relations) experience entropy, decay, deterioration, and decomposition due to the ecosystemic forces working against them. In systemic terms, to renew is to revitalize and re-energize an organism's structures and functions in ways that will assure its continuity in space and time.

A couple's "oneness" needs boundaries in order to establish a corporate differentiation and individuation in relation to its surrounding social systems. The establishment of these boundaries serves vital functions, acting as a protective defense against unwanted or toxic intrusions to their intimacy, as well as a perimeter within which the partners can engage in a positive revitalization of their intimate transactions. The nuclear family needs boundaries as well, as attested by systems theory research and practice, facilitating the interactional patterns that take place between the components of the system and their extended family networks, friends, and community. Chapter 13 presented an analogy derived from cytology, illustrating the fact that in order to survive and be functional, a living cell has to engage in four processes: 1.) The ingestion of nutrients; 2.) The exclusion of toxicity; 3.) The digestion of nutrients; 4.) The expelling of the resulting waste; and 5.) The sharing of nutrients with other cells. These transactions happen at the semipermeable membrane (boundary) that surrounds each cell.

A living organism may experience renewal and revitalization continually until entropic forces, built-in aging mechanisms, and gradual decay win the battle, resulting in a final death. The human spirit yearns to be free from this natural tendency, hoping for a glorified state into which the resurrected believer will enter in order to enjoy God's presence and fellowship as Scripture reminds us (see the chapters in Rom 7—8; 1 Cor 15; 2 Cor 5).

Much debate has surrounded the mind-brain phenomena, and new investigations in the fields of cognitive science, neurobiology, and biochemistry may add to the complexities of the physical-metaphysical dilemma. The tension between empirical observations and faith-based propositions pertaining to the mind-brain dilemma poses a challenge. In this work, the human mind is a scriptural construct that denotes a person's cognitive-emotive and motivational functions—exuding properties of being a creature made in the image of God. The human engages in cognitive processes—he/she thinks, reasons, attributes meaning to reality, and defines things by name. The human mind is capable of learning, storing semantic and episodic memories, retrieving these events, and exercising judgment in a decision-making process. The mystery of how the mind actually connects and works as relating to the brain is one of the puzzles of our times. Data emerging from neurobiological, biochemical, and electromagnetic properties and functions of the human brain is shedding more light as these domains in science advance in their research efforts. Needless to say, these scientific fields need to grow even more to begin to elucidate the frontiers of consciousness.

As human beings, we have been created in the image of God, including our reason, intellect, sensibility, and will. We are endowed with an ethical and moral capacity, reflecting or exuding virtues after God. Our mindful processes can be regarded as emergent properties that can actualize God's truth by virtue of being connected to and empowered by God. As the *Imago Dei,* we also possess a relational, dialogical capacity. Scripture depicts the mind as being created, fallen, naturally depraved and corrupt, regenerated, transformed, and in need of constant renewal. To renew our minds is to infuse a new perspective, to consciously reframe reality, to be mindfully aware of possibilities, to re-uptake new attitudes, and to adopt new stances. Renewal, in human relations, may be enacted in stances, behaviors, cognitive and affective processes, and underlying motivations.

The natural mind develops in a context, in a given age (*aion:* god of time in pagan mythology), marked by social currents and cultural trends that affect a person's cognitive-emotive processes, motivations, and lifestyle. A mindset may be described as a conglomerate of ideas, attitudes, and motivations underlying behavioral patterns subject to the pressures of the surrounding context. This context is transduced by means of philosophies and trends (e.g., materialism, atheism, agnosticism, hedonism, narcissism, mysticism, existentialism) and represents the medium in which the mind is "soaked"—the vinegar in which cucumbers become pickles. Relationships do not escape the pressures to conform to these trends. The believer's relationships are affected by the myriad of ideas springing from secular sources, embedded in relativism, abandonment of God-given guidelines, and a search for narcissistic fulfillment.

The postmodern trends present a challenge in which the absence of metanarratives and absolutes emphasizes a relative stance subject to personal knowledge framed within a different context: a multiverse versus a universe with a sort of tribalism guiding a hermeneutic of a participatory, intersubjective nature.

The natural mindset may be squeezed into the mold of this age and deviate from God's truth and will. It may be blinded by sinful filters and become reprobate, denying access to God's guidelines for faith and conduct. A constant deviation from, and transgression of, God's will results in a desensitized state that obliterates God's appeals to human conscience. The natural mind (without renewal) is described in Scriptures as being corrupt (Titus 1:15); depraved (Rom 1:28); vain, futile (Eph 4:17); obtuse, slow, bogged down (Luke 24:45); unable to know God or to understand His ways (1 Cor 2:14); captive to the law of sin (Rom 7:25); following the dictates of the flesh (Rom 8:6); and hostile toward God (Rom 8:7). Furthermore, it is presented as living in futility (Eph 4:17); sensual (Col 2:18); corrupted and deprived of the truth (1 Tim 6:5); and warped at the core (2 Tim 3:8). In sum, no matter how sophisticated, insightful, or brilliant a natural mind is, it does not know God, does not obey God, does not engage in dialogue with the Spirit, and is unable to know his will.

The propensity of the natural (unrenewed) mind is to engage in arbitrary inferences, false generalizations, and subjective attributions of a negative, pessimistic nature. In the natural realm, without the illuminating action of God's Spirit, a sort of blindness to God's truth exists in which the mind establishes its own version, based on sensorial, inaccurate, and partial experience—both personal and social. Thus, idiosyncratic logic with false conclusions derived from faulty premises serves as the principle of cognitive functioning that is of a selfish, subjective nature.

The natural mind minimizes the truthful aspects of God's revelation, as well as God's commandments. It magnifies the need to pursue selfish goals, focuses upon inconsequential aspects, and gives power to those things that have no real value before God. It develops inadequate images of God with projections of a "father" characterized by socialized, dysfunctional, and natural tones. These negative attributions are due to distorted, experiential perceptions.

A metacognitive outlook is necessary—a top-down perspective of spiritual insight—in order to ascertain whether a mindset is being molded and trapped into the patterns of this age. A person embedded in these trends is not necessarily aware of his or her entrapment. Naturally speaking, entropy prevails, and the propensity to go on in a customary fashion does not allow for deep reflection of our own predicament. Thus, ascertaining before God our state of being, our thoughts, feelings, and motivations, is a crucial process that must be constantly renewed in order to develop insights into who we are and what we are supposed to do, according to God's will and purpose.

Part II: Principles Derived from the New Covenant in Marital Transactions

THE TRANSFORMATION OF BEING BY THE RENEWAL OF THE MIND

In his letter to the Romans, after a long theological discourse (Romans 1—11), Paul urges believers to engage in a process of transformation and renewal. His appeal—based upon the mercies of God—addresses us as well: we are to present our bodies as living sacrifices and not be conformed to the patterns of this age; rather, we are to be transformed through the renewal of our minds, so as to prove what the will of God is for our lives (Rom 12:1–2).

The ultimate goal in Christian striving is to be transformed into the likeness of Jesus—to be "transformed by the renewing of your mind" (Rom 12:2). Paul's employment of the term *metamorphosis* reminds us of the radical change in structures and functions found in some living organisms. An example from nature may illustrate the point: a caterpillar hanging in a cocoon becomes a butterfly. This radical transformation (metamorphosis) follows a meta-epigenetic principle, which allows for developmental changes that unfold and restructure the original form, actualizing new potentials present in the essence or substructure of the organism.

The transformation of our being is effectuated when we surrender to God and present ourselves as living sacrifices in order to experience a transformation with our mindful processes becoming subject to the person of the Holy Spirit, whose presence and power coparticipates with our human endowments. Cognitive processes such as thinking, reasoning, perception, attribution of meaning, memory, learning, and the formation of attitudes, values, and beliefs are all intertwined with God's personal presence in the mind and the heart. These processes may experience a realignment with, a redirection, and a honing in on God's will and purpose. Emotive aspects and motivational endeavors follow the same transformation, moving along the same lines.

The process of mindful renewal may be framed in a dialogical context in which both stability and flexibility are factors at work, representing the interaction between steadfastness and creativity. The freedom to take spontaneous, off-the-beaten-paths of a purposive nature may enhance a relationship without losing sight of a targeted destination. Creative renewal is fostered in a climate of divergent thinking and open-ended inquiry. Yet, these expanding dimensions have to be framed by ethical and moral boundaries. At times, a given partner may take a less than ethical or moral "off-the-road" detour (i.e., unfaithful to the path jointly agreed on) that proves to be detrimental to a marriage's stability, harmony, or peacefulness. Off-the-road experiences often lead to muddy, dirty experiences that are enjoyed by the person who delights in the freedom to roam this planet—something that the partner that stays faithful to the path jointly agreed on does not appreciate, nor is willing to tolerate. Thus, it is desirable to be zesty, creative, and unpredictable with these renewing endeavors, while remaining faithfully clean and mindfully predictable in maintaining harmony and peace.

Renewal is not necessarily an invitation to be *avant-garde* to the point of upsetting the peace, harmony, or faithfulness characterizing a long-standing commitment. Renewal is the process by which a partner may enact his or her capacity to invite the transcending to the trivial, to rearrange mindful configurations and styles in approaching challenges, to reattribute a fresh meaning to ongoing reality, and to remain open to God's empowering presence in order to be free, open, and energized to behave in a loving fashion. Creativity and spontaneity in enacting desirable interpersonal behaviors, and flexibility in approaching conflicts are some of the ways in which such renewal may be actualized.

Partners who become aware of being trapped in a tedious box may consider the possibility of renewing their covenantal deal. Thinking "out of the box" (defined in terms of a status quo of a steady, predictable ethos, characterized by sameness and repetitiveness) is desirable and necessary to revitalize intimate relations. Their life under the sun—a contingent order—needs the infusion of a supra-ordinate order, which enhances the meaning of their covenantal deal as experienced in the sight of God. Once they are endowed with a renewed, creative thrust, they may perceive their relationship as being subject to a bigger box—God's eternal order and design, applicable to human relations.

It is in light of living in the sight of God that believers understand and experience the fact that it is God who works all things together for good through all contingencies, vicissitudes, and events (Rom 8:28), so that they would be aligned and shaped into the likeness of Jesus (v. 29). The character, conduct, and interpersonal influence of each partner experiences a power-assisted energy that transforms what God has reformed, and is conforming, into the likeness of his Son. With this transformation, God empowers partners to be his witnesses in a fallen world (Acts 1:8) and to offer praises, thanksgiving, and service to others in the world by means of his Spirit (1 Pet 2:9; Heb 13:15). The pouring of the Holy Spirit upon all flesh signals that God has accepted us in Christ, and that this gift has been provided in order that we may live a zesty, empowered, and meaningful lifestyle. It is the Holy Spirit who empowers partners in covenants to live this kind of life.

In sum, to renew our minds is to take something that customarily grows old and decays—that is subject to entropy—and restructure its basis, processes, and functions to foster its revitalization. It is to realign the styles of thinking and the attributions of meaning to events that deviated from their original intention and purpose, setting them back on course with a new, empowered vision. It is to re-establish passion, recovering the original zest and meaning in life. It is to realign the cognitive, affective, motivational, and enactive processes to be in tune with God's will for our lives, rendering it more functional, free, open, flexible, and mature.

The process of mind renewal is effectuated by the coparticipation between the human and the Spirit, allowing the Word to have ample room in our hearts and minds. It is necessary to obey by faith what God says, living by every word that comes from God. The proactive aspects of believing, meditating, and engaging the Word as a cleansing agent are necessary in order to yield to the Holy Spirit along the restructuring, resocializing process following His promptings, allowing all cognitive processes to be illustrated, illuminated, and directed by the Spirit.

The apostle Paul admonishes the Ephesian believers to "be renewed in the spirit of your mind" (Eph 4:23). Through this endeavor, one may believe, grow, and establish a dialogue with God in communion. Furthermore, one may be occupied in the things of God (Rom 8:5); love God above all things and seek to have an ongoing affinity with God (Col 3:2); understand God's purposes, without questioning so much His will (Rom 11:34); and reframe, restructure, and re-attribute meaning to reality according to God's definitions as one has "the mind of Christ" (1 Cor 2:16).

THE CAPACITIES OF A RENEWED MINDSET

The renewed mind is stable, but not rigid nor stagnant; it develops good habits, but is not trapped into deadly routines, stereotyped boxes, or a lifestyle devoid of zest, vitality, and novelty. It does not get hopeless or helpless; it does not give in to pessimism, lethargy, or intropunitive stances, but remains in faith and in hope, challenging the status quo, vanity, and futility. It has the capacity to remain open, free, and dialogical with God.

The renewed mind has consciousness of the Holy Spirit's presence and focuses on the things of God. In arguing this point, the apostle Paul states,

> Those who live according to the sinful nature have their minds set on what that nature desires; but those who live in accordance with the Spirit have their minds set on what the Spirit desires. The mind of sinful man is death, but the mind controlled by the Spirit is life and peace; the sinful mind is hostile to God. It does not submit to God's law, nor can it do so. Those controlled by the sinful nature cannot please God. You, however, are controlled not by the sinful nature but by the Spirit, if the Spirit of God lives in you. (Romans 8:5–9, NIV)

A renewed mindset is capable of honing in on God's definitions of reality: "Gird up the loins of your mind [your understanding of reality]" (1 Pet 1:13, NKJV). A brief exploration of the terms used may be helpful. The Greek verb ἀναζώννυμι, translated as "I gird up, tuck in the loose folds of my garment, brace up" (with a view to active exertion), conveys a metaphor referring to the fastening of a flowing tunic to prevent it from hampering active work. In other words, it means to tighten the cognitive belt—to exercise the Spirit-empowered, metacognitive-executive control mechanisms of the top-down agency in order to have a grip on cognitive processes: thinking, reasoning, perception, attribution of meaning, learning capacity, memory, intentions, and motivation. It is to be mindfully aware of the need to be sober, insightful, and ready.

Covenantal Renewal as a Way of Life

In writing to the Colossians, the apostle's emphasis may be framed in metacognitive mindfulness. Colossians 3:1 says, "Keep seeking the things above" (NET); "seek the things that are above" (ESV); "set your hearts on things above" (NIV). Verse 2 reads, "Keep thinking about things above, not things on the earth" (NET); "set your minds on things that are above, not on things that are on earth" (ESV). The terms used by Paul to convey this notion may be further explored.

1. *Zeteitē* (ζητεῖτε, from ζητέω = I seek, search for, desire, require, demand) conveys a sense of seeking by *inquiring* or investigating to reach a *binding* (*terminal*) resolution; to search, "getting to the bottom of a matter." That is, the mindset may be purposefully (mindfully) directed toward an object of inquiry—a construct, idea, principle, or revealed truth expressed in a propositional fashion by God. Having the context in mind—that is, being endowed with peripheral awareness of historical and cultural issues, language (genre, style, semiotics), intended audience, and theological thrust—helps us to have a better focus on the main purpose in life: to live in the sight of God. The interpenetration of both peripheral and focal aspects of cognitive processing may be subsumed under a metacognitive perspective. This vantage point may allow for both detached and purposeful mindfulness, as if observing the abstracted configuration from a higher plane by means of a top-down executive agency involved in parallel processes.

2. *Phroneite* (φρονεῖτε, from *φρονέω*, "the midriff or diaphragm; the physiological parts around the heart")—that is, to regulate from within, as inner perspective (insight) shows itself in corresponding, outward behavior. The notion derived from this term (*phronéō*) is difficult to translate into English because it combines the *visceral* and *cognitive* aspects of thinking. Perhaps, the metacognitive-executive function of the empowered believer is able to amalgamate the multiple codes conveying data—physiological, sensory, perceptual, super-conscious—and process these in a dialogical (bottom-up and top-down) fashion, chunking them into passionate knowing, or cognitive passion, in honing in on God and beholding his presence.

A renewed mindset allows for the development of accurate empathy, acceptance, and validation of others as the "mind of Christ" (Phil 2:5) is enacted. The expression "Let the mind of Christ be in you" may refer to attitudes, motivation, intention, and directionality in interpersonal dealings, framed in a New Covenant fellowship. Respect and mutuality in fellowship are a possibility as everyone whose mind is renewed can engage in sane, sober decision-making and getting along with others . . . having the "same mind set" (Phil 2:2).

A renewed mindset is sober. The same passage (1 Pet 1:13) also includes the term *nēfontes* (νήφοντες = being sober minded, not drunk or intoxicated; [figuratively] free from illusion, i.e., from the intoxicating influences of sin [like the impact of selfish

Part II: Principles Derived from the New Covenant in Marital Transactions

passion, greed, etc.]). Peter's admonition is to have *presence of mind* (clear judgment), to be *temperate* (self-controlled), to have "one's wits" (faculties), and to be rational. Other passages allude to the same notion (1 Thess 5:6, "stay alert and sober"; 1 Thess 5:8, "but since we are [of the day], we must stay sober"; 2 Tim 4:5, "be self-controlled in all things"; 1 Pet 4:7, "be self-controlled and sober-minded for the sake of prayer"; and 1 Pet 5:8, "be sober and alert"). Still another term in the verse is *elpisate*, (ἐλπίσατε) used in the phrase "to fully set your hope on the grace"; that is, to actively wait upon God's promises, or to mindfully hone in on what is already real in God's will. Finally, Peter admonished disciples to live "as obedient children, not conforming yourselves to the former lusts, as in your ignorance" (1 Pet 1:14, NKJV).

One of the key elements of a renewed mind is its capacity to be armed or inoculated in order to be able to face eventual suffering (1 Pet 4:1–2). The expression "arm yourself with the same attitude" may allude to a paradigm resembling what is known in psychology as "stress inoculation training," in which a person anticipates dreadful events proactively while in a state of relaxation, calmness, and soberness, preparing a mindset to face eventual stressful situations. In this way, the renewed Christian is not naïve or unprepared, but sober, watchful, and ready for any vicissitude that may challenge him or her. Parallel to the Pauline warning directed to those who marry and who will face difficult circumstances (1 Cor 7:28), Peter's admonition may apply to those entering covenantal dealings: they need to "arm themselves" with the thought of encountering possible sufferings and anticipate what they need to do in order to conquer their challenges.

The renewed mind is proactive (Phil 4:8). In his appeal to the Philippians, St. Paul states, "Finally . . . whatever is true [versus untrue, deceitful, lies]; whatever is worthy of respect [versus ignominious, brute]; whatever is just; whatever is pure; whatever is lovely [versus odious, hateful, irascible]; whatever is commendable [versus lowly, trivial, disrespectful]; if something is excellent [versus mediocre] or praiseworthy [versus shameful], think about these things." In other words, target and occupy your mind with such things. The capacity to direct thoughts and to have purposeful "comebacks" against automatic, natural, unregenerated thoughts is possible under the auspices of the Spirit's empowering of the human mind.

To the Colossians, the same apostle wrote, "Set your hearts on things above" (Col 3:1, NIV), as well as "Set your minds on things above" (Col 3:2, ESV). Thus, directional and purposeful aspects are ascribed to the renewed mind, and these features prevent the person from being trapped in sinful predicaments or mindlessly following automatic, irrational, or dysfunctional patterns. Paul engages in behavioral prescriptions, such as "put to death . . . whatever belongs to your earthly nature," which includes immorality, impurity, evil desires, and greed (NIV). These are not legalistic injunctions aimed at human efforts to be holy, but consequential aspects of having been treated by God with grace and being empowered to do so.

A cognitive appraisal of God's will becomes possible as we present our bodies as living sacrifices and are transformed by the renewal of our minds. The renewed mind is directed to ascertain the will of God—the internal witness of the Spirit aligning with the indwelling Word of God—and corroborate God's desires, plans, and purposes as these unfold in the experience of the believer. There is a veridical basis that provides an internal witness to God's truth about our new status as God's children (Rom 8:16), allowing for certainty and security in his presence. We are able to assess our discernment of God's will in accordance with the supportive scriptural data, which conveys God's revealed truth—and to experience an internal witness of the Holy Spirit to our spirit, which corroborates God's intentions for us.

Hopefully, marriage covenants are enacted between two individuals experiencing these processes—both regenerated and being transformed and conformed to God's ideal. All covenants established among humans experience the tendency to grow old and become routine oriented, diminishing in meaning, intensity, zest, or satisfaction. Decreased reinforcement, attention, and dedication to one another along routines need to be addressed to transform and renew the level of interest, fostering the eagerness to promote love and good works. Thus, the necessary influx of life and Spirit is stressed in order to be in tune with God's paradigm for being and doing what he desires.

Renewal, in human relations, may be ascertained as being enacted in stances, behaviors, cognitive and affective processes, and underlying motivations. The ingredients of renewal may be stated in terms of flexibility, creativity, spontaneity, tolerance for frustration amidst changes, and the emergence of an array of novel, off-the beaten-path avenues taken in addressing everyday issues. Renewal is not a just another concept, but the capacity to invite the transcending to the trivial, to rearrange and reattribute meaning to reality, and to remain open to God's empowering presence, allowing for a constant readiness to be free, open, and energized to behave lovingly. Creativity in dealings, spontaneity in enacting desirable behaviors, and flexibility in approaching conflicts represent some of the ways in which this renewal may be actualized.

THE RENEWAL OF A COVENANTAL COMMITMENT: DEGREE OF STABILITY AND SATISFACTION

The promise embedded in God's good news is that our covenantal relationship is not just for the here and now, but forever—we are partakers of an eternal life with God. On the human side, marriage is a created order; couples do not enter eternity as such, but as children in the family of God, relating in a new economy and style yet to be grasped and experienced. Nevertheless, marriages are framed in lasting terms as couples enter a covenantal transaction that hopefully will last until death separates them. The longevity and stability of believers' marriages need an infusion of life and

Part II: Principles Derived from the New Covenant in Marital Transactions

energy to be renewed and revitalized in an ongoing fashion. The currents, customs, and forces of this present time (*aion*) militate against covenantal relations, which we are considering as living organisms, subject to natural entropy and decay, routines and repetitive patterns, etc. These stressors tend to diminish, mitigate, and erode the degree of commitment—to God, to a partner, to the relationship, to an ideal, and to the contextual community. These factors may be placed under two major categories: stability and satisfaction of partners engaged in intimate deals.

Marriage may be assessed in terms of two main factors: the *degree of stability* of the relationship and the *level of satisfaction* of the relationship. Yet, these global factors may be further qualified as personal, interpersonal, and cultural expectations enter into play. Idealistic, functional, and pragmatic aspects enter the scene as well. Thus, the *stability* of a marital relationship may be perceived from five different angles, related to a person's values and reflected in degrees of adhesion and commitment to:

- Self-fulfillment, gratification, achievement, a sense of security, validation, etc.;
- A partner—his or her gratification, achievement, sense of security, validation, etc.;
- The marital union, the relationship itself;
- The marital institution as a social/spiritual/ideal structure;
- The norms and expectations of a tight community of believers.

In terms of *satisfaction*, the contentment and happiness of a person may be perceived as being dependent on the same set of variables: a sense of self-fulfillment of some sort; the fulfillment of some need or state of well-being of the partner; the serving, preserving, or enhancing of the marital relationship; the serving, preserving, or enhancing of marriage as a social/spiritual structure or institution; and the harmonious fitting into a community of believers surrounding the couple with given expectations and norms.

By now, the reader realizes that it is simply difficult to present an encompassing model of transactions that represents this complexity, as interactions happen in a convoluted, cyclical fashion. Personal, interpersonal, cultural, and spiritual factors contribute to a unique system. The multiplicity of factors interacting within a particular context render the definition of what an ideal marriage should be difficult to elucidate.

From the considerations above, we may ask concrete questions. As a husband or a wife, *are you satisfied in your marriage? Why? Why not? Also, is your marriage stable? And if so, why is it?* In postmodern times, a person's answers to these questions may reflect several postures and provide a variety of reasons. Even if the person's answer is affirmative, we do not necessarily have a full picture of his or her experience. The person may offer several qualifying explanations about his or her perceived fulfillment and satisfaction. These may depend on his attribution of value and meaning to the variables depicted:

- High self-fulfillment and satisfaction with high commitment to the partner, the relationship, and the marital institution, aiming at high stability—a functional, optimal condition;
- High self-satisfaction, but low commitment to the partner (who experiences low self-fulfillment and satisfaction) with high commitment to the marital stability established by means of legalistic impositions, demands of submission to authority, church expectations, etc.;
- High self-fulfillment and satisfaction with low commitment to both the partner and the relationship, but high commitment to the institution of marriage—a self-righteous narcissist preoccupied with theological definitions of headship and external appearances or image conveyed to the community;
- High self-fulfillment and satisfaction, and high regard for the marriage institution (in principle), but low commitment to the relationship, failing to meet the needs, expectations, and desires of the partner—a selfish, or un-empathic person, or a highly cognitive person who experiences difficulties in processing emotional data;
- High self-satisfaction with low commitment to the partner, fostering low stability—as in the case of a pleasure-seeking individual not committed to either the partner, the relationship, or the marriage as an institution;
- High self-fulfillment and satisfaction, and high commitment to the relationship and its stability, but low commitment to the institution of marriage, living together with the partner in a postmodern arrangement or a common-law agreement by mutual consent;
- High self-fulfillment and satisfaction, but no commitment to the relationship or the institution, as in the case of predators, abusers, or victimizers who regard the trapped, abused "partner" as an object of self-gratification;
- Low self-fulfillment and satisfaction, but seeking the fulfillment and satisfaction of the partner, considering marriage as an obligatory trapping, yet shaping, sanctifying, and perfecting of his character through present-day suffering, bearing the yoke of martyrdom or witness for a higher cause—the partner's well-being and the institution of marriage to be supported at the cost of personal losses;
- Low self-fulfillment and satisfaction experienced by both partners, but suffering "for God's sake" and putting up with one another for legalistic, convenient, financial, or social reasons—based on concerns such as what the community or the church would say.

An orthogonal illustration with stability and satisfaction as the variables may bolster the readers' understanding of the possibilities mentioned.

Part II: Principles Derived from the New Covenant in Marital Transactions

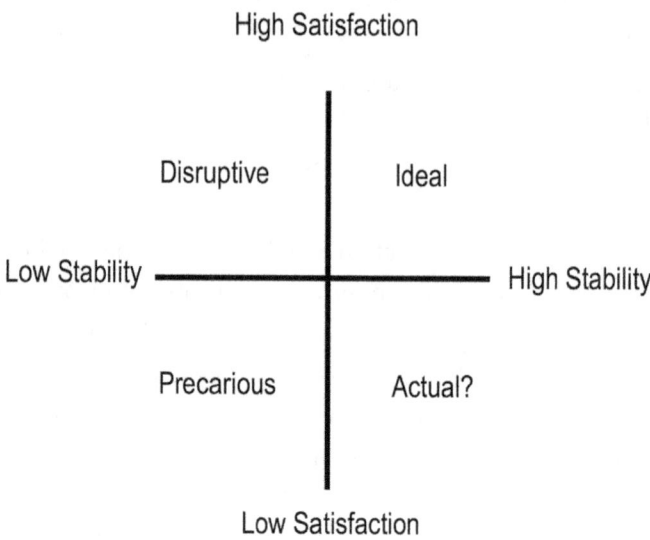

Fig. 16.1: Degree of Stability and Satisfaction in Marriage

In ideal terms, a Christian marriage may be experienced as being highly satisfied and highly stable, represented in the first quadrant. Unfortunately, many Christian couples find themselves in a quadrant representing an actual state: highly stable but not satisfied. They are committed to God and to personal ideals and values; they make every effort to stay together in spite of disappointments, lack of fulfillment, or contentment. A feeling of martyrdom, suffering, and bearing with one another seems to permeate their system, bound to the letter of the law. A third possibility may explain why many marriages do not last, as both partners experience lack of both satisfaction and stability and tend to give up rather than engage in renewing or restorative endeavors. The fourth possibility renders the marriage an "open system" of a precarious, unstable, and undesirable nature, destined to fail. Postmodern currents fostering hedonistic, narcissistic, or swapping-and-swinging mindsets do not allow for any permanence or stability in marriage.

The emphasis placed on the stability of marital relationships and the injunctions against divorce have characterized Christian teachings for centuries. Unfortunately, the emphasis on marital satisfaction has not received the same attention. The lack of satisfaction that characterizes many stable marriages is worth exploring: a highly stable, yet unsatisfactory, marriage may lead a couple to experience their covenant as a burden to bear. If marriage could be compared to either a heavenly or hellish state experienced on Earth, we need to be reminded that both heaven *and* hell are *very* stable. The main difference is that heaven is more satisfying than hell. Therefore, there is nothing wrong with emphasizing both aspects in marriage: stability and satisfaction in the here and now, while we wait for heaven to happen.

The second commandment—to love our neighbor as we love ourselves—points to the mutual privilege to be dispensed toward one another: to desire the same, satisfying benefits for one's partner as one desires for oneself. Security, stability, and satisfaction are often reflected in covenantal intimacy involving emotional closeness and sexuality. Sex is a feature that in traditional marriages was considered the obligation of a wife to please her partner—a duty supported by passages designed to enforce this "right" by males. On the other side, postmodern unions seem to emphasize sex as a flexible feature determined by the idiosyncratic desires of each partner.

Scripture places the sexual union within a frame of reference in which a couple experiences an intimate union—one flesh, in an expressive movement of private and exclusive ecstasy. The security, stability, and longevity of a covenantal commitment foster an expressive freedom actualized in the sexual relationship, which was designed to be a mutually enjoyable experience through time. The renewal of the mind of both partners may foster a creative, fresh, and satisfying sexual life. An expression from a psychiatrist friend may make sense to the reader: "If you renew your mind, you never go to bed with the same partner." That is, partners may re-uptake and re-experience one another in a creative, ongoing array of existential impressions as if every encounter is a new opportunity to express love.

PRACTICAL WAYS OF RENEWING A MINDSET

The new covenantal terms are much more satisfying than the old ones. The Holy Spirit infuses the capacity to experience satisfaction embedded in love, grace, and mercy—beyond the satisfaction resulting from the obedience to duties and obligations framed in a covenantal union. Applying this principle to human transactions in order to renew a mindset and experience satisfaction in relations, a person must be willing and able to experience an insightful, "kairotic" process in an ambiance of love, grace, and mercy. For the Greeks, *kairos* represented a teaching moment, a frame of mind that was open to experience and to new input, as well as the production of new insights. In this way, *kairos* is the "aha" moment that results as a person adopts a disposition and willingness to have the eyes of the understanding open to see, ascertain, and apprehend truth. This understanding and insight facilitate the growth of a wise mindset. In order to experience these "aha" moments, a creative and open disposition endowed with the desire to know and be known is necessary—to be willing and able and to mindfully engage in the new covenantal terms described in this work.

Partners that experience low levels of satisfaction or stability may "come to their senses" and become aware of their situational contingencies. They may call things by name (define their problem, state their needs); then, they jointly engage in communication, exchanging impressions and concerns, and conveying requests and

Part II: Principles Derived from the New Covenant in Marital Transactions

expectations from each other. They may express their hopes and desires in a mutual fashion and set commonly envisioned goals. Specific avenues along this initiative may be outlined in the following suggestions:

- Practice being open to explore new possibilities with a flexible stance; avoid being squeezed into impossible dilemmas, unsolvable aspects of life, or situational constraints that are not so changeable;

- Realize that you cannot control things that escape your areas of responsibility, nor be responsible for things that fall out of your control. Yet, with a renewed mindset you may engage in unilateral, unconditional, and proactive behaviors that may empower and encourage your partner—beyond your limits, control, or responsibility—with grace and mercy;

- Reframe the meaning of what is going on, adopting a metacognitive stance and seeing things as if from the top, objectively. Cast a new outlook, a new redefinition, or a new way of painting the picture; try to avoid somber tones in doing so;

- Renegotiate covenantal terms. Even God-given covenants were renewed at times to bring again the awareness of the higher ground of transacting before God as the basis for stability and satisfaction;

- Refresh the appraisal of routines to engage in creative changes—bringing something old to new endeavors, something new to old routines;

- Regain momentum to behave in a more purposeful, mindful, and exciting way; recapture yourself "on the spot" as a person who, in a free, open, spontaneous, and creative fashion, sings to self: "This is the day that the Lord has made, I will be glad and rejoice in it";

- Engage in a metacognitive capacity to see from a different perspective—considering yourself as a participant-observer of your own attitudes, intentions, and processes, etc. From an observer's perspective, re-engage as a participant with purposeful mindfulness, consciously aware of your proactive intentions to bless your partner;

- Engage in self-talk—your dialogical capacity to modulate your inner deliberations, musings, conjectures, and expressions; these may be meditated about and rehearsed in the mind and heart to be delivered in a more sensitive, empathic manner as you communicate with your partner;

- Be mindful of developing new attitudes toward your partner—whatever is good, worthy of praise, empowering, and reinforcing, etc. Set your mind on those things;

- Plan proactively new behaviors toward your partner. Decide to eliminate your excessive behaviors (things you do too much, which are regarded as unnecessary, offensive, maladaptive, dysfunctional, or negative, etc., by your partner). Assess and decide to increase those behaviors that seem to be lacking in your repertoire. Augment your positive expressions, your attentive care, and your anticipatory planning—or just do the things that are pending: finish your unfinished projects or deliver the promised goods, etc.;

- Engage in internal rhetoric. After deliberative dialogues of an internal nature, shift to inner persuasion, commanding yourself to be the person you need to be and to do the things you ought to do in order to engage in desirable behaviors. Foster new perceptions and attributions of meaning; be positive about the attributes of your partner to augment new, positive feelings;

- Make it a priority to spur—to provoke intentionally, proactively, purposefully—one another on to love and good works (Heb 10:24). These are the emergent properties of the Spirit acting in coparticipation with believers in order to align their mindset and passion with the same dispositional attitude that was in Christ;

- Create a joint bank of new memories in order to obliterate and superpose a feed-forward control over detrimental aspects of the past that may linger and affect present dealings (old memories, especially those of a negative nature). These new memories (both semantic and episodic) may be established and consolidated proactively as you engage in further good works, promoting positive experiences.

As those engaged in the new field of interpersonal neurobiology have put it, "Neurons that fire together wire together." Let your mirror neurons align with each other along experiences of a positive nature, resonating with one another amidst ideas, feelings, and behaviors. Joint experiences of fun, relaxation, pleasure, and mutuality foster an excellent attachment at deep levels of neural processing within the plasticity of your brain. New research points to the possibilities of augmenting your capacity for intimate behaviors (affecting one another's brains), allowing the empathic firing of your neural pathways to myelinate (mix proteins and phospholipids, forming a whitish insulating sheath around many nerve fibers and increasing the speed at which impulses are conducted), consolidate, and establish new pathways in your brain. These repeated features of an interpersonal nature foster not only the renewal of your mind, but also the positive transformation of your brain.

A graphic illustration is provided (Fig. 16.2), which emphasizes a believer's meta-cognitive mindfulness—a top-down executive agency that allows for personal awareness and insight in processing one's own processes. Thus, capacity emerges from and is activated by the infusion of the Holy Spirit and the indwelling Word, empowering the potential to persuade one's self to engage in love and good works with purposeful mindfulness. The concrete manifestations of these efforts are depicted at the bottom with a number of cognitive, emotive, and behavioral events enacted as imitators of God as beloved children.

Part II: Principles Derived from the New Covenant in Marital Transactions

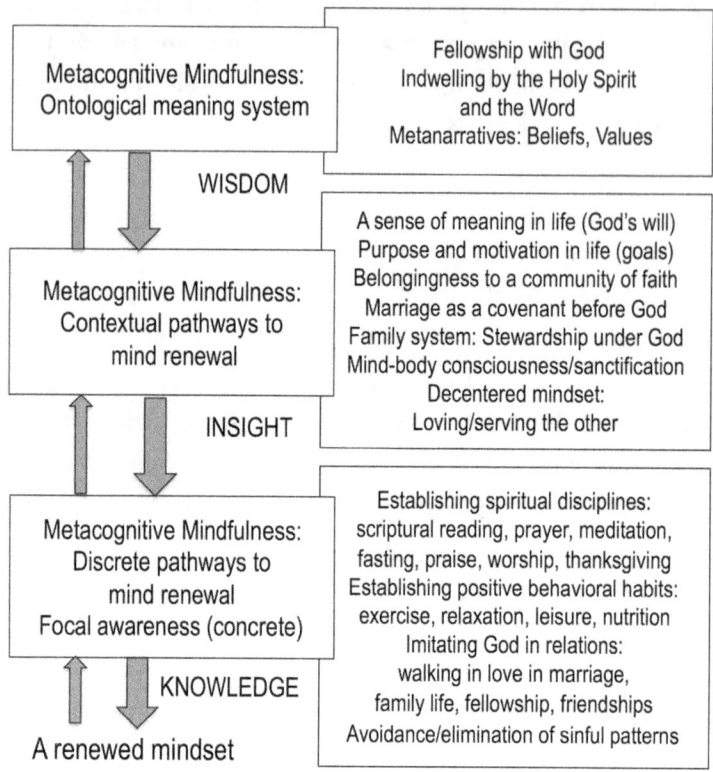

Fig. 16.2: Pathways to Mind Renewal

EXISTENTIAL ZEST IN LIFE

A creative mindset registers reality in sober fashion, yet it may go beyond the empirical data—what actually is there—and instead of replicating the observed perception, visualize a creative impression of this reality. Monet was an impressionist whose art was characterized by capturing scenes in a few minutes, finishing them later at his studio. He would paint the same landscape (e.g., lilies on the pond, a Japanese bridge, haystacks) numerous times. His art is an example of an artist renewing his own mindset: in spite of painting thirty replicas of the same landscape, he offered multiple renderings of the same reality. No picture was exactly the same: what varied was the depiction of light, shading, tones, and impressions gathered from each captured moment. His bold strokes and brush marks on canvas give us analogical impressions—not actual correspondence or depictions of reality as expressed in a digitalized version.

Applying this impressionistic example to marriage, phenomenologically speaking, a husband (if possessed of a creative, open, artistic mindset) may capture and convey a fresh, new, exciting, and existential rendering of the same reality (his wife of many years) in a number of ongoing, successive impressions. If both partners renew their minds, they will "see" and regard each other in a new light, being willing and able to approach each other in creative, proactive, graceful, and loving initiatives. In order to recapture one's "first love" feelings (Rev 2:4–5) and avoid boredom, routines, or satiation, a partner needs to "repaint and thin no more."

The last book of the Bible deals with the revelation of Jesus Christ, the redeemer husband coming back for his wife. A sevenfold warning is provided to seven churches to be ready for such an encounter at all times. Addressing the church in Ephesus, Jesus reminds his departed bride-to-be that she needs to recapture her first love, to go back and regain momentum and sight of the original basis of the covenant—the high ground of being-in-relation. Revelation 2:4 states (translated from the Greek, τὴν ἀγάπην σου τὴν πρώτην ἀφῆκε), "You have *abandoned* your first love" [emphasis mine]. The verb *aphemi*, from the Greek ἀφίημι (I send away, I let go, release, permit to depart, I divorce), can be actually used to denote divorce, so the imagery employed is very strong. The image conveys a spouse who slacks off, diminishes her zest and zeal, falls victim to the currents of her age, and becomes detached, estranged, and cold. In a way, she acts as a divorced person while still conducting business as a spouse. To such a spouse Jesus offers a loving, yet strong admonition: he charges her to renew her mind and her commitment, to engage in the deeds she did at first, and to engage in good works, accompanying her stated faith and vows.

The capacity to renew our minds may be actualized in existential living, adopting a metacognitive perspective, and seeing God's Spirit provide a new perception of his empowering presence animating our lives. The indwelling of God's presence and power may illuminate and provide meaning and zest to our life, in spite of the challenges we may face or experience. A picture is provided as a reinforcing visualization of this proposition.

Part II: Principles Derived from the New Covenant in Marital Transactions

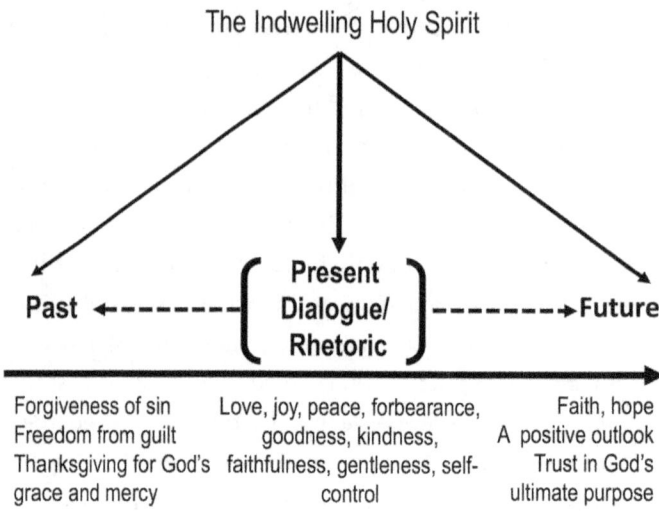

Fig. 16.3: Existential Bracketing of Reality and Mind Renewal

Our past has been dealt with, and our future has been secured in God's hands. Inviting and realizing God's presence, we may engage in dialogue with God and ourselves—and persuade ourselves with internal rhetoric to live by faith, actualizing God's transcending perspective and finding meaning in our natural life under the sun.

The reader may choose to consider the option to stop here, and regard the content of this book as a theme ending at this point. Covenantal renewal may be considered a concluding capstone placed on the theological exposition of the New Covenant paradigm, proposed as a heuristic model for intimate relations. Those interested in the author's model—employed in his clinical practice integrating biblical-theological principles to psychological ones—may further explore the musings rendered in theoretical propositions and illustrated with several diagrams and illustrations that appear in chapter 17. This model—not a static version, but in process—deals in particular with the process of forgiveness, and may be regarded as a metacognitive-dialogical approach that relies on the empowering of the Holy Spirit and the indwelling, living Word. It relies on the "thirdness" that encompasses therapeutic encounters and interactions—the trialogues involving the person, the presence, and the power of the Holy Spirit in coparticipation with the internal dialogues and rhetoric of those searching for emotional well-being and freedom.

Chapter 17

A Metacognitive-Dialogical Model of Forgiveness

FORGIVENESS HAS BEEN TREATED as a covenantal transaction in which a person dispenses grace and mercy toward a partner, empowered with a unilateral, unconditional, and proactive intention to imitate the Father's ways. This process allows for better dealings to be established and renewed on a more functional bilateral, conditional, and transactional basis. To forgive from this higher perspective, a model is proposed that is metacognitive and dialogical in nature. The model builds on the concepts of a dialogical self,[1] engaged in metacognitive processes,[2] and employing insightful feedback, empowered feedforward control systems, and internal rhetoric.[3] The model is framed in a biblical and theological Christian perspective—regarding the forgiver as a person empowered by the Holy Spirit and imitating the Father's ways, exemplified in terms of the New Covenant.

The model may serve as a heuristic device for psychotherapists, counselors, or pastors engaged in helping people along the process of forgiveness. It may also provide insights into the forgiveness process to readers interested in the ontological, psychological, theological, and functional aspects of this process.

Starting with a conscious realization and account of the offenses committed against the self, the mindful awareness of the processes that enter into play may be described in a diagrammatic fashion. The process is depicted as flowing clockwise in a feedback loop. Although the diagram shows a linear, coplanar feedback loop, the reality of the experiential flow dealing with a forgiving process moves along a more convoluted, multidimensional, parallel process, as we will see from various levels of analysis.

When counseling a person who has decided to forgive, the metacognitive components may be defined, elaborated, fostered, trained, or coached in a sort of collaborative empiricism, coupled with the person's spiritual understanding and application of scriptural principles. Furthermore, the internal dialogue is postulated as a process occurring in the mindset of the offended person engaged in a process of forgiveness. The "intramural" maneuvers of the ambivalent self have to deal with both aspects:

---

1. Hermans et al., "The Dialogical Self"; Hermans, "Voicing the Self"; Polischuk, "Perspectives on the Self."
2. Wells, *Metacognitive Therapy*.
3. Nienkamp, *Internal Rhetorics*; Polischuk, "A Metacognitive Perspective."

Part II: Principles Derived from the New Covenant in Marital Transactions

the natural, offended, and retaliatory self—resentful, hurt, angry, etc., yet under the conviction infused by the indwelling Word and the Holy Spirit—on the one side; and the empowered self—capable of dispensing grace and mercy under the auspices of the same indwelling agents—on the other.

Metacognitive strategies are sequential processes that a person may use to control cognitive activities and to ensure that a cognitive goal (e.g., understanding the process of forgiveness and knowing how to apply it) has been met.[4] These processes help 1.) To regulate and oversee the learning of functional avenues (attentiveness to one's reactionary processes, ascertaining one's true emotions at work, controlling the autonomic nervous system (ANS) by means of relaxation exercises, engaging in detached and purposeful mindfulness, etc.); and consist of 2.) Planning and monitoring cognitive-behavioral activities (e.g., as outlined in a practical guide extracted from scriptural data, accounts in a personal journal, anger workbooks, etc.); as well as checking 3.) The outcomes of those activities (e.g., verbal feedback in therapy; reading one's own notes about changes in frequency, intensity, or duration of retaliatory versus forgiving thoughts, feelings, and behaviors registered in a journal).

The process starts with the awareness and attention to the cost of dealing with the offense committed against the person, its impact, and its consequences as registered in cognitive, emotive, and behavioral terms. The process that follows is depicted in diagrammatic form.

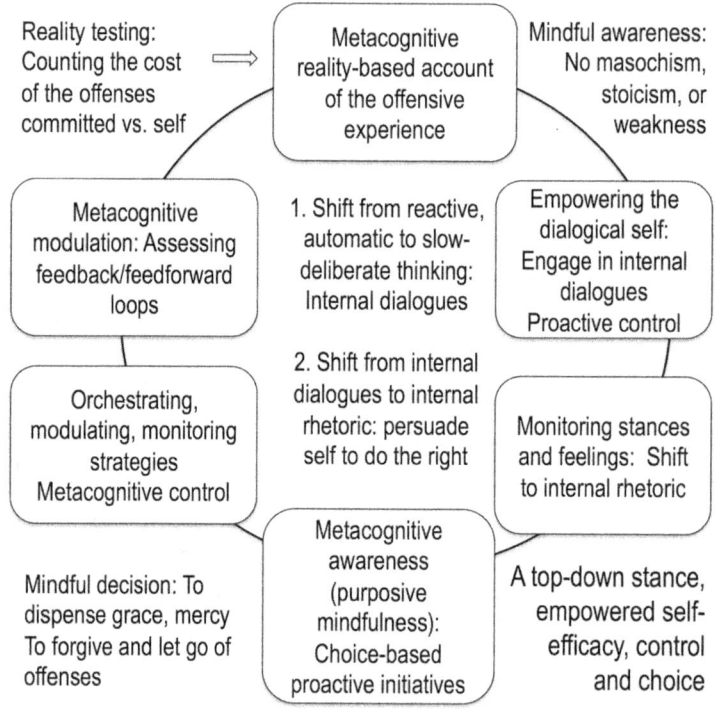

4. Wells, *Metacognitive Therapy*.

Fig. 17.1: Metacognitive Processes in Forgiveness

The internal dialogues of the offended-forgiving self include a third interlocutor—the Holy Spirit—who brings to mind the allocated, indwelling, and consolidated truth of God residing in the "inner being." The command to forgive is brought to life, coparticipating with cognitive and emotive processes (mind and heart), based upon the revealed truth about God's forgiveness of the struggling self. The forgiver's assessment of the impact of the offense (e.g., hurts, losses, experiences of anger) that saturate his or her dialogical styles of thinking (e.g., rumination, negative deliberations, conjectural musings) take place. Another diagram may help to elucidate the trialogical concept.

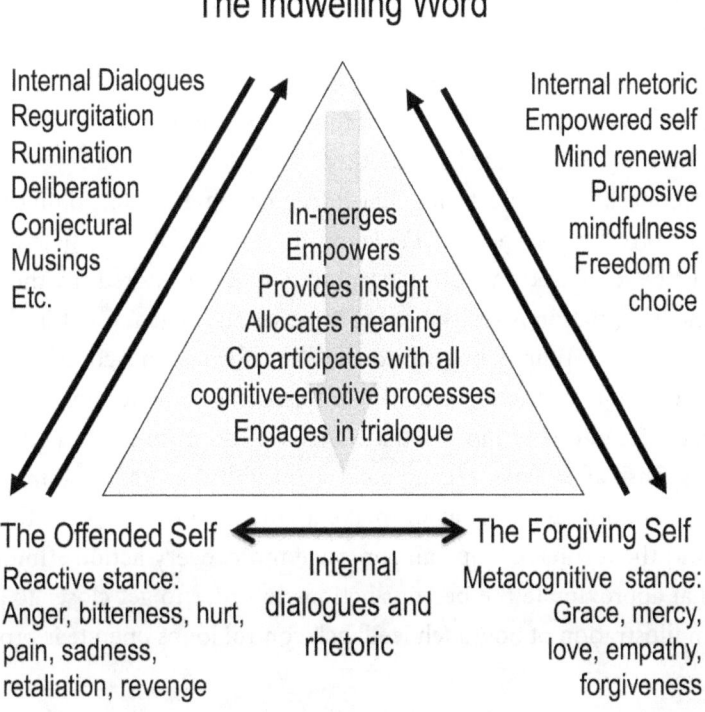

Fig. 17.2: Trialogue: The Internal Dialogues of the Self and the Holy Spirit

The person who forgives needs to count the cost of this endeavor. The forgiving person must sit first and count the cost of dispensing grace and mercy; even more, he or she must count the cost of letting go and having no more claims over the transgressor. What appears as an unjust, unfair deal, subject to a secondary loss (the primary loss being the sense of devastation created by the impacting transgression on the person's self-image, esteem, or lifestyle), needs to be reframed, recast, and seen metacognitively. The self must see the freedom, disposition, and control on his or her side in order to act in unilateral, unconditional, and proactive ways toward the offender—as God did.

The process of forgiveness arises from the need to attend to some disturbances in the natural flow of events. The referential input is upset by some offending stressor, which activates a series of processes. These include feedback loops, sensors, regulators, and other features of a system in need of regulation and control. We may now dissect these processes in some detail.

FEEDBACK LOOPS AT WORK

Disturbances in the natural flow of events being processed by the person provoke stress and evoke reactions. These stimuli are captured by the senses and transduced to conscious awareness with an appeal to process control loops to remediate and control the effect of these disturbances. Feedback control loops, represented by arrows going backward, will eventually serve as mechanisms employed to regulate and control the disturbance and lead it to a normal level of functioning, but not until there has been a significant deviation in the systems awareness.

These feedback loops are functional in regulating and controlling human behavior and involve four stages: 1.) *Evidence:* the impact of an activator (stimulus, stressor) must be registered (measured, captured, and data stored) by the person; 2.) *Relevance:* the information is relayed to the top-executive agency, not in the raw-data form in which it was captured, but transduced/transformed in a context that makes it emotionally resonant; 3.) *Consequence:* the information provides options to respond, employing a choice of one or more paths available to do so; and 4.) *Action:* the enactment of a response after experiencing a clear, insightful moment (*kairos*), in which the person can recalibrate a behavior, make a choice, and act. Then, that action is measured, and the feedback loop can run once more, every action stimulating new behaviors that approximate the person's actions in order to get closer to a desirable outcome. An illustration of how such feedback control loops operate is provided.

A Metacognitive-Dialogical Model of Forgiveness

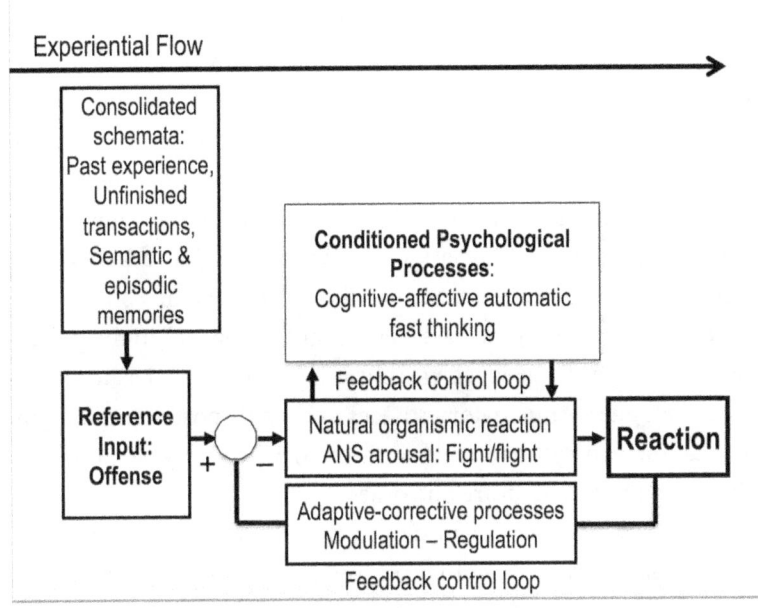

Fig. 17.3: Processes at Lower Levels: A Feedback Control System

The lower level depicted in the diagram also includes conditioned psychological processes. Focal attention emerges as an abstracted aggregate of sensory, peripheral input and directs the organismic capacity of the person to evoke a psychological reaction—cognitive-emotive in nature. The model regards these tacit sensations as superconsciously abstracted data, comprised of emergent thoughts and feelings that are evoked as reactions arising from the multiple codes being automatically processed—neurobiological and physiological substrata coupled to mindful awareness. These are endowed with the potential of the person to engage in fast thinking, which, when triggered by stress, assumes an emotional and reactionary nature.[5] The negative, automatic thoughts postulated by Beck and the internal dialogues described by Hermans may emerge at this junction in this model.[6]

Internal sources of stress (interoceptive triggers associated with an offense) may be pointed out: being anxious or depressed, having a negative flashback, evoking mentally an unfinished transaction, bringing a semantic or episodic memory of a bothersome nature to mind, or dialoguing (altercating, debating, quarreling) internally with someone "as if being there" as a sort of "presence in absence," among many other possibilities, all constitute a trigger capable of eliciting a reaction. Both external and internal triggers are processed by the organismic valuing system in an automatic, unconscious manner (in psychoanalytic terms) or in a super-conscious fashion (in cognitive science terms). What follows as a consequence is a fight-or-flight reaction.

5. Kahneman, *Thinking, Fast and Slow*.
6. Beck, *Cognitive Therapy*; Hermans, "Voicing the Self."

This reaction may be coupled with fear, anger, anxiety, or any feeling associated with the ongoing contingency, integrated into the experience.

The past is postulated as being a major influence on a person's behavior. Guilt, shame, anger, and other negative emotions may well be associated with the person's recapitulations (feedback loops) of the past, evoked by the present offending event. Reactive behaviors may occur in function of their antecedents—sensory, semantic, or episodic memories of a negative nature. These antecedents may be tapped and interact by means of neurobiological, associational networks—and as additive components, they may trigger the person's automatic reactions to any evoking stressor in the present. Unfinished transactions of the past "revisit" and "show up" in the present interaction—the so-called Zeigarnick effect—acting as a "presence in absence" transferred to the partner in dialogue.[7] Anticipatory stances and predisposed mindsets may add to a given provocation; ego-syntonic, self-confirmatory bias may also influence present behaviors in view of negative future outcomes.

The reacting person may unconsciously project, displace, or blame his or her interlocutor in negative ways. The other person may be there as an actual partner engaged in dialogue, but also represent someone else of significant emotional impact—a transference, in psychoanalytical terms—being superposed upon the actual interlocutor in dialogue. The person processing this interaction may not be necessarily aware of these negative projections being cast upon the interlocutor, as his or her unconscious filters channel all perceptions into negative attributions of meaning. The partner in dialogue—being experienced as an "it" versus a "thou"—may become the recipient of inordinate negative feelings that far exceed the natural expectations that may apply at the present interaction.

The upsurge of negative reactions of an exaggerated, augmented, or unfair nature toward a partner may "show up" if any conscious or unconscious triggers exert their influence when partners are engaged in a small argument or dealing with a trivial matter. Projection, transference, and displacement could be at work in these cases. In psychoanalytical work, it is the analysis of negative transference that promotes insight and freedom. In metacognitive-dialogical work, it is the top-down, metacognitive insight that helps in the process—elucidating intrapsychic, as well as interpersonal issues—and guides the interactive dialogue. An existential analysis of the impacting reality provoking angst may help, considering how this dread spreads throughout the experiential flux, bracketed in the here and now of the person.

---

7. Zeigarnick, "On Finished and Unfinished Tasks."

FEEDFORWARD CONTROL SYSTEMS

In contrast to feedback control, a feedforward control system is engaged at the moment a disturbance occurs without having to wait for a registered deviation in the process variables of the system. The disturbance engages a proactive, feedforward loop, postulated as a mechanism that quickly and directly cancels out the effects of a disturbance. Usually, feedforward control is an additional feature to feedback control and needs to be developed, elaborated, and consolidated as a proactive and anticipatory mechanism—a predisposed metacognitive stance, an empowered readiness to cope as needed—in order to enable the person to take care of everything else that may cause the processes to deviate from an intended way of being and responding.

In this work, such feedforward control is postulated as being empowered by the infusing, indwelling Holy Spirit, who coparticipates with the endeavors emerging on the believer's part. Besides this, the Spirit activates, reminds, and guides the believer along the capacity to resort to the indwelling Word (John 16:13). The allocated and consolidated law of the life-giving Spirit (Rom 8:2) at work in the substructural levels of the inner being is a feature promised in the New Covenant: "I will put my laws in their minds and I will inscribe them on their hearts" (Heb 8:10). Feedforward control systems may be invoked, following the line of reasoning employed in chapter 8, which dealt with the believer's self-efficacy empowered by the Holy Spirit.[8] The bottom level represents the natural flow of events triggered by an offense. The processes that take place along this level result in natural reactions involving feedback systems. The top-down infusion engaged by the MEC flows downward, splitting into parallel lines involving both, proactive monitoring and superposed feedforward control, acting on both sides of the naturally reactive processes involving feedback loops. Note that the employment of a superposed executive control system may override the ongoing process of reactive nature, with a proactive, purposive response to the provoking event. A schematic representation of what a feedforward control may do in a superposed fashion, as it pertains to the process of forgiveness, is depicted here.

---

8. Phillips and Harbor, *Feedback Control Systems*.

Part II: Principles Derived from the New Covenant in Marital Transactions

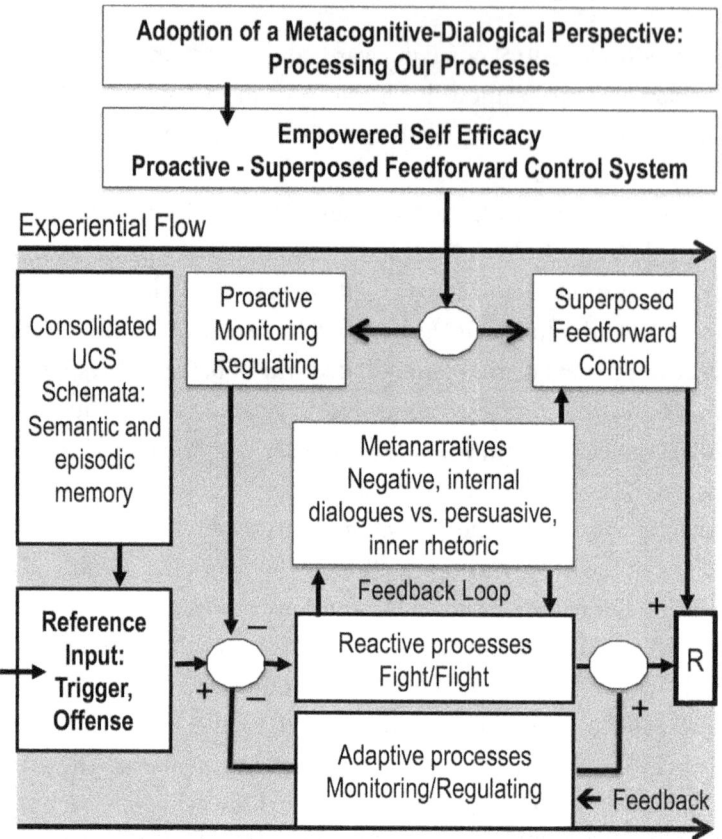

Fig. 17.4: Feedback and Empowered Feedforward Control

As stated before, information about past events, added to present contingencies, influence the ways in which the impact of a challenge is processed in view of present or future consequences. A chain of cause-and-effect (a circuit or "loop") allows for an event to feedback to itself. Arrows flowing up and down levels, as well as going sideways within a level, represent the flow of sensory-cognitive-emotive information amongst structures, processes, and events. Data is transported, transduced, and transformed—conveying interactive processes taking place between upper and lower levels of cognitive-affective, spiritual, and enactive functioning—as well as within-level processes. Although the experiential flow is from left to right, feedback loops in the processing organism may feed information back to the sending source to align, correct, enhance, and control the responses of a person. A diagram is provided (Fig.17.5), aimed at elucidating feedback and feedforward processes at work, regulated by a top-down, metacognitive-executive control system adapted to illustrate the changes from reactions to responses that enter into play in the process of forgiveness.

A Metacognitive-Dialogical Model of Forgiveness

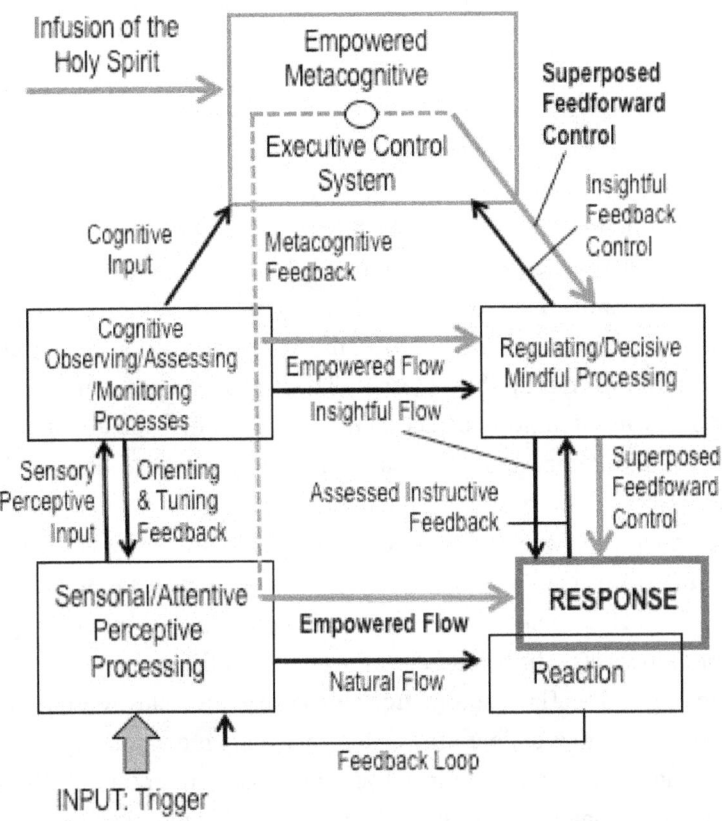

Fig. 17.5: Feedback and Feedforward Control Systems, Reactions, and Responses

The whole configuration represents a dynamic information processing system, a way of hypothetically capturing phenomena occurring within the mindset of a person facing an offensive challenge, and the need to forgive. The person may be activated by both natural and metaphysical sources (e.g., a triggering offense coming from a spouse or the nudging of the Spirit, prompting the person to respond in a unilateral, unconditional, or proactive fashion).

Usually, as processes go, the internal dialogues generated by feedback loops seem to be reinforced by an ongoing flow of a negative nature. Rumination, brooding, and the regurgitation of offenses are relentlessly fueled by feedback loops. The disturbances created by the offenses provoke the person to entrench her or his unforgiving and retaliatory feelings. What is needed is the intromission and infusion of an empowering, enabling agent—the Holy Spirit—who enters in coparticipation with the person's metacognitive-executive control agency. In this way, the person may engage a feedforward control that, in a superposed fashion, preempts and engages a self-controlled response instead of reacting in anger.

To adopt a transcending, metacognitive-dialogical perspective requires a faithful reliance on the person, the presence, and the power of the Holy Spirit, as well as the

Part II: Principles Derived from the New Covenant in Marital Transactions

ascertaining of the emergent appeal of lodged and consolidated Scripture, engaged with in a coparticipatory fashion. Such an encompassing, higher view of reality allows for a detached, as well as a purposive mindfulness, to be utilized. It is from this vantage point that a person will never feel destitute or alone in the process of forgiving, but empowered and able to proceed with the full knowledge that God not only is in control of circumstances, but is also a witness of the ongoing process. Being an imitator of God, acting in his sight, and having the certainty of his witnessing and empowering presence are the best anchor points to rely on as we engage in the process of forgiveness. We know that God knows that we are trying to walk in love.

The ruminations, conjectures, negative memories, and brooding that characterize the styles of thinking employed in internal dialogues are metacognitively caught and disengaged by means of mindful detachment. This mindful detachment is activated by the person's conscious engagement of his/her metacognitive-executive control system (MEC). In the opinion of the author, the detaching mechanism postulated—inserted in the diagram with the label MCE$_1$—is empowered by the indwelling Word and the Holy Spirit (provided that the person appropriates by faith this powerful metacognitive stance). The MEC$_1$ enters into play, disengaging the elicited, ongoing automatic reactions, and, in a regulating-modulating way, allows the person to slow down his/her fast-thinking styles. Thus, automatic snowballing and catastrophic thinking may be "converted" into slow deliberations—internal dialogues, musings, conjectures—amenable to monitoring and scrutiny. These processes are crucial in the attempt to shift from internal dialogues to internal rhetoric—self-talk with a persuasive tone, endowed with purposeful mindfulness. It is at this junction that feedforward control systems enter into play, superposing a conscious, deliberate decision to act in responsive, not reactive, fashion.

The New Covenant promises to allocate the will of God in the heart and mind of the believer seeking to imitate God's ways. As noted in the top box in Figure 17.6 (the substructural, ontological level), the interpenetration of both the Word and the Spirit is signaled as a "packaged deal" as far as the whole box goes—with arrows going down to the middle-level processes. Yet, within this box, the reader may notice arrows going up and down with a regulatory mechanism at the center. That is, the Word and the Spirit act in an interpenetrated fashion coparticipating with the human substructures (located in the upper box), where the core metanarratives are cast in values and beliefs affecting the consolidated schemata of a cognitive, affective, and enactive nature. The empowered internal persuasion of the self enters into play: the person is able to control, regulate, and command a decision to act in a forgiving fashion, dispensing forgiveness as God did.

Elaborating on the abstract notions and illustrations provided so far, the graph below may serve as a heuristic device in understanding the process as an integrated contingency and in coaching a person along this metacognitive-dialogical perspective on forgiveness.

A Metacognitive-Dialogical Model of Forgiveness

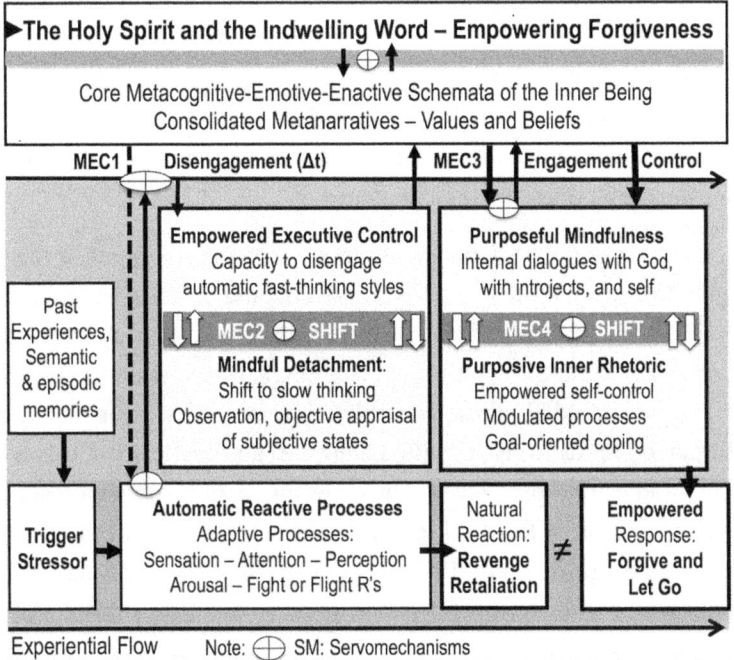

Fig. 17.6: Empowered Metacognitive-Executive Processes in Forgiveness

A final diagram depicting the proposed paradigm recapitulates all the processes that have been elaborated to this point. The nomenclature and definition of the model's elements—boxes, labels, levels, processes—are described as follows:

1. *The upper level box.* The model starts with the forgiver at the top, the person who happens to be offended—and who may be regarded as the processor-protagonist engaged in the process of the forgiveness of offenses. The diagram depicts the substructural, ontological level of the person in which the indwelling Holy Spirit and the Word of God may enter into a coparticipation with the higher cortical functions of a human being. The empowering and enabling of natural endowments takes place when the person engages his or her spiritual resources in order to think and act in a top-down fashion, enacting the executive functions that regulate all the processes described in the mediating level below. At the core of the inner being, the cognitive-emotive-enactive schemata of consolidated metanarratives are lodged and serve as the basis to start from in the process depicted. It is from this basis that values and beliefs emerge and affect the person's attitudes and behaviors that enter into play in the process of forgiveness.

2. *Bottom-up processes.* Having established the premises that enter into play from a top-down perspective, we may draw our attention to the bottom-up process that starts with the impact or stress evoked by challenging contingencies. An offense is registered (whether this stressor is an external provoking or an internally

evoked stimulus/event) by the attentive-sensory capacity of a person—depicted as a box at the bottom level, on the left corner—starting the process that runs across the diagram. At the lower level, the person's natural processes involve automatic (conditioned, adaptive) capacities. These involve several coding processes—attentive, sensory, perceptive, attributive, emotive, and enactive—and register the event as an abstracted offense.

3. *The organismic system* is depicted as a box receiving the input of the provoking stimuli. The impact of the sensed/perceived offense activates automatic processes at a base level—conditioned and reactive in nature, mediated by the autonomic nervous system (ANS), evoking fight-or-flight responses and triggering emotionally coded rapid thinking relayed to the central nervous system. The offended person tends to react immediately and automatically at this level, except that the middle and upper levels may enter into action so that a reaction may be changed by means of feedback control. The intervention of middle and upper levels engage the postulated MEC mechanisms that enter into play and modulate the process outcome.

4. *The middle level of analysis.* Running across the diagram, this level depicts the mediational processes, including the relay stations conveying coded information and activating servomechanisms and metacognitive-control mechanisms that allow for disengagement, engagement, and shifting between cognitive-emotive-behavioral processes occurring between the upper level and the bottom level, described as follows.

    a. The box that appears on top of the offending trigger (located at the middle level at the left) represents the added contributions stemming from the consolidated schemata of past experiences, comprised of unconscious (UCS), unfinished transactions negative in nature, implicit (pre-verbal, sensory) memories, and explicit (semantic and episodic) memories. This negative intrusion into the present may affect the person in a subceptive fashion (*subceptive phenomena* refers to the sense of having some awareness of what is happening, but no cognitive grasp or label to define it consciously) and become an obstacle to the process of forgiveness. On the other hand, positive memories of experiences of a forgiving nature may run in parallel and act in the opposite fashion, facilitating the process of regulating the outcome.

    b. The activation of higher processes (upper level) offers the reader a theological/natural, interactive challenge: Is it the person being offended who initiates or invokes the living Word and the Holy Spirit, or does God's prompting from above first elicit the person's capacity to engage? In the diagram, the author gives credit to the Holy Spirit for initiating the prompting;

A Metacognitive-Dialogical Model of Forgiveness

the person's "capacity within incapacity" is activated with the arrow going up—appealing to the first engagement of the metacognitive-executive control (MEC1). The MEC is a top-down mechanism that enters into action in a top-down fashion to disengage the reactive processes coming from the bottom-up (automatic, conditioned), fast-thinking processes. This allows for a mindful detachment (as if the person was pressing a clutch to disengage natural reactions from their driving automaticity).

c. The person who is able to stop the automatic, snowballing effects of a reactive nature that run along the experiential flow may engage the metacognitive-executive control (MEC2) again. This time, the endowed capacity allows one to shift from fast to slow thinking and engage in deliberate, objective mindfulness; it also promotes the detached assessment of the impacting situation/offense without the need to engage in fight-or-flight reactions, enabling the person to stay calm, collected, and objective.

d. Being endowed with a controlled, detached mindfulness, the person may further activate the metacognitive-executive control (now labeled MEC3) and regulate the flow of cognitive-emotive-behavioral processes. The person may engage his or her purposive mindfulness and deliberate with internal dialogues—with God, with introjects, and with self. Dialogues with God may be described as existential interactions between the person's middle and upper levels (the heart/mind/soul appealing to God and listening to God's voice embedded in lodged Scripture, coupled with the promptings of the Holy Spirit) with feedback and feedforward control loops entering into play. Internal dialogues with introjects and self may be empowered with objective aspects under the influence and guide of the Word and the Spirit as well, besides the naturally prompted dialogues involving themes of hurt, pain, anger, revenge, and retaliation, etc.

e. The appeal to the metacognitive-executive control (now labeled MEC4) enables the self to shift from internal dialogues (rumination, threat monitoring, brooding, deliberative arguments, counting the cost of forgiveness, and musings about losses in self-image and esteem, etc.) to internal rhetoric—persuading him- or herself to engage in judgment and decision-making in order to regulate and enact purposive behaviors leading to a mindful response (a controlled output versus the natural reaction that may occur if the empowered metacognitive-dialogical processes are not invoked). At this junction, Scripture—the Word of Christ that dwells abundantly in the inner being (Col 3:16)—may emerge, superpose, and infuse the inner rhetoric of the self with persuasive power (e.g., "forgiving one another, as God forgave you in Christ" Eph 4:32; Col 3:13). The empowered person is able to self-admonish with scriptural content and thrust, i.e., "be an imitator of God," (Eph 5:1, personalized) and decide to act on this basis.

5. *Enacting the act of forgiving.* From the inner being (top-down executive agency, or the ontological, essential, empowered self), the empowered processes follow. These involve the person's triggered attention, perception, and fast-thinking reactions. The appeal to the metacognitive-executive control system allows for a mindful detachment and cessation of the triggered automatic processes. The detached yet mindful monitoring of the offenses may take place in a dialogical fashion. Then, the ongoing appeal to the executive control allows for a feedforward shift to internal rhetoric with the persuasion to engage in a proactive, willful, and controlled response. Note the contrast between the lower-level boxes at the right, indicating a natural reaction versus an empowered response at the end of the experiential flow. This change is possible, and with repeated "training in godliness," it becomes part of the repertoire of the forgiving person.

CONCLUSION

The model presented in this chapter is an example of the possibility that exists to live the terms of the New Covenant in intimate relations, exemplified in one of its main clauses: forgiving one another as God forgave us in Christ. The same model may apply to the rest of the principles enunciated in this work: to be and act in unilateral, unconditional, and proactive fashion; to dispense grace and mercy; to promote intimacy; and so on. As this chapter indicates, in order to forgive as God forgave us in Christ, we need to consider the challenging option to imitate God as empowered persons. Human effort and willpower are essential qualities that enter into this process, but as experience goes, these qualities come short or are not enough to obey such a high command. The infusion of the Holy Spirit at an ontological level, permeating the middle level depicting cognitive-emotive and motivational-enactive processes, is essential.

This book has emphasized the biblical-theological basis to be employed in elaborating models of integration in the field of Christian psychotherapy and counseling. This metacognitive-dialogical model may serve as a heuristic device in considering the ways in which psychotherapists, counselors, and pastors may assist, guide, coach, or empower the capacities of a believer in dealing with offenses, engaged in a Spirit-empowered, metacognitive-dialogical process of forgiveness. The same approach may be employed to encourage believers to accept the challenge—to be imitators of God, as dearly beloved children, and walk in love—in full: to enact *all* the principles derived from the New Covenant elaborated on in this work. After all, it is the best, God-given paradigm for human relations available.

Bibliography

Ackerman, Nathan W. *The Psychodynamics of Family Life.* New York, NY: Basic, 1958.

Adams, Jay E. *Competent to Counsel.* Nutley, NJ: Presbyterian and Reformed, 1975.

———. *Marriage, Divorce, and Remarriage in the Bible.* Grand Rapids, MI: Zondervan, 1986.

Allis, Oswald T. "Modern Dispensationalism and the Doctrine of the Unity of Scripture." *The Evangelical Quarterly* 8 (1936) 22–35.

Allport, Gordon W. *The Nature of Personality.* Westport, CT: Greenwood Press Reprint. Facsimile of 1950 edition. Reading, MA: Addison-Wesley, 1975.

Anderson, Raymond. *On Being Human: Essays in Theological Anthropology.* Grand Rapids, MI: Eerdmans, 1982.

Anderson, Raymond, and Dennis Guernsey. *On Being Family: Essays on a Social Theology of the Family.* Grand Rapids, MI: Eerdmans, 1985.

Atkinson, David J. *To Have and to Hold: The Marriage Covenant and the Discipline of Divorce.* Grand Rapids, MI: Eerdmans, 1981.

Augsburger, David W. *Caring Enough to Forgive.* Ventura, CA: Regal, 1981.

———. *Cherishable: Love and Marriage.* Scottdale, PA: Herald, 1971.

———. *Helping People Forgive.* Louisville, KY: John Knox, 1996.

———. *The New Freedom of Forgiveness.* Chicago, IL: Moody, 2000.

Azrin, Nathan H., et al. "Reciprocity Counseling: A Rapid Learning-Based Procedure for Marital Counseling." *Behaviour Research and Therapy* 11 (1973) 365–82.

Baab, Otto J. "Marriage." *The Interpreter's Dictionary of the Bible,* ed. by George Arthur Buttrick, 284. New York, NY: Abingdon, 1962.

Bacchiocchi, Samuele. *The Marriage Covenant: A Biblical Study on Marriage, Divorce, and Remarriage.* Berrien Springs, MI: Biblical Perspectives, 2006.

Bach, George R., and Peter Wyden. *The Intimate Enemy: How to Fight Fair in Love and Marriage.* New York, NY: Avon, 1968.

Baker, Charles. F. *A Dispensational Theology.* Grand Rapids, MI: Grace Bible College, 1971.

Ball, John. *A Treatise of the Covenant of Grace.* Facsimile of 1645 edition. Liskeard: Exposure, 2006.

Balswick, Jack O. *Men at the Crossroads: Beyond Traditional Roles and Modern Options.* Downers Grove, IL: InterVarsity, 1992.

Balswick, Jack O., and Judith K. Balswick. *The Family: A Christian Perspective on the Contemporary Home.* Grand Rapids, MI: Baker, 1991.

———. *A Model for Marriage: Covenant, Grace, Empowerment, and Intimacy.* Downers Grove, IL: IVP Academic, 2006.

———. "A Theological Basis for Family Relationships." *Journal of Psychology and Christianity* 6.3 (1987) 37–49.

Bandura, Albert. *Self-Efficacy: The Exercise of Control.* New York, NY: W. H. Freeman, 1997.

———. *Social Learning Theory.* Englewood Cliffs, NJ: Prentice Hall, 1977.

Bibliography

Barth, Karl. *Church Dogmatics III / 1*, ed. by George W. Bromiley and Thomas F. Torrance. Edinburgh: T & T. Clark, 1969.

Barth, Markus. *Ephesians: Translation and Commentary on Chapters Four to Six*. Garden City, NY: Doubleday, 1974.

Beavers, Robert W. *Successful Marriage: A Family Systems Approach to Couples Therapy*. New York, NY: Norton, 1985.

Beatty, Melody. *Codependent No More: How to Stop Controlling Others and Start Caring for Yourself*. 2nd rev. ed. Center City, MN: Hazelden, 1987.

Beck, Aaron. T. *Cognitive Therapy of Depression*. New York, NY: Guilford, 1987.

Beck, Judith, S. *Cognitive Therapy: Basics and Beyond*. 2nd ed. New York, NY: Guilford, 2011.

Bem, Daryl. *Beliefs, Attitudes, and Human Affairs: Basic Concepts in Psychology*. Belmont, CA: Brooks/Cole, 1970.

Benson, Herbert. *The Relaxation Response*. New York, NY: Avon, 1976.

Berg, Insoo K. *Family Based Services: A Solution-Focused Approach*. New York, NY: W.W. Norton., 1994.

Binswanger, Ludwig. "The Existential Analysis School of Thought." In *Existence*. New York, NY: Basic, 1958.

Blomberg, Craig L. *Matthew: An Exegetical and Theological Exposition of Holy Scripture*. The New American Commentary 22. Nashville, TN: Broadman, 1992.

Bogue, Carl. "Jonathan Edwards on the Covenant of Grace." *Soli Deo Gloria: Essays in Reformed Theology*, ed. by John H. Gerstner and R. C. Sproul. Nutley, NJ: Presbyterian and Reformed, 1976.

Bonhoeffer, Dietrich. *The Cost of Discipleship*. New York, NY: MacMillan, 1963.

———. *Life Together: The Classic Exploration of Faith in Community*. San Francisco, CA: Harper, 1978.

Bornstein, Philip H., and Marcy Bornstein. *Marital Therapy: A Behavioral- Communications Approach*. New York, NY: Pergamon, 1986.

Boszormenyi-Nagy, Ivan, and Barbara R. Krasner. *Between Give and Take: A Clinical Guide to Contextual Therapy*. New York, NY: Brunner/Mazel, 1986.

Bowen, Murray. *Family Therapy in Clinical Practice*. New York, NY: J. Aronson, 1978.

Bowlby, John. *A Secure Base: Parent-Child Attachment and Healthy Human Development*. London: Routledge, 1988.

Brebner, J. T., and A. T. Welford. "Introduction: An Historical Background Sketch." In *Reaction Times*, ed. by A. T. Welford, 1–23. New York, NY: Academic, 1980.

Bright, Vonette Z., and Bill Bright. *Managing Stress in Marriage*. San Bernardino, CA: Here's Life, 1990.

Brown, Kirk W., et al. *A Handbook of Mindfulness*. New York, NY: Guilford, 2015.

Bruce, Frederick F. *The Epistle to the Hebrews*. Rev. ed. Grand Rapids, MI: Eerdmans, 2004.

Brueggemann, Walter. *The Covenanted Self*, ed. by Patrick D. Miller. Minneapolis, MN: Fortress, 1999.

———. *The Psalms of Life and Faith*, ed. by Patrick D. Miller. Minneapolis, MN: Fortress, 1995.

Brunner, Emil. *Love and Marriage*. London: Fontana/Collins, 1972.

Buber, Martin. *Between Man and Man*. London: Fontana/Collins, 1963.

——— *I and Thou*. New York, NY: Scribner, 1958.

Burke, Cormac. *Covenanted Happiness: Love and Commitment in Marriage*. Princeton, NJ: Scepter, 1999.

Burrows, M. "The Basis for Israelite Marriage." *American Oriental Society* 15 (1938) 53–71.

Calvin, Jean. *Calvin: Institutes of the Christian Religion.* Vols. 1–2, ed. by John T. McNeil. Philadelphia: Westminster John Knox, 1960.

———. *Hebrews and 1 & 2 Peter.* Vol. 12. Grand Rapids, MI: Eerdmans, 1994.

Cautela, Joseph R., and Patricia A. Wisocky. "The Thought-Stopping Procedure: Description, Applications, and Learning Theory Interpretations." *Psychological Record* 2 (1977) 255–64.

Chapman, Gary. *Covenant Marriage: Building Communication and Intimacy.* Nashville, TN: Broadman & Holman, 2003.

Chartier, Myron. "Parenting: A Theological Model." *Journal of Psychology and Theology* 6 (1978) 54–61.

Clark, Stephen B. *Man and Woman in Christ.* Ann Arbor, MI: Servant, 1980.

Clinebell, Howard. *Growth Counseling for Marriage Enrichment.* Philadelphia, PA: Fortress, 1975.

Cloud, Henry, and John Townsend. *Boundaries.* Grand Rapids, MI: Zondervan, 1992.

———. *Boundaries in Marriage.* Grand Rapids, MI: Zondervan, 2002.

Collins, Gary R. *The Biblical Basis of Christian Counseling for People Helpers.* Colorado Springs, CO: NavPress, 1993.

———. *Christian Counseling: A Comprehensive Guide.* Rev. ed. Dallas, TX: Word, 1988.

———. (Ed.) *Resources for Christian Counseling.* Dallas, TX: Word, 1986–1991.

Cook, Kay V., and Lance Lee. *Man and Woman: Alone and Together.* Wheaton, IL: Victor, 1992.

Cosgrove, Lisa. "When Labels Mask Oppression: Helping Counselors in Training to Think Critically about Psychiatric Diagnosis." *Journal of Mental Health Counseling* 27 (2005) 283–96.

Cosgrove, Lisa, and C. Flynn. "Marginalized Mothers: Parenting without a Home." *Analysis of Social Issues and Public Policy* 5 (2005) 127–43.

Cosgrove, Lisa, and Varda Konstam. "Forgiveness and Forgetting: Clinical Implications for Mental Health Counselors." *Journal of Mental Health Counseling* 30.1 (2008) 1–13.

Covey, Stephen R. *The Seven Habits of Highly Successful People.* Rev. ed. New York, NY: Free Press, 2004.

Crabb, Lawrence J. *Connecting.* Nashville, TN: Word, 1997.

———. *Effective Biblical Counseling.* Grand Rapids., MI: Zondervan, 1977.

———. *The Marriage Builder: A Blueprint for Couples and Counselors.* Grand Rapids, MI: Zondervan, 1982.

Cross, Frank M. *Canaanite Myth and Hebrew Epic: Essays in the History of the Religions of Israel.* Cambridge, MA: Harvard University Press, 1997.

———. *From Epic to Canon: History and Literature in Ancient Israel.* Baltimore, MD: Johns Hopkins University Press, 2000.

Davenport, Donna S. "The Functions of Anger and Forgiveness: Guidelines for Psychotherapy with Victims." *Psychotherapy: Theory, Research, Practice, Training* 28 (1991) 140–44.

Deary, Ian J., et al. "A Free, Easy-to-Use, Computer-Based Simple and Four-Choice Reaction Time Programme: The Deary-Liewald Reaction Time Task." *Behavioral Research Methods* 43 (2011) 258–68.

Decker, Rodney J. *Christian Scholarship and the Church.* Greenville, SC: Bob Jones University, 2008.

Bibliography

———. "The New Covenant and the Church." *Bibliotheca Sacra* 152 (1995) 290–305; 431–56.

De Jong, Peter, and Insoo K. Berg. *Interviewing for Solutions*. 2nd ed. Pacific Grove, CA: Brooks/Cole, 2002.

Denton, Roy T., and Michael W. Martin. "Defining Forgiveness: An Empirical Exploration of the Process and Role." *American Journal of Family Therapy* 26 (1998) 281–92.

Der, G., and Ian J. Deary. "Age and Sex Differences in Reaction Time in Adulthood: Results from the United Kingdom Health and Lifestyle Survey." *Psychology and Aging* 21.1 (2006) 62–73.

De Shazer, Steve. *Clues: Investigating Solutions in Brief Therapy*. New York, NY: W. W. Norton, 1988.

Dobson, James. *The Complete Marriage and Family Home Reference Guide*. Wheaton, IL: Tyndale, 2000.

———. *Dare to Discipline*. Wheaton, IL: Tyndale House, 1970.

———. *Love for a Lifetime: Building a Marriage That Will Go the Distance*. Portland, OR: Multnomah, 2004.

Dumbrell, William J. *Covenant and Creation: A Theology of Old Testament Covenants*. Rev. ed. Eugene, OR: Wipf & Stock, 2009.

Dunstan, Gordon R. "The Marriage Covenant." *Theology* 78 (1975) 244–52.

Edwards, Jonathan. *The Works of Jonathan Edwards*. Vols. 1–2, ed. by Sereno Edwards Dwight and Edward Hickman. First published in 1834. Carlisle, PA: Banner of Truth, 1974.

Eichrodt, Walther. *Theology of the Old Testament*. Translated by John Austin Baker. Philadelphia: Westminster, 1961.

Emmerson, Grace I. "Women in Ancient Israel." In *The World of Ancient Israel: Sociological, Anthropological Perspectives*, ed. by Ronald E. Clements, 371–84. Cambridge, UK: Cambridge University Press, 1989.

Engelsma, David J. *Marriage: The Mystery of Christ and the Church*. Grandville, MI: Reformed Free, 1998.

Enright, Robert D. *Forgiveness Is a Choice*. Washington, DC: American Psychological Association, 2001.

Enright, Robert D., and Richard P. Fitzgibbons. *Helping Clients to Forgive: An Empirical Guide for Resolving Anger and Restoring Hope*. Washington, DC: American Psychological Association, 2000.

Enright, Robert D., and Robert L. Zell. "Problems Encountered When We Forgive One Another." *Journal of Psychology and Christianity* 8 (1989) 52–60.

Erikson, Erik. *Childhood and Society*. New York, NY: W. W. Norton, 1978.

Fee, Gordon. *The First Epistle to the Corinthians*. Grand Rapids, MI: Eerdmans, 1987.

Fennel, David L. "Characteristics of Long-Term First Marriages." *Journal of Mental Health Counseling* 15 (1993) 446–60.

Filley, Alan C. *Interpersonal Conflict Resolution*. Glenview, IL: Scott, Foresman, 1975.

Finch, John B. *A Christian Existential Psychology: The Contributions of John G. Finch*, ed. by H. Newton Malony. Washington, DC: University Press of America, 1980.

Fine, M. *Disruptive Voices: The Possibilities of Feminist Research*. Ann Arbor, MI: University of Michigan Press, 1992.

Framo, Joseph L. *Family-of-Origin Therapy: An Intergenerational Approach*. New York, NY: Brunner/Mazel, 1992.

Franklin, Clyde W. *The Changing Definition of Masculinity*. New York: Plenum, 1984.

Freud, Anna. *The Ego and the Mechanisms of Defense.* 10th ed. New York, NY: International Universities Press, 1957.

Friesen, Deloss D., and Ruby M. Friesen. *Counseling and Marriage.* Resources for Christian Counseling. Vol. 19. Dallas, TX: Word, 1989.

Fromm, Erich. *The Art of Loving.* New York, NY: Bantam, 1956.

———. *Escape from Freedom.* New York, NY: Avon, 1969.

Fruzzetti, Alan E., and Marsha M. Linehan. *The High-Conflict Couple: A Dialectical Behavior Therapy Guide to Finding Peace, Intimacy, and Validation.* Oakland, CA: New Harbinger, 2006.

Gangel, Kenneth O. "Toward a Biblical Theology of Marriage and Family." *Journal of Psychology and Theology* 5 (1977) 55–59; 150–62; 247–59; 318–31.

Gardner, Howard. *Truth, Beauty, and Goodness Reframed: Educating for the Virtues in the Twenty-First Century.* New York, NY: Basic, 2011.

Goldenberg, Irene, and Herbert Goldenberg. *Family Therapy: An Overview.* 7th ed. Belmont, CA: 2008.

Gordon, Kristina C., et al. "The Use of Forgiveness in Marital Therapy." In *Forgiveness,* ed. by Michael McCullough, et al. New York, NY: Guilford, 2000.

Gottsdanker, R. "The Attaining and Maintaining of Preparation." In *Attention and Performance.* Vol. 5, ed. by P. M. A. Rabbitt and S. Dornic, 33–49. London, UK: Academic, 1975.

Gottman, John M. *Marital Interaction: Experimental Investigations.* New York, NY: Academic, 1979.

Gottman, John, et al. "Behavior Exchange Theory and Marital Decision Making." *Journal of Personality and Social Psychology* 34.1 (1976) 14–23.

Gottman, John M., and Nan Silver. *The Seven Principles for Making Marriage Work: A Practical Guide from the Country's Foremost Relationship Expert.* New York, NY: Three Rivers, 2000.

Gottman, John M., et al. *Ten Lessons to Transform Your Marriage.* New York, NY: Three Rivers, 2007.

Grace, Mike, and Joyce Grace. *A Joyful Meeting.* St. Paul, MN: International Marriage Encounter, 1980.

Greenberg, Leslie S., and Rhonda N. Goldman. *Emotion-Focused Therapy: The Dynamics of Emotion, Love, and Power.* Washington, DC: American Psychological Association, 2008.

Greenberg, Leslie S., and Susan M. Johnson. *Emotionally Focused Therapy for Couples.* New York, NY: Guilford, 1988.

Grenz, Stanley J. *The Social God and the Relational Self.* Louisville, KY: Westminster John Knox, 2001.

Grudem, Wayne. *Biblical Foundations for Manhood and Womanhood.* Wheaton, IL: Crossway, 2002.

———. "The Meaning of κεφαλη ("Head"): An Evaluation of New Evidence, Real and Alleged." *Journal of the Evangelical Theological Society* 44.1 (2001) 25–65.

Gruenler, Royce. *The Trinity in the Gospel of John: A Thematic Commentary on the Fourth Gospel.* Grand Rapids, MI: Baker, 1986.

Guernsey, Dennis B. *The Family Covenant: Love and Forgiveness in the Christian Home.* Pasadena, CA: Hope, 1999.

Guinness, Os. *Time for Truth: Living Free in a World of Lies, Hype, and Spin.* Grand Rapids, MI: Baker, 2002.

Bibliography

Haeri, Shahla. *Law of Desire: Temporary Marriage in Shi'i Iran.* Syracuse, NY: Syracuse University Press, 1989.

Hafemann, Scott. J., and Paul R. House, eds. *Central Themes in Biblical Theology: Mapping Unity in Diversity.* Grand Rapids, MI: Baker, 2007.

Hahn, Scott W. "Covenant in the Old and New Testaments: Some Current Research (1994–2004)." *Currents in Biblical Research.* 3.2 (2005) 263–92.

———. *Kinship by Covenant: A Canonical Approach to the Fulfillment of God's Saving Promises.* Rev. ed. New Haven, CT: Yale University Press, 2009.

Haley, Jay. *Problem-Solving Therapy.* San Francisco, CA: Jossey-Bass, 1976.

———. *Strategies of Psychotherapy.* New York: Grune & Straton, Inc., 1976.

Hall, Gary. "Origin of the Marriage Metaphor." *Hebrew Studies* 23 (1982) 169-71.

Hanson, Paul D. *Isaiah 40—46.* Louisville: John Knox, 1995.

Harakas, Stanley S. "Covenant Marriage: Reflections from an Eastern Orthodox Perspective." In *Covenant Marriage in Comparative Perspective,* ed. by John White Jr. and Eliza Ellison, 92–123. Grand Rapids, MI: Eerdmans, 2005.

Hardacre, Helen. "The Impact of Fundamentalisms on Women, the Family, and Interpersonal Relations." In *Fundamentalisms and Society,* ed. by Martin E. Marty and R. Scott Appleby. Chicago, IL: University of Chicago Press, 1993.

Hargrave, Terry D., and James N. Sells. "The Development of a Forgiveness Scale." *Journal of Marital and Family Therapy* 23.1 (1997) 41–62.

Harley, Willard. *His Needs, Her Needs.* Old Tappan, NJ: Flemming H. Revell, 1986.

Harris, Alexander H. S., and Carl E. Thoresen. "Forgiveness, Unforgiveness, Health, and Disease." In *Handbook of Forgiveness,* ed. by E. L. Worthington, Jr. New York, NY: Brunner-Routledge, 2005.

Harris, Alexander H. S., et al. "Spiritually and Religiously Oriented Health Interventions." *Journal of Health Psychology* 4.3 (1999) 413–33.

Harrison, Roland K. *Introduction to the Old Testament.* Grand Rapids, MI: Eerdmans, 1969.

Hartman, William E., and Marilyn Fithian. *Treatment of Sexual Dysfunction.* Kanham, MD: Jason Aronson, 1994.

Hebb, Donald O. *The Organization of Behavior.* New York, NY: Wiley & Sons, 1949.

Hermans, Hubert J. M. "Voicing the Self: From Information Processing to Dialogical Interchange." *Psychological Bulletin* 119.1 (1996) 31–50.

Hermans, Hubert J. M., et al. "The Dialogical Self: Beyond Individualism and Rationalism." *American Psychologist* 47 (1992) 23–33.

Hillers, Delbert R. *Covenant: The History of a Biblical Idea.* Baltimore, MD: Johns Hopkins University Press, 1969.

Holmes, Arthur F. *All Truth Is God's Truth.* Grand Rapids, MI: Eerdmans, 1977.

Horton, Michael. *God of Promise: Introducing Covenant Theology.* Grand Rapids, MI: Baker, 2006.

Huber, Charles H. *Ethical, Legal, and Professional Issues in the Practice of Marriage and Family Therapy.* 2nd ed. New York, NY: Merrill, Macmillan Co, 1994.

Hugenberger, Gordon. *Marriage as a Covenant.* New York, NY: E. J. Brill, 1994.

Humphrey, Frederick G. *Marital Therapy.* Englewood Cliffs, NJ: Prentice-Hall, 1983.

Inhelder, Bärbel. *Piaget Today.* London: Erlbaum, 1987.

Intrater, Keith. *Covenant Relationships: A More Excellent Way.* Shippensburg, PA: Destiny Image, 1989.

Ironside, Henry A. *The Great Parenthesis: Timely Messages on the Interval between the 69th and 70th Weeks of Daniel's Prophecy.* Grand Rapids, MI: Zondervan, 1943.

Jackson, Don. "Family Rules: Marital Quid Pro Quo." *Archives of General Psychiatry* 12 (1965) 389–94.

Jacobson, Neil S. "Behavioral Marital Therapy." In *Handbook of Marital Therapy*, ed. by Alan S. Gurman and D. P. Kniskern. New York, NY: Brunner / Mazel, 1981.

Jacobson, Neil S., and Gayla Margolin. *Marital Therapy: Strategies Based on Social Learning and Behavior Exchange Principles.* New York, NY: Brunner / Mazel, 1979.

Jakobs, O., et al. "Effects of Timing and Movement Uncertainty Implicate the Temporo-Parietal Junction in the Prediction of Forthcoming Motor Actions." *NeuroImage* 47.2 (2009) 667–77.

Johnson, James T. "Marriage as Covenant in Early Protestant Thought: Its Development and Implications." In *Covenant Marriage in Comparative Perspective*, ed by. John Witte Jr. and Eliza Ellison, 124–52. Grand Rapids, MI: Eerdmans, 2005.

Johnson, Susan M. *The Practice of Emotionally Focused Couple Therapy: Creating Connection.* 2nd ed. New York, NY: Brunner-Routledge, 2004.

Jones, Lynn K. "Emotionally Focused Therapy with Couples: The Social Work Connection." *Social Work Today* 9.3 (2009) 18.

Kafka, Franz. *In the Penal Colony.* Translated by Willa and Edwin Muir. New York, NY: Schocken Books, 1948.

Kahneman, Daniel. *Thinking, Fast and Slow.* New York, NY: Farrar, Straus and Giroux, 2011.

Kaiser, Walter C. Jr. "The Old Promise and the New Covenant: Jeremiah 31:31–34." *Journal of Evangelical Theological Society* 15 (1974) 11–23.

———. *Toward an Old Testament Theology.* Grand Rapids, MI: Zondervan, 1991.

Kaplan, Helen S. *Disorders of Sexual Desire.* New York, NY: Simon & Schuster, 1979.

Karpel, Mark A. *Evaluating Couples: A Handbook for Practitioners.* New York, NY: Norton, 1994.

Katz, J., et al. "Individual Differences in Self-Appraisals and Responses to Dating Violence Scenarios." *Violence and Victims* 12.3 (1997) 256–76.

Keller, Timothy, and Kathy Keller. *The Meaning of Marriage: Facing the Complexities of Commitment with the Wisdom of God.* New York, NY: Dutton, 2011.

Kierkegaard, Søren. *The Concept of Anxiety.* Chester, West Sussex: Princeton University Press, 1981.

———. *The Sickness unto Death.* Chester, West Sussex: Princeton University Press, 1983.

Kippley, John F. *Sex and the Marriage Covenant: A Basis for Morality.* San Francisco, CA: Ignatius, 2005.

Kitchen, Kenneth A. *Ancient Orient and Old Testament.* Chicago, IL: InterVarsity, 1966.

———. "The Fall and Rise of Covenant, Law, and Treaty." *Tyndale Bulletin* 40.1 (1989) 118–35.

Klein, Melanie. *Love, Guilt, and Reparation, and Other Works.* In *The Writings of M. Klein, 1921–1945.* Vol. 1. New York, NY: Delacorte, 1975.

Kline, Meredith G. *Images of the Spirit.* Grand Rapids, MI: Baker, 1980.

———. *Kingdom Prologue: Genesis Foundations for a Covenantal Worldview.* Rev ed. Eugene, OR: Wipf & Stock, 2006.

———. *The Structure of Biblical Authority.* Rev. ed. Eugene, OR: Wipf & Stock, 1997.

———. *Treaty of the Great King: The Covenant Structure of Deuteronomy.* Grand Rapids, MI: Eerdmans, 1963.

Konstam, Varda, et al. "Toward Forgiveness: The Role of Shame, Guilt, Anger, and Empathy." *Counseling and Values* 46 (2001) 26–39.

Köstenberger, Andreas J., and David W. Jones. *Marriage and the Family: Biblical Essentials.* Wheaton, IL: Crossway, 2012.

Kramer, Samuel N. *The Sumerians: Their History, Culture, and Character.* Chicago, IL: University of Chicago Press, 1963.

L'Abate, Luciano, and Sherry McHenry. *Handbook of Marital Interventions.* New York: Grune and Stratton, 1983.

Ladd, George. *The Gospel of the Kingdom.* Repr. Grand Rapids, MI: Eerdmans, 1959.

Lajoie, Y., and S. P. Gallagher. "Predicting Falls within the Elderly Community: Comparison of Postural Sway, Reaction Time, the Berg Balance Scale, and the Activities-Specific Balance Confidence (ABC) Scale for Comparing Fallers and Non-Fallers." *Archives of Gerontology and Geriatrics* 38.1 (2004) 11–25.

Lakatos, Imre. "Falsification and the Methodology of Scientific Research Programmes." In *Criticism and the Growth of Knowledge,* ed. by Imre Lakatos and Alan Musgrave, 192–94. Cambridge, UK: Cambridge University Press, 1970.

Lamb, Sharon. "Forgiveness Therapy: The Context and Conflict." *Journal of Theoretical and Philosophical Psychology* 25 (2005) 61–80.

Lamb, Sharon, and Jeffrie G. Murphy, eds. *Before Forgiving: Cautionary Views of Forgiveness in Psychotherapy.* New York, NY: Oxford University Press, 2002.

Lawler, Michael G. "Marriage as a Covenant in the Catholic Tradition." In *Covenant Marriage in Comparative Perspective,* ed. by John Witte Jr. and Eliza Ellison, 70–91. Grand Rapids, MI: Eerdmans, 2005.

Lederer, William, and Don Jackson. *The Mirages of Marriage.* New York, NY: Norton, 1968.

Lerner, Harriet. *The Dance of Anger: A Woman's Guide to Changing Patterns of Intimate Relationships.* New York: Harper and Row, 1985.

Levy, David. *Love and Sex with Robots: The Evolution of Human-Robot Sex Relationships.* New York, NY: Harper Perennial, 2008.

Lincoln, Andrew T. *Ephesians.* World Biblical Commentary. Vol. 42. Nashville, TN: Nelson, 1990.

Linehan, Marsha M. *DBT Skills Training Manual.* New York, NY: Guilford, 2014.

———. *Skills Training Manual for Treating Borderline Personality Disorders.* New York, NY: Guilford, 1993.

Lowery, Fred. *Covenant Marriage: Staying Together for Life.* West Monroe, LA: Howard, 2002.

Luskin, Frederic. *Forgive for Good: A Proven Prescription for Health and Happiness.* San Francisco, CA: Harper, 2002.

Luther, Martin. *Concerning Christian Liberty.* Translated by R. S. Grignon. Charlottesville, VA: University of Virginia Library, 2001.

MacAdams, Dan P. *The Stories We Live By: Personal Myths and the Making of the Self.* New York, NY: Guilford, 1997.

Mace, David R. *Getting Ready for Marriage.* Nashville, TN: Abingdon, 1985.

Mace, David R., and Vera Mace. *How to Have a Happy Marriage.* Nashville, TN: Abingdon, 1984.

Madanes, Cloe. *Strategic Family Therapy.* San Francisco, CA: Jossey-Bass, 1981.

Mahler, Margaret. *The Psychological Birth of the Human Infant: Symbiosis and Individuation.* New York, NY: Basic, 1975.

Mahoney, Michael J., and Bobby G. DeMonbreun. "Confirmatory Bias in Scientists and Non-Scientists." *Cognitive Therapy and Research*. (1977).

Maldonado, Jorge. *Even in the Best Families: The Family of Jesus and Other Biblical Families Like Ours*. New York, NY: World Council of Churches, 1997.

Malony, H. Newton. *Christian Existential Psychology*. Washington: University Press of America, 1980.

———. *Integration Musings: Thoughts on Being a Christian Professional*. Pasadena, CA: Integration, 1986.

———. *Win-Win Relationships: 9 Strategies for Settling Personal Conflicts without Waging War*. Nashville, TN: Broadman & Holman, 1995.

Margalit, Avishai. *The Ethics of Memory*. Cambridge, MA: Harvard University Press, 2002.

Margolin, Gayla. "Behavior Exchange in Happy and Unhappy Marriages: A Family Cycle Perspective." *Behavior Therapy* 12.3 (1981) 329–43.

Martin, Grant R. *Counseling for Family Violence and Abuse*. Vol. 6. Resources for Christian Counseling. Waco, TX: Word, 1987.

Maslow, Abraham H. "A Theory of Human Motivation." *Psychological Review* 50 (1943) 370–96.

Masters, William H., and Virginia Johnson. *Human Sexuality*. New York, NY: HarperCollins, 1991.

May, Rollo. *The Discovery of Being: Writings in Existential Psychology*. New York, NY: Norton, 1983.

———. *Existence: A New Dimension in Psychiatry and Psychology*. New York, NY: Basic, 1958.

———. *Psychology and the Human Dilemma*. Princeton, NJ: Van Nostrand, 1967.

McCarthy, Dennis J. *Old Testament Covenant: A Survey of Current Opinions*. Richmond, VA: John Knox, 1972.

———. *Treaty and Covenant: A Study in Form in the Ancient Oriental Documents and in the Old Testament*. 2nd ed. Rome: Biblical Institute, 1981.

McCoy, Charles S. *The Covenant Theology of Johannes Cocceius*. New Haven, CT: Yale University Press, 1956.

McCullough, Michael E. *Beyond Revenge: The Evolution of the Forgiveness Instinct*. San Francisco, CA: Jossey-Bass, 2008.

McCullough, Michael E., and Jo-Ann Tsang. "Forgiveness, Forbearance, and Time: The Temporal Unfolding of Transgression-Related Interpersonal Motivation." *Journal of Personality and Social Psychology* 84 (2003) 540–57.

McCullough, Michael E., et al. "Vengefulness: Relationships with Forgiveness, Rumination, Well-Being, and the Big Five." *Journal of Personality and Social Psychology* 27 (2001) 601–610.

McCullough, Michael E., and Charlotte V. O. Witvliet. "The Psychology of Forgiveness." In *Handbook of Positive Psychology*, ed. by C. R. Snyder and Shane J. Lopez, 446–58. New York, NY: Oxford University Press, 2002.

McGrath, Alister. *The Twilight of Atheism: The Rise and Fall of Disbelief in the Modern World*. New York, NY: Galilee Trade, 2006.

McKenzie, Steven L. and Howard N. Wallace. "Covenant Themes in Malachi." *CBQ* 45 (1983) 549–63.

McLean, Stuart "The Language of Covenant and a Theology of the Family." Paper presented at seminar. *Consultation on a Theology of the Family*. Fuller Theological Semnary, 1984.

Bibliography

McMinn, Mark R. *Cognitive Therapy Techniques in Christian Counseling.* Dallas, TX: Word, 1991.

Meichenbaum, Donald. *Stress Inoculation Training.* Elmsford, NY: Pergamon, 1985.

Mendenhall, George E. "Covenant Forms in Israelite Tradition." *Biblical Archaeologist* 17.3 (1954) 50–76.

———. "Law and Covenant in Israel and the Ancient Near East." *Biblical Archaeologist* 17.2 (May 1954) 26–44; 17.3 (September 1954) 49–76.

Milgrom, Jacob. *Cult and Conscience: The Asham and the Priestly Doctrine of Repentance.* Leiden: Brill, 1976.

Miller, Geoffrey D. *Marriage in the Book of Tobit.* Berlin: Walter de Gruyter, 2011.

Minuchin, Salvador. *Families and Family Therapy.* Cambridge, MA: Harvard University Press, 1974.

Monk, Gerald, et al. *Narrative Therapy in Practice: The Archaeology of Hope.* San Francisco, CA: Jossey Bass, 1997.

Morgan, Edmund S. The *Puritan Family: Religion and Domestic Relations in Seventeenth-Century England.* New York, NY: Harper & Row, 1966

Murray, John. "Covenant Theology." *Collected Writings of John Murray.* Vol. 4. Carlisle, PA: Banner of Truth, 1982.

Nadelson, Carol C. "Marital Therapy from a Psychoanalytical Perspective." In *Marriage and Marital Therapy,* ed. by Thomas J. Paolino and Barbara S. McCrady. New York, NY: Brunner-Mazel, 1978.

Naylor, Peter J. *The Language of Covenant: A Structural Analysis of the Semantic Field of Berit in Biblical Hebrew, with Particular Reference to the Book of Genesis.* Oxford: Oxford University Press, 1980.

Neidig, Peter H., and Dale H. Friedman. *Spouse Abuse: A Treatment Program for Couples.* Champaign, IL: Research, 1984.

Neufeld, Ephraim. *Ancient Hebrew Marriage Laws: With Special References to General Semitic Laws and Customs.* London: Longmans, Green and Co., 1944.

Newell, William R. *Hebrews, Verse by Verse: A Classic Evangelical Commentary.* Grand Rapids, MI: Kregel Classics, 1995.

Nicholson, Ernest W. *God and His People: Covenant and Theology in the Old Testament.* New York: Oxford University Press, 1988.

Niehaus, Jeffrey J. *God at Sinai.* Grand Rapids, MI: Zondervan, 1995.

———. "An Argument Against Theologically Constructed Covenants." *Journal of Evangelical Theological Studies* 50.2 (2007) 259–73.

———. "Covenant: An Idea in the Mind of God." *Journal of the Evangelical Theological Society* 52.2 (2009) 225–46.

———. "Covenant and Narrative, God and Time." *Journal of the Evangelical Theological Society* 53.3 (2010) 535–59.

Nienkamp, Jean. *Internal Rhetorics: Toward a History and Theory of Self-Persuasion.* Carbondale, IL: Southern Illinois, 2001.

Norwood, Robin. *Women Who Love Too Much.* Repr. New York, NY: Pocket Books, 2008.

Novak, David. "Jewish Marriage: Nature, Covenant, and Contract." In *Covenant Marriage in Comparative Perspective,* ed. by John White Jr. and Eliza Ellison, 26–52. Grand Rapids, MI: Eerdmans, 2005.

Olson, David H. *Building a Strong Marriage.* Minneapolis, MN: Prepare-Enrich, 1987.

Olson, David H., et al. *Prepare/Enrich Counselor's Manual*. Minneapolis, MN: Prepare-Enrich, 1982.

Oswalt, John N. *The Book of Isaiah, Chapters 40–66*. Grand Rapids, MI: Eerdmans, 1998.

Owen, John. *Hebrews*. Wheaton, IL: Crossway Classical Commentaries, 1998.

Paolino, Thomas J., and Barbara S. McCrady. *Marriage and Marital Therapy: Psychoanalytic, Behavioral, and Systems Theory Perspectives*. New York, NY: Brunner/Mazel, 1978.

Palmer, Gail, and Don Efron. "Emotionally Focused Family Therapy: Developing the Model." *Journal of Systemic Therapies* 26.4 (2007) 17–24.

Palmer, Paul F. "Christian Marriage: Contract or Covenant?" *Theological Studies*, 33.4 (1972) 617–65.

Paul, Norman L., and Betty B. Paul. *A Marital Puzzle*. New York, NY: Gardner, 1986.

Panneberg, Wolfhart. *Anthropology in Theological Perspective*. Translated by M. J. O'Connell. Philadelphia, PA: Westminster, 1985.

Paxson, Ruth. *Life on the Highest Plane: God's Plan for Spiritual Maturity*. Repr. Grand Rapids, MI: Kregel Classics, 1996.

Payne, Leanne. *Listening Prayer: Learning to Hear God's Voice and Keep a Prayer Journal*. Grand Rapids, MI: Baker, 1999.

Penn-Lewis, Jesse. *The Battle for the Mind*. Fort Washington, PA: CLC, 2012.

Penner, Clifford, and Joyce Penner. *The Gift of Sex*. Waco, TX: Word, 1981.

Pentecost, J. Dwight. *Faith that Endures: A Practical Commentary on the Book of Hebrews*. Grand Rapids, MI: Kregel, 2000.

Philips, Dietrich. "The Church of God." In *Spiritual and Anabaptist Writers*, ed. by George H. Williams and Angel M. Mergal, 226–60. Philadelphia, PA: Westminster, 1981.

Phillips, Charles L., and Royce D. Harbor. *Feedback Control Systems*. Hemel Hempstead: Prentice Hall, 1999.

Phillips, Charles L., and John M. Parr. *Signals, Systems, and Transforms*. 5th ed. Upper Saddle River, NJ: Prentice-Hall, 2014.

Piaget, Jean, and Bärbel Inhelder. *The Psychology of the Child*. New York, NY: Basic, 1969.

Polanyi, Michael. *Personal Knowledge: Towards a Post-Critical Philosophy*. Chicago, IL: University of Chicago Press, 1962.

Polischuk, Pablo. *Llamemos las Cosas por Su Nombre*. Miami: Editorial Vida/Zondervan, 2005.

———. "A Metacognitive Perspective on Internal Dialogues and Rhetoric: Derived from the Details of the Prodigal Son's Parable." *Journal of Psychology and Theology* 43 (2015) 60–72.

———. "A New Covenant: Paradigm for Family Progress." *The Judson Journal*. Newton Centre, MA: Andover Newton School of Theology, 1994.

———. "Perspectives on the Self: Substantial and Dialogical Aspects." *Perspectives in Faith and Science*. 50.2 (1998) 95–107.

Pritchard, James B., ed. "Summerian Sacred Marriage Texts." *The Ancient Near East: Supplementary Texts and Pictures Relating to the Old Testament*, 637–45. Princeton, NJ: Princeton University Press, 1969.

Rabinowitz, Joseph J. "Marriage Contracts in Ancient Egypt in the Light of Jewish Sources." Cited in Gordon P. Hugenberger, *Marriage as a Covenant*, 73. New York, NY: Brill, 1994.

Radner, Karen, and Eleonor Robson, eds. *The Oxford Handbook of Cuneiform Culture*. Oxford: Oxford University Press, 2011.

Ratcliff, Roger. "Group Reaction Time Distributions and an Analysis of Distribution Statistics." *Psychological Bulletin* 86 (1979) 446–61.

Reed, Gayle L., and Robert D. Enright. "The Effects of Forgiveness Therapy on Depression, Anxiety, and Posttraumatic Stress for Women after Spousal Emotional Abuse." *Journal of Consulting and Clinical Psychology* 74 (2006) 920–29.

Rekers, George. *Counseling Families*. Resources for Christian Counseling. Vol. 14. Waco, TX: Word, 1988.

Reid, Charles J. *Marriage Covenant*. Louisville, KY: John Knox, 1967.

Rendtorff, Rolf. *The Covenant Formula: An Exegetical and Theological Investigation*. Old Testament Studies. Edinburgh: T. & T. Clark, 1998.

Reymond, Robert L. *A New Systematic Theology of the Christian Faith*. Nashville, TN: Nelson, 1998.

Ripley, Janet S., et al. "Covenantal and Contractual Values in Marriage: Marital Values Orientation Toward Wedlock or Self-Actualization (Marital VOWS) Scale." *Personal Relationships* 12 (2005) 317–36.

Robertson, O. Palmer. *Christ of the Covenants*. Phillipsburg, PA: Presbyterian & Reformed, 1980.

Rogers, Carl R. "Toward a Modern Approach to Values: The Valuing Process in the Mature Person." *Journal of Abnormal and Social Psychology* 68 (1964) 160–7.

———. *On Becoming a Person: A Therapist's View of Psychotherapy*. Boston, MA: Houghton Mifflin, 1995.

Rosenthal, Robert. 1973. *On the Social Psychology of the Self-Fulfilling Prophecy: Further Evidence for Pygmalion Effects and Their Mediating Mechanisms*. New York, NY: MSS Modular, 1973.

Ryrie, Charles C. *Basis of the Premillennial Faith*. Neptune, NJ: Loizeaux, 1953.

———. *Dispensationalism*. Chicago, IL: Moody, 1965.

Sager, Clifford. *Marriage Contracts and Couple Therapy*. New York, NY: Brunner/Mazel, 1976.

———. "Transference in Conjoint Treatment of Married Couples." *Archives of General Psychiatry* 16 (1967) 185–93.

Sandage, Steven J., et al. "Toward a Multicultural Positive Psychology: Indigenous Forgiveness and Among Cultures." *The Counseling Psychologist* 31 (2003) 564–92.

Satir, Virginia. *Conjoint Family Therapy*. Palo Alto, CA: Science and Behavior, 1967.

Satir, Virginia, et al. "Family Reconstruction: The Family Within—A Group Experience." *The Journal for Specialists in Group Work*. 13.4 (1988) 200–208.

Schaumburg, Harry W. *False Intimacy: Understanding the Struggle of Sexual Addiction*. Colorado Springs, CO: NavPress, 1992.

Scofield, Cyrus I., ed. *The Scofield Reference Bible*. New York, NY: Oxford University Press, 1917.

Segal, Zindel, et al. *Mindfulness-Based Cognitive Therapy for Depression*. New York, NY: Guilford, 2013.

Seligman, Martin. *Helplessness: On Depression, Development, and Death*. San Francisco, CA: W. H. Freeman, 1992.

———. (2002). "Positive Psychology, Positive Prevention, and Positive Therapy." In *Handbook of Positive Psychology*, ed. by C. R. Snyder and Shane Lopez, 3–9. New York, NY: Oxford University Press, 2002.

Sells, James, and Mark A. Yarhouse. *Counseling Couples in Conflict: A Relational Restoration Model.* Downers Grove, IL, InterVarsity, 2011.

Selvini-Palazzoli, Mara, et al. *Paradox and Counterparadox: A New Model in the Therapy of the Family in Schizophrenic Transaction.* New York, NY: Jason Aronson, 1978.

Scharff, David E. and Jill S. Scharff. *Object Relations Family Therapy.* Northvale, NJ: Jason Aronson, 1997.

Sharf, Richard S. *Theories of Psychotherapy and Counseling: Concepts and Cases.* 4th ed. Belmont, CA: Thomson Brooks/Cole, 2008.

Shatz, Carla J. "The Developing Brain." *Scientific American.* 267.3 (1992) 60–7.

Shipp, Glover. *Marriage Is a Covenant, Not a Contract.* Joplin, MO: College, 1995.

Showers, Renald E. *There Really Is a Difference!: A Comparison of Covenant and Dispensational Theology.* Bellmawr, NJ: Friends of Israel Gospel Ministry, 1990.

Siegel, Daniel J. *The Developing Mind: How Relationships and the Brain Interact to Shape Who We Are.* New York: NY: Guilford, 1999.

Simon, Herbert A. "Explaining the Ineffable: AI on the Topics of Intuition, Insight, and Inspiration." *Proceedings of the Fourteenth International Joint Conference on Artificial Intelligence.* 1 (1995) 939–48.

———. "How Big Is a Chunk?" *Science* 183 (1974) 482–88.

Skynner, A. C. Robyn. "An Open-Systems, Group Analytic Approach to Family Therapy." In *Handbook of Family Therapy,* ed. byAlan S. Gurman and David P. Kniskern. New York: Brunner/Mazel, 1981.

Smalley, Gary. *The Covenant Marriage.* Focus on the Family Series. Bloomington, MN: Bethany House, 2003.

Smedes, Lewis B. *The Art of Forgiving.* New York: Ballantine, 1996.

———. *Forgive and Forget: Healing the Hurts We Don't Deserve.* NY: Harper Collins, 1984.

———. *Sex for Christians.* Rev. ed. Grand Rapids, MI: W. Eerdmans, 1994.

Smolarz, Sebastian R. *Covenant and the Metaphor of Divine Marriage in Biblical Thought: A Study with Special Reference to the Book of Revelation.* Eugene, OR: Wipf & Stock, 2011.

Spaht, Katherine S. "Covenant Marriage Seven Years Later: Its as Yet Unfulfilled Promise." *Lousiana Law Review* 65 (2005) 605–34.

Spencer, Aída B. *Beyond the Curse: Women Called to Ministry.* Peabody, MA: Hendrickson, 1989.

Spencer, Aída B., et al. *Marriage at the Crossroads: Couples in Conversation about Discipleship, Gender Roles, Decision Making and Intimacy.* Downers Grove, IL: InterVarsity, 2009.

Sproul, Robert C. *Knowing Scripture.* Downers Grove, IL: InterVarsity, 1977.

———. *What Is Reformed Theology?: Understanding the Basics.* Grand Rapids, MI: Baker, 2005.

———. *When You Rise Up: A Covenantal Approach to Homeschooling.* Phillipsburg, NJ: P. & R., 2004.

Stackouse, Max L. "Covenantal Marriage: Protestant Views and Contemporary Life," In *Covenant Marriage in Comparative Perspective,* ed. by John Witte Jr. and Eliza Ellison, 153–81. Grand Rapids, MI: Eerdmans, 2005.

Stahmann, Robert F., and William J. Hiebert. *Premarital Counseling: The Professional's Handbook.* 2nd ed. Lexington, MA: Lexington, 1987.

Stenberg, Robert J. *Cognitive Psychology.* Cenage Learning. 6th ed. Belmont, CA: Wadsworth, 2011.

———. *Mechanisms of Cognitive Development.* New York, NY: W. H. Freeman, 1984.

Bibliography

Stewart, Charles W. *The Minister as Marriage Counselor.* Nashville, TN: Abingdon, 1970.

Stuart, Richard B. *Helping Couples Change: A Social Learning Approach to Marital Therapy.* New York, NY: Guilford, 1980.

———. "Operant-Interpersonal Treatment of Marital Discord." *Journal of Consulting and Clinical Psychology* 33 (1969) 675–82.

Stuart, Richard, and Barbara Jacobson. *Couple's Therapy Workbook.* Champaign, IL: Research, 1987.

Stuart, Richard B., and Freide Stuart. *Premarital Counseling Inventory.* Champaign, IL: Research, 1975.

Sullivan, Harry S. *The Interpersonal Theory of Psychiatry.* New York, NY: Norton, 1953.

Tan, Siang-Yang. *Counseling and Psychotherapy: A Christian Perspective.* Grand Rapids, MI: Baker Academic, 2011.

Tangney, J. P., et al. "Assessing Individual Differences in the Propensity to Forgive." Paper presented at the annual meeting of the American Psychological Association. Boston, MA (1999).

Taylor, Robert M., and Lucille P. Morrison. *Taylor-Johnson Temperamental Analysis Manual.* Los Angeles, CA: Psychological, 1984.

Thielicke, Helmut. *Life Can Begin Again.* Philadelphia, PA: Fortress, 1963.

Thoresen, Carl E.; et al. "Forgiveness and Health: An Unanswered Question." In *Forgiveness: Theory, Research, and Practice,* ed. by Michael E. McCullough, et al., 254–80. New York, NY: Guilford, 2000.

Torrance, E. P. "Creativity Research in Education: Still Alive." In *Perspectives in Creativity,* ed. by I. A. Taylor and J. W. Getzels, 278–96. Chicago, IL: Aldine, 1975.

Treggiari, Susan. *Roman Marriage: Iusti Coniuges from the Time of Cicero to the Time of Ulpian.* Oxford: Clarendon, 1993.

Trotzer, James D. *Marriage and Family: Better Ready Than Not.* Muncie, IN: Accelerated Development, 1986.

Tweedie, Donald F. "Contract Therapy and Behavior Modification." *Journal of Psychology and Theology* 1.3 (1973) 50–55.

———. "Contract Therapy and the Christian Covenant." *Journal of Psychology and Theology* 1.2 (1973) 73–76.

———. "Contract Therapy: The Renegotiation of Marriage and the Family." *Journal of Psychology and Theology* 1.1 (1973) 76–78.

Tutu, Desmond. *No Future without Forgiveness.* New York, NY: Doubleday, 2000.

Vande Kemp, Hendrika. *Family Therapy: Christian Perspectives.* Grand Rapids, MI: Baker, 1991.

Van Leeuwen, Mary S. *Gender and Grace: Love, Work, and Parenting in a Changing World.* Downers Gove, IL: InterVarsity, 1990.

———. *The Person in Psychology: A Contemporary Christian Appraisal.* Grand Rapids, MI: Eerdmans, 1985.

Viscott, David. *I Love You, Let's Work It Out.* New York: Simon and Schuster, 1987.

Vos, Geerhardus. *Biblical Theology: Old and New Testaments.* Eugene, OR: Wipf & Stock, 2003.

Wade, Nathaniel G., et al. "Helping Clients Heal: Does Forgiveness Make a Difference?" *Professional Psychology: Research and Practice* 36.6 (2005) 634–41.

Wade, Nathaniel G., and Everett L. Worthington. "In Search of a Common Core: A Content Analysis of Interventions to Promote Forgiveness." *Psychotherapy: Theory, Research, Practice, and Training* 42.2 (2005) 160–77.

Walsch, Neal D., and Gerald G. Jampolski. *Forgiveness: The Greatest Healer of Them All*. Hillsboro, OR: Beyond Words, 1999.

Walvoord, John F. "The New Covenant with Israel." *Bibliotheca Sacra* (1946) 25.

———. *The Millennial Kingdom*. Grand Rapids, MI: Zondervan, 1983.

———. *Prophecy in the New Millennium*. Grand Rapids, MI: Kregel, 2001.

Waring, E. M., and Reddon, J. R. "The Measurement of Intimacy in Marriage: The Waring Intimacy Qurestionnaire." *Journal of Clinical Psychology* 39.1 (1983) 53–57.

Warren, Neil C. *Finding the Love of Your Life: Ten Principles for Choosing the Right Marriage Partner*. Colorado Springs, CO: Focus on the Family, 1992.

———. *The Triumphant Marriage: 100 Extremely Successful Couples Reveal Their Secrets*. Colorado Springs, CO: Focus on the Family, 1995.

Watzlawick, Paul. *The Situation Is Hopeless but not Serious: The Pursuit of Unhappiness*. New York, NY: W. W. Norton, 1993.

Watzlawick, Paul, et al. *Change: Principles of Problem Formation and Problem Resolution*. New York, NY: Norton, 1974.

Weinfeld, Moshe. *Deuteronomy and the Deuteronomic School*. Repr. Winona Lake: IN: Eisebrauns, 1992.

Weiss, Robert L. "The Conceptualization of Marriage from a Behavioral Perspective." In *Marriage and Marital Therapy: Psychoanalytic, Behavioral, and Systems Perspectives*, ed. by Thomas J. Paolino and Barbara S. McCrady. New York: Brunner/Mazel, 1978.

Welford, A. T. "Choice Reaction Time: Basic Concepts." In *Reaction Times*, ed. by A. T. Welford, 73–128. New York, NY: Academic, 1980.

Wellhausen, Julius. *Prolegomena to the History of Ancient Israel*. Eugene, OR: Wipf & Stock, 2003.

Wells, Adrian. *Metacognitive Therapy for Anxiety and Depression*. New York, NY: Guilford, 2009.

Wells, David F. *God in the Wasteland: The Reality of Truth in a World of Fading Dreams*. Grand Rapids, MI: Eerdmans, 1994.

———. *Losing Our Virtue: Why the Church Must Recover Its Moral Vision*. Grand Rapids, MI: Eerdmans, 1998.

———. *No Place for Truth, or Whatever Happened to Evangelical Theology?* Grand Rapids, MI: Eerdmans, 1993.

Westcott, R. S. *The Concept of Berit with Regard to Marriage in the Old Testament*. Dallas, TX: Dallas Theological Seminary, 1985.

Wheat, Ed. *How to Save Your Marriage Alone*. Grand Rapids, MI: Zondervan, 1983.

Whitaker, Carl. *Midnight Musings of a Family Therapist*. New York, NY: W.W. Norton, 1989.

White, Michael. *Maps of Narrative Practice*. New York, NY: W.W Norton, 2007.

Williamson, Paul R. *Sealed with an Oath: Covenant in God's Unfolding Purpose*. Downers Grove, IL: IVP Academic, 2007.

Witte, John, and Eliza Ellison. *Covenant Marriage in Comparative Perspective*. Grand Rapids, MI: Eerdmans, 2005.

Witsius, Hermann. *The Economy of the Covenants Between God and Man*. 2 vols. Repr. Phillipsburg, NJ: Presbyterian & Reformed, 1990.

Bibliography

Wood, Julia T. *Gendered Lives: Communication, Gender and Culture.* Belmont, CA: Wadsworth, 1994.

Worthington, Everett L., ed. *Christian Marital Counseling: Eight Approaches to Helping Couples.* Grand Rapids, MI: Baker, 1996.

———. *Counseling Before Marriage.* Resources for Christian Counseling 23. Dallas, TX: Word, 1990.

———. (Ed.) *Dimensions of Forgiveness: Psychological Research and Theological Perspective.* Philadelphia, PA: Templeton Foundation, 1998.

———. *Forgiveness and Reconciliation: Theory and Application.* New York, NY: Routledge, 2006.

———. (Ed.) *Handbook of Forgiveness.* New York, NY: Routledge, 2005.

———. *Hope-Focused Marriage Counseling: A Guide to Brief Treatment.* Downers Grove, IL: InterVarsity, 2005.

———. *Hope for Troubled Marriages.* Downers Grove, IL: Intervarsity, 1993.

———. *Marriage Counseling: A Christian Approach to Counseling Couples.* Downers Grove, IL: InterVarsity, 1989.

Worthington, Everett L., and F. A. DiBlasio. "Promoting Mutual Forgiveness within Fractured Relationships." *Psychotherapy* 27 (1990) 219–23.

Worthington, Everett L., and N. G. Wade. "The Psychology of Unforgiveness and Forgiveness and Implications for Clinical Practice." *Journal of Social Science and Clinical Psychology* 18 (1999) 385–418.

Wright, H. Norman. *Marital Counseling: A Biblical, Behavioral, Cognitive Approach.* New York, NY: Harper and Row, 1981.

———. *Premarital Counseling.* Chicago, IL: Moody, 1981.

Wright, Nicholas T. "The Climax of the Covenant: Christ and the Law in Pauline Theology." *Westminster Theological Journal* 56.1 (1994) 197–201.

Yancey, Philip D. *What's so Amazing about Grace?* Grand Rapids, MI: Zondervan, 1997.

Zeigarnick, Bluma. "On Finished and Unfinished Tasks." In *A Sourcebook of Gestalt Psychology,* ed. by William D. Ellis. New York, NY: Humanities, 1967.

Zizioulas, John. *Being as Communion: Studies in Personhood and the Church.* Crestwood, NY: St Vladimir's Seminary Press, 1997.

———. "Human Capacity and Human Incapacity: A Theological Exploration of Personhood." *Scottish Journal of Theology* 28 (1974) 41–48.

www.ingramcontent.com/pod-product-compliance
Lightning Source LLC
Chambersburg PA
CBHW080406300426
44113CB00015B/2414